MODERN

MARKETING THEORY

Critical Issues in the Philosophy

of Marketing Science

SHELBY D. HUNT

Paul Whitfield Horn Professor of Marketing
Texas Tech University

SS62AA
PUBLISHED BY
SOUTH-WESTERN PUBLISHING CO.
CINCINNATI, OH

Publisher: James R. Sitlington, Jr.
Production Editor: Thomas E. Shaffer
Production House: CompuText Productions
Cover and Interior Designer: Jim DeSollar
Marketing Manager: David L. Shaut

1 2 3 4 5 6 7 D 5 4 3 2 1 0

Printed in the United States of America

Library of Congress Cataloging-in-Publication Data

Hunt, Shelby D.
  Modern marketing theory : critical issues in the philosophy of marketing science / Shelby D. Hunt.
      p.   cm.
  "SS62AA."
  Includes bibliographical references.
  ISBN 0-538-81221-4
  1. Marketing.   2. Marketing research.   3. Philosophy, Modern.
  4. Positivism.   I.   Title.
  HF5415.122.H86 1991
  658.8—dc20   90-9617
                                                                                CIP

*This book is dedicated
to my brothers,
Bill, Larry, and Ken.*

PREFACE

For the philosopher, clarity is a matter of good faith.

Marquis de Vauven

Modern Marketing Theory: Critical Issues in the Philosophy of Marketing Science differs markedly from its predecessors, *Marketing Theory: Conceptual Foundations of Research in Marketing* (1976) and *Marketing Theory: The Philosophy of Marketing Science* (1983). Both of those works focused on applying the philosophy of science "tool kit" to marketing theory and research. Part I of *Modern Marketing Theory* continues this applications tradition. Part II, on the other hand, adopts an historical perspective. Specifically, Part II traces the historical development of the philosophy of science and then uses this historical material to investigate certain critical issues in contemporary marketing theory. The reason for Part II's shift in orientation stems from marketing's "crisis literature."

In the 1960s and 1970s a phenomenon known as the "crisis literature" developed in the philosophy of science and spread to the social sciences. In the 1980s it reached marketing. Briefly, this literature questions whether there can possibly be genuine progress in the development of knowledge in any science and challenges the appropriateness of the existing philosophical foundations of contemporary social science and marketing. Unfortunately, although the crisis literature is often highly provocative, much of the discussion—both in the social sciences and marketing—has been ill-informed and misguided. In fact, much of the debate has lapsed into simple name-calling rather than informed discussion on substantive issues. For example, many of those who are currently ranting about the "evils of positivism" are remarkably ill-informed about who the logical positivists were and the nature of their fundamental beliefs. (Indeed, many writers attribute views to the positivists that are actually *antipositivist*. See reference 497a.)

The overriding objective of Part II is to raise the level of the debate in marketing's crisis literature. Thus, its underlying premise is that much of the unproductive nature of the crisis literature has its origins in factual misunderstandings of the nature of various philosophical "isms," e.g., logical positivism, logical empiricism, classical empiricism, classical rationalism, classical realism, idealism, relativism, and so forth. Part II identifies the fundamental tenets of these major "isms" in the philosophy of science and traces their historical development from the time of Plato to the present. Hopefully, this historical treatment of the philosophy of science will at least help separate the truly substantive issues in marketing's crisis literature from the purely semantical ones.

All those who have attempted to find publishers for works that have small markets know the difficulty of the task. Therefore, I should like to thank South-Western Publishing Co. for agreeing to publish this work and, in particular, Michael V. Needham, Senior Vice President and General Manager, and James R. Sitlington, Jr., Publisher.

How does one even begin to give proper acknowledgment for a book containing over six hundred references? Obviously, any work that attempts to chronicle the historical development of the philosophy of science would be impossible without the original contributions of those whose works are chronicled. If I acknowledged all those philosophers of science whose works are discussed, the list would be indeed long. On the other hand, it is difficult to narrow the list to a "chosen few." Therefore, I find I must opt for the (admittedly unsatisfactory) procedure of a "collective thanks" to all those philosophers of science whose works are detailed herein. Nevertheless, equity theory absolutely demands that an exception be made for Professor Harvey Siegel (Philosophy Department, University of Miami). My own work has benefited enormously from Professor Siegel's many writings. His incisive analyses of extraordinarily complex issues in the philosophy of science are paradigm examples of true scholarship.

In an extraordinary display of intercollegial generosity, numerous philosophers of science graciously reviewed drafts of Part II, including: Robert L. Causey (University of Texas-Austin), Martin Hollis (University of East Anglia, United Kingdom), Evan K. Jobe (Texas Tech University), John Kekes, (State University of New York at Albany), Michael Krausz (Bryn Mawr College), Jarrett Leplin (University of North Carolina at Greensboro), Michael E. Levin (City College, City University of New York), Steven Lukes (Oxford University), Paul E. Meehl (University of Minnesota), Jack W. Meiland (University of Michigan), Dennis C. Phillips (Stanford University), Hilary Putnam (Harvard University), Israel Scheffler (Harvard University), and David Stove (University of Sydney). Given the ambitious nature of Part II's task, their encouraging comments have been most appreciated. Moreover, they significantly improved the book by correcting numerous errors. Although any remaining errors are my responsibility, alone, I gratefully thank all these philosophers for their help.

I should also like to acknowledge that my work has benefited greatly from the efforts of several marketing scholars whose perspectives differ greatly from my own: Professors Paul F. Anderson (Penn State University), the late Johan Arndt (Norwegian School of Management), Jerry Olson (Penn State University), J. Paul Peter (University of Wisconsin, Madison), and Gerald Zaltman (University of Pittsburgh). Consistent with the "critical discussion" tradition in philosophy, I often find I learn more from those with whom I disagree than from those who share my views. Throughout Part II, I discuss and evaluate many aspects of these authors' works. I have earnestly attempted to characterize their views (and all others' views) in a fair manner, rather than developing straw man caricatures. In my judgment, a major problem in marketing's crisis literature (not unlike other social sciences) has been the caricaturizing of others' perspectives. Toward the end of fairness, I adopt a procedure that is, most unfortunately, uncommon in marketing—the extensive use of direct quotations, rather than paraphrasing. Hopefully, this procedure will be a positive step toward raising the level of the debate.

Professor Dale Duhan used a draft of Part II when he taught the Marketing Theory seminar at Michigan State University in the spring quarter, 1989. Both he and his students provided encouraging feedback and detailed comments. I thank them for their assistance.

I gratefully acknowledge the support that Texas Tech University has provided in this project and my colleagues' help in particular. Professors Larry M. Austin, Patrick M. Dunne, Roy D. Howell, James B. Wilcox, and Robert E. Wilkes have improved this work by their comments. Furthermore, over the years both my own doctoral students and those who have used my previous books on marketing theory at other universities have provided numerous helpful suggestions and I thank them all. Most especially, I thank Kenneth R. Bartkus and Robert M. Morgan for their help in preparing *Modern Marketing Theory*. Finally, but very importantly, thanks go to Joyce S. Marsh and Heather R. Skiles for their excellent typing assistance.

S. D. Hunt

CONTENTS

PART 1
THE PHILOSOPHY
OF MARKETING
SCIENCE

1
INTRODUCTION

Question: Prove to me I should study logic!
Answer: How would you know that it was a good proof?

Epictetus

Marketing research books usually contain sections on issues such as experimental research designs, data collection procedures, the availability and desirability of secondary data, sampling methods, data analysis, and the writing of research reports. Since this monograph discusses none of these topics, how can it claim to be about "marketing research"? Most books on *advanced* research topics in marketing discuss items such as factor analysis, multiple discriminant analysis, cluster analysis, multiple regression, dummy variable regression, canonical correlation, and covariance analysis. Since the page numbers represent the most sophisticated use of quantitative tools in this monograph, why have graduate students referred to this work as *advanced* issues in marketing research? Finally, students often describe most contemporary works on marketing theory as "impractical," with no relevance to the real world. How can this monograph concern marketing theory and further assert that the study of theory is the most *practical* intellectual pursuit of anyone interested seriously in marketing research? Is this entire monograph an inherent contradiction in terms? Let's examine these contradictions and determine whether they are real or only apparent.

1.1   THREE CONTRADICTIONS?

Few students of marketing would deny that much marketing research attempts to explain, predict, and understand marketing phenomena. Thus, much research is directed at explaining why some products have failed and attempting to predict which new products will succeed; explaining why certain retail institutions have declined and predicting which retail institutions will emerge; explaining why some promotional programs have succeeded and predicting the characteristics of successful future programs; and explaining why consumers have allocated

1

their vast expenditures according to certain patterns and predicting how consumers will purchase in the future. Thus, explanation, prediction, and understanding are fundamental to marketing research.

Care should be taken to distinguish between *marketing* research and *market* research. Marketing research (or, alternatively, scholarly research in marketing) always seeks to expand the total knowledge base of marketing. In general, market research attempts to solve a particular company's marketing problem. To evaluate a particular department store's image would be a market research problem. To explore whether department stores have images *at all* is a marketing (scholarly) research problem. To attempt to determine the best location for a particular warehouse is a market research problem. To attempt to develop a model for locating warehouses *in general* is a marketing research problem. The following question can serve as a litmus test for differentiating *market* research from *marketing* research: "After conducting this research project, what will we then know about marketing *in general* that we do not know now?" In short, "What will be the contribution of this research to knowledge about marketing?" Unfortunately, many dissertation research proposals and even some completed dissertations fail this test. Although the line differentiating marketing research from market research may sometimes be fine, the distinction is useful and conceptually important.

Myers, Massy, and Greyser [461] have drawn similar distinctions among basic research, problem-solving research, and what they refer to as "problem-oriented" research. They suggest that problem-oriented research lies between basic research and problem-solving research and "may be fundamental or highly applied, but its driving force is the desire to make a contribution to the solution of an important practical problem." [462, p. 157] Does problem-oriented research "lie between" basic research and problem-solving research? If "basic" research is considered to be roughly synonymous with "marketing" research and "problem-solving" research is considered to be roughly synonymous with "market" research, then problem-oriented research is *not* "between" the two. Problem-oriented research is a subclass of *marketing* research because it is research directed at general *classes* of marketing problems and because it is generalizable *across* different firms. Problem-oriented research is, simply, a kind of basic research in marketing that is normative-driven rather than positive-driven (see Section 1.3.1). It seeks answers to normative questions such as "How *should* retail establishments price their merchandise?" rather than answers to positive questions such as "How *do* retail establishments price their merchandise?" Both questions are appropriate for "basic" or "marketing" research.

The first apparent contradiction dissolves if we note that this monograph is substantially concerned with exploring the basic methodological issues attendant on the explanation, prediction, and understanding of marketing phenomena. These basic methodological issues are customarily given only cursory treatment, at best, in most marketing research texts. Such texts focus primarily (and probably justifiably, given their target markets) on the conventional topics previously mentioned (data collection, sampling, etc.). Fortunately for the present endeavor, many of the basic methodological issues in research and scientific inquiry have been extensively developed in the philosophy of science and are applicable to marketing research. *The major purpose of this monograph will be to draw upon the vast storehouse of analytical methods in the philosophy of science in order to systematically explore the basic methodological issues underlying marketing research.* The philosophical orientation of this monograph can be described as modern empiricism, which is an eclectic blend of scientific realism, logical empiricism, critical rationalism (falsificationism), and pragmatism. As such, the orientation is decidedly fallibilistic (but not cynical, skeptical, or relativist) and absolutist (but not dogmatist or "Absolutist"). See Part II for more on these "isms."

The second apparent contradiction is (*a*) that "advanced" topics in marketing research universally seem to be quantitatively sophisticated and (*b*) that quantitative techniques are conspicuous by their absence in this monograph, yet (*c*) students who have previewed this work generally consider it advanced. The contradiction is illusory. Quantitative techniques represent a tool kit for conducting research. Many mathematical and statistical models are difficult to understand and, hence, *advanced*. Similarly, the philosophy of science is a tool kit which students may perceive as being relatively advanced. Students may find the tool kit of moderate difficulty for two reasons. First, few students have been formally exposed to the philosophy of science, and the first exposure to new material is always the most difficult. The reader must not only comprehend the *substance* of the tool kit but must also learn the *vocabulary*. Every effort has been made to "dejargonize" the presentation. Nevertheless, just as students must understand such terms as *differentiation* and *integration* to learn the role of calculus in marketing research, so must they understand such terms as *retrodiction* and *deductive-nomological explanation* to appreciate the usefulness of the philosophy of science tool kit in marketing research.

Some marketing commentators have observed that the history of marketing (not unlike the history of other social sciences) can be best understood as a history of marketing fads. Every few years some group comes along with a tool kit which promises to be the key to marketing problems. Thus, marketing has been blessed with motivation research, operations research, Markov processes, systems analysis, the behavior sciences, mathematical models, multidimensional scaling, psychographics, conjoint analysis, structural equation models, and multiattribute models. Although each tool kit has value in conducting research in marketing, advocates of the various tool kits often tend to oversell and overpromise. Therefore, a caveat concerning the philosophy of science seems appropriate. Just as marketing research problems are not solved by restating our ignorance in mathematical symbols, so too the present philosophy of science tool kit provides no panaceas, no magic formulas.

The second reason some students may find this presentation moderately difficult is that we shall attempt to rigorously analyze an area (often referred to as "the scientific method") about which students have some notoriously nonrigorous (though often firmly held) notions. Unfortunately, rigor and difficulty often travel in tandem. If the analysis is both complete and clear (rigorous), this will maximize the opportunity for others to point out errors. When analyses are incomplete and ambiguous, the temptation is often strong for authors to dismiss their errors as misinterpretations. Since ambiguity should never be confused with profundity, I plead guilty to the charge of attempted rigor.

The last apparent contradiction is that (a) students believe that theory is impractical, yet (b) this book concerns theory while (c) claiming to be devoted to a practical intellectual pursuit. The fallacy lies in the false dichotomy of *theoretical-practical*. Almost all marketing practitioners, most marketing academicians, and, sadly, too many marketing researchers perceive *theoretical* and *practical* as being at the opposite ends of a continuum. This perception leads to the conclusion that as any analysis becomes more theoretical, it must become less practical. To puncture this misperception, one need only note that *a theory is a systematically related set of statements, including some lawlike generalizations, that is empirically testable. The purpose of theory is to increase scientific understanding through a systematized structure capable of both explaining and predicting phenomena.* Thus, any structure which purports to be theoretical must be capable of explaining and predicting phenomena. Any structure that has neither explanatory nor predictive power is not a theory. Since the explanation and prediction of marketing phenomena are eminently practical concerns, the study and generation of marketing theory are practical pursuits of the first order.

The *theoretical-practical* issue is not the only false dichotomy in marketing. Consider the *behavioral-quantitative* classification. Incredibly, some marketing educators still inquire of prospective faculty whether they are quantitative *or* behavioral. This false dichotomy automatically presumes that no one can be both behaviorally oriented and at the same time be well-grounded in quantitative methodology. The presumption is, of course, unfounded. The *rigor-relevance* dichotomy has also been shown to be false. [332a]

1.2   OBJECTIVES OF MONOGRAPH

The primary objective here will be to systematically explore some of the basic methodological issues underlying marketing research. The analytical methods that will be developed and employed will be drawn from the modern empiricist tool kit. Numerous other tool kits exist in the philosophy of science: classical empiricism, pragmatism, phenomenalism, rationalism, instrumentalism, logical positivism, conventionalism, relativism, constructivism, and, recently, *"Weltanschauungen-ism."* The differentiating characteristics of these various "isms" need not detain us, since Part I of this work is not *on* the philosophy of science, but rather, attempts to *use* philosophy of science. This is not a philosophy of science book disguised in the trappings of marketing research. Much of the philosophy of science is not even mentioned, let alone developed, in this work. Philosophy of science issues and methods are introduced and discussed only when they are deemed useful for explicating some particular methodological issue in marketing research.

One way to clarify the purpose of this work is to give some examples of the basic methodological issues that will be explored. Although certainly not exhaustive, the following list should prove reasonably representative of these issues:

1. How does one scientifically explain marketing phenomena?
2. Is it possible to be able to explain marketing phenomena without being able to predict them?
3. Is functionalism a different method of explaining phenomena?
4. How does explanation differ from causation?
5. Can one understand marketing phenomena without being able to explain or predict them?
6. What is the role of laws and lawlike generalizations in marketing research?
7. How do empirical generalizations differ from laws?
8. Are the axioms in a theory "assumed to be true"?
9. Can Weber's law be extended to marketing phenomena?
10. How do universal laws differ from statistical laws?
11. What is theory, and what is its role in marketing research?
12. How can formalization help in analyzing marketing theory?
13. Why must theories contain lawlike generalizations?
14. Why must theories be empirically testable?
15. How can marketing phenomena best be classified?

Before analyzing these questions, some preliminary matters require attention. These preliminary issues can be best examined in the context of the so-called "Is marketing a science?" controversy. The controversy was sparked by an early *Journal of Marketing* article written by Converse and entitled "The Development of a Science of Marketing." [129] Prominent writers who then entered the debate included Bartels, Hutchinson, Baumol, Buzzell, Taylor, and Halbert. [37, 313, 51, 101, 614, 243] After raging throughout most of the 1950s and 1960s, the controversy has since (apparently) waned. The waning may be more apparent than real because many of the substantive issues underlying the marketing science controversy overlap with the more recent "broadening the concept of marketing" debate. Fundamental to both controversies are some radically different perspectives on the essential characteristics of both *marketing* and *science*. An exploration of the basic nature of both these notions will provide a frame of reference for the rest of this monograph.

1.3   THE NATURE OF MARKETING

What is marketing? What kinds of phenomena are appropriately termed marketing phenomena? How do marketing activities differ from nonmarketing activities? What is a marketing system? How can the marketing process be distinguished from other social processes? Which institutions should one refer to as marketing institutions? *In short, what is the proper conceptual domain of the construct labeled "marketing"?*

Prior to 1985, the American Marketing Association defined marketing as "the performance of business activities that direct[s] the flow of goods and services from producer to consumer or user." [128] This position has come under attack from various quarters as being too restrictive. The attacks have prompted one textbook on marketing to note, "Marketing is not easy to define. No one has yet been able to formulate a clear, concise definition that finds universal acceptance." [529, p. 3]

Although vigorous debate concerning the basic notion of marketing has alternately waxed and waned since the early 1900s, the most recent controversy probably traces back to a position paper by the marketing staff of the Ohio State University in 1965. The paper suggested that marketing be considered "the process in a society by which the demand structure for economic goods and services is anticipated or enlarged and satisfied through the conception, promotion, exchange, and physical distribution of goods and services." [419, p. 43] Note the conspicuous absence of the notion that marketing consists of a set of business activities (as in the AMA definition). Rather, marketing is viewed as a *social process*.

Next to plunge into the semantic battle were Kotler and Levy. Although they did not specifically propose a new definition of marketing, Kotler and Levy in 1969 suggested that the concept of marketing be broadened to include nonbusiness organizations. They observed that nonbusiness organizations, including churches, police departments, and public schools, have products and customers and use the normal tools of the marketing mix. Therefore, Kotler and Levy concluded that these organizations perform marketing activities, or at least marketing-like activities. Thus, "the choice facing those who manage nonbusiness organizations is not whether to market or not to market, for no organization can avoid marketing. The choice is whether to do it well or poorly, and on this necessity the case for organizational marketing is basically founded." [345, p. 15] In the same issue of the *Journal of Marketing,* William Lazer discussed the changing boundaries of marketing. He pleaded that "what is required is a broader perception and definition of marketing than has hitherto been the case—one that recognizes marketing's societal dimensions and perceives of marketing as more than just a technology of the firm." [383, p. 9] Thus, Kotler and Levy desired to broaden the notion of marketing by including not-for-profit organizations, and Lazer called for a definition of marketing that recognized marketing's expanding societal dimensions.

David Luck took sharp issue with Kotler and Levy by insisting that marketing be limited to those business processes and activities which ultimately result in a *market* transaction. [402, p. 54] Luck noted that even thus bounded, marketing would still be a field of enormous scope and that marketing specialists could still render their services to non-marketing causes. Kotler and Levy then accused Luck of a new form of myopia and suggested that "the crux of marketing lies in a *general idea of exchange* rather than the narrower thesis of market transactions." [346, p. 57] They further contended that defining marketing "too narrowly" would inhibit students of marketing from applying their expertise to the most rapidly growing sectors of the society.

Other marketing commentators began to espouse the dual theses that (1) marketing be broadened to include nonbusiness organizations and (2) marketing's societal dimensions deserve scrutiny. Thus, Ferber prophesied that marketing would diversify into the social and public policy fields. [178] And Lavidge sounded a similar call to arms by admonishing marketers to cease evaluating new products solely on the basis of whether they *could* be sold. Rather, he suggested that they evaluate new products from a societal perspective, that is, *should* the products be sold?

> The areas in which marketing people can, and must, be of service to society have broadened. In addition, marketing's functions have been broadened. Marketing no longer can be defined adequately in terms of the activities involved in buying, selling, and transporting goods and services. [380, p. 27]

The movement to expand the concept of marketing probably became irreversible when the *Journal of Marketing* devoted an entire issue to marketing's changing social/environmental role. At that time, Kotler and Zaltman coined the term *social marketing,* which they defined as "the design, implementation, and control of programs calculated to influence the acceptability of social ideas and involving considerations of product planning, pricing, communication, distribution, and marketing research." [347, p. 5] In the same issue, marketing technology was applied to fund raising for the March of Dimes [448], health services [648], population problems [171], and the recycling of solid waste. [650]

Further, Dawson chastised marketers for ignoring many fundamental issues pertaining to the social relevance of marketing activities:

> Surely, in these troubled times, an appraisal of marketing's actual and potential role in relation to such [societal] problems is at least of equal importance to the technical aspects of the field. Yet, the emphasis upon practical problem-solving within the discipline far outweighs the attention paid to social ramifications of marketing activity. [147, p. 71]

Kotler has since reevaluated his earlier positions concerning broadening the concept of marketing and has articulated a "generic" concept of marketing. He proposes that the essence of marketing is the *transaction*, defined as the exchange of values between two parties. Kotler's generic concept of marketing states, "Marketing is specifically concerned with how transactions are created, stimulated, facilitated, and valued." [348, p. 49] Empirical evidence indicates that, at least among marketing educators, the broadened concept of marketing represents a *fait accompli*. A study by Nickels has shown that 95 percent of marketing educators believe that the scope of marketing should be broadened to include nonbusiness organizations. Similarly, 93 percent agree that marketing goes beyond just economic goods and services, and 83 percent favor including in the domain of marketing many activities whose ultimate result is not a market transaction. [475, p. 142]

Although the advocates of extending the notion of marketing have won the semantic battle, their efforts may not have been victimless. Carman notes that the definition of marketing plays a significant role in directing the research efforts of marketers. He believes that many processes (e.g., political processes) do not involve an exchange of values and that marketing should not take such processes under its "disciplinary wing." [105, p. 14] Bartels has also explored the so-called identity crises in marketing and has pointed out numerous potential disadvantages to broadening the concept of marketing. These potential disadvantages include (1) turning the attention of marketing researchers away from important problems in the area of physical distribution, (2) emphasizing methodology rather than substance as the content of marketing knowledge, and (3) developing an increasingly esoteric and abstract marketing literature. Bartels concluded, "If 'marketing' is to be regarded as so broad as to include both economic and noneconomic fields of application, perhaps marketing as originally conceived will ultimately reappear under another name." [41, p. 76] Similarly, David J. Luck decries the "semantic jungle" that appears to be growing in marketing. [404] Citing conflicting definitions of *marketing* and *social marketing* in the current literature, Luck suggests that this semantic jungle has been impeding the efforts of marketers to think clearly about their discipline. He challenged the American Marketing Association to create a special commission to clear up the definitional problems in marketing. Finally, Robert J. Eggert, a past president of the American

Marketing Association, stated that the development of a consistent standard definition of marketing was a primary goal of the association. [163]

Three questions appear to be central to the definition (broadening the concept) of marketing controversy. First, what kinds of phenomena and issues *do* the various marketing writers perceive to be included in the scope of marketing? Second, what kinds of phenomena and issues *should* be included in the scope of marketing? Third, how can marketing be defined both to systematically encompass all of the phenomena and issues that should be included and, at the same time, to systematically exclude all other phenomena and issues. That is, a good definition of marketing must be both properly inclusive and exclusive. All three questions cry out for rigorous analysis. However, since a complete explication of Questions 2 and 3 depends in part on a satisfactory exposition of Question 1, the present analysis will begin by examining the various kinds of phenomena and issues that marketing writers often seem to put within the confines of marketing. In short, what is the scope of marketing?

1.3.1   The Scope of Marketing

The scope of marketing is unquestionably broad. Often included are such diverse subject areas as consumer behavior, pricing, purchasing, sales management, product management, marketing communications, comparative marketing, social marketing, the efficiency/productivity of marketing systems, the role of marketing in economic development, packaging, channels of distribution, marketing research, societal issues in marketing, retailing, wholesaling, the social responsibility of marketing, international marketing, commodity marketing, and physical distribution. Though lengthy, this list of topics does not exhaust the possibilities. Not all writers would include all of the topics under the general rubric of marketing. However, the point deserving emphasis here is that different commentators on marketing would *disagree* as to which topics should be excluded. The disagreement stems from fundamentally different perspectives and can be best analyzed by attempting to develop some common ground for classifying the diverse topics and issues in marketing.

During a presentation at the 1972 fall conference of the American Marketing Association, Philip Kotler made some observations concerning how to classify marketing phenomena using the concepts *micro, macro, normative,* and *positive.*[1] These observations spurred the development of the classificatory schema detailed in Table 1-1. The schema proposes that all marketing phenomena, topics, and issues can be

---

[1] Some of the observations of Professor Kotler were apparently extemporaneous since they were not included in his published paper. [349]

Table 1-1   The Three Dichotomies Model of Marketing

Positive	Normative

Profit sector
Micro
1. Problems, issues, theories, and research concerning:
  a. Individual consumer buyer behavior
  b. How firms determine prices
  c. How firms determine products
  d. How firms determine promotion
  e. How firms determine channels of distribution
  f. Case studies of marketing practices
	2. Problems, issues, normative models, and research concerning how firms *should:*
	  a. Determine the marketing mix
	  b. Make pricing decisions
	  c. Make product decisions
	  d. Make promotion decisions
	  e. Make packaging decisions
	  f. Make purchasing decisions
	  g. Make international marketing decisions
	  h. Organize their marketing departments
	  i. Control their marketing efforts
	  j. Plan their marketing strategy
	  k. Apply systems theory to marketing problems
	  l. Manage retail establishments
	  m. Manage wholesale establishments
	  n. Implement the marketing concept

Macro
3. Problems, issues, theories, and research concerning:
  a. Aggregate consumption patterns
  b. The institutional approach to marketing
  c. The commodity approach to marketing
  d. Legal aspects of marketing
  e. Comparative marketing
  f. The efficiency of marketing systems
  g. Whether the poor pay more
  h. Whether marketing spurs or retards economic development
  i. Power and conflict relationships in channels of distribution
  j. Whether marketing functions are universal
  k. Whether the marketing concept is consistent with consumers' interests
	4. Problems, issues, normative models, and research concerning:
	  a. How marketing can be made more efficient
	  b. Whether distribution costs too much
	  c. Whether advertising is socially desirable
	  d. Whether consumer sovereignty is desirable
	  e. Whether stimulating demand is desirable
	  f. Whether the poor should pay more
	  g. What kinds of laws regulating marketing are optimal
	  h. Whether vertical marketing systems are socially desirable
	  i. Whether marketing should have special social responsibilities

Table 1-1 The Three Dichotomies Model of Marketing (continued)

Positive	Normative

Nonprofit sector
Micro
5. Problems, issues, theories, and research concerning:
  a. Consumers' purchasing of public goods
  b. How nonprofit organizations determine prices
  c. How nonprofit organizations determine products
  d. How nonprofit organizations determine promotion
  e. How nonprofit organizations determine channels of distribution
  f. Case studies of public goods marketing
	6. Problems, issues, normative models, and research concerning how nonprofit organizations *should*:
	  a. Determine the marketing mix (social marketing)
	  b. Make pricing decisions
	  c. Make product decisions
	  d. Make promotion decisions
	  e. Make packaging decisions
	  f. Make purchasing decisions
	  g. Make international marketing decisions (e.g., CARE)
	  h. Organize their marketing efforts
	  i. Control their marketing efforts
	  j. Plan their marketing strategy
	  k. Apply systems theory to marketing problems

Macro
7. Problems, issues, theories, and research concerning:
  a. The institutional framework for public goods
  b. Whether television advertising influences elections
  c. Whether public service advertising influences behavior (e.g., Smokey the Bear)
  d. Whether existing distribution systems for public goods are efficient
  e. How public goods are recycled
	8. Problems, issues, normative models, and research concerning:
	  a. Whether society should allow politicians to be "sold" like toothpaste
	  b. Whether the demand for public goods should be stimulated
	  c. Whether "low informational content" political advertising is socially desirable (e.g., 10-second "spot" commercials)
	  d. Whether the U.S. Army should be allowed to advertise for recruits

categorized using the three categorical dichotomies of (1) profit sector/ nonprofit sector, (2) micro/macro, and (3) positive/normative. The three categorical dichotomies yield 2 x 2 x 2 = 8 classes or cells in the schema. Thus, the first class includes all marketing topics that are micro-positive and in the profit sector. Similarly, the second class includes all marketing activities that are micro-normative and in the profit sector, and so on throughout the table. This model of the scope of marketing was first proposed in an article entitled "The Nature and Scope of Marketing." [301] The model has come to be known as the Three Dichotomies Model.

Some definitions are required to properly interpret the schema presented in Table 1-1. *Profit sector* includes the study of organizations or other entities whose stated objectives include the realization of profit. Also included are studies that adopt the *perspective* of profit-oriented organizations. Conversely, *nonprofit sector* includes the study and perspective of all organizations and entities whose stated objectives do not include the realization of profit. *Positive* marketing adopts the perspective of attempting to describe, explain, predict, and understand the marketing activities and phenomena that actually exist. This perspective examines what *is*. In contrast, *normative* marketing adopts the perspective of attempting to prescribe what marketing organizations and individuals ought to do or what kinds of marketing systems a society ought to have. That is, this perspective examines what *ought to be* and what organizations and individuals *ought to do*.

Of the three dichotomies proposed to organize the total scope of marketing, the micro-macro dichotomy is probably the most ambiguous. Drawing upon the distinction between microeconomics and macroeconomics, the original paper distinguished between micromarketing and macromarketing on the basis of aggregation: *micro* referred to the marketing activities of individual units (firms and consumers or households), while *macro* referred to a higher level of aggregation, either marketing systems or groups of consumers. However, as has been pointed out, such topics as "Does marketing have special social responsibilities?" would not fit the macro label on the basis of a level of aggregation criterion. Given that most marketers desire to classify topics similar to the "social responsibilities" issue as *macro*, how should the specification of *macro* be modified?

Some marketers have suggested an "internalities versus externalities" classification. That is, micromarketing focuses on the internal marketing interests of firms; whereas macromarketing focuses on the interests of society with regard to marketing activities. Specified in this way, macromarketing would include such topics as "social responsibilities," efficiency, productivity, and whether "the poor pay more." And this is all to the good. However, the specification would not encompass such topics as the legal aspects of marketing, comparative marketing, and power relationships in channels of distribution. None of these topics necessarily focuses on the "interests of society," yet many marketers would like to include them under the *macro* rubric because the topics are very different from such *micro* topics as "How do (or should) firms determine their advertising budgets?" Therefore, an "interests of society" criterion is not sufficient.

Thus, it would appear that macromarketing is a multidimensional construct and that a complete specification would (should) include the following criteria:

> Macromarketing refers to the study of (1) marketing systems, (2) the impact of marketing systems on society, and (3) the impact of society of marketing systems.

Criterion (1) is a level of aggregation criterion that allows the inclusion of such topics as comparative marketing, the institutional structure of marketing, and power relationships in channels of distribution. Criterion (2) is a generalized "interests of society" criterion that brings in such topics as "social responsibilities" and the role of marketing in economic development. Criterion (3) recognizes that society impacts on marketing and would include such topics as the legal aspects of marketing and the consequences for marketing of different political and social value systems. This is the perspective that has been officially adopted by the *Journal of Macromarketing*. [204a, p. 3]

An examination of Table 1-1 reveals that most of the early (circa 1920) approaches to the study of marketing reside in cell 3, profit sector/macro/positive. The institutional, commodity, and functional approaches analyzed existing (positive) business activities (profit sector) from a marketing systems (macro) perspective. However, not all of the early marketing studies were profit/macro/positive. L.D.H. Weld's 1920 classic, *The Marketing of Farm Products* [631], not only examined existing distribution systems for farm commodities but also attempted to evaluate such normative issues as "Are there too many middlemen in food marketing?"[2] Thus, Weld's signally important work was both profit/macro/positive and profit/macro/normative. Similarly, the Twentieth Century Fund study, *Does Distribution Cost Too Much?* [601], took an essentially profit/macro/normative perspective. Other important works that have combined the profit/macro/positive and the profit/macro/normative perspectives include those of Harold Barger, Reavis Cox, and Neil Borden. [33, 138, 73]

Although the profit/micro/normative (cell 2) orientation to marketing can be traced at least back to the 1920s and the works of such notables as Reed and White [524, 634], the movement reached full bloom in the early 1960s with proponents of the managerial approach to marketing such as McCarthy. [427] The managerial approach adopts the perspective of the marketing manager, usually the marketing manager in a large manufacturing corporation. Therefore, the emphasis is micro and in the profit sector. The basic question underlying the managerial approach is: "What is the optimal marketing mix?" Consequently, the approach is unquestionably normative.

During the middle 1960s, writers such as Lazer, Kelley, Adler, and Fisk [382, 8, 201] began advocating a *systems approach* to marketing.

---

[2] Every generation of marketing students needs to be reminded that hostility to marketing activities and institutions is as ancient as marketing itself. Thus, Plato has Socrates say, "In well-ordered states, [retail traders] are commonly those who are the weakest in bodily strength, and therefore of little use for any other purpose." [498, p. 271]

Sometimes the systems approach used a profit/micro/normative perspective and simply attempted to apply to marketing certain sophisticated optimizing models (such as linear and dynamic programming) developed by the operations researchers. Other writers used the systems approach in a profit/macro/positive fashion to analyze the complex interactions among marketing institutions. Finally, some used the systems approach to include the profit/macro/normative:

> The method used in this book is called the general systems approach. In this approach the goals, organization, inputs, and outputs of marketing are examined to determine how efficient and how effective marketing is. Constraints, including competition and government, are also studied because they affect both the level of efficiency and the kinds of effects obtained. [201, p. 3]

During the late 1960s, the *environmental approach* to marketing was promulgated by writers such as Holloway, Hancock, Scott, and Marks. [277, 278, 570] This approach emphasized an analysis of the environmental constraints on marketing activities. These constraints included consumer behavior, culture, competition, the legal framework, technology, and the institutional framework. Consequently, this approach may be classified as profit/macro/positive.

Two trends are evident in contemporary marketing thought. The first is the trend toward *social marketing* as proposed by Kotler, Levy, and Zaltman [345, 347, 348] and as promulgated by others. [448, 171, 650, 105, 534] Social marketing, with its emphasis on the marketing problems of nonprofit organizations, is nonprofit/micro/normative. The second can be termed the *societal issues* trend. It concerns such diverse topics as consumerism, marketing and ecology, the desirability of political advertising, social responsibility, and whether the demand for public goods should be stimulated. [383, 147, 1, 330, 628, 456, 641, 230, 228, 384] All of these works share the common element of *evaluation*. They attempt to evaluate the desirability or propriety of certain marketing activities or systems and, therefore, should be viewed as either profit/macro/normative or nonprofit/macro/normative.

In 1985, two decades after the Ohio State University position paper, the debate within the American Marketing Association culminated in a new "official" definition: "Marketing is the process of planning and executing the conception, pricing, promotion, and distribution of ideas, goods, and services to create exchanges that satisfy individual and organizational objectives." Although the new definition does not completely satisfy all those who participated in the debate, most agree that it is a substantial improvement over its predecessor. We should note in particular the emphasis on *exchange* and the "broadening" of marketing to include "ideas." Thus, suitably interpreted, the definition accommodates all eight cells of the Three Dichotomies Model.

In conclusion, it is possible to classify all the approaches to the study of marketing and all the topics usually considered within the scope of marketing by using the three categorical dichotomies of profit sector/nonprofit sector, positive/normative, and micro/macro. This does not imply that reasonable people cannot disagree as to which topics should fall within the scope of marketing. Nor does it even imply that reasonable people cannot disagree as to which cell in Table 1-1 is most appropriate for each topic. (For example, the study of the efficiency of marketing systems may have both positive and normative aspects.) Rather, Table 1-1 provides a useful analytical framework, as shall be demonstrated in the next section.

1.3.2   Is Marketing a Science?

The previous discussion on the scope of marketing now enables us to clarify some of the issues with respect to the definition (broadening the concept) of marketing controversy and the "Is marketing a science?" debate. Most marketing practitioners and some marketing academicians perceive the entire scope of marketing to be profit/micro/normative (Cell 2 of Table 1-1). That is, practitioners often perceive the entire domain of marketing to be the analysis and improvement of the decision-making processes of marketers. This perspective is exemplified by the definition of marketing suggested by Canton [104] and, somewhat surprisingly, by the definition proffered by Kotler in the first edition of *Marketing Management:* "Marketing is the analyzing, organizing, planning, and controlling of the firm's customer-impinging resources, policies, and activities with a view to satisfying the needs and wants of chosen customer groups at a profit." [343, p. 12]

Most marketing academicians would chafe at delimiting the proper subject matter of marketing to simply the profit/micro/normative dimensions. Most would, at the very least, include all the phenomena, topics, and issues in the top half of Table 1-1 (that is, Cell 1 through 4). Kotler and others now wish to include in the definition of marketing *all* eight cells in Table 1-1.

Now, returning to the "Is marketing a science?" controversy, the preceding analysis suggests that a primary factor explaining the nature of the controversy is the widely disparate notions of marketing held by the participants. The common element shared by those who hold that marketing is not (and cannot be) a science is the belief that the entire conceptual domain of marketing is Cell 2—profit/micro/normative. Hutchinson clearly exemplifies this position:

> There is a real reason, however, why the field of marketing has been slow to develop a unique body of theory. It is a simple one: marketing is not a science. It is rather an art or a practice, and as such much more closely resembles engineering, medicine, and architecture than it does physics, chemistry, or biology. The medical profession sets us an excellent example, if we would but follow it; its members are called "practitioners" and not scientists. It is the work of physicians, as it is

of any practitioner, to apply the findings of many sciences to the solution of problems. . . . It is the drollest travesty to relate the scientist's search for knowledge to the market research man's seeking after customers. [313]

Note first that Hutchinson confuses problem-solving or *market* research (seeking after customers) with problem-oriented, basic or *marketing* research (expanding the knowledge base of marketing). And no one would deny that the "seeking after customers" is not science. Second, if, as Hutchinson implies, the entire conceptual domain of marketing is profit/micro/normative, then marketing is not and (more importantly) probably *cannot* be a science. However, if the conceptual domain of marketing is expanded to include both micro/positive and macro/positive phenomena, then marketing *could* be a science. That is, if phenomena such as consumer behavior and systems of distribution are included in the conceptual domain of marketing, there is no reason why the study of these phenomena could not be deserving of the designation "science."

Other disciplines, including economics, psychology, sociology, and philosophy, have experienced similar discipline-definitional controversies. It is not at all uncommon for an economist to review a colleague's work and proclaim, "This isn't *really* economics." Several decades ago, a definitional debate raged in philosophy. Some philosophers preferred a narrow approach, confining the philosophy of science to the method of investigating ordinary language systems. Other philosophers, including Karl R. Popper, rebelled at such an emasculation of philosophy of science. Popper noted that all definitions of disciplines were largely arbitrary in content. That is, they primarily represented an agreement to focus attention on some problems, issues, and phenomena, to the exclusion of others. [503, p. 19] Popper believed that to so define philosophy of science would almost, *by definition*, preclude philosophy from making substantive contributions to the total body of scientific knowledge.

Narrowly circumscribing the appropriate subject matter of a discipline can seriously trammel research and other scientific inquiry. Kaplan refers to the problem as "premature closure." [332, p. 70] When some marketers confine their conceptualization of the total scope of marketing to its micro-normative dimensions, they *prematurely close* their thinking and the thinking of others over which they have influence. This may be a particularly pernicious process for marketing because studies which attempt to describe, classify, explain, and predict the micro-positive and macro-positive aspects of marketing will probably do more for the micro-normative dimension of marketing in the long run than will studies that are specifically restricted to micro-normative marketing. As Kaplan has observed, "Tolerance of ambiguity is as important for creativity in science as it is anywhere else." [332, p. 71]

Is marketing a science? Differing perceptions of the scope of marketing have been shown to be a primary factor in the controversy over this question. The second factor contributing to the controversy has been differing perceptions concerning the basic nature of science, a subject that will now occupy our attention.

1.4 THE NATURE OF SCIENCE

The question of whether marketing is a science cannot be adequately answered without a clear understanding of the basic nature of science. So what is a science? Some writers claim that there is nothing which distinguishes science from any other societal institution: "[S]cience is whatever society chooses to call science" [13, p. 26]. This irrationalistic perspective is discussed and evaluated briefly in Section 10.2.2 and more extensively in Hunt [311]. Other writers cite the perspective proposed by Buzzell. A science is:

... a classified and systematized body of knowledge,
... organized around one or more central theories and a number of general principles,
... usually expressed in quantitative terms,
... knowledge which permits the prediction and, under some circumstances, the control of future events. [101, p. 37]

Buzzell then proceeded to note that marketing lacked the requisite theory and principles to be termed a science.

Although the Buzzell perspective on science has much to recommend it, the requirement "organized around one or more central theories" seems overly restrictive. This requirement confuses the successful culmination of scientific efforts with *science itself.* Was the study of chemistry not a science before such discoveries as the periodic table of elements? Analogously, would not a pole-vaulter still be a pole-vaulter even if he could not vault 15 feet? The major purpose of science is to develop laws and theories to explain, predict, understand, and control phenomena. Withholding the label "science" until a discipline has "central theories" would not seem reasonable.

The previous comments notwithstanding, requiring a science to be organized around one or more central theories is not completely without merit. There are strong honorific overtones in labeling a discipline a science. The label often signifies that the discipline has "arrived" in the eyes of other scientists. In large part, the label "science" is conferred upon a discipline only when the discipline has matured enough that it contains several "central theories." Thus, physics achieved the status of a science before psychology, and psychology achieved it before sociology. However, the total conceptual content of the term "science" is decidedly not just honorific. Marketing does not, and should not, have to wait to be knighted by others to be a science. How, then, do sciences differ from other disciplines, if not by virtue of having central theories?

Consider the discipline of chemistry—unquestionably a science. Chemistry can be defined as "the science of substances—their structure, their properties, and the reactions that change them into other substances." [490, p. 15] Using chemistry as an illustration, three observations will enable us to clarify the distinguishing characteristics of sciences. First, a science must have a distinct subject matter, a set of phenomena which serves as a focal point for investigation. The subject matter of chemistry is *substances*, and chemistry attempts to understand, explain, predict, and control phenomena related to substances. Other disciplines, such as physics, are also interested in substances. However, chemistry can meaningfully lay claim to be a separate science because physics does not *focus on* the reactions of substances.

What is the basic subject matter of marketing? Most marketers now perceive the ultimate subject matter of marketing to be the *transaction*. Harking back to the chemistry analogue, marketing might then be viewed as the science of transactions—their structure, their properties, and their reactions with other phenomena. Given this perspective, the subject matter of marketing would certainly overlap with that of other disciplines, notably economics, psychology, and sociology. The analysis of transactions is considered in each of these disciplines. Yet, only in marketing is the transaction the *focal point*. For example, transactions remain a tangential issue in economics, where the primary focus is on the allocation of scarce resources. [385, p. 2] *Therefore, the first distinguishing characteristic is that any science must have a distinct subject matter.* To the extent that the transaction is the basic subject matter of marketing, marketing would seem to fulfill this requirement.

A distinct subject matter alone is not sufficient to distinguish sciences from other disciplines because all disciplines have a subject matter (some less distinct than others). The previously cited perspective of chemistry provides a second insight into the basic nature of science. Note the phrase "their structure, their properties, and their reactions." Every science seeks to describe and classify the structure and properties of its basic subject matter. Likewise, the term *reactions* suggests that the basic subject matter of chemistry is presumed to be systematically interrelated. Thus, the second distinguishing characteristic: *Every science presupposes the existence of underlying uniformities or regularities among the phenomena which comprise its subject matter. The discovery of these underlying uniformities yields empirical regularities, lawlike generalizations, laws, principles, and theories.*

The basic question for marketing is not whether there now exist several central theories that serve to unify, explain, and predict marketing phenomena. Rather, the following should be asked: "Are there underlying uniformities and regularities among the phenomena that constitute the subject matter of marketing?" This question can be answered affirmatively on two grounds—one *a priori* and one empirical. Marketing is a discipline investigating human behavior. Since numerous uniformities and regularities have been observed in other behavioral sciences, there is no *a priori* reason for believing that the subject matter of marketing is devoid of uniformities and regularities. The second ground for believing that the uniformities exist is empirical. In the past three decades, the quantity of scholarly research conducted on marketing phenomena probably exceeds the total of *all* prior research in marketing. Efforts in the consumer behavior dimension of marketing have been particularly prolific. Granted, some of the research has been less than profound, and the total achievements may not be proportionate to the efforts expended. Nevertheless, who can deny that *some* progress has been made or that *some* uniformities have been identified? In short, who can deny that there exist uniformities and regularities in the subject matter of marketing? I, for one, cannot.

The task of delineating the basic nature of science is not yet complete. Up to this point, we have utilized chemistry to illustrate that all sciences involve (1) a distinct subject matter, (2) the description and classification of the subject matter, and (3) the presumption that underlying the subject matter are uniformities and regularities which science seeks to discover. The chemistry example provides a final observation. Note that "chemistry is the *science* of . . ." This suggests that sciences can be differentiated from other disciplines (and pseudo-sciences) by the method of analysis. At the risk of being somewhat tautologous, sciences employ a set of procedures that are commonly referred to as the scientific method. The historical significance of the development and acceptance of the method of science cannot be overstated. The scientific method has been called "the most significant intellectual contribution of western civilization." [453, p. 63] Is the method of science applicable to marketing?

One way of interpreting the entire remainder of Part I of this monograph is to view it as an articulation of the application of the scientific method to marketing, and Part II an examination of its history. Therefore, comments here on the scientific method should be viewed as strictly introductory in nature. One immediate observation is that there is no reason whatsoever to presume that the scientific method of analysis is any less appropriate to marketing than to other disciplines. Similarly, scholarly researchers in marketing, although often holding rather distorted notions concerning such topics as the role of laws and theories in research, seem to be at least as technically proficient as researchers in other areas.

The second observation concerning the scientific method involves the "unity of scientific method controversy." Three questions frame this issue: Is there a single scientific method? Do different sciences require different methods? Are several scientific methods appropriate for the same science? Zaltman states that *the* scientific method is a myth. [647, p. 93] Conversely, Bergman states that "there is one and only one scientific method." [56, p. 164] Similarly, whole volumes have been written on the unity of the scientific method. [472a, 318] The unity of scientific method controversy has far-reaching implications for marketing. In fact, a basic understanding of the foundations of this controversy is an absolute precondition to fully comprehending the rest of this monograph. Consequently, the next section will be devoted to an exposition of this issue. The analysis will draw heavily from the works of Rudner, Salmon, Kyburg, Hempel, and Bergman. [542, 547, 361, 264, 56]

1.5 THE UNITY OF SCIENTIFIC METHOD

The claim is sometimes made that marketing and other social sciences require a scientific method which differs somewhat from the method of the physical sciences. Do the various sciences require different scientific methods? Are there several equally appropriate methods for any particular science? Those who respond affirmatively to these questions support the Multi-Scientific-Method (MSM) thesis. Those who respond negatively support the Single-Scientific-Method (SSM) thesis. Such is the substance of the unity of science issue. Analyzing it requires an appreciation for (1) the differences between the *methodology* of a discipline and the *techniques* of a discipline and (2) the importance of carefully distinguishing between issues in the context of discovery versus issues in the context of justification. (The context of justification is sometimes referred to as the context of validation.)

The techniques of a discipline are the specific tools and apparatus, both conceptual and physical, that researchers in a discipline have found useful in the conduct of inquiry. Marketing uses such devices as consumer panels, questionnaires, pupillometers, Likert scales, multiple regression, multidimensional scaling, surveys, random sampling, and multiple classification analysis. Some of these tools are conceptual, and some are physical. The tools used encompass the *techniques* of marketing research. Chemistry employs test tubes, thermocouples, spectrometers, and cyclotrons. Some techniques, such as strictly experimental research designs, are much more common in the physical sciences than in marketing or most of the social sciences. Unfortunately, many advocates of the MSM thesis point to these differences in techniques to support their position. However, the scientific method is not restricted to certain kinds of hardware (test tubes, cyclotrons, pupillometers), to techniques of gathering data (experiments, surveys), to techniques of measuring phenomena (thermometers, Likert scales), or, most certainly, to techniques of analyzing data (regression, multiple classification analysis, canonical correlation). Astronomy is certainly a science, and yet its techniques are in some respects closer to those of marketing than to those of physics (note the conspicuous lack of laboratory experimentation in astronomy). To the extent that advocates of the MSM thesis rely on these differences in *techniques* for evidential support, their position becomes either (*a*) trivial or (*b*) untenable: trivial, because different sciences obviously use different techniques in research; untenable, because the *techniques* of a science should not be confused with the *methodology* of a science.   What, then, is the methodology of science?

Philosophers of science agree that *the methodology of science is its logic of justification.*   That is, the scientific method consists of the rules and procedures on which a science bases its acceptance or rejection of its body of knowledge, including hypotheses, laws, and theories. [542, p. 5; 547, p. 10; 56, p. 164; 361, p. 5]   To the extent that advocates of the MSM thesis are not simply referring to different techniques, they are really claiming that different sciences have (or should have?) different bases on which to assess the truth content of their disciplines. This, indeed, is a radical claim and one which has been thoroughly discredited. [542, p. 4]   As Hempel has observed:

> The thesis of the methodological unity of science states, first of all, that, notwithstanding many differences in their techniques of investigation, all branches of empirical science test and support their statements in basically the same manner, namely by deriving from them implications that can be checked intersubjectively and by performing for those implications the appropriate experimental or observational tests. This, the unity of method thesis holds, is true also of psychology and the social and historical disciplines. In response to the claim that the scholar in these fields, in contrast to the natural scientists, often must rely on empathy to establish his assertions, logical-empiricist writers stressed that imaginative identification with a given person often may prove a useful heuristic aid to the investigator who seeks to guess at a hypothesis about that person's beliefs, hopes, fears, and goals. But whether or not a hypothesis thus arrived at is factually sound must be determined by reference to objective evidence: the investigator's emphatic experience is logically irrelevant to it. [266, p. 191]

The unity of science stems from the common acceptance by the sciences of a methodology for the justification (confirmation, validation, corroboration) of knowledge. One of the primary objectives of this monograph will be to systematically explore this logic of justification as applied to marketing. That is, we shall explore the basic nature of the scientific understanding, explaining, and predicting of marketing phenomena.   In the process, the unique roles of hypotheses, laws, lawlike generalizations, empirical generalizations, and theories will be developed.

This section began by delineating two rival theses: the Multi-Scientific-Method (MSM) thesis and the Single-Scientific-Method (SSM) thesis. Supporters of the MSM thesis have been shown to often confuse the techniques of a science with its methodology. A second short-coming of the MSM thesis is even more important. *Advocates of the MSM thesis often confuse the context of discovery with the context of justification.*

1.5.1   Discovery Versus Justification

How does one go about discovering scientific hypotheses, laws, and theories? What kinds of tools and procedures will assist the researcher in uncovering them? Are some procedures better than others? Are some procedures correct and others incorrect? Is there a single procedure that is guaranteed to produce results? Should a theory or law be evaluated on the basis of how that theory or law was generated? What was the genesis of Reilly's Law? How did John Howard and Jagdish Sheth create their theory of buyer behavior? All these issues and questions should be considered in the *context of discovery*. If there existed a set of systematic rules and procedures which were optimal for the discovery of hypotheses, laws, and theories, that set of rules and procedures would constitute a *logic of discovery*.

How does one scientifically *explain* marketing phenomena? Can one explain marketing phenomena without being able to *predict* them? What are the roles of laws and theories in explaining and predicting phenomena? Must theories be empirically testable? Are the axioms of a theory assumed to be true? Must theories contain lawlike generalizations? These issues and questions belong in the *context of justification*. As previously noted, the set of rules and procedures that delineate the criteria for accepting or rejecting knowledge (hypotheses, laws, and theories) in science constitutes its *logic of justification*.

Salmon has observed that treating issues that appropriately belong in the context of discovery as if they belong in the context of justification often leads one to commit the "genetic fallacy." Salmon offers the following statement as an extreme illustration of the genetic fallacy: "The Nazis condemned the theory of relativity because Einstein, its originator, was a Jew." [547, p. 12] Obviously, in this extreme example, the fact that Einstein was a Jew should have been ignored in assessing the validity of the theory of relativity. Unfortunately, in the literature of science, dividing issues into discovery and justification is frequently much more difficult and, thus, a trap is laid for the unsuspecting researcher.

Bergman has noted that many philosophers of science, including Hegel and John Dewey, have confused the discovery of scientific knowledge with its justification. [56, p. 51] The confusion of discovery with justification seems widespread in all the sciences, and marketing is no exception. This writer has previously observed that Robert Bartels' "General Theory of Marketing" should perhaps be evaluated in the context of discovery, rather than justification. [296] Similarly, Bartels has offered a metatheory of marketing comprising seven axioms. [40] To what extent are these seven axioms proposed as rules for *discovering* marketing theory, and to what extent are they to be used to *evaluate* marketing theory? Likewise, William Lazer believes that there are two approaches for developing models and theories in marketing— *abstraction* and *realization*. Abstraction begins with "perceptions of marketing situations," whereas realization begins with "theoretical and abstract statements about marketing." [381] Which aspects of these approaches belong in the context of discovery, and which in the context of justification? Similarly, in discussing the scientific method, Zaltman, Pinson, and Angelmar propose a paradigm of the research process composed of the following nine states [647, p. 12]:

1. Assessment of relevant existing knowledge
2. Concept formation and specification of hypotheses
3. Acquisition of meaningful data
4. Organizing and analyzing data in relevant ways
5. Evaluation of and learning from results
6. Dissemination of research information
7. Providing explanations
8. Making predictions
9. Engaging in necessary control activities

The reader should attempt to determine which of these stages should be evaluated in the context of discovery, and which in the context of justification. Hopefully, the chart in Figure 1-1 will be of some assistance.

Figure 1-1 attempts to provide guidance as to which issues are in the context of discovery and which are in the context of justification. The top half of the chart shows four procedures for generating (discovering) empirical generalizations, laws, and theories. These procedures are simply illustrative and by no means exhaust the possibilities. The bottom half details a variety of issues in justification, and again, the issues by no means exhaust the subject. Since the entire remainder of this monograph will be devoted to exploring the issues in the bottom half of Figure 1-1, our attention here will be directed to the top half, that is, the alternative routes to the discovery of scientific knowledge.

One route in Figure 1-1 shows that dreams sometimes play an important role in scientific discovery. Hempel relates the story of how the chemist Kekulé discovered the structure of the benzene molecule:

> He had long been trying unsuccessfully to devise a structural formula for the benzene molecule when, one evening in 1865, he found a solution to his problem while he was dozing in front of his fireplace. Gazing into the flames, he seemed to see atoms dancing in snakelike arrays. Suddenly, one of the snakes formed a ring by seizing hold of its own tail and then whirled mockingly before him. Kekulé awoke in a flash: he had hit upon the now famous and familiar idea of representing the molecular structure of benzene by a hexagonal ring. [264, p. 16]

Similarly, it is claimed that the goddess of Namakkal visited the great Indian mathematician Ramanujan (1887-1920) and revealed mathematical formulas to him. [547, p. 10] Thus, sometimes a dream can prompt a scientific discovery.

Figure 1-1   Discovery versus justification

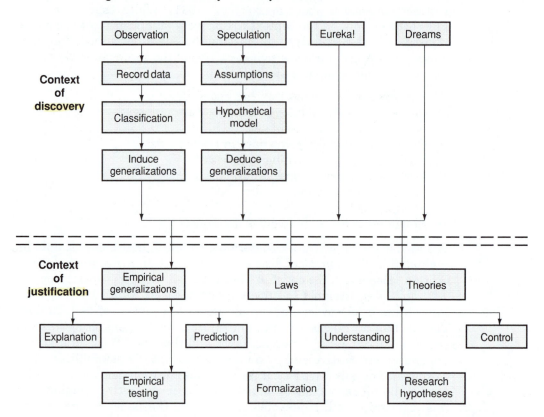

A second path to discovery, the eureka route, can be illustrated by Archimedes' (287-212 B.C.) principle. Supposedly, Archimedes noticed that his bathwater rose in height when he immersed himself. Shouting "Eureka," he proclaimed that any body immersed in a fluid would be "buoyed up" with a force equal to the weight of the displaced fluid. Likewise, schoolchildren are told the story of how Newton discovered the universal law of gravitation when an apple dropped on his head. The point of these examples (fables?) concerning the dream and eureka routes is that serendipity plays a prominent role in scientific discovery. *Many, if not most, major scientific discoveries are flashes of perceptual insight and are not the result of following some rigorously prescribed procedure.*

Consider, now, the first route in Figure 1-1, which starts with *observation*, and the second route, which starts with *speculation*. The first route is a variant of the generalized *inductivist* route, and the second is a form of the generalized *deductivist* route. The deductivist route plays a prominent role in much economic theory, while marketing theoreticians seem to advocate an inductivist route. Thus, McGarry notes that the "scientific method" in marketing involves the four steps of (1) selecting facts, (2) registering these facts, (3) rearranging the facts so as to bring order out of chaos, and (4) finding a formula or conclusion [431]. Similarly, Schwartz observes that "there appears to be no way of avoiding the laborious empirical method in discovering marketing theory." [567, p. 135] Conversely, Fisk notes that "the first step in applying the scientific method is to think of an hypothesis." [202, p. 10] Is the *inductivist* route the preferred procedure for marketing, as many marketing theorists suggest? To answer this question, we must examine more carefully the basic nature of this route.

Let us suppose that a marketing theorist desires to explore phenomena relating to consumer purchase behavior. In particular, let us suppose that the theorist has decided to focus on the phenomenon of brand loyalty as the "dependent" variable. The inductivist route suggests that the first steps for the theorist would be observation and the recording of data. What would the theorist observe? "Everything," the strict inductivist might reply. Yet, we might then point out that observing and recording everything would be impossible because the number of potential phenomena that could be observed and recorded at any point in time is virtually infinite (phase of the moon, height of the tides, temperatures, etc.). The inductivist would probably then become somewhat defensive, chastise us for taking his statement "too literally," and respond, "Of course, you should not observe and record all phenomena! Just observe and record all data *relevant* to the problem of brand loyalty." The reader should attempt to put himself in the place of the bewildered research assistant who has just been instructed to observe and record all data *relevant* to the problem of brand loyalty and ignore all phenomena *irrelevant* to brand loyalty. By what criterion is the research assistant to separate relevant phenomena from the irrelevant variety? The strict inductivist will finally admit that the charge to the research assistant must be to first think of some *a priori* hypotheses concerning which phenomena might be systematically related to brand loyalty and then to make observations and record data *relevant* to those hypotheses. That is, data are never *a priori* relevant or irrelevant to a *problem* such as brand loyalty. Rather, data can only be *a priori* relevant or irrelevant to hypotheses (however crude or tentative) concerning certain phenomena and brand loyalty.

After observation and the recording of data comes the classification stage in the inductivist route. By now the reader should recognize that the appropriate question is, "On what basis should the data be classified?" Again, since the number of ways a set of data can be classified is virtually unlimited, the data must be classified on some basis that is likely to be useful for exploring *a priori* hypotheses. In conclusion, the strict inductivist approach to theory building is untenable, because speculation and the creation of *a priori* hypotheses are absolutely essential parts of any *systematic procedure* of theory discovery and creation. Actual research does not proceed according to the stages suggested by the strict inductivists, and the inductivist route certainly cannot be defended as the *preferred* procedure.

Given the previous analysis of the strict inductivist route for generating theory, why do so many marketing theorists tout its virtues? Perhaps many marketing theorists have reacted (overreacted?) to certain perceived deficiencies in conventional economic theory. Economic theory is perceived to be deductive in nature. Economic theory is also often perceived to be unrealistic and divorced from the real world. As Alderson has noted, "economists have shown a notable preference for elegance over relevance." [10, p. 18] Nevertheless, it is erroneous to believe that the deficiencies of economic theory are to be found in the context of discovery. That is, to the extent that economic theory is deficient, the cause lies not in the economists' deductive procedures for generating theory. Rather, the "received truth" of economic theory must be analyzed and evaluated in the context of justification. To what extent has economic theory been tested and found to accurately depict the real world? These and other questions that are appropriate to the context of justification will be discussed in Chapter 6.

This section began by proposing that advocates of the Multi-Scientific-Method thesis often confuse issues and procedures in the context of discovery with issues and procedures in the context of justification. Proponents of MSM point out the wide variety of "methods" for the discovery of laws and theories in science. We must grant their premise, but not their conclusion. Granted, there exists no single set of procedures that is guaranteed to lead to the discovery of laws and theories. Also, there exists no single set of procedures that can be defended as optimal. *Therefore, there is no single logic of discovery.* Nevertheless, the conclusion that many scientific methods exist does not necessarily follow, because the scientific method concerns the context of justification, not discovery, and *there does exist a single logic of justification which is common to all science.* The reader should clearly recognize the difference between *discovery* and *justification* because we shall be referring to it on numerous occasions throughout this monograph. (See also, the contexts of "acceptance" and "pursuit" in Section 11.1.1.)

1.6   CONCLUSIONS ON MARKETING SCIENCE

The purpose of this introductory chapter has been to detail the objectives of this monograph and to discuss some preliminary issues. The primary objective has been stated to be the utilization of the tool kit of the philosophy of science for systematically exploring some of the basic methodological issues underlying marketing research. The preliminary issues that have been explored have been in the context of the "Is marketing a science?" controversy. In attempting to explore this controversy, we have found it necessary to delve into the basic nature of both marketing and science and to distinguish between methodology and techniques and between discovery and justification. The analysis suggests several conclusions.

The scope of the area called marketing has been shown to be exceptionally broad. Marketing has micro/macro dimensions, profit sector/ nonprofit sector dimensions, and positive/normative dimensions. Reasonable people can disagree as to which combination of these dimensions (refer to the eight cells in Table 1-1) represents the *appropriate* total scope of marketing. If marketing were restricted to the profit/micro/normative dimension (as many practitioners would do), then marketing would not be a science and could not become one. Sciences involve the explanation, prediction, and understanding of phenomena, and, therefore, any discipline which is purely evaluative (normative) is not a science. At least for marketing académe, restricting the scope of marketing to its profit/micro/normative dimension is unrealistic, unnecessary, and, without question, undesirable.

Once the appropriate scope of marketing has been expanded to include at least some *positive* dimensions (Cells 1, 3, 5, and 7 in Table 1-1), then the explanation, prediction, and understanding of these phenomena could be a science. The question then becomes whether the study of the positive dimensions of marketing has the requisite characteristics of a science. Aside from the strictly honorific overtones of *nonmarketers* accepting marketing as a science, the substantive characteristics differentiating sciences from other disciplines have been shown to be (1) a distinct subject matter, (2) the description and classification of the subject matter, (3) the presumption of underlying uniformities and regularities in the subject matter, and (4) the adoption of the method of science for studying the subject matter. The *positive* dimensions of marketing have been shown to have a subject matter properly distinct from that of other sciences. The marketing literature is replete with description and classification. There have been discoveries (however tentative) of uniformities and regularities in marketing phenomena. Finally, although Kenneth Longman deplores "the rather remarkable lack of scientific method employed by scientists of marketing" [399, p. 10], I suggest that marketing researchers are at least as committed to the method of science as are researchers in other disciplines. Therefore, we can conclude that the study of the *positive* dimensions of marketing can be appropriately referred to as *marketing science*.

1.7   THE THREE DICHOTOMIES MODEL: AN EVALUATION

Since its first publication in 1976, the Three Dichotomies Model of Marketing has evoked substantial interest and significant controversy. For a review and analysis of the controversy, see Arndt [21]. Many marketing academicians have expressed views such as "I basically agree with the model except for the following characteristic . . ." This section will address the major "except fors" that have been proposed. Although the positive/normative dichotomy has sparked the most spirited comments, it is fair to say that all aspects of the model have been questioned. And this is as it should be, since models in general are not (a positive observation) and should not be (a normative observation) inscribed in stone for all time.

Although numerous colleagues have volunteered their observations on the Three Dichotomies Model, the "except fors" discussed here have come primarily from the participants at the first Macro-Marketing Conference [542] and from letters to the editor of the *Journal of Marketing* by Donald P. Robin [535, 536] and Michael Etgar [168]. These writers have charged that the positive/normative dichotomy is (1) false, (2) dangerous, (3) unnecessary, (4) meaningless, and (5) useless. Each charge will be discussed, in turn.

1.7.1   Is the Positive/Normative Dichotomy False?

Some writers have suggested that *the positive/normative dichotomy is a false dichotomy because we cannot escape from our own value systems*. This premise is probably true: We probably cannot escape from our value systems. Nevertheless, the premise does not imply that the positive/normative dichotomy is false. To accede to this conclusion would be to capitulate to despair and to commit the "philosophers' fallacy of high redefinition" (see Section 9.6.2).

There is an analogous problem in the discipline of journalism. Journalism stresses *objectivity* in reporting: journalists attempt to keep their personal value systems out of their "news" writing. All knowledgeable people recognize the impossibility of keeping the "news" columns completely free of editorializing. Nevertheless, the goal of separating news from opinion remains one of the ethical pillars of journalism. It does so because the credibility of journalists would be irreparably damaged if they abandoned the *goal of objectivity* simply because they found its complete achievement to be unattainable.

So it is in marketing. Granted, marketing research cannot be value-free. But this does not imply that we should not *attempt* to separate the positive issue of whether marketers perceive themselves as having "social responsibilities" from the normative issue of whether marketers *should* have social responsibilities. Nor does it imply that we should not attempt to clearly separate the issue of whether the poor do in fact "pay more" from the issue of whether it is *wrong* for them to pay more. Nor, finally, does it imply that we should not attempt to separate how managers do in fact make marketing decisions from how they *should* make those decisions. The importance of the positive/normative dichotomy as a goal for clear thinking and analysis is in no way impaired because that goal is, in principle, not completely attainable.

1.7.2   Is the Positive/Normative Dichotomy Dangerous?

A few colleagues have proposed that *the positive/normative dichotomy is dangerous because it may lead people to downgrade the importance of micro/normative marketing.* However, the model does not imply that micro/normative marketing is unimportant or unworthy of attention. On the contrary, the study of how marketing decisions *should* be made is extremely important. To believe otherwise is to grossly misinterpret the model. Unquestionably, some people, now that they have a taxonomic schema showing the various dimensions of marketing, may choose to de-emphasize micro/normative marketing. Further, this de-emphasis *may have* unfortunate consequences. Nevertheless, many marketers *still* consider the entire scope of marketing to be its micro-normative dimension, and this *has had* demonstrably unfortunate consequences.

The positive/normative dichotomy puts micro/normative marketing "in its place." It does not imply that "place" is unimportant. The potential advantages of awakening people to the fact that there are dimensions to marketing *beyond* the micro/normative dimension greatly outweigh any possible dangers of downgrading the importance of micro/normative marketing.

1.7.3   Is the Positive/Normative Dichotomy Unnecessary?

Robin [535, p. 136] charges that *the positive/normative dichotomy is "unnecessary" for considering the "Is marketing a science?" controversy because "using scientific explanation in marketing simply requires that the normative statements be used as antecedent conditions."* To illustrate his point of using normative statements in scientific explanations, Robin offers the following "explanation" as an example:

Antecedent conditions

C_1 = Long-run profit maximization is the primary objective of the organization.

C_2 = One or more competitors of approximately equal economic strength exist in the market.

C_3 = The organization has the opportunity of offering several different variations of a new product, at varying prices, with different promotional possibilities, and through a variety of channels.

C_4 = The products of the firm are such that buyers can adequately determine their value (functional and/or psychological).

Generally accepted propositions

L_1 = Strong competitors can and will produce products desired by buyers if a large enough number desire them.

L_2 = Buyers purchase goods in a manner that they perceive to be in their best interest at the time of the purchase.

Thus:

Given C_1, C_2, C_3, C_4, L_1, and L_2, the firm must organize the controllable variables available to it (i.e., the marketing mix) so as to develop and maintain a satisfied group of buyers.

Robin concludes, "It should be noted that the antecedent condition C_1 represents an assumed organizational objective which is, as previously explained, a *normative judgment*." [535, p. 138]

Is the positive/normative dichotomy unnecessary? Do normative statements play a role in scientific explanation? To evaluate these questions, we must refer to the meaning of *positive statements* versus *normative statements*. Recall that the positive/normative dichotomy provides categories based on whether the focus of the analysis is primarily descriptive or prescriptive. Positive marketing adopts the perspective of attempting to describe, explain, predict, and understand the marketing activities, processes, and phenomena that actually exist. This perspective examines *what is*. In contrast, normative marketing adopts the perspective of attempting to prescribe what marketing organizations and individuals ought to do or what kinds of marketing systems a society ought to have. That is, this perspective examines what *ought to be* and what organizations and individuals *ought to do*. Thus, one signal (but not the *only* one) of a normative statement is the existence of an *ought* or *should* or some similar term.

Returning to Robin's "explanation," are there any normative statements? In particular, is C_1 normative, as Robin indicates? Clearly, it is a *positive* statement, not a normative one. C_1 states that "long-run profit maximization is the primary objective of the organization." If C_1 were normative, it would state, "Long-run profit maximization *ought to be* the primary objective of the organization." As a matter of fact, there are *no* normative statements in Robin's "explanation." Note that C_2 states that "competitors of approximately equal economic strength *exist*," not that they "ought to exist." Further, C_3 and C_4 state that "the organization *has*" and that "products of the firm *are*"—both are positive statements.

There are no normative statements in Robin's "explanation" precisely because (as Robin himself points out) in scientific explanation "the explanandum [the statement to be explained] must be logically derivable from the explanans [the statements doing the explaining]." And any statement with an "ought" *cannot* be an antecedent condition in a logically valid scientific explanation. Thus, far from showing that the positive/normative dichotomy is *unnecessary*, Robin's "explanation" gives powerful justification for considering the dichotomy to be *necessary*.

1.7.4   Is the Positive/Normative Dichotomy Meaningless?

Robin [535, p. 136] also suggests that *the positive/normative dichotomy is "meaningless" because the information derived from a positive "study is of little interest unless it is given prescriptive overtones. . . . That is, the positive issues are barren except where they have prescriptive implications."* We can begin our analysis of this comment by asking: To *whom* are positive studies "of little interest" unless there are prescriptive implications? Is it to the marketing manager? Are all positive studies "barren" unless they provide immediate guidance as to how the marketing manager can make better decisions? This seems to be the "meaningfulness" criterion that Robin is proposing.

No one would dispute that much of the positive study in marketing has managerial implications. There is no doubt that the explanations and predictions from positive studies frequently serve as useful guides for developing normative decision rules and normative models. However, the view that all positive studies are "meaningless" unless they assist the marketing manager is exactly the kind of narrow perception of the scope of marketing that has for so long caused so much mischief in our discipline. The discipline of marketing does not exist solely and exclusively to serve the needs of the marketing manager, just as the discipline of psychology does not exist solely to serve the needs of the clinical psychologist. Research in marketing has many aims. Fortunately, the American Marketing Association now specifically acknowledges that there are numerous "constituencies" for marketing research. The A.M.A. Task Force on the Development of Marketing Thought identified five such groups: academicians (including students), managers, public policy members, special interest groups, and consumers. [452]

The prime directive for scholarly research is the same for marketing as for all sciences: *to seek knowledge*. The knowledge must be inter-subjectively certifiable and capable of describing, explaining, and predicting phenomena. At some times, the knowledge may assist marketing managers in making decisions. At other times, the knowledge may guide legislators in drafting laws to regulate marketing activities.

At still other times, the knowledge may assist the general public in understanding the functions that marketing activities perform for society. Finally, at the risk of "waxing philosophical," the knowledge may simply assist marketing scholars in *knowing*, a not inconsequential objective.

1.7.5   Is the Positive/Normative Dichotomy Useless?

In a restatement of his position, Robin agrees that "normative statements are not part of scientific explanatory models." [536, p. 6] Nevertheless, he still concludes that *"any attempt to classify marketing phenomena on the basis of a positive/normative dichotomy will lead either to confusion or a useless set of relationships."* His conclusion is based in part on the observation that the positive and normative "parts of our world are so inseparably intermingled." Robin in this case seems to be echoing Etgar's observation that "Hunt's classification fails to pass a major test by which categorical schemes should [please note: normative statement] be judged: namely, self-exclusivity—the principle that under a specific classificatory scheme such as normative/positive, a given phenomenon should be classified as falling into one category only." [168, p. 146]

Is lack of self-exclusivity a fatal flaw? I think not. First of all, it is unnecessary to concede the *positive* issue of whether the P/N dichotomy is completely lacking in self-exclusivity. Many studies in marketing are either overwhelmingly positive (such as descriptive analyses of the channels of distribution for farm products) or overwhelmingly normative (such as models for the optimal allocation of media expenditures). Thus, it is clear that the classification in the model of many, if not most, marketing studies and phenomena is not in doubt; and this is all that is required for a taxonomic schema to be viable. [623, p. 16]

Second it is unnecessary to concede the *normative* issue of whether lack of self-exclusivity would render the P/N dichotomy "useless." Many useful classificational schemata lack self-exclusivity. For example, most universities evaluate their faculties on the dimensions of teaching, research, and service. Please note that these dimensions are closely related; some would even believe them to be "inseparably intermingled." Research activities often carry over into teaching and service activities. Likewise, teaching activities impact on research and service. Is this a "fatal flow" of the teaching/research/service trichotomy, making it "useless"? Since normative economics is not independent of positive economics, should all economic thought be lumped into one side? Certainly, economists think not. [213] So it is with the positive/normative dichotomy in marketing. The positive dimensions impact on the normative dimensions. The normative dimensions impact on the positive dimensions. The results are synergistic and thus useful to the discipline of marketing.

1.8   THE THREE DICHOTOMIES MODEL AS A GENERAL PARADIGM FOR MARKETING

All disciplines must have general paradigms. These paradigms represent a loose consensus among the participants in a discipline concerning its fundamental nature. Among other things, the general paradigm of a discipline plays a central role in guiding the research efforts of scholars. Some of these general paradigms are *taxonomical* in nature. (This is one of the many uses of the term "paradigm," as will be discussed in Section 10.2.1.)

The Three Dichotomies Model of Marketing would seem to be a general paradigm that could help resolve some of the critical problems in marketing. The paradigm is (1) properly inclusive, (2) analytically useful, (3) pedagogically sound, and (4) conceptually robust. The paradigm is *inclusive* and healing rather than *exclusive* and divisive. It succeeds in including within the scope of marketing a wide range of perceptions. Those who view marketing with a traditional *managerial* perspective have a "home" in the profit sector/micro/normative cell. Those who prefer a "broadened" perspective have the nonprofit half of the model. Those, like Dawson, who wish to have more attention paid to the societal impact of marketing have the macro-positive and macro-normative cells. Finally, those who desire to focus their attention on the science of marketing have the micro/positive and macro/positive cells. As can be noted, the Three Dichotomies paradigm brings the various perspectives of marketing *together* rather than attempting to *exclude* people with pejorative statements such as "What you are interested in is not *really* marketing." The model recognizes that marketers are a diverse group with different perspectives, different "homes," and *different contributions to make.*

The Three Dichotomies paradigm of marketing is *analytically useful.* It has been used to analyze the various approaches to the study of marketing: the functional, commodity, institutional, managerial, systems, and environmental approaches. The paradigm has also been used to explore the "broadening of the concept of marketing" debate. Finally, the paradigm has been instrumental in resolving the "Is marketing a science?" controversy.

The Three Dichotomies model is *pedagogically sound:* It is useful as a teaching device. Students can readily understand the model. They are familiar with the micro/macro dichotomy from economics, and the profit sector/nonprofit sector dichotomy is straightforward. Only the positive/normative dichotomy is outside the average business student's vocabulary and requires substantial elaboration. Distressingly, many beginning business students, both at the bachelor's and master's levels, perceive marketing to be exclusively advertising and personal selling. Salutary effects on students' views of marketing can be generated by demonstrating the broad scope of marketing with the aid of the model.

Finally, the Three Dichotomies paradigm is *conceptually robust*. The preceding sections have been devoted to analyzing and evaluating various comments and observations concerning specific aspects of the model. The paradigm has absorbed the blows with surprisingly little damage. Although the ultimate test of both its conceptual robustness and its desirability as a general paradigm for marketing is *time*, the performance of the model to date warrants optimism.

1.9   PLAN OF MONOGRAPH

The plan or organization of a monograph is second in importance only to its content. The organization of Part I of this monograph posed a dilemma. In order to truly comprehend the nature of laws and theories in marketing, one must first understand and appreciate their usefulness in explaining and predicting marketing phenomena. However, in order to understand the problem of scientific explanation, one must first comprehend the nature of laws and theories. The dilemma parallels the micro/macro teaching problem in economics. Should microeconomics be taught before macroeconomics, or vice versa? This book discusses explanation before laws and theories, on the ground that it is sometimes desirable to demonstrate the usefulness of concepts, such as laws and theories, before delving into their basic nature. However, the chapters on laws and theories are relatively self-contained, and readers may, at their discretion, start with the latter chapters first.

Chapter 2 explores the morphology of scientific explanation. That is, how does one go about *explaining* marketing phenomena? Various explanatory models are developed, including the deductive-nomological, deductive-statistical, inductive-statistical, pattern, and functionalist models. Chapter 3 discusses some issues in explanation, such as the relationships among explanation, prediction, and causation. Marketing explanations, such as the product life cycle and consumer behavior, are then analyzed. Chapter 4 investigates the nature of laws in marketing and evaluates the four criteria for lawlike generalizations—generalized conditionals, empirical content, nomic necessity, and systematic integration. Chapter 5 delineates the characteristics of the various kinds of laws: equilibrium laws, laws of atemporal coexistence, laws of succession, process laws, axioms, fundamental laws, derivative laws, bridge laws, statistical laws, and universal laws. Chapter 6 begins by noting some misconceptions concerning the nature of theory. A perspective on theory is presented, and the three major criteria for theories are detailed. These criteria reveal that theories must (1) contain systematically related sets of statements, (2) contain some lawlike generalizations, and (3) be empirically testable. Chapter 7 examines the role of classification in theory development, contrasts positive theory with normative theory, and explores whether deterministic theory in marketing is possible.

APPENDIX, CHAPTER 1
MARKETING RESEARCH:
PROXIMATE PURPOSE AND
ULTIMATE VALUE

By: **Shelby D. Hunt**
Paul Whitfield Horn Professor of Marketing
Texas Tech University

INTRODUCTION

Historically, the American Marketing Association has defined marketing research as the "systematic gathering, recording, and analyzing of data about problems relating to the marketing of goods and services" (American Marketing Association 1961). Recently the Board of Directors of the AMA approved the following definition:

> Marketing research is the function which links the consumer, customer, and public to the marketer through information—information used to identify and define marketing opportunities and problems; generate, refine, and evaluate marketing actions; monitor marketing performance; and improve understanding of marketing as a proc-

ess. Marketing research specifies the information required to address these issues; designs the method for collecting the information; manages and implements the data collection process; analyzes the results; and communicates the findings and their implications.

Several academic members of the Board of Directors voted against the definition, believing it to be too managerial in orientation.

Definitions are "rules of replacement" (Hempel 1970, p. 654). That is, a definition means that a word or group of words (the definiens) is proposed to be truth-functionally equivalent to the word being defined (the definiendum). *Good* definitions exhibit inclusivity, exclusivity, differentiability, clarity, communicability, consistency and parsimony.

The purpose of the present paper is to explore the *inclusivity* of the AMA

Source: Reprinted by permission from *Marketing Theory*, eds., Russell W. Belk, *et al.*, Chicago: American Marketing Association, 1987, pp. 209-213.

definition of marketing research. That is, to what extent does the definition *include* all the activities and phenomena that marketers would *want* to be labeled "marketing research"? In doing so we shall generate six prototypical research questions in marketing, examine the characteristics of these research questions, and inquire whether research conducted about these questions would be properly called "marketing research" under the new definition. Hopefully, such a procedure will shed light on whether the new definition is properly inclusive.

RESEARCH QUESTIONS IN MARKETING

Table 1 displays six prototypical research questions that researchers commonly explore when they contend they are doing "marketing research." Although each question examines the same substantive area (advertising), the kinds of research projects designed to explore these questions will vary greatly. The table categorizes each research question according to the "Three Dichotomies Model" (Hunt 1976) and (1) identifies whether such research is primarily conducted by practitioners or academicians, (2) indicates whether such research would be publishable, (3) states the proximate (immediate) purpose or objective of the research, (4) shows the ultimate potential value or consequences (intended or unintended) of the research, and (5) indicates whether the research would be considered "marketing research" under the new AMA definition.

Research Question One

The first research question asks, *"How should the Jones Toy Co. allocate its advertising budget amongst the various media to reach its primary target market, children under 12 years of age?"* A research project addressing this question would be profit/micro/normative, since it takes the perspective of an individual firm and attempts to provide specific guidance for its marketing problem. Academicians in their consulting activities sometimes develop research projects to answer this kind of question. However, the overwhelming majority of these projects are done by practitioners, be they "in-house" marketing researchers or those in marketing research agencies. This kind of project has been called "market" research by Hunt (1976), "problem-solving" research by Myers, Massy and Greyser (1980), and "applied" research by countless others.

The results of a research project directed at question one would in general not be publishable in journals like the *Journal of Marketing* or the *Journal of Marketing Research*. These journals have adopted the value system of scholarly journals, requiring all accepted manuscripts to make some new contribution to marketing knowledge that is *generalizable* to some extent. Therefore, research projects that simply *apply* existing marketing knowledge to the solution of a firm's problem would be unacceptable.

In researching question one, the immediate objective of the researcher is to help the manager make a better decision, thereby increasing the firm's efficiency through a better allocation of scarce resources. However, the consequences do not necessarily stop there. Society also benefits since individual firm efficiency can lead to greater efficiency for society as a whole.

A research project designed to explore question one would obviously fit comfortably within the AMA

Appendix Table　Prototypical Research Questions in Marketing

Research Question	Category[a]	Primary Researchers[b]	Publication of Knowledge[c]	Proximate Purpose[d]	Ultimate Potential Value	Consistency with AMA Definition
1. How should the Jones Toy Co. allocate its advertising budget among the various media to reach its primary target market, children under 12 years of age?	Profit/micro/normative	Practitioners	No	Better decisions for a firm	Firm efficiency Societal efficiency	Yes
2. How should firms *in general* allocate their advertising budgets among the various media in an optimal fashion?	Profit/micro/normative	Academicians	Yes	Better decisions for firms in general	Firm efficiency Societal efficiency	No
3. To what extent does television advertising in general shape children's beliefs about products and consumption?	Profit/micro/positive or Profit/macro/positive	Academicians	Yes	K.f.K.S.[e]	Firm efficiency Societal efficiency Better public policy Better informed citizenry	No
4. To what extent is television's shaping of children's beliefs about products and consumption injurious to society?	Profit/macro/normative	Academicians	Yes	K.f.K.S.[e]	Socially responsible firms Better public policy Better informed citizenry	No
5. To what extent should the federal government restrict or regulate the amount or content of advertising directed at children?	Profit/macro/normative	Academicians	Yes	Better public policy	Better public policy	No
6. What are the best research methods to explore questions one through five?	Not applicable	Academicians	Yes	Better research	Firm efficiency Societal efficiency Socially responsible firms Better public policy Better informed citizenry	No

[a]Using the "Three Dichotomies Model," (Hunt 1976).

[b]Emphasis on "primary." That is, it is recognized that on occasion both practitioners and academicians conduct all kinds of research.

[c]In scholarly journals such as the *Journal of Marketing* and the *Journal of Marketing Research.*

[d]The immediate objective of the inquiry.

[e]"Knowledge for Knowledge's Sake."

definition. This is the type of research that is routinely and regularly conducted by corporate marketing research departments and marketing research agencies. What might surprise some people is the fact that this is precisely the kind of marketing research project that is most often conducted by marketing academicians.

There are no accurate figures on the total number of marketing professors in the United States. Nevertheless, given that there are 1,288 four-year institutions offering bachelor's degrees in business and 626 such institutions offering a major in marketing, an estimate of 5,000 marketing academicians in four-year institutions would not seem unreasonable (*Peterson's Annual Guide to Undergraduate Study* 1986). Again, although no "hard" numbers are available, probably 90% of the 5,000 marketing academicians (to the extent that they do research at all) do almost *exclusively* these kinds of "consulting" research projects. Many marketers, both practitioners and academicians, seem to believe that the remaining 10% should *also* focus exclusively on consulting research. Put another way, to what extent should *any* marketing academician explore research questions similar to the following five, and to what extent should such projects be considered "marketing research"?

Research Question Two

The second research question asks, *"How should firms in general allocate their advertising budgets among the various media in an optimal fashion?"* Like research question one, question two is also profit/micro/normative. However, question two calls for

research that attempts to generate a procedure or model to solve a particular *class* of marketing problem. The procedure or method would presumably be applicable across many firms in many different contexts. Such context-free research is conducted primarily by academicians. To the extent that practitioners conduct these kinds of projects, the results of such studies are generally held to be proprietary in nature and not disseminated to the larger marketing community.

Unlike research projects directed toward question one that focus on a particular firm, projects directed at question two attempt to improve the decision making of firms *in general* in a particular decision area. Like question one, the ultimate consequences are higher levels of efficiency for both firms and society. Given that the procedure or model developed by the researcher makes a significant "enough" contribution to marketing knowledge and is perceived to be generalizable across contexts, the results of such a project would be potentially publishable in *JM* and/or *JMR*.

Research projects directed at addressing questions such as question two are what Myers, Massy, and Greyser call "problem-oriented" research (1980). Consistent with the objectives of the Marketing Science Institute, they recommend that marketing academicians focus more of their attention on these kinds of research projects. On the other hand, writers such as Anderson (1983) and Arndt (1985) believe that academic marketing researchers spend too much of their time working on "problem-oriented" research and that too much of our journal space is devoted to reporting the results of such projects. Curiously, the proposed AMA definition of marketing research would seem to exclude research projects directed at these kinds of questions from being considered "marketing" research. This anomaly would appear to be either an error of interpretation on my part or a gross oversight on the part of the definitions committee.

Research Question Three

The third research question asks, *"To what extent does television advertising in general shape children's beliefs about products and consumption?"* Research projects directed at this question would be either profit/micro/positive or profit/macro/positive, depending on the nature of the specific research design. Such projects are almost exclusively the province of academicians and would be considered "basic" marketing research (Meyers, Massy, and Greyser 1980) or "pure" consumer research (Holbrook 1986). The results of such research projects would be potentially acceptable for publication in *JM, JMR* and the *Journal of Consumer Research*.

The proximate purpose of such "basic" research projects is "knowledge for knowledge's sake." Ultimately, the results of such projects might be useful in guiding decision-makers in their efforts to determine the "best" solutions to research questions like one and two, thus impacting on firm and societal efficiency. Likewise, such research efforts might be useful to government officials in their efforts to develop better public policy. (Please note that better public policy may also be in the best interests of firms). Finally, the results of such research projects may simply result in a "better informed citizenry."

Marketing practitioners routinely decry the emphasis on basic research

projects (like number two) by marketing academicians, and this negative attitude toward such research may be responsible for the apparent exclusion of such research projects from the official AMA definition. Many marketing academicians share the practitioners' disdain for any research that does not have a predictable, observable, relatively direct benefit to marketing management (Enis 1986, Parasuraman 1982, Peters 1980, Westing 1979). For example, Meyers, Massy, and Greyser propose that "although much basic research in marketing is generated for 'its own sake,' the Commission's view was that if marketing knowledge over the long run is to be considered 'effective,' it should contribute something to improved decision making or other aspects of marketing management practice in the industrial sector" (1980, p. 145). Similarly, Parasuraman contends that "the *raison d'etre* for any marketing theory is its potential application in marketing practice" (1982, p. 78).

Needless to say, there have always been academicians (and practitioners) advocating the legitimacy and desirability of basic research in marketing. The *Journal of Marketing* in its first few decades published *primarily* basic research. In fact, the very first article in the very first issue of *JM* examined whether the interests of the consumer were being well served by the Agricultural Adjustment Administration (Anderson 1936). Over a decade ago, Levy called for splitting the "basic" side of marketing from its "applied" side, referring to the former as "marcology" (1976). More recently, Anderson has called for more basic research, pointing out that "it is clear that marketing must be more concerned with the pursuit of knowledge as knowledge" (1983,

p. 27).   My own position on this issue was stated in 1978:

> The prime directive for scholarly research in marketing is the same as for all sciences: *to seek knowledge.* The knowledge must be intersubjectively certifiable and capable of describing, explaining, and predicting phenomena. Sometimes the knowledge will assist the managers in making decisions. Other times the knowledge will guide legislators in drafting laws to regulate marketing activities. At still other times the knowledge may assist the general public in understanding the functions that marketing activities provide society. Finally, at the risk of "waxing philosophical," *the knowledge may simply assist marketing scholars in knowing,* a not inconsequential objective (1978, p. 109).

Most interestingly, while the Definitions Committee of the AMA was busy drafting a definition of marketing research that excluded basic research efforts, another committee of AMA was specifically recognizing the legitimacy of such research. The special task force on the development of marketing thought noted that research in marketing has many "clients" and identified the following five "audiences of marketing knowledge" (Monroe, *et al.* 1986, p. 8):

1. managers of enterprises ("practitioners")
2. educators/teachers, scholars and students
3. public policy makers
4. special interest groups (includes hostile groups such as consumer interest groups, as well as supportive groups)
5. consumers (all of us)

As with many large institutions, the "left hand" seems oblivious of the "right".

Research Question Four

The fourth research question asks, *"To what extent is television's shaping of children's beliefs about products and consumption injurious to society?"* Research projects directed at this question would be profit/macro/normative, conducted almost entirely by academicians, and publishable in journals such as *JM* and, more recently, the *Journal of Macromarketing.*

Research projects directed at answering this question are pursued "for the sake of knowledge." Some commentators contend that the knowledge generated by such a project should not influence marketing management decisions (Friedman 1970, Levitt 1958). Others believe that such information should be used by "socially responsible" managers (Gray 1968, Morell 1956). In any respect, such knowledge might result in better public policy and, of course, a better informed citizenry. Although "better public policy" would seem to be in the best interests of *all* marketing practitioners, and socially responsible decisions are definitely an objective of at least *some* (Wood, Chonko, and Hunt 1986), this kind of research project would, again, not be "marketing" research under the new definition.

Research Question Five

The fifth research question asks, *"To what extent should the federal government restrict or regulate the amount or content of advertising directed at children?"* Efforts directed at answering this question would be categorized as profit/macro/normative, conducted almost exclusively by academicians, and would be potentially publishable in the *Journal of Marketing,* the *Journal of Macromarketing,* and the *Journal of Public Policy and Marketing.*

The proximate purpose of research conducted here would be the same as its ultimate value: better public policy. Please note that such research efforts could be significantly informed by the results of projects designed to answer questions three and four. Also, this kind of research would not be, officially, "marketing research" according to the definition.

Research Question Six

The sixth research question asks, *"What are the best research methods to explore questions one through five?"* Research directed at this question cannot be classified within the Three Dichotomies Model because it is a *substantive*, rather than a *methodological*, model. Research efforts dealing with methodological issues on a fundamental or philosophical level (such as modern empiricism vs. relativism) would potentially be publishable in the *Journal of Marketing*. Similarly, research efforts on research techniques (such as factor analysis, multidimensional scaling, etc.) would potentially be publishable in the *Journal of Marketing Research*. Historically, the *Journal of Marketing Research* has devoted between fifty percent and sixty percent of its pages to the development of better marketing research techniques. The emphasis on "esoteric" research techniques has been criticized by many practitioners and academicians. For example, Arndt (1985) has claimed our discipline suffers from "instrumentitis."

The proximate purpose of methodological research efforts is "better" research on *all* marketing research problems. To the extent that "better" methods are used in the conduct of marketing research, all the clients of

marketing knowledge are better served. Nevertheless, research on methodological issues would appear not to be "marketing" research as per the definition.

CONCLUSION

Is the new AMA definition of marketing research *properly* inclusive? Quite obviously, the definition specifically addresses only one of the preceding prototypical marketing research questions, i.e., research directed at solving a specific firm's marketing problem. Research directed at providing new knowledge for solving general *classes* of marketing management problems, or for providing *basic* knowledge that might be *ultimately* useful in solving marketing management problems, or for informing public-policy decisions, or for addressing the interests of society in having a well-informed citizenry, do not seem to find a "home" within the new definition.

For the purposes at hand, *I personally believe the new definition is in fact properly inclusive.* It seems to me that the definition was never meant to be a good definition of marketing research in all its aspects. Rather, the purpose of the definition was to articulate for students and the public at large what practitioner marketing researchers actually do (or ought to do) in corporate and agency research organizations. This is quite clearly the case when words like "the function" are used in the definition.

Rather than changing the *definiens* to make it include a broader array of research issues under the rubric of marketing research, it would be simpler and just as appropriate to change the definiendum. That is, rather than change the *definition*, we should delimit the construct being *defined*. We should clearly state that we are defining marketing research of the "problem-solving" or "applied" variety. Changing the first part of the first sentence in the definition to read: "Marketing research is the function *within the firm* that links the consumer ..." would succinctly accomplish this objective.

Definitional issues aside, our discussion implicitly raises numerous fundamental questions about research in the marketing academic discipline. To what extent should marketing academicians focus exclusively on consulting research (should the ten percent join the ninety percent)? To what extent should more marketing academicians be encouraged to conduct scholarly research (should the ninety percent be encouraged to join the ten percent)? What are the institutional mechanisms that encourage/discourage research of a consulting/scholarly nature? Should specific institutional mechanisms be developed to encourage/discourage more research of a consulting/scholarly nature?

My own views on the preceding questions are that marketing academicians should not do just consulting research—the ten percent should not join the ninety percent. Rather, we should encourage more scholarly research—the 90 percent should be encouraged to become more professionally active in scholarly activities. It seems to me that there are numerous institutional mechanisms that tend to encourage consulting research and discourage scholarly research and that changes in these institutional mechanisms would be desirable from the perspective of both marketing practitioners and academicians, alike. The myopic view of the American Marketing Association's definition of marketing research represents a small, but potentially significant, institutional mechanism discouraging scholarly marketing research. Must forward progress in a discipline *always* be preceded by first stepping backward?

REFERENCES

Anderson, Don S. (1936), "The Consumer and the A.A.A.," *Journal of Marketing*, 1 (July), 3-8.

Anderson, Paul F. (1983), "Marketing, Scientific Progress, and Scientific Method," *Journal of Marketing*, 47 (Fall), 18-31.

Arndt, Johan (1985), "On Making Marketing Science More Scientific: Roles of Orientation, Paradigms, Metaphors, and Puzzle Solving," Journal of Marketing, 49 (Summer), 11-23.

Enis, Ben M. (1986), "Comments on Marketing Education in the 1980's and Beyond: The Rigor/Relevance Rift," in *Marketing Education: Knowledge Development, Dissemination, and Utilization*, Joseph Guiltinan and Dale Achabal, eds., Chicago: American Marketing Association, 1-4.

Friedman, Milton (1970), "The Social Responsibility of Business Is to Increase Its Profits," *The New York Times Magazine*, September 13, 658-669.

Gray, Elisha (1968), "Changing Values in the Business Society," *Business Horizons*, 11 (August), 26.

Hempel, Carl G. (1975), "Fundamentals of Concept Formation in Empirical Science," in *Foundations of the Unity of Science,* Vol. 2, Otto Neurath, Rudolf Carnap, and Charles Morris, eds., Chicago: University of Chicago Press, 651-745.

Holbrook, Morris B. (1986), "The Place of Marketing Research on the Business-Research Continuum," in *Marketing Education: Knowledge Development, Dissemination, and Utilization,* Joseph Guiltinan and Dale Achabal eds., Chicago: American Marketing Association, 11-15.

Hunt, Shelby D. (1976), "The Nature and Scope of Marketing," *Journal of Marketing,* 40 (July), 17-28.

_____ (1978), "A General Paradigm of Marketing: In Support of the Three Dichotomies Model," *Journal of Marketing,* 42 (April), 107-110.

Levitt, Theodore (1958), "The Dangers of Social Responsibility," *Harvard Business Review,* 36 (September-October), 41-50.

Levy, Sid (1976), "Marcology 101 or the Domain of Marketing" in *Marketing: 1776-1976 and Beyond,* Kenneth L. Bernhardt, ed., Chicago: American Marketing Association, 577-581.

Maiken, Jeffrey M., John G. Myers, William H. Peters, George Schwartz, and J. Howard Westing (1979), "What is the Appropriate Orientation for the Marketing Academican?" in *Conceptual and Theoretical Developments in Marketing,* O. C. Ferrell, Stephen W. Brown, and Charles W. Comb, eds., Chicago: American Marketing Association, 49-75.

Monroe, Kent B., William C. Wilkie, Linda J. McAleer, and Albert R. Wildt (1986), "Report of the AMA Task Force on the Development of Marketing Thought," in *Marketing Education: Knowledge Development, Dissemination, and Utilization,* Joseph Guiltinan and Dale Achabal, eds., Chicago: American Marketing Association, 8-9.

Morrell, Ben (1956), *The Role of American Business in Social Progress,* Indianapolis: Clarendon Press.

Myers, John G., Stephen A. Greyser, and William F. Massy (1980), *Marketing Research and Knowledge Development: An Assessment for Marketing Management,* Englewood Cliffs, N.J.: Prentice Hall.

Parasuraman, A. (1982), "Is a 'Scientist' versus 'Technologist' Research Orientation Conducive to Marketing Theory Development?" in *Marketing Theories: Philosophy of Science Perspectives,* Ronald A. Bush and Shelby D. Hunt, eds., Chicago: American Marketing Association, 78-79.

Peters, William H. (1980), "The Marketing Professor-Practitioner Gap: A Possible Solution," *Journal of Marketing Education,* Fall, 4-11.

Peterson's Annual Guide to Undergraduate Study: Four Year College (1986), Princeton, New Jersey: Peterson's Guides.

Report of Definitions Committee of the American Marketing Association (1961), Chicago: American Marketing Association.

Wood, Van R., Lawrence B. Chonko, and Shelby D. Hunt (1986), "Social Responsibility and Personal Success: Are They Compatible?" *Journal of Business Research,* 14, 193-212.

Westing, J. Howard (1979), Comments in "What is the Appropriate Orientation for the Marketing Academician?: A panel discussion," originally appearing in *Conceptual and Theoretical Developments in Marketing,* ed., O. C. Farrell, Stephen W. Brown, and Charles W. Lamb, Jr., Chicago: American Marketing Association, 49-75.

QUESTIONS FOR ANALYSIS AND DISCUSSION

1. Do the social sciences and marketing require a different methodology than the physical sciences? If yes, how would it differ? If no, why do so many social science researchers claim that their methodology must be different?

2. Lazer suggests that there are two approaches to model building in marketing—abstraction and realization [381] (see illustration). Are these approaches two different *methodologies*? Do they belong in the context of discovery or in the context of justification? Which is more *deductive*? Which is more *inductive*? Evaluate the usefulness of models. Which is superior for marketing? Why?

Model building by abstraction

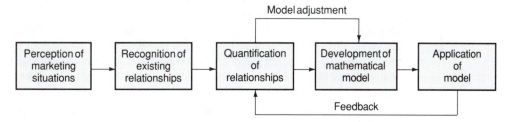

Model building by realization

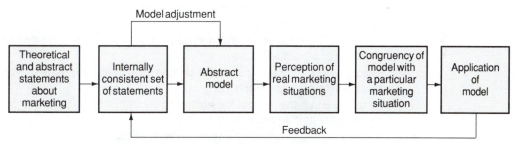

3. Differentiate between *marketing research* and *market research*. Can both result in possible publications for scholarly journals in marketing? Should they? Would marketing practitioners enjoy reading a journal that was exclusively devoted to results of *market* research studies? Would academicians? Is *marketing* research impractical?

4. Many of the articles in the *Journal of Marketing Research* can be classified as very quantitatively sophisticated profit/micro/normative in content. At the same time, *JMR* is often criticized as being too scientific. Are the preceding two statements contradictory? Is the discipline called management science a *science*? Could it possibly be a science? Is marketing *management* a science? Is accounting a science? *Could* accounting be a science?

5. Table 1-1 purports to be a classificational schema which encompasses the entire scope of marketing. Examine several issues of the *Journal of Marketing* and the *Journal of Marketing Research*. Determine which articles fall into

which categories.   Can some fall into several categories simultaneously? Conduct the same procedure for the chapters and major issues in a marketing textbook.   Whenever an article, chapter, or issue cannot be classified satisfactorily, propose a modification of the schema to accommodate it.

6. What is the optimal combination of cells and topics in Table 1-1 for a basic course in marketing?   A marketing management course?   A marketing research course?   MBA courses?   Ph.D. courses?   What were your criteria for optimality?

7. Why is it important to differentiate the *discovery* of theories and laws from the *justification* of theories and laws?   Are the processes of discovery different in marketing than in the physical sciences?   Should they be different?

8. Why is the "Is marketing a science?" issue important?   Does it have implications for the kind of research that is done in marketing?   For how marketing is taught?   For the standards for acceptance or rejection of manuscripts by the marketing journals?   For marketing practitioners?

9. Why is the "broadening the concept of marketing" issue important?   What are the implications of this issue for the areas in Question 8?

10. This chapter began with a headnote which quoted the Greek philosopher Epictetus.   What is the relevance of the headnote to the body of the chapter?

11. Bartels proposes that seven axioms comprise his metatheory [40]:
    a. Theory proceeds from a concept of its subject and should be consistent with it.
    b. Theory is built upon basic concepts derived from the concept of the subject and from related disciplines.
    c. By subdivision of basic concepts, their range and qualities may be shown in intraconcept differences.
    d. Concepts in a dependent-independent relationship are the bases of explanation or prediction.
    e. Theory based on presumed relationships is valid to the degree that those relationships have generality.
    f. As theory bears the mark of the marketing theorist, individuality and diversity are normal characteristics of theory.
    g. All theories of a discipline, however diverse, should be embraceable, implicitly or explicitly, in a general theory, either by grouping or synthesis.

    Evaluate this metatheory.   Is it a *logic* of discovery?   Should it be evaluated entirely in the context of discovery?   Which of the statements are normative, and which are positive?

12. Some marketers believe that marketing is an art, not a science.   Others have observed that marketing people have been neither good artists nor good scientists.   Finally, some have pointed out that truly great scientists have also been great artists, since genius in both science and art emanates from the taking of great care.   Evaluate these positions.   Be sure to carefully define what you mean by "art," "science," "artist," and "scientist".   (Turn to the headnote at the beginning of Chapter 5 for another point of view.)

13. Some writers believe that a necessary condition for scientific progress is that scientists must ask important questions.   This position emphasizes the

importance of the logic of discovery because no matter how good our process of validation, if the question is trivial, nothing can save it. Evaluate this position. How does one separate "important" questions from "unimportant" questions? Does current research in consumer behavior ask important questions? Does research in channels of distribution? Can the answers to "trivial" questions sometimes become important?

14. "If science is the body of knowledge obtained by methods based on observation, then painting is a science since it is based on observation." Evaluate.

15. Westing [in 179 and 306a] claims that marketing academia is "moving farther and farther away from our clients who are the businessmen of the country." What is a "client"? Is marketing academia "moving farther away"? Westing claims that marketing is a professional discipline like medicine. Are the "clients" of medical schools the practicing physicians or people who are sick? Does marketing have any *other* clients? Who are they, and how would these clients influence the nature of the market discipline? Is society in general a client?

16. Westing [in 170 and 306a] claims that "we are not a discipline. Economics is the discipline of study in business." Further, he observes that economics is the "mother science of marketing." He then proposes that the application of economics to marketing has been largely unsuccessful because "economics has never paid much attention to demand creation" and the theory of pricing was not "much of a contribution to the field." Evaluate the consistency of these views. What does the concept "mother science" imply?

17. Many writers claim that "marketing is a professional discipline, not an academic discipline." Others refer to marketing as an "applied" rather than a "basic" discipline. Are these positive or normative statements? Differentiate among these kinds of disciplines. What are the consequences for marketing teaching and research if it is a professional or academic or applied or basic discipline? What is the nature of the marketing discipline?

18. A colleague once observed:

    Economics, not marketing, is the professional discipline because economics is much more of a profession than marketing. After all, there are far more professional economists than professional marketers, and economics has far more professional status.

    Evaluate.

19. Peters [in 179 and 306a] suggests that the "fast-track research schools are influencing the other types of schools so that everyone now, or almost everyone, is setting up 'publish or perish' requirements." Do you agree? Estimate the total number of colleges and universities that teach marketing. What percentage do you think really "publish or perish"? Estimate the number of faculty that teach marketing. Now estimate the percentage of faculty who have published one or more journal articles in *JM, JMR,* or *JCR* in the last three years. Does this suggest that there must be a whole lot of perishing going on?

20. Peters [in 179 and 306a] indicates that his school gives "credit for unpublished, applied research studies if they truly make a contribution to the applied

area of the discipline." What is an "applied research study"? If such a study is unpublished, how could one decide whether it makes a contribution or not? What does "make a contribution" mean?

21. Myers, Greyser, and Massy [461] believe that

> the objectives of knowledge generation in our field should be to improve marketing management practice. Thus, even basic research if it is to be considered "effective" should, over the long run, contribute something to improved decision making or other aspects of management practice.

Evaluate. Before research is undertaken, what clues are there that a piece of research would "over the long run" contribute to management practice? How long is the "long run"?

22. Myers, Greyser, and Massy [461] decry the lack of "problem-oriented" research in marketing. Examine the last two volumes of the *Journal of Marketing* and the *Journal of Marketing Research.* What percentage of the articles were "problem oriented"? What are the factors that influence the kinds of research that academicians will pursue? Which of these factors encourage and which discourage the pursuit of "problem-oriented" research?

23. Myers, Greyser, and Massy [461] conclude:

> What the commission in effect rediscovered in the management science/model-building area was a reaffirmation of what many model-builders themselves have long believed—comparatively few firms or practicing management people seem to be using their models.

Why is this the case? Is it reasonable to expect line managers to extensively use sophisticated marketing models?

24. Accounting practitioners have historically been very generous in supporting academic accounting departments. Marketing practitioners provide very little support to academic marketing departments. Why is this the case? What steps could be undertaken by marketing academia to encourage marketing practitioners to be more supportive.

25. Differentiate between the study of consumer behavior and the study of buyer behavior. Is consumer behavior a subset of marketing? Is buyer behavior? Ought they to be? What were your criteria for inclusion/exclusion?

26. "Studying the exchange process is the province of economics, not marketing. That [the exchange process] is the whole purpose of supply and demand analysis."

Evaluate.

2
THE MORPHOLOGY OF EXPLANATION

Science has not the monopoly of truth but only the monopoly of the means for checking truth and enhancing it.

Mario Bunge

The term *explanation* plays a prominent role in all kinds of scientific inquiry. Although the observation, description, and classification of phenomena are important in science, the *explanation* of phenomena remains the *sine qua non* of science; without explanation, there is no science. As will be shown later, the systematic explanation of phenomena is a logical requirement for the scientific *understanding* of phenomena.

Ernest Nagel suggests that "the distinctive aim of the scientific enterprise is to provide systematic and responsibly supported explanations." [464, p. 15] However, terms such as *systematic, responsibly supported,* and *explanation* are remarkably compressed concepts, and much of this monograph will be devoted to unpacking them. The objective of this chapter will be to unpack the concept of explanation. That is, how does one go about explaining the occurrence of some phenomenon? What general characteristics do all satisfactory explanations have? How can various explanations be evaluated? Are some explanations better than others? Before turning to these questions, the next section will explore the purpose of explanations in marketing.

2.1 EXPLANATIONS IN MARKETING

Carl Hempel suggests that scientific explanations should be viewed as scientific answers to "why" questions. [262, p. 334] Why did phenomenon X occur? Phenomenon X occurred because .... Thus, marketers might want to know: Why have the sales of product X been decreasing rapidly? Why do newspapers charge lower rates to local advertisers than to national advertisers? Why have budget motels recently entered the hotel/motel industry? Why do people purchase particular brands of detergents? Possible explanations for these "why" questions might involve, in turn, the product life cycle, price sensitivity, the "wheel of retailing," and a consumer behavior model. These specific marketing explanations will be evaluated in detail in the next chapter. At this point, we need only emphasize that marketing research is vitally concerned with explaining marketing phenomena and that answers to "why" questions usually serve as precursors to "what will happen if" questions. For example, if one can explain why people buy particular detergents, one can predict "what will happen if I produce a particular brand of detergent."

Rigby suggests that a model is any structure which purports to *represent* something else. [531, p. 109] Aeronautical engineers use miniature models of airplanes to represent full-sized airplanes in wind tunnel tests. A road map is a model of a highway system. *Mathematical* models use mathematical symbols to represent certain characteristics of phenomena. A poem is a kind of *verbal* model using words to represent phenomena. A photograph or statue is an *iconic* model which *looks like* what it is supposed to represent. Most marketing models are *verbal* models, although mathematical and statistical models are becoming more common. All theories are models because (as Chapter 6 will reveal) all theories purport to represent some aspects of real-world phenomena. However, the converse is not true: All models are not theories, since many models will not have all the requisites of theoretical constructions. *An explanatory model is any generalized procedure or structure which purports to represent how phenomena are scientifically explained.*

Subsequent sections of this chapter will analyze six different kinds of explanatory models: deductive-nomological explanations, deductive-statistical explanations, inductive-statistical explanations, statistical relevance explanations, pattern explanations, and functionalist explanations. These various kinds of explanatory models are structurally dissimilar. That is, they employ fundamentally different kinds of logic and evidence to explain phenomena. Before analyzing and comparing them, we need to develop some normative criteria for evaluating the adequacy of purportedly explanatory structures.

2.2   CRITERIA FOR EVALUATING EXPLANATORY MODELS

Generally, most philosophers of science agree that to seek an answer as to why a phenomenon occurred is to at least show that, given some antecedent conditions, the phenomenon was somehow *expected to occur*. Thus, any explanation of the decreased sales of a product must show that, given certain conditions, one would have *expected* the decreased sales. If one seeks to explain the growth of budget motels, one must show that, given certain other phenomena, the growth of budget motels could be *expected*. So the first criterion is that any model which purports to be explanatory must somehow show that the phenomenon to be explained was expected. Three other normative criteria seem equally appropriate for assessing the explanatory adequacy of a model. Explanatory models should be *pragmatic, intersubjectively certifiable,* and have *empirical content.*[1]

Pragmatism, the second criterion, can best be illustrated with an example. Suppose a particular analysis logically *precluded* Newton's Laws of Motion as qualifying as explanatory. Since Newton's Laws are prime examples of what would almost universally be considered explanations in the sciences, simple pragmatism would suggest that the analysis was too restrictive and that we should go back to the drawing board. Thus, *pragmatism* dictates that models incorporating devices structurally similar to Newton's Laws should be considered explanatory.

The third criterion provides that explanations, like all scientific knowledge, must be objective in the sense of being *intersubjectively certifiable.* That is, different investigators (hence, *intersubject*) with different opinions, attitudes, and beliefs must be able to check the logic and make observations or conduct experiments to determine the truth content of the purported explanation. The intersubjectively certifiable criterion implies that *explanatory structures must be testable.* In this regard, one criticism of cognitive dissonance theory in social psychology is that the proponents of dissonance theory generally find results favorable to the theory; whereas nonbelievers in dissonance theory generally find no evidence to support the theory. Cognitive dissonance researchers have had problems in attempting to intersubjectively certify dissonance theory.

The fourth criterion requires explanations to have *empirical content.* Not only must an explanation be testable, it must be *empirically* testable. This rules out so-called purely analytic explanations, where statements are true, not by recourse to empirical (real-world) phenomena, but just because of the way terms are defined. There is something uncomfortable about the claim that one can explain the high market share of a brand by pointing out that more people buy it than any other brand. Such explanations would be purely analytic: true by definition alone. Explanations using extra empirical statements are also ruled out by the empirical content criterion. As Lambert and Brittan point out, "Appeals to God's will, for instance, although satisfying to many people, are not generally held to be explanatory; that the Lisbon earthquake occurred because God willed it is not really an assertion open to scientific investigation." [365, p. 26]

---

[1]Lambert and Brittan [365, p. 26] have an excellent discussion of normative criteria for evaluating explanations.

The preceding criteria do not exhaust the possibilities. However, they do appear to be a minimal set of desirable attributes for scientific explanations. Given these criteria, we can begin exploring the structure of various explanatory models.

2.3   DEDUCTIVE-NOMOLOGICAL EXPLANATION

The classical model of explanation is the deductive-nomological (D-N) model. Suggested by Hempel [262, p. 335], the terms literally mean "to deduce from laws." The D-N model, referred to as hypothetic-deductive [332, p. 10; 81, p. 385], covering law [151], and, simply, deductive [332, p. 336], is classical in the sense that early philosophers such as Hume [293] and Kant [331] implied the D-N model in their writings when referring to explaining phenomena. For example, in discussing the nature of science, Kant refers to "the laws from which reason explains the facts." [331, p. 18] Rigorous explication of the D-N model has been developed by Stallo, Campbell, Cohen and Nagel, and Hempel. [599, 103, 123, 262]

The deductive-nomological model of explanation has the following structure:

$$\left.\begin{array}{l} C_1, C_2, \ldots C_k \\[4pt] L_1, L_2, \ldots L_r \end{array}\right\} \; \text{Explanans } S$$

$$\overline{}$$

$$E \quad \} \; \text{Explanandum}$$

The $C_1, C_2, \ldots C_k$ refer to the characteristics or facts of the particular situation, and the $L_1, L_2, \ldots L_r$ refer to certain laws of strictly universal form. These laws state that *every* time some particular set of phenomena $(C_1, C_2, \ldots C_k)$ occurs, then some other phenomenon *(E)* will also occur). Together, the characteristics and the laws jointly make up the explanans. The explanans deductively implies (this is the meaning of the solid horizontal line) the explanandum E, which represents the phenomenon to be explained. The D-N model suggests that to scientifically explain a phenomenon is to deductively subsume the phenomenon under a set of laws and, therefore, to show that the phenomenon could be *expected to occur.* [123, p. 397] Note that in the D-N model *if* the explanans is true, then the explanandum *must* be true because the laws are of strictly universal form. That is, the laws state that *every* time characteristics $C_1, C_2, \ldots C_k$ occur, then E must occur.

A simple example of D-N explanation should make the model clearer. Why does a cube of ice with dimensions 1 foot x 1 foot x 1 foot float in water? The characteristic facts are that the cube of ice weighs approximately 56.2 pounds and that a cubic foot of water weighs approximately 62.4 pounds. Archimedes' Law states that a body in a fluid will displace an amount of that fluid equal to the weight of the body and that the fluid will exert an upward force on the body equal to the weight of the displaced fluid. Also, Newton's First Law of Motion states (essentially) that every time the result of all the forces acting on a body equals zero, the body will remain at rest. The characteristics (the weight of ice versus the weight of an equal volume of water) in conjunction with the laws (Archimedes' and Newton's) logically imply (predict) that the cube of ice will float in the water.

Many explanations of why ice floats in water will mention Archimedes' Law but neglect to explicitly state Newton's Law. A logician would refer to such explanations as *enthymemes* (or elliptical explanations [262, p. 414]) because one of the laws necessary to deduce the explanandum was suppressed or skipped over.

The D-N model of explanation certainly satisfies the four criteria in Section 2.2 for evaluating purportedly explanatory structures. The classical explanations of the sciences are unquestionably consistent with it. If the terms have empirical content (refer to real-world phenomena), then the model assures us that the explanation will be testable (at least testable in principle), which means that the explanation will be intersubjectively certifiable. The beauty of the D-N structure is that the explanandum is a logical consequence of the explanans, which greatly simplifies empirical testing. To the extent that the explanandum is verified by empirical observation, evidence is provided that reality is actually isomorphic (structurally similar in essential respects) with the proposed explanans. Thus, *scientific understanding* of the real world is increased. Some philosophers of science accept only the D-N model as satisfactorily explanatory. [154, p. 132] This tunnel view of explanation may be too restrictive, as our analysis of statistical explanations will show.

2.4   STATISTICAL EXPLANATION

Statistical explanation differs markedly from deductive-nomological explanation. Fundamentally, whereas D-N explanations employ only laws of strictly universal form, all statistical explanations contain at least one law in the probabilistic or statistical form:

$$P(G, F) = r$$

The law states that "the probability of G, given F, is r." An interpretation of this law suggests that in the long run the expected proportion of those cases of F which are also G is r.

We say an interpretation of the statistical law because there are basically three different theories of probability: mathematical probability, relative frequency, and subjective probability. [332, p. 225] Some familiarity with these three theories is necessary to analyze the basic nature of statistical explanations.

2.4.1   Theories of Probability

Roughly speaking, mathematical probability is an *a priori* notion where probabilities can be assigned to events without observation of the frequencies with which those events actually occur. To mathematical probability advocates, the probability of an event is determined by simply dividing the number of "favorable" cases of an event by the total number of all alternatives, provided that all cases are equally likely (equipossible).   Therefore, the probability of throwing an "ace" with a "fair die" is 1/6 since there are six equally likely alternatives, of which an "ace" is one.   The major problem with mathematical probability is that not all statistical situations are *a priori* deterministic.   Thus enter the relative frequency advocates.

The relative frequency approach also divides events into favorable and unfavorable cases, but it does so on the basis of actual observation of historical data rather than *a priori* judgment. Here the desirability or necessity of equipossible events vanishes. What is the probability that Jones Steel Company will get the next order from Smith? Since Smith historically has given Jones 20 percent of his steel orders, the probability is 0.2. Unfortunately, there often is no sound basis for assuming that past frequencies will continue into the future, as there is for mathematical probability, and, also, many events *have* no historical frequencies. What is the probability of total nuclear war next year? What is the probability that Joseph Parker will get a Ph.D.? Now enter the subjectivists.

The subjectivists claim that if the statement "Nuclear war is more likely during crisis periods than during detente periods" has meaning, then ascribing probability numbers to phrases such as "more likely" might prove a useful enterprise. For example, a group of leading scientists has estimated a probability of 0.5 that total nuclear war will break out before the year 2000. [196] Obviously, a probability of this kind cannot be estimated from either historical frequency or mathematical *a priori* reasoning. Here the term *probability* stands for the subjective degree of belief or certitude concerning the occurrence of an event, rather than its historical frequency. Although initially viewed with horror by traditional statisticians, the so-called Bayesian approach to probability has gradually gained widespread respectability because of its admitted usefulness. [564]

The preceding discussion of the theories of probability is meant to be suggestive rather than exhaustive. Each theory is useful, given a particular kind of problem. However, the notion of statistical explanation which follows presumes a mathematical or relative frequency interpretation of probability.

2.4.2   Statistical Explanation and the Social Sciences

Gustav Bergman points out that statistical laws and statistical explanations gain in importance when our knowledge is imperfect because we do not know all of the variables which influence the phenomenon to be explained. [56] Although the terms *perfect* and *imperfect* may have unfortunate connotations, the basic notion seems reasonable.   May Brodbeck amplifies the view by succinctly stating the reasons why statistical explanation has such importance in the social sciences.

> Without some abstraction or selection from all the possibilities the world presents[,] there can be no science at all. By their very nature scientific laws describe only certain features of the kinds of things or events they hold to be connected. How much can safely be ignored depends upon the way things are. . . . To say, in consequence, that abstraction is all very well for the physical sciences but will not do for the study of man and society is the counsel of desperation; that is, no solution at all. The social scientist, striving to merit the honorific half of that title, settles for something less than perfection. . . . The use of the statistical concept [in the physical sciences] marks our ignorance of all the influencing factors, a failure in either completeness or closure or, usually, both. Similarly, the social scientist, deliberately selecting for study fewer factors than actually influence the behavior in which he is interested, shifts his goal from predicting individual events or behaviors to predicting a random variable, that is, to predicting the frequency with which this kind of behavior occurs in a large group of individuals possessing the circumscribed number of factors. This is the price. The reward, of course, is that instead of helplessly gazing in dumb wonder at the infinite complexity of man and society, he has knowledge, imperfect rather than perfect, to be sure, but knowledge not to be scorned nonetheless, of a probability distribution rather than of individual events. After all, while we might much prefer to know the exact conditions under which cancer develops in a particular person, it is far from valueless to know the factors which are statistically correlated to the frequency of its occurrence. [81, pp. 293-94]

It is important to clearly differentiate between the assertion that some explanations are statistical in form and the assertion that since no scientific explanation is *known* to be true, all scientific explanations are only more or less *probable.* This would be confounding the nature of the structure of explanations with the quantity and quality of the evidence in support of those explanations. As Hempel points out, "The distinction between lawlike statements of strictly universal form and those of probabilistic form pertains, not to the evidential support of the explanation in question, but to the claims made by them: roughly speaking, the former attribute (truly or falsely) a certain characteristic to all members of a certain class; the latter to a specified proportion of its members." [262, p. 379]

A similar confusion sometimes surrounds the terms *deduction* and *induction* as they relate to statistical explanation. As we shall see in the following section, not all statistical explanations are inherently inductive (that is, some are deductive). Likewise, not all inductive processes are inherently statistical.

2.4.3   Deductive-Statistical Explanation

In the deductive-statistical model (D-S) the explanandum E is deduced from the explanans in exactly the same fashion as in the D-N model; that is, the phenomenon to be explained is a logical consequence of the explanans. Therefore, if the explanans is true, then the explanandum must be true. If the explanandum is false, then the explanans is false. However, the explanandum may be true and the explanans false. The reader is advised to review the preceding three statements as many times as is necessary to see that they are logically true.

The D-S explanatory model can best be illustrated by an example. Assume the following definitions and statistical laws:

C_1 = Purchasing agent J sees no difference between the offerings of suppliers X and Y.

C_2 = Purchasing agent J desires to split his orders between suppliers X and Y approximately evenly.

C_3 = Purchasing agent J does not want his suppliers to become complacent.

C_4 = Purchasing agent J decides to flip a fair coin to decide which supplier gets each order.

C_5 = Successive tossings of the coin are "independent."

O_k = Supplier k gets an order.

$O_k{}^*$ = Supplier k gets two orders in succession.

SL_1 = $P(O_k, C_1 \cdot C_2 \cdot C_3 \cdot C_4) = 0.5$. The probability of k getting any order is a statistical law with probability 0.5, given $C_1, C_2, C_3,$ and C_4.

SL_2 = $P(m + n) = P(m) \times P(n)$. This is a statistical law that if two events, m and n, are independent, then the probability of both events occurring $(m + n)$ equals the probability of m times the probability of n.

The schema for a deductive-statistical explanation can now be formed:

$$C_1, C_2, C_3, C_4, C_5$$

$$\text{} \quad\quad \} \text{ Explanans } S$$

$$\frac{SL_1, SL_2}{P(O_k{}^*, S) = 0.25} \quad\quad \} \text{ Explanandum } E$$

The D-S model states that, given S (the characteristics C_1, C_2, C_3, C_4, and C_5 and the two statistical laws SL_1 and SL_2), the probability that supplier k will get two orders in succession is precisely 0.25 (that is, 0.5 x 0.5). Just as in the D-N model, the explanandum is a deductive, logical consequence of the explanans.

Note that the explanandum in the example is a statement in statistical form. This is important and no accident. *The D-S model can explain only other statistical laws; the only statements that are deductive, logical consequences of statistical laws are other statistical laws.* Section 2.4.4 will demonstrate that *all other* kinds of explananda are inductively inferred from the explanans and not strict logical consequences of the explanans.

The D-S model is reasonably consistent with our normative criteria for explanations in Section 2.2. If the terms in the explanandum have empirical counterparts, the D-S model is intersubjectively confirmable by empirical testing. That is, we can observe real-world phenomena to determine whether the explanandum actually occurs. Many of the classical explanations in genetics are fundamentally of the D-S variety. Likewise, the decomposition of radioactive materials in physics (the "half-life" statistical laws) can be used to explain other statistical laws. Nevertheless, most statistical explanations in the social sciences are not D-S in nature. Most statistical explanations are *inductive,* not *deductive.*

2.4.4   Inductive-Statistical Explanation

Unlike with the D-S and D-N models, with the inductive-statistical (I-S) model the phenomenon to be explained is *not* a logical consequence of (is not necessarily implied by) the explanans. In the I-S model the explanans only confers a certain likelihood that the phenomenon will occur.

To put I-S into schematic form we need to add two items to the example in Section 2.4.3:

$O_k{}^{**}$ = Supplier k gets at least one order in the next 10 orders.
SL_3 = $P(O_k{}^{**}, C_1 \cdot C_2 \cdot C_3 \cdot C_4 \cdot C_5 \cdot SL_1 \cdot SL_2) = 1 - (0.5)^{10} = 0.999 \ldots$
  The statistical law that the probability of supplier k getting at least one order in the next 10 orders is extremely high, given $C_1 \ldots C_5$ and SL_1 and SL_2.

Following Hempel's [262, p. 383] procedure, the schema for the inductive-statistical explanation can now be formed:

$$C_1, C_2, C_3, C_4, C_5 \qquad \} \text{ Explanans } S$$

$$SL_1, SL_2, SL_3,$$

$$\overline{\overline{}} \qquad \text{[it is very likely that]}$$

$$O_k^{**} \qquad \} \text{ Explanandum } E$$

Given that the circumstances $(C_1 \ldots C_5)$ and the appropriate statistical laws (SL_1, SL_2, SL_3) are true, O_k^{**} is *very likely* to occur. Instead of a single line indicating that O_k^{**} is deductively subsumed under the explanans, we show a double line indicating that the explanans only confers *inductive* support to O_k^{**}. The conclusion E is not a logical consequence of the premises S in the sense that it is possible for E not to occur and the premises still be true. That is, the negation of E does not logically imply the negation of S.

An Evaluation of I-S Explanatory Model. Evaluating the I-S model via the criteria of Section 2.2 reveals substantial conformity. For example, "Why were 51 percent of all babies born last year in General Hospital male?" This phenomenon would classically be explained by the use of an I-S model referring to certain statistical laws in genetics. The model also makes predictions of a sort, thus making the model testable and, hence, intersubjectively confirmable. Finally, the explanans would lead one to *expect* the explanandum to occur.

Three problems sharply demarcate the fundamental differences between the D-N and I-S explanatory models. First, consider the consequences of testing a particular D-N model.

Test 1

D-N model K implies A.
A is false.
_____
D-N model K is false.

Test 2

D-N model K implies B.
B is true.
_____
D-N model K is supported.

Test 3

D-N model K implies B_1, B_2, B_3, B_4.
B_1, B_2, B_3, B_4 are true.
_____
D-N model K is strongly supported.

Test 1 shows that *if* D-N model K does imply A (that is, if our logic is correct) and *if* A is in fact false (that is, if our measurements are accurate), then all or some part of model K is false. The D-N model is *falsifiable* in a very strong sense because the D-N model incorporates laws of strictly universal form. The laws in the D-N model state that every time certain circumstances prevail, then some phenomenon will occur. Therefore, if we observe the required circumstances, and if phenomenon *A* does *not* occur, there exist only three possibilities: (1) there has been an error in logic (model *K* does not really imply that *A* will occur); (2) there has been an error in measurement (the characteristics $C_1 \ldots C_k$ were not present, or phenomenon *A* occurred but the measurements did not detect it); or (3) all or part of model *K* is false. So, the researcher must check the logic, check the measurements, and then draw the appropriate conclusions.

Now examine Tests 2 and 3 of the D-N model. Note that it is never appropriate to conclude that a particular D-N explanation is true. Rather, repeated empirical testing can only confer more or less empirical *support* or corroboration that a particular D-N explanation is true.

Now examine the consequences of testing a particular I-S model:

Test 1	*Test 2*
I-S model *J* suggests *A*. *A* is false.	I-S model *J* suggests *B*. *B* is true.
I-S model *J* is not supported.	I-S model *J* is supported.

Test 3

I-S model *J* suggests B_1, B_2, B_3, B_4.
B_1, B_2, B_3, B_4 are true.

I-S model *J* is strongly supported.

I-S model *J* suggests (makes more or less very likely) that if certain circumstances occur, then phenomenon *A* will occur. Empirical Test 1 shows that, in fact, *A* does *not* occur; that is, A is false. Once again, just as with the D-N model, the researcher should check both the logic and the measurements. However, in contrast with the D-N model, if the logic and measurements are found to be correct, the researcher cannot claim that I-S explanation *J* is false. Rather, because of the statistical nature of the laws in model *J*, the researcher can only conclude that the model is *not* supported. An example may serve to clarify the preceding observation.

Consider the I-S example previously discussed in this section that had the statistical law $SL_3 = P(O_k^{**}, C_1 \ldots)$. The law suggests that O_k^{**} (getting at least one order in the next 10 orders) is very likely to occur. Suppose we observe that O_k^{**} does *not* occur; *X* fails to get a single order 10 times in succession. The apologist for the I-S model might say, "Isn't that just my luck? Every time *I* test a model, the observation winds up in the tail of the distribution!" Or the researcher might ascribe the poor results to "noisy data." The preceding implies a fundamental difference between D-N and I-S explanations: *I-S models are fundamentally not falsifiable.* Further, if falsifiability is a reasonable normative criterion for explanatory models, then I-S models cannot be considered *explanatory*. This is exactly the conclusion of those holding the strict deductivist position.

Is there another sense of the word *falsifiable* that might admit I-S explanations? Yes, there is. Consider the following test.

Test 4

I-S model J suggests A_1, A_2, A_3, A_4.
A_1, A_2, A_3, A_4 are all false.

It is very likely that I-S model J is false.

Test 4 shows that a whole series of observations have failed to support I-S model J. This might be considered very strong evidence that model J is probably false and could be called the *weak falsifiability criterion*. In the previous example, if X loses 40 orders in a row, this is strong evidence that the underlying statistical law in model J is false.

If strict falsifiability is demanded, then I-S models cannot be deemed satisfactory explanations. If a weak falsifiability criterion suffices, then I-S models should be considered acceptable explanations. Is the weak falsifiability criterion justified? I believe the answer is yes. Even the strict deductivist Carl Hempel has moved toward the acceptance of statistical explanations as explanatory. He suggests, however, that we probably need to change our thinking to a different interpretation of the word *because*. [262, p. 393] If weak falsifiability were rejected, then almost all explanations in marketing and other social sciences would also have to be rejected. As will be shown in Chapter 5, almost all the laws (hence, all the explanations) in the social sciences are basically statistical in nature.

The second problem of the I-S model concerns how to ascertain the amount of inductive support that the premises confer upon the conclusion; for example, in Test 4 precisely what do we mean by the phrase "it is very likely that"? What is needed is a system of *inductive logic* to quantify the amount of inductive support, and this has been an intractable problem for centuries. Carnap's system of inductive logic suggests that for simple I-S models with only one statistical law, the likelihood of (degree of inductive support for) the occurrence of an event is the statistical probability of the event. [110] Therefore, since SL_1 and SL_2 combine to form SL_3 in the previous example, the structure would be:

$$
\begin{array}{l}
C_1, C_2, C_3, C_4, C_5 \\
SL_3 \\
\hline
O_k^{**}
\end{array} \quad [r = 0.999\ldots]
$$

Unfortunately, Carnap's system has not been extended to more complicated statistical systems with multiple statistical laws. *The degree of inductive support that a series of statistical laws confers upon the occurrence of an event remains unresolved except where all the laws can be compressed into a single law.*

The third problem with the I-S model concerns its ambiguity. [262, p. 394] Consider the following I-S argument:

C_1 = Jones is a black.
C_2 = Jones drinks alcoholic beverages.
SL_1 = 90 percent of all black drinkers drink Scotch.
_____ [very likely]
Jones drinks Scotch.

However, suppose the following premises are also true:

C_3 = Jones is a Southerner.
SL_2 = 90 percent of all Southerners do *not* drink Scotch.
_____ [very likely]
Jones does not drink Scotch.

The preceding two arguments (whose premises we assume to be true only for expository purposes) yield contradictory conclusions. It is psychologically uncomfortable to note that *ex post* we can always find a model consistent with the observation. If Jones is observed drinking Scotch, the I-S model builder says, "Aha, he drinks Scotch because he is a black." And if Jones is observed drinking bourbon, the I-S model builder says, "Indeed, as I always said, very few Southerners drink Scotch."

Carnap suggests resolving the ambiguity problem with *the requirement of total evidence:* "In the application of inductive logic to a given knowledge situation, the total evidence available must be taken as a basis for determining the degree of confirmation." [106, p. 211] Similarly, Hempel [265] proposes *the requirement of maximal specificity:* "In formulating or appraising an I-S explanation, we should take into account all the information . . . which is of potential explanatory relevance to the explanandum event." (See Cooke [94] for an evaluation of this criterion.) The criterion implies that an acceptable statistical explanation of why Jones drinks Scotch must be based on a statistical law using as a reference class the most narrowly defined class which our total evidence suggests as relevant. In this case we need a statistical law concerning the proportion of black Southerners who drink Scotch. Using any other reference class may yield poor results.

2.5   ARE LOGICAL EMPIRICIST MODELS OF EXPLANATION ADEQUATE?

Suppe [607] has observed that the modern empiricist treatment of science has been subject to significant and sustained attack in the last two decades. In particular, the "Received View" concerning the nature of scientific theories and explanations has been assaulted, and Suppe concludes that "the last vestiges of positivistic philosophy of science are disappearing from the philosophical landscape." [607, p. 619] Therefore, he proposed, "Positivism truly belongs to the history of the philosophy of science, and its influence is that of a movement historically important in shaping the landscape of a much-changed philosophy of science." [607, p. 632] The purpose here is to review and evaluate the attacks on the logical empiricist models of explanation. Both the deductive-nomological model and the inductive-statistical model will be examined.

2.5.1   Is the D-N Model Dead?

Attacks on the D-N model have generally been prefaced by showing that some "explanation" may "fit" the D-N model and yet be regarded as unsatisfactory by most people. A well-known illustration is the "flagpole" explanation proposed by Bromberger [85] and cited by Suppe:

> Using geometric optics, we can form a law of coexistence which correlates the height of a flagpole, the angle of the sun to the horizon, and the length of the shadow cast by the flagpole. Using this law and initial conditions about the height of the flagpole and the sun's angle, we can explain the length of the shadow in accordance with the D-N model. However, if we take our initial conditions as being the length of the shadow and the sun's angle, using the law the D-N model allows us to (causally!) explain the height of the flagpole. But only the former case is a genuine explanation, the latter being spurious; since the D-N model sanctions both as genuine, the D-N model is defective. [607, p. 621]

Bromberger concludes that only explanations which employ causal laws can be satisfactory. Similarly, Jobe [324] uses examples such as Ohm's Law and concludes that satisfactory D-N explanations must use "genuine laws of nature." Finally, Brody uses the following illustrations (adapted from Aristotle):

(A)   *a.* The planets do not twinkle.
     b. All objects which do not twinkle are near the Earth.
     c. Therefore, the planets are near the Earth.
(B)   *a.* The planets are near the Earth.
     b. All objects near the Earth do not twinkle.
     c. Therefore, the planets do not twinkle. [83, p. 20]

Brody proposes that both (A) and (B) are "acceptable" D-N explanations but that only (B) *should* be considered as explanatory. He concludes that "a deductive-nomological explanation of a particular event is a satisfactory explanation of that event when, besides meeting

Hempel's requirements, its explanans essentially contains a description of the cause of the event described in the explanandum." [83, p. 23]

The preceding attacks do seem persuasive. To suggest that "lack of twinkling" *explains* the distance of the planets from the Earth clearly will not do, just as the length of women's hemlines will not *explain* stock market purchases. In other words, as will be shown in Section 3.1, predictive adequacy is not sufficient for explanatory adequacy.

The position here is that any *satisfactory* explanation must contain in its explanans some mechanisms or laws or lawlike generalizations which are *purportedly* causal (see Section 3.2 for more on causality). This position coincides with the views of advocates of *scientific realism,* the closest thing today to a "school" to supersede logical empiricism. For example, the realists Keat and Urry point out that the D-N model fails "to distinguish between providing the grounds for expecting an event will occur, and explaining *why* it will occur." [334, p. 13] Nevertheless, scientific realism should be viewed less as a *replacement* for logical empiricism and more as the next most reasonable step for philosophy of science, since both movements share substantial common ground:

> Both share a general conception of science as an objective, rational enquiry which aims at true explanatory and predictive knowledge of an external reality.... First, the idea that scientific theories must be objectively assessed by reference to empirical evidence. This evidence is such that all scientists who are competent, honest, and lacking in perceptual deficiencies can agree upon it, though not necessarily with total certainty. Second, there is the idea that there are "objects," in the broadest sense of the term, which exist independently of our beliefs and theories about them.... This means a rejection of the view that scientific theories determine that reality, rather than make genuine discoveries about it.... Both hold that there are general standards of scientificity, of what counts as an adequate explanation, of what it is that we must try to achieve by scientific theories, of the manner in which empirical evidence should be used to assess their truth or falsity, and so on. Whilst disagreeing about what these standards are, both believe that they exist.... They are external and universal standards, independent of particular, substantive theories and explanations, and applicable to all periods in the historical development of science [334, p. 44]

Curiously, Hempel himself, in his early work on the D-N model, ascribed a role for causal mechanisms. [262, p. 250] However, his later works dropped the requirement. [262, pp. 351-54] Dropping any reference to causal mechanisms from the D-N model resulted from the desire of the logical positivists and their successors, the logical empiricists, to expunge all metaphysical concepts from their analyses. And, since causality can never *be conclusively* verified, it was considered too metaphysical. What the logical empiricists never completely realized (or never could bring themselves to admit) is that if the *conclusive verification* criterion were applied to all concepts in science, the domain of scientific inquiry would be dangerously close to an empty set!

Is the D-N model dead? Not at all! The attack discussed in this section simply reveals that the model is not restrictive enough. The D-N model should be modified to require the specific inclusion of purportedly causal mechanisms or causal laws in the explanans.

2.5.2   Is the I-S Model Dead?

Leading the charge against the I-S model have been Salmon, Jeffrey, and Greeno. [548, 318, 237] Recall that both the D-N and I-S models of explanations are, fundamentally, *arguments*. That is, premises (the explanans) and a conclusion (the explanandum) are joined by a "therefore." With the D-N model the premises deductively imply or entail the conclusion. With the I-S model the premises suggest the conclusion with "high probability." Salmon, Jeffrey, and Greeno deny that explanations are arguments, leading Suppe to conclude that "one will have to give up the requirement that statistical explanations are 'correct' arguments. . . . The important point is that Hempel's I-S model is defective, hence by implication so is his D-N model." [607, p. 623]

If explanations are not arguments, what are they? Salmon [548] proposes the "statistical relevance" (S-R) model of explanations. By this account, an explanation "is an assembly of facts statistically relevant to the explanandum regardless of the degree of probability that results." [607, p. 623] Note that the S-R model violates the "high probability" requirement of the I-S model.

Writers cite numerous examples of satisfactory explanations which do not accord a high probability to the explanandum. Three examples can illustrate the procedure: (1) Half-life laws can be used to explain the emission of an electron from a radioactive substance where the probability of the electron emission at the time is very low. (2) The fact that a person gets lung cancer is often explained by noting that the person smokes two packs of cigarettes per day, even though only a small percentage of cigarette smokers contract cancer. (3) Finally, an injection of penicillin may legitimately be thought to explain why a patient gets a rash even though only a few patients have this reaction. These kinds of examples have led writers to propose that "it is not the high probability conferred on the explanandum which makes an account explanatory, but rather the specification of a so far unnoticed factor which changes this probability to a value which differs from the value ascribed to it on the basis of the information that was available before the explanation had been given." [352, p. 131]

Now, the S-R model does not propose that *any* assembly of facts will qualify as explanatory, only an assembly of those facts that are *relevant;* and most analyses of the model have been directed at separating the "relevant" from the "irrelevant." Criteria such as "homogeneous reference classes" and "screening-off relations" have been proposed to help solve the problem of separating "causal" relevance relations from "merely" statistical relevance relations. We shall not evaluate these issues here. Interested readers should consult Shrader [578] and Meixner [439] for reviews. The purpose here is to evaluate the following line of reasoning implied by advocates of the S-R model:

1. S-R explanations are adequate.
2. S-R explanations are *not* arguments.
3. I-S explanations are arguments.
4. Therefore, I-S explanations and, by implication, D-N explanations are defective.

To evaluate whether S-R explanations are adequate, consider the S-R explanation "cigarette smoking causes lung cancer in a person." Suppose scientists someday discover a "cancer gene" such that 50 percent of all the people who have this gene will ultimately contract cancer. Suppose further research yields the finding that "98 percent of all people who smoke two packs of cigarettes daily *and* have the cancer gene will ultimately develop lung cancer." Note that the "98 percent" statistical generalization enables one to *explain* the incidence of lung cancer by way of an I-S explanation, since 98 percent would provide "high probability."

The preceding example enables us to draw several conclusions. First, *if* the original cigarette S-R is "adequate," then the 98 percent I-S explanation *must be* adequate, since the 98 percent I-S explanation contains all the information of the S-R explanation and *more*. Further, if adequacy is considered a relative concept, then no one would dispute that the 98 percent I-S explanation is *better than* the S-R explanation. (See Watkins [627, pp. 239-40] for more.)

Second, the fact that the 98 percent I-S explanation is *better* than the S-R explanation suggests that the goal of all scientists employing S-R explanations should be to upgrade these explanations to I-S types. Third, if the goal of scientists should be to upgrade S-R explanations (which are not arguments) to I-S types (which are all arguments), one cannot claim that I-S explanations are "defective" because they are arguments. *If anything, S-R explanations are defective because they are not correct arguments.*

Are S-R explanations adequate? If "adequate" is construed as "useful," then the answer must be yes. It is certainly useful to know that although only a small percentage of smokers will contract lung cancer, heavy smokers are 5-10 times more likely to develop lung cancer than are nonsmokers. However, as a goal for developing explanations of phenomena, S-R explanations are *inadequate* because they should be viewed as intermediate explanations directed toward the development of I-S explanations or D-N explanations. The original "cigarette" S-R explanation was "adequate" only because it was the best that science could provide at the time. This is as it should be, since all explanations must be evaluated given our knowledge base at a point in time. [225]

Although "hard core" critics of logical empiricism continue to cite Salmon's work as evidence of the inadequacies of the D-N and I-S models, Salmon's most recent work has, essentially, abandoned the S-R model. He has adopted a realist view (see Section 11.3) of scientific explanation and writes:

> It seemed obvious at the time [of writing the 1971 book] that statistical relevance relations had some sort of explanatory power in and of themselves. As I have said repeatedly throughout this [1984] book, that view seems utterly mistaken.... Their fundamental import lies in the fact ... that they constitute evidence for causal relations. [552, pp. 191-2]

In conclusion, the logical empiricist models of explanation remain the most viable models available for explaining phenomena. This is not to say that there are no unresolved issues with respect to the models. The D-N model should be made *more* restrictive by requiring causal mechanisms or causal laws in the explanans. The I-S model should be made *less* restrictive by relaxing the "high-probability" requirement and recognizing that sometimes the best that science can provide at a point in time is an "explanation" of the S-R variety. Nevertheless, these modifications neither suggest that the logical empiricist models of explanation are "fundamentally defective" nor that the S-R model should be the goal of science, as Salmon himself now admits.

2.6   THE PATTERN MODEL

The pattern model (P-M) purportedly constitutes a fifth distinctive kind of explanation. Abraham Kaplan, an advocate of the pattern model, views P-M explanations as extremely important in the methodology of the behavioral sciences. [332, p. 332] Kaplan defines and discusses the pattern model:

> Very roughly, [in the pattern model] we know the reason for something when we can fit it into a known pattern.... something is explained when it is so related to a set of other elements that together they constitute a unified system. We understand something by identifying it as a specific part in an organized whole.... in the pattern model we explain by instituting or discovering relations ... These relations may be of various different sorts: causal, purposive, mathematical, and perhaps other basic types, as well as various combinations and derivatives of these. The particular relations that hold constitute a pattern, and an element is explained by being shown to occupy the place that it does occupy in the pattern....

> The perception that everything is just where it should be to complete the pattern is what gives us the intellectual satisfaction, the sense of closure, all the more satisfying because it was preceded by the tensions of ambiguity. [332, pp. 332-35]

Is the P-M explanatory? Does it meet the normative criteria set forth in Section 2.2? Certainly, many so-called explanations in the behavioral sciences and marketing simply show how the phenomenon fits into a distinctive pattern; thus pragmatism favors the pattern model. Also, many of the concepts employed in pattern explanations have empirical content; that is, their terms have empirical referents. As we shall see, however, the criterion of *intersubjective confirmability* poses problems for P-M explanations. The potential for the intersubjective confirmability of pattern models can be best explored by analyzing an example of a P-M explanation by Kaplan:

> According to the pattern model, then, something is explained when it is so related to a set of other elements that together they constitute a unified system. We understand something by identifying it as a specific part in an organized whole. There is a figure consisting of a long vertical straight line with a short one branching upwards from it near the top, and a short curved line joining it on the same side near the bottom; the figure is meaningless until it is explained as representing a soldier with fixed bayonet, accompanied by his dog, disappearing around the corner of a building (the curved line is the dog's tail). We understand the figure by being brought to see the whole picture, of which what is to be explained is only a part. [332, p. 333]

Is the preceding P-M explanation intersubjectively certifiable? To analyze it, let's designate the soldier-with-dog P-M explanation as *J*. Consider now a second P-M explanation, *K*, for the figure in Kaplan's example. Pattern model *K* proposes that the figure actually is a dead tree with small branches at the top and the bottom. Which explanation is correct? If two subjects perceive different patterns which encompass the same phenomenon, what objective criteria can be used to confirm one pattern over the other? Kaplan mentions "intellectual satisfaction" as a criterion. [332, p. 335] But intellectual satisfaction is an irretrievably individual phenomenon. Model *K* may be more intellectually satisfying to me, whereas model *J* may be more intellectually satisfying to you. A criterion such as familiarity suffers from the same weakness. A familiar pattern to a Western European might be totally unfamiliar to the East Asian.

The intersubjective confirmability criterion for the D-N, D-S, and I-S models is overcome via empirical testing. All of these models employ laws which make predictions that are susceptible to testing. Choosing between rival explanatory constructions can be accomplished by examining multiple tests of the models where the rival constructions predict different outcomes. At present, there are no similar "tests" for pattern models. *Therefore, the pattern model fails the criterion of inter-subjective confirmability and cannot be considered as having explanatory power.*

It can be shown that all of the examples discussed by Kaplan either (1) fail the intersubjective confirmability criterion or (2) are actually D-N explanations in disguise. Kaplan discusses a P-M to explain thunder: "[A] bolt of lightning heats the air through which it passes, which then expands, disturbing the air around it and thus setting up sound waves." [332, p. 334] This particular pattern model has explanatory power *only* because it presumes some lawlike relationships: (1) lightning heats air; (2) heated air expands; (3) expanding air will disturb surrounding air; and (4) disturbed air creates sound waves. That D-N explanations will have "patterns" is undoubtedly true, but that *patterns alone* have explanatory power is an entirely different assertion.

The true value of pattern models may lie, not in the context of justification (with the notion of explanation), but rather, in the context of discovery. Since explanatory schemata frequently have distinctive patterns and since these patterns may be consistent across different kinds of phenomena, the theorist searching for tentative explanations might start his search by first looking for a familiar pattern. Kaplan himself admits that "the pattern model may more easily fit explanations in early states of inquiry." [332, p. 332]

2.7   FUNCTIONALIST EXPLANATION

No one even remotely familiar with the social sciences can avoid being exposed to functionalism, and the advocates of functionalism as a distinct methodology are legion. [517, 416, 445, 487, 602] Some students of marketing, notably the late Wroe Alderson [9, 10], have also taken up the functionalist banner. Is functionalist explanation fundamentally different from other forms of explanation? First, we would note that functionalism belongs in the general class of philosophical inquiry known as *teleology* (literally, the study of purposes). No one would deny that much animal and human behavior seems purposive, leading analysts such as Taylor, Grene, and Wright [613, 240, 646] to conclude that the explanation of human behavior may be irreducibly teleological. Others, such as Utz and Clark [621, 119], propose that all purportedly teleological explanations can be recast as D-N or I-S explanations (as in Section 2.7.2). The most prominent of the teleologically oriented writers have been the functionalists.

Despite the popularity of functionalism, there are tremendous logical difficulties with functionalism and functional explanation. First, despite all the writings on functionalist methodology, the meanings of the terms *function, functional,* and *functional explanation* lack both specificity and universal consensus, even among advocates of functionalism.

Before analyzing the basic logic of functional explanations, we must first explore the different usages of the term *function*.

2.7.1   Uses of the Terms *Function* and *Functional Explanation*

Ernest Nagel suggests that functionalists use the term *function* in at least six different ways. [464, p. 522]   These different usages alone account for substantial confusion in functionalist literature, and four of them seem particularly appropriate for our analysis.

1. The first use of the term *function* is when it simply signifies the **dependence or interdependence between variables**; that is, X is a function of Y. For example, "the incidence of purchase of major brand gasoline is a function of the generalized self-confidence of the subjects." However, such lawlike locutions are precisely the kinds of statements that are found in nonfunctionalist approaches. Hence, if the entire functionalist procedure were so construed, then functionalism could not be considered a distinctive mode of inquiry. That is, funtionalist explanations would not be different from other kinds of explanations.

2. Biologists and others use the term function to refer to **certain organic processes** ("vital functions") such as reproduction and respiration that are considered indispensable for the continued life of the organism or the maintenance of the species. Similarly, in anthropology, Malinowski asserts that "in every type of civilization, every custom, material object, idea, and belief fulfills some vital function." [415, p. 132] Thus, functionalists sometimes use the term *function* as synonymous with "indispensable role."

3. A third use of the term signifies some generally recognized **use or utility** of a thing. "The function of salesmen's call reports is to transmit intelligence," or "the function of advertising is to create sales." However, if all uses of the term *function* were confined to relatively simple assertions about the intended use of certain phenomena, then functional explanations would be weak, if not impotent.

4. Finally, the term *function* often signifies the **contribution that an item makes or can make toward the maintenance of some stated characteristic or condition in a given system to which the item is assumed to belong.** *Thus, functional analysis seeks to understand a behavior pattern or a sociocultural institution by determining the role it plays in keeping the given system in proper working order or maintaining it as a going concern.* [262, p. 305] If functionalism is to lay claim to being a distinct method of inquiry, it will do so on the basis of this final interpretation of function.

This last view of functions and functional explanation (which we shall adopt and analyze) seems reasonably consistent with Wroe Alderson:

> Functionalism is that approach to science which begins by identifying some system of action, and then tries to determine how and why it works as it does. Functionalism stresses the whole system and undertakes to interpret the parts in terms of how they serve the system. Some writers who are actually advocates of functionalism prefer to speak of the holistic approach because of emphasis on the system as a whole. [9, p. 16]

Similarly, Radcliffe-Brown discusses his version of functionalism:

> [In] social life, if we examine such a community as an African or Australian tribe, we can recognize the existence of a social structure. Individual human beings, the essential units in this instance, are connected by a definite set of social relations into an integrated whole. The continuity of the social structure, like that of an organic structure, is not destroyed by changes in the units. Individuals may leave the society, by death or otherwise; others may enter it. The continuity of structure is maintained by the process of social life, which consists of the activities and interactions of the individual human beings and of the organized groups into which they are united. The social life of the community is here defined as the *functioning* of the social structure. The *function* of any recurrent activity, such as the punishment of a crime, or a funeral ceremony, is the part it plays in the social life as a whole and therefore the contribution it makes to the maintenance of the structural continuity. [517, p. 179]

Lastly, Malinowski presents his view of functionalism:

> [Functionalism] aims at the explanation of anthropological facts at all levels of development by their function, by the part which they play within the integral system of culture, by the manner in which they are related to each other within the system, and by the manner in which this system is related to the physical surroundings.... The functional view of culture insists therefore upon the principle that in every type of civilization, every custom, material object, idea, and belief fulfills some vital function, has some task to accomplish, represents an indispensable part within a working whole. [415, p. 132]

Although we shall adopt the fourth interpretation of the term *function* for analytical purposes, a caveat is warranted. A proper evaluation of any author's functionalist theoretical construction requires the reader to carefully consider how the author uses the term *function*. Not only do different authors use the term differently, but individual authors (perhaps unknowingly) also slip back and forth in their usage of the term. This can create considerable problems for anyone attempting to analyze functionalist explanations.

2.7.2   Preliminary Problems of Functional Explanation

Before we attempt a formal analysis of functional explanation, two minor issues need resolving.[2] One logical requirement for *causal* explanations (see Chapter 3 for a discussion of causality) is temporal sequentiality: If *A* is supposed to cause *B,* then *A* must occur before *B* in time. Functionalist explanations, like all teleological explanations, make liberal use of the concepts "goals" and "purposes." Since goals and purposes refer to *future* events, does not this ascribe causal efficacy to future events? That is, does not this mean that future phenomena can cause present phenomena? For example, can the goal of an increased market share (a future event) *cause* a firm to increase advertising effort and have explanatory power? Is this not contradictory? The reader will note that a simple resolution to this apparent contradiction lies in the manner of phrasing. Future events do not cause or explain present actions; the *desire* for a future event may cause or explain present actions. Here the desire temporally precedes the behavior that one seeks to explain, and the apparent contradiction dissolves.

A similar teleological problem confronts the user of explanations of this sort: "The chameleon has the ability to change its skin color in order to blend in with its varying backgrounds, thus protecting it from natural enemies." The phrase "in order to" signifies a teleological emphasis in the explanation. However, using Darwinian theory, such covertly teleological explanations can be entirely avoided. A skeletal outline of such an explanation might include statements along these lines: (1) An early mutant lizard had the ability to change colors. (2) This ability increased the likelihood of its survival and the survival of those of its progeny which also carried the mutant gene. (3) Through time the proportion of the species carrying the mutant gene rose due to "survival of the fittest." Note that no reference to purposive or teleological factors is required. Most such covertly teleological explanations can be recast in other, nonteleological, forms. Similarly, some purportedly functionalist explanations can also be recast. These two minor problems resolved, we are now in a position to explore the formal logic of functional explanation.

2.7.3   The Logic of Functional Explanation

The best way to evaluate the logic of functional explanation is (1) to present a classical functional explanation in the fourth sense of the term *function,* (2) to dissect the explanation so as to lay bare its logical

---

[2] The analysis that follows in this section draws to varying degrees on the writings of Ernest Nagel [464, pp 520-34], Richard Rudner [542, pp. 84-111], and Carl Hempel. [261]

structure, and (3) to evaluate that structure. Malinowski's well-known explanation of the function of mourning in primitive cultures provides just such a typical illustration:

> The ritual despair, the obsequies, the acts of mourning, express the emotion of the bereaved and the loss of the whole group. They endorse and they duplicate the natural feelings of the survivors; they create a social event out of a natural fact. Yet, though in the acts of mourning, in the mimic despair of wailing, in the treatment of the corpse and in its disposal, nothing ulterior is achieved, these acts fulfill an important function and possess a considerable value for primitive culture.

What is this function?

> The death of a man or a woman in a primitive group, consisting of a limited number of individuals, is an event of no mean importance. The nearest relatives and friends are disturbed to the depth of their emotional life. A small community bereft of a member, especially if he be important, is severely mutilated. The whole event breaks the normal course of life and shakes the moral foundations of society. The strong tendency on which we have insisted in the above description: to give way to fear and horror, to abandon the corpse, to run away from the village, to destroy all the belongings of the dead one—all these impulses exist, and if given way to would be extremely dangerous, disintegrating the group, destroying the material foundations of primitive culture. Death in a primitive society is, therefore, much more than the removal of a member. By setting in motion one part of the deep forces of the instinct of self-motivation, it threatens the very cohesion and solidarity of the group, and upon this depends the organization of that society, its tradition, and finally the whole culture. For if primitive man yielded always to the disintegrating impulses of his reaction to death, the continuity of tradition and the existence of material civilization would be made impossible. [417, p. 52]

What is the basic structure of the preceding functional explanation? Basically, the structure is as follows:

Functional Model 1

1. At some time t, a system s (a primitive society) is in state k (proper working order).
2. The class of systems S (primitive societies) of which s is a member must have condition n (group cohesiveness and solidarity) in order to maintain state k (proper working order).
3. Phenomenon j (death of a member) has negative effects on condition n (group cohesiveness and solidarity).
4. If characteristic c (mourning and other acts of bereavement) were present in system s at time t, then c would counter the effect of j and condition n would be satisfied.
5. Therefore, Statements 1 through 4 explain why characteristic c is present in system s at time t.

Several observations on the morphology (structure) of Functional Model 1 (FM1) are apparent. First, FM1 shows that functional explanations belong to a class of explanations called *homeostatic* or *equilibrating.* FM1 suggests that there are certain preferred states in the system (e.g., survival) and that if the existence of these preferred states is threatened (e.g., by a death), the system will adopt certain mechanisms to return to these preferred states. Thus, FM1 is an equilibrating model of explanation.

Second, the FM1 explanatory structure incorporates certain laws or lawlike statements. Note the verb "must have" in statement 2, the phrase "has negative effects on" in Statement 3, and the verb "would counter" in Statement 4. All of these statements can be construed as having essentially lawlike form (see Chapter 4). Statement 5, the explanandum, is thus derived from Statements 1 through 4 (the explanans) in precisely the same way as in the D-N, D-S, and I-S explanatory models. *Therefore, FM1 is neither a fundamentally different kind of explanation nor a different methodology. To the extent that it is an explanation at all (see next paragraph), FM1 is a special case of deductive-nomological or statistical explanation where certain of the lawlike statements involve homeostatic mechanisms.*

Third, as Hempel has observed [262, p. 310], the explanandum (Statement 5) in FM1 is not a logical consequence of the explanans (Statements 1 through 4). Statement 4 essentially provides that *if c* were present, then condition n would be satisfied; that is, c is sufficient for n. However, what is required is a statement of the following variety: *If n is to be satisfied, then c* must be present; that is, c must be necessary or indispensable for n. Logicians would refer to this logical error as affirming the consequent [547, p. 27] This fallacy can be illustrated by the following incorrect syllogism:

All men are mortal.
Fido is mortal.
——————————
Fido is a man.

Note that the preceding syllogism and FM1 have the same structure. *Therefore, the host of functional explanations which have the basic structure of FM1 are logically false—the premises do not imply the conclusion.*

Since there are almost no circumstances where a characteristic c is functionally indispensable for condition $n,$ can any form of functional explanation by salvaged? Is it possible to reconstruct a functional model which both captures the essence of functionalism and at the same time is logically correct? Functional Model 2 (FM2) attempts to do just that. Note that although Statements 1 through 3 are identical to those of FM1, Statements 4 and 5 are different.

Functional Model 2

1. At some time *t*, a system *s* (a primitive society) is in state *k* (proper working order).
2. The class of systems *S* (primitive societies) of which *s* is a member must have condition *n* (group cohesiveness and solidarity) in order to maintain state *k* (proper working order).
3. Phenomenon *j* (death of a member) has negative effects on condition *n* (group cohesiveness and solidarity).
4. Set *C* is the set of all sufficient items which, if any one were present in the system *s*, would counter phenomenon *j* and maintain condition *n* and thus system state *k*.
5. Therefore, Statements 1 through 4 explain why some item in set *C* will be in system *s* at time *t*.

A functional explanation such as FM2 can now predict only that some item in the set *C* will occur. When sociologists Merton and Parsons discuss *functional equivalents,* they are in our terms exploring the nature of set *C* [445, p. 34; 487, p. 58]. Even thus salvaged, constructing sound functionalist explanations is no small task. The staggering job of identifying the complete set of functional alternatives and then tying the set into functionalist lawlike generalizations is seldom achieved. All too often, functional explanations of phenomena degenerate into one or more of the following: (1) *ad hoc ex post* rationalizations of why some phenomenon has occurred, (2) pseudo-explanations that are empirically empty, (3) logically fallacious explanations, or (4) hopelessly circular explanations, such as:

(a) Why does *X* do *Y?*
(b) Because *X* has goal *J,* and
(c) *Y* leads to the satisfaction of goal *J.*
(d) Therefore, *X* does *Y.*
(e) How do you know *X* has goal *J?*
(f) Because *X* does *Y!*

These observations have led many analysts of functionalism to believe that the major importance of functionalism lies not in the context of justification but in the context of discovery. [332, p. 365; 542, p. 109; 262, p. 329]

2.7.4 Functionalism in the Context of Discovery

The claim that functionalism has a unique *methodology* implies that the *logical apparatus* for confirming or falsifying functional explanations, theories, and laws is distinct from the logical apparatus used in other branches of scientific inquiry. As discussed in Chapter 1, the methodology (as contrasted with the techniques) of a discipline concerns the very bases or criteria on which to test the truth content of the discipline's claims about knowledge. On the other hand, the assertion that the importance of functionalism for the social sciences lies primarily in the context of discovery implies that functionalism may have heuristic value to scholars in searching for fundamental relationships among social phenomena. Presumably, Robert Bartels was suggesting that marketers adopt a functionalist "set" in his "theory of social initiative."

> Different societies attain similar ends (in relative measure) by different means. The level of technology, the values of the group or nation, even the relative importance attached to economic, intellectual, religious, or leisure activity are factors which must be considered in interpreting the marketing process and institution of a people. *Ecological orientation, in other words, is the starting point in marketing analysis.* [39, p. 32, emphasis added]

Under what circumstances might adopting a functionalist perspective be desirable for a researcher? Arthur Stinchcombe has proposed these criteria, "Whenever we find *uniformity of the consequences* of action but *great variety of the behavior causing those consequences,* a functional explanation in which the consequences serve as causes is suggested. [602, p. 80, Stinchcombe's emphasis] He has further proposed several situations in which the researcher should consider functional explanations [602, p. 82]: (1) If, when subjects experience increased difficulty in achieving their goals, they increase their activity, functional explanations are indicated. (2) If a variety of explanations or purposes, or inadequate and inconsistent purposes, are offered by people behaving to explain their behavior, a functional explanation is indicated. (3) If it is known that some causal process is operating which selects patterns of behavior according to their consequences, a functional explanation is indicated. That is, when we know that processes are selecting out certain functional behavior, it is strategic to look for those functions in any bit of behavior which we find in that selective context.

In the context of discovery, the value of functionalism is primarily an empirical question: "Is it likely that adopting a particular perspective or mode of exploration will lead to the discovery of new knowledge?" The study of discovery lies in the domain of the psychology or sociology of science rather than in the domain of the philosophy of science. If we are to evaluate the scientific worth of functionalism on the basis of the quantity and quality of scientific knowledge that a functionalist "set" generates, then the jury on functionalism is still out in both marketing and the other social sciences.

2.8   SUMMARY AND CONCLUSIONS

Explanations play a crucial role in scientific inquiry. A major task of science is to explain the phenomena which constitute its basic subject matter. In general, explanations are scientific answers to *why* questions. Any proposed explanation of a phenomenon must at least (1) show that somehow the phenomenon was expected to occur, (2) be intersubjectively certifiable, and (3) have empirical content. Generalized procedures or structures which purport to show how phenomena can be explained are called explanatory models. Of the six purportedly explanatory models that have been examined, only the deductive-nomological (D-N), deductive-statistical (D-S), and inductive-statistical (I-S) models meet the criteria for satisfactory explanations. The pattern model (P-M) fails the intersubjectively certifiable criterion, and functionalist explanations, to the extent that they are satisfactory explanations at all, are simply special cases of deductive-nomological explanations or statistical explanations. The greatest value of functionalism probably lies in the context of discovery rather than justification.

QUESTIONS FOR ANALYSIS AND DISCUSSION

1. Zaltman *et al.* (drawing upon Harvey [255]) suggest two alternative routes to scientific explanation—one by Bacon and one by Harvey. [647, p. 6] The "Baconian" route has the following order: (1) perceptual experiences; (2) unordered facts; (3) definition, classification, measurement; (4) ordered facts; (5) inductive generalizations; (6) laws and theory construction; and (7) explanation.

    The "Harvey" route has this order: (1) perceptual experiences, (2) image of real-world structure, (3) *a priori* model, (4) hypotheses, (5) experimental design, (6) data, (7) verification procedures, (8) laws and theory construction, and (9) explanation. Both 7 and 8 feed back into 2.

    Are these two different *models* of explanation? What are the essential differences between these models? Do the models fall within the scope of the logic of justification or the logic of discovery? Which model is superior? Why?

2. Find three other definitions of the term *model* in the marketing literature. How do the perspectives of these definitions differ from the perspective herein presented? Would the other definitions allow someone to distinguish between models and laws, theories, explanations, and hypotheses? Would a road map be a *model* using these other definitions? If not, would you rather choose to declare (1) that a road map is not a model or (2) that the definition of the term *model* is inadequate? Evaluate the usefulness of the varying perspectives on models.

3. How does an explanation of some phenomenon differ from an *explanatory model?*

4. What phenomena does marketing science seek to explain? Assess the current "state of the art" of our ability to explain each phenomenon you identify. Which phenomena do we seem to be making the most progress in explaining?

5. Find an explanation of some phenomenon in the marketing literature. Evaluate the nature, adequacy, and usefulness of the explanation.

6. Succinctly summarize the nature of the D-N, D-S, and I-S models of explanation. What are the essential differences among these models? Does *induction* play any role at all in the D-N and D-S models?

7. The notion of *Verstehen* suggests that the only way to understand and explain some human process is to be a *participant* in that process. [3] For example, only blacks could possibly teach black studies courses. Only marketing practitioners could possibly understand marketing phenomena. Would such a procedure and such knowledge pass the *intersubjectively certifiable* criterion?

8. Are explanations in marketing a *means* or an *end,* or both? That is, *why* are we interested in "why" questions? Would your answer depend on who you are, that is, a practitioner, student, or academician?

9. From the works of Wroe Alderson [9, 10], select what purports to be a *functionalist* explanation of some marketing phenomenon. Evaluate the adequacy of this explanation.

10. How does requiring explanations to be *falsifiable* differ from requiring them to be *confirmable?* Why are confirmability and falsifiability important?

11. In analyzing the work of Wroe Alderson, Hostiuck and Kurtz state:

    > Functionalism, for example, is mostly an analytical-conceptual schema. But, there is increasing evidence that it may also qualify as a theoretical structure. It is a "systematically related set of statements" that certainly includes "some lawlike generalizations." The aspects of "empirical testing" may admittedly have to wait for further developments in qualitative analysis. [284, p. 150]

    Evaluate their conclusion.

12. It is often suggested that to explain a phenomenon is to make the "unfamiliar become familiar." Is *making familiar* a necessary condition for explanation? Is it sufficient? Is it desirable?

13. Louch [in 401 and 306a] suggests that "when we say that a man . . . kills his father because he has been cut out of the will . . . we are offering [an explanation of a case that does] not require the support of general or theoretical statements." How satisfactory is this explanation, given the fact that only an infinitesimal fraction of all children who are cut out of their parents' wills subsequently kill their parents? What were your implicit or explicit criteria for "satisfactory?"

3
EXPLANATION: ISSUES AND ASPECTS

> Whenever we propose a solution to a problem we ought to try as hard as we can to overthrow our solution rather than defend it. Few of us, unfortunately, practice this precept; but other people, fortunately, will supply the criticism for us if we fail to supply it ourselves.
>
> *Karl R. Popper*

The purpose of this chapter is to explore certain issues in explanation and to evaluate several marketing explanations. The issues include the interrelationships among prediction, explanation, and scientific understanding. The nature of causal explanations will be explored, and the ways in which explanations are incomplete will be investigated. The fundamental explananda of marketing science are next proposed. The chapter concludes with a formal analysis of four different explanations in marketing: a product life cycle explanation, a consumer behavior explanation, a price discrimination explanation, and a wheel of retailing explanation.

3.1 EXPLANATION, PREDICTION, AND RETRODICTION

Does having an acceptable explanation for a phenomenon imply that we could have predicted it? That is, does being able to explain market share imply that we could have predicted market share? Conversely, does being able to predict market share imply that we can explain it? The issue has relevance to marketing because many marketing theorists apparently believe that explanation and prediction are not systematically interrelated. Robert Bartels suggests, "Explanation, however, rather than prediction is generally the objective of theory in the social and behavioral sciences." [40, p. 9] In their text on marketing research, Luck, Wales, and Taylor likewise seem to believe that explanation does not imply prediction. [403, p. 4] Hempel refers to the issue at hand as the thesis of structural identity or structural symmetry: *(1) Every adequate explanation is potentially a prediction, and (2) every adequate prediction is potentially an explanation.* [262, p. 367] Let's explore each half of the thesis, in turn. (See, also, Section 9.3.2.)

3.1.1   Explanations as Potential Predictions

To writers such as May Brodbeck and Karl Popper, the thesis of structural identity seems to be not an issue but a fact. First, May Brodbeck:

> Prediction has the same logical form as explanation. In predicting something as yet unknown, we deductively infer it from particular facts and laws that are already known. This deductive tautological connection among statements also shows why observations confirm or refute hypotheses. If a prediction inferred from a set of premises turns out to be true, then the generalization is further confirmed. If it turns out to be false, then we know that either the generalization or the individual fact used in making the prediction *must* be false. Because we are less likely to be mistaken about individual facts, in most cases the failure of a prediction means that the generalization is thereby refuted.
>
> It makes no difference whether the premises are statistical or deterministic, as nonstatistical generalizations are called. If they are deterministic, we may predict an individual event; if they are statistical, only statements about classes of events may be either explained or predicted. [81, pp. 9-10]

Popper comes to similar conclusions concerning the basic way in which explanations, predictions, and testing are interrelated. Popper suggests that explanations, predictions, and testing do not differ in logical structure. Rather, the differences are related to what is considered *known* or *given* and what is considered *unknown* or to be *uncovered*. [504, p. 133] With *explanation,* certain phenomena are known and what is to be uncovered are the laws and theories that can explain the phenomena. For example, if we know that many consumers are brand loyal, our task in marketing may be to *explain* their brand loyalty by uncovering certain laws and theories. With *prediction,* certain laws and theories are known, and we wish to apply our scientific knowledge by predicting certain phenomena. For example, if certain laws and theories concerning brand loyalty are known, a marketing practitioner may apply these constructions to predict the characteristics of consumers who might be brand loyal to his particular product. Finally, with *testing,* certain laws and theories are proposed, and we compare the actual phenomena with the phenomena that the laws and theories predicted would occur. To the extent that the laws and theories predict correctly or incorrectly (that is, the test results are positive or negative), we have corroborative or noncorroborative evidence that the real world is actually constructed as our laws and theories would suggest.

To Brodbeck and Popper, every explanation implies an *ex post facto* prediction. Thus, the explanation-implies-prediction argument is:

The E-P Argument

(a) The explanation of phenomenon X at time t_n implies that

(b) *if* person A had been present at time t_{n-2}, and

(c) *if* A had known circumstances $C_1, C_2, C_3, \ldots C_k$, and

(d) *if* A had applied laws $L_1, L_2, L_3, \ldots L_j$

(e) *then* A could have predicted that X would occur at time t_{n-1}.

(f) Therefore, all explanations are potentially predictive.

Careful examination of the premises (statements *a* through *d*) of the E-P argument shows them to be true. All of the models that do explain phenomena—the D-N, D-S, and I-S models—are consistent with the premises. Models which do *not* explain phenomena, such as the pattern model, are *not* consistent with the premises of the E-P argument. Finally, the conclusions (statements *e* and *f*) of the E-P argument do seem to be logically implied by the premises. Therefore, we must conclude that the E-P argument is true: Every adequate explanation is potentially a prediction. That is, if we could not have predicted the occurrence of a phenomenon, we cannot now satisfactorily explain it.

The preceding discussion provides insight into a common circumstance in the social sciences and marketing. Someone creates a model or theory. A critic evaluates the model and concludes that it is not empirically testable since the model has no predictive capacity. The apologist for the model then claims, "The fact that my model makes no predictions is irrelevant because my purpose is to *explain* the phenomenon, not predict it!" In light of this analysis, the apologist's defense becomes vacuous since *all adequate explanations must have predictive capacity*.

Dubin struggles at length with his "Power Paradox," and although he refers to *understanding* rather than *explanation*, the issue is similar to the thesis of structural identity. Dubin states the Power Paradox in terms of a question: "Why is it that we can create models of social behavior that are powerful in contributing to understanding, without providing, at the same time, precision in prediction?" [160, p. 17] Since Dubin uses the term *model* as synonymous with our term *theory*, we can reconstruct the premises and conclusions of Dubin's paradox for analysis:

a. Many social science theories do not provide precision in prediction.

b. Many of these same theories contribute powerfully to understanding.

c. The preceding seems paradoxical.

Many marketing theorists believe that their theories and models contribute to the understanding of marketing phenomena, while at the same time admitting the predictive impotence of their theories. Bettman and Jones evaluated several models of consumer behavior, including those proposed by Farley, Ring, and Nicosia. After observing the lack of predictive power of many of these models, Bettman and Jones conclude, "The main use of these models may lie in attempting to understand behavior rather than predict it." [61, p. 556]   Can we understand behavior without being able to predict it?   Perhaps an analysis of Dubin's Power Paradox will shed light on the issue.

Since paradoxes are created by man, not nature, we should explore whether the premises *(a* and *b)* of the paradox are true.   Even a casual observer of the social sciences would conclude that *a* is true; many social science and marketing models and theories do not predict.   However, is *b* true?   Do these nonpredictive models contribute powerfully to understanding?   The answer depends on the meaning of the term *understanding*.   Bunge suggests that two usages are common, (1) *intuitive understanding* and (2) *scientific understanding*.   Intuitive understanding of a phenomenon suggests that we are *psychologically comfortable* or *familiar* with the phenomenon. [96, p. 30]   Scientific understanding of a phenomenon implies, at least, that we can *scientifically explain* the phenomenon. [96, p. 31]   Now, intuitive understanding does not imply scientific understanding; many people are psychologically comfortable with a rainbow but cannot explain how rainbows occur.   Also, intuitive understanding is inescapably individual in kind.   Phenomena that may be psychologically comfortable to one person (e.g., thunder) may be psychologically uncomfortable to another person.   Therefore, just as we found with the pattern model (Section 2.6), intuitive understanding fails the criterion of being intersubjectively confirmable and cannot be considered as a part of scientific knowledge.

Clearly, Dubin does not mean *understanding* in the intuitive sense, but rather, in the scientific sense.   However, since scientific understanding (in order to be intersubjectively confirmable in the context of Section 2.2) implies explanatory power, and since explanatory power implies being potentially predictive, *the Power Paradox disappears. Premise b is false; marketing and other social science theories which do not predict do not make powerful contributions to (scientific) understanding.*

3.1.2   Predictions as Potential Explanations

The second half of the thesis of structural identity asserts that every adequate prediction is potentially an explanation.   The case favoring the second half of the structural identity thesis usually rests on this kind of argument:

The P-E Argument

(a) The prediction that phenomenon X will occur at time t_{n+1} means that

(b) *if* person A observes certain circumstances $C_1, C_2, C_3, \ldots C_k$ at time t_n, and

(c) *if* A applies laws $L_1, L_2, L_3, \ldots L_j$ at time t_n,

(d) *then* A can predict that X will occur at time t_{n+1}.

(e) Furthermore, if A waits until time t_{n+1}, and

(f) *if* A observes that phenomenon X occurs,

(g) *then* A can explain phenomenon X by reference to statements *b* and *c*.

(h) Therefore, all adequate predictions are potential explanations.

Many people who readily accept the explanation-implies-prediction argument totally reject the prediction-implies-explanation argument. Critics claim that they can predict the business cycle by measuring the length of hemlines on women's skirts, but no reasonable person would argue that women's hemlines *explain* business cycles. Similarly, one can accurately predict the birthrate in Oslo, Norway by observing the temperatures of the sidewalks in Madison, Wisconsin, but reasonable people would not claim to *explain* the former by the latter.[1]

The critic's claim can be supported and the P-E Argument broken by attacking statement *c*, "if A applies laws $L_1, L_2, L_3, \ldots L_j$ at time t_n." Are there statements which can be used to make accurate predictions but which are not *laws*? Since the subject of "laws" is the topic for Chapter 4, the treatment here will be brief in the extreme. However, consider the following statement: "All desks in room 201 that have the initials S.D.H. also have the initials S.E." The statement has universal form (all X are Y) and can generate a prediction of a sort; that is, if you go to room 201, and if you find any desk with S.D.H. on it, you will also find S.E. on it. Nevertheless, such statements are not properly considered *laws*, but rather, are *accidental generalizations*. Therefore, since accidental generalizations have predictive capacity, and since explanations must contain laws, and since accidental generalizations are not laws, *the P-E Argument is false*. Contrary to the thesis of structural identity, *all adequate (accurate) predictions are not potential explanations*. This conclusion is consistent with scientific realism but contrary to logical empiricism (see Section 9.3.2).

3.1.3   Are Explanations and Predictions Potential Retrodictions?

Although the terms *explanation* and *prediction* are familiar words in common English, the term *retrodiction* belongs strictly to the scientific vocabulary. The term *retrodiction* as used by Ryle [546, p. 124] implies making inferences about the past on the basis of present observations.

---

[1] Yes, it can be done. The sidewalk temperature in Madison is correlated with the ambient temperature in Madison. The latter is correlated with the ambient temperature in Oslo. The temperature in Oslo is related to the rate of conception in Oslo (higher in winter). QED.

Hempel [262, p. 173] and Hanson [249, p. 193] use the term *postdiction* to imply the same procedure.

Note the significant difference between retrodiction and both explanation and prediction. With explanation, the phenomena which do the *explaining* occur in time before the phenomenon to be explained. Likewise, with prediction, the phenomena which do the *predicting* antecede the phenomenon to be predicted. In contrast, with retrodiction, the phenomena which accomplish the *retrodicting* occur *after* the phenomenon to be retrodicted.

An example of retrodiction should show how it differs from both explanation and prediction. Carbon 14 dating of objects classically illustrates the retrodiction of when an animal died. By measuring the amount of Carbon 14 contained in the bone structure of a deceased animal and by employing certain (statistical) laws concerning radiocarbon decay, the date when the animal died can be *retrodicted* within an accuracy of ±50 years. [68, p. 315] Thus, retrodiction has this formal structure:

(a) Certain circumstances C_1, C_2, C_3, ... C_k are observed (e.g., the amount of Carbon 14 in the bones of a deceased animal), and

(b) certain laws L_1, L_2, L_3, ... L_j (e.g., laws governing radiocarbon decay) are then applied to

(c) *retrodict* the occurrence of some past phenomenon (e.g., date of death) which anteceded C_1, C_2, C_3, ... C_k.

Must we be able to retrodict in order to adequately explain or predict? Hanson argues affirmatively: "Every prediction, if inferentially respectable, must possess a corresponding postdiction, [retrodiction]." [249, p. 193] Unfortunately, Hanson uses as his model for explanatory adequacy certain models such as Newtonian mechanics that are deterministic in a very strong sense. That is, the relationships in the models are reversible with respect to their time variables. Hanson confuses necessary conditions with sufficient conditions. Many very useful explanations need only show that condition C_1, C_2, C_3, ... C_k are *sufficient* to predict X. Retrodiction requires that conditions C_1, C_2, C_3, ... C_k were *necessary* for X to occur; that is, X could not have occurred without C_1, C_2, C_3, ... C_k also occurring. It is one thing to be able to predict that certain circumstances will be sufficient to assure the early demise of a new product. It is an entirely different thing to be able to take a dead product and retrodict the circumstances that killed it. Although retrodiction would be a desirable characteristic of any model, neither explanatory nor predictive adequacy implies the ability to retrodict.

3.2   CAUSAL EXPLANATIONS

Are all explanations *causal?* Can an explanation be adequate and yet noncausal? The Paradox of Causation: Although the term *cause* is widely used in both everyday language and scientific language, for centuries the notion of *causality* has steadfastly resisted definitive explication.

In everyday language we ask, "Why did the window break?" And we are satisfied with the explanation: *"Because* little Jimmy threw a ball into it!" Also, "What caused the house to burn down?" "Little Jimmy caused it by playing with matches." Likewise, physical scientists remain comfortable with such assertions as "the force of gravity *causes* the missile to fall to the earth" and "the rays of the sun *cause* the ice to melt." Marketers seem comfortable with such statements as "lack of promotion caused the product to fail" and "high prices caused the recent sales decline." However comfortable both laymen and scientists are with the terms *cause* and *causal explanation,* the next section shows how methodologically troublesome the notion of causality has been.

3.2.1   The Notion of Causality

Exactly what is meant by the assertion *"X* causes *Y,"* and precisely what kinds of evidence can be gathered to support the assertion? In particular, the fundamental problem of causation is: *What evidence can empirically or logically separate the assertion "X causes Y" from the assertion "X and Y occur regularly in the same pattern"?* Perhaps the best place to start would be with a review of some historical perspectives on causation.

Most of the perspectives on causation invoke two common themes. To illustrate the first theme, in 1840 William Whewell suggested that "by cause we mean some quality, power, or efficacy by which a state of things produces a second state." [633, p. 67] He then espouses his version of the law of universal causation:

> We assert that "Every event must have a cause": and this proposition we know to be true not only probably, and generally, and as far as we can see; but we cannot suppose it to be false in any single instance. We are as certain of it as of the truths of arithmetic or geometry. We cannot doubt that it must apply to all events past and future, in every part of the universe, just as truly as to those occurrences which we have ourselves observed. [633, p. 67]

Although not necessarily subscribing to the law of universal causation, modern-day adherents to scientific realism believe that causation must involve the powers and capacities of things. Scientific realism holds that "the long-term success of a scientific theory gives reason to believe that something like the entities and structure postulated by the theory actually exists." [434, p. 26] (See Section 11.3.) The realists Harré and Madden [251, pp. 86-87] discuss causal powers:

The proper analysis of the ascription of a power to a thing or material (and, with some qualifications, also to a person) is this:

"X has the power to A" means "X $\genfrac{}{}{0pt}{}{(will)}{(can)}$do A, in the appropriate conditions, *in virtue of its intrinsic nature.*"

In ascribing powers to people, "can" must be substituted for "will." Whether he will or no has to be explained by considerations other than the extrinsic conditions for action. It is the reference to the nature of the potent thing that marks the difference between the ascription of powers and of mere dispositions.

From this analysis of power ascriptions two important points follow.

1. To ascribe a power to a thing or material is to say something specific about what it *will* or *can do,* but it is not to assert any specific hypotheses about the nature of that thing. To ascribe a power to a thing asserts only that it can do what it does in virtue of its nature, whatever that is. It leaves open the question of the exact specification of the nature or constitution in virtue of which the thing, person, or material has the power. It leaves it open to be discovered by later empirical investigation, should that prove to be possible.

2. But to ascribe a power is to say that what the thing or material does or can do is to be understood as brought about not just by the stimuli to which it may be subject or the conditions which it finds itself in, i.e., by extrinsic conditions, but in some measure by the nature or constitution of that thing or material, i.e., by intrinsic conditions. (In a sense the ascription of a power is a schema for an explanation of the manifestation of the power.)

William Stanley Jevons illustrates the second theme: "A cause is defined as the necessary or invariable antecedent of an event, so that when the cause exists, the effect will also exist or soon follow." [320, p. 140] A modern version of this kind of analysis is the "INUS condition" proposed by Mackie. [413] INUS stands for "insufficient-necessary-unnecessary-sufficient." Mackie proposes that "A is an INUS [causal] condition of a result P if and only if, for some X and some Y, $(AX$ or $Y)$ is a necessary and sufficient condition of P, but A is not a sufficient condition of P and X is not a sufficient condition of P." [413, p. 17] That is, a cause may be an insufficient but necessary part of a condition that is itself unnecessary but sufficient for the result. As Sosa [598, p. 4] has pointed out, an INUS condition is very little different from a condition which is, *ceteris paribus,* sufficient. Bagozzi proposes that many of the causal relations proposed by marketers are INUS conditions and offers the following example [29, pp. 17-18]:

As an example, let us examine the claim sometimes made by marketers that brand image (measured by the brand name) affects the perception of quality. When marketers make this claim they are not saying that the brand image is a necessary cause or condition for the attribution of quality.   One may judge a product as high or low in quality without knowing the brand.   Similarly, marketers are not claiming that the brand image is sufficient for the perception of quality since one must at least attend to, be aware of, and evaluate the brand name before such an attribution can be made.   Rather, the brand image may be regarded as an INUS condition in that it is an insufficient but necessary part of a condition that is itself unnecessary but sufficient for the result.   Many of the causal relations investigated by marketers are of this sort.

Therefore, by "X causes Y" writers usually mean that "X has the power to produce Y," or X is an invariable antecedent of Y, or "X is *necessary* for Y," or "X is *sufficient* for Y."   But how can we *know* that "X has the power to produce Y" or any of the other conceptualizations of cause?   What are the kinds of evidence or criteria?   So far we have synonyms for *cause* but no objective criteria.   In short, what are the necessary and sufficient conditions to enable one to label a relationship *causal?*   Many philosophers of science have attempted to generate the necessary and sufficient conditions for causality, including J. S. Mill with his canons of induction.

The logical positivists and logical empiricists believed that "cause" was a metaphysical concept that could (and should) be avoided.   Thus, following Hume, Kyburg questions whether the concept of "cause" is "of scientific interest." [361, p. 236]   May Brodbeck contends that "as we learn more about the laws of temporal processes, the notion of cause tends to be eliminated." [81, p. 672]   As we shall see in Section 9.6.2, these writers have fallen victim to the "philosophers' fallacy of high redefinition," as has Dubin:

> Empirically relevant theory in the social sciences is built upon an acceptance of the notion of relationship rather than the notion of causality. . . . The *operations* by which we test [a] relationship between theoretically predicted values and empirical values differ in *absolutely no respect* whether we label the relationships among units of a model as *laws of interaction* or as *causal laws.* . . . The temptation is strong to interpret sequential laws of interaction as though they were causal in structure.   This gratuitous assumption of causality adds nothing to social science, however much it satisfies psychological needs. [160, pp. 91, 94, 106]

3.2.2   Evidence for Causation

So the term *causation* is firmly ensconced in common English and the technical languages of both the social and physical sciences.   At the same time, sufficient conditions to apply the term do not exist (in fact may be logically impossible to attain).   Dubin and other "Humeans" suggest throwing the term out.   Much less drastic, yet much more pragmatic and consistent with contemporary social science, would be to attempt the more modest task of setting forth certain *necessary* or *minimal* conditions for causality. This procedure could at least point out some patently noncausal explanations. *Pragmatically speaking, we may refer to causal explanations as those explanations that employ nonspurious, theoretically supported, sequential laws in their explanans.* Using the preceding definition as a guide, we can identify four criteria for classifying an explanation as causal.[2]

1. *Temporal sequentiality.* If changes in factor *A* are to be used to causally explain factor *B*, then the occurrence of the changes in *A* must precede in time the occurrence of changes in *B*. That is, *A* and *B* must be related by a *law of succession.* Not all laws are laws of succession (see Chapter 5). Many laws, such as Boyle's Law of Gases, are *laws of atemporal coexistence;* they show a relationship that must be realized and contain no time variable.

   The direction of the sequentiality of phenomena is not always intuitively obvious. For years, it was presumed that attitude changes preceded behavior changes. Recent evidence suggests that behavior changes often precede attitude changes. [636, 199, 523] However, the notion of temporal sequentiality suggests that if the introduction of additional salesmen is to be considered a *cause* of increased sales, then the salesmen must be added before the observed increase in sales. Similarly, if a new volume discount policy is to be considered a *cause* of better channel relations, then the discount policy must precede in time the improved channel relations.

2. *Associative variation.* If factor *A* is a cause of factor *B*, then changes in the level or presence of factor *A* must be systematically associated with changes in the level or presence of factor *B*. Although it is true that "correlation does not imply causation," the observation that two factors are systematically associated (correlation being a measure of the degree of this association) is evidence *in support of* causation. Conversely, the *absence* of association is very strong evidence that the two factors are *not* causally related. If market shares are caused by advertising, then we could expect to find differences in market shares systematically associated with differences in the quantity or quality of advertising.

3. *Nonspurious association.* If *A* causes *B*, then there must be no factor *Z* which, if introduced into the explanation, would make the systematic association between *A* and *B* vanish. Green and Tull refer to the criterion as the "absence of other possible causes." [236, p. 81] If one diligently explores for other factors which might possibly have caused changes in *B* and can find no such factor, then this evidence supports the assertion that the association between *A* and *B* is a true causal relationship rather than a spurious one.

---

[2] See Simon [589, p. 454] for a somewhat different treatment of criteria for causality. Also, see Green and Tull. [236, p. 79 ff.]

The nonspurious criterion emphasizes the tremendous scientific value of experimental research designs as opposed to nonexperimental designs. Although definitions of "experimental design" differ, most experimental designs either systematically exclude from the research setting, or carefully monitor and control, factors other than the independent variable (the one doing the "causing") which might influence the dependent variable (the one being "caused"). Discounting the possibility that other factors cause changes in B becomes much more difficult in *nonexperimental* designs. Causal imputations in marketing are particularly likely to fail the nonspuriousness criterion since most research in marketing has traditionally relied upon nonexperimental designs.   Some publications suggest that this situation may be changing. [135, 624]

4. *Theoretical support.*   The fourth criterion suggests that well-confirmed theories can be used to support the assertion that A causes B.   That is, if A causes B is consistent with theory X, and if theory X has been successfully used to explain other phenomena, then theory X provides theoretical support for the assertion that A causes B.

Suppose someone says, "The length of women's skirts *causes* our market share to rise or fall." Suppose further that an examination of the evidence reveals (1) the general rising of women's skirts has preceded the rising of marketing shares, (2) the correlation between the two factors has been very strong, and (3) no third factor can be found which makes the correlation vanish. That is, the evidence accords with the temporal sequentiality, associative variation, and nonspuriousness criteria. Clearly, most people would *still* view as ridiculous the claim that "the length of women's skirts *causes* market share." The causal claim in question is ridiculous precisely because it has no theoretical support; that is, it does not fit into all the rest of the things we "know" about factors associated with the lengths of skirts and market share.

The criterion of theoretical support must not be pushed too far. Poor Galileo paid a heavy price because his notions concerning the movements of celestial bodies did not fit with the "known" theological fact that the Earth was the center of the universe. Also, recall that Einstein's Theory of Relativity did not fit with Newtonian mechanics. Nevertheless, the burden of proof must lie with the proposer of new "nonfitting truths."

Many marketing researchers are now using the so-called *Granger conditions* as a means of testing for causal relationships. Using the techniques of Granger [234], Sims [590], and Pierce and Haugh [494], Jacobson and Nicosia [314] explored for causal relationships between advertising and various measures of aggregate demand. Bass and Pilon [46a] used similar techniques to evaluate their time-series model of market share behavior. Granger's definition of causality suggests that a variable X is causally related to Y if we are better able to predict Y by using all of the available variables, including X, than by using the same set of variables without X. Using this definition, Granger, Sims, and Pierce and Haugh propose a wide range of specific tests. These tests are cross-correlational in nature and use time-series data. All of the tests use as evidence of causality what is referred to here as "temporal sequentiality" and "associative variation."

Other marketing researchers are vigorously pursuing the structural equations approach to causal modeling. Originally conceptualized by Bock and Borgman [71] and later developed by Joreskog [322, 323], this approach uses the maximum likelihood method for estimating parameters. Bagozzi [29] has developed the approach most completely for marketing and has used it to examine for causal relationships between performance and satisfaction among industrial salespeople.

This section on causation concludes with a personal observation. I have no objection to the use of the terms *cause* and *causation* in marketing and, in fact, believe the search for true causal relationships to be central to the mission of marketing science. However, we must never delude ourselves into believing that we can ever know any causal relationship with certainty. Purportedly causal relationships are always only more or less probable, and we should always diligently explore the possibility that the relationships are actually spurious. The very essence of science is that all statements are tentative and subject to change and revision on the basis of future evidence.

3.3 EXPLANATION CHAINS AND INFINITE REGRESS

All explanations are incomplete in a fundamental way; something is always left unexplained. Phenomenon K (e.g., the path of a celestial body) is explained by subsuming it under laws L_1 and L_2 (Newtonian mechanics). But the critic rightly complains that L_1 and L_2 are unexplained. The theorist responds that L_1 and L_2 can be explained by subsumption under L_3 and L_4 (Einstein's Special Theory of Relativity), and the critic demands the explanation chain of L_3 and L_4. The theorist stops his *explanation chain* at the most basic lawlike statements known at the time (Einstein's General Theory of Relativity), prompting the critic to note that the explanation is still incomplete.

Since all explanatory structures involve potentially infinite regresses of the preceding variety, explanations are incomplete in this sense. Thus, the critic's point must be admitted. Fortunately, the problem poses no insurmountable conceptual barrier when placed in proper perspective. Surely, no one would seriously propose that in order to explain *anything* we must explain *everything*. Such nihilism would place ludicrous requirements on scientific explanations in light of the admitted usefulness of explanations that involve potentially infinite regresses. Also, the admission that the most basic laws underlying explanations are left unexplained must be clearly differentiated from the assertion that the basic laws are *unsupported*. Even though the basic laws at the end of the explanation chain may be unexplained by other laws, there may well exist tremendous empirical support for the veracity of the laws.

3.3.1   Marketing Explanation Chains

Explanation chains abound in marketing. For example, many studies in consumer behavior [45, 287, 576] at least implicitly employ variants of the A-P-I-B chain:

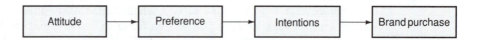

The chain implies that attitude can be used to explain preference and preference can be used to explain intentions and, thus, intentions can be used to explain brand purchase. The chain can be stated even more simply by starting at the other end. Consumers are more likely to purchase brands they intend to buy than brands they do not intend to buy; consumers are more likely to intend to buy brands they prefer than brands they do not prefer; finally, consumers are more likely to prefer brands toward which they have a favorable attitude than brands toward which they do not have a favorable attitude.

Bunge has suggested that explanation chains be evaluated according to their explanatory depth. [96, p. 29] Some explanation chains remain at a shallow, superficial, or trivial level, even though they involve several stages. Other explanations seem deep, relying on profound or fundamental lawlike statements. Returning to the A-P-I-B chain, there is something intellectually disquieting about its depth. The chain seems to regress no further than a seemingly superficial level.

How deep an explanatory chain must go to reach respectability remains an open issue. Indeed, even chains as shallow as A-P-I-B have found usefulness in short-range predictions (explanations) of the purchase of consumer durables. [333, p. 52] Unfortunately, the A-P-I-B chain is usually of limited usefulness to practitioners because it is not deep enough to provide most marketers with guidance as to *how* and *where* to *influence* the chain. The marketer contends, "Don't tell me that people who have a favorable attitude toward my brand are likely to purchase it; tell me what factors that I control can influence attitude!" Therefore, from the marketing practitioner's perspective, the respectability of an explanatory chain is directly proportional to the guidance it gives to the marketer in his attempts to influence the chain.

From the marketing academician's perspective, the issue of how deep an explanatory chain must be for *scientific respectability* is even more ambiguous. Such academic norms are essentially set by peer group consensus. These norms are strongly influenced by the editors and reviewing staffs of the major professional journals. It is incumbent upon these groups to maintain high standards.

3.4   OTHER FORMS OF EXPLANATORY INCOMPLETENESS

Besides the problem of the infinite regress of explanation chains, numerous other ways in which explanations may be incomplete have been suggested. [262, p. 415] Three in particular seem worthy of note: enthymemes, partial explanations, and what Hempel refers to as explanation sketches. [262, p. 424]

3.4.1   Enthymemes

Many explanations are incomplete in that they are elliptically formulated, or what the logician refers to as *enthymemes*. [365, p. 29] To be elliptically incomplete implies that certain necessary statements or laws are skipped over or suppressed in the explanation. The person offering the explanation presumably *assumes* that the reader will either consciously or unconsciously fill in the missing statements. Most narrative explanations are elliptically formulated because both writer and reader would perceive fully articulated explanations as tedious and unnecessary. This form of incompleteness is usually harmless enough, provided the writer is certain that the reader can fill in the explanation with the appropriate statements. Refer to the structural analysis of the consumer behavior explanation later in this chapter for an illustration of an enthymeme (see Section 3.7.1).

3.4.2   Partial Explanations

Often a proposed explanation is *partial* in the sense that the explanation does not explain why k occurred, but only that some phenomenon of type G occurred and that k is a subclass of G. For example, using the construct "generalized self-confidence," it might be possible to explain why a person purchased a "major brand" of gasoline but not which *specific* brand. Recall that FM2 in Section 2.7.3 was a partial explanation and in this sense incomplete. Naturally, we would prefer all explanations to be complete, but the importance of partial explanations should not be minimized.

3.4.3   Explanation Sketches

The last form of explanatory incompleteness is suggested by the term *explanation sketch*. Here, the proposed explanation is neither *elliptically* formulated nor is it *partial* in the sense of the previous section. An explanation sketch implies that only a general outline of the explanation is offered. ("Here are some variables which might be related to brand preference.") Explanation sketches need substantial elaboration and development before they can qualify as complete explanations.

Explanation sketches probably belong more in the context of discovery than in the context of justification. They are meant to suggest fruitful areas of inquiry for researchers exploring the phenomena in question. Most explanations in both marketing and other social sciences may come closer to being explanation sketches than fully articulated explanations.

3.5   THE FUNDAMENTAL EXPLANANDA OF MARKETING

If the distinctive aim of science is to explain phenomena, what phenomena does marketing theory attempt to explain? That is, what are the fundamental explananda of marketing science? Alternatively, what are the fundamental "dependent variables" of marketing science? Consistent with the perspective of most marketing theorists [10, 26, 27, 28, 345], this writer has proposed that the basic subject matter of marketing is the exchange relationship or transaction. The discipline of marketing has its normative or "applied" side which is not science. The positive or "basic" side houses the science of marketing. *Therefore, marketing science is the behavioral science which seeks to explain exchange relationships.* Given this perspective of marketing science and adopting the customary (albeit somewhat arbitrary) convention of designating one party to the exchange as the "buyer" and one party as the "seller," the fundamental explananda of marketing can be logically derived. The four sets of fundamental explananda (FE) of marketing science are:

FE1.   The behaviors of buyers directed at consummating exchanges.

FE2.   The behaviors of sellers directed at consummating exchanges.

FE3.   The institutional framework directed at consummating and/or facilitating exchanges.

FE4.   The consequences for society of the behaviors of buyers, the behaviors of sellers, and the institutional framework directed at consummating and/or facilitating exchanges.

The first set of fundamental explananda indicates that marketing science seeks to answer this question: *Why do which buyers purchase what they do, where they do, when they do, and how they do?* The "which buyers" seeks to explain why certain buyers enter into a particular exchange relationships and others do not. The "what" indicates that different buyers purchase different product/service mixes. The "where" is the institutional/locational choice of buyers. That is, why do some buyers purchase at discount department stores and others at full-service department stores, and why do some buyers purchase in neighborhood stores and others in shopping centers? The "when" refers to the timing decisions of buyers. Why do buyers purchase differently at different stages in the family life cycle? Finally, the "how" refers to the processes that consumers use in making their purchasing decisions. That is, what are the identifiable stages in consumer decision making? The "how" also refers to any organizational systems that buyers develop to accomplish the purchasing task, for example, the sharing of buying responsibilities among various members of the household.

The second set of fundamental explananda of marketing concerns the behaviors of sellers. As Lutz [407, p. 5] has pointed out, "It has been extremely unfortunate that the vast bulk of theory-based behavioral research in marketing has been on consumer behavior." He then concludes that "if we truly believe that exchange is the fundamental building block of marketing, then we have virtually ignored (in a scientific sense) the behavior of the party selling to the consumer." The guiding question is, *Why do which sellers produce, price, promote, and distribute what they do, where they do, when they do, and how they do?* The "which" points out that not all sellers participate in all exchanges. The "what" seeks explanations for the kinds of products produced, prices charged, promotions used, and distributors employed. The "when" seeks explanations for the timing of the behaviors of sellers. The "where" refers to the locations chosen by sellers to do business. The "how" refers to the processes involved and to the organizational frameworks developed by sellers when they engage in exchange relationships.

The third set of fundamental explananda suggests that marketing science seeks answers to these questions: *Why do which kinds of institutions develop to engage in what kinds of functions or activities to consummate and/or facilitate exchanges, when will these institutions develop, where will they develop, and how will they develop?* The "which" points out that not all kinds of institutions participate in the consummation and/or facilitation of all kinds of exchanges, and seeks to identify the kinds of institutions and "what" specific kinds of activities (functions) will be performed by each. The "when" refers to the evolution or changing of the kinds of institutions through time and "where" these changes will take place. The "how" refers to the processes that bring about these institutional changes.

As used here, the term *institution* refers both to the intermediaries which either take title to goods or negotiate purchases or sales, such as wholesalers and retailers, and to purely facilitating agencies such as those which are solely engaged in transportation, warehousing, advertising, or marketing research. As suggested by Arndt [21, p. 37], marketing institutions can also be considered as "sets of conditions and rules for transactions and other interactions." Note that the study of *marketing systems* can be considered the study of collections of interacting marketing institutions. In short, the third set of explananda seeks to explain the nature and development of all kinds of marketing systems.

The fourth set of fundamental explananda concerns the consequences of marketing for society. The guiding question is, *Why do which kinds of behaviors of buyers, behaviors of sellers, and institutions have what kinds of consequences for society, when they do, where they do, and how they do?* The "which" directs the theorists to focus on specific kinds of behaviors and/or institutions and explain "what" kinds of consequences these behaviors or institutions will have for society. Again, the "when" refers to the timing of the consequences and the "where" focuses on *those on whom* the consequences will fall. For example, will the consequences fall disproportionately on the disadvantaged members of society? Finally, the "how" focuses on the processes and mechanisms by which various parts of society are impacted by marketing activities. The study of the kinds of consequences discussed here is generally subsumed under the term *macromarketing*. The preceding four sets of explananda are proposed to be *fundamental* in the sense that every phenomenon that marketing science seeks to explain can ultimately be reduced to a phenomenon residing in one of the four sets.

3.6   A PRODUCT LIFE CYCLE EXPLANATION

As samples of "why" questions in marketing, Section 2.1 asked (1) why the sales of product X have been decreasing rapidly, (2) why consumers purchase particular brands of detergents, (3) why budget motels have recently entered the hotel/motel industry, and (4) why newspapers charge lower rates to local advertisers than to national advertisers? This section and the three subsequent sections will offer typical marketing explanations of these phenomena and then systematically explore the underlying structure of the explanations.

Why are the sales of product X decreasing rapidly? A marketing explanation of this phenomenon might include reference to the product life cycle (PLC) concept. The product life cycle suggests that products go through four stages: introduction, growth, maturity, and decline. [344, p. 430] During the introductory stage, sales increase very slowly and profits are usually negative. During the growth stage, the product catches on and both sales and profits increase rapidly. At the maturity stage, sales begin to level off and profits start a gradual decline.

Finally, both sales and profits decrease precipitously during the decline stage. *The decrease in sales of product* X *can be explained by noting that* X *is in the decline stage of its life cycle where rapidly decreasing sales and profits are to be expected.*

Product life cycle explanations of the preceding variety frequently turn out to be vacuous. The crucial part of the explanans is the statement "X is in the decline stage," since this statement carries the burden of explaining the decreasing sales. Yet, how do we know that "X is in the decline stage"? Kotler has observed that "the stages, if stages there are, [of the product life cycle] are too variable in length to permit a prediction of when the next one will occur." [344, p. 438] Since the lengths of the stages are too variable, the primary factor determining the stage of the life cycle is sales. But the explanans then turns into a *tautology* or an *analytic* explanation because if the level of sales determines the stage of the life cycle, then the stage in the life cycle cannot be used to explain the level of sales. Unless and until the product life cycle can be refined to the point where the stages can be identified independent of the sales variable, the life cycle concept will remain impotent and void of explanatory power.

Recognizing the essentially tautologous nature of the product life cycle, Tellis and Crawford [615] have developed a substitute notion, the product evolution cycle (PEC). Drawing upon the theory of biological evolution, they propose that sales are an evolutionary function of three motivating forces: market factors, managerial effectiveness, and government mediation. Unlike the PLC, the PEC does not assume that sales is a function of time. Rather, the evolution of sales proceeds within the dimension of time. The evolution proceeds in the direction of greater efficiency, greater complexity, and greater diversity. The PEC would appear to resolve some of the troublesome tautological problems of the PLC. However, it has yet to be subjected to empirical testing.

3.7   A CONSUMER BEHAVIOR EXPLANATION

The next explanation attempts to answer the question *"Why do consumers purchase particular brands of detergents?"* Engel, Kollat, and Blackwell in their book *Consumer Behavior* present a model of habitual decision-process behavior and in a following section, entitled "Using the Model to Explain Consumer Behavior," they provide an explanation for detergent purchasing. [167, p. 67] Both the model and the explanation are reproduced for analysis (see Figure 3-1).

3.7.1   A Reconstruction of the Explanation

The explanation provided by Engel, Kollat, and Blackwell uses a narrative format which is pedagogically appropriate for a textbook but which

Figure 3-1   Habitual decision-process behavior

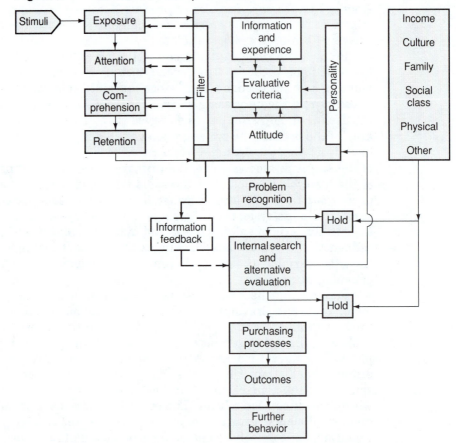

Source: James F. Engel, David T. Kollat, and Roger D. Blackwell, *Consumer Behavior* (New York: Holt, Rinehart & Winston, 1973), p. 60. Reprinted by permission from Holt, Rinehart & Winston, Inc.

The purchase of a laundry detergent

Laundry detergents generally are purchased on the basis of habit rather than extended problem solving. A problem is recognized when the housewife runs out of detergent, and her decision usually calls for purchase of a preferred brand on her next visit to the grocery store. There is no need to engage in conscious weighing of alternatives or external search for information. The situation changes, of course, when a significant new product comes on the market, but innovations of that magnitude are a rarity in this industry.

Survey results showed that women evaluate a detergent on the following bases: (1) cleaning ability (96 percent), (2) low suds (54 percent), (3) safety to colors (48 percent), (4) whitening and brightening ability (44 percent), (5) price (31 percent), and (6) fresh smell (20 percent). In addition to these evaluative criteria, 86 percent favored a powdered form and 60 percent preferred to use warm water. Several major brands were found to rate highest on these criteria, with Tide being the dominant favorite. These ratings of brand attitude closely paralleled market shares. The result is strong loyalty toward one or two preferred brands and only relatively small incidence of permanent brand switching. If the housewife does switch, it tends to be a temporary action to take advantage of a price reduction.

Those who were interviewed, for the most part, evidenced satisfaction with their present alternative. Postdecision evaluation, therefore, seldom takes place. [167, pp. 66-67] makes evaluation difficult. The following reconstruction (1) captures the essence of the explanation, (2) shows specifically how the explanation relates to the model, and (3) lends itself more readily to structural analysis and evaluation.

a. Most people do not engage in conscious weighing of alternatives or external search for information when purchasing detergents.

b. Therefore, for most people, and except for unusual circumstances, the purchase of detergents can be classified as habitual in nature.

c. Therefore, the habitual decision-process behavior model can be applied to the purchasing of detergents.

d. The *stimulus* occurs when the housewife runs out of detergent.

e. The *evaluative criteria* for detergents (surveys show) are in rank order of most often mentioned to least often mentioned: (1) cleaning ability, (2) low suds, (3) . . .

f. Additional evaluative criteria suggest that 86 percent of women prefer detergent in powder form, and 60 percent prefer to use warm water (survey results).

g. The model suggests that the components of *attitude* are the evaluative criteria. That is, people are likely to *prefer* brands that they *rate highly* on specific attributes considered *important* in that generic product.

h. The model suggests that people are more likely to purchase brands they prefer (favorable attitude) than brands they do not prefer.

i. Therefore, the model suggests that people are likely to purchase brands rated highly on the evaluative criteria.

j. Therefore, the preceding suggests that with high likelihood the ratings of each brand on the evaluative criteria should match closely with the market share of each brand.

k. Survey results show that ratings of brand attitude closely parallel market shares.

l. This explains the market shares of different brands of detergents.

The preceding reconstruction, which hopefully, accurately reflects the underlying logic of the explanation, shows in graphic relief the basically different kinds of statements in the explanatory structure. Taken in order, statement *a* is an *assumption* that probably could be validated empirically if challenged. Statement *b* is *classificatory;* however, the underlying classificatory schema is not given explicitly. Therefore, determining the acceptability of the classificatory schema is not possible. Statement *c* is a *logical* classificatory statement. Given *b*, then *c* must be true. Statement *d* is another assumption which probably could be empirically verified, if necessary. Statements *e* and *f* are both *observation* statements; here the authors bring in "real-world" evidence. The next three statements contain the heart of the explanation; *g, h,* and *i* are the *laws* or *lawlike* statements that carry the brunt of the explanation. Statement *j* is a *hypothesis* suggested by the preceding arguments. Finally, *k* is an *observation* sentence and *l* is the *explanandum,* or conclusion.

3.7.2   Structural Analysis of the Explanation

What is the basic form of the explanation? As reconstructed, the nature of the lawlike statements *g, h,* and i makes the explanation inductive-statistical. The qualifier, "with high likelihood," in *j* suggests an I-S model. The conclusive test, however, is the following question, "Can *k* be false and *j* still be true?" The answer must be yes; even with no measurement error, a nonrepresentative sample might give us the wrong results.

The reconstruction also shows that the original narrative explanation was an *enthymeme* (elliptical); some necessary statements were skipped over or suppressed. For example, the logical equivalent of statement *h* was suppressed. Although often heuristically unimportant, the suppression of premises can frequently impede analysis.

Next, note the *teleological* character of the explanation. That is, the lawlike generalizations are heavily purposive in kind. Statements *g, h,* and *i* suggest that the brand purchase decision is purposive to the extent that people seek brands that they perceive will correspond most closely to their evaluative criteria.

Consider the depth of the explanation chain. The most basic statements in the chain concern components of the evaluative criteria that are product-specific, for example, cleaning ability and low suds. These components are presumably under the control of the detergent firms. Therefore, the explanation attempts to explain a phenomenon (market share) by relying on factors (cleaning ability, etc.) that potentially enable the firm to *influence* the explanation chain. This suggests that, pragmatically speaking, the explanation is respectably deep.

An examination of causal considerations casts a shadow on the pragmatics of the explanation. The explanation implies that a firm might increase its market share by changing its product and promotion along lines suggested by the evaluative criteria. This presumes that changes in the evaluative criteria will cause subsequent changes in purchase and market share. However, the *temporal* sequence in this instance may be counterintuitive. Studies suggest that the "real" causal chain may be the reverse: Changes in purchase (market share) cause subsequent changes in the evaluative criteria. [636, 62, 199, 523] Empirical evidence in the explanation provides no clue as to the true temporal sequence. Therefore, policy decisions based on such explanations may prove faulty.

Finally, consider the underlying habitual decision-process behavior (H-D-P-B) model. Many of the concepts in the model are not explicitly included or discussed in the explanation, for example, personality, information, experience, income, culture, and family. What was the role of the H-D-P-B model in generating the explanation? Essentially, the H-D-P-B model provided numerous constructs that fit together in a theoretical manner and that the authors suggest might be useful in explaining habitual purchase behavior. The *users* of the model then select several constructs as potentially explanatory. Therefore, at this stage, the H-D-P-B construction might be considered a *model* which would have its greatest value in the *context of discovery*.

3.8   A PRICE DISCRIMINATION EXPLANATION

Firms often engage in price discrimination; they charge different prices to different customers for the same product or service. Theaters charge different prices for adults than for children. Universities charge brilliant students less than average students by providing scholarships. For the services provided by the federal government, wealthier citizens are charged more than poorer citizens, since the income tax rate is progressive. The same phenomenon occurs in newspaper advertising. *Why do newspapers charge lower rates to local advertisers than to national advertisers?* Simon states one possible explanation:

> *Factual problem.* It is an observed fact that newspapers charge lower advertising rates to local retailers than to nationally advertised brands of goods. To explain why they do is a research problem.
>
> *Assumptions.* We *assume,* first, that businessmen (newspaper owners, in this case) will charge that price to each group of people that will result in *maximum profit.* (This is the "economic man" assumption . . .).
>
> Second, we *assume* that businessmen know how groups of customers (retailers and national advertisers) react to various prices. (This is the "perfect knowledge" assumption . . .).
>
> *Deduction.* We *deduce* that, if one customer group is *less sensitive* to a price increase than another group is, it will be profitable to charge a higher price to the less sensitive customer. (This can be shown with a standard logical chain of economic deduction . . .).
>
> *Hypothesis.* We then hypothesize that, if the deduction is correct, the newspaper publishers believe that national advertisers are less sensitive to price changes. This hypothesis can be tested by finding out what the newspaper advertisers believe about the relative sensitivity of local and national advertisers. A questionnaire study found that publishers do indeed believe that national advertisers are less sensitive to price changes and thus confirmed the hypothesis. [589, p. 38]

Simon's proposed explanation is well formed, succinct, and rigorous. It thus requires little elaboration or analysis. Some of the terminology differs in minor ways from the present treatment. For example, his *factual problem* would be our *explanandum;* this is the phenomenon to be explained. His *assumptions* would be our *laws,* since these are generalized statements that do most of the explaining. The term *assumption* carries unfortunate connotations in the social sciences, such as "cannot be tested," "should not be tested," and "need not conform to reality." Since formal analysis of axioms and assumptions will be deferred to the next chapter, we need here only observe that few terms have been so thoroughly abused in the social sciences as have the terms *assumption* and *axiom.* They should definitely be labeled "handle with care."

A final observation concerning Simon's excellent explanation of newspaper price discrimination focuses on his *hypothesis* section. Simon deduces certain predictions which should occur *if his explanation is correct.* He then tests these predictions. Thus, Simon provides a graphic illustration of what it means to require explanations to be empirically testable and intersubjectively verifiable.

3.9   A WHEEL OF RETAILING EXPLANATION

A recent institutional innovation in the hotel/motel field has been the rise of so-called budget motels. These motels lack many of the amenities (room service, bellhops, chandeliers, and posh wallpaper) but feature very low prices on rooms [455]. *Why have budget motels been such a successful retail innovation?* A seemingly appropriate marketing explanation might involve the Wheel of Retailing first proposed by McNair [437].

Stanley Hollander's conceptualization of the Wheel of Retailing holds that "new types of retailers usually enter the market as low-status, low-margin, low-price operators. Gradually they acquire more elaborate establishments and facilities with both increased investments and higher operating costs. Finally, they mature as high cost, high-price merchants, vulnerable to newer types who, in turn, go through the same pattern." [275]

A Wheel explanation of budget motels would start with the observation that the original motels began as cabins along the highways. They were low-cost, low-margin, low-price, and emphatically low-status operations. Through time, motels added many services and upgraded their facilities to the point where today the distinguishing features between motels and hotels are difficult to find. Concomitant with the added services and upgraded facilities have been increases in costs and prices. Therefore, the entry of budget motels can be explained by demonstrating that it is another instance of the Wheel of Retailing.

The Wheel constitutes a form of inductive-statistical explanation because of the phrase "new retailers *usually* enter the market." Hollander acknowledges that *not all* new retailers enter as low-cost, low-margin, and so on. [275, p. 337] Vending machine retailing, department store branches, and convenience grocery stores are retail institutions whose entries have not conformed with the Wheel notion. Unfortunately, no one has been able to suggest the particular conditions that must prevail for new retail institutions to enter in accordance with the Wheel.

Essentially, the Wheel attempts to explain the entry of budget motels by demonstrating that the history of the motel industry is consistent with an *empirical regularity* (see Chapter 4) observed in other industries, that is, the upgrading of services and facilities and, therefore, the increasing of costs and prices. The explanation seems incomplete because it does not explain *why* the motel industry continually increased services, facilities, costs, and prices. Perhaps, integrating the Wheel notion with the theory of competition for differential advantage might make the explanation more complete.

3.9.1   The Wheel of Retailing and Competition for Differential Advantage

The economist J. M. Clark has promulgated a theory of competitive interaction called the theory of competition for differential advantage. [120] Clark holds that new firms or institutions enter an industry when they believe they will have some differential advantage over existing firms in serving some subset of customers. Competition consists of a series of initiatory moves by some firms to gain a differential advantage and of subsequent countermoves by rivals to neutralize that advantage. Wroe Alderson captures the essence of the concept:

> Every business firm occupies a position which is in some respects unique. Its location, the product it sells, its operating methods, or the customers it serves tend to set it off in some degree from every other firm. Each firm competes by making the most of its individuality and its special character. It is constantly seeking to establish some competitive advantage. Absolute advantage in the sense of an advanced method of operation is not enough if all competitors live up to the same high standards. What is important in competition is differential advantage, which can give a firm an edge over what others in the field are offering. [9, p. 101]

We can now attempt to integrate the Wheel of Retailing into the theory of competition for differential advantage.[3]

1. All new retail institutions enter the market because the participants perceive that they will have some form of differential advantage over existing retail forms. The basis for differential advantage may be some innovation that yields greater convenience in location to certain customers (e.g., vending machines), speedy service (e.g., fast-food restaurants), low prices (motels), or some other benefit to a subset of potential customers. The particular differential advantage of early motels, when competing against hotels, was both convenient locations along the highway and low prices. Motels were low cost, low price, and low status, and they competed primarily against existing *hotels*.

2. The number of motels increased rapidly as a large segment of the market desired both convenient locations away from downtown areas and the low prices. As the number of motels increased, the nature of competition changed from motel versus hotel to motel versus motel. That is, the primary thrust of competition for motels changed from trying to lure customers from hotels to trying to lure customers from *other motels*. Then, individual motels began to seek some differential advantage over other motels.

3. Price reductions are the form of differential advantage that would be neutralized most easily and quickly. Therefore, the upgrading of services and facilities would be the most common means used to gain differential advantage. For example, most motels followed the following progression: no television, pay television, free television, color television. Each motel attempted to neutralize the differential advantage of its competitors by matching its competitors' services and facilities.

4. Therefore, through time the motel industry gradually increased its costs, margins, and prices. The motel industry thus became a tempting target for budget motels stressing low costs, margins, and prices.

The preceding integration of the Wheel with competition for differential advantage shows why the Wheel must state that new types of retailers *usually* enter as low cost, low price, and so on. There is no basis for supposing that *all* new forms of retailing would seek low price as their basis for differential advantage. Also, the revised structure appears at least testable in principle. In particular, the generalization that as a new form of retailing matures, the thrust of competition will change in the directions noted seems amenable to empirical

---

[3] This analysis parallels in part the integration of the Wheel into the concept of intertype competition; see Bucklin. [92, p. 120 ff.]

confirmation. Finally, integrating the Wheel of Retailing into the theory of competition for differential advantage has made the explanation of the phenomenon of budget motels substantially deeper and more complete.

3.10   SUMMARY AND CONCLUSIONS

This chapter has explored a variety of issues in explanation and has utilized the tools developed so far to analyze several explanations of marketing phenomena. The thesis of structural symmetry was examined and found to be half correct: All adequate explanations of phenomena must be potentially predictive. However, all adequate predictions of phenomena are not necessarily adequate explanations because predictions can be made without the use of lawlike generalizations. And lawlike generalizations are necessary for the scientific explanation of phenomena. Finally, the ability to *retrodict* phenomena is *not* a necessary condition for explanation.

The relationships between scientific *understanding, explanation,* and *prediction* were explored via an analysis of Dubin's Power Paradox. The paradox disappears upon the realization that prediction is necessary for explanation and that explanation is necessary for understanding. Therefore, models and theories in marketing that do not explain and predict do not contribute to scientific understanding.

The epistemologically troublesome notions of causality and causal explanations were shown to be intractable with respect to generating *sufficient* conditions for classifying an explanation as *causal.* However, various kinds of evidence can be introduced to *suggest* that a particular relationship or explanation is causal. These include temporal sequentiality, associative variation, nonspurious association, and theoretical support.

All explanations are incomplete in one way or another. In principle, all explanations involve an explanation chain and are, therefore, incomplete. Some explanations are incomplete because they are enthymemes; that is, they skip over or leave out some premise. Some explanations are better termed partial explanations or explanation sketches.

The product life cycle has been explored as an explanatory device and has been found to lack explanatory power. A consumer behavior model was found to be useful in the context of discovery. Simon's price discrimination explanation was found to be well formed and illustrated how explanations can be empirically testable. Finally, the Wheel of Retailing was integrated into the theory of competition for differential advantage and used to explain the phenomenon of budget motels.

QUESTIONS FOR ANALYSIS AND DISCUSSION

1. Summarize the thesis of structural symmetry. Why have so many marketing and social science theorists been reluctant to accept the conclusion that every acceptable explanation is a potential prediction?
2. Find an instance in the marketing literature where the author used the term *cause,* and evaluate the appropriateness of the author's usage. What criteria,

either explicit or implicit, did the author use to justify his causal assertion? Evaluate those criteria.

3. Can there be any such thing as a "final explanation" of any marketing phenomenon?

4. Find an example of an explanation chain in the marketing literature.   Is it acceptably deep? Evaluate the explanation.

5. How do enthymemes, partial explanations, and explanation sketches differ? Are there other ways in which explanations can be incomplete?

6. This chapter found the product life cycle to be explanatorily impotent. If this is so, why does the product life cycle receive so much attention in the marketing literature? Is the attention justified?

7. The explanation of marketing phenomena is the cornerstone of research in marketing. Yet, the term *explanation* is not in the index of any of the following prominent marketing research texts [236, 74, 136, 261]. How can this paradox be reconciled?

8. A *Journal of Marketing Research* reviewer of the article "A Crucial Test for the Howard-Sheth Model of Buyer Behavior" [297] commented:

> A more thorough study of the philosophy of science literature might have led the authors to realize that this "criterion of simplicity" is not always appropriate, e.g., when your theory development is primarily aimed at *explanation* rather than *prediction*.

Evaluate this charge. The criterion of simplicity states that, roughly speaking, if two theories generate the same hypotheses and have equivalent empirical support, accept the simpler theory. (For more on the criterion of simplicity, see "Simplicity, Parsimony, and Model Building" by Pinson and Roberto [495].)

9. Empirical studies frequently cite the coefficient of determination (R^2), and they discuss the percentage of the dependent variable "explained" by the independent variable(s). When used in this context, why is the term *explained* usually enclosed in quotation marks?

10. What does it mean to propose that all marketing phenomena can "ultimately be reduced" to one of the four sets of fundamental explananda? Chapter 1 proposed that one dimension of macromarketing is the "consequences of society for marketing systems." Could this dimension be "reduced"? Go through a recent issue of *JMR*. See whether all of the dependent variables can be "reduced." If not all of them can, what additional fundamental explananda are required?

11. Bagozzi [in 306a] suggests that marketing researchers want to understand and control marketing behavior. He contends that "both objectives—understanding and control—rest fundamentally on the identification and analysis of causal relationships." Could not understanding come about through the use of, simply, regularity relationships? Similarly, could not control come about by way of regularity relationships? Evaluate.

12. Chapter 3 identifies four criteria for classifying explanations as potentially causal: (1) temporal sequentiality, (2) associative variation, (3) nonspurious association, and (4) theoretical support. John Stuart Mill suggests the methods of agreement, difference, residues, and concomitant variation. Compare and contrast these two sets of criteria.

4
THE MORPHOLOGY OF SCIENTIFIC LAWS

Several kinds of statements about behavior are commonly made. When we tell an anecdote or pass along a bit of gossip, we report a single event—what someone did upon such and such an occasion. . . . These accounts have their uses. They broaden the experience of those who have not had firsthand access to similar data. But they are only the beginnings of a science. The next step is the discovery of some sort of uniformity.

B. F. Skinner

Commentators on the history of science have found that the notion of descriptive or scientific laws evolved from the older conception of prescriptive or normative laws. [81, p. 673] The earliest laws were normative commandments that asserted rules for proper (moral) conduct: "Thou shalt not kill." Whether these normative laws were sanctioned by the established church or civil government, or frequently both, all people were universally obliged to obey them. From this genesis, the term *law* has been extended to descriptive regularities in science because these, too, apply "universally" to all phenomena. However, at that point the similarity ends. Normative laws *prescribe* what people *ought* to do; scientific laws in human behavior *describe* what people actually do.

When a citizen fails to *obey* a normative law, the appropriate authorities may invoke sanctions, for example, excommunication, public humiliation, failing the marketing theory course, imprisonment, flogging, or even death. As the electrical machinery conspirators found out, when a marketer disobeys a governmental normative law such as "Thou shalt not conspire to fix prices," both fines and imprisonment may ensue. On the other hand, the consequences of finding behaviors that "disobey" a descriptive or scientific law suggest a reexamination of the law in question rather than punishment. If behaviors do not follow the law, then either the law should be rejected or the conditions under which the law is believed to be true should be modified. When the term *law* is used in this book, we refer to scientific laws and not normative laws.

Both normative laws and scientific laws should be carefully distinguished from normative decision rules or normative decision models. Normative decisions rules or models prescribe the most appropriate courses of action to follow in order to rationally attempt to achieve some stated objective. Thus, linear programming can provide a set of normative decision rules for optimally allocating the advertising budget among the various media. The so-called marketing concept is not a *concept* in the normal sense of the term. Rather, it is a philosophy of doing business based on a set of three normative decision rules: (1) firms should be customer oriented; (2) all marketing activities of the firm should be integrated; and (3) profit rather than sales should be the orientation of the firm. Although many normative decision rules are nothing more than crude *rules of thumb,* some are firmly based on scientific laws. Bunge suggests that normative decision rules that are based or founded on some set of scientific laws be referred to as *grounded rules.* [96, p. 132] In summary, normative laws prescribe what people *morally* or *legally* ought to do; normative decision rules or models prescribe what people ought to do to *rationally achieve some stated objective;* scientific laws in human behavior describe what people actually do.

This chapter concerns the morphology of scientific laws and their role in scientific inquiry. First, we shall explore the role of laws in marketing research; then, we shall provide some criteria for separating lawlike generalizations from ordinary conversational generalizations and evaluate some marketing lawlike generalizations.

4.1   ROLE OF LAWS IN MARKETING RESEARCH

Laws and lawlike statements play vital roles in marketing inquiry. As indicated in Chapter 2, the development of laws in marketing is an absolute requirement for explaining marketing phenomena. All of the models discussed in Chapter 2 that have explanatory power (deductive-nomological, deductive-statistical, and inductive-statistical) explain phenomena by deductive or inductive subsumption under lawlike generalizations. That is, we can *explain* the market shares of various detergents by showing that the shares are consistent with certain lawlike statements relating brand purchases with the components of brand attitudes (Section 3.7).

In addition to explaining marketing phenomena, lawlike statements in marketing facilitate the *prediction* of marketing phenomena. All models that can provide satisfactory scientific explanations of *past* marketing phenomena must be potentially capable of predicting future marketing phenomena; or, as Chapter 3 indicated, all satisfactory explanations are potential predictions. The laws in the models provide the predictive power. Taken together, the ability to systematically explain marketing phenomena and the ability to predict marketing phenomena lead to the *scientific understanding* and *control* of marketing phenomena. If by employing certain laws, the marketer can predict the consequences of changing certain resources under his control, then the marketer has at least some ability to *control* the system. Thus, the intellectual goal of all scientific endeavor is scientific understanding, and the pragmatic consequence of scientific endeavor is increased control over man's environment.

The next section will discuss the basic form of laws, that is, generalized conditionals. Also, some distinctions will be made concerning laws, lawlike generalizations, and principles. One caveat prefaces our discussion: The term *law* is another slippery term (like the term *explanation*) that seems intuitively clear at first glance but provides stout resistance to rigorous analysis.

4.2   THE FIRST CRITERION: GENERALIZED CONDITIONALS

All laws specify a relationship in the form of a generalized conditional.[1] *Conditional* implies some kind of "if—then" relationship. Thus, a common basic form is: "Every time *A* occurs, then *B* will occur." Or, in slightly more developed form, "For any *x*, if *x* is *A*, then *x* is *B*" (or, alternatively, "All *A* are *B*"). For example, "All consumers who systematically avoid purchasing private label merchandise are low in generalized self-confidence." Note that this statement can be recast in generalized conditional form: "For any *x* (consumer), if *x* is *A* (systematically avoids purchasing private label merchandise), then *x* is *B* (low in generalized self-confidence)." Not all statements of generalized conditional form constitute laws. In particular, we have previously suggested that *accidental generalizations,* although having the form of generalized conditionals, are not usually recognized as laws. The criteria for according lawlike status to statements will occupy the rest of this chapter after an examination of principles, laws, and lawlike generalizations.

Confusion often arises concerning the differences among the following concepts: "principles," "laws," and "lawlike generalizations." First, let's differentiate between laws and lawlike generalizations. Lawlike generalizations (or "lawlike statements" or "lawlike propositions") are statements in generalized conditional form which fulfill all the criteria of laws but have not yet been tested and confirmed or corroborated.[2]

---

[1] For excellent discussions of laws, see Nagel, Hempel, Lambert and Brittan, Kaplan, and Bunge. [464, pp. 47-73; 262, p. 264 ff.; 365, p. 37 ff.; 332, p. 84 ff.; 94].

[2] Many writers use the term *confirmed* instead of the term *corroborated*. Popper [503, p. 251 ff.] suggests that confirmed, more than corroborated, is likely to indicate that the lawlike statement is known to be absolutely true, which is not a requirement for a law.

Although the subject of criteria for corroboration (or confirmation) of laws and theoretical constructions will be extensively investigated in Chapter 6, a few preliminary observations can be made here. To say that a lawlike statement is highly confirmed, or corroborated, or believed to be true, is different from saying that it is absolutely true, or true-with-certainty, or "True" (with capital "T"). (See Section 11.3.4 for further discussion on this issue.) Therefore, we do not require lawlike statements to be "True" to be a law. Rather, we require them to be highly confirmed or corroborated by the evidence, which gives us reason to believe them to be true or isomorphic with the real world.

A second distinction is between laws and principles (sometimes referred to as "high-level laws," "most fundamental laws," or, simply, "Laws" with an uppercase "L"). The distinction is largely honorific. In any discipline a *law* becomes a *principle* when it is widely held to be of extreme significance or importance to that discipline and when the evidence corroborating it is overwhelming. Thus, we have the Law of Demand in economics, the First Law of Thermodynamics in physics, and Weber's Law in psychology.

Simon seems to have blurred the distinction between *law* and *principle:* "If an empirical test of the hypothesis confirms the hypothesis, the generalization might be called a *law,* provided that the finding is sufficiently *important.*" [589, p. 38, Simon's emphasis] The unfortunate consequences of this confusion have led many writers to decry the absence of *laws* in the behavioral sciences and marketing when what they have really observed is the absence of *principles* (or *Laws* with uppercase "L") in those areas. Berelson and Steiner have documented a host of reasonably well-supported generalizations worthy of being called *laws* in the behavioral sciences [54], and Schuette has suggested the development of a similar "propositional inventory" in marketing. [566] Schuette's use of the term *proposition* is roughly synonymous with our term *law.*

4.3　THE SECOND CRITERION: EMPIRICAL CONTENT

What kinds of statements that have the basic form of generalized conditionals should be characterized as *lawlike?* Alternatively, what criteria should be applied to distinguish lawlike statements from nonlawlike statements? One extremely desirable criterion is that *all lawlike statements must have empirical content.* [365, p. 38] The empirical content criterion rules out both nonsense statements and strictly analytical statements. An example of a nonsense generalized conditional might be: "All marketing maloglops are high priced." Clearly, according lawlike status to such statements would be patently ridiculous since maloglops are nonexistent.

Much more important than just ruling out nonsense laws, the empirical content criterion also excludes strictly analytical statements from being considered lawlike. Before discussing the importance of excluding strictly analytical statements, we need to distinguish between two basic kinds of statements: analytic and synthetic.

Consider the following two statements: (1) marketing activities consume a large portion of the consumer's dollar; and (2) either marketing activities consume a large portion of the consumer's dollar, or marketing activities *do not* consume a large portion of the consumer's dollar. Both statements are true, yet they are true for different reasons. The first statement is known to be true because of studies conducted by Reavis Cox, Harold Barger, and others. [138, 23] That is, Statement 1 is known to be true only after we examine the facts in the real world. Such statements are called *synthetic*. [56, p. 26] Conversely, Statement 2 is true no matter what the "real-world facts" are. Statement 2 is true because it makes no assertion about the real world: It does not say anything at all! Such statements are called *purely analytic,* and, strictly speaking, they are true only because of the order and nature of the logical terms (such as *either* and *or)* and the way in which they define certain descriptive terms (such as *marketing)*. True analytic statements are *tautologies,* and false ones are *contradictions.*

Bergman suggests that in tautologies the descriptive words appear only vacuously; that is, the truth content of tautologies is independent of the descriptive words. [56, p. 27] Therefore, to show that Statement 2 is really tautological, we need to define the descriptive words:

p = Marketing activities
q = Consume a large portion of the consumer's dollar

As constructed, Statement 2 then merely asserts that "either p is q, or p is not q." We could then insert any descriptive terms for p or q that we desire, and the statement would still be true. Therefore, the descriptive terms in Statement 2 appear only *vacuously*. A similar reconstruction of Statement 1 will reveal it to be a synthetic statement. (Try it!)

So the *empirical content* criterion successfully weeds out strictly analytic statements from lawlike statements because we want our laws to "say something" about the real world. We want lawlike statements to be empirically testable. However, the analytic/synthetic distinction may not always be as clear-cut as has been implied. Consider this assertion: "No consumer can be brand loyal to more than one brand at a time in the same product class." The statement is certainly a generalized conditional of the form *"If* for any X, if X is a consumer, and if she is loyal to brand A, and *if* brands A and B are in the same product class, *then* she cannot at the same time be loyal to brand B." Does the statement pass the empirical content criterion for being considered lawlike? Is the statement analytic or synthetic?

Whether the brand loyalty assertion is analytic or synthetic depends primarily on how brand loyalty is defined. Consider the following definition: "Consumer X is considered to be brand loyal to brand A if, and only if, the consumer purchases over 50 percent of his/her requirements of the product class from brand A." Given this definition, the brand loyalty assertion is obviously analytic, since it would be mathematically impossible for a consumer to purchase in excess of 50 percent of his/her requirements from brand A and at the same time purchase over 50 percent from brand B. Therefore, given this definition, the "brand loyalty" generalization would fail the empirical content criterion.

On the other hand, Tucker suggests denoting a consumer as brand loyal if he or she makes three successive choices of the same brand. [618] Consider the following sequence of purchases over a 12-month period:

CBAAACABBBAB

Using Tucker's definition, the consumer would be brand loyal to *both* brands A and B during the same 12-month period, and the assertion that a consumer will be brand loyal to only one brand in a single time period becomes synthetic, not analytic. That is, with the revised definition, it is now *possible* to show that the brand loyalty generalization is empirically false. Therefore, the statement would pass the *empirical content* criterion.

Halbert has observed that many of the generalizations in the marketing literature seem to be "either tautologies, truisms, or so overly general that they are of very limited use in developing marketing science." [243, p. 66] As one example, Halbert points out a generalized statement by Jastrom: "If it appears to be profitable to plan advertising at all, there will be some one rate of outlay for which it will be most profitable to plan." [317] Readers should decide for themselves whether the statement is a tautology.

In his "Theory of Social Initiative," Robert Bartels states, "Society, not the business entrepreneur, is the basic undertaker of all activity." [39, p. 32] Is this analytic or synthetic? Would it pass or fail the empirical content criterion for lawlikeness? As previously illustrated, the key depends on how certain terms (such as *basic undertaker*) are defined and, unfortunately, Bartels provides no definitions. However, since innumerable "basic" activities do seem to be undertaken by business entrepreneurs, *if* the statement is intended to be synthetic, it is probably false. Therefore, there would probably be a strong temptation to define the term *basic undertaker* in such a way that the truth content of the statement would be assured. Consequently, to the extent that the statement is synthetic, it is probably false. And to the extent that the statement is analytic, it will fail the empirical content criterion. In either case, the statement should not be considered lawlike.

4.4   THE THIRD CRITERION: NOMIC NECESSITY

The previous discussion suggests that lawlike statements must have (1) the basic form of generalized conditionals and (2) empirical content. Criterion 3 states that *all purportedly lawlike statements must possess nomic* (nō´mǐk) *necessity* (sometimes referred to as "nomological universality" or "nomic universality"). The purpose of the nomic necessity criterion is to systematically prevent *accidental* generalizations from being considered laws. Nomic necessity implies that the occurrence of some phenomenon *must* be associated with some other phenomenon; the relationship cannot be, simply, by *chance*. The classic illustration of an accidental generalization has been provided by Nagel: "All the screws in Smith's current car are rusty." [464, p. 52] Note that the statement is a generalized conditional with empirical content. Nevertheless, few people would like to accord lawlike status to such a generalization precisely because it somehow seems to describe an *accidental* relationship.

As Rescher has observed, although there is widespread agreement that scientific laws involve a necessity that transcends simple accidental regularity, the issue of explicating what exactly is meant by nomic necessity remains a major problem. [527, p. 103] A few examples of generalizations might help to clarify the issue. Consider the following five generalizations: (1) all the coins in my pocket are half-dollars; (2) all products produced by Procter & Gamble are distributed through supermarkets; (3) all products with the trade name Maxwell House have a coffee base; (4) two cities attract retail trade from an intermediate town in the vicinity of the breaking point (where 50 percent of the trade is attracted to each city) in direct proportion to their populations and in inverse proportion to the square of the distances from the two cities to the intermediate town; [130, p. 379] and (5) in any survey, the percentages of people who express intentions to purchase a brand are directly proportional to the square roots of the percentages of informants who currently use the brand. [164, p. 34]

Note that all five of the statements in the previous paragraph are generalized conditionals of the "all *A* are *B*" variety and that all five have empirical content. Nevertheless, most scholars would find it intellectually disquieting to accord lawlike status to the first three and would be more than willing to consider the last two as suitable candidates for lawlike status. (Remember, this does not necessarily mean that we have enough empirical evidence to consider 4 and 5 to be *laws* but only that they pass muster for consideration as *lawlike*.) Intuitively, the generalizations embodied in the first three statements seem qualitatively different, more *accidental*, than those embodied in the last two. But precisely how do we analytically (rather than intuitively) separate accidental from nonaccidental generalizations? The answer lies in the fact that *generalizations exhibiting nomic necessity have a kind of hypothetical power which is different from that of accidental generalizations.*

The major purposes of scientific laws are to explain and predict phenomena. To accomplish these tasks, laws must have the power to generate hypotheses such as "If phenomenon X occurs, then phenomenon Y will occur." To demonstrate that accidental generalizations lack hypothetical power, consider the following statements:

A. If this coin (which is not in my pocket) were placed in my pocket, it would be a half-dollar.
B. If this product (which is not labeled Maxwell House) were labeled Maxwell House, then it would have a coffee base.
C. If this automobile were produced by Procter & Gamble (which it is not), it would be distributed through supermarkets.

Statements A, B, and C are all called *counterfactual conditionals* because the premises of the statements are not true.[3] That is, the premises are "counter to the facts": The coin is not in my pocket, the product is not labeled Maxwell House, and the automobile is not produced by Procter & Gamble.

Referring to the five generalizations, none of the first three generalizations support their respective counterfactual conditionals. No reasonable person would believe that Statements A, B, C were true *even though* he or she knew that Generalizations 1, 2, and 3 were true. The generalization "All the coins in my pocket are half-dollars" does *not* support (i.e., give someone good reason to believe) Statement A. The generalization "All products with the trade name Maxwell House have a coffee base" does *not* support Statement B. Finally, the generalization "All products produced by Procter & Gamble are distributed through supermarkets" does not support Statement C because there is nothing to prevent Procter & Gamble from distributing a product through another channel of distribution if it chooses to do so. The Procter & Gamble generalization (like the others) thus lacks the element of *must*. Alternatively, the Procter & Gamble generalization lacks the nomic necessity required of true lawlike statements because it lacks the *hypothetical power* to support counterfactual conditionals. As the next paragraph will show, true lawlike statements will exhibit nomic necessity by supporting counterfactual conditionals.

Consider the following statements:

D. If city K had four times the population of city J (K actually has only twice the population of J), then city K would double the percentage of retail trade that it draws from intermediate city I.

---

[3]The classic treatment of counterfactual conditionals is in Goodman. [231] For a good discussion of counterfactual conditionals in marketing, see Gaski [221].

E. If the usership of brand X had been 16 percent (it actually was only 4 percent), then in this survey the percentage of people who expressed an intention to purchase brand X would have doubled.

Note, once again, that both D and E are counterfactual conditionals like A, B, and C. However, this time the generalizations *can support* their respective counterfactual conditionals if in fact the generalizations accurately represent the real world (a strictly empirical question). That is, Generalization 4, "Two cities attract retail trade from an intermediate town . . . ," can support Statement D if Generalization 4 accurately depicts the real world. Similarly, Generalization 5 can support Statement E. *Therefore, in order for a statement to be considered lawlike, our third criterion is that it must exhibit nomic necessity, which rules out accidental generalizations. Accidental generalizations can be identified by their lack of hypothetical power as evidenced by their inability in principle to support counterfactual conditionals.*

4.5   THE FOURTH CRITERION: SYSTEMATICALLY INTEGRATED

The analysis thus far has shown that lawlike statements have the form of generalized conditionals that have empirical content and exhibit nomic necessity. The final requirement provides that *all purportedly lawlike statements must be systematically integrated into a body of scientific knowledge.* Stated negatively, a simple empirical regularity (even a well-confirmed one) is not a lawlike generalization. An empirical regularity does not qualify as a lawlike statement until it is systematically integrated into a coherent scientific structure or framework.

An empirical regularity is a statement summarizing observed uniformities of relationships between two or more concepts or variables. That empirical regularities should not be classified as lawlike until they have found a niche in a systematic framework has been observed both by philosophers of science and by theoreticians. Lambert and Brittan suggest, "What leads us to reject the red sky in the morning/rain in the afternoon as a law, is that it is an isolated assertion having no apparent theoretical ramifications." [356, p. 45] Kaplan believes that a "nomic generalization must be derivable from other laws, that is, play a part in scientific theory. Otherwise, we obtain what might be called an empirical generalization rather than a law." [332, p. 92] Robert K. Merton has commented that the literature in sociology abounds with isolated propositions which have not been assimilated into sociological theory. [445, p. 149] Finally, Rescher plainly states the systematically integrated criterion:

> An empirical generalization is not to be viewed as fully adequate for explanatory purposes until it can lay claim to the status of a law. Now a law is not just a summary statement of observed-regularities-

to-date; it claims to deal with a universal regularity purporting to describe how things inevitably are: how the processes at work in the world must invariably work, how things have to happen in nature. Such a claim has to be based upon a stronger foundation than any mere observed regularity-to-date. The *coherence of laws* in patterns that illuminate the "mechanisms" by which natural processes occur is a critical element—perhaps the most important one—in furnishing this stronger foundation, this "something more" than a generalization of observations. An "observed regularity" does not become a "law of nature" simply by becoming better established through observation in additional cases; what is needed is *integration* into the body of scientific knowledge. [527, pp. 15-16]

The requirement that generalizations must be systematically integrated with other statements in the total corpus of knowledge points out the importance of theories. Since theories are systematically related sets of statements that include some lawlike generalizations, theories provide a crucial mechanism for according lawlike status to empirical regularities and other isolated propositions.

Consider Ehrenberg's "Duplication of Viewing" (hereafter referred to as "D-V") relationship: $d_{ts} = kr_t r_s \pm 1$. [164, p. 33] Ehrenberg was interested in determining what percentage of the audience would be duplicated if X percentage of the population viewed a television program on Monday night and Y percentage of the population viewed a program on Tuesday night. This information, of course, would be of great value to potential sponsors of the programs. Ehrenberg suggested that a wide range of empirical conditions support the relationship $d_{ts} = kr_t r_s \pm 1$ where:

d_{ts} = The audience (in rating points) that is duplicated at two times, s and t, on two different days of the week
r_t = The rating of the program at time t
r_s = The rating of the program at time s
k = A constant

Is the D-V relationship an empirical regularity, or is it a lawlike generalization? Certainly, the relationship is in the basic form of a generalized conditional and it also has empirical content. Ehrenberg indicates that several hundred cases examined support the relationship. [164, p. 34] (The cases cited are proprietary studies, the actual data and results of which are not provided. However, we can still explore the structural nature of the proposed relationship independent of an evaluation of the body of empirical evidence brought forward to corroborate the relationship.)

As noted previously, if the D-V relationship is to be considered a lawlike statement, it must be *systematically integrated* into a body of scientific knowledge. Ehrenberg provides no clues as to how the relationship fits existing knowledge. Actually, it appears to run *counter* to known "facts" about television viewing. For example, we "know" that different kinds of television programs attract different kinds of viewers, and that similar kinds of programs attract similar kinds of viewers. Nevertheless, the D-V relationship would lead one to conclude that the duplication of audience between a western on Monday and a western on Tuesday would be identical to the duplication between the same western on Monday and a Wednesday documentary on the political situation in Brazil (provided that the appropriate ratings are the same). On the other hand, the notion that similar programs draw similar audiences suggests that the duplication between the two westerns would be greater than the duplication between the western and the documentary. Therefore, the D-V relationship runs counter to our existing body of knowledge about television viewing.

Headen, Klompmaker, and Rust [256] tested the D-V law in the United States. They conclude:

> The authors attempted to examine the major conclusions of Goodhardt and Ehrenberg in terms of a national sample of U.S. data. The basic conclusions are that, because of the differences between the U.S. and U.K. media environments, the simplifying assumptions of Goodhardt and Ehrenberg (i.e., the use of only within- and between-channel K-values) cannot be used if accuracy is desired. For example, because of the longer broadcast day in the U.S., duplication patterns should take into account the daypart in which audience flow patterns are being studied. Also, whereas, there seems to be no program-type loyalty in the U.K., the authors' results show positive evidence of this phenomenon. [256, p. 340]

Is the D-V relationship a lawlike generalization? The previous analysis suggests that it is not. The D-V relationship (to the extent that it is true) is an empirical regularity because (a) it has not been systematically integrated into a body of knowledge about television viewing and (b) it actually contradicts a well-corroborated existing body of knowledge. It is important to note that classifying the relationship as an empirical regularity in no way disparages the importance or value of the discovery (if it is true). Requiring a relationship to be systematically integrated into a body of knowledge in order to be considered lawlike is one way of ensuring that we focus on the scientific explanation of phenomena (answering "why" questions), not simply the prediction of phenomena. And, we have found, prediction does not imply explanation.

In contrast with the D-V relationship, consider the sources of price reliance proposed by Benson P. Shapiro. [575] Shapiro investigated the phenomenon of consumers using the price of a product as an indicator of the perceived quality of the product. He found that the tendency of consumers to rely heavily on price (price reliance) as an indicator of quality was a generalized mental construct, an attitude or trait. He found that some people seemed price reliant regardless of the product under consideration and that some people were not price reliant.

Shapiro then tested hypotheses regarding the relationships that determined the existence of price reliance. Both personal and situation-specific factors were examined. Among the relationships tested were:

1. Price reliance increases as the *credibility* of the source of price information increases.
2. Price reliance increases as the *perceived risk* in the purchasing situation increases.
3. Price reliance increases as the *specific self-confidence* of the consumer decreases.

Shapiro empirically tested these relationships (and others) and found corroborative evidence. [575]

Are these determinants of price reliance to be considered empirical regularities or lawlike statements? They do have the basic form of generalized conditionals, and they do have empirical content—both requirements for lawlike status. However, are the observed relationships systematically integrated into a body of scientific knowledge? An affirmative reply seems justified. Shapiro demonstrates that all three relationships logically flow from the previous theoretical and empirical work of Bauer [47, 48, 49, 50], Brody and Cunningham [84, 140], Cox [134], and Janis and Field. [316] Therefore, in contrast with Ehrenberg's duplication of viewing relationship, the determinants of price reliance relationships should be accorded lawlike status. Note that this does not necessarily imply that the price reliance relationships are *laws*. Lawlike statements become laws only after substantial empirical corroboration. What is meant by "substantial empirical corroboration" is a subject for Chapter 6, where we discuss the criteria for confirmation of lawlike and theoretical constructions.

The criterion that statements must be systematically integrated into a coherent body of knowledge in order to be considered lawlike raises some possibly dangerous problems, the most obvious of which is conservatism. There is no question but that the *systematically integrated* criterion casts a conservative bias on scientific inquiry—newly discovered relationships that do not fit into some overall framework may unfortunately be automatically categorized as "spurious." Some observed regularities may then not receive the careful attention and further exploration that they deserve. Similarly, the systematically integrated requirement may be drastically distorted. Rescher speaks to this problem:

> The law must certainly fit into *some* pattern, but this need not of course necessarily be *the presently accepted* pattern. It is a convenient but unwarranted step to condemn the unfamiliar as unscientific, and to bring to bear the whole arsenal of scientific derogation (as "occult," "supernatural," "unscientific") that one sees, for example, orthodox psychologists launch against parapsychology.
>
> But the fact that the requirement of coherence [systematic integration] for explanatory laws can be abused does not show that it

should not be used. (Every useful instrument can be misapplied.) And, of course, the proper use of this requirement must always be conditioned by reference to the primary requirement of correspondence—the evidence of tested conformity to fact. [527, pp. 16-17]

Therefore, although researchers in marketing should require their lawlike statements to systematically fit into some larger framework, we must consciously avoid either ignoring "nonfitting" empirical regularities or rejecting them because they do not fit into some currently accepted framework or theory.

4.5.1   Role of Empirical Generalizations

The preceding section should not be interpreted as in any way minimizing the importance of empirical generalization. Unquestionably, empirical generalizations or empirical regularities play a prominent role in science. As noted previously, empirical regularities may become lawlike statements after they are systematically integrated into a body of scientific knowledge. A second prominent role of empirical generalizations lies within the *context of discovery*. How the laws of science are discovered is primarily the domain of the sociology and psychology of science. Undoubtedly, the observation of empirical regularities by scientists is a frequent stimulus for scientific inquiry, research, and the discovery of corroborated lawlike generalizations.

Edward Jenner's development of a vaccine for smallpox can be cited as just one example of an empirical regularity leading to the discovery of scientific knowledge. Jenner observed that, although almost the entire population of 18th-century England at one time or another had smallpox, milkmaids almost never had smallpox. This observed empirical regularity sparked his scientific curiosity and led him to observe that milkmaids did contract a mild disease known as cowpox. He theorized that, somehow, the contraction of cowpox kept the milkmaids from being susceptible to smallpox. Thus, an observed empirical relationship led directly to the ultimate discovery of a vaccine for smallpox. The process that led Jenner to develop a smallpox vaccine illustrates the frequently important role that empirical regularities play in the context of discovery. (See Section 11.3.1 for further discussion.)

It would appear that some of the work of early synthesizers of marketing thought was spurred by observed empirical regularities. In recounting the origins of Arch W. Shaw's marketing writings, Joseph C. Seibert comments:

Mr. Shaw's intellectual curiosity led him to devote a great deal of his time to the discovery of [business systems] and brought him conferences with leaders of many different types of industries. The outstanding discovery of these meetings, to Mr. Shaw, appeared to be the uniformity of procedures in spite of the variety of products produced and the outward differences of the separate organizations. [38, p. 234]

In the preceding case, the development of Shaw's concepts can be traced to his observation of an empirical regularity concerning the similarity of business systems across various different kinds of industries and products.

A final caveat on the role of empirical generalizations seems desirable. We must carefully distinguish between asserting that observing empirical regularities may often be a first step toward establishing lawlike relationships and asserting that the *only* way to discover lawlike relationships is to first observe some empirical regularities. Unfortunately, the latter assertion seems to be implied in much recent marketing literature. As was demonstrated in Chapter 1, it is certainly possible that lawlike statements may be discovered by first amassing data on hundreds of different variables and then continuously sifting the data through ever more sophisticated mathematical and statistical sieves. However, to state that this is the *only* procedure or even the most preferable procedure seems totally unwarranted.

4.6   SUMMARY

We are now in a position to build a comprehensive framework for principles, laws, and lawlike statements. This framework is illustrated in Figure 4-1, which suggests that all statements which purport to be of lawlike form must specify a relationship in the form of a *generalized conditional*. Common examples of generalized conditionals are: "All instances of *A* are also instances of *B*," and "Every time *X* occurs, then *Y* will occur."

Figure 4-1   Laws and lawlike statements

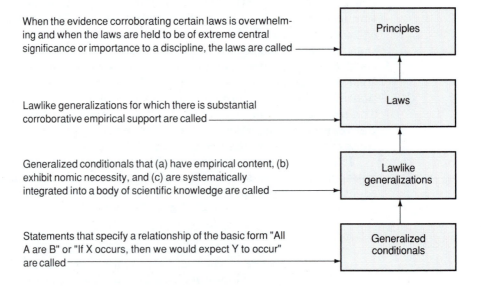

When the evidence corroborating certain laws is overwhelming and when the laws are held to be of extreme central significance or importance to a discipline, the laws are called ⟶ **Principles**

Lawlike generalizations for which there is substantial corroborative empirical support are called ⟶ **Laws**

Generalized conditionals that (a) have empirical content, (b) exhibit nomic necessity, and (c) are systematically integrated into a body of scientific knowledge are called ⟶ **Lawlike generalizations**

Statements that specify a relationship of the basic form "All A are B" or "If X occurs, then we would expect Y to occur" are called ⟶ **Generalized conditionals**

In order for a generalized conditional statement to be a *lawlike generalization* or, alternatively, a lawlike statement, it must *(a)* have empirical content, *(b)* exhibit nomic necessity, and *(c)* be systematically integrated into a body of scientific knowledge. The empirical content criterion successfully weeds out strictly analytic statements, tautologies, and nonsense generalizations from being considered lawlike. The nomic necessity criterion serves the useful purpose of distinguishing lawlike statements from accidental generalizations such as "All products with the trade name Maxwell House have a coffee base." Finally, the systematically integrated criterion enables us to differentiate lawlike statements from strictly empirical regularities. Empirical regularities have been shown to play an important role in the context of scientific discovery.

Lawlike generalizations become *laws* when a substantial body of corroborative empirical evidence has been developed. Exactly what is meant by a "substantial body of corroborative empirical evidence" will be the topic of Chapter 6. Lastly, a law becomes a *Principle* or *Law* (note uppercase "L") when the evidence corroborating the law is overwhelming and the law is held to be of extreme significance or importance to the scholars in a particular discipline.

QUESTIONS FOR ANALYSIS AND DISCUSSION

1. A "perfect system" for playing blackjack would destroy the game of blackjack, which would therefore render useless the "perfect system." Similarly, the discovery of marketing "laws" would be self-defeating. Evaluate.

2. John D. C. Little suggests that good normative decision models should be: *(a)* simple, *(b)* robust, *(c)* easy to control, *(d)* adaptive, *(e)* complete on important issues, and *(f)* easy to communicate with. [397] Shouldn't normative decision models, like scientific laws, be required to be empirically testable? If no, why not? If yes, how would you empirically test a normative decision model? Is the distinction between normative decision models and scientific laws a useful one? How about the distinction between normative laws and normative decision models?

3. Someone has said, "It is curious that marketing practitioners disclaim any interest in marketing laws since every time they make a strategic decision, they must rely either explicitly or implicitly on a presumed marketing law." Evaluate.

4. Wroe Alderson's principle of postponement "requires that changes in form and identity occur at the latest possible point in the marketing flow; and changes in inventory location occur at the latest point in time." [9, p. 424] Is this a principle, law, lawlike generalization, empirical regularity, theory, or what? Is it empirically testable?

5. Suppose Congress, in its infinite wisdom, passed a law making it illegal for Procter & Gamble to distribute products through any channel other than supermarkets. Would the generalization "All products produced by Procter & Gamble are distributed through supermarkets" then pass the nomic necessity criterion?

6. Schwartz suggests, "A law is a former theory which over time, and for the geographic area to which it is supposed to apply, has been demonstrated to yield perfectly accurate predictions each time it is used." [568, p. 8] Evaluate the

usefulness of this conceptualization of law. Why did Schwartz insert his "geographic area" qualifier but not others (e.g., he could have qualified his conceptualization with reference to a particular culture or industry)?

7. Economic theory is sometimes criticized because its lawlike statements are supposed to only be true, *ceteris paribus*. The phrase *ceteris paribus* is seldom found in the physical science or marketing literature. What does *ceteris paribus* imply? Is it a "defect" in economic theory? Should the physical sciences use it more often? Should marketing? Could the use of *ceteris paribus* be abused? How?

8. If the distinction between laws and principles (or Laws) is strictly honorific, is it therefore, unimportant?

9. Ehrenberg suggests that "the *validity* of a scientific law depends only on its range of empirical generalization, i.e., on the different conditions for which it is known to hold or not to hold, as shown by direct observation and analysis." [164, p. 32] Evaluate this perspective of *validity*. Does the concept of *ceteris paribus* relate to Ehrenberg's statement?

10. Evaluate the following argument:
    a. No purely analytic statement can be a lawlike generalization (such statements fail the empirical content criterion).
    b. The statement "2 + 2 = 4" is purely analytic.
    c. *All* mathematical statements have a basic form similar to "2 + 2 = 4."
    d. Therefore, all statements in mathematics are purely analytic.
    e. Since no analytic statement can be lawlike, no mathematical statement can be lawlike.
    f. All theories contain lawlike generalizations.
    g. Therefore, mathematics contains no theory.
    h. All sciences must contain theory.
    i. Therefore, mathematics is not a science.
    j. Mathematicians will dislike statement *i*.

11. "The nomic necessity criterion is really only requiring that laws be theoretically supportable since it is really theories which enable us to 'support' counterfactual conditionals." Evaluate.

12. Bunge [94, p. 260] proposes that "a proposition is a law statement if and only if it is *a posteriori* (not logically true), general in some respect (does not refer to unique objects), has been satisfactorily corroborated for the time being in some domain, and belongs to some theory (whether adult or embryonic)." Evaluate.

13. Is empirical evidence alone necessary and sufficient for according the status of law to a generalization? Is it necessary but not sufficient? Is it sufficient but not necessary? Is it neither necessary nor sufficient?

5

SCIENTIFIC LAWS: ISSUES AND ASPECTS

Nothing could be more absurd than the attempt to distinguish between science and art. Science is the noblest of the arts and men of science the most artistic of all artists. For science, like art, seeks to attain aesthetic satisfaction through the perceptions of the senses; and science, like art, is limited by the impositions of the material world on which it works. The lesser art accepts those limitations; it is content to imitate or to describe Nature and to follow where she leads. The greater refuses to be bound; it imposes itself upon Nature and forces her to submit to its power.

Norman Robert Campbell

The previous chapter examined the basic nature of laws and lawlike statements. Lawlike statements were found to be generalized conditionals that *(a)* have empirical content, *(b)* exhibit nomic necessity, and *(c)* are systematically integrated into a body of scientific knowledge. Laws are lawlike generalizations for which there is substantial corroborative support. The challenge of the present chapter will be to explore the various kinds of scientific laws and to examine certain issues relating to them. First, we shall explore how different kinds of laws incorporate *time* as a variable and, thus, examine equilibrium laws, laws of atemporal coexistence, laws of succession, and process laws. Second, we shall systematically inquire into the nature of, and the proper role for, axioms or "assumptions" in theory construction. Third, lawlike statements will be shown to differ as to their extension and universality. In this context we shall examine singular statements, existential statements, statistical laws, and universal laws. Lastly, the importance of carefully delimiting the extension of laws will be discussed, along with an evaluation of an extension of Weber's Law and the so-called psychophysics of prices controversy.

5.1   THE TIME ISSUE

One way of exploring the various kinds of laws and lawlike statements is to analyze the manner in which the time dimension is handled.

Figure 5-1 shows four kinds of laws that differ with respect to the time dimension: process laws, laws of succession, laws of atemporal coexistence, and equilibrium laws. Some very powerful lawlike statements not only explicitly incorporate time variables to facilitate the prediction of *future* phenomena but also permit the retrodiction of *past* phenomena. Bergman refers to these powerful statements as *process laws.* [81, p. 416] Following Hempel, lawlike statements which incorporate time-dependent relationships and allow the prediction of future phenomena but *not* the retrodiction of past phenomena can be called *laws of succession.* [262, p. 352] In contrast with process laws and laws of succession, *laws of atemporal coexistence* do not specifically incorporate time as a real variable at all. [262, p. 352] Finally, certain kinds of laws of atemporal coexistence state relationships that occur only when the system is "at rest." Such statements are called *equilibrium laws.* [81, p. 417] The next sections will systematically explore and elaborate on the unique characteristics of each of the previously mentioned kinds of laws that differ with respect to the time dimension. First, let's start with an analysis of laws of equilibrium.

Figure 5-1   Laws and the time variable

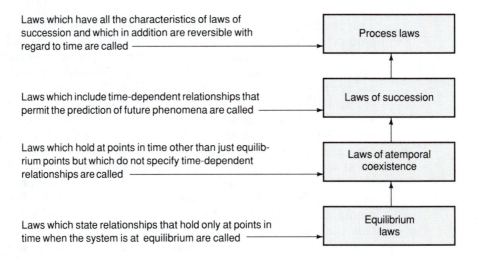

Laws which have all the characteristics of laws of succession and which in addition are reversible with regard to time are called ——————————————→ Process laws

Laws which include time-dependent relationships that permit the prediction of future phenomena are called —————→ Laws of succession

Laws which hold at points in time other than just equilibrium points but which do not specify time-dependent relationships are called ————————————————→ Laws of atemporal coexistence

Laws which state relationships that hold only at points in time when the system is at equilibrium are called ————→ Equilibrium laws

5.1.1   Equilibrium Laws

Equilibrium laws are laws of atemporal coexistence stating that certain specified relationships in a particular system will be true *only* if the values of the variables are not changing through time; i.e., the system must be at rest. Thus, the basic form of such laws is:

$$Y_{t(e)} = f\,[X_{t(e)}]$$

That is, specified values of Y are associated with specified values of X only when the system is at a point in time e when X and Y are not changing (the definition of equilibrium).

Conventional demand theory analysis prescribes that, at *equilibrium,* the consumer will purchase the particular combination of goods X and Y where the marginal rate of substitution of good X for good Y equals the ratio of the price of X to the price of Y. The marginal rate of substitution shows the rate at which the consumer is willing to substitute X for Y, and the price shows the rate at which he can substitute X for Y. Note that the relationship holds only if the system is at equilibrium. Of equal importance, the converse is true: If the relationship does not hold, the system is not at equilibrium.

Equilibrium laws play an important part in the scheme of science proposed by functionalists. As discussed in Chapter 2, functional analysis seeks to understand a behavior pattern or sociocultural institution by determining the role it plays in keeping the given system in "proper working order" (an equilibrium kind of notion) or maintaining it as a going concern. [262, p. 205] Wroe Alderson, as a functionalist, suggested that marketers recognize that there are three different levels of equilibrium in organized human activities:

> First, there is market equilibrium which pertains to the network of external relations among organized behavior systems. Secondly, there is an organizational equilibrium which is a form of internal balance within an individual system. Finally, there is the more embracing concept of ecological equilibrium pertaining to the adjustment between a society and its environment. [10, p. 304]

Other marketing theorists have also extolled the virtues of viewing the markets for products as illustrations of equilibrating systems. Lawrence C. Lockley unequivocally advocates this position:

> The concept of an equilibrium is a universal natural concept. The populations of fish and food tend to reach an equilibrium in each stream or body of water. The action of osmosis brings about an equilibrium between separated bodies of liquids. Human populations tend to reach a point of equilibrium in terms of their sources of support. Whatever organization of natural phenomena we consider, we see a tendency for forces ultimately to come to rest in an equilibrium.
>
> Strangely, this same tendency is apparent in the marketplace. Consider the case of staple foods (as will be discussed in more detail later) offered in cans. Some products are promoted by food packers as nationally advertised brands and some offered by wholesalers or retailers as private brands. Many years ago, when canned foods were relatively new in the market, some of the well-advertised brands had a disproportionate share of the market. But as time has passed, there seems to have developed a sort of rough equilibrium in this field, an equilibrium which is only temporarily upset by special promotional efforts.

This same type of equilibrium is present, actually or incipiently, among competitors in many individual consumer markets. Men's shoes, household mechanical appliances, breakfast cereals, soaps and detergents, and bed sheets and blankets illustrate the tendency toward equilibrium. Among dentifrices, for example, the advertising, the point-of-purchase promotional material, the package design, the product formulation, and the channels of distribution have come to be about the same. Share of the market may have reached a point of stability. In the absence of any marked modification of these forces, we may have an excellent illustration of a market equilibrium. [398, p. 39]

Lockley then goes on to show how the notion of equilibrium led to the conceptualization of several lawlike statements, including the principle of *drift*. "There will always be a tendency for merchandise to drift down from a 'specialty' to a 'shopping' to a 'convenience' goods classification. This is another way of saying of course that an equilibrium tends to be reestablished as soon as it is disturbed." [398, p. 44]

Is the principle of drift an equilibrium law? The answer must depend on whether the stated relationship has time as a real variable and whether the relationship holds only at an equilibrium position. Clearly, time *does appear* as a real variable in the principle of drift, since we can restate the principle as, "There will always be a tendency *as time passes* for merchandise to drift..." To state that an equilibrium will appear is not the same thing as specifying certain lawlike relationships that will hold *at equilibrium*. It is the latter requirement which separates equilibrium laws from laws of succession. Therefore, to the extent that the principle of drift is lawlike, it should be considered as a kind of law of succession.

A caveat seems desirable here concerning equilibrium laws and equilibrating systems. Students of marketing should carefully distinguish between (1) the assertion that there exist equilibrium laws concerning marketing phenomena and (2) the assertion that all (or even most) marketing processes and systems are inherently equilibrating (i.e., marketing systems universally tend toward the establishment of equilibrium positions). Note that Statement 1 is a positive existential statement (see Section 5.3.2) which in principle can be verified by finding examples of equilibrium laws in marketing. However, Statement 2 appears to have an essentially metaphysical quality. The usefulness of believing in Statement 2, as Lockley appears to do, may lie more in the context of discovery. Therefore, the appropriate question would be, "To what extent has the belief that marketing processes are inherently equilibrating led to the discovery of well-supported lawlike statements?" If this is truly the appropriate question, then there would appear to be insufficient evidence to either accept or reject the assertion that marketing systems universally or even commonly tend toward the establishment of equilibrium positions.

5.1.2   Laws of Atemporal Coexistence

The previous section explored one specific type of coexistence law, that is, equilibrium laws. Now, all equilibrium laws are laws of atemporal coexistence, but not all laws of atemporal coexistence are equilibrium laws. That is, many laws of atemporal coexistence state relationships that occur at points in time other than just equilibrium positions. Therefore, the basic form of laws of atemporal coexistence would be:

$$Y_t = f(X_t)$$

Specified values of Y at any time t are associated with specified values of X at the same time t.

Bergman refers to all laws of atemporal coexistence as *cross-sectional laws* and states that "cross-sectional is taken from the metaphor that considers a state a temporal cross-section of a process. Such laws state functional connections obtaining among the values which several variables have at the same time." [56, p. 102]

Dubin takes a slightly different position on atemporal coexistence laws. Identifying these laws as *categoric laws*, Dubin says:

The recognition of a categoric law of interaction is facilitated by noting that its typical form employs the words *is associated with*. Synonyms for this phrase serve, of course, to provide the same identification. . . . Categoric laws are symmetrical. It does not matter whether one or the other of the units comes first in the statement of the law. Thus, "juvenile delinquency and broken homes are positively related" is identical with "broken homes and juvenile delinquency are positively related." The symmetry of categoric laws is emphasized, for this fact buttresses that a law of interaction is not a statement of causality. What, indeed, is the meaning of cause if the units *juvenile delinquency* and *broken homes* can be interchanged without restriction in the law of interaction between them? [160, pp. 100-101]

Dubin then goes on to admonish the reader to avoid jumping to the conclusion that the broken-home condition preceded in time the juvenile delinquency and, therefore, *caused* it.

Dubin's caveat merits the close scrutiny of marketing students. Extreme caution must be exercised when attempting to infer the temporal sequence of a relationship from data that are strictly cross-sectional or associative. For example, the temptation may be strong to infer that high advertising expenditures cause high sales. Such an inference may be unwarranted if the supportive data are cross-sectional because it is common knowledge that many firms set their advertising budgets at specified percentages of sales. Thus the data may equally support either of the two assertions "Advertising causes sales" and "Sales cause advertising." There are numerous instances where the temporal sequentiality of the relationships remain in doubt. Are changes in attitude lawfully related to subsequent changes in purchase behavior? Or, are changes in purchase behavior lawfully related to subsequent changes in attitude? Or, does the relationship go in both directions depending on the situation? The major conclusion to be drawn from the preceding discussion would appear to be: If the data base which is used to test lawlike statements is cross-sectional (that is, all data are drawn from the same time period), adopt the agnostic position of treating any corroborated or confirmed lawlike statements as *laws of coexistence* rather than *sequential laws* (or even more strongly, *causal laws*). Adopting this agnostic position is scientifically most respectable because the researcher will, hopefully, remain alert to the possibility that the actual direction of the temporal sequence may be opposite to intuition.

5.1.3   Laws of Succession

The preceding sections have discussed the two kinds of laws which do not include time as a real variable. *Laws of succession,* however, provide that specified values of one or more variables will be succeeded in time by specified values of one or more other variables. [262, p. 352] Dubin refers to such laws as *sequential laws* [160, p. 100], and Kaplan uses the term *temporal laws.* [332, p. 109] The basic form of such laws is:

$$Y_{t+n} = f(X_t)$$

One extremely useful perspective for evaluating laws of succession is to examine the *level of specificity* of the time variable in the proposed relationships. Varying degrees of specificity are found in the relationships in marketing models and theories. Many marketing theorists only minimally specify the time variable in their theoretical constructions. Others are much more explicit in identifying which variables are hypothesized to influence other variables through time.

Consider the Engel-Kollat-Blackwell model of consumer behavior reproduced in Figure 5-2. The authors, in their discussion, often do not explicitly state which relationships are time-dependent and which are not. There is little doubt about some of the proposed relationships. For example, the authors clearly imply that changes in exposure precede changes in attention, preceding changes in comprehension and retention. But what about the relationships among these constructs: attitude, evaluative criteria, and personality? What is the proposed temporal sequence of changes in these constructs? Possibly the authors mean to propose that these relationships be considered laws of atemporal coexistence. The ambiguity results from the minimal specification of the time variable. Unfortunately, many marketing models only

Figure 5-2   Complete model of consumer behavior showing purchasing processes and outcomes

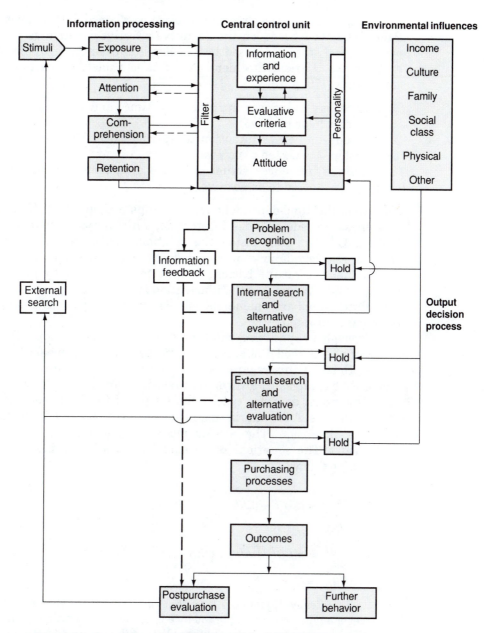

Source: From James F. Engel, David T. Kollat, and Roger D. Blackwell, *Consumer Behavior*, 2d ed. (New York: Holt, Rinehart & Winston, 1973), p. 58. Reproduced by permission of the publisher.

minimally specify the time-dependent relationships. Sometimes, the *implied* time-dependent relationships are intuitively clear; at other times, they are not.

Next, consider the "hierarchy of effects" model investigated by Palda [484] and based on the cognitive-affective-conative sequence of psychological states proposed by Lavidge and Steiner. [379] As stated by Terrence O'Brien, the hierarchy of effects model consists of three statements [479, p. 284]:

1. Awareness influences attitude over time, and the relationship is expected to be positive.
2. Attitude influences intention to purchase over time, and the relationship is expected to be positive.
3. Intention influences actual purchase over time, and the relationship is expected to be positive.

Note that the time-dependent relationships are specified: Changes in awareness precede changes in attitude, which precede changes in intention. O'Brien then tested the relationships using the method of cross-lagged correlations on panel data on 636 housewives and concluded that the results basically supported the hierarchy predictions. [479, p. 289] The point of the illustration is that when the time-dependent relationships are unambiguously specified, the process of empirical testing is facilitated.

Although in specifying the time-dependent relationships, the hierarchy of effects model is superior to many marketing models, it is far from optimal in this regard. Note that the hierarchy of effects model states that changes in awareness precede changes in intention. However, the model does *not* specify the length of time between these expected changes. A few marketing models are very specific in identifying the time dimension. The Nicosia model of consumer behavior is one such model. The equations composing Nicosia's linear model and his explanation follow:

1. $\dfrac{dB(t)}{dt} = b[M(t) - \beta B(t)]$

2. $M(t) = mA(t)$

3. $\dfrac{dA(t)}{dt} = a[B(t) - \alpha A(t)] + cC(t)$

4. $C(t) = C$

Specifically, Equation 1 says that the time rate of change in the level of buying of a certain brand by a consumer of a certain type is directly proportional to the difference $[M(t) - \beta B(t)]$. Equation 2 states a dependence of motivation M upon attitude A. Then, Equation 3 says that the time rate of change in level of attitude is directly proportional to the difference $[B(t) - \alpha A(t)]$ plus a constant multiple of the advertising level C. Finally, the level of C is defined by Equation 4 to be constant with respect to time. [476, p. 209]

Thus, the nature of the time-dependent relationships is very clearly specified in the Nicosia model. Once again, this should greatly facilitate testing the model. However, this should not be interpreted as meaning that the entire model is easily testable. Severe measurement and parameter estimation problems exist with the Nicosia model. In evaluating the falsifiability of the Nicosia model, Zaltman, Pinson, and Angelmar conclude that "one can even fear that no test of the model will be possible without a significant alteration of its very nature." [647, p. 108]

5.1.4   Process Laws

Up to this point, we have considered equilibrium laws, laws of atemporal coexistence, and laws of succession, and how each of these kinds of laws incorporates the time variable. However, laws of succession are not the final way to deal with time. Bergman uses the term *process law* to refer to lawlike statements that have all the characteristics of laws of succession and in addition are reversible with regard to time. [61, p. 416] Laws of succession enable one to predict future phenomena; process laws enable one to both predict future phenomena and retrodict past phenomena. This is the meaning of *reversible* with regard to time. Thus, if we know the position and velocity of a planet at a single instant in time, the laws of Newtonian celestial mechanics enable us not only to predict the position and velocity of the planet in the future but also to retrodict the position and velocity of the planet at points of time in the past.

As the reader will note, process laws are very powerful kinds of statements. To the best of the writer's knowledge, at present there exist no examples of process laws in marketing. This should not be too depressing since, in fact, there probably exist no examples of process laws in *any* of the social sciences. The development of process laws, and, hence, the accumulation of what Bergman calls "process knowledge," would still be a useful goal or ideal point for marketing and the social sciences, even if the objective were never to be reached.

5.2   AXIOMS, FUNDAMENTAL, AND DERIVATIVE LAWS

Few issues in the methodology of the social sciences have spawned as much controversy as the nature of, and the proper role for, axioms or "assumptions" in scientific inquiry. The debate has been especially lively in economics, with Friedman, Samuelson, and other writers [214, 554, 555, 556, 222, 412, 391, 423, 465] expressing sharp differences of perspective. Although all of the major issues in the so-called Friedman-Samuelson debate cannot be specifically evaluated at this point, two aspects of the controversy are appropriate here: (1) What are axioms or assumptions? and (2) What does it mean to say that "the axioms of a theory are assumed to be true"?

To appreciate the nature and role of axioms in scientific inquiry requires some elaboration of the notions of *fundamental laws* versus *derivative laws*. Hempel suggests that all lawlike statements in any theory can be categorized as either fundamental or derivative. [262, p. 267] The set of derivative laws in a theory consists of all those laws that can be deduced from other laws *in the same theory*. Thus, Kepler's laws concerning the motions of planets can be deduced or derived from the more fundamental Newton Laws. In marketing, the "square root law," which states that to double the attention-getting power of an advertisement the size of the advertisement must be increased fourfold, can be derived from the more fundamental Weber's Law. [447, p. 13]

The fundamental laws of a theory are those that (1) are used to deduce other laws and (2) cannot themselves be deduced from other laws in that same theory. The fundamental laws of a theory are the axioms of that theory, and the derived laws are often called theorems. As Bergman has observed, "The laws of a theory are deduced from its axioms." [56, p. 131]

Two observations need emphasizing with regard to fundamental versus derivative laws. First, laws that are fundamental (axioms) in one theory can be derived (theorems) in some other theory. [94, p. 268] For example, Newton's Laws are fundamental in Newtonian mechanics but are derived laws vis-à-vis Einstein's Theory of Relativity. This implies that the categorization of fundamental versus derived is *theory specific*. Second, for some theories there may be a choice between which laws should be considered fundamental and which should be considered derived. Consider a hypothetical theory composed of five laws, L_1, L_2, L_3, L_4, and L_5. One construction of the theory may consider L_1 and L_2 to be fundamental, since they can be used to derive L_3, L_4, and L_5. On the other hand, a rival construction may consider L_1 and L_3 to be fundamental and use them to derive L_2, L_4, and L_5. In such cases the theorist has a choice of which statements should be considered as fundamental.

So, if the axioms of a theory are the fundamental laws of the theory, what does it mean to assert that "the axioms of a theory are *assumed* to be true"? Unfortunately, the preceding assertion seems often to be interpreted as meaning either that the axioms *should not* be empirically tested to see whether they are consistent with reality or that the axioms cannot be so tested. Nothing could be further from the truth! The selection or recognition that certain lawlike statements in a theory are fundamental and, thus, to be called "axioms," convey to them no privileged sanctuary from the criterion that all purportedly lawlike statements must be empirically testable. Empirically testing the axioms of a theory is both possible and desirable. The assertion that the axioms are assumed to be true does not mean that the axioms are assumed to be true *empirically*. Rather, the axioms of a theory are assumed to be true *analytically*.

Understanding the difference between assuming that axioms are true empirically and assuming that axioms are true *for strictly analytical purposes* is crucial for clearing up many of the misconceptions about the proper role of axioms in theory construction and evaluation. Therefore, what does the phrase "for strictly analytical purposes" imply? Recalling our distinction between fundamental and derivative laws, the statement that axioms are assumed to be true for strictly analytical purposes implies that we assume axioms to be true *only* for the purpose of generating derivative laws and other statements. Therefore, "for strictly analytical purposes" comprises the following kinds of processes: "If these statements (the axioms) are true or false, then the following statements (theorems or hypotheses) are true or false." The preceding discussion can be summarized by noting that we assume that axioms are true for the purpose of *constructing* theory rather than for the purpose of *evaluating* theory.

5.2.1   Bridge Laws

One set of derivative laws deserving special attention are *bridge laws,* or what Hempel refers to as *bridge principles:*

> [Bridge laws] indicate how the processes envisaged by the theory are related to empirical phenomena with which we are already acquainted, and which the theory may then explain, predict, or retrodict.... Without bridge principles, as we have seen, a theory would have no explanatory power.... Without bridge principles, the internal principles of a theory would yield no test implications, and the requirement of testability would be violated. [264, pp. 72-75]

Bridge laws, then, are derivative laws that "bridge the gap" between the general laws in any particular theory and the specific classes of empirical phenomena under investigation. Sometimes when researchers refer to the so-called "guiding hypotheses" or even "hypotheses" of their research, they are implicitly referring to bridge laws.

An example will better serve to illustrate the nature and function in theory of fundamental laws, derivative laws, and bridge laws. The marketing implications of Leon Festinger's theory of cognitive dissonance provide an excellent vehicle to illustrate these concepts. [181] Before discussing the lawlike statements in Festinger's theory, four definitions are necessary:

Definition 1. Cognitions are the bits of knowledge one has about himself, about his behavior, and about his surroundings.

Definition 2.   Two cognitions are in a *dissonant* state if, considering these two alone, the obverse of one cognition would follow from the other.

Definition 3.   Two cognitions are *consonant* if one cognition does follow from the other.

Definition 4.   Two cognitions are *irrelevant* if one cognition implies nothing at all concerning the other.

With the preceding four definitions in mind, the core of the theory of cognitive dissonance can be stated in terms of three *fundamental lawlike (FL)* statements:

FL_1:   After a decision is made, there may exist dissonant or "nonfitting" relations among cognitive elements.

FL_2:   The existence of dissonance gives rise to pressures to reduce the dissonance and to avoid increases in dissonance.

FL_3:   Dissonance can be reduced by *(a)* changing one or more of the cognitive elements, *(b)* adding new consonant elements, and *(c)* decreasing the importance of the elements in the dissonant relations.

Scores of dissonance theorists have used these fundamental lawlike statements to generate derivative laws. While conducting research on appliance purchases [295], the present writer used the fundamental laws of dissonance theory to derive the following bridge laws *(BL):*

BL_1:   Consumers will experience cognitive dissonance after the decision to purchase a major appliance.

BL_2:   If retailers provide information to recent purchasers of major appliances, and if the information reassures the consumers that they made wise decisions, then the information will assist the consumers in their efforts to reduce cognitive dissonance.

The first bridge law can be derived from the set of fundamental laws on the basis that the purchase of a major appliance would be an important decision for consumers. Further, consumers would have dissonant cognitions since it is unlikely that the chosen brand model would be rated the best on all relevant characteristics, for example, style, color, and price. The second bridge law follows from the notion that the posttransaction reassurances provided to the consumer would be perceived as adding consonant cognitions, which is one method for reducing the dissonance of the consumer. Note that both bridge laws enable the researcher to span the gap between the general relationships in the fundamental laws and the specific relationships in real-world phenomena.

The writer then used the preceding bridge laws, a sample of 152 recent purchasers of refrigerators, and an experimental research design to test, among other things, the following *research hypothesis:* The subjects who received the posttransaction reassurances will have lower perceived dissonance scores (i.e., will be less dissonant) than the subjects in the control group. The results of the study provided modest support for the research hypothesis and, therefore, the underlying bridge laws and, finally, the entire theory in general.

All research which purports to test some theoretical construction will employ bridge laws. They may be either explicitly stated or implicitly implied. The more explicitly the bridge laws are stated, the less chance there is that the researcher will make a logical error. Often the hypotheses that are actually tested in a research project are not derivable from the theory which is supposedly being evaluated, simply because the researcher did not specifically state the bridge laws. Such research is useless at best and misleading at worst.

In summary, Figure 5-3 shows that the fundamental laws or axioms of a theory (1) are used to deduce other laws and (2) cannot themselves be deduced from other laws in that same theory. Axioms are not assumed to be true empirically; rather, they are assumed to be true for the analytical purpose of deriving other statements. The derivative laws in a theory are deduced from the fundamental laws. Bridge laws are derivative laws that bridge the gap between the general laws of a theory and the specific classes of phenomena under investigation. As the cognitive dissonance example illustrated, bridge laws are needed to derive the research hypotheses for testing purposes. Researchers often do not specifically state the bridge laws and, instead, jump directly from other more general derived laws or even fundamental laws to the directly testable research hypotheses. Such procedures run the risk of testing research hypotheses that cannot in fact be derived from the set of lawlike statements that the theory comprises.

Figure 5-3 Fundamental and derivative laws

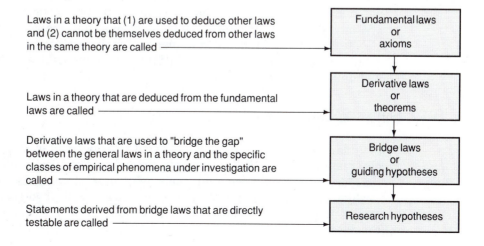

Laws in a theory that (1) are used to deduce other laws and (2) cannot be themselves deduced from other laws in the same theory are called ——————→ **Fundamental laws or axioms**

Laws in a theory that are deduced from the fundamental laws are called ——————→ **Derivative laws or theorems**

Derivative laws that are used to "bridge the gap" between the general laws in a theory and the specific classes of empirical phenomena under investigation are called ——————→ **Bridge laws or guiding hypotheses**

Statements derived from bridge laws that are directly testable are called ——————→ **Research hypotheses**

5.3   EXTENSION AND UNIVERSALITY

Bunge suggests that both lawlike and nonlawlike statements should be categorized by their extension or range. [94, p. 266] The *extension* of a statement consists of the set of all possible objects (past, present, and future) covered by the statement. The work of Weitz [630] illustrates the importance of carefully delineating the extension of theories and propositions. Weitz reviews the research that has been conducted on salesperson performance using variables such as sales behaviors, behavioral predispositions, and salesperson capabilities. He concludes that past research results were contradictory or inconclusive in part because the researchers were attempting to uncover universal characteristics or behaviors that would be predictive of performance over too wide a range of situations. That is, the researchers were seeking generalizations with an *extension* that was unlikely. Weitz then suggests a contingency framework for sales effectiveness based on the following basic postulate: "The effectiveness of sales behaviors across customer interactions is contingent upon or moderated by *(a)* the salesperson's resources, *(b)* the nature of the customer's buying task, *(c)* the customer-salesperson relationship, and interactions among *(a)*, *(b)*, and *(c)*." [630, p. 91]

Knowledge of the extension of a statement is valuable both because statements differing in extension have different roles in theory construction and because statements differing in extension vary with respect to their confirmability and falsifiability. *Confirmable* means the extent to which a statement is capable of being shown to be empirically true; that is, does the statement accurately describe the real world? *Falsifiable* means the extent to which a statement is capable of being shown to be empirically untrue; that is, how conclusively can we show that the real world is not arranged in accordance with the statement? As will be demonstrated, not all statements that are confirmable are at the same time falsifiable. Likewise, some statements are falsifiable but not confirmable; some are *neither* confirmable nor falsifiable. Others are only *weakly* confirmable or falsifiable. We shall restrict the discussion to four basic kinds of statements that have differing degrees of extension: singular statements, existential statements, statistical laws, and universal laws.

5.3.1   Singular Statements

Singular statements, sometimes referred to as particular [503, p. 27] or observation [262, p. 103] statements, extend only to specific phenomena that are bound in time and space. Singular statements are never lawlike statements since they do not have the form of generalized conditionals, which is a basic requirement for any statement to be considered lawlike. Singular statements play a crucial role in the confirmation or validation of theories and laws because the research hypotheses that are used to test theories and laws are usually singular statements.

The research hypothesis concerning cognitive dissonance discussed in the preceding section is illustrative of singular statements in marketing research: "The subjects who received the posttransaction reassurances will have lower perceived dissonance scores (i.e., will be less dissonant) than the subjects in the control group." That the statement is singular is evident from the fact that it refers to specific subjects in specific groups and specific scores taken at identifiable points in time. The dissonance hypothesis also shows the tremendous value of singular statements in testing theories. The statement is *(a)* derived from dissonance theory and *(b)* both confirmable and falsifiable. If the actual data show that the dissonance scores of the subjects in the experimental group are lower than the scores of the subjects in the control group, then the hypothesis (singular statement) is *confirmed*. Because the hypothesis is derived from the theory, the confirmation of the hypothesis is evidence in support of dissonance theory; that is, it *corroborates* (or tends to confirm) dissonance theory. Conversely, if the data show the opposite results, then the hypothesis is *falsified*, and thus we have evidence noncorroborative of dissonance theory. It is in this sense that singular statements are generally both confirmable and falsifiable and, consequently, play such a vital role in theory validation.

5.3.2   Existential Statements

Existential statements are statements which propose the existence of some phenomenon. "There exist products that have life cycles." "Man has psychological needs." "The abominable snowman exists!" All of the previous statements are existential in basic form. Even though their extension is greater than that of singular statements, note that existential statements are not lawlike because they do not have the form of generalized conditionals.

Zaltman et al. suggest that all existential statements are purely confirmable but not falsifiable. [647, p. 66] To illustrate their point they cite Martilla as an example of an existential statement: "There are opinion leaders in industrial firms." [421, p. 173] The position taken here is that although all existential statements are purely confirmable, only those statements whose extension or range is unqualified or unbounded are not falsifiable. Qualified or bounded existential statements are both confirmable and falsifiable. Zaltman's example is actually a bounded existential statement and, hence, is capable, at least in principle, of being falsified. That is, there is a bounded or finite number of industrial firms. Therefore, one could in principle examine the entire set of industrial firms and potentially falsify the statement

"There are opinion leaders in industrial firms." Contrast the preceding with the unqualified existential statement, "There are opinion leaders." Finding a single opinion leader would confirm the statement, but, because of the unbounded extension of the statement, it is not falsifiable.

In attempting to explore the foundations of consumer behavior, Tucker asserted two "propositions":

> Proposition 1.   Someone goes through some process and acquires something with some effect.
>
> Proposition 2.   Someone uses something in some way with some effect. [619, p. 134]

These "propositions" are in reality unqualified existential statements, and thus are confirmable but not falsifiable. The first proposition can be confirmed as true if one can discover a single person who has gone through some process and acquired something with some effect. Nevertheless, no possible research design could possibly show the statement to be false.

The primary role of these "propositions" and other existential statements in marketing research is probably heuristic. For example, if one adopts the existential belief that there exist lawlike relationships among marketing phenomena, then one may attempt to discover the relationships. On the other hand, if one holds firmly the belief that the relationships among marketing phenomena are nonlawlike, then why conduct research? It is precisely in this context that the belief or nonbelief in existential statements plays a heuristic role in research.

5.3.3   Statistical Laws

The nature and form of statistical laws were first broached in the evaluation of various methods of scientific explanation in Chapter 2. Laws of basically statistical form gain prominence when there are a large number of variables (many of which are often unknown) that influence the phenomenon to be explained or predicted. Therefore, the exact specification of the relationship between changes in the phenomenon to be explained or predicted and any other single variable is thwarted by other variables. Under such conditions, theoreticians frequently rely on statistical laws that state an indeterministic relationship between variables. Such lawlike statements have substantially greater extension than either singular statements or existential statements because statistical laws *do* have the form of generalized conditionals. That is, the relationships implied in statistical laws extend to a far greater number of objects and phenomena than do singular or existential statements.

Kaplan refers to one particular subset of statistical laws as *tendency* laws. [332, p. 97] Such laws state that there *tends* to be a relationship, usually rather loosely specified, between two variables. Commentators on laws in marketing would probably agree that *most of the lawlike statements in marketing are (explicitly or implicitly) tendency laws.* Examples of tendency laws abound in marketing: "Opinion leaders [tend to] meet more salesmen than nonleaders." [563, p. 50] "Brand loyalty [tends to vary] directly with perceived satisfaction with the old brand." [471, p. 406] "Lower income consumers [tend to] prefer credit contracts that include the lowest monthly payments." [625, p. 73] "The greater the cost of the product considered, the greater the tendency for two or more family members to be involved in the decision process." [233, p. 196] A final illustration: "Audiences tend to expose themselves selectively to those messages which best fit their existing predispositions or inclinations." [72, p. 53]

Unlike singular statements, tendency laws (like all statistical laws) are neither *strictly* confirmable nor *strictly* falsifiable. To see this, consider how one would test the "opinion leader" statement mentioned in the previous paragraph. The procedure would probably involve obtaining a sample of opinion leaders and nonleaders and then measuring their respective contact with salesmen. No matter how strong the relationship found, the evidence would never be *conclusive* in favor of or against the "opinion leader" statement. If the data contradicted the statement, defenders could always claim that the data base was too small, or was biased, or that the data were "contaminated" or "noisy." For example, Farley and Ring found very low coefficients of determination in their test of the Howard-Sheth theory of buyer behavior. They then postulated that "noisy data" was the problem, rather than the low explanatory power of the theory. [170, p. 435]

If, on the other hand, the results of a research project *supported* the "opinion leader" statement, attackers could claim that the observed relationship was "spurious" and that the relationship could disappear with a larger sample or a different kind of test. Therefore, tendency laws are neither *strictly* confirmable (that is, able to be proved conclusively true) nor *strictly* falsifiable (that is, able to be proved conclusively false). Rather, test results can be shown to be either *consistent* or *inconsistent* with the tendency law in question and thus *corroborative* or *noncorroborative.*

Observations of the preceding kind lead many scholars to debunk the whole notion of statistical laws. Bunge suggests that this would be a mistake:

> Some die-hard classical determinists claim that stochastic statements do not deserve the name of law and are to be regarded, at their best, as temporary devices. This anachronistic view has no longer currency in physics, chemistry, and certain branches of biology (notably genetics), especially ever since these sciences found that all molar laws in their domains are stochastic laws deducible (at least in principle) from laws concerning single systems in conjunction with definite

statistical hypotheses regarding, e.g., the compensation of random deviations. Yet the prejudice against stochastic laws still causes some
harm in psychology and sociology, where it serves to attack the stochastic approach without compensating for its loss by a scientific
study of individuals. [95, p. 336]

The preceding advice by Bunge is also wise counsel for marketing.
Tendency laws have played, do play, and will continue to play a central
role in marketing theory. The fact that such laws are only *weakly* confirmable and *weakly* falsifiable should be no cause for methodological
alarm.

There are other kinds of statistical laws besides tendency laws, the
most prominent of which is the *probability* law. Recall that the relationship between the variables in a tendency law is usually very loosely
specified. In contrast, the relationship between the variables in a
probability law is clearly specified in the form of a probability or relative frequency statement:

$$P(G, F) = r$$

That is, the probability of event G, given that event F has occurred, is r.
Or, alternatively, in the *long run* the proportion of cases of F which are
also G is r. "The probability of throwing an 'ace' given a 'fair die' is 1/6."
The reader may want to review the section on theories of probability in
Chapter 2 at this point.

Although, as Popper has pointed out [503, p. 189], probability laws
are not falsifiable, they are in general more powerful than tendency
laws precisely because the relationships between the variables are more
clearly specified. This increases their predictive and explanatory power,
and thus their susceptibility to empirical testing and corroboration.

Probability laws are less common in marketing than tendency laws
because the existence of a probability law between two variables presupposes that the other variables which influence the process interact
either in a random manner or at least in a consistent way with the phenomenon in question. That is, the law that the probability of throwing
an ace with a fair die equals 1/6 presupposes that such factors as initial
velocity and the direction of the throw, which do in fact influence the
results of each single toss of the die, will be randomly distributed
through time. Therefore, the factor determining the probability of an
ace on any throw will be the geometry of the cube. The lack of probability laws in marketing can be ascribed to the fact that in most marketing
processes the other variables which might influence the phenomenon in
question do not exert random or consistent interactions through time.

The work of Bass on the rate of diffusion of innovations illustrates a
probability law in marketing. [44, p. 215 ff.] Bass classified the initial
purchasers of new consumer durable goods into innovators and imitators, where the latter group included early adopters, the early majority,

the late majority, and laggards. From the basic notion that imitators are primarily influenced in their purchase of durables by other buyers, Bass proposed the following probability law: "The probability that an initial purchase will be made at T, given that no purchase has yet been made, is a linear function of the number of previous buyers." Bass then tested his probability law on purchasers of 11 consumer durable goods and found substantial corroborative support. The reader can satisfy himself that the Bass proposition is in fact a probability law by observing that it has the basic form $P(G, F) = r$. In this case, the probability r is a linear function of the number of previous buyers rather than a simple constant.

The probability law proposed by Bass, like many statistical laws, is perhaps more significant for what it excludes than for what it includes. The law excludes certain variables from playing significant roles in determining the rate of purchase of new durable goods. For example, one might propose *a priori* that different levels of advertising would influence the rate of purchase. However, since this variable is not explicitly included in the relationship, then, *if the probability law is true,* we must conclude that either *(a)* advertising does not influence (or only minimally influences) the rate of purchase or *(b)* advertising influences the rate of purchase, but it does so in a consistent manner across different products. In the latter case, advertising would be *implicitly* incorporated in the probability statement.

5.3.4   Universal Laws

Laws of *strictly universal form* take the form of universal generalized conditionals and constitute the prototypes of all laws. Universal laws state: "Every time A occurs, then B will occur," or "All A are B," or "For any x, if x is an instance of A, then x is an instance of B." Note that universal laws do *not* simply state that "B exists," as would an existential statement. Neither do they state that "B tends to be associated with A," as would a tendency law. Nor do universal laws state that "the probability of B happening, given A, is r," as would a probability law. Since laws of strictly universal form extend to all instances of A, they have greater extension than singular statements, existential statements, or statistical laws.

The tremendous power of universal laws lies in their being falsifiable in a very strict sense. As Popper has observed, laws of universal form can be alternatively expressed as negative existential statements or "there-is-not statements." [503, p. 69] An example from Newtonian mechanics will illustrate this point. Newton's Third Law of Motion states that for every action there is a reaction equal in magnitude and opposite in direction. Note that this law can be stated alternatively as a negative existential statement, "There exists *no* action for which there is *not* a reaction equal in magnitude and opposite in direction." All laws of strictly universal form can be similarly reconstructed as negative existential statements.

As previously discussed, positive existential statements are strictly confirmable. That is, to confirm the statement "Opinion leaders exist," one need only find a single opinion leader. Similarly, negative existential statements are strictly falsifiable. The negative existential statement "Opinion leaders *do not* exist" can be falsified by finding a single opinion leader. *Therefore, since all universal laws can be alternatively expressed as negative existential statements, all universal laws are strictly falsifiable.*

Universal laws have greater explanatory and predictive power than statistical laws. Recall that the deductive-nomological (D-N) model of scientific explanation, discussed in Chapter 2, has the following structure:

$$C_1, C_2, \ldots C_k$$
$$ \Big\}\ \text{Explanans } S$$
$$\frac{L_1, L_2, \ldots L_k}{E} \qquad \Big\}\ \text{Explanandum } E$$

In this model, the characteristics $(C_1, C_2 \ldots)$ of the situation and the strictly universal laws $(L_1, L_2, \ldots)$ *deductively imply* the phenomenon to be explained, E. Thus, the D-N model explains the occurrence of a phenomenon E by invoking a universal law stating that certain antecedent circumstances C_k are invariably followed by phenomenon E and then noting that circumstances C_k had, indeed, occurred.

The most common form of statistical explanation is the inductive-statistical (I-S) model:

$$C_1, C_2, \ldots C_k$$
$$ \Big\}\ \text{Explanans } S$$
$$\frac{SL_1, SL_2, \ldots SL_k}{E} \qquad \begin{array}{l} \text{[it is very likely that]} \\ \Big\}\ \text{Explanandum } E \end{array}$$

In the I-S model of explanation, unlike the D-N model, the phenomenon to be explained is not a logical, deductive consequence of the explanans. The I-S model states that, given circumstances C_k and certain statistical laws SL_k, then *it is very likely* that E would have occurred (or would tend to occur). Because the laws are statistical, not universal, the explanandum E is not a logical consequence of the premises S, in the sense that even if E does not occur, S could still be true. Therefore, universal laws have greater explanatory power than statistical laws, and a structurally similar argument could be developed to demonstrate that they have greater predictive power as well.

To the best of this writer's knowledge, there currently exist no marketing laws of strictly universal form. In this regard, marketing does not differ from the other social or behavioral sciences, none of which contain laws of strictly universal form. [332, p. 97] The previous statements do not mean that no theorist in marketing or any of the other behavioral sciences states his lawlike generalizations in universal forms. Rather, even though some theorists *state* their lawlike generalizations in universal form, they expect their readers to *interpret* the laws statistically. Readers should ask themselves the following question when they confront any lawlike generalization which is stated in strictly universal form: "Would the theorist be willing to accept the conclusion that his law is false if he were shown the results of a *single experiment* where the law did not predict correctly and where the theorist was convinced that there were neither methodological nor observational errors in the experiment?" If the answer to this question is affirmative, then the theorist truly wants his law to be interpreted in a strictly universal manner, since the essence of this question is whether the law being examined is *strictly falsifiable*. Strict falsification is a requirement of all laws of truly universal form. However, most theorists would probably reply in the negative to the previous question and then defensively retort, "Don't take my words so literally!"

We may conclude that no existing laws in marketing have the form of strictly universal, generalized conditionals. Indeed, some would take the position that marketing phenomena (like other behavioral phenomena) are *inherently* indeterministic, and thus the best that can ever be accomplished will be laws of basically statistical form.[1] *If* marketing phenomena were assumed to be inherently indeterministic, this should not be intellectually discomforting to marketing researchers. Although strictly universal laws have greater explanatory and predictive power than statistical laws, in many situations statistical laws perform quite adequately.

5.4   SUMMARY AND CONCLUSIONS

This chapter has attempted to explore the extension and universality of both lawlike and nonlawlike statements. The reader may wish to consult Figure 5-4, on page 142, which delineates the various kinds of statements that have differing extension and gives hypothetical examples of each kind. The examples were specifically constructed so that each would involve the common construct of the "maturity phase of the product life cycle." Singular statements have the least extension of all statements because they refer to specific phenomena that are bound in time and space. Singular statements are both strictly confirmable and strictly falsifiable.

---

[1] The reader should be analyzing all statements by now and should recognize that this statement is falsifiable but not strictly confirmable. Can the statement be alternatively constructed as a negative existential statement?

Figure 5-4   Extension and universality

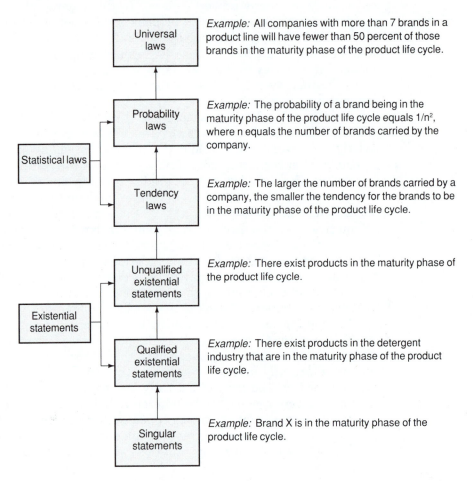

Universal laws
Example: All companies with more than 7 brands in a product line will have fewer than 50 percent of those brands in the maturity phase of the product life cycle.

Probability laws
Example: The probability of a brand being in the maturity phase of the product life cycle equals $1/n^2$, where n equals the number of brands carried by the company.

Tendency laws
Example: The larger the number of brands carried by a company, the smaller the tendency for the brands to be in the maturity phase of the product life cycle.

Unqualified existential statements
Example: There exist products in the maturity phase of the product life cycle.

Qualified existential statements
Example: There exist products in the detergent industry that are in the maturity phase of the product life cycle.

Singular statements
Example: Brand X is in the maturity phase of the product life cycle.

Note: All examples are hypothetical and are for illustrative purposes only.

Thus, their primary role in research lies in the *testing* of laws and theories. Existential statements propose the existence of some phenomenon. Bounded or qualified existential statements are both confirmable and falsifiable, whereas unqualified existential statements are confirmable but not strictly falsifiable. Tendency laws are a kind of statistical law stating that two variables tend to vary together in a systematic way. Most lawlike statements in marketing are tendency laws. Probability laws are a genus of statistical law where the relationship between two variables is clearly specified in the form of a probability or relative frequency statement. Both tendency laws and probability laws are neither confirmable nor falsifiable. Universal laws state a relationship between two variables in the form of a strictly universal generalized conditional. Such laws have the greatest extension and universality and are falsifiable but not strictly confirmable.

5.5   PROBLEMS IN EXTENSION: THE PSYCHOPHYSICS OF PRICES

The previous sections have attempted to classify various kinds of statements according to their differing extension. The extension of a statement was defined as the set of all possible objects (past, present, and future) covered by the statement. That is, what is the statement referring to: apples, oranges, attitudes, or preferences? A careful delimitation of the extension of statements is essential to systematic, scientific inquiry. Unfortunately, the marketing discipline as an applied area of investigation has been awash with lawlike statements that have been borrowed from other disciplines and then extrapolated to fit marketing problems. This extrapolation often extends the lawlike statement far beyond its legitimate domain or "universe of discourse." To illustrate the problems of questionable extension or extrapolation, we shall consider some of the issues raised by the so-called "psychophysics of prices and Weber's Law" controversy.

Kamen and Toman used preference behaviors of consumers concerning various pricing combinations of major branded gasolines and independent branded gasolines to attempt to test their "fair price" theory versus Weber's Law. [327] The research sparked critical comments by Monroe and by Gabor et al. and a reply by Kamen and Toman. [451, 220, 329] Although many issues were raised during the controversy, only the issue of the extension of Weber's Law will be explored here.

The crux of the fair price theory of Kamen and Toman (hereafter referred to as K-T) is that consumers have specific notions as to what constitutes a fair price for a product and that when the actual price exceeds this fair price, consumers will take courses of action in an attempt to maintain the fair price. Thus, for their gasoline data, K-T suggest:

> According to the "fair price" theory, as the price of major brand gasoline exceeds the perceived fair price, more and more motorists will turn to the Independents. Thus, suppose that the price difference between Majors and Independents is two cents. This theory would predict that when the price of gasoline is high—for example, 42 cents for Majors and 40 cents for Independents—more people would be attracted to the Independents than when the price of gasoline is low—for example, 28 cents for Majors and 26 cents for Independents. This prediction is exactly opposite to the one inferable from Weber's Law. [327, p. 27]

K-T thus imply that the following *bridge law* is inferable from Weber's Law: When the price of gasoline is high, more people will be attracted to the majors than to the independents than when the price of gasoline is low, if the same price *differential* is maintained at both price levels. Since K-T's results supported that fair price prediction, the major issue is whether their bridge law was a valid inference from

Weber's Law. That is, can Weber's Law be extended to cover K-T's concepts in the predicted relationship?

First, a review of Weber's Law and its original extension seems desirable. All participants in the controversy agree that Weber's Law states:

$$\Delta I / I = K$$

where ΔI equals the smallest increase in the intensity of a stimulus that will be just noticeably different from the previous intensity of the stimulus, I equals the original intensity of the stimulus, and K equals a constant which varies according to the nature of the stimulus. Substantial research has confirmed that the relationship *extends* to the following stimuli: pressure, visual brightness, lifted weights, tone, smell, and taste. [54, p. 96] K-T concede that they have extrapolated Weber's Law beyond its original extension [329, p. 253] but claim that their extrapolations are consistent with the current marketing literature. They cite, as an example, Engel, Kollat, and Blackwell:

> Assume, for example, that a price increase of $1 is to be put into effect. That increase would be highly apparent on a 50-cent item, whereas it probably would escape detection on an $80 item. [327, p. 27]

Are K-T just testing current and reasonable extensions or extrapolations of Weber's Law? To this issue we now turn.

The original extension of Weber's Law concerned people's ability to discriminate between different intensities of selected stimuli (smell, taste, etc.). The current marketing literature, like the above quotation from Engel, Kollat, and Blackwell, has extended Weber's Law to a different stimulus, that is, *price*. K-T, on the other hand, have extended Weber's Law beyond the current literature in at least two other respects.

The current literature has retained the notion of discriminability (note that E-K-B use the phrases "highly apparent" and "escape detection"). K-T extend Weber's Law to *consumer preferences* instead of *discriminability*. K-T recognize that they have done this [329, p. 253] but provide no logic to justify the extension. Perhaps the logic exists, but it was not presented. K-T state that "any price difference is discriminable" and that "there simply is no JND (just noticeable difference) for price." [329, p. 253] These statements seem curious in light of K-T's own research, which appears to indicate that some price changes for some people were not discriminable. To wit, K-T's following paragraph is presented:

> An opportunity for a cleaner validation study arose a little less than a year after general gasoline price levels rose slightly over one cent in the same 24 markets mentioned previously. Approximately 1,500 motorists, randomly selected from city directories, were interviewed

by telephone on their reactions to the price increase. Approximately 47 percent believed that the general gasoline price level went up during the past year, 2 percent believed that it went down, 44 percent that it remained the same, and 7 percent did not know or failed to answer this question. [327, p. 34]

In any respect, even if it were true that all price changes were discriminable, this would be insufficient reason to extend Weber's Law from *discriminability* to *preferences*. To repeat, there may be a logic available to justify extending discriminability to preference, but K-T did not present it.

The third major extension of Weber's Law by K-T concerns the notion of ΔI, the *differential*. In the original extension of Weber's Law, the differential referred to different intensities of the *same stimulus* (smell, taste, etc.). However, the differential that K-T refer to is different intensities of *different stimuli*. That is, the K-T differential is the difference in price between major branded gasoline and independent gasoline (not a difference for the same gasoline). Once again, K-T provide no logic to show that this is a reasonable extension.

In summary, K-T extended the original version of Weber's Law (1) to a different stimulus (price), (2) from discriminability to preferences, and (3) from different intensities of the same stimulus to different intensities of different stimuli. Taken in total, and without any justifying logic, these extensions (especially 2 and 3) seem unwarranted since they so drastically alter the basic statement of the law. The "fair price" theory of K-T is intriguing; K-T's research is interesting; and their data base is sound. Unfortunately, it is difficult to see what any of their results have to do with Weber's Law. They certainly did not test Weber's Law in any meaningful sense of the word *test*. Hopefully, if the "psychophysics of prices" controversy has done nothing else, it has underscored the tremendous importance of carefully delimiting the extension of lawlike statements. One must always stop to ask, "What is this statement really saying?" Also, "To which kinds of circumstances and situations does this statement apply, and to which does it not?"

QUESTIONS FOR ANALYSIS AND DISCUSSION

1. "Models are really the bases for marketing theories since they are the *axioms* on which marketing theories are founded." [381] Evaluate the view that models are axioms.

2. Find a theory or model in the marketing literature. Determine which statements purport to be lawlike. How do the statements handle the time dimension? Examine the extension of the statements.

3. Laws are "hypotheses that are empirically corroborated to a degree regarded as satisfactory at a certain point in time." [647, p. 71] To what extent is this perspective consistent or inconsistent with the treatment presented herein?

4. All lawlike statements have empirical content. Any statement which has empirical content can be empirically tested. Any statement which can be empirically tested can be shown to be true or false. Therefore, all lawlike statements can be shown to be empirically true or false. Evaluate.

5. Alderson proposed "a research agenda for functionalism" which included 150 falsifiable propositions. "For a proposition to be falsifiable, it must make a flat assertion with no authority behind it except its apparent consistency with other propositions that have already been accepted into the body of theory." Further, "a proposition is not falsifiable, or testable, if it has been hedged and qualified until it is almost certainly true under some circumstances." [10, p. 345] Analyze a sample of Alderson's propositions. What kinds of lawlike statements are they? What is their extension? To what extent are they *falsifiable?*

6. "As the degree of extension of a lawlike generalization increases, its accuracy of prediction will decrease." Evaluate.

7. Pinson et al. take great issue with the term *lawlike generalization:*

> The term "lawlike generalization" . . . is not commonly used in the philosophy of science literature. Instead, most authorities use the term "lawlike statement." . . . The reason for preferring the term "lawlike statement" over "lawlike generalization" relates to the redundance of the latter term [since] a minimum necessary condition of any scientific statement proposed as lawlike is that it can be a universal generalization. [496, p. 67]

Evaluate the charge made by Pinson et al. Are all generalizations *lawlike?* Are all lawlike statements *universal?*

8. Lockley proposes the following tendency law in marketing, which he calls the principle of nonprice competition: "For products for which product or marketing differentiation becomes difficult, there will be an increasing tendency toward nonprice competition, and the extent of nonprice competition will tend to be in proportion to the size and resources of the competing vendors." [398, p. 48] Does this imply that for products for which differentiation is *easy* there will be a *decreasing* tendency for nonprice competition? Evaluate.

9. The channels of distribution literature increasingly centers on the notions of power and conflict. A major problem has been to get an adequate definition of conflict. The following two perspectives are typical: (1) "The term conflict refers neither to its antecedent conditions, nor to individual awareness of it, nor certain affective states, nor its overt manifestations, nor its residues of feeling, precedent, or structure, but to all of these taken together as the history of a conflict episode." [502, p. 319] (2) "Conflict in our scheme refers to overt behavior arising out of a process in which one unit seeks the advancement of its own interests in its relationship with others." [565, p. 363]

Are these *definitions* of conflict, *explanations* of conflict, *lawlike generalizations* involving conflict, or what? Is it possible for a statement to be both a lawlike generalization and a definition at the same time? How useful would the two preceding perspectives be in conducting research on conflict in channels of distribution?

10. Is it possible to have a set of nontrue theorems which are derived from a set of true axioms? Does your answer differ depending on whether the axioms were universal or statistical in nature?

6

THE MORPHOLOGY OF THEORY

Once upon a time two explorers came upon a clearing in the jungle. In the clearing were growing many flowers and many weeds. One explorer says, "Some gardener must tend this plot." The other disagrees, "There is no gardener." So they pitch their tents and set a watch. No gardener is ever seen. "But perhaps he is an invisible gardener." So they set up a barbed-wire fence. They electrify it. They patrol with bloodhounds. (For they remember how H. G. Wells's The Invisible Man *could be both smelt and touched though he could not be seen.) But no shrieks ever suggest that some intruder has received a shock. No movements of the wire even betray an invisible climber. The bloodhounds never give cry. Yet still the Believer is not convinced. "But there is a gardener, invisible, intangible, insensible to electric shocks, a gardener who has no scent and makes no sound, a gardener who comes secretly to look after the garden which he loves." At last the Sceptic despairs, "But what remains of your original assertion? Just how does what you call an invisible, intangible, eternally elusive gardener differ from an imaginary gardener or even from no gardener at all?"*

A. G. N. Flew

This chapter will attempt to explicate the nature and role of theory in scientific inquiry and research. After discussing various perspectives on the concept of theory, a consensus conceptualization of theory will be offered. A review of some basic misconceptions of the nature of theory will show that as a result of these misconceptions marketing theory has taken a "bum rap." The body of the chapter will be devoted to developing in some detail the full import of the three key ideas embodied in the consensus conceptualization of theory. First, let's explore some perspectives on the notion of theory.

6.1   THE NOTION OF THEORY

What constitutes a theory? Is the term *theory* synonymous with *law*? How does a *theory* of X differ from an *explanation* of X? How do theories differ from hypotheses? Is a theory simply a model? Strangely enough, although *theory* would have to rank high among the most abused terms in marketing, there is probably more unanimity among philosophers of science as to what constitutes a theory than there is agreement among them concerning the nature of laws and explanations. This is not to say that there is a universal consensus concerning the nature of theoretical constructions. Rather, different uses of the term *theory* in philosophy of science are more apparent than real, more superficial than substantive, as a representative sample of perspectives will demonstrate.

Kaplan defines theory thus: "We may say to start with that a theory is a system of laws. But the laws are altered by being brought into systematic connection with one another, as marriage relates two people who are never the same again." [332, p. 297] Similarly, Bergman notes, "If there has to be a formula again, one might say that a theory is a group of laws deductively connected." [56, p. 31] Blalock suggests:

> It has been noted that theories do not consist entirely of conceptual schemes or typologies but must contain lawlike propositions that interrelate the concepts of variables two or more at a time. Furthermore, these propositions must themselves be interrelated. [65, p. 2]

Bunge is much more specific and detailed in his description of theory:

> In ordinary language and in ordinary metascience "hypothesis," "law," and "theory" are often exchanged; and sometimes laws and theories are taken to be the manhood of hypotheses. In advanced science and in contemporary metascience the three terms are usually distinguished: "law" or "law formula" designates a hypothesis of a certain kind—namely, non-singular, non-isolated, referring to a pattern, and corroborated; and "theory" designates *a system of hypotheses, among which law formulas are conspicuous*—so much so that the core of a theory is a system of law formulas. In order to minimize confusions we will provisionally adopt the following characterization: A set of scientific hypotheses is a scientific theory if and only if it refers to a given factual subject matter and every member of the set is either an initial assumption (axiom, subsidiary assumption, or datum) or a logical consequence of one or more initial assumptions. [95, p. 381], emphasis added]

In his classic work *The Logic of Scientific Discovery,* Popper metaphorically suggests that "theories" are nets to catch what we call 'the world': to rationalize, to explain, and to master it. We endeavor to make the mesh finer and finer." [503, p. 59] Braithwaite believes that "a scientific theory is a deductive system in which observable consequences logically follow from the conjunction of observed facts with the set of the fundamental hypotheses of the system." [76, p. 22] Finally, the marketing theoretician Wroe Alderson proposes that a "theory is a set of propositions which are consistent among themselves and which are relevant to some aspect of the factual world." [9, p. 5]

Although the previous perspectives on theory differ, a careful examination will reveal that the differences are noteworthy primarily for their superficiality. Note how often these similar terms and phrases are repeated: "system of laws," "systematic connection," "interrelated lawlike propositions," "set of scientific hypotheses," "factual subject matter," "group of laws," and "deductively related." All of these key concepts can be incorporated into a consensus definition of theory which will serve as the focal point for this chapter and which was originally proposed by Richard S. Rudner [542, p. 10]:

> *Definition:* **A theory is a systematically related set of statements, including some lawlike generalizations, that is empirically testable. The purpose of theory is to increase scientific understanding through a systematized structure capable of both explaining and predicting phenomena.**

Much of the rest of this chapter will be devoted to fully explicating the import of this conceptualization of the nature and role of theory. In the process we will show that a full articulation of the three key criteria of theory— (1) systematically related, (2) lawlike generalizations, and (3) empirically testable—will demonstrate that this conceptualization can be truly described as consensus. Concurrently, we will show that the correct application of the three key criteria will both systematically *exclude* all constructions that should not be given the status of *theory* and, at the same time, will systematically *include* all constructions that should be referred to as theories. However, before we proceed further, a brief analysis of theoretical misconceptions will reveal that careless usage of the term *theory* has resulted in much mischief in marketing.

6.2   MISCONCEPTIONS OF THEORY

No marketing academician would dispute this assertion: The term *marketing theory* is often viewed with disfavor by both marketing students and marketing faculty. Few criticisms in academia are more damning than "This course is too theoretical!" A suggested opening gambit for a course in marketing theory is to ask the students to try to think of another course they have had which they disliked because it was "too theoretical." The instructor then begins to probe the students to determine exactly what each meant when he or she thought some particular course was *too theoretical*. After some discussion the students' criticisms begin to center on four recurring themes:

1. The too theoretical course was difficult to understand.
2. The too theoretical course was conjectural rather than factual. ("That's just a theory, not a fact.")
3. The too theoretical course was not related to the real world.
4. The too theoretical course was not practical enough. ("It's all right in theory but not in practice.")

Although the complaint that *too theoretical* courses are difficult to understand is often justified, this complaint should be met with sympathy and compassion but not with alarm. Theories often deal with abstract concepts and complicated relationships, and thus they may be difficult to comprehend. Simplicity is a desirable characteristic of theory, but reality is often complex and theoretical constructions used to explain reality must often be complex. However, the theory presented in courses is sometimes difficult to understand because of the theorist's obtuse and nonlucid manner of writing, rather than because of the inherent difficulty of the theoretical relationships. Even great theorists (such as J. M. Keynes) have often expressed their ideas in a manner susceptible to great variance in interpretation. While discussing Wroe Alderson's theoretical constructions, Hostiuck and Kurtz note that "the authors have heard even recognized scholars of marketing groan at the mere mention of Alderson and intimate that they never really understood him." [284, p. 141] Perhaps it is just too much to expect a creative theorist to present his theoretical constructions lucidly, but a nonlucid articulation of a theory will make students groan that it is difficult to understand and will also retard the testing and future development of the theory.

The second complaint states that too theoretical courses are *conjectural* rather than *factual*. One characteristic of the scientifically immature mind is to be uncomfortable in the presence of uncertainty. The true scientist is always ready to revise his beliefs in the light of fresh evidence. The really important issues in any discipline are always conjectural rather than factual. To recognize that consumers' preferences are shifting toward smaller automobiles is useful, but the real challenge is to develop theories, which by their very nature will be conjectural, to explain past shifts in consumer preferences and to predict future shifts. Likewise, knowing that distribution channels are now shorter is less useful than theorizing *why* they are now shorter and attempting to predict what will happen to the length of distribution channels in the future. Although theories must be empirically testable (hence, not "purely conjectural") because of the nature of any theory's constituent lawlike generalizations, a theory can never be *confirmed* in the same sense that simple descriptive or singular statements can be confirmed. Nevertheless, except for people who just like to read telephone books or census data, the most interesting issues in a discipline are usually more conjectural than factual.

The charges that the content of courses is "not related to the real world" or is "not practical" are serious indeed. In fact, these charges are perhaps the most common and serious of all the charges that are made against theoretical courses. *The resolution of these charges lies in the realization that all purportedly theoretical constructions must be empirically testable and must be capable of explaining and predicting real-world phenomena.* Two conclusions immediately follow: (1) All purportedly theoretical constructions *must* be related to the real world. (2) All purportedly theoretical constructions *must* be practical, since the explanation and prediction of real-world phenomena must rank high on any list of practical concerns. Rather than "it's all right in theory but not in practice," the truth of the matter is that *if it is not all right in practice, it cannot be alright in theory!* Courses filled with complex mental gymnastics (often couched in mathematical terms) that have no relevance to the real world and no explanatory or predictive power are not *too theoretical* at all. On the contrary, such courses are completely devoid of theoretical content.

Unfortunately, all too many marketing students and academicians have tended to bestow the term *theory* on locutions that are nothing more than obtuse armchair philosophy or mathematical mental gymnastics with no explanatory or predictive power. It is little wonder that the label "too theoretical" has truly become an epithet. One of the objectives of this book is to challenge marketing theorists to cull out the obtuse armchair philosophy and to ensure that their purportedly theoretical constructions are empirically testable and have explanatory and predictive power. For too long, marketing theory has taken a "bum rap" because it has been awash in nontheoretical constructions masquerading as theory.

In summary, since the real world is often complex, the theoretical constructions with which we attempt to explain reality will often be complex. Since by their very nature theories cannot be conclusively shown to be *true* (in the sense that a singular statement can be shown to be true), theories are, of necessity, *conjectural*. But the most important issues (such as explanation and prediction) in any discipline are always of the conjectural variety. Finally, the notion that *theoretical* and *practical* are at opposite ends of a continuum is nonsense. Any construction which purports to be a theory must be capable of explaining and predicting real-world phenomena. And the explanation and prediction of phenomena are eminently *practical* concerns. With these misconceptions of theory disposed of, we can now turn our attention to the three criteria distinguishing theoretical from nontheoretical constructions.

6.3   THE "SYSTEMATICALLY RELATED" CRITERION

So, a theory is a *systematically related* set of statements, including some lawlike generalization that is empirically testable. This section will explore two basic questions: (1) Why should the statements in a theory be required to be systematically related? (2) Precisely in what way should the statements in a theory be systematically related? Rudner provides one response to the first question:

We are all familiar with the view that it is not the business of science merely to collect unrelated, haphazard, disconnected bits of information; that it is an ideal of science to give an *organized* account of the universe—to connect, to fit together in relations of subsumption, the statements embodying the knowledge that has been acquired. Such organization is a necessary condition for the accomplishment of two of science's chief functions, explanation and prediction. [542, p. 11]

Robert K. Merton addresses the same issue in sociology:

[A] miscellany of . . . propositions only provides the raw materials for sociology as a discipline. The theoretic task, and the orientation of empirical research toward theory, first begins when the bearing of such uniformities on a set of interrelated propositions is tentatively established. The notion of directed research implies that, in part, empirical inquiry is so organized that if and when empirical uniformities are discovered, they have direct consequences for a theoretic system. [445, p. 149]

The view taken here is that we require theories to contain systematically related sets of statements in order to increase the *scientific understanding* of phenomena. To scientifically understand the occurrence of a phenomenon requires more than simply being able to explain and predict it using *isolated* lawlike generalizations. Also, we must be able to show how the statements used to explain and predict a phenomenon are incorporated into the total body of scientific knowledge. The view that the *systematically related* criterion represents a consensus position can be supported by a careful examination of the previously cited perspectives on theory. For example, Kaplan mentions "systematic connection," Bergman talks about "deductively connected," Blalock requires "interrelated propositions," and Braithwaite discusses a "set of fundamental hypotheses." Therefore, all of these writers allude to what we are calling the systematically related criterion.

The second question asks, "In *what precise way* should the statements in a theory be systematically related?" As Dubin has observed, to simply have a collection of propositions is not necessarily to have a theory. [160, p. 16] The propositions or statements in a theory must have a high degree of internal consistency. To check for internal consistency, all of the *concepts* in each statement in the theory must be clearly defined, all of the *relationships* among the concepts in each statement must be clearly specified, and all of the *interrelationships* among the statements in the theory must be clearly delineated.

Complete articulation of the nature of the "systematically related" criterion requires an elaboration of the notion of "full formalization" in the philosophy of science. The essence of the full formalization of a theory is the complete, rigorous articulation of the entire syntactic and semantic structure of the theory. Bergman suggests, "One formalizes a scientific theory by replacing its descriptive words by 'marks on paper.' The logical words, which remain, are the only ones we 'understand.'"

[56, p. 38] But full formalization implies much more than simply replacing descriptive words with "marks on paper." Figure 6-1 illustrates that a *fully formalized theory consists of a formal language system that has been axiomatized and appropriately interpreted.*[1] We must now turn to an examination of (1) formal language systems, (2) axiomatized formal systems, and (3) appropriately interpreted, axiomatized formal systems because to require theories to contain systematically related sets of statements implies that theories must, in principle, be amenable to formalization.

Figure 6-1   The full formalization of a theory

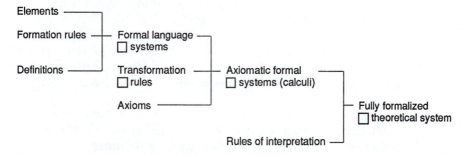

6.3.1   Formal Language Systems

Formal language systems must first be differentiated from natural language systems such as English. Both formal language systems and natural language systems include (1) elements, (2) formation rules, and (3) definitions. The English language elements are the *words* of English, and the formation rules (the grammar or syntax) state the permissible ways in which words can be combined to form correct English sentences. For example, the statement "marketing advertising beneficial" is not a correct English sentence because it violates the *formation rule* that each English sentence must contain a verb.

In addition to elements and formation rules, both natural languages and formal language systems must have sets of definitions. The kinds of definitions that are required here are *nominal* definitions [258, p. 654] or *rules of replacement.* [542, p. 15] These types of definitions should be carefully distinguished from definitions of the so-called *operational* variety. Roughly speaking, nominal definitions have to do with relationships among *terms alone* (syntactic considerations) and operational definitions have to do with relationships between terms and the *real world* (semantic considerations). We will treat operational

---

[1]The succeeding discussion follows, in part, Rudner and Kyburg. [542, pp. 10-18; 361]

definitions in the section probing the "empirically testable" criterion of theoretical constructions and will focus our present attention on nominal definitions.

A nominal definition states that one term, the definiendum, is equivalent to another term or groups of terms, the *definiens*. So, Alderson defines assortment:

$$\text{assortment} =_{df} \text{meaningful heterogeneous collection}$$

In this instance, "assortment" is the definiendum and "meaningful heterogeneous collection" is the definiens. The significance of calling nominal definitions "rules of replacement" is that the truth value of any statement which includes the definiendum is maintained if the definiendum is replaced by the definiens. [542, p. 16] That is, any statement which is true and which contains the term *assortment* will likewise be true if "assortment" is replaced by "meaningful heterogeneous collection." Similarly, any false statement which contains the term *assortment* will remain false if "meaningful heterogeneous collection" is substituted for it.

But how does one define *meaningful heterogeneous collection?* We must either introduce other terms to define *meaningful heterogeneous collection,* or we must suffer circularity by defining:

$$\text{meaningful heterogeneous collection} =_{df} \text{assortment}$$

In either case, a little reflection reveals that in any language system there will be a set of *primitive* elements or terms. These primitive elements will be undefined within that system but will not necessarily be undefined within some other system. Also, all of the nonprimitive elements within the given language system can be defined by means of the primitives. Alderson suggested that in his conceptualization of marketing all of the subject matter could be ultimately reduced by a series of definitions to three primitive terms: sets, behavior, and expectations. [10, p. 25] Although this conclusion may be open to question, Alderson clearly realized that all language systems contain primitive or undefined elements.

We require theories to contain systematically related sets of statements. The *systematically related* criterion implies a kind of systematization that is, at least in principle, amenable to formalization. A fully formalized theory implies, among other things, a formal language system. Since both formal language systems and so-called natural languages include (1) elements, (2) formation rules, and (3) definitions, how do formal language systems differ from natural languages? Formal language systems differ from natural languages in that they identify all of the primitive elements, and they develop a complete "dictionary" which shows how all of the nonprimitive terms are derived from the primitive elements. Further, rather than having the loose and continually evolving formation rules of natural languages, such as English, formal language systems rigorously and exhaustively specify the formation rules delineating the permissible ways to combine elements to form statements.

Summarizing, the full formalization of a theory requires the construction of a formal language system which includes a complete list of the primitive elements of the system, a "dictionary" showing how all of the system's nonprimitive terms are derived from the primitive elements, and a complete explication of the formation rules specifying how elements can be combined to form permissible statements (often called "wff's" or "well-formed formulations" in the philosophy of science literature). Nevertheless, the full formalization of a theory requires more than just a formal language system. The system must also undergo *axiomatization,* a subject to which we now turn.

6.3.2   Axiomatic Formal Systems

Figure 6-1 indicates that a fully formalized theory includes a formal language system that has been axiomatized. An axiomatized formal language system is referred to as a *calculus* in the philosophy of science. Axioms and their role in theory construction have already been discussed in Section 5.2, which the reader might find helpful to review. The axiomatization of a formal language system requires (1) the adoption of rules of transformation and (2) the selection of appropriate fundamental statements or axioms. Recalling that formation rules detail the permissible ways in which elements can be combined to form statements, *transformation rules detail how statements can be combined to deduce other statements in the system.* A syllogistic example of a transformation rule from consumer demand theory should illustrate the kinds of rules that are required:

1. Bundle of goods *A* contains four oranges and two apples.
2. Bundle of goods *B* contains three oranges and three apples.
3. Bundle of goods *C* contains two oranges and four apples.
4. Consumer *X* indicates a preference for bundle *A* over bundle *B*.
5. Consumer *X* indicates a preference for bundle *B* over bundle *C*.
6. Therefore, consumer *X* will indicate a preference for bundle *A* over bundle *C*.

In consumer demand theory, Statement 6 is deducible from Statements 1-5 because demand theory assumes that consumer preferences follow the logical transformation rule known as *transitivity.* That is, if *A* is preferred to *B,* and *B* is preferred to *C, then A* is preferred to *C.* Therefore, to axiomatize a formal language system requires first that we adopt a series of transformation rules that dictate how some statements can be deduced from other statements.

After the permissible ways in which certain statements can be deduced from other statements have been delineated, the axiomatization of a formal language system requires the selection of appropriate fundamental statements or axioms to separate fundamental statements from derived or deduced statements. According to Popper [503, p. 71], the criteria for selecting the *appropriate* fundamental statements for axiomatization are four: (1) free from contradiction, (2) independent, (3) sufficient, and (4) necessary. The first criterion requires that the fundamental statements be internally consistent to the extent that mutually exclusive outcomes or statements cannot be deduced from the fundamental statements. That is, if an appropriate set of transformations on the fundamental statements produces the statement that "*X* will occur," then there must *not* be some other permissible set of transformations that will produce the statement that "*X* will *not* occur." Thus, the first requirement is an internal consistency criterion. The second requirement, that the fundamental statements be *independent*, implies that no statement in the final set of fundamental statements can be deducible from the other statements. That is, the axioms must truly be *fundamental* in the system. The third requirement, *sufficient*, implies that all of the statements which are part of the theory proper can be derived from the set of fundamental statements. Lastly, to be *necessary* implies that all the statements in the fundamental set are *used* to derive other statements; that is, there are no superfluous statements.

Two points should be reemphasized here. First, as discussed in Section 5.2, the fundamental statements or axioms of a theory are assumed to be true for *analytical* purposes only. That is, they are assumed to be true for the purpose of deriving other statements. The axioms are *not* assumed to be true for *empirical* purposes. Therefore, it is entirely appropriate and desirable to empirically test the axioms of a theory. Second, at least some of the fundamental or derived statements in the axiomatic formal system must have the characteristics of lawlike generalizations. Otherwise, the axiomatic formal system would not be a theoretical construction.

In summary, the axiomatization of a formal language system requires (1) the specification of the transformation rules that state the permissible ways in which statements can be combined in order to derive or deduce other statements and (2) the delineation of a set of fundamental statements or axioms that are free from contradiction, independent, sufficient, and necessary. Every theory is, at least in principle, susceptible to axiomatization because every theory is composed of statements, and it should be possible to classify the statements as to whether they are (1) derived or (2) fundamental *within that theory*. For an excellent axiomatization of consumer demand theory, the reader is urged to consult the first 50 pages of Peter Newman's *Theory of Exchange*. [472] This writer knows of no strictly marketing theory that has been axiomatized.   Whether marketing theorists should attempt to axiomatize and formalize their theories will be discussed later in this chapter.

6.3.3   Rules of Interpretation

Recapitulating, a fully formalized theoretical structure will include a formal language system that has been axiomatized. Recall, however, that the essence of the full formalization of a theoretical system is a complete, rigorous articulation of *both* the syntactic and semantic structure of the theory. The analysis, so far, has been purely syntactic; that is, only the requirements for the logical relationships among elements and combinations of elements (statements) have been articulated. We have developed the requirements for a formalized analytical-conceptual schema.   Since everything up to this point has dealt solely with Bergman's "marks on paper," it is now time to bring in the meanings of the marks on paper. Alternatively stated, it is now time to bring in the real world by discussing the semantic rules of interpretation.

Referring again to Figure 6-1, an axiomatic formal language system becomes a fully formalized theoretical system when a complete set of appropriate semantic rules of interpretation for the elements or terms in the formal language system have been developed. Since theoretical systems are used to explain and predict phenomena, the elements in the theories must somehow be linked to observable entities and the properties of observable entities in the real world. The semantic rules of interpretation that accomplish this linkage are variously referred to as measures, indicants, operational definitions, coordinating definitions, correspondence rules, or epistemic correlations. [464, p. 93]

Although a complete analysis of semantic rules of interpretation will be deferred to the section on the "empirically testable" criterion of theories, the *ideal goal* of these semantic rules should be stated here. The semantic rules of interpretation are optimal when for each possible interpretation of the axiomatized formal system by semantic rules that makes the fundamental statements (or axioms) true, all of the derived statements (or theorems) will likewise be true. Such a set of optimal semantic rules of interpretation would thus achieve a kind of *isomorphism* or "one-to-one correspondence" between the marks on paper of the theory and the real world.

Summarizing the last three sections, a theory is a systematically related set of statements, including some lawlike generalizations, that is empirically testable. To be *systematically related* is a desirable and consensus criterion of theory because science endeavors to increase scientific understanding by giving an organized account of the universe. A set of statements will fulfill the *systematically related* criterion when it exhibits a kind of systematization that is, at least in principle, amenable to full formalization. A fully formalized theoretical system consists of a formal language system that has been axiomatized and completely interpreted. Formal language systems contain (1) elements, (2) formation rules, and (3) a set of definitions (all three are rigorously specified). An axiomatic formal language system includes a set of transformation rules showing how some statements can be derived from other statements and a set of fundamental statements that are (1) free from contradiction, (2) independent, (3) sufficient, and (4) necessary. An axiomatized formal language system becomes a fully formalized theoretical system when a complete set of semantic rules of interpretation has been developed.

6.3.4   Issues in Formalization

Although theories are required to have a kind of systematization that is susceptible to formalization, four points need to be made regarding formalization. First, the preceding discussion of *full formalization* in no way attempts to capture or describe the actual processes that theorists use to discover or create a theoretical structure. The formalization of a theory is *ex post*. That is, the process of formalization customarily begins in earnest only *after* the theory has been proposed. Second, some writers warn against the premature formalization of theories on the ground that formalization may actually inhibit scientific creativity. Thus, Kaplan suggests:

> The demand for exactness of meaning and for precise definition of terms can easily have a pernicious effect, as I believe it often has had in behavioral science. It results in what has been aptly named the *premature closure* of our ideas. That the progress of science is marked by successive closures can be stipulated; but it is just the function of inquiry to instruct us how and where closure can best be achieved. . . . There is a certain kind of behavioral scientist who, at the least threat of an exposed ambiguity, scurries for cover like a hermit crab into the nearest abandoned logical shell. But there is no ground for panic. That a cognitive situation is not as well structured as we would like does not imply that no inquiry made in that situation is really scientific. On the contrary, it is the dogmatisms outside science that proliferate closed systems of meaning; the scientist is in no hurry for closure. Tolerance of ambiguity is as important for creativity in science as it is anywhere else. [332, p. 70]

Third, the complete formalization of any theory is an arduous task requiring great effort. Finally, few theories in *any* of the sciences have been fully formalized.

Many philosophers of science have questioned the role of formalization in theory development. Suppe [606, pp. 110-15] has summarized their arguments. First, the systematic interconnections among the concepts of many theories are insufficiently specified to enable *fruitful* axiomatization. Suppe cites such examples as Darwin's theory of evolution, Hoyle's theory on the origin of the universe, Pike's theory of language structure, and Freud's psychology. Second, the formalization of a theory often leaves untouched many of the truly interesting philosophical problems. This is because formalization usually emphasizes syntactic rather than semantic considerations. Third, formalization is a static analysis revealing at best a "snapshot" of a theory at a point in time. Thus, formalization ignores the dynamics of theory development.

Suppe then replies to these criticisms by pointing out that the fact that some theories cannot be completely formalized ignores the possibility (and usefulness) of *partial* formalization. Also, for studying the fine details of a structure, a "snapshot" is often to be much preferred to a "videotape." Suppe concludes, "Rather surprisingly the various criticisms of the Received View have left this claim [that theories should be formalized] essentially unchallenged." [606, p. 62] Suppe's conclusion coincides with that of most current writers. For example, MacKinnon suggests:

> Perhaps the most basic and obvious question to be asked concerning rational reconstructions of scientific theories is "Why bother?" Rational reconstructions have contributed little if anything either to the understanding of historically developing theories or to advancing their future development. The rather pragmatic point of view that I will adopt, but not defend, here is that in a rational reconstruction a scientific theory becomes an object of study, rather than a tool for studying some other domain. Reconstructing a theory is a help to understanding it, at least in the sense that we have some understanding of anything we can take apart and put back together. [414, p. 510]

The preceding analysis implies that the primary purpose of formalization lies in *evaluating* theoretical structures, not in discovering or creating them. Often, the attempt to even partially formalize a theory, by baring its essential structure or morphology, can sharpen the discussion of the theory and put it into a framework suitable for testing. *For many marketing theories, the partial formalization of the theory is an absolutely necessary precondition for meaningful analysis.* Two examples should illustrate this point. First, we shall consider the so-called "general theory of marketing" proposed by Robert Bartels [39], and second, we shall explore the partial formalization of the Howard-Sheth "theory of buyer behavior" [287] that was generated by Farley and Ring. [170]

6.3.5   The "General Theory of Marketing": A Partial Formalization

An article by Robert Bartels on marketing theory [39] generated substantial debate concerning the nature of theoretical constructions in general and the components of a general theory of marketing in particular. Bartels proposed a general theory of marketing which included seven subtheories: (1) theory of social initiative; (2) theory of economic (market) separations; (3) theory of market roles, expectations, and interactions; (4) theory flows and systems; (5) theory of behavior constraints; (6) theory of social change and marketing evolution; and (7) theory of social control of marketing. In order to analyze the basic nature of these seven "theories," the present writer found it necessary to partially formalize them. The reconstructions or partial formalizations of the seven theories were then used for evaluative purposes. [296] A review of two of Bartels' theories will help to illustrate the process used for partial formalization. Bartels states his theory of flows and systems as follows:

> Flows are the movements of elements which resolve market separations. Marketing does not occur as a single movement, but rather as a number of movements, in series, parallel, reciprocal, or duplicatory. They occur in the complex relations among the individuals who have found an economic basis for their existence and for their participation in the marketing process. [39, p. 33]

Similarly, Bartels states his theory of behavior constraints in this way:

> Action in the marketing system is not determined wholly by any one individual or set of participants. It is governed by many determinants and occurs within constraints defined by society. Some of these constraints are economic in nature. Only that can be done which can be done within the bounds of economic feasibility. This may be determined through experience in the profitable combining of economic factors of production. However, much feasibility is predetermined and set forth in the form of marketing technology, know-how, or generalizations for behavior. This is reason for having thorough knowledge of marketing mechanics, or the relations of commodities-functions-institutions as set forth in conventional marketing theory.
>
> Constraints are also social, rather than economic or technical, in nature. These may be of an ethical nature, as that term is used broadly, indicating what is "right" to do under certain circumstances. Rightness may be determined by personal, legal, societal, and theistic standards, and each of these may differ from one society to another. As marketing is viewed more as a personal process rather than only a physical one, such constraints play a more prominent role in marketing theory. [39, p. 33]

The first steps in the formalization of any theory are to generate the basic statements of the theory in precise, succinct fashion and to array the statements in an orderly manner to facilitate theoretical analysis. One such reconstruction or (very) partial formalization of the first "theory" would be:

1. The elements in marketing can be classified into those that flow and those that do not flow.

2. The flowing elements of marketing can be further classified by type—series, parallel, reciprocal, and duplicatory.
3. a. The marketing flows are very important and should be studied by marketing students.
   b. The relationships among marketing flows are very complex.

Similarly, one possible reconstruction of the second "theory" would be:

1. Marketing behavior is constrained behavior.
2. a. Some of the constraints are designed by society.
   b. The societal constraints may be classified as economic, social, ethical, or technical.

As can easily be seen, these reconstructions, *even though they represent only the first modest steps toward formalizations,* are much more amenable to rigorous analysis than the original narrative discussions of the "theories." The present writer analyzed these reconstructions and concluded that none of the seven "theories" were theories at all. Rather, the seven "theories" were shown to be an assemblage of classificational schemata, some intriguing definitions, and exhortations to fellow marketing students to adopt a particular marketing perspective in attempting to generate marketing theory. [296, p. 68] Pinson et al. then analyzed these same partial formalizations and came to different conclusions regarding their theoretical adequacy. [496] Pinson et al.'s discussion prompted a rebuttal which concluded that Bartels' "theory" was neither a theory of marketing, nor a 'general' theory of marketing." [296, p. 73]

The point to be emphasized here is not whether Bartels' theory is or is not really a theoretical construction. Rather, the partially formalized reconstructions greatly facilitated theoretical analysis. Also, a *caveat* is needed at this point; if the reconstructions do not accurately capture the basic structure, then, of course, any subsequent analysis will not do justice to the theory. In conclusion, in response to the question "Why formalize?" we respond, "In order to facilitate the analysis of theoretical and purportedly theoretical constructions." A second example of a partial formalization will reveal another benefit.

6.3.6   The Theory of Buyer Behavior: A Partial Formalization

Few theories in marketing have sparked more scholarly interest and excitement than the Howard-Sheth theory of buyer behavior. [287] Figure 6-2 reproduces a summary of this theory. As can be observed, the theory consists of a large number of constructs, both exogenous and endogenous to the system. The constructs are interconnected by both direct causal linkages (the solid lines) and by feedback effects (the dashed lines).

Figure 6-2   The Howard-Sheth theory of buyer behavior

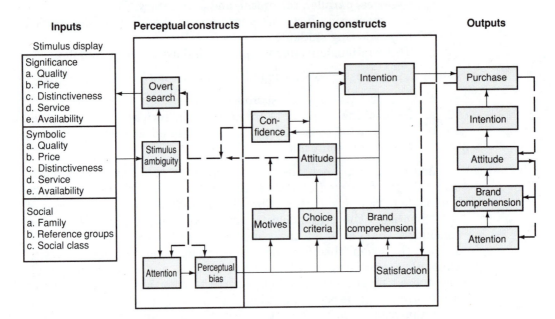

Source: John A. Howard and Jagdish N. Sheth, *The Theory of Buyer Behavior* (New York: John Wiley & Sons, 1969) p. 30.   Reprinted by permission from John Wiley & Sons, Inc.

Now, the fundamental question to be asked of any theoretical structure is: *How well does this theory represent the real world by explaining and predicting real-world phenomena?* To answer this question requires that the theory undergo empirical testing. Unfortunately, the theory as depicted in Figure 6-2 is not constructed in a form suitable for testing. Both the syntactic and semantic structure of the theory must first be reconstructed in at least partially formalized form to make the structure amenable to empirical testing. Farley and Ring addressed themselves to this task in their trailblazing study, "An Empirical Test of the Howard-Sheth Model of Buyer Behavior." [170]

Farley and Ring's partial formalization of the H-S theory required the rigorous specification of the exact nature of the linkages among the constructs. They lament, "Indeed, in its [the model's] present form, the functional relationships among the variables are generally unspecified, although their directions are known." [170, p. 427] The formalization of the theory culminated in a series of 11 simultaneous equations, each having the basic form:

$$Y_{(i)} = \sum_{\substack{j=1 \\ (j \neq i)}}^{11} \beta_{i,j} Y_{(j)} + \sum_{k=1}^{K} Y_{i,k} X_{(k)} + Y_{i,o} + u_{(i)}; \ i = 1, \ldots, 11.$$

Farley and Ring then obtained operational measures (the semantic rules of interpretation previously discussed) and conducted a test of the theory using both ordinary least squares and two-stage least squares regressions. Their results can be interpreted as weakly supporting the H-S theory.

Farley and Ring's efforts also sparked a critical appraisal of the basic structure of the H-S model by Hunt and Pappas. [297] This appraisal found that, since the actual variables used in the H-S model had been common knowledge in consumer behavior for some time, the major substantive contribution of the H-S theory was the postulation of certain *developmental linkages*. For example, Howard and Sheth propose the developmental linkage that attitude influences purchase only *through* intention to purchase. Any complete test of the H-S model must test for the existence or nonexistence of these developmental linkages. A method using partial correlation coefficients was suggested as a possible procedure for testing the developmental linkages in the H-S model. [297, p. 347]

Subsequent empirical research by Lehmann, O'Brien, Farley, and Howard has specifically tested for the developmental linkages postulated by the H-S model. [386] Using the partial correlation coefficient procedure and cross-lagged correlation analysis, they concluded:

> Confidence levels for the Howard-Sheth model, as well as for the other two structures, were high enough to conclude that they are statistically significant, if yet very imperfect, representations of consumer information processing and decision making over time. In terms of finding strong support for the model, however, the results were disappointing. [386, p. 51]

Because of the weak support for the H-S version, Lehmann et al. constructed a revised model with different developmental linkages.

The pioneering efforts of Farley, Ring, Lehmann, O'Brien, and Howard conclusively demonstrate the desirability of formalization. Without their partial formalization of the Howard-Sheth theory, it would still be largely untested. Their partial formalization led to empirical testing [170], then to theoretical appraisal and evaluation [297], and then to retesting and redevelopment. [386] In conclusion, the bogeyman of premature closure should deter no one from the formalization of theories, at least to the extent that formalization facilitates both theoretical analysis and empirical testing.

6.4   THE "LAWLIKE GENERALIZATIONS" CRITERION

The preceding sections have discussed the import of requiring the statements comprised by a theory to be systematically related. Nevertheless, not all systematically related sets of statements are theoretical in nature. For example, definitional schemata, purely analytical schemata, and classificational schemata all contain systematically related statements, but they are not theories. For systematically related sets of statements to be a theory, at least some of them must be in the form of lawlike generalizations. A discussion of the nature of lawlike generalizations need not be repeated here, since Chapter 4 has already explored this topic. It will suffice to recall that lawlike generalizations are statements having the basic form of generalized conditionals (statements of the "If X occurs, then Y will occur" variety) that (a) have empirical content, (b) exhibit nomic necessity, and (c) are systematically integrated into a body of scientific knowledge.

Why must theories contain at least some statements taking the form of lawlike generalizations? Because the purpose of theory is to increase scientific understanding through a systematized structure capable of both *explaining* and *predicting* phenomena. Being able to scientifically explain a phenomenon implies logically the ability to predict that phenomenon (see Chapter 3). Now, all of the models discussed in Chapter 2 that have explanatory power require lawlike generalizations to explain phenomena. That is, the deductive-nomological, deductive-statistical, and inductive-statistical models all rely on lawlike generalizations for their explanatory power. Models which do not include lawlike generalizations, for example the pattern model, have been shown to yield inadequate scientific explanations of phenomena. *Therefore, all purportedly theoretical constructions must contain lawlike generalizations because a major purpose of theory is to explain phenomena, and all scientific explanations of phenomena contain lawlike generalizations.*

Once again, the *lawlike generalizations* criterion represents a consensus position in the philosophy of science. Thus, Kaplan requires a "system of *laws*" [332, p. 297]; Bergman suggests a "group of *laws*" [56, p. 31]; Blalock demands that theories contain "*lawlike* propositions" [65, p. 2]; and finally, Bunge insists on "a system of hypotheses, among which *law* formulas are conspicuous." [95, p. 381] All of these authors are requiring theoretical constructions to contain what is referred to here as "lawlike generalizations."

Unfortunately, marketing theorists seem often to ignore the lawlike generalizations criterion in their efforts to develop marketing theory. Theorists create elaborate structures of systematically related statements composed exclusively of definitional and classificational schemata. As previously noted, a definition is a rule of replacement whereby an element (the definiendum) in a statement can be replaced by another element or elements (the definiens) without losing the truth value of the statement. A *definitional schema* is simply a systematically related set of definitions. All theories will contain definitional schemata, but a definitional schema is, by itself, not a theory.

Also frequently confused with theoretical schemata, a classificational schema is a kind of system which sets forth the conditions for the applicability of its categorial or classificatory terms. Classificational schemata always attempt to *partition* some universe of elements or statements into homogeneous groups.

6.5   THE "EMPIRICALLY TESTABLE" CRITERION

Having established that theories must contain systematically related statements, that at least some of these statements must be lawlike generalizations, and that classificational schemata should not be confused with theoretical schemata, there remains the task of exploring (1) what it means to require theories to be *empirically testable* and (2) why they must be so required. First, why must theories be empirically testable? One powerful reason has been suggested by K. R. Popper. Scientific knowledge, in which theories are primal, must be *objective* in the sense that its truth content must be *intersubjectively certifiable*. [503, p. 44] Requiring a theory to be empirically testable ensures that it will be intersubjectively certifiable since different (but reasonably competent) investigators, with differing attitudes, opinions, and beliefs, will be able to make observations and conduct experiments to ascertain the truth content of the theory. Hempel concurs, "Science strives for objectivity in the sense that its statements are to be capable of public tests with results that do not vary essentially with the tester." [258, p. 695] Scientific knowledge rests on the bedrock of empirical testability which makes it intersubjectively certifiable. Most other kinds of knowledge (for example, theological knowledge, whose cornerstone is "faith") lack the capacity to be intersubjectively certifiable.

The second reason for requiring theories to be empirically testable springs from the purpose of theory itself. As previously discussed, the major purpose of theory is to increase scientific understanding through a systematized structure capable of both explaining and predicting phenomena. Any systematized structure which is *not* empirically testable will suffer from explanatory and predictive impotence. It will not be able to explain and predict phenomena. Hence, any structure that is not empirically testable will not be able to perform the tasks expected of genuine theoretical structures. Many purportedly theoretical constructions in marketing seem to lack explanatory and predictive power.

A final justification for requiring theories to be empirically testable lies in the desirability of distinguishing between theoretical schemata and what Rudner refers to as *purely analytical schemata*. [542, p. 28] An analytical schema contains a systematically related set of statements, all of which are purely *analytic* rather than *synthetic*. "Products have life cycles" is a synthetic statement. "Either products have life cycles or products do not have life cycles" is purely analytic. Whether a synthetic statement is true or false can be ascertained only by examining the "real-world facts." In contrast, whether a purely analytical statement is true or false can be determined solely by examining the order and nature of the logical terms (such as *either* and *or*) and the way in which certain descriptive terms (such as *products*) are defined. The real-world facts are completely irrelevant to the truth value of a purely analytical statement. Therefore, requiring theories to be empirically testable will screen out purely analytical schemata from being considered theories, which is desirable because we want the truth value of our theoretical construction to be relevant to the real would.

Summarizing, theories are required to be empirically testable in order that they be *(a)* intersubjectively certifiable, *(b)* capable of explaining and predicting phenomena, and *(c)* differentiated from purely analytical schemata. So far we have been using the expression "empirically testable" as if it had perfect antecedent clarity. It's time to explore much more carefully exactly what it means to empirically test a theory.

6.5.1   The Nature of Empirical Testing

When confronted with any theory, ask the basic question, "Is the theory true?" Less succinctly, ask the questions: "To what extent is the theory isomorphic with reality? Is the real world actually constructed as the theory suggests, or is it not? To what extent has the theory been empirically confirmed?" Numerous criteria have been proposed to evaluate the adequacy of theoretical constructions. Popper has proposed the four criteria of internal consistency, logical form, comparison with other theories, and empirical testing. [503, p. 32] Dodd reviewed the literature regarding criteria to evaluate theories and recorded 70 commonly used criteria, including accuracy, applicability, brevity, brilliance, and clarity. [152, p. 31] He then reduced the 70 to 24 criteria considered most relevant, including verifiability, predictivity, consistency, and reliability. [152, p. 49] Clark proposes the criteria of clarity, explanatory power, simplicity, and confirmation. [121, p. 109] Bunge suggests 20 criteria to evaluate theories, grouped into (1) formal criteria, (2) semantic criteria, (3) epistemological criteria, (4) methodological criteria, and (5) metaphysical criteria. [96, pp. 352-54] Zaltman et al. used essentially the Bunge groupings to develop their set of 16 criteria, which they then employed to evaluate the Nicosia model of consumer decision processes, the Howard-Sheth theory of buyer behavior, and the Engel-Kollat-Blackwell model of consumer behavior. [647, p. 104]

What may be getting *lost* in all this generating of evaluative criteria is the realization that one criterion stands supreme over all others: *Is the theory true? To what extent has it been empirically confirmed?* Bunge clearly wanted his nonempirical criteria to be applied *only* for empirically equivalent theories: "Experience will be weighty, perhaps decisive at one point, in the evaluation of empirically *inequivalent* theories. But how does one proceed in the presence of one or more empirically equivalent theories?" [96, p. 347]   Kaplan expresses the same belief:

> Norms of validation can be grouped according to the three major philosophical conceptions of truth: correspondence or semantical norms, coherence or syntactical norms, and pragmatic or functional norms. The first set is the basic one somehow; the others must be regarded as analyses or interpretations of correspondence. Science is governed fundamentally by the reality principle, its thought checked and controlled by the characteristics of the things it thinks about. [332, p. 312]

The way to determine the truth content of any theory is to empirically test it. Figure 6-3 represents one (grossly compacted) conceptualization of the process of empirical testing. For a different and much more detailed conceptualization, see Bunge. [96, p. 309]

6.5.2   The Empirical Testing Process

Figure 6-3 shows that the first step in empirically testing a theory is to derive some bridge laws or guiding hypotheses from the theory proper. As discussed in Section 5.2.1, a bridge law is a kind of derivative law whose function is to bridge the gap between a theory and the specific classes of phenomena under investigation. A researcher desirous of testing the role of *risk* in consumer behavior might develop bridge laws dealing specifically with the perceived risk involved in purchasing new homes. Similarly, the "fair price" theory is couched in terms of the prices of goods in general. To test the "fair price" theory one must develop bridge laws concerning *specific* stimuli, e.g., the prices of gasoline used by Kamen and Toman. [327]

Neither theories nor bridge laws are directly testable; they are only *indirectly* testable. Because both theories and bridge laws are composed of statements in the form of generalized conditionals, neither can be tested by a direct confrontation with data. To illustrate, consider the bridge laws mentioned in Section 5.2.1:

BL_1:   Consumers will experience cognitive dissonance after the decision to purchase a major appliance.

BL_2:   If retailers provide information to recent purchasers of major appliances, and if the information reassures the consumers that they made wise decisions, then the information will assist the consumers in their efforts to reduce cognitive dissonance.

As stated, these bridge laws are not susceptible to a direct comparison to data; they are not *directly* testable. In contrast, research

Figure 6-3   The empirical testing process

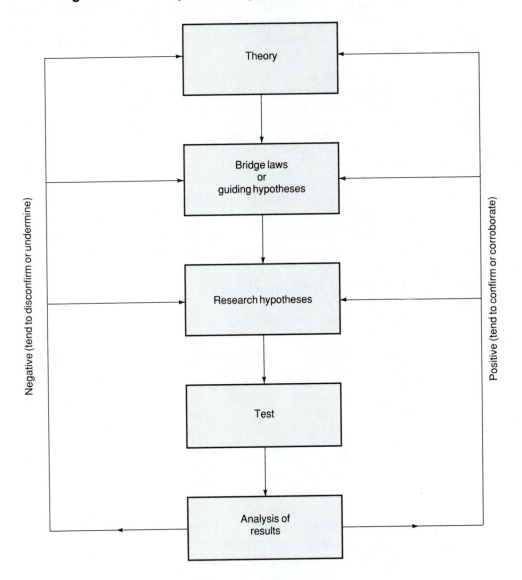

hypotheses are directly testable. These are predictive-type statements that are *(a)* derived from the bridge laws and *(b)* amenable to direct confrontation with data. For example, a research hypothesis derived from the preceding bridge laws and actually tested was: "The subjects who received the posttransaction reassurances will have lower perceived dissonance scores (i.e., will be less dissonant) than the subjects in the control group." [295] The research hypothesis is directly testable because it refers to specific subjects in specific groups (rather than consumers in general) and to specific scores on a measuring instrument (rather than dissonance in general).

The requirement that research hypotheses be predictive-type statements that are amenable to direct confrontation with data implies that all of the descriptive terms in the statements must have rules of interpretation containing empirical referents (sometimes referred to as operational definitions, empirical indicators, or epistemic correlations). This does *not* mean that all of the terms in the theory proper must be "observables" or that every term in the theory must have an empirical referent. Rather, to require theories to be empirically testable implies that they must be capable of generating predictive-type statements (hypotheses) whose descriptive terms have empirical referents.   The notion of empirical referents deserves some elaboration, especially since it is closely intertwined with the school of thought commonly known as *operationalism.*

The position taken here should be carefully distinguished from the early forms of logical positivism or what Hempel refers to as the *narrow thesis of empiricism.* According to the narrow thesis, "Any term in the vocabulary of empirical science is definable by means of observation terms; i.e., it is possible to carry out a rational reconstruction of the language of science in such a way that all primitive terms are observation terms and all other terms are defined by means of them." [258, p. 675] This *radical empiricist* position has been adopted by the school of thought known as *operationalism,* which was originated by P. W. Bridgman. [78] Three key propositions seem central to the doctrine of operationalism:

1. Only terms that have operational definitions are "meaningful." Terms without operational definitions are "meaningless" and, hence, have no value in scientific endeavor. [79]
2. Operational definitions always make reference ultimately to an instrumental operation. [80] That is, there must be some experiment or manipulation involved.
3. There must be only one operational definition for each scientific term. [78, p. 6]

The three propositions embodying the radical empiricism of the operationalists have been successfully challenged by Hempel [258, 182] and others. [56, p. 58] Hempel suggests that Proposition 1 is untenable because (among other reasons) *theoretical constructs* play a vital role in science. These highly abstract concepts, for example, "channel of distribution," "self-image," "transvection," and "utility," often stoutly resist direct operational definitions. Such terms are not introduced piecemeal into a theory. "Rather, the constructs used in a theory are introduced jointly, as it were, by setting up a theoretical system formulated in terms of them and by giving this *system* an experiential interpretation, which in turn confers empirical meaning on the theoretical constructs." [258, p. 684] Thus, Proposition 1 of the operationalists seems much too restrictive.

Hempel suggests that Proposition 2 is also overly restrictive. Requiring direct experimenter manipulations is unnecessary to give experiential import to a term. Operational definitions based on unobtrusive observations will often yield equally satisfactory results, maintaining intersubjective reliability. The important requirement is that different investigators be able to observe the phenomenon with reasonable agreement as to whether the requisite test conditions have been realized and the appropriate response obtained. [262, p. 126]

Concerning Proposition 3, Bergman notes that some researchers refused "to 'generalize' from one instance of an experiment to the next if the apparatus had in the meantime been moved to another corner of the room or if the experimenter had, in the one case but not the other, blown his nose." [56, p. 58] The replication of an experiment would be logically impossible if Proposition 3 were interpreted literally, since each instance would be a "different" operational definition. Also, testing a theory under a variety of circumstances of application is extremely desirable in the process of confirmation. Yet, testing a theory under different circumstances may entail using different operational definitions for key constructs. The adoption of Proposition 3 would imply that each time we change the circumstances in the testing of a theory we must consider ourselves to be testing a "new" theory. Science seems hardly to be advanced by the adoption of such a position. A much more viable position seems to be to acknowledge that alternative and equally valid operational definitions or measures may exist for the same concept, while maintaining constant vigil to ensure that the alternative operational definitions or measures are, indeed, equally valid.

In conclusion, the preceding analysis suggests that the position of the radical empiricists is untenable. At the same time, metaphysical excesses are to be avoided. *Consequently, the requirement that theories be empirically testable shall be construed as being satisfied when a theory is capable (at least in principle) of generating predictive-type statements (hypotheses) whose descriptive terms have empirical referents, thus ensuring that the statements are amenable to a direct confrontation with real-world data.* This requirement is similar to the criterion of significance for theoretical terms suggested by Carnap. [107]

6.5.3   On Confirmation

Wartofsky has observed that

> No term in science suffers a greater ambiguity than does *hypothesis*. One could make up a list of contradictory statements about hypotheses and their status and use in scientific discussion which would make

the scientific community look like something on the other side of Alice's looking glass. [626, p. 183]

Alas, the term *hypothesis* is commonly used as a general-purpose label synonymous with such concepts as law, lawlike generalization, derived law, theory, explanation, model, axiom, and theorem.   The term *hypothesis* is overworked, overused, overbroad.   Such abuse may result in little harm in ordinary conversation but may have serious, unintended consequences in research and scientific writing.   Therefore, this writer suggests using the term *hypothesis* (or *research hypothesis)* to represent statements that are derived from laws or theories and are susceptible to direct testing by confrontation with real-world data.   This usage is by no means a consensus position because there is no consensus concerning the term.   However, the viewpoint expressed here is similar to Dubin's position: "An hypothesis may be defined as the predictions about values of units of a theory in which empirical indicators are employed for the named units in each proposition." [160, p. 212]

The important consequence of reserving the label "hypothesis" for directly testable statements is that it highlights the notion of the empirical confirmation of theories.   Because theories are not directly testable, they are not *strictly confirmable*.   Theories cannot be shown to be conclusively true in an empirical sense.   One can only say that certain research hypotheses have been derived from a theory and that these hypotheses have been directly tested.   If the hypotheses are confirmed, then this provides empirical support that the theory is, indeed, empirically true; that is, the theory has been empirically corroborated by the confirmation of the research hypotheses.   If the hypotheses are rejected by the data, then this provides empirical evidence that *(a)* the theory is false (reality just isn't constructed as the theory suggests), *(b)* errors have been made in the empirical testing procedures, or *(c)* the rejected hypothesis was not properly derived from the theory.

The preceding discussion of the empirical testing procedure suggests that both *deduction* and *induction* play vital roles in the process of empirical confirmation. Since theories are not directly testable, one must *deduce* from them research hypotheses that are susceptible to direct confrontation with data. Once the tests of the research hypotheses have been conducted, the procedure of empirical confirmation is inherently *inductive*. To claim that empirically confirming a research hypothesis thus strictly confirms a theory is to fall prey to the logical fallacy of *affirming the consequent*. It would be claiming the following to be a valid syllogism:

> If theory X is true, then hypothesis h is true.
> Hypothesis h is empirically true.
> _____
> Therefore, theory X is true.

Obviously, hypothesis h could be true and yet theory X could be false.   Therefore, when a theory has been tested many times and its hypotheses have been confirmed, we cannot say that the theory is empirically true; rather, we can say that the empirical tests have provided strong *inductive* support for the truth of the theory. In a sense, we are "weighing" the empirical evidence. [96, p. 319] The "heavier" the weight of the empirical evidence, the more likely it is that the theory accurately represents reality and, thus, the more highly "confirmed" the theory is.

6.6   SUMMARY

This chapter has attempted to explicate the fundamental underpinnings of the nature and role of theory in scientific inquiry. The treatment here has proposed that the major role of theory is to *increase scientific understanding through a systematized structure capable of both explaining and predicting phenomena*. Consequently, theories become systematically related sets of statements, including some lawlike generalizations, that are empirically testable. Theories must contain a systematically related set of statements because science seeks to give an organized account of phenomena. Theories must contain lawlike generalizations because it is precisely these statements that give theories their explanatory and predictive power. Theories must be empirically testable in order that they may be *(a)* intersubjectively certifiable, *(b)* capable of explaining and predicting real-world phenomena, and *(c)* differentiated from purely analytical schemata. A theory is capable of being empirically testable when it is possible to derive from the theory certain predictive-type statements (hypotheses) that are amenable to direct confrontation with real-world data.

QUESTIONS FOR ANALYSIS AND DISCUSSION

1. Define and differentiate: theories, laws, hypotheses, models, generalizations, empirical regularities, propositions, and concepts. Show how these terms are related.
2. Do theories generate hypotheses, or do hypotheses lead to theories? How are theories generated?
3. Would marketing theory be useful to a marketing practitioner? To a government official? To a teacher of a basic marketing course?
4. "A theory is a systematically related set of statements, including some lawlike generalizations, that is empirically testable." We may therefore conclude that all theories can be shown to be either "true" or "false." Discuss.
5. Someone has said: "The problem with marketing research is the lack of an isomorphic relationship between concepts and their respective operational definitions." Evaluate.
6. Robert K. Merton makes a plea for "theories of the middle range" in sociology:

    Throughout this book, the term *sociological theory* refers to logically interconnected sets of propositions from which empirical uniformities can be derived. Throughout we focus on what I have called theories of the middle range: theories that lie between minor but necessary working hypotheses that evolve in abundance during day-to-day research and the all-inclusive systematic efforts to develop a unified theory that will explain all the observed uniformities of social behavior, social organization, and social change. [445, p. 39]

Is Merton actually pleading for theories in sociology with greater extension? (See Chapter 5.) Evaluate the current work in marketing theory. How much of it appears to be in the middle range? Give examples of works that are in the middle range, more specific than the middle range, and more general than the middle range. Does Merton's plea also apply to marketing?

7. A major issue in marketing theory concerns the development of a general theory of marketing. Bartels suggests that "the broadest statement of marketing thought in any period is the 'general theory' of that day." [39] Similarly, the subtitle of Alderson's last book [10] was *A Functionalist Theory of Marketing*. Do you agree with Bartels' definition of a general theory of marketing? If yes, why? If no, suggest an alternative definition and show how it is superior to Bartels' definition. Will we ever have (i.e., is it possible to have) a general theory of marketing? What would be the role or purpose of a general theory of marketing if we did have one?

8. What is the relevance of the "garden in the jungle" headnote at the beginning of the chapter to the content of the chapter?

9. Evaluate Bartels' perspective on the nature of theory:

   Theory is a form in which knowledge is expressed, and the term is used with two meanings. First, it designates a tentative, speculative, or unproven generalization concerning a subject. In this sense, it is synonymous with "hypothesis" and presents an early stage in the logical process. Second, it means a summary of considered conclusion reached after analysis and synthesis of information, and, as such, it represents a mature stage in the development of thought. This second concept of theory is the sense in which the term is used hereafter. [40, p. 2]

10. Many theories or models in marketing consist primarily of a diagram with little boxes, each having a single concept or construct and various arrows connecting the boxes. Is this a theory proper or a pictorial representation of a theory? To what extent is this procedure appropriate or inappropriate? Can it be abused?

11. Evaluate the following three characteristics of a good theory proposed by Baumol [51]:

    1. The model should be a sufficiently simple version of the facts to permit systematic manipulation and analysis.
    2. It must be a sufficiently close approximation to the relevant facts to be usable.
    3. Its conclusions should be relatively insensitive to changes in its assumptions.

12. In "Lawlike Generalizations and Marketing Theory" [298] Hunt contends that "in order for generalizations to be considered lawlike, the *minimum* necessary conditions are that the generalizations specify a relationship in the form of a universal conditional (such as my example in the original note) which is

capable of yielding predictive statements (hypotheses) which are composed of terms that have empirical referents and, thus, permit empirical testing." Are these the minimum necessary conditions?

13. El-Ansary in his "General Theory of Marketing: Revisited" [165] proposed that "a vertical marketing system, distribution channel, is a key integrative concept in marketing." Evaluate the contention that in a general theory of marketing the marketing channel would be the key integrative concept.

14. El-Ansary [165] suggests that a major section of a general theory of marketing would be "a theory of micromarketing." Apparently, he believes that such a theory would include subtheories of product and brand management, pricing, promotion, physical distribution management, marketing research, financial aspects, and marketing program productivity. What would these subtheories attempt to explain and predict? Would such a collection of subtheories be appropriately referred to as a theory of micromarketing? Would a theory of micromarketing be positive or normative? Would it be possible to have a general theory of marketing which included both positive and normative components?

15. There is a famous paradox on how theories and laws are confirmed or corroborated by empirical testing. First proposed by Hempel [257], the paradox is usually referred to as the "Raven paradox" and can be roughly stated as:

   a. The statement P "All ravens are black" is logically equivalent to the statement P^* "All nonblack things are nonravens."

   b. One may empirically explore the validity of P by examining ravens and seeing whether they are black (tend to confirm) or nonblack (tend to disconfirm).

   c. One may empirically examine P^* by looking at nonblack objects (e.g., roses) and determining whether they are nonravens (tend to confirm) or ravens (tend to disconfirm).

   d. Any evidence which tends to confirm P^* *must* logically tend to confirm P.

   e. Therefore, the fact that a rose may be red tends to confirm that ravens are black.

   f. Statement e is intellectually disquieting.

   Gardner [224] discusses the paradoxical nature of ravens thus:

   > We look around and see a yellow object. Is it a raven? No, it is a buttercup. The flower surely confirms (albeit weakly) that all nonblack objects are not ravens, but it is hard to see how it has any *relevance* at all to the statement "All ravens are black." If it does, it equally confirms that all ravens are white or any color except yellow. [224, p. 121]

   Evaluate. (Remember that logic, like nature, is often surprising, sometimes fascinating, but never paradoxical).

16. Do you agree that logic, like nature, is never paradoxical? If yes, why? If no, why not?

17. Alderson's "Law of Exchange" states: If X is an element in the assortment A and Y is an element in the assortment B, then X is exchangeable for Y if, and only if, the following three conditions hold:

   1. X is different from Y.

   2. The potency of the assortment A is increased by dropping X and adding Y.

   3. The potency of the assortment B is increased by adding X and dropping Y.

Evaluate the Law of Exchange. To what extent does the Law of Exchange differ from conventional microeconomic demand theory? To what extent does the Law of Exchange have empirical content?

18. "In order for an economy to be characterized by many variations of the same basic product, it is necessary and sufficient that there be heterogeneity of demand." True? False? Why?

19. What is a transvection? Discuss the actual and potential usefulness of Alderson's transvection concept in marketing. Develop a hypothetical example of a transvection.

20. What is Alderson's "discrepancy of assortments"? How does this concept attempt to explain the existence of intermediaries? Why is a wholesaler "most vulnerable when it purchases only a part of what the manufacturer supplies and sells to retailers only a small portion of what their customers demand"? Do you agree?

21. Bagozzi in "Toward a Formal Theory of Marketing Exchanges" [28] proposes that "in their interactions with each other and with other social actors, the parties to an exchange are presumed to maximize"

$$U_d = U(Z_a, Z_c, Z_{mb})$$

where U_d is the utility for the dyad and Z_a = affect, Z_c = cognitions, and Z_{mb} = moral beliefs. To what extent does this equation differ from Alderson's Law of Exchange? Do you agree that the parties to an exchange maximize U_d?

22. Ferrell and Perrachione [180] contend that "one of Bagozzi's recurring goals or self-imposed criteria is to construct a theory that will go beyond description to explanation (and eventually prediction and control). Yet the models he has proposed, in spite of their frequent descriptive richness, are consistently insufficient when measured against the explanation criterion." Do you agree or disagree with this criticism?

7
THEORY: ISSUES AND ASPECTS

A science is served in many ways: by intelligent discussion and fresh proposals, by the extension or completion of previously presented theories, by the fair-minded and unflinching evaluation of current proposals, by justly protesting, blowing the whistle, and pointing out that this kingly theory or that is not wearing a shred of evidence, by sometimes synthesizing and sometimes isolating, by daring to be explicit and—ironically—by daring to be suggestive. It is when scientists and philosophers of science cannot make up their minds as to which role they are playing or—what is worse—try to fill several roles at once, that matters go awry. Then the Ivory Tower and the Tower of Babel sound disturbingly alike.

Paul Surgi Speck

The preceding chapter explored the nature of theoretical constructions. The purpose of this chapter is to examine several specific issues in marketing theory. Since classificational schemata are often confused with theoretical schemata, we shall begin by analyzing the nature of classifications in marketing. Next we shall delineate the differences between positive theory, normative theory, deterministic theory, and stochastic theory. The chapter concludes with an examination of a major philosophy of science controversy: Is/can science be objective?

7.1 CLASSIFICATIONAL SCHEMATA

Marketing is replete with classificational schemata. There are classificational schemata for different kinds of goods (convenience, shopping, etc.), stores (department stores, limited line stores, etc.), wholesalers (general merchandise, general line, etc.), pricing policies (cost-plus, demand-oriented, etc.), and numerous others. Classificational schemata play fundamental roles in the development of a discipline since they are the primary means for *organizing* phenomena into classes or groups that are amenable to systematic investigation and theory development. Nevertheless, classificational schemata, no matter how elaborate or complex, are not by themselves theoretical, although most theoretical constructions will contain classificational schemata as components. As previously noted, an analysis of the seven subtheories of Bartels' general theory of marketing revealed them to be primarily classificational schemata which lacked the requisite lawlike generalizations to be considered as theories. [296, p. 68]

In the last chapter of their book *Consumer Behavior,* Engel, Kollat, and Blackwell evaluate the present position of consumer behavior research. One of the major deficiencies of present research, they point out, is the lack of standardized classification systems. [167, p. 659] For example, they note the wide variation of categories of "stage in the family life cycle" and the fact that almost every researcher uses a different schema for determining social class. They conclude, "The lack of standardized variable categories also makes it difficult to compare and integrate research findings. Instead of improving, this problem has also intensified during the last five years." [167, p. 659]

If having a variety of nonstandard classificational schemata for the same phenomenon is dysfunctional, how does one select the *best* classificational schema from the available alternatives? Since classificational schemata help to organize the elements of the universe, and since organizing phenomena often represents the first step in theory development, how can one differentiate the good classificational schema from the bad? This section will attempt to answer these questions, first by discussing the two basic approaches to generating classificational schemata and then by developing some criteria for evaluating any classificational schema.

Classificational systems always involve a partitioning of some universe of objects, events, or other phenomena into classes or sets that are homogeneous with respect to some categorical properties. There are two distinctly different procedures or methods for generating classificational schemata. Following the essence of Harvey's terminology, one procedure is *logical partitioning* and the second is *grouping.* [255, p. 334] The procedure here referred to as logical partitioning is sometimes called "deductive classification," "a priori classification," or "classification from above." Grouping is probably a less satisfactory label for the second procedure (more accurately, second *set* of procedures). The grouping procedures are often called "inductive classification," "*ex post* classification," "classification from below," "numerical taxonomy," or "quantitative classification." The essential difference between the logical partitioning and grouping procedures is that with the former the classificational schema is always developed *before* the researcher analyzes any specific set of data (hence, "deductive," "a priori," and "from above"). In contrast, when using grouping procedures, the researcher generates his schema only *after* he analyzes some specific set of data (hence, "inductive," *"ex post,"* and "from below"). With logical partitioning, the researcher *imposes* a classificational system on the data; with grouping, the researcher lets the data suggest the system. Both kinds of procedures are used in marketing, and both have their strengths and weaknesses. After a (very) modest elaboration on the two procedures, we shall explore some criteria for evaluating any classification system.

7.1.1   Logical Partitioning

Logical partitioning starts with the careful specification of the marketing phenomena to be categorized—families, retailers, wholesalers, types of goods, brands of goods, etc. Next comes the delineation of the categorial terms. These are the properties or characteristics of the phenomena on which the classificational schema is to be based—for families this might be age, marital status, number of children, etc.; for retailers it might be number of units and type of ownership. Finally, labels are given to the various categories that emerge from applying the categorial terms to the phenomena—thus, for families we have "newly married couples," the "full nest I," "empty nest," etc., and for retailers we have independents, chain stores, etc.

Several observations concerning logical partitioning are important to keep in mind. First, Sokal and Sneath point out that logical partitioning usually results in *monothetic* classifications. [597, p. 13] With monothetic classification systems, *all* members of a category possess *all* of the characteristics or properties used to identify the category. To illustrate this point, consider the commonly used stage in the family life cycle schema reproduced in Table 7-1. This schema is an example of logical partitioning with monothetic classifications. In order for a family to be classified as "full nest III," the family must satisfy *all* of the criteria; that is the couple must be over 45 years old, married, and have the youngest child be 6 years or older. If the couple satisfied the age and marital status criteria but had, by chance, a child under 6 years old, then it could not be classified as "full nest III." (In fact, it would not fit any category in the schema, a point to be discussed later.) Now, it may intuitively appear that all classificational schemata would be monothetic. But such is not the case, as will be shown when we discuss grouping procedures.

The second observation concerning logical partitioning is that the procedure can result in either single-level or multilevel schemata. Prominent among multilevel schemata are *hierarchical* classification systems which involve the ordering relation ⊂ from set theory. Thus A ⊂ B should be read, "The class of phenomena designated as A are contained in the class of phenomena designated as B." Hierarchies can be displayed by means of Euler-Venn diagrams from set theory or by *trees*.

Table 7-1   The stage in the family life cycle schema

Category	Age		Marital status		Children			
	Less than 45 years	45 years or older	Single	Married	No Children	Youngest child under 6 years	Youngest Child 6 years or over	No dependent children
1. The bachelor stage	X		X					
2. Newly married couples	X			X	X			
3. The full nest I	X			X		X		
4. The full nest II	X			X			X	
5. The full nest III		X		X			X	
6. The empty nest		X		X				X
7. The solitary survivors		X	X					X

Source: Adapted from a version originally proposed by the Survey Research Center, University of Michigan.

Figure 7-1 illustrates the common hierarchical classification of whole-salers by means of a tree. The ordering relation ⊂ is both asymmetri-cal and transitive. Thus, A ⊂ B, being asymmetrical, implies that B ⊄ A (brokers are a subset of the class known as agent wholesalers, but agent wholesalers are *not* a subset of the class called brokers). Simi-larly, A ⊂ B and B ⊂ C implies, by transitivity, A ⊂ C (if a mail-order wholesaler is a kind of limited function wholesaler, and if a limited

Figure 7-1   Classification of wholesalers

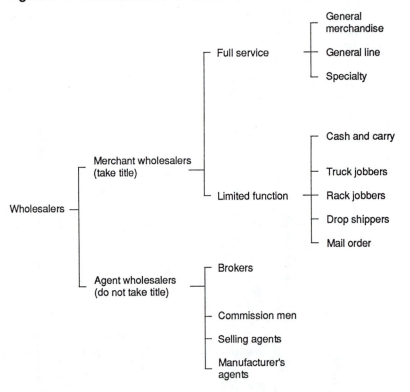

function wholesaler is a kind of merchant wholesaler, then a mail-order wholesaler is a kind of merchant wholesaler). Hierarchical classifica-tions are preferable (other things equal) to single-level classifications because of their greater systemic power. That is, hierarchical classifi-cations have greater power to systematically organize the phenomena under investigation.

The third observation about logical partitioning is that there may exist *empty classes*. That is, a proper application of the categorial terms may generate a class to which no phenomenon belongs. The importance of empty classes lies in the context of discovery; observing that empty classes exist may spur the researcher to inquire as to the circumstances under which phenomena might be classified into the now empty set. For example, the existence of holes or empty classes in Mendeleev's periodic table of elements in chemistry suggested the existence of, and spurred the search for, previously unknown elements.

A final observation is suggested by Harvey. Logical partitioning "presupposes a fairly sophisticated understanding of the phenomena being investigated, else the classifications involved may be totally unrealistic, nothing better than an inspired guess." [255, p. 366] Any universe of phenomena can be classified in an infinite variety of ways. Which properties or characteristics are the important ones to use for classificatory purposes? Which classes would be most meaningful for research? Logical partitioning assumes substantial *a priori* knowledge about how to answer these questions. The procedures referred to previously as grouping procedures (which will be discussed next) require much less *a priori* knowledge about the phenomena to be classified.

7.1.2   Grouping Procedures

Like logical partitioning, all grouping procedures for classification start with the specification of the phenomena to be classified and the properties or characteristics on which the categorizing is to be done. However, grouping procedures are designed to conveniently accommodate larger numbers of properties than is logical partitioning. As Frank and Green point out:

> Almost every major analytical problem requires the classification of objects by several characteristics—whether customers, products, cities, television programs, or magazines. Seldom are explicit classification systems with some combination of attributes, such as those used for measuring a customer's social class or stage in life cycle, found. Such classification systems typically represent self-imposed taxonomies; that is, taxonomies the researcher believes to be relevant because of a theory or prior experience. Although this approach [logical partitioning] can be useful, it has limitations. Regardless of the complexity of reality, it is difficult to classify objects by more than two or three characteristics at a time. If reality requires greater complexity, researchers are severely constrained by their conceptual limitations. [210, p. 84]

So, the first difference between logical partitioning and grouping is that the grouping procedures are better equipped to handle large numbers of categorial terms or properties. The second difference, and perhaps the most significant from a methodological perspective, is that *all grouping procedures share the common characteristic that they determine categories or classifications by an analysis of a specific set of data.* Consequently, they are referred to as "inductive," "*ex post*," or "classification from below" procedures.

Although all grouping procedures determine classifications by analyzing data, numerous basic models have been developed to accomplish the classificatory task, and many computer programs have been generated for each model. Among the most commonly used models are factor analysis, multiple discriminant analysis, multidimensional scaling, and cluster analysis. Thus, factor analysis has been used to classify liquor preferences, advertising readership, and coffees. [604, 620, 457] Multiple discriminant analysis has been used to classify brands of beer. [325] Both pharmaceuticals and colors of automobiles [470, 153] have been classified by multidimensional scaling. Cluster analysis has generated classifications of cities for test marketing and market survey respondents. [235, 326] Finally, gasoline brands were classified by Kamen using "quick clustering" [328] and by Aaker using "visual clustering." [2] Although some of these models are often used for purposes other than classification, researchers are ever more frequently using them to organize phenomena for classification. The tremendous differences among the models notwithstanding, they share the common property of separating phenomena into groups that maximize both the degree of "likeness" *within* each group and the degree of differences *between* groups according to some objective function.

A detailed exposition of the specific models for grouping phenomena need not concern us here; interested readers are advised to consult the previously cited references for guidance as to which specific grouping model would be most appropriate for their needs. What shall concern us from a methodological perspective are certain fundamental characteristics of grouping procedures contrasted with logical partitioning. First, Sokal and Sneath observe that classificational schemata that are developed by grouping procedures usually have classes that are *polythetic*. [597, p. 13] Recalling that logical partitioning usually results in monothetic classes, with *polythetic* classes the phenomena in any given class may share many characteristics in common; however, no individual phenomenon need possess *all* of the characteristics of the class. One simple example will illustrate this point. W. A. K. Frost used a clustering program to classify different television programs. [217] One cluster contained the following programs: *World of Sport, Football, Sportsview, Horse Racing, Motor Racing, Boxing,* and *News.* All of the programs, save one, share (among other things) the common characteristic of being either sporting events (boxing, etc.) or solely concerned with sporting events (*Sportsview*). The *News* program must be perceived by viewers as being similar to the other members of its cluster *in toto*; yet, it does not share the *sports* characteristic common to its companions. It is in this respect that grouping procedures are polythetic.

A second characteristic of grouping models is that they usually result in single-level rather than multilevel classifications. Hierarchical clustering routines are available [162] and have been discussed in the marketing literature [210]; yet, procedures that generate single-level classifications are most commonly employed.

Third, unlike logical partitioning, grouping procedures do not generate empty classes since classes can only be formed from existing observations. To the extent that empty classes serve the heuristic function of suggesting fruitful avenues for research, the inability to generate empty classes might be disadvantageous. Also, at the risk of sounding tautologous, if researchers use a clustering program, they will get clusters. Aaker emphasizes this point when he advocates "visual clustering":

> [The results] indicate that the structure is not very well defined and that an unambiguous set of clusters does not exist. This observation, it should be noted, is not insignificant. Often an output which lists several clusters fails to convey this type of conclusion to those not intimate with the program. [2, p. 331]

Finally, grouping procedures require substantially less a priori knowledge concerning which specific properties are likely to be powerful for classifying phenomena than does logical partitioning. Also, grouping procedures are uniquely equipped to accommodate large numbers of potentially useful categorial properties. These are powerful advantages for grouping procedures. Nevertheless, these procedures have not yet produced many *general* classificational schemata. Classifications developed through grouping procedures seldom are generalized beyond their original data base. Rather than developing classification systems for marketing phenomena in general, the use of these procedures has been restricted to problems that are highly situation specific. Perhaps this is what Frank and Green are implying when they suggest that we refer to grouping procedures as "preclassification techniques":

> These taxonomic procedures may be called preclassification techniques since their purpose is to describe the natural groupings that occur in large masses of data. From these natural groupings (or clusters) the researcher can sometimes develop the requisite conceptual framework for classification. [210, p. 302]

Irrespective of the procedure used for classifying, either logical partitioning or grouping, the resultant classificational schema can be evaluated using the same criteria. The next section will attempt to systematically develop such criteria.

7.1.3   Criteria for Evaluating Classificational Schemata

Numerous criteria have been suggested for evaluating alternative classificational schemata. Although the following five criteria do not exhaust the possibilities, they would seem to make a useful starting point for any researcher who has a classification problem:

1. Does the schema adequately specify the phenomenon to be classified?
2. Does the schema adequately specify the properties or characteristics that will be doing the classifying?
3. Does the schema have categories that are mutually exclusive?
4. Does the schema have categories that are collectively exhaustive?
5. Is the schema useful?

Criterion 1 inquires whether the schema adequately specifies the phenomenon to be classified. That is, *exactly* what is being categorized? What is the universe? An analysis of the familiar classification of goods schema should help to explicate this criterion. Table 7-2 reproduces three versions of the classification of goods schema: the American Marketing Association definition (which closely follows the original version by Copeland [133]), the version suggested by Richard H. Holton [281], and the version suggested by Louis P. Bucklin in his classic article "Retail Strategy and the Classification of Goods." [91]

What is the universe that is being partitioned by the classification of goods schema? Is it products, brands of products, consumers' perceptions of products, or consumers' perceptions of brands of products? The answer is not altogether unambiguous. The AMA definition of convenience good appears to be referring to *products*, yet both the Holton and Bucklin versions of convenience goods appear to be classifying consumers' *perceptions* of products. Holton observed, "A given good may be a convenience good for some consumers and a shopping good for others." [281, p. 54] This would clearly imply that the universe consists of perceptions of goods rather than goods per se. Thus, E. J. McCarthy suggests that the approach a marketing manager should take is to determine the proportion of consumers who perceive the product as a convenience good and compare this with the proportion who perceive it as being either a shopping good or a specialty good. [428, p. 305] This approach implies that there will seldom, if ever, be anything that could be classified as a *convenience good;* rather, there are only a certain proportion of consumers who *perceive* a good to be a convenience good.

Similar ambiguity surrounds the specialty goods category where people commonly cite specific *brands* as examples of specialty goods. Thus, for some consumers a particular *brand* of coffee would be a specialty good, and the universe being partitioned would be consumers' perceptions of brands of goods and not simply goods. Perhaps some of the debate that has centered on the classification of goods schema during the past 50 years can be explained by pointing out that this schema does not do well on Criterion 1; it does not clearly specify the universe to be classified. Readers should ask themselves whether other classification schemata in marketing, such as the *product life cycle* schema,

TABLE 7-2   The classification of goods schema

Category	Definition		
	American Marketing Association*	Richard H. Holton**	Louis P. Bucklin***
Convenience goods	Those consumers' goods which the customer purchases frequently, immediately, and with a minimum of effort	Those goods for which the consumer regards the probable gain from making price and quality comparisons as small compared to the cost of making such comparisons	Those goods for which the consumer, before his need arises, possesses a preference map that indicates a willingness to purchase any of a number of known substitutes rather than to make the additional effort required to buy a particular item
Shopping goods	Those consumers' goods which the customer in the process of selection and purchase characteristically compares on such bases as suitability, quality, price, and style	Those goods for which the consumer regards the probable gain from making price and quality comparisons as large relative to the cost of making such comparisons	Those goods for which the consumer has not developed a complete preference map before the need arises, requiring him to undertake search to construct such a map before purchase
Specialty goods	Those consumers' goods on which a significant group of buyers are habitually willing to make a special purchasing effort	Those convenience or shopping goods which have such a limited market as to require the consumer to make a special effort to purchase them	Those goods for which the consumer, before his need arises, possesses a preference map that indicates a willingness to expend the additional effort required to purchase the most preferred item rather than to buy a more readily accessible substitute

* Definitions Committee, American Marketing Association *Marketing Definitions* (Chicago: AMA, 1960), pp. 11, 21, and 22.
** Richard H. Holton, "The Distinction Between Convenience Goods, Shopping Goods and Specialty Goods," *Journal of Marketing*, 23 (July 1958), pp. 53–56.
*** Louis P. Bucklin, "Retail Strategy and the Classification of Goods," *Journal of Marketing*, 27 (January 1963), pp. 50–55.

suffer from the same ambiguity. Does the product life cycle schema refer to an industry's product or to an individual company's product?[1]

Criterion 2 inquires whether the properties or characteristics that have been chosen to do the classifying have been adequately specified. Implicit in Criterion 2 is the question "Are these properties the *appropriate* properties for classificatory purposes?" One clue that the chosen properties may be inappropriate is when different properties are used throughout the schema, "changing horses in midstream," so to speak. Mario Bunge addresses this issue: "One of the principles of correct classification is that the characteristics or properties chosen for performing the grouping should be stuck to throughout the work; for example, a shift from skeletal to physiological characteristics in the classification of vertebrates will produce not only different classes but also different systems of classes, i.e., alternative classification." [95, p.75]

Referring once again to the classification of goods schema in Table 7-2, note that the AMA schema uses three properties to identify convenience goods: purchased *(a)* frequently, *(b)* immediately, and *(c)* with a minimum of effort. This would lead one to expect some other category to contain goods purchased *(a)* infrequently, *(b)* not immediately, and *(c)* with great effort. Yet, shopping goods are classified on the basic property of *comparison* and specialty goods are classified on the basis of *willingness to expend effort*. The shifting from one set of properties for the classification of convenience goods to other properties for specialty goods and shopping goods is a strong sign that the schema is structurally unsound.

Consider, now, the revision suggested by Holton and detailed in the second column of Table 7-2. Holton uses the same two properties for classifying convenience goods and shopping goods: the consumer's perceptions of *(a)* the probable *gain* for making comparisons versus *(b)* the probable *cost* of such comparisons. Unfortunately, Holton then scraps these properties and uses the size of the market to classify specialty goods. Only the Bucklin version of the classification of goods schema consistently uses the same properties to do the job of classifying. These properties are *(a)* the existence of a preference map and *(b)* the nature of the preference map if one exists. To see that this is indeed the case, refer to Figure 7-2, which reformulates the essence of Bucklin's schema by means of a tree diagram. Bucklin's efforts are unique in terms of classifying goods because only his schema retains the conceptual richness of Copeland's original concepts, while at the same time rigorously and consistently explicating the properties used for classificatory purposes. Bucklin's version has much to recommend it.

So one aspect of Criterion 2 is whether the chosen properties are appropriate for classification. Second, one should ask whether the operational procedures for applying the classificatory properties are

---

[1] Polli and Cook discuss this issue. [499]

Figure 7-2 Bucklin's classification of goods schema

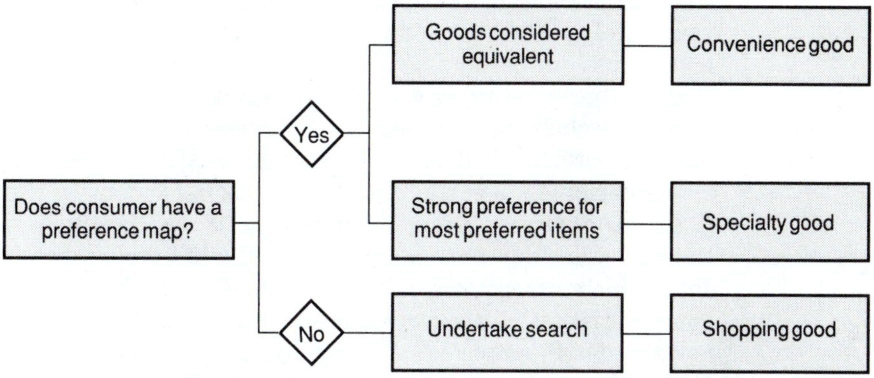

Source: Adapted from Louis P. Bucklin, "Retail Strategy and the Classification of Goods," *Journal of Marketing*, January 1963.

rigorous. *The procedures should be intersubjectively unambiguous,* a characteristic which is sometimes referred to as "high interjudge reliability." The procedures should be such that different people would classify the phenomena in the same categories. For example, the family life cycle schema in Table 7-1 has "marital status" as a categorial property with two categories, single and married. To be intersubjectively unambiguous, the schema must have rigorous procedures to enable different people to reliably classify widows, widowers, and divorcees.

Is the product life cycle schema intersubjectively unambiguous? Will different people categorize the same product in the same stage? A randomly selected group of a dozen products given to a group of students familiar with the product life cycle notion is hereby guaranteed to produce sobering results.

The third criterion for evaluating classificational schemata suggests that all the categories at the same level of classification should be *mutually exclusive.* That is, if an item fits one category or class, it will not fit any other class. No single item may fit two different categories at the same level. "At the same level" must be emphasized because, of course, in a hierarchical classificational schema the same item will fit different categories at different levels. Therefore, in Figure 7-1, a general line wholesaler is both a full-service wholesaler and a merchant wholesaler.

Many classifications in marketing do not meet the mutually exclusive criterion. The normal distinction between industrial goods and consumer goods typifies the problem. Common usage in marketing suggests, "Consumer goods are those goods and services destined for the ultimate consumer. These contrast with industrial goods, which are those goods and services destined for use in producing other goods and services." [428, p. 300] Holloway and Hancock have commented that this partitioning of goods does not result in mutually exclusive categories. "Relatively few goods are exclusively industrial goods. The same article may, under one set of circumstances, be an industrial good and under other conditions a consumer good." [279, p. 683] Although the lack of exclusivity may not be a mortal blow to any classificational schema, it certainly does violence to the basic notion of classification.

Criterion 4 suggests that classificational schemata should be *collectively exhaustive.* Every item that is to be classified should have a "home." Consider, once again, the family life cycle schema in Table 7-1. Into which category would a couple fall if they had the following characteristics: *(a)* over 45 years old, *(b)* married, and *(c)* youngest child under 6 years old? Obviously, there is no home for this family. Now, all classification systems can be made collectively exhaustive by the simple expedient of adding that ubiquitous category "other." However, the size of this category should be monitored carefully. If too many phenomena can find no home except other, then the system should be examined carefully for possible expansion by adding new categories.

Criterion 5 simply asks, "Is the schema useful?" Does it adequately serve its intended purposes? How well does it compare with alternative schemata? Of the five criteria, this one is "first among equals." Researchers do not create classificational schemata because they are possessed by some taxonomic devil. Rather, classifications are devised to attempt to solve some kind of problem. Harvey reminds us that we must keep in mind the purpose of the classificational system when evaluating it.

> Classification may be regarded as a means for searching reality for hypotheses or for structuring reality to test hypotheses. It may also be regarded as a beginning point or the culmination of scientific investigation. We possess, therefore, no means of assessing the adequacy or efficiency of a given classification independently of the job it is designed to do. [255, p. 326]

Therefore, the ultimate criterion is usefulness. How useful is the schema for helping marketing managers solve problems? In this regard, the product life cycle schema may pass muster if it simply reminds managers to constantly monitor their product line, since a company cannot afford to have all of its products in the "decline" stage. How *theoretically fruitful* is the schema? Have the concepts embodied in the schema been useful for developing lawlike generalizations? Many popular classificational schemata in marketing (e.g., the product life cycle) have exhibited extremely limited usefulness in generating lawlike statements. Much work remains to be done in this area.

In conclusion, classificational schemata are important in theory development because they are our primary means for organizing phenomena. Generating useful classificational systems frequently represents one of the first steps in theorizing. For this reason, we have spent considerable time analyzing classificational schemata. Nevertheless, classificational systems are a kind of nontheoretical construction because they lack the requisite lawlike generalizations that all theoretical constructions must contain. To develop useful systems for classifying is an endeavor worthy of any researcher, but this should not be confused with the construction of theory proper.

7.2   POSITIVE VERSUS NORMATIVE THEORY

Most of this book has focused on the nature of positive theories: systematically related sets of statements, including some lawlike generalizations, that are empirically testable and that increase scientific understanding through the explanation and prediction of phenomena. However, much of the theorizing in marketing is normative, not positive. How do normative theories differ from positive theories? As we shall see, these two kinds of theories differ as to (1) structure, (2) purpose, and (3) validation criteria. First, what is the nature of normative theories?

Normative theories are of at least two kinds. One embodies an *ethical* "ought"; the other, a *rational* "ought." There are normative theories which are essentially *ethical theories* that prescribe morally "correct" behavior. Such theories are found in the branch of philosophy generally known as "ethics," which has been a subject of philosophical inquiry since time immemorial.

However, when marketers discuss "normative theory," we are usually *not* referring to theories of ethical behavior. Rather, we are usually referring to some kind of model which assists a decision maker in rationally or systematically choosing from among a limited set of alternative actions or strategies, given certain (1) objectives, (2) consequences or payoffs, and (3) states of nature. As an example, consider the well-known "high-assay model" originally developed by the advertising agency of Young and Rubicam and reproduced in Figure 7-3.

The high-assay model attempts to assist the advertising decision maker in scheduling media. The model incorporates the method of steepest ascent, which proposes that the user should purchase the insertion at each step which provides the greatest increase in effectiveness for the money expended.

Statements 2 and 3 are typical of the statements in normative decision theories: "Specify market segments and their ratings" and "Cycle through all media to find lowest cost medium per rated prospect." Note

Figure 7-3 High-assay model

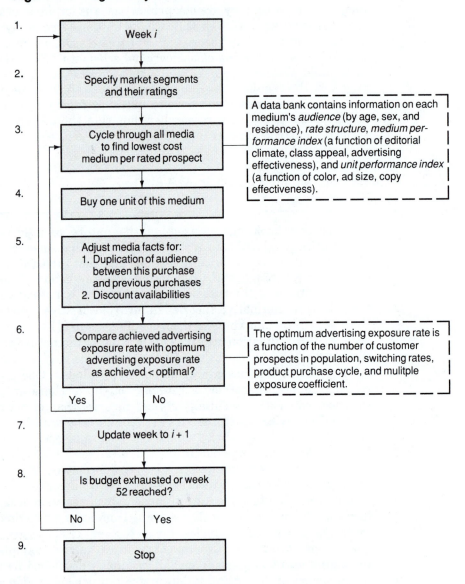

Source: From Philip Kotler, *Marketing Decision Making* (New York: Holt, Rinehart & Winston, 1971), p. 457.

the *prescriptive* nature of these statements. The basic form of these statements is: "Under circumstances $X_1, X_2, X_3, \ldots X_k$, one should do Y in order to achieve G." All normative decision theories must contain such prescriptive statements.

On the other hand, all positive theories must contain, not prescriptive statements, but lawlike generalizations. This is the fundamental *structural* difference between normative and positive theory. Since theories that are purely normative contain no lawlike generalizations, such structures are explanatorily impotent. Recall that it is precisely the lawlike generalizations in positive theories that carry the brunt of the load of explaining and predicting phenomena.

A second difference is one of purpose. The purpose or objective of positive theory in marketing is to increase our understanding of marketing phenomena. Positive theories enable us to do this by providing systematized structures capable of explaining and predicting phenomena. It is true that, because of their ability to explain and predict phenomena, positive theories are often extremely useful aids to decision making. Nevertheless, aiding decision making remains a favorable consequence of *using* theories. The *objective* of theory is to explain, predict, and understand. To say that the purpose of positive theory in marketing is to aid in making marketing decisions is analogous to saying that the purpose of the theory of gravitation is to aid us in sending rockets to the moon.

Consider the purpose of the high-assay normative decision theory. Its objective is to help the advertising decision maker to better schedule media. Such is the situation with all normative decision theories. *The entire purpose of creating normative decision models in marketing is to assist marketers in making better decisions.* As another example, Massey and Weitz [424] have developed a normative theory of market segmentation. The purpose of their theory is to provide specific guidelines for allocating marketing expenditures among various market segments.

The final distinction between positive theory and normative decision theory lies in their differing validation criteria. How does one go about determining whether the theories are valid? The validity of a positive theory is determined by (1) checking the internal logic and mathematics of the theory and then (2) exposing it to empirical tests in the real world. Roughly speaking, we develop testable hypotheses of the following kind: "If theory X is valid, then every time we see circumstances $C_1, C_2, C_3, \ldots C_k$ in the real world, we would expect to also find phenomena $P_1, P_2, P_3, \ldots P_k$." Note that it is the existence of lawlike generalizations in positive theory that enables us to derive testable hypotheses.

Consider the appropriate validation procedures for normative decision theories. The internal logic and mathematics of such a theory can be checked and verified. Further, the *usefulness* of the theory can be evaluated. That is, compared with other relevant theories, to what extent are the necessary data available, how expensive is the theory to use, how much time does it take to use the theory, and does the theory use the "best" objective function?

Although the usefulness and logic of normative decision theories can be validated, such theories cannot be empirically tested in the real world in the same sense as positive theories. Because normative decision theories do not contain lawlike generalizations, they cannot explain and predict phenomena and, therefore, they cannot generate empirically testable hypotheses. As MacDonald has observed:

> Let it be admitted that all or most human beings are intelligent or rational. And that what is known by reason is certainly true. But, also, what can be known by unaided reason is what *must* be true, and perhaps what *ought* to be but never what *is* true of matter of fact. And statements which are logically certain are tautological or analytic and are neither verified nor falsified by what exists. *Statements about what ought to be are of a peculiar type which will be discussed later, but it is certain that they say nothing about what is.* [409, p. 724, emphasis added]

It is precisely because normative decision theories are not empirically testable that many writers, including this one, prefer the label "normative decision *model*" instead of the label "normative decision theory." The label "theory" is often reserved only to those schemata that are empirically testable.

7.3 DETERMINISTIC VERSUS STOCHASTIC THEORY

Unquestionably, much marketing theory uses tendency laws or tendency relationships, for example, "Salesmen tend to be more satisfied with their jobs when they perceive that their immediate supervisor closely directs and monitors their activities." [114, p. 331] It would seem that such relationships are inherently stochastic. Bass has been a proponent of the view that *all* marketing behavior may well be *fundamentally* stochastic:

> Despite growing evidence that individual consumer choice behavior is characterized by substantial randomness, the underlying premise or rationale which guides most of the current research in individual consumer behavior is that, in principle, behavior is caused and can therefore be explained. Thus, works such as those by Howard and Sheth and Engel, Kollat, and Blackwell, however valuable they may have been in providing structure and framework for empirical research, may have misdirected research by implicitly overemphasizing deterministic models of behavior. [46, p. 1]

Nevertheless, over the past 15 years several authors have expressed discomfort at or criticism of the use of stochastic instead of deterministic models as bases for marketing theory [454, p. 5]:

> These models have been and can continue to be useful devices for describing and sometimes predicting consumer behavior, but there are many inherent factors which greatly limit the ability of [stochastic] brand switching models to help develop a theory of consumer behavior.

Is marketing theory *inherently* stochastic? To evaluate this issue requires an exact specification of the characteristics of deterministic theory.[2]

7.3.1   The Nature of Deterministic Theory

Intuitive conceptions of determinism connote some type of certainty—that is, if *A,* then *B, always.* The discussion here will attempt to make this notion more precise. Since the determinism of almost any current marketing theory might be open to dispute, we look to the physical sciences for an instructive example. We will begin, then, by considering Newtonian mechanics as the prototypical example of deterministic theory.

The theory of classical mechanics derives from the three laws promulgated by Newton, which are of strictly universal form. Under these laws, the mechanical state of a particle is completely specified by its position and momentum. Position and momentum are, therefore, the state variables of the theory. For a system of point masses, the mechanical state of the system is given by the mechanical states of all the particles in the system. With this information concerning a system at an arbitrary point in time, we need only specify the force function applying to the system in order to completely, uniquely specify the mechanical state of the system at any future time. *This ability to predict a unique state over time is the essence of the determinism of classical mechanics.* This discussion draws heavily on one by Nagel in his argument against the claimed indeterminacy of quantum mechanics. [464, pp. 277-335]

It is important to note that classical mechanics is deterministic only with respect to the mechanical state of the particle system, that is, its state variables. It says nothing, for example, about the chemical and electromagnetic states, nor does it deal with changes caused by these unspecified factors. *Thus, it is not necessary that a deterministic theory completely specify all aspects of a system.*

Moreover, in classical mechanics the positions and momenta of all particles are assumed to be known precisely at an instant in time. Obviously, in practice such perfect measurements can never be made. This imperfect knowledge of the initial state of the system causes mechanical equations to yield values for variables at a future time that are only approximate, that is, probabilistic. Again, uncertainty due to measurement does not damage the determinism of the theory.

In order to maintain that classical mechanics is a deterministic theory, it is necessary to treat it as an ideal state construct which is approximated in experiments. This is equivalent to stating that,

---

[2] Parts of the following analysis are drawn from Nakamoto and Hunt. [468]

ignoring experimental error, classical mechanics is deterministic because of the logical relationships between statements of the theory. Formally stated, "a theory is deterministic if, and only if, given the values of its state variables for some initial period, the theory logically determines a unique set of values for those variables for any other period." [464, p. 292]

This idea of determinism is quite inclusive. For example, there is no loss of uniqueness in allowing an infinite number of state variables. Furthermore, the state variables might be defined in terms of classes of individuals rather than individuals, for example, in terms of statistical parameters. If the state description of a theory is defined by the values of a set of statistical parameters, and if those parameters can be uniquely specified through the theoretical laws, given their values at some initial time, the theory would be deterministic.

7.3.2   Uncertainty in Explanation

As a prelude to analyzing the sources of uncertainty that lead to indeterminism in theory, we shall explore the sources of uncertainty in scientific explanations. The issues are the same since scientific explanations contain exactly the same kinds of laws and lawlike generalizations as scientific theories. The analysis focuses on deductive-nomological (D-N), deductive-statistical (D-S), and inductive-statistical (I-S) explanations.

All three types of explanation suffer some kinds of uncertainty. However, this does not mean that all of the theories built on all three explanatory models are indeterministic. The definition of deterministic theory denotes uncertainty only in a specific sense. If the logical structure of the theory predicts two or more states of the system at a point in time based on the same initial conditions, this uncertainty with respect to prediction makes the theory indeterminate.

As noted earlier, one result of this restriction is that no form of measurement error affects the determinism of a theory. Such error does not affect the logic of the theory, only the ability of the scientist to test the predictions of the theory. The precision with which these predictions can be confirmed is a problem in determining the empirical adequacy of the theory, that is, its "correctness," a separate problem from that of logical analysis.

Since measurement error is the only form of uncertainty present in a deductive-nomological explanation, theories cast in this form must be deterministic. The explanandum is logically subsumed under the explanans, and the laws, universal in form, are assumed to be consistent. Therefore, the theory cannot predict two inconsistent versions of the explanandum.

In deductive-statistical explanations, the variables of the explanation are statistical parameters. The explanandum is logically subsumed and mathematically derived from the explanans. Given a fairly reasonable set of assumptions, a statistical parameter mathematically derived from another will be uniquely specified. Thus, with respect to statistical variables of state, any theory based on this type of explanatory model will be deterministic.

The deductive form of the explanatory models in the deductive-nomological and deductive-statistical cases guarantees that any theory based on these models will be deterministic. The same reasoning does not apply to inductive-statistical explanations.

As noted earlier, inductive-statistical explanations confer some level of logical probability on the occurrence of the explanandum phenomenon. Conversely, they confer some likelihood of the nonoccurrence of the explanandum as well; that is, both the occurrence and the nonoccurrence of the explanandum are consistent with the truth of the explanans. In light of the definition given above, inductive-statistical explanations are not deterministic.

The preceding discussion is summarized in Table 7-3, which shows the three sources of uncertainty in the three kinds of explanations. The three sources of uncertainty result from (1) errors in measurement, (2) the logical relationships between statements in the explanans and the explanandum, and (3) the inability to predict the occurrence of individual phenomena. D-N explanations are deterministic because the only source of uncertainty arises from measurement error. D-S explanations have both measurement error and uncertainty resulting from their inability to predict the occurrence of individual phenomena. Yet, D-S explanations are deterministic because their explananda (a statistical parameter) are logically subsumed under the explanans. I-S explanations are indeterministic since they contain all three sources of uncertainty.

Table 7-3   Sources of uncertainty in scientific explanation

Type of explanation	Measurement	Prediction	Logical relationship
Deductive-nomological	Yes	No	No
Deductive-statistical	Yes	Yes	No
Inductive-statistical	Yes	Yes	Yes

7.3.3   Determinism and Marketing Theory

The foregoing discussion of the nature of deterministic theory, the relationship of deterministic theory to explanatory models, and the uncertainty inherent in explanation can be used to assess the role of deterministic theory in marketing. Bass [46] has argued that the presence of a stochastic element in consumer behavior makes it impossible to construct deterministic marketing theory. His argument centers on the claim that the stochastic element inherent in the individual actions of consumers makes it impossible to construct laws of universal form. Bass notes that even if this assumption were incorrect, the number of variables affecting consumer behavior might be so large that it would be pragmatically impossible to build deductive-nomological explanations of buyer behavior. Granting the assumption, it is true that it would be impossible to construct a deterministic theory predicting each consumer purchase, that is, deductive-nomological explanations of consumer behavior.

However, one could consider the long-run behavior of consumers toward a product or the behavior of a group of consumers toward a product and construct theories explaining brand loyalty, market share, or other statistical parameters or probabilities. Such theories, predicting particular values for the statistical variables of state, would be deterministic since they would be based on a deductive-statistical paradigm.

Thus, deterministic theory of some type is a legitimate goal of research in marketing. The critical question arising from this discussion is whether deterministic marketing theory is a desirable goal. And, if so, what implications does such a theoretical focus have for the conduct of theory construction and testing? In order to analyze this issue, it is necessary to return to the fundamental motivations for theory development in marketing.

Consider the buying behavior of a consumer. The "ideal" theory of consumer behavior would explain such behavior completely. Regarding a consumer facing a buying decision, the theory would allow one to predict the decision outcome with probability 1.0. Failing this, the theory might predict the outcome of the decision with some high likelihood—for example, "The consumer in this situation will buy with probability .9." This is an inductive-statistical explanation. As noted earlier, most marketing theory to date has been of this type.

Alternatively, by changing the focus of our considerations from one to many decisions, for example, the buying decision of an aggregate of consumers in a particular situation, the theory might predict market share. Depending on the precision of the estimate, the theory could be a deterministic one. Many so-called stochastic models of consumer choice provide exact predictions of such parameters as market share. To the extent that these models have a systematic basis, they represent deterministic theories. Again, the restriction of the determinism might be relaxed and a theory of inductive-statistical form developed to provide a range of estimates with varying probabilities.

The essential notion embodied in the above examples is that deterministic theory is an ideal toward which marketing theory is moving in a natural fashion. The implication is that, from a structural perspective, both the "deterministic" and "stochastic" schools of research in marketing are developing theory whose ultimate objective is deterministic.

7.4   SCIENCE AND OBJECTIVITY

This book has been about marketing science. The word *science* has its origins in the Latin verb *scire,* meaning "to know". Now, there are many ways to know things. The methods of tenacity, authority, faith, intuition, and science are often cited. The characteristic that separates scientific knowledge from other ways to "know" things is the notion of intersubjective certification.

Scientific knowledge, in which theories, laws, and explanations are primal, must be objective in the sense that its truth content must be intersubjectively certifiable. Requiring that theories, laws, and explanations be empirically testable ensures that they will be intersubjectively certifiable since different (but reasonably competent) investigators with differing attitudes, opinions, and beliefs will be able to make observations and conduct experiments to ascertain their truth content. Scientific knowledge thus rests on the bedrock of empirical testability.

Some philosophers of science have vigorously attacked the notion that science differs from astrology and palmistry on the basis that the former is intersubjectively certifiable, whereas the latter two are not. Chief among these attacks are the *Weltanschauungen* (comprehensive interpretation) analyses of Hanson [248], Kuhn [355], and Feyerabend [187]. (See Section 10.2.) The position of these writers at various times has been that science is not an objective enterprise since competing theories cannot be tested against each other. Most of the radical positions of these writers have been repudiated by most modern philosophers of science, leading Suppe [607, p. 634] to conclude, "The *Weltanschauungen* views, in a word, are *passé,* although some of their authors continue to develop them and they continue to be much discussed in the philosophical literature." Although the *Weltanschauungen* views have been rejected in the philosophy of science for several years, these views are now creeping into the marketing literature (often with uncritical acceptance). So, let's examine the "objectivity-comparability" issue.[3]

The attack on the objectivity of science usually proceeds as follows:

1. When there is a shift from one theory to another, the very meanings of the terms shared by the two theories will change.
2. For example, the concept "mass" in Newtonian theory is different from the concept "mass" in Einstein's theory of relativity.

---

[3] Parts of the following analysis are drawn from Levin. [394]

3. Since the meanings of the terms are different, the two theories are not comparable.
4. Since the theories are not comparable, empirical testing cannot provide grounds for accepting one theory over the other.
5. Therefore, the acceptance of one theory over another must be made on nonempirical grounds.
6. Therefore, when scientists engage in empirical testing they are not attempting to determine whether their propositions and theories accurately depict the real world. Rather, the scientists are playing a type of game.

First of all, consider the example in Statement 2. It is true that mass in Newtonian theory is different from mass in Einsteinian theory: In the first case the mass of an object is independent of its velocity, and in the second case mass increases with velocity. But this does not necessarily make the theories incomparable. As a matter of fact, the Newtonian concept of *mass* is exactly the same thing as the Einsteinian concept of *rest mass*. Therefore, the theories are comparable and empirically differentiable since, even though some terms in one theory may have different meanings in the other theory, the terms that have different meanings are expressible in some combination of terms in the other theory. As long as the meanings of all terms in each theory are clearly articulated (a straightforward logical empiricist requirement), the problem of "meaning change" poses no difficulty for empirical testing and the "objectivity" argument falls.

Suppose, however, that the shift from one theory to another theory is so radical that it is *impossible* to translate the terms in one theory into the terms of the other? Levin [394] proposes an extreme illustration: It is impossible to translate the term *angular momentum* into Papuan since there is no possible combination of Papuan terms that has the required properties. Similarly, Priestley theorized that "fire" was the consumption of the substance phlogiston, and there is no equivalent for the word *phlogiston* in modern oxidation theory.

In reply, it *is* possible to translate the term *angular momentum* into Papuan by teaching the Papuan physics from the ground up and introducing each new term one at a time. One might contend that such a procedure would change the language so that it would no longer be "Papuan." This contention would be without merit. In an effort to cleanse the French language of Anglicisms such as *le drugstore*, the French government routinely creates new words and no one seriously contends that the resultant language is not truly French.

The same argument holds for the phlogiston example. Phlogiston can be defined in terms of oxidation theory by the following exercise: "Place exactly one gram of steel in an oven and burn it. Weigh the residue. If the residue weighs less than one gram, refer to the escaped substance as phlogiston." This is precisely the kind of experiment which falsified the phlogiston hypothesis (the residue will weigh more, not less). In short, even if a theory lacks terms that are equivalent to some terms in another theory, there is absolutely no reason to believe that new terms cannot be created to make the theories comparable for empirical testing.

However, continues the argument, even if the problem of meaning shift can be resolved, the entire empirical testing process is *theory-laden*. That is, when one tests a theory, it is the theory itself which directs the investigation as to what kinds of observations to make and what kinds of tests to run. Therefore, the argument goes, the *theory-testing* process cannot be objective. For example, when a theory is tested by regression, it is the theory itself that specifies which variables should be included as independent variables so that the observations are "tainted" by the theory.

The argument that the empirical testing process is theory-laden is curious since it takes the advantages of science and seemingly turns them into disadvantages. A major advantage of science is that it requires its theories to be empirically testable. That is, if theory X proposes that variables A, B, and C are causally related to D, then there must be some way to empirically examine this proposition. To then conclude that the testing process is tainted because the theory tells the researcher to focus attention on variables A, B, and C, is absurd.

Recall the original argument: Science is not objective *because competing theories are not comparable*. Even if we grant that theory X is tainted because it directs us to attempt to explain D by way of A, B, and C, does this mean that theory X is not comparable to theory Y, which suggests that E, F, and G will best explain D? Clearly not—both theory X and theory Y share the same dependent variable, D. In fact, as long as two competing theories share a common set of dependent variables, the two theories are comparable and in principle empirically differentiable. What if the two theories do not share a common set of dependent variables? Then, of course, they are noncompeting and the issue of objectively differentiating between the two by empirical testing neither arises nor should arise.

The final version of the argument: Observations are always interpreted in the context of *a priori* knowledge. As Kuhn [355, p. 113] points out, "What a man sees depends both upon what he looks at and also upon what his previous visual-conceptual experience has taught him to see." Therefore, the very observations used to test theories, not just the *process* of choosing variables, are theory-laden. Since the observations used to test each theory are theory-laden, competing theories are noncomparable. Because of the absence of a theory-neutral observation language, objectivity in science is lost.

There are at least two possible responses to the argument that the absence of a theory-neutral observation language makes competing theories noncomparable and science nonobjective. The first is to simply deny that all of the observation languages used to test theories are theory-laden. That is, this response proposes that most theories can be tested by means of observations that are not contaminated but are theory-neutral. Many philosophers of science hold this view. [394, p. 414]

The second possible response, the one to which this writer subscribes, is to accept the *premise* that all observation is potentially contaminated, whether by our theories or our worldview or our past experiences, but to deny the *conclusion* that science cannot, therefore, objectively choose from among rival theories on the basis of empirical testing. Two issues underlie the reply: (1) What does "theory-laden" really imply? and (2) what does "objectively choose" really mean?

The term *laden* suggests some heavy load, some crushing burden. Therefore, when our observations and measurements are theory-laden, they are contaminated by such a crushing burden of theory that they can no longer function effectively. Can serious observers of science accept such a view? Consider the incredible advances in measurement in the physical sciences in the last 100 years: from measuring time by means of a simple pendulum to measuring it by means of the atomic clock. Perhaps it could be claimed that even the atomic clock is "contaminated" by modern quantum mechanics. Yet, to claim that time measurements via an atomic clock are laden seems disingenuous.

But how about the social sciences? Aren't all measurements in the social sciences theory-laden? Here, admittedly, our response must be more circumspect. The measurement problems of the social sciences are at least different from, if not greater than, the measurement problems of the physical sciences. Intuitively, there seems to be much greater opportunity and likelihood for measures of ego strength, achievement motivation, attitude, and brand loyalty to be laden with the theories and value structures of researchers than for measures of time, velocity, distance and mass to be thus "laden." Nevertheless, even the most casual observer of the social sciences would have to admit that the last 30 years have brought about enormous improvements in the measurement of social science constructs. Standardized measures with demonstrated construct validity and reliability are becoming commonplace. There are grounds for optimism concerning continuing progress in developing better measures and, certainly, no grounds for the nihilism implicit in the claim that social science measures are so laden that they cease to function in their role of assisting us in objectively differentiating among competing theories on an empirical basis.

Lastly, what does "objectively choose" really mean in the claim that observations are so theory-laden that we cannot *objectively choose* from among competing theories? Unfortunately, supporters of the value-laden thesis seem to confuse "objectively choose" with "choose with certainty" and, thus, commit the "philosophers' fallacy of high redefinition" (see Section 9.6.2). Obviously, if objectivity requires that the choice between rival theories be made with certainty (no possibility for error), then science is not objective. But such a construal of the concept of objectivity would be exactly the opposite of the essence of knowledge claims in science. In science, all knowledge claims are tentative, subject to revision on the basis of new evidence. The concept "certainty" belongs to theology, not science.

In conclusion, are knowledge claims based on intuition, authority, theology, faith, astrology, and palmistry to be placed on an equal epistemological footing with the knowledge claims of science? Are all of these areas equally objective/nonobjective? Clearly, the answer must be no. Does science make mistakes? Of course—science does not even pretend to be infallible. However, science is the most, if not the only, objective game in town.

7.5   FINAL NOTE TO PART I

Unfortunately, much of the so-called theory in marketing falls substantially short of fulfilling the requirements detailed in this monograph. Substantial evidence exists which suggests that the shortcomings of marketing theory can be attributed in large measure to misperceptions by marketing theorists as to the fundamental nature of theoretical constructions. It is the modest hope of this writer that the preceding analysis can play a constructive role in assisting theorists in their efforts to develop theory in marketing. The task of theory development is arduous, but the rewards are commensurate with the challenge.

The philosophy of science tool kit that has been presented in Part I of this monograph provides the theoretical analyst with a set of powerful instruments for analyzing theoretical and purportedly theoretical constructions in marketing. The evaluative criteria that have been developed are stringent. Therefore, a caveat for the would-be theoretical analyst: It is much easier to criticize someone else's theory than it is to develop one's own. Be constructive, not destructive, in your analysis. Finally, a note to existing and would-be marketing theorists. Obtuse armchair philosophy does not constitute theory. Keep in mind that your theory must contain a systematically related set of statements, including some lawlike generalizations, that is empirically testable. And that the purpose of developing your theory is to increase scientific understanding through a systematized structure capable of explaining and predicting marketing phenomena.

QUESTIONS FOR ANALYSIS AND DISCUSSION

1. Evaluate the classificational schema discussed in Chapter 1 which used the three dichotomies of profit/nonprofit, micro/macro, and positive/normative to classify issues in marketing. Would the schema be a useful pedagogical tool? How well does it satisfy our criteria for classificational schemata?

2. Distinguish between normative and positive theory. Is price theory normative or positive? Is it appropriate for economists to use price theory to recommend that General Motors be broken up?

3. How would you classify (i.e., as a theory, law, definition, etc.) the statement "Effort in marketing takes two primary forms—either sorting or transformation"? [10, p. 49] Why?

4. Differentiate between *normative* theory and *positive* theory. Must the development of positive theory necessarily precede the development of normative theory? Do all normative theories rest upon an essentially positive base?

5. Someone has said, "We should always carefully distinguish between developing criteria for evaluating what constitutes a theory and developing criteria for evaluating what constitutes a good theory." Are these really two different notions? Could any single criterion be used for both purposes?

6. Halbert suggests a very normative approach to theory:

   > A theory, then, must include an explanation of its own uses, that is, how one can make decisions with it. Thus, a theory exists for a set of phenomena when all the possible decisions to be made involving those phenomena can be explained. These explanations must fit all possible individuals who make these decisions, and the fitting must be satisfactory to the theorist. [243, p. 5]

   Would a physicist agree with Halbert? Evaluate Halbert's position.

7. Sauer, Nighswonger, and Zaltman [557] observe that marketing research seems to be moving "away from issues of substantive significance" and toward issues of narrow technological significance. Do you agree or disagree? To what extent could the tenets of logical empiricism be a causal factor in this shift? Do you believe they *have* been a causal factor?

8. What is the difference between *science* and the *philosophy of science?* Sauer, Nighswonger, and Zaltman [557] contend that logical empiricism includes the idea that "the primary focus of *scientific* effort should be placed on the testing of hypotheses (justification) rather than their discovery." Do you agree with their contention?

9. Sauer, Nighswonger, and Zaltman [557] propose that two of the central tenets of logical empiricism are: (1) that concepts (theory) must be connected with observation by logical operations and (2) that explanation and prediction are basically the same, and thus all propositions should be testable. Do you agree that logical empiricism has these two central tenets? What would be the consequences of having a "science" with the following two tenets: (1) it is unnecessary for our theories to be connected with the real world; and (2) it is unnecessary to have the propositions be derived from our theories be capable of empirical testing?

10. One commentator on Olson's 1981 A.C.R. presidential address [480] lamented as follows:

    > I am confused. First, Olson attacked my research because I test a theory against the "null hypothesis" straw man. He wants me to test two competing theories against each other. Good grief! It's difficult enough to find one theory to test, let alone competing theories. Anyway, I find it curious that Olson rejects logical empiricism and then

says we should test competing theories. What he is asking for is nothing more than the old "crucial tests," a cornerstone of the very logical empiricism that Olson says has been one of the major problems of consumer behavior research.

Evaluate.

11. "The ultimate issue in the justification/discovery controversy was never whether there was a difference between the context of justification and the context of discovery. Rather, the controversy was really over the domain of the philosophy of science. In this respect the controversy is very similar to the broadening of the concept of marketing debate in the early 1970s. The philosophy of science discipline, like the marketing discipline, took an imperialistic turn in the early 1970s." Evaluate.

12. Brodbeck [82] contends that the meaning of some terms or concepts and the truth of some sentences do not depend upon the meaning or truth of other terms or sentences. Otherwise we would be faced with a "vicious regress" in which language is a self-contained system with no contact with the world it is presumably about. Evaluate.

13. Brodbeck [82] proposes that a statement is meaningful if we know to what its descriptive terms refer and can therefore directly or indirectly determine by experience whether the statement is true or false. Meaning precedes verification or confirmation. This is not a verification theory of meaning. Brodbeck contends that a statement is verifiable because it is meaningful, not vice versa. Evaluate this position.

14. In evaluating the logical empiricist approach to science, J. Paul Peter agrees with the criticisms of Suppe.[607]. One of Suppe's criticisms is that "there is no natural division between observable and nonobservable terms." [607, p. 83] That is, the original logical empiricist position was that there was a reasonably sharp distinction between empirically observable concepts and theoretical concepts. Many philosophers of science now propose that there are no *purely* observable concepts: All concepts have a significant amount of theoretical content.   Peter then proposes that, "although one could digress through a seemingly endless number of *internal constructs* which are assumed to be causes of behavior, eventually one would have to resort to something outside the individual as the cause of the internal process and hence the behavior" (emphasis added). [in 306a, p. 386] What are "internal constructs"? How do they differ from "theoretical constructs"? Is it possible to argue that the distinction between theoretical constructs and observable constructs is untenable because all "observable constructs" have a theoretical content, and then to argue that all "internal constructs" should be avoided?

15. J. Paul Peter proposes that "positivism focuses on the verifiability of theories, whereas falsification may be more accepted in consumer research." [in 306a, p. 384] What is verifiability? What is falsification? Is it necessary to *choose* between these procedures in science?

16. J. Paul Peter concludes that "to the degree that academic consumer research does have an impact on the distribution of wealth in ways which are not in the best interest of society, serious consideration should be given to whether scientific or societal goals take precedence." He continues: "One fruitful area for future *academic* consumer research would be to develop normative or ideal

systems of consumer, business, and government interactions which would better serve society and to investigate how such systems could be implemented." Evaluate.

17. What is the relevance of the headnote at the beginning of this chapter to the issues discussed in Section 7.4?

18. In advocating the use of historicism, Anderson in the panel discussion at the 1982 Theory Conference [99] proposed the following:

> Basically, what this means [historicism] is that philosophers and sociologists of science have decided to look at actual science and to test the norms that they derive for scientific processes against the actual history of science. It seems a reasonable thing to do. If I'm going to suggest to you that I have a scientific method, then I ought to be able to state that I have taken these norms, I have put them up against what we could consider to be exemplary episodes in the actual history of science, and I have demonstrated that these norms were followed. In fact, these are the norms which caused science to progress.

What is a "norm" of science? How could one "test" a norm of science? Evaluate Anderson's proposition that the norms of science, as developed by philosophers of science (or others, presumably), should be tested by placing "them up against what we could consider to be exemplary episodes in the actual history of science." How would one separate the "exemplary" episodes from the "nonexemplary" variety?

19. Anderson [99] also posed what he considered to be the "real question" of science and the "job" of scientists.

> Basically, I think that the work in the past 20 years in the history, sociology, and philosophy of science has shown us that the process of science is a consensus generation process. The real question is: "How can I convince my colleagues in the scientific community that my theory is correct?"
>
> Latour and Woolgar, for example, conceptualize the scientific process as a kind of investment activity—we all invest in credibility. Our background knowledge, the theories that we are committed to, the facts that we take as given, are the investments that we make. Our job as scientists is to enhance that credibility to reinvest our credibility capital, and to advance our own status within the field.

Is the "real question" the one that Anderson suggests? Ought it to be a real question? Why? If you disagree with Anderson, then what is or ought to be, the real question? If a scientist adopts Anderson's real question, how well could he or she perform the "job" of enhancing credibility? What would be the consequences for society if science in general agreed with Anderson and adopted his concept of the real question and job of science? How would society view science? What would be the consequences for science and the scientific community?

20. Lutz [99] in the panel discussion advocated historicism focusing on the behaviors of scientists:

> Most of us ascribe to the notion that, in the behavioral sciences, description precedes explanation of behavior, which in turn permits prescriptions regarding appropriate behavior. Historicism is the only

school of thought which seemingly follows the same logic in deriving its prescriptions for appropriate conduct of scientific inquiry; hence, I believe that some form of historicism (or any other approach which relies on the description and explanation of scientists' behaviors as the basic input to prescriptions) is most likely to prove fruitful in the long run.

What kinds of *behaviors* did Lutz have in mind? How could the *description* of these behaviors lead to the *prescription* of "appropriate conduct of scientific inquiry?" What would be the norms for determining which behaviors were appropriate? If the subject matter of the philosophy of science is the behaviors of scientists, is the philosophy of science a behavioral science? Ought it to be?

21. Anderson [99] in the panel discussion argued that sociological criteria play a role in scientific knowledge:

> But I think we would be closing our eyes to the evidence that has been developed in the history and the sociology of science if we didn't also recognize that sociological criteria play an important role in the actual construction of knowledge, things like the conjunction of a particular theory with professional interests—even class interests (if you can believe that some of the sociologists will go that far). The social acceptability of the results plays an important role in determining the kinds of theories that scientists are willing to propose and the kinds of theories that scientists are willing to defend.

Do factors such as "class interests" play a role in scientific knowledge? Should they? Evaluate.

22. Olson [99] in the panel discussion presents his philosophy of research:

> Some people—realists—believe in an objectively knowable world that exists independently of themselves. If you believe this, it will lead you to certain kinds of methods and research issues (such as logical empiricism). If you don't believe in an independent reality (or for purposes of doing science, you pretend that you don't believe in that), then your idealistic perspective will probably lead you in entirely different directions. Your philosophy and approach to research will be different from the "realists." Even the issues you select for study may be different. Since I believe in the latter perspective, I guess I am a relativist.
>
> This point of view leads us to recognize that there is no one "right way" to do science. I think Feyerabend is correct in suggesting that no rule, no prescriptive method, will ensure success. However, this doesn't mean that there are no rules whatsoever. Instead, we can consider that certain methods and rules may be appropriate and useful in certain circumstances, but as circumstances change (e.g., the theory develops or measurement techniques improve), different rules may be required. There are rules—many of them—but no single rule applies universally.

Brodbeck discusses hers:

> In one sense, method means the various techniques of laboratory research, experimental research, field observation, or just observing how people behave. There are as many different kinds of methods

as there are sciences, and within sciences there are different kinds of methods. In that sense, there is no unitary method. Another sense of method regards the principles (you might call it methodology or what I call the philosophy of science), in which we talk about what the criteria are that we use in order to introduce concepts. What are the criteria for a good, meaningful concept? What are the criteria we use for acceptance or rejection of a hypothesis? How do we go about theory construction, and how do we validate or justify a theory? I tend to use that sense of method measuring broad general principles. I am an empiricist, and I think all sciences, if they are to be sciences, are empirical; that is, they recognize that concepts have to have a relationship with reality. We have to be able to tell whether what we say is true or false. We try to test hypotheses by means of observations, directly or indirectly, and as our ambition grows, we try to develop theories of wider and wider scope that will explain more and more phenomena. In that sense, I think all sciences are alike.

What are the major issues Olson and Brodbeck are discussing? Evaluate their respective positions.

PART 2

THE PHILOSOPHY

OF SCIENCE:

HISTORICAL

PERSPECTIVES,

CURRENT STATUS,

AND IMPLICATIONS

FOR MARKETING

INTRODUCTION

Formal marketing education began in the United States in 1902 when the University of Michigan offered a course entitled "The Distributive and Regulative Industries of the United States," taught by Professor E. D. Jones. The beginning of marketing's formal literature is often ascribed to Arch W. Shaw and his 1912 article entitled "Some Problems in Market Distribution." The institutionalization of marketing took place in 1937 with the formation of the American Marketing Association. As formal marketing education enters its tenth decade, our formal literature its ninth, and our major professional association, its seventh, we find many marketing scholars posing significant and fundamental questions for the marketing discipline. Many of these questions concern the nature of research conducted by the marketing academic community. Almost everyone seems to believe that there are many problems and deficiencies in marketing research, but the list of problems and their proposed "solutions," vary tremendously.

Many critics of contemporary marketing research contend that it is "too." It is *too* quantitative, managerial, parochial, empirical, trivial, research methods-oriented, or "numbers crunching" oriented. Such critics emphatically claim that marketing research should be "more." It should be *more* theoretical, interesting, provocative, dialectical, critical, Marxist-oriented, creative, or international. Although critics certainly do not speak with a single voice, many believe that the cause of all the ills of marketing research is that it is "dominated" by either logical positivism or logical empiricism. Some even contend that marketing is "imprisoned" by these philosophical "isms." [22] Again, although critics have no single solution to the deficiencies of marketing research, many propose that marketing should "adopt." It should *adopt* qualitative research methods, historical methods, case studies, relativism, constructivism, naturalistic methods, humanistic methods, or interpretive techniques.

As a result of the criticisms directed at contemporary marketing research, many writers have begun to debate numerous fundamental questions concerning the marketing discipline, marketing research, and marketing science. In particular, the following fundamental questions are, either explicitly or implicitly, often discussed:

1. What is the long-range goal or mission of marketing research? What should it be?
2. What are the short-range specific objectives of marketing research? What should they be?
3. Who are the clients, or constituencies, of marketing research? Who should they be?
4. What are the most appropriate methods of inquiry for marketing research? What should they be?
5. What are our beliefs about the nature of reality in marketing research? What should they be?
6. What are our procedures for justifying knowledge-claims in marketing research? What should they be?
7. Is marketing research objective? Should it be?
8. Is marketing research cumulative? Should it be?
9. Is marketing research rational? Should it be?
10. Is marketing research just an academic "game"? Should it be?
11. Is knowledge in marketing research "constructed," rather than "discovered"? Should it be?
12. Are rival knowledge-claims in marketing research evaluated objectively, neutrally, or non-arbitrarily? Should they be?

As a point of departure for addressing the preceding questions, many writers have turned to the philosophy of science literature. And this is as it should be. For over two thousand years both philosophy in general and philosophy of science in particular have been developing "isms," or perspectives, on these kinds of questions. Among others, these "isms" include: Platonism, classical empiricism, classical rationalism, idealism, classical positivism, classical realism, pragmatism, logical positivism, logical empiricism, critical rationalism, falsificationism, historicism, relativism, constructivism, instrumentalism, and scientific realism (see Part II, Figure 1). All these "isms" address the many "ogies" of science, including: methodology (the study of procedures in inquiry), ontology (the study of "being"), and epistemology (the study of how we "know").

Marketing has certainly not been alone in asking these kinds of questions and searching the philosophy of science literature for answers. Extensive discussions throughout the social sciences parallel the debates in marketing. For example, Shweder and Fiske, in an article entitled "Uneasy Social Science," note the following paradox throughout all social science: Many individual researchers believe that "progress is being made on the problem on which I am working," while at the same time they have "a vague sense of unease about the overall rate of progress of their discipline." [579, p. 1] Moreover, several critics of contemporary social science are beginning to question whether "progress" is possible and, as a result, have developed what is called the "crisis literature." Most interestingly, Shweder and Fiske point out four common reactions of many in the social sciences to this "crisis literature," and these reactions have been much the same in marketing.

The first and perhaps most common reaction to the crisis literature has been one of extreme indifference: "Most practicing social scientists do not want to be bothered by the crisis literature in the social sciences or worry about abstract formulations about the possibility of a social science." [579, p. 2] So it is in marketing. It is always distressing to the participants in any disciplinary debate to find out that many of their colleagues are sublimely indifferent to the issues in question. However, marketing has become a very broad discipline with a radically heterogeneous literature and many marketers are content to focus exclusively on, say, mathematical modeling of promotion decisions. Therefore, believing (probably incorrectly) that the issues in the crisis literature do not affect them personally, they have a "ho hum" reaction. Such a reaction is easy to understand, according to Shweder and Fiske, because "the gloom-and-doom message that sometimes emerges in the crisis literature is not that difficult to oppose." [579, p. 3]

A second reaction to the crisis literature is supreme joy and elation. Some academicians see themselves as participating in glorious revolutions that will overthrow "the establishment," establish new agendas for their disciplines, and turn them in directions more consistent with their philosophical beliefs. Therefore, such individuals are busily engaged within their disciplines in various political activities to ensure the success of their revolutions.

A third reaction to the crisis literature is one of a mixture of fear and dismay. Some academicians look with dismay at the level of the debate, believing the discussions to be misguided, shallow, or factually in error. They fear the (explicit or implicit) skepticism, relativism, and irrationalism that often overwhelm attempts at rational discussion in the debate.

A fourth and final reaction to the crisis literature is a sense of bewilderment. Many academicians simply do not *understand* the debate. They perceive the participants to be talking in such strange language that they find it difficult to separate genuine, substantive issues from purely semantical ones. One bewildered marketing academician turned to me at a recent conference and said: "Over the last two days I have heard people use the term 'paradigm' in at least eight different ways. How am I supposed to understand what is going on here?" Similarly, many of the debates in the crisis literature seem to have degenerated into *ad hominem* and "name-calling." Consider the label "positivist." Phillips [497a] has chronicled the ongoing diatribe being conducted by a host of writers against contemporary social science. In a section of his book entitled "Rampant Anti-Positivism," he concludes:

> There have been many exaggerated claims about the evils of positivism, and about the beneficial effects of its demise. . . . First, many

Part II Figure 1 Philosophy of Science Time Chart

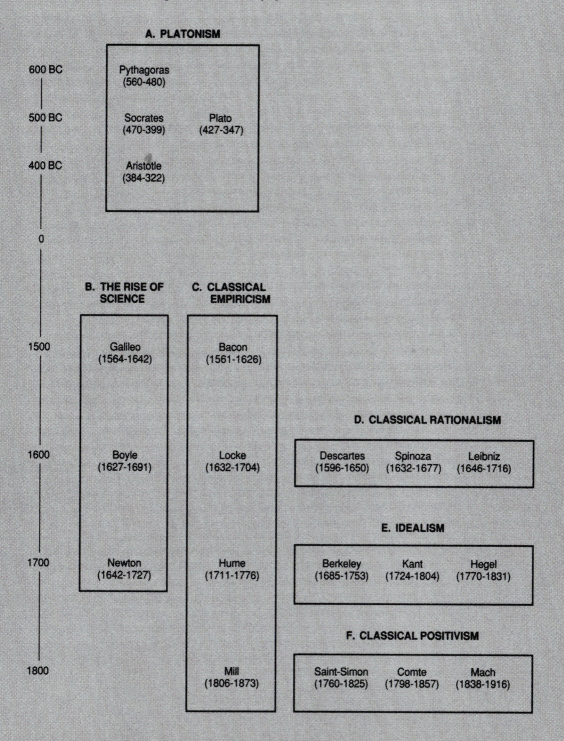

Part II Figure 1   Philosophy of Science Time Chart

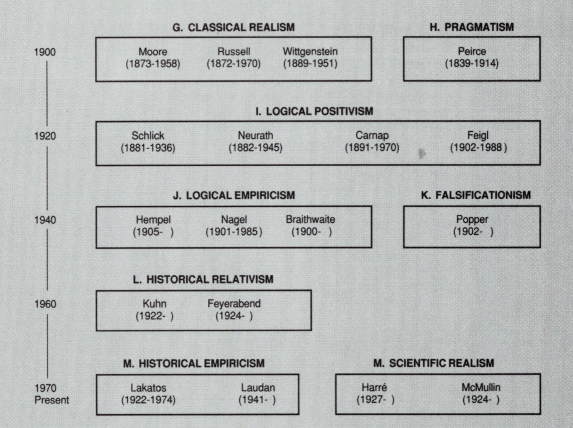

factual errors are made when researchers refer to positivism. Indeed, without suggesting that those who make the errors are dishonest, it seems as if the word "positivism" arouses such negative feelings that it is often used in a blanket way to condemn any position at all that the writer in question disagrees with, irrespective of how positivistic that position really is...[For example,] there is nothing in the doctrines of positivism that necessitates a love of statistics or a distaste for case studies. [497a, pp. 94 and 96]

In addition to sinking to the level of simple name-calling, many of the discussions in the crisis literature are factually ill-informed about the nature of the various "isms" in the philosophy of science. For example, Phillips notes that "some of the most boisterous celebrants at positivism's wake are actually more positivistic than they realize, or have more in common with the positivists than they would care to admit." [497a, p. 44]

It is fair to say that the crisis literature in the marketing discipline has been no better informed about the various "isms" in the philosophy of science than the social sciences in general. For example, Sheth, Gardner, and Garrett do an exemplary job of describing and evaluating twelve major "schools of thought" in marketing. [577] However, in a section entitled "Is Marketing a Science or, at Best, a Standardized Art?" they discuss the "vigorous debate" that "is currently raging in marketing regarding metatheoretical criteria." They claim, "while some notable scholars, led by Shelby Hunt, maintain that *logical positivism* is the proper foundation for theory development, another growing group, led by Paul Anderson, has recently begun to argue that marketing theory should be judged with relativistic criteria." [577, pp. 184-5] Thus, Sheth, Gardner, and Garrett (quite unintentionally) confuse logical positivism with modern empiricism. Although both logical positivism and modern empiricism are opposed to relativism, the differences between logical positivism and modern empiricism (as we shall see) are great. Much more importantly, informed discussion about the most appropriate philosophy for marketing science will be impossible as long as all those who oppose relativism are lumped together under the, highly misleading, label of "positivist."

Our mission in Part II of this book shall be to raise the debate in the crisis literature in marketing to a more informed level. When I originally planned this part of the book, I intended to restrict the discussion to the fundamental tenets of logical positivism, logical empiricism, historical relativism, historical empiricism, and scientific realism. However, I found it very difficult to explain these various "isms" without at least briefly discussing classical realism and Hegelian idealism. Unfortunately, I could find no way to enable the reader to comprehend Hegelian idealism without discussing classical rationalism and classical empiricism. At last, I recognized that I might as well start at "the beginning" of philosophy, i.e., Platonism.

The next four chapters will chronicle the history of the philosophy of science from the time of Plato to the present. I have taken extraordinary measures in the two-year research project that led to these chapters to make them as historically accurate as possible. Obviously, however, these four short chapters omit much detail. I sincerely urge all readers to take advantage of the numerous references throughout the chapters to study each of the various topics in greater depth. At the very least, those readers who, heretofore, have been "bewildered" about the crisis literature should be able to understand the debate after reviewing its history. Hopefully, some may even choose to participate. To all, I say, welcome!

8

NATURAL PHILOSOPHY AND THE RISE OF SCIENCE: FROM PLATO TO HEGEL

The need for justifying rationality arises out of the context of a longstanding conflict between faith and reason. Some defenders of faith contend that in the last analysis no belief or action can be rationally justified. They argue that the standards upon which the supposed justifications rest do, themselves, need justification. But this justification cannot be provided because the processes of justifying one standard by another must lead either to infinite regress, or to nonrational commitment to some standard. Opposed to this is the view to be defended here: that the rational justification of beliefs and actions is possible.

If it were true that nothing could be justified by reason, then all honestly held convictions would have an equal claim upon general acceptance, and argument would, indeed, be replaced by "passionate intensity." This would be a dangerous and undesirable situation, for the inevitable conflicts could then be settled only by force. The civilizing restraint of debate and criticism would disappear. If rationality is abandoned, then either "anarchy is loosed upon the world," or dogmatism supported by brute force would prevail.

John Kekes

This chapter traces the history of the philosophy of science and the scientific method from its Grecian origins with Platonism to the latter part of the 19th century and the triumph of German idealism. Figure 1 shows the various "isms" to be discussed. As we shall see, philosophy and science were "one" throughout most of this 2500-year period. Furthermore, we shall see that many of the current debates in marketing and the social sciences were argued (perhaps better) in Plato's time. Thus, we begin with Platonism.

8.1   PLATONISM

Any history of the philosophy of science (at least, Western philosophy of science) must begin with the ancient Greeks.[1] Indeed, the very word "philosophy" comes from the two Greek words *philo*, meaning "love," and *sophia*, meaning "wisdom." Therefore, the term "philosophy" has its origins in the "love of wisdom." However, *sophia* in ancient Greek had a slightly different meaning than the English "wisdom." *Sophia*, when combined with *philo*, actually connoted something closer to the "love of intellectual curiosity" than to the love of wisdom in the sense of "sage" philosophy (see Section 8.1.2).

8.1.1   Pythagoras

Although Thales of Miletus, founder of the Ionian school of philosophy in about 580 B.C., is often referred to as the "father of philosophy," little about him is known. Therefore, our study begins with Pythagoras (570-520 B.C.) who was the first scholar to actually refer to himself as a "philosopher." [242] Much of what we know about Pythagoras comes from Plato. We know that Pythagoras founded a school of scholars in southern Italy that required all members to take vows of secrecy. The school taught its members to spurn such things as fame and worldly possessions and to focus, instead, on seeking "truth by contemplation."

The Pythagoreans made significant contributions to the development of mathematics. In fact, they believed that numerals had an almost mystical significance and were the keys to understanding the universe. Even today, when one speaks of a philosopher as having a "Pythagorean orientation," one implies that the person believes there is a "mathematical harmony" present in nature. Thus, the 16th century astronomer Kepler believed that God had created the solar system in a regular mathematical pattern, and Kepler "explained" the internal radii of each of the six planets (known at that time) by showing that within each planet would fit just one of the five "regular" solids. For example, a regular cube fits within the sphere of Saturn, a tetrahedron within Jupiter, a dodecahedron within Mars, and so on in a "nest." [400, p.46] To the Pythagoreans, experience and observation played an inconsequential role in inquiry.

---

[1]For an introduction to Eastern science and philosophy of science, see Snyder, especially Chapter Six. [596]

8.1.2   Plato

The philosophy of Plato (427-347 B.C.) was very consistent with that of Pythagoras. The historian, John Losee, notes that "Plato described the creation of the universe by a benevolent Demiurge, who impressed a mathematical pattern upon a formless primordial matter." [400, p. 18] Plato's significance to Western philosophy cannot be overemphasized. Plato defined knowledge as "justified true belief," and for him, the method of "truth by contemplation" (in the manner of Pythagoras) fell far short of the goal. Rather, true philosophical wisdom, according to Plato, must pass the "test of critical discussion." That is, truth will reveal itself through the Socratic method of vigorously critical questions and equally thoughtful answers (the Socratic dialogues). In Plato's Greece, these dialogues or debates had formal rules governing permissible conduct for both questioner and answerer. Furthermore, critical discussion through the Socratic method was to be conducted for the purpose of the pursuit of truth, in contrast to the Sophists who, Plato claimed, were interested solely in the pursuit of victory in argument.

In essence, Plato's views on the nature of philosophy (the pursuit of truth) and its method (critical discussion) have dominated the Western philosophical world for over two thousand years. As Popper noted in his classic work, *The Logic of Scientific Discovery,* "there is a method which might be described as 'the one method of philosophy'. . .*rational discussion . . .* stating one's problem clearly and examining its various proposed solutions *critically.*" [503 p. 16 (emphasis in original)]

Recall that the meaning of *sophia* in ancient Greek was closer to "intellectual curiosity" than the English "wisdom." It is worth noting that Eastern philosophy, instead of adopting a critical discussion method, developed along "sage" lines. [53] In sage philosophy, true knowledge is to be obtained by studying and interpreting the pronouncements of the master, or "sage." If there is to be critical discussion in sage philosophy, it is on how to most appropriately interpret the truths of the master. Sage philosophy, by its very nature, cannot be cumulative or progressive, since the knowledge of the student cannot go beyond that of the master. Also, it has the distressing tendency to deteriorate into cultism or mysticism. The dominance of truth-through-critical-discussion in Western philosophy, in contrast to the dominance of sage philosophy in the East, is one reason why science became institutionalized in 17th century Europe, rather than countries such as China and Russia. [53, p.28] We shall return to the subject of the institutionalization of science in 17th century Europe in Section 8.2.

Plato's philosophical inquiry focused on issues such as the nature of justice, human pleasure, values, politics, and ethics. He did not delve into topics that would normally be included today within the natural or physical sciences. Nevertheless, one of his most controversial theories, the "theory of forms," has implications for science. Enamored with the abstract nature of mathematics and numerals, Plato theorized that there was an independent realm of "forms" (abstract ideas or essences) that had a real existence outside space and time. These "forms," he theorized, had an ultimate reality independent from being perceived by any human mind. The objects that we perceive through our senses are just imperfect copies of these ultimate forms. For example, there is an ultimate "form" called "man" that exists in some autonomous realm. Individual men in the perceived world are simply "imperfect copies" of this ultimate form. Given that knowledge is "justified true belief" and that objects in the external world are only imperfect copies of these perfect forms, *genuine* knowledge was possible only about Plato's idealized "forms" and not about the existing world as revealed by our senses. Today, we may note, the modern relativist/constructionist view claims that scientists "construct" the idealized "reality" they seek to explain. [492, 481] Since Plato's idealized "forms" were *independent* of the human mind, his theory was very different from the modern relativist/constructivist view, but both share the common element called "idealism" (see Section 8.4).

8.1.3   Socrates on Relativism

The position that truth could be gleaned from critical discussion earned Plato the enmity of the Sophists, who had a relativist conception of truth that differs very little from the versions of our modern-day relativists. Protagoras of Abdera was a Sophist who earned his livelihood by going from city to city in the Greek world offering instruction to the young on rhetoric and politics. In *Theaetetus*, Plato presents a dialogue between Protagoras and Socrates that analyzes and evaluates the notion of "relativist truth" that Protagoras put forward. According to the dialogue, Protagoras held that:

> Man is the measure of all things ... [and that any given thing] is to me such as it appears to me, and is to you such as it appears to you ... [Then] each one of us is a measure of what is and what is not ... to the sick man his food appears sour and is so; to the healthy man it is and appears the opposite. Now there is no call to represent either of the two as wiser—that cannot be—nor is the sick man to be pronounced unwise because he thinks as he does, or the healthy man wise because he thinks differently ... in this way it is true ... that no one thinks falsely. [246, pp. 152a, 160c, 166d, 167d, and 170a]

Following Siegel [586], the relativism proposed by Protagoras "denies the existence of any standard or criterion higher than the individual by which claims to truth and knowledge can be adjudicated," since "knowledge and truth are relative to the person contemplating the proposition in question." [586, p. 226] For Protagoras a proposition is true if it seems so to the observer; and false, if it so seems to the observer, and "that is the end of that."   Socrates attacks relativism through several arguments, including:

> If what every man believes as a result of perception is indeed to be true for him; if, just as no one is to a better judge of what another experiences, so no one is better entitled to consider whether what another thinks is true or false, and . . . every man is to have his own beliefs for himself alone and they are all right and true—then . . .where is the wisdom of Protagoras, to justify his setting up to teach others and to be handsomely paid for it, and where is our comparative ignorance or the need for us to go and sit at his feet, when each of us is himself the measure of his own wisdom?. . .To set about overhauling and testing one another's notions and opinions when those of each and every one are right, is a tedious and monstrous display of folly, if the Truth of Protagoras is really truthful. [246, p. 162a]

Thus, Socrates contends that Protagorean relativism is self-defeating, making it incoherent (the various claims are inconsistent). Siegel [586, p.226] paraphrases the argument of Socrates in the following succinct fashion:

1. Protagoras claims to show his students how to assess the warrant and justification of knowledge-claims ("overhauling and testing one another's notions and opinions").
2. The thesis of Protagoras (that "man is the measure of all things") undermines the task Protagoras sets out to do since, if his thesis is correct, no proposition can ever be judged unjustified or unwarranted.
3. Consequently, if knowledge is relative, then it is useless to ever engage in the task that Protagoras is engaging in ("overhauling and testing one another's notions and opinions").
4. Therefore, "if Protagoras' thesis is right, it cannot be right, for it undermines the very notion of rightness."

Although Plato may have thought that the various arguments in *Theaetetus* conclusively destroyed the doctrine of relativist truth, in hindsight we know that such was not to be the case. Nevertheless, both Siegel [586] and other writers maintain that the arguments of Socrates are as powerful and definitive now as they were in the time of Plato. For example, Vallicella (following Socrates) notes that a "consistent relativist, on pain of contradiction, must hold that the thesis of relativism is itself only relatively true." [622, p. 462] That is, a consistent relativist cannot hold that *it is absolutely true* that "all truths are relative (to social classes, historical epochs, whatever)." Therefore, a consistent relativist must hold that "it is *relatively true* that all truths are relative." But what does it mean to say that "it is relatively true that all truths are relative?" Such a statement is highly ambiguous and quickly degenerates into incoherent assertions like "it is true that for everyone (for every class, epoch, group) that all truths are relative" or that "*it is only true for relativists* that all truths are relative." Vallicella closes with "we must conclude, then, that relativized relativism is just as incoherent as absolute relativism." [622, p. 463]

As an aside, analysts of *ethical* relativism have also questioned whether a coherent (i.e., not self-refuting) version of *it* is possible. Lyons analyzes the various forms of ethical relativism and concludes: "The only clear reason that we seem to have for resorting to relativistic analyses of moral judgments is that this will save the vulnerable forms of relativism from the scrap heaps of incoherence. As I suggested earlier, a theory that avoids incoherence by arbitrary modifications, that lacks independent theoretical justification, cannot command our respect." [408, p. 224] (See Section 10.1.1 for more on moral relativism.)

The version of relativism advocated in marketing by Anderson, "critical relativism," has been found also to be self-refuting. Siegel examines critical relativism and notes that "we can be *critical* relativists only if we can utilize standards to evaluate the claims, beliefs, standards, and methods of others and ourselves. If we can so utilize standards, we give up relativism, because we commit ourselves to standards that can be appropriately appealed to in the assessment of disciplinary knowledge claims." [587, p. 130] Briefly, Siegel is claiming (as Calder and Tybout have pointed out [102a, p. 203]) "critical relativism" is an oxymoron. That is, to be relativistic implies that there are no standards of appraisal across theories, or paradigms, or whatever: "[T]ruth is a subjective evaluation that cannot be properly inferred outside of the context provided by the theory." [492, p. 119] On the other hand, if one is to be "critical" of a theory, paradigm, or whatever, one must either restrict oneself solely to the appraisal criteria within that theory or paradigm, or *necessarily* commit oneself to appraisal criteria that transcend the theory or paradigm.

Anderson defends his critical relativism from these charges by pointing out that " 'truth' plays no role in the ontology of critical relativism." Rather, "it is a relativism with respect to an axiology that lies at the heart of critical relativism." [16, p. 134] Here, "axiology" refers to the goals and aims of a particular research program. We shall return to this issue later in Section 11.3.4. For now, however, we might note that when one appraises the axiology or aims of a research program, one will normally make some putative knowledge-claims like: This research program can (cannot), or probably will (will not), achieve (or come close to achieving) its goals and aims. However, such knowledge-claims would have to be justified by good reasons, and such reasons would seem to *necessarily* transcend the research program a person is evaluating. In other words, critical relativism attempts to give warrant for people to believe its knowledge-claims, and therefore, it seems to just avoid the word "truth," not its substantive content. Since we will extensively discuss these issues in Chapters 10 and 11 (see, especially 11.3.4), we will now return to our historical narrative.

8.1.4   Aristotle

Plato's greatest student was undoubtedly Aristotle (384-322 B.C.). Whereas Plato restricted the study of philosophy to a narrow range of topics, Aristotle expanded philosophical inquiry into the study of virtually everything. Not only did he study and write on such topics as ethics, politics, rhetoric, and metaphysics, but also on areas such as astronomy, physics, zoology, psychology, and the formal nature of logic. [53, p. xvi] Thus, Aristotle added the study of all the elements of "natural philosophy" to the traditional subjects of moral philosophy, political philosophy, and metaphysics. Stated differently, Aristotle expanded philosophy to include what we now call *science*. In fact, the English word "science" was coined in the latter half of the 19th century. Prior to that time the closest English word to "scientist" was "natural philosopher." [53, p. xii]

Aristotle disagreed vigorously with Plato's theory of forms. In today's terms, Aristotle was both an *empiricist* and a *realist*. Plato's extreme distrust of any claims to knowledge stemming from sense-perceptions (observations) led him to postulate the existence of an independent, autonomous realm of objectively perfect "forms." Not only did this autonomous realm include perfect forms such as "man" and "tree," but also, perfect forms such as "good" and "beauty." The nature of these transcendent forms could not be grasped by observation but only by the power of intellectual intuition.

Aristotle argued that Plato had committed the logical error of treating the *property* of an object as the object itself. That is, the fact that it is meaningful to claim that a woman is *beautiful* (an attribute of a woman) is logically different from claiming that "beauty" has an existence independent of the object (the woman). Thus, Aristotle adopted a form of *realism*, proposing that the outside world consists only of individual objects, such as women (who may have the attribute "beauty") and trees, and *not* the idealized perfect forms of "woman" and "tree." It is easy to see how Aristotle's rejection of Plato's theory of forms was a necessary prerequisite for his empirical work in natural philosophy, which was heavily observation-based.

Aristotle not only *did* science, he was also the first *philosopher* of science. As Losee notes, Aristotle "created the discipline [of the philosophy of science] by analyzing certain problems that arise in connection with scientific explanation." [400, p. 6] In fact, much of Aristotle's philosophy of science survives to this day in one form or another. First,

Aristotle is usually credited with developing what is now referred to as "syllogistic" logic. He proposed that science *begins* with observations in the real world, progresses through inductive processes to explanatory principles, and then uses these explanatory general principles to deduce (syllogistically) observations. These views presaged by almost 2000 years those of Sir Francis Bacon.

Aristotle also analyzed the nature of scientific explanations and mathematics. He proposed that satisfactory explanations must be developed in syllogistic form, with *true* general premises, deductive logic and conclusions. Thus, the Deductive-Nomological model of scientific explanation developed by Hempel has its origins in Aristotle. [367, p. 12] Aristotle also recognized that there was something fundamentally different between mathematics and empirical science. In today's terms, he was interested in a "demarcation" issue. Aristotle maintained that, whereas the subject matter of empirical science *changes* in character through time, the subject matter of mathematics is "that which is unchanging." [400, p. 12] The change/unchanging demarcation of Aristotle bears a striking similarity to today's analytic/synthetic distinction between mathematics and empirical science.

Most importantly, Aristotle merged Plato's method of knowledge-through-critical-discussion with the empiricist method of careful observation. However, Aristotle's method of inquiry did not include the testing of hypotheses through *experimentation*. He was an observer of nature, not an intervenor or experimenter. As Durant puts it: "It is again the absence of experiment and fruitful hypothesis that leaves Aristotle's natural science a mass of undigested observations." [161, p. 71] Nevertheless, many claim that Aristotle's works remain:

> [T]he most marvelous and influential system of thought put together by a single mind. It may be doubted if any other thinker has contributed so much to the enlightenment of the world. Every later age has drawn upon Aristotle, and stood upon his shoulders to see the truth. [161, p. 72]

8.1.5   Philosophy after Aristotle

After the death of Aristotle in 322 B.C., Greek philosophy was heavily influenced by several strains of cultism and mysticism. For example, the Phoenician merchant Zeno introduced Stoic philosophy into Athens about 310 B.C. Unlike the optimistic philosophy of Aristotle, Stoicism emphasized the apathetic acceptance of defeat. The study in Greece of subjects like natural philosophy and the philosophy of science virtually disappeared. Nor did the situation improve with the subjugation of Greece by Rome in 146 B.C. As Durant eloquently puts it:

> The glory that had been Greece faded now in the dawn of the Roman sun; and the grandeur that was Rome was the pomp of power rather

than the light of thought. Then that grandeur decayed, that little light went almost out. For a thousand years darkness brooded over the face of Europe. All the world awaited the resurrection of philosophy. [161, p. 74]

The reawakening of philosophy in Western civilization began within the Roman Catholic church. Over a period of several hundred years, the wealth and power of the Church had been growing steadily. In fact, it was the single unifying institution in Europe and by the 13th century owned approximately one third of the landmass of Europe [161, p. 79]. Returning from the Middle East, the Church's Crusaders brought back copies of Aristotle's works in Latin, Greek, Arabic, and Hebrew. At first, the Church resisted Aristotle's philosophy and forbade its teachers to lecture on his works. However, primarily through the efforts of Thomas Aquinas, the works of Aristotle were absorbed gradually into official Church teaching. As a result, "by 1260 A.D. he was *de rigueur* in every Christian school, and Ecclesiastical assemblies penalized deviations from his views." [161, p. 73]

Alas, the Church had turned Aristotle into the Western equivalent of an Eastern sage. Now, knowledge about the world was not to be had through methods of Platonian critical discussion or Aristotelian observation. Rather, truth about the world was to be found through properly *interpreting* the works of Aristotle. (Thirteenth century scholars are known to have consulted Aristotle's writings to determine whether oil would congeal if left out in the cold at night.) The pursuit of knowledge degenerated into scholastic interpretation. Though the Church had revived *philosophy*, the revival of the philosophy of *science* awaited the scientific revolution that occurred in 17th century Europe. We turn now to the nature of this revolution and its causes.

8.2   THE RISE OF MODERN SCIENCE

The period beginning in approximately 1550 A.D. and stretching through 1700 A.D. encompasses the rise of modern science. In fact, the achievements of science were so spectacular and their impact on society so great that the label "Scientific Revolution" aptly applies. Butterfield claims that the Scientific Revolution "outshines everything since the rise of Christianity and reduces the Renaissance and the Reformation to the rank of mere episodes, mere internal displacements, within the system of Medieval Christendom."[100, p. vii]

Consider the enormous achievements during the "short" span of only 150 years: Kepler (1571-1630) developed his Laws of Planetary Motion (among them, that the orbits of the planets around the sun are elliptical); Gilbert (1544-1603) did his pioneering work in the areas of magnetism and electricity; Vesalius (1514-1564) expanded the frontiers of knowledge in anatomy; Harvey (1578-1657) discovered and demonstrated that blood circulates throughout the human body; Boyle's (1627-1691) experiments on gases showed that the pressure of a gas and its volume are inversely related (Boyle's Laws); Galileo's (1564-1642) experiments with falling bodies demonstrated the "Law of Descent" (i.e., the distance that a body falls is directly proportional to the square of the time of its descent); finally, and most importantly, Newton (1642-1727) developed his laws with respect to the motions of all physical objects and published them in *Principia* in 1687. *Principia* provided a theoretical framework for synthesizing the works of Kepler, Galileo and others. In Newton's Laws, scientists for over 200 years believed that they had discovered genuine *episteme* (proven knowledge or knowledge-with-certainty), similar to the certainty previously provided by the authority of the Church.

The rise of modern science in Europe in the 17th century has been well studied. One of the most authoritative works on the subject was written by Ben-David (originally published in 1971 and revised in 1984 [53]). Ben-David explores the lack of continuous scientific growth throughout the world before 17th century Europe:

> Rapid accumulation of knowledge, which has characterized the development of science since the 17th century, had never occurred before that time. The new kind of scientific activity emerged only in a few countries of Western Europe, and it was restricted to that small area for about two hundred years. (Since the 19th century, scientific knowledge has been assimilated by the rest of the world.) This assimilation has not occurred through the incorporation of science into the cultures and institutions of the different societies. Instead it has occurred through the diffusion of the patterns of scientific activity and scientific roles from Western Europe to the other parts of the world. [53, p. 21]

Four features characterize the rise of modern science in the 17th century. First, there was a *rapid growth* in knowledge. The rapidity in the growth of knowledge justifies calling it a "revolutionary," rather than an "evolutionary" phenomenon. Second, the rapid growth in knowledge occurred across many different areas, including medicine, biology, anatomy, electricity, mechanics, and astronomy. Third, rather than natural philosophers (scientists) "starting from scratch" and building free-standing, complete philosophical systems, they took the works of other philosophers and built upon them. The *cumulative* nature of their work was (in today's terms) both verificationist and falsificationist in nature. The work of Galileo built upon the efforts of Kepler and Copernicus (verificationist), and *refuted* the work of Ptolemy (falsificationist). Similarly, the work of Newton built upon Galileo, and the discoveries of Vesalius in anatomy refuted the official Church position of Galen (129-200 A.D.). (The Church endorsed the Galenic view that the heart, brain, and liver have their own *independent* systems of arteries, nerves and veins.)

The fourth feature characterizing the rise of modern science was its *method*. The "new philosophy" emphatically rejected the position that knowledge was to be restricted to the proper interpretation of the ancient canonical trio of Aristotle, Ptolemy and Galen. First, the new philosophy brought back the *knowledge-through-critical-discussion* criterion of Plato. Second, the new philosophy retained the strong emphasis on *logic* and *observation,* as expounded by Aristotle. Third, it resurrected the notion from Pythagoras that much of the external world can be expressed in terms of *mathematical relationships.* To the methods of Plato, Aristotle, and Pythagoras, the method of the new philosophy added a new and key component: the belief in *experimentation.* Not only was the knowledge generated by the new philosopher-scientist to be logical, consistent with observation, and capable of passing the tests of critical discussion, but also, the truth-content of the knowledge should be capable of empirical testing through experimentation, as with Galileo.

The importance of adding experimentation to the natural philosopher's methodological "tool kit" in the 17th century cannot be overestimated. Experimentation plays a significant role both in the discovery of hypotheses about the world and in their justification. For example, Galileo's experiment leading to the Law of Descent has been described as one of the twenty "great scientific experiments" that changed our world. [253] Galileo used a polished bronze ball rolling down a groove in an inclined wooden beam to determine that the distance a freely moving object would travel would be directly proportional to the square of the duration of time. (Interestingly, one of Galileo's "clocks" was his pulse rate.) Historians differ as to whether Galileo's experiment was *only* a test of his hypothesis (justification) or whether Galileo actually derived his "time-squared" hypothesis from observing balls rolling down inclined planes (discovery). Galileo's own working notes suggest that he conducted numerous (over one hundred) experiments with balls rolling down inclined planes. Some of them he used to inductively generate the "time-squared" relationship, and other experiments demonstrated and tested it. [253, p. 78]

The preceding paragraphs on the rise of modern science adopt a rationalist perspective that there has been a *genuine* accumulation of knowledge as a result of the rise of modern science. The opposite position, or irrationalism, claims the contrary. For example, Stove reviews the works of those he calls the "modern irrationalists," including Kuhn and Feyerabend, and notes:

> Much more is known now than was known fifty years ago, and much more was known then than in 1580. So there has been a great accumulation or growth of knowledge in the last four hundred years. This

is an extremely well-known fact, which I will refer to as (A). . . . So a
writer whose position inclined him to deny (A), or even made him at
all reluctant to admit it, would almost inevitably seem, to the philosophers who read him, to be maintaining something extremely implausible. . . . Everyone would admit that if there has *ever* been a growth of
knowledge it has been in the last four hundred years, so anyone reluctant to admit (A) must, if he is consistent, be reluctant to admit that
there has ever been a growth of knowledge at all. But if a philosopher
of science takes a position which obliges him, on pain of inconsistency,
to be reluctant to admit *this*, then his position can be rightly described
as irrationalism . . . [603, pp. 3,4]

Stove goes on to explore the literary devices that modern irrationalists use to seduce even highly trained philosophers (not to mention un-
wary, casual readers) into the relativistic thesis that our knowledge of
the external world has not truly progressed in the last four hundred
years. The subjects of irrationalism, relativism, and scientific progress
will be returned to later in Chapters 10 and 12. For now, we need to
explore the rather formidable barriers in the 17th century that inhibited the development of modern science.

8.2.1   Opposition to the Rise of Modern Science

Four institutions and societal groupings vigorously fought the development of modern science: organized religion, the universities, mechanicians (engineers) and the speculative metaphysicians. Each will be
discussed, in turn.

The antipathy of organized religion toward the development of modern science is well-documented and has been much discussed. The rise
of modern science with its claims to produce knowledge about the external world through critical discussion, observation, logic, and experimentation challenged the authority of the Roman Catholic Church over
temporal things. By challenging the *authority* of the Church concerning sources of knowledge about how the world "works," science threatened to weaken the Church's power as the dominant institution in
Europe.

The most celebrated case of the religious suppression of science
was, of course, the silencing of Galileo in 1633. In his dialogue on *The
Two Great World Systems,* Galileo compared the relative merits of the
Copernican universe (with the planets revolving around the Sun) and
the Ptolemaic system (with the Sun revolving around the Earth). Galileo's book was harshly critical of the Church-approved Ptolemaic system and, consequently, the Inquisition found him guilty of heresy. He
spent the last nine years of his life under house arrest (which was a
rather lenient sentence, since he could, like countless others, have been

burned at the stake). Only in 1820 did the Church admit that Copernicus was right. [644, P. 6] And only within the last decade has the
Church begun to admit that it may have made a mistake in silencing
Galileo. In 1980, Pope John Paul II commissioned a panel of scholars to
reexamine the evidence and verdict. As yet, the Church has not formally rehabilitated Galileo.

Many current writers forget that the uneasy truce between science
and religion is primarily a product of the 20th century. Not only have
religious leaders distrusted science, but as recently as 1874, the Catholic University in Ireland refused to allow the physical sciences to be
taught at all! [227, p. 784] Similarly, in the late 1800s, it was still the
practice of the Prime Minister of England when facing a national crisis
such as a cholera epidemic or a cattle plague to primarily seek the
assistance of Anglican church leaders, rather than science. The church
leaders would then call for a "national day of prayer" to ask for divine
intervention to solve the crisis. Such practices prompted the Superin-
tendent of the Royal Institution (of science) in London to challenge
church leaders to conduct a "prayer gauge" experiment. [227] The proposed experiment involved selecting a hospital that would be the focus
of national prayer and comparing the mortality rate before and after
the day of supplication. Although the experiment was never conducted,
the fact that the challenge caused such an uproar illustrates the high
tension and distrust between the religious and scientific communities
that existed as recently as the latter-half of the 19th century. [227]

The universities in the 17th century constituted a second institution openly hostile to the development of modern science. Formal universities emerged in Europe in the 13th century with the University of
Paris (about 1210) and Oxford University (in 1284). One obvious reason for their hostility to science was that almost all universities were
sectarian in nature. For example, it was not until 1870 that a non-
Anglican could study at either Oxford or Cambridge. [88]

Although natural philosophy was taught in the universities, the
curriculum was oriented primarily toward the humanities and the professions of law, politics, and medicine. Further, the dominant method
of inquiry was Scholasticism; that is, knowledge was to be found
through the proper interpretation of the writings of others, primarily
the ancient Greeks. In fact, the modern notion of the university professor as a scholar engaging in original research that creates new knowledge is of very recent origin. The first universities to emphasize science
and research were those in Germany in the early part of the 19th century, with the University of Berlin in 1810 being the forerunner. Only
much later was the concept of the professor-as-researcher accepted in
England. Oxford University granted its first Ph.D. in 1917! [88]

The Scholasticism of the Middle Ages survives today in the form of
"hermeneutics." Hermeneutics in the 19th century focused on the
interpretation of Holy and Sacred writings with the intent of finding

their "real meaning." However, in the 20th century, following the works of Heidegger, proponents of hermeneutics expanded its scope to include the interpretation of all literary works and have generally abandoned the belief that there is any such thing as the "real meaning." Rather, they now emphasize the "meaning for the subject." [485]

Although the universities were openly hostile to the development of science and refused to disseminate the knowledge that science generated, this does not imply that they had absolutely no positive impact. On the contrary, most of the natural philosophers who engaged in empirical science in the 17th century were university trained. The university training in logic and mathematics was definitely beneficial to the 17th century natural philosophers. Not surprisingly, Hall analyzed the backgrounds of those who were members of England's Royal Society (of science) in 1663 and found that fifty-seven percent definitely had attended a university, and another thirty percent had probably done so. [245, p.5]

The mechanicians (engineers) also resisted the development of science. [53, p. 26] The mechanicians were nonuniversity educated people who saw little relationship between the explorations of science and their own practical problems of building bridges, constructing buildings, and designing machinery. Many doubted that science would ever contribute anything to practical technology. [227, p. 785] Even by the time of the Industrial Revolution in 18th century England, the link between science and technology had not yet been firmly established, leading one prominent engineer to conclude: The scientist's "deep thinking [is] quite out of place in a world of railroads and steamboats, printing presses and spinning-jennies." [285, p. 114] (Of course, the debate over "theory" and "practical research" continues today in marketing; the reader should note the parallels.)

The speculative metaphysicians of the 17th century also resisted the development of science. [522, p. 18] The speculative metaphysicians sought to develop comprehensive philosophies through reasoning alone, unaided by observation, measurement, or experiment. The hostility of metaphysicians toward empirical science continues to this day, largely influenced by Hegel (1770-1831), whose works will be examined later (see Section 8.4.3).

The question "Why did science develop in Western Europe in the 17th century and not elsewhere?" is often asked. Ben-David proposes that the question is ill-formed. Recalling the powerful institutions that vigorously opposed the development of science, he notes that these institutions would exist in *all* societies and would probably have similar animosities toward science. He notes that religious institutions provided purpose and meaning to people's lives and therefore, were *needed*. Mechanicians provided buildings, roads, and machines; all *needed*. Metaphysicians provided grand philosophies of the universe to all who required grandiose explanations of the world. Magicians and astrologers provided wonderment and sweeping prophesy. Universities provided training for physicians, lawyers, and ministers. Against the backdrop of these groups and institutions, the activities, methods, and objectives of 17th century science must have seemed pale, indeed. In short, empirical science was, simply, "not needed." The properly formed question, Ben-David suggests, is not "Why didn't science develop in places other than 17th century Europe?" Rather, he insists, "What needs explanation is the fact that science ever emerged [anywhere] at all." [53, p.31]

But, we know that science *did* successfully take root in 17th century Europe. The scientific revolution *did* succeed. Those institutions and groups that resisted the rise of modern science *were* unsuccessful. Why?

8.2.2   Factors Contributing to the Rise of Modern Science

Several factors combine to explain the, almost miraculous, success of the scientific revolution. Chronologically, the first factor is the Renaissance. The Renaissance is a label usually applied to the period 1350-1600 when there was in Europe a rebirth of interest in art, literature, and learning. Furthermore, there was a dramatic increase in general economic activity and in trade with the East. Through this interaction, the East played a critical role in the development of science in the West. Trading ships brought back not only Eastern goods, but also copies of ancient manuscripts. In particular, Renaissance scholars rediscovered the works of Plato and, through him, Pythagoras. From reading Plato, Renaissance scholars reintroduced the concept that knowledge could be gained through "critical discussion," rather than *only* from authority. Stimulated by Pythagoras, Renaissance scholars made significant achievements in the development of both pure and applied mathematics. For example, it was during this period of time that the concept of the "equals sign" in mathematics was formally developed.

The European traders also brought back cheap paper from Egypt, which, when combined with the development of printing presses, made books no longer the sole province of monks in monasteries. In fact, numerous technological achievements both contributed to, and were absolutely necessary for, the rise of modern science. The achievements of Galileo would have been impossible without the invention of the telescope in the early 17th century. [545, p.535] Similarly, the invention of the microscope in the latter part of the 17th century was a necessary precursor for the study of microbiology.

In addition to the Renaissance, contacts with the East, and the rise of technology, the Protestant Reformation gave significant impetus to the development of modern science. The Reformation did so by breaking the hegemony of the Roman Catholic Church over intellectual activity throughout Europe. Of the many Protestant sects, the beliefs of the Puritans were particularly hospitable to modern science. First, the Puritans believed in social welfare, or the good of the many, as an important *religious* objective. Further, they believed that "the experimental study of Nature to be a most effective means of begetting in men a veneration for God." [444, p.232] Not surprisingly, many Puritans were prominent members of England's Royal Society (of science) in the 17th century. [444, p. 30]

However, not all Protestant sects were equally tolerant. In fact, many small, self-contained Protestant communities had no appreciable class of intellectuals except their clergymen and, therefore, "would not tolerate anything approaching Heresy." [53, p. 71] Fortunately, in most of Europe Protestants were not able to effectively form closed religious communities and, therefore, there was no single religious authority to enforce religious dogma. Moreover, Protestant leaders began to realize that the persecution of scientists (such as Galileo) by the Roman Catholic Church offered them excellent opportunities to gain converts: "As a result, official Protestant authorities on several occasions adopted policies of supporting science, and eventually in Commonwealth England they came very near to the acceptance of the scientistic utopia as a basis for their official educational policy." [53, p. 71] Thus, one answer to the problem of science being "not needed" is that the Protestants needed science in their struggle with the Roman Catholic Church.

Another answer to the "not needed" problem can be found in the political and social structures of 17th century Europe. At that time there were numerous groups throughout Europe seeking to change European political and social structures by making them more pluralistic, open, and future-oriented. These groups became benefactors and supporters of science since, Ben-David suggests, they "needed" science to provide a "cognitive structure consistent with their interests." That is, they viewed the scientist as:

> ... a person studying nature rather than the ways of God and man, and using as his intellectual tools mathematics, measurements and experiment instead of relying on the interpretation of authoritative sources, speculation, or inspiration. He was a person viewing the state of knowledge in his time as something to be constantly improved on in the future rather than something to be brought up to the standards of a golden age in the past. [53, p. 170]

So, the Renaissance gave science Plato's method of "critical discussion" and improvements in mathematics. The rise of technology gave science instruments with which to conduct experiments. The Protestant Reformation "needed" science, as did those who wanted to change the political and social structures of Europe. In addition, the specific behaviors and activities of the practitioners and proponents of the new philosophy also contributed to the successful rise of modern science. Although the new philosophy was inherently concerned with *understanding* (theory) rather than *doing* (practice), many scientists attempted to demonstrate the science-technology link by working on problems having practical consequences. For example, Merton [443] quantitatively analyzed the papers offered to England's Royal Society in the 17th century and found a preponderance of papers focusing on practical problems in mining, navigation, and warfare.

Scientists also attempted to assuage the fears of the clerics by demonstrating that the knowledge gained through science was not necessarily antithetical to religion in general or to the existence of God in particular. Such efforts are unsurprising because most natural philosophers in the 17th century were confirmed deists. For example, Newton's First Law (a body will remain at rest unless acted upon by an outside force) denies that motion is *inherent* to matter and, therefore, retains for God the role of "Prime Mover." In fact, standard attacks by Marxists on Newton, such as those by Hessen (in Werskey [632]) include the criticism that Newton "left room" for God.

Also, the development of scientific academies also helped assure the success of the scientific revolution. Scientists formed England's Royal Society (of science) in 1660 and France's *Acadèmie des Sciences* in 1666. With the inception of the academies, science now became institutionalized in the sense of having its own set of procedures and norms and in "the acceptance in a society of a certain activity as an important social function valued for its own sake." [53, p. 75]

The most important factor favoring the success of the scientific revolution (though, most certainly, not *assuring* it) was the very power of the idea of the "scientific method," itself. The scientific method of combining critical discussion, logic, and mathematics with observation and experimentation was definitely an idea whose time had come. It has been referred to by many writers as "the most significant intellectual contribution of Western civilization." [453, p.63] Natural philosophers in the 17th century were truly inspired when they conjoined (1) the emphasis on logic and speculation implicit in Plato's method of "critical discussion," (2) the powerful tool of mathematics, as proposed by Pythagoras, (3) the belief in systematic observation and syllogistic logic of Aristotle, and, most importantly, (4) the reliance on experimentation advocated by Galileo (and subsequently articulated by Sir Francis Bacon). As long as societies were mired in the morass of purely speculative philosophy, "sage" philosophy, and knowledge from interpreting authority, genuinely cumulative knowledge about the external world was unlikely.

Given the rise of the "new philosophy," with its emphasis on the development of knowledge through the scientific method, there was a need to articulate and explicate the characteristics of this method. That is, there was a need for the activity we refer to now as the philosophy of science. The first "great debate" over the fundamental nature of the scientific method was between two groups, one group called "empiricists," the other "rationalists."

8.3   THE EMPIRICISM-RATIONALISM DEBATE

The Empiricism-Rationalism Debate focused on the scientific method and the best procedures to insure scientific progress. We shall use the term "classical empiricism" to identify a group of philosophers (most notably Bacon, Hume, Locke, and Mill) who believed that science should start from observations of the real world and inductively develop its generalizations, laws, and theories. The modifier "classical" is used to remind the reader that we are examining the specific beliefs of a specific philosophical movement. Although all current philosophers who refer to themselves as "empiricists" would hold observation and experience in high regard, few would completely embrace all the positions of the classical empiricists. All the classical empiricists shared the following fundamental tenet: *Experience and observation are the fundamental sources or "foundations" of our knowledge of the external world.*

Opposing the empiricists were the classical rationalists, as exemplified by Descartes, Spinoza and Leibniz. The fundamental tenet of the classical rationalists was that *a priori reason alone is the fundamental source or "foundation" of our knowledge of the external world.* Again, the modifier "classical" is used to indicate that we are referring to a specific philosophical movement and to differentiate it from other forms of rationalism. Although there are numerous uses of the term "rationalism" (both in general philosophy and the philosophy of science), they all share the common concept of "reason." For example, the Age of Enlightenment, usually associated with certain developments in Europe in the 18th century, is often called the "Age of Reason." The rationalism of the Enlightenment implied a deep conviction that mankind, through human reasoning (contrasted with superstition, mysticism, and religious faith) could comprehend the nature of the world and that this comprehension would result in cumulative progress toward a better life for all mankind. Therefore, the rationalism of the Enlightenment in the 18th century was a distinctly optimistic and uplifting philosophy that drew in part upon the success of science in the 17th century. What was necessary for mankind to progress was the release of the power of reason from the shackles of superstition, mysticism, and religious and political dogma.

As previously mentioned in Section 8.2, Stove notes that the works of Kuhn and Feyerabend necessarily imply an extreme form of "irrationalism." [603, p. 4] In doing so, Stove does *not* mean that Kuhn and Feyerabend are opposing what we are referring to here as "classical rationalism" (reason is the *primary* source of knowledge). Rather, Kuhn and Feyerabend are irrationalists to Stove and others because they believe that mankind's reasoning ability is incapable of gaining knowledge about the nature of the world. Irrationalism contends that reason (combined with anything) is incapable of producing genuine knowledge about the world at all, in the past, present, or future! It is in this sense that such standard reference books as the *Dictionary of the History of Science* use Kuhn and Feyerabend as typical examples of prominent irrationalists. [150, p. 360]

Both the classical empiricists and the classical rationalists were very sympathetic toward the development of science. Indeed, unlike today where most academic philosophers of science are not practitioners of science [373, p.7], *all* the classical empiricists and rationalists were *both* philosophers and practitioners. Although sharing a positive view toward science and its progress, the different fundamental tenets of the classical empiricists and rationalists led them along very different paths.

8.3.1 Classical Empiricism

Many scholars refer to Sir Francis Bacon (1561-1626) as England's first great philosopher. Left penniless at an early age by the death of his father, Bacon studied the law and earned a seat for himself in the House of Commons, after which he was knighted and became Lord Chancellor of England. [12] Although Bacon (as a practitioner of science) made no great scientific discoveries, his literary skills made him a powerful advocate of both science and the scientific method. His most important work, *Novum Organum*, was published in 1620. In it, Bacon propounded his theory of "inductive ascent," which holds that science starts with observations and inductively proceeds (like bricks in a pile) in a steady, gradual process to general principles that would be known-with-the-certainty of their foundations, i.e., simple, direct observations. What is generally not recognized is that Bacon was firmly committed to the inductive-deductive scientific procedure advocated by Aristotle. [400, p.62] That is, the *inductively* developed generalizations were to be tested through *deductively* generated hypotheses.   Bacon bitterly opposed the Aristotelian scholasticism of his day, which used only deductive logic to properly interpret the truths of the "master," Aristotle. Bacon decried the fact that even when practitioners of Aristotelian science relied on observation, they did so in an entirely too casual fashion (generalizing too quickly and avoiding systematic experimentation). Bacon emphasized that the "first principles" from which useful deductions can be made should be arrived at through his "inductive ascent," rather than from Church authority.

Given Bacon's belief that experience and observation are the fundamental sources of knowledge of the external world, he devoted much of his writings on the scientific method to developing procedures for careful observation and experimentation. Primary among these procedures were his three Tables of Investigation. After amassing large quantities of observational and experimental data on a given phenomenon, Bacon suggested that the data be categorized in Tables of Affirmation, Negation, and Degrees. Basically, these three tables would reveal when one phenomenon was positively associated with another phenomenon (Affirmation), or negatively associated with the existence of another phenomenon (Negation), or changes in one phenomenon were associated with changes in another phenomenon (Degrees). To help investigators further analyze the Tables of Investigation, Bacon offered twenty-seven techniques for finding important relationships in the data. Of these so-called "Prerogative Instances," the most important was the "Instance of the Fingerpost," to which he gave the label "crucial experiment." Such an experiment could be decisive in choosing between two hypotheses. Finally, to do good research, Bacon urged investigators to purge themselves of their own biases and prejudices about the phenomenon under investigation. He called these biases and prejudices "Idols" and urged investigators to rid themselves of Idols of the "Tribe," "Den," "Market Place," and "Theater." The Idols of the Theater earned for Bacon the enmity of philosophers, for these Idols included the metaphysical philosophical systems of his day, which, he contended, were like "stage plays" and did not give a true picture of the real nature of the world.

Consistent with the Enlightenment, Bacon sought to encourage scientists to work on projects that would lead to control over nature for the betterment of mankind and a higher quality of life. He likened the speculative metaphysicians to "spiders," spinning webs of marvelous ingenuity out of their own bodies, but having no contact with reality: "Bacon's hostility [towards the scholastics and metaphysicians] reflects *moral* outrage—Aristotle's philosophy not only had not led to new works to benefit mankind, but also had thwarted those few attempts that had been made." [400, p. 68]

John Locke.   Our second empiricist, John Locke (1632-1704), was an English physician and lecturer on philosophy at Oxford University. His primary contribution to the empiricism-rationalism debate came with the publication of his *Essay Concerning Human Understanding,* published in 1690. In it, Locke vigorously attacked the rationalist conception of "innate ideas." The rationalists argued that many of our concepts or ideas (both within and outside of science) are present at birth. Locke powerfully and persuasively argued the empiricist position that all ideas come from either "sensation" (the interaction of the senses with the environment) or "reflection" on sensations. Therefore, all knowledge of the external world must come from experience and observation, or reflection on the same. Not only did his *Essay* further the empiricist cause in science, but it also provided a major philosophical foundation for the Enlightenment of the 18th century. Locke's view that the human mind at birth is truly a *tabula rasa* on which experience is imprinted justifies the liberal view of the Enlightenment that the education of the young can improve society and the quality of life.

David Hume. David Hume (1711-1776), our third empiricist, was a Scottish philosopher who dropped out of Edinburgh University at the age of fifteen to devote full time to the pursuit of philosophy. His first major work, *A Treatise of Human Nature* (1739), was very poorly received and, therefore, he published a revised version in 1748 entitled *An Enquiry Concerning Human Understanding*. Whereas Bacon and Locke had extensively analyzed science from the viewpoint of the coexistence of the *properties* of various phenomena, Hume extended the empiricist approach to the investigation of the *sequences* of phenomena in time. He also attacked the rationalist belief that science could produce so-called "necessary truths" about the external world.

Hume divided all knowledge statements into two, mutually exclusive, categories: "relations of ideas" and "matters of fact." Consistent with Locke (and contrary to the views of the rationalists), Hume claimed that "matters of fact" can be known only from sense impressions. On the other hand, some kinds of "relations of ideas" are "necessary truths" because they are "intuitively certain." For example, the axioms of Euclidean geometry were to Hume intuitively certain and, therefore, any theorems deductively derived from the axioms of Euclidean geometry were "necessary truths" because they were demonstrably certain through deductive logic.

Hume next proceeded to analyze the kinds of relations of ideas called "causal relations." He concluded that, unlike geometrical relations, causal relations cannot reach the status of "necessary truths," since they cannot be known with certainty. In other words, the observation that phenomenon "X" has always in the past been succeeded by phenomenon "Y" does not *deductively* imply that phenomenon "X" will always in the future be *necessarily* succeeded by phenomenon "Y." Given that all our knowledge of the external world comes from sense impressions, there is no way to establish the "necessary connection" between the phenomena.

The preceding argument on "necessary truths" is usually referred to as "Humean skepticism," or in Laudan's terms, the "Plebeian Problem of Induction." [373, p. 80] Hume's argument was devastating to the rationalist position that science *could* produce and *did* produce "certain" knowledge through "pure reason" alone. However, to those who were content with science producing "highly probable" knowledge or "highly warranted" knowledge, Humean skepticism posed no insurmountable problem. Indeed, Hume himself summarily dismissed his own skepticism, believing that inductively inferring causality was essential for scientific knowledge and was justified by custom and habit:

> Custom, then, is the great guide of human life. It is that principle alone which renders our experience useful to us—without the influence of custom we should be entirely ignorant of every matter of fact beyond what is immediately present to the memory and senses. [292, p. 45]

As we shall see later, although Hume saw no problem with Humean skepticism, many subsequent writers have either explicitly or implicitly adopted his skeptical position. Prominent among these adopters of skepticism have been Popper, Kuhn, and Feyerabend. (See Sections 9.2.3, 9.3.4, and 9.6.2.)

John Stuart Mill.   Our final empiricist, John Stuart Mill (1806-1873) authored *The System of Logic* (1843) and *Utilitarianism* (1863) and was probably the most influential philosopher (empiricist or otherwise) in the English-speaking world during the 19th century. All his writings were driven by a deep commitment to foster both scientific and social progress. The "intuitionism" of the classical rationalists, he held, inhibited the progress of science toward understanding the true nature of the world. Similarly, intuitionism in ethics, by inhibiting progress toward the liberal ideal of individual freedom and human happiness, should be replaced with his utilitarianism.

With respect to our sources of knowledge, Mill took empiricism to its logical extreme. Rejecting the Humean dichotomy of knowledge about "matters of fact" and "relations of ideas," Mill claimed that even the fundamental axioms of geometry were simply highly confirmed generalizations from experience. [367, p. 31] (He did, however, recognize that the *theorems* of geometry were "necessary truths" by deductive logic.) Thus, all genuine knowledge in science came from inductively generalizing from experience. Mill's justly famous "canons of induction" included the methods of: agreement, difference, concomitant variation, residues, and the "joint method" of agreement and difference. Mill made the incredibly strong (and demonstrably incorrect) assertion that all the causal laws in science had historically been generated from the application of one or more of his methods. Of the five methods, Mill held the "method of difference" to be most important, since he claimed that only the method of difference could conclusively separate true causal laws from merely accidental regularities. Unfortunately, like his contemporaries, Mill constantly confused *discovery* with *verification*. Thus, he writes that *induction* is "the operation of *discovering* and *proving* general propositions." [Mill, as quoted in 367, p. 33] (See Bagozzi [28] for a discussion of the application of Mill's methods to marketing.)

But if all the laws of science are to be inductively generated from experience, what is the *justification* for these inductive procedures? Mill's answer to Humean skepticism was to postulate a principle of universal causation, which provided that every phenomenon is invariably and unconditionally preceded by some particular set of antecedent circumstances. Recognizing that his principle of universal causation could be justifiably attacked as metaphysical speculation, Mill claimed that the principle could be empirically justified by "simply enumerating" the enormously large number of cases that affirmed his principle and the complete lack of contradictory instances.

8.3.2   Rationalism

Both the classical empiricists and rationalists opposed scholasticism and were generally sympathetic toward the development of science. Nevertheless, whereas the empiricists criticized scholasticism for its lack of empirical foundations, the rationalists criticized the implausibility of the underlying laws or "first principles" of scholasticism. They believed that the knowledge-claims of empirical science could be made with the same degree of certainty as the claims of mathematics (which for them were indeed certain) if science would but emulate Euclidian geometry and start with first principles whose truth-status was incontrovertible. Science would then contain "necessary truths" in the sense that the claims would be true in both this world and all possible worlds. That is, the nature of the world could be nothing other than the way science claims it to be.

René Descartes.   The first great rationalist was the Frenchman René Descartes (1596-1650). Although university trained in the law, his inherited wealth enabled him to spend a lifetime on philosophical inquiry. His pioneering works on theoretical mathematics lay the foundations for modern analytic geometry, and his most famous work was his 1641 *Meditations on First Philosophies* (often referred to as, simply, "Meditations").

Descartes' procedure for developing his "first principles" was the "method of doubt." He started by introspectively examining all the things that he thought to be true and then proceeded to systematically eliminate all beliefs about which he had any doubt at all. Finally, he was left with one, absolutely incontrovertible, undeniably true, belief: *cogito ergo sum* (I think, therefore I am). The fact that he was thinking *necessarily* implied that he existed, and he could not possibly be in error about his thinking because "to be in error" would necessarily imply that he was thinking. From *cogito ergo sum* Descartes attempted to deductively derive the existence of God. Maintaining that God was the "first cause" of all motion, he deduced that a Perfect Being would necessarily want the motion in His creation to continue in perpetuity (otherwise, like a human clock, the universe would run down). From the principle that a Perfect Being would want to conserve all of the motion in His universe, Descartes derived his three general laws of motion and seven rules governing the impact of objects when they collide.

Unfortunately, several of his laws and rules could be (and were) easily refuted by empirical tests. For example, his fourth rule of impact states that, regardless of the speed of an object, a body of smaller size cannot move a body of larger size. Such easily refuted principles caused massive problems for both Descartes' science and his philosophy. Although Descartes retained for experience and observation a minor role in determining such things as the "boundary conditions" for the general laws, empirical refutation of such general laws was impermissible since the principles were *necessary truths*. Further, since "God is no deceiver," the world of sense perceptions could only be consistent with his deductively derived laws of science. Therefore, empirical testing was unnecessary.

Descartes believed that many of our "ideas," such as "tree," "flower," and "table," stem directly from sense-perceptions. A second genus of ideas is *formed* by the human mind as a result of reflecting on our sense-perceptions. For example, some trees are "larger" than other trees. However, Descartes maintained that a third group of ideas had to be "innate," since they did not exist in the world of sense-perceptions and were used by people temporally *prior* to the opportunity for people to generate them by "reflection." An example would be the concept of "infinity." As will be recalled, Descartes' claim for the existence of innate ideas was attacked by Locke. His *Essay* refuted Descartes by noting that, as a matter of fact, small children have no conceptualization of ideas like "infinity" until they receive instruction on the topic. Therefore, Lock argued, such concepts cannot be innate but must come from "reflection" on sensation.

Benedict de Spinoza.   The second great rationalist philosopher was the Dutch metaphysician, Benedict de Spinoza (1632-1677). Trained as a rabbi, he was expelled from his synagogue for his unorthodox beliefs and had to earn his living by grinding and polishing lenses. His principal philosophical works include *Tractatus Theologico-politicus* (1670) and *Ethics* (published posthumously in 1677).

Spinoza's philosophy was a completely self-contained, deductive metaphysical system, which used the structure of Euclidian geometry as its model. Like Hegel after him, Spinoza claimed that his system came to him through a mystical experience. As with Descartes, the starting point for Spinoza's system was theological in character. Completely rejecting the Judeo-Christian concept of anthropomorphic God, Spinoza proclaimed that God and nature are "one" (*Deus sive Natura*).

All of Spinoza's beliefs about science, ethics, and politics derive from his belief that "God" and "nature" are simply two different terms applied to the same infinite, eternal, and self-sufficient reality. Spinoza's pantheism, thus, led him to proclaim as "absurd" the belief of Descartes and the Scholastics in "divine teleology," the notion that God had purposes for the world. Divine teleology would imply that God wished to bring about some state of affairs in the world which did not yet exist. However, such a situation would necessarily imply, Spinoza reasoned, the absurdly contradictory belief that there was something God lacked, but which He needed or desired. It is easy to understand how Spinoza's pantheism was decried as a thinly-disguised atheism by his clerical critics and why he was expelled from his synagogue.

Spinoza's philosophical system included a severely deterministic perspective both in natural science and in the areas of ethics, political economy, and social science. All physical and mental activities are strictly determined; nothing can be other than it is. In *Ethics*, Spinoza contended that authors of conventional moral codes fallaciously believed in free will. In *Politics*, Spinoza accepted the Hobbesian belief that "have the right to" means the same as "have the power to." Thus, Spinoza's works, along with those of Hegel, provided a philosophical/historical foundation for Marxist social philosophy. The Russian historian Georgi Plekhanov [1940] viewed Spinozism as one of the direct, historical forerunners of Marxist dialectical materialism.

Gottfried Leibniz. The last of the great trio of classical rationalists was Gottfried Leibniz (1646-1716). A German philosopher, mathematician, lawyer, and diplomat, Leibniz was a tireless worker for scientific cooperation throughout the nations of Europe. He maintained active memberships in all three of the major European scientific academies: the Royal Society (of England), the French Academy, and the Prussian Academy.

Consistent with the liberal views of the Enlightenment, Leibniz was an optimist with respect to human reasoning and scientific progress. [505, p. 69] Although he was a great reader and admirer of Spinoza, Leibniz, being a confirmed deist, emphatically rejected Spinoza's pantheism: God and nature, for Leibniz, were *not* simply two different "labels" for the same "thing." Leibniz held that the world was a harmonious whole produced by God for divine ends and could be described and understood in a clear and consistent way through the "language" of mathematics. Extending Descartes' view of innate ideas, Leibniz proposed that we are also born with "innate principles." For example, since the most fundamental principles of syllogistic logic can neither be inferred from experience and observation, nor deduced (by definition) from more fundamental principles of logic, they must necessarily be with us at birth, or *innate*.

In addition to God, the other fundamental entity in Leibniz's philosophy was the "monad." Like the original conceptualization of "atom," monads were the smallest, indestructible units of the cosmos. Yet, unlike the materialistic conceptualization of the atom, monads contained their own distinct, divinely inspired purposes. Therefore, each monad is not only *distinct*, but also *unique*. Leibniz developed a complete philosophical system using the tools of logic and mathematics and his fundamental entity, the monad. Although his philosophical system based on monads has not survived in modern science, his work on mathematics endures. For many centuries, mathematicians had struggled with procedures to handle processes and problems that contained units of change that were infinitesimally small. Inspired by the work of his predecessors on summations of series and differences, Leibniz proposed both the basic procedure and the specific notation for modern differential and integral calculus. He also tackled the problem of reducing mathematics to logic and provided the basis for the later work in this area by Frege in the 19th century and Russell in the twentieth. (See Sections 8.5.2 and 9.1.2.)

8.3.3   The Quest for Certainty and the Grand Synthesis

Understanding the empiricism-rationalism debate requires an appreciation of the aims or objectives of the participants. Both the empiricists and the rationalists accepted "foundationalsim" as their objective—i.e., the development of a method for producing knowledge from foundations that would *invariably* produce *certain* knowledge. This infallibilist orientation had characterized philosophy since the time of Aristotle and Plato [373, p. 185] As Popper put it, the science of Galileo wanted to establish the truth of its theories "beyond all reasonable doubt." [505, p. 103] Indeed, epistemology, the branch of philosophy that studies the warrant for knowledge-claims, has its roots in the Greek word *episteme,* meaning "indubitable knowledge," as contrasted with *doxa,* meaning "opinion." However, since the time of Aristotle and Plato, philosophers also knew of the "fallacy of affirming the consequent" (the truth of the consequence or predictions of a theory or law does not, according to deductive logic, imply that the theory or law is true). Therefore, the so-called "method of hypothesis" (what would now more commonly be called the "hypothetico-deductive" method of verification) was highly suspect, since it could not yield *certain* knowledge.

In medieval times the Church provided the necessary authority for those seeking knowledge-with-certainty in both things-spiritual and things-temporal. Both the empiricists and the rationalists sought a method or logic for producing knowledge with certainty equal to that previously provided by the authority of the Church. The empiricists (many strongly influenced by Sir Issac Newton) recognized the fallacy of affirming the consequent and believed that knowledge with certainty could be produced by inductively generalizing from observations. The rationalists in their quest for certainty were highly suspicious of the accuracy of observational processes and also recognized the fallacy of affirming the consequent. Therefore, seeing in mathematics and geometry a kind of certainty similar to that of the Church, they earnestly searched for indubitably true first premises on which to base their scientific knowledge (e.g., the *cogito ergo sum* of Descartes). As Nickles phrases it, for both the empiricists and rationalists, "the correct method of discovery = correct method of verification." [474, p. 180]

The empiricist's logic of discovery (inductive generalizations) began to crumble when it became apparent that many scientific discoveries were being made through conjectural, rather than inductive-empirical means. For example, the wave theory of light and the theory of the atom involved inherently unobservable entities that were not and could not have been produced through inductive generalizations. [373, p. 187] The rationalists' logic of discovery (start from indubitable first principles) was damaged by the development of non-Euclidian geometry. (Since Euclidian geometry is not true-with-certainty, i.e. "True", how can geometrical methods produce infallible truths ("Truth") in empirical science?) Furthermore, the rationalists could not rely exclusively on mathematical methods, given Hume's analysis of the purely analytical or formal nature of mathematics. As Einstein later phrased it: "As far as the laws of mathematics refer to reality, they are not certain; and as far as they are certain, they do not refer to reality." [164a, p. 28]

The empiricism-relativism debate resolved into what has been described by van Fraassen [116, p. 263] as the "Grand Synthesis" of John Herschel (1792-1871) and William Whewell (1794-1866). Herschel's *Preliminary Discourse on Natural Philosophy* (1830) has been described as "the most comprehensive and best balanced work on the philosophy of science" at that time. [400, p. 115] Herschel was the first to clearly distinguish between the "context of discovery" and the "context of justification" in science. He noted "we must not, therefore, be scrupulous as to *how* we reach a knowledge of such general facts, i.e., laws and theories; provided only we verify them carefully when once discovered, we must be content to seize them wherever they are to be found." [269, p. 164]

Herschel stressed that the quest for certainty of the earlier empiricists and rationalists was hopeless. The best that science can do is to produce fallibilistic knowledge that is highly likely or very probable. Furthermore, there was no single logic of discovery. Rather, both inductive and hypothetico-deductive methods can be fruitful in developing the hypotheses, generalizations, and theories of science.

Nevertheless, "Herschel emphasized that agreement with observations is the most important criterion of acceptability for laws and theories." [400, p. 118] That is, with respect to the contexts of discovery and justification, Herschel's views correspond well to those prevailing today. Nevertheless, although the grand syntheses of Herschel and Whewell were highly influential, they did not dominate philosophical thought in the 19th century. Philosophy turned its back on science and embraced the philosophy of *idealism*.

8.4   THE ASCENDANCE OF IDEALISM

Although the classical rationalists and empiricists disagreed vigorously over the best procedures for ensuring scientific progress, each was decidedly sympathetic toward both the works of scientists and their developing social institution. We turn now to a group of philosophers who, with the exception of Kant, were generally hostile to science. The common characteristic of these philosophers is a commitment to *idealism*, whose central tenet is that *the external world does not exist independently of its being perceived.*

Basically, idealism is an ontological position relating to what philosophers usually refer to as the "mind-body problem." That is, to what extent is the conscious, perceiving mind separate from the material body within which it is housed? At one extreme lies *materialism,* which holds that *only* material objects (the mind being one such object) constitute "reality." At the other extreme lies *idealism*, holding that the only things that are "real" are the ideas housed in some perceiving mind.

As an aside, some may note that many writers advocating the relativist/constructivist position in marketing and the social sciences seem unaware that they are advocating a form of idealism. Such is not the case, however, with Olson. He states:

> Some people—realists—believe in an objectively knowable world that exists independently of themselves.... If you don't believe in an independent reality (or for purposes of doing science, you pretend you don't believe in that), then your *idealistic* perspective will probably lead you in entirely different directions.... Since I believe in the latter perspective, I guess I am a relativist. [Olson, in 99, p. 14, emphasis added]

Versions of idealism can be traced back at least to the works of Plato. As will be recalled, his theory of forms postulated an independent realm of abstract ideas or essences that had a real existence outside space and time. However, in contrast with the views of the major idealist philosophers we shall discuss (Berkeley, Kant, and Hegel), Plato's idealized "forms" did not depend for their existence on the perceiving mind, a most important difference.

8.4.1   Berkeley

George Berkeley (1685-1753), whose name is pronounced as if it were "Barkley," was an Irishman of English heritage who, after studying at Trinity College in Dublin, became an Anglican bishop and founded a college on the island of Bermuda. His major philosophical writings include the *Treatise Concerning the Principles of Human Knowledge* (1710) and *Three Dialogues Between Hylas and Philonous* (1713). Berkeley is often acknowledged as the originator of philosophical idealism, even though he gave the label "immaterialism" to the central thesis of his philosophy. Bishop Berkeley was alarmed by the theological skepticism implicit in many scientific works and in other writings of those associated with the Enlightenment, as is evidenced by the following subtitle of his first book: *Wherein the chief causes of error and difficulty in the sciences, with the grounds of skepticism, atheism, and irreligion, are inquired into.*

A summarized version of Berkeley's idealism is his phrase "to be is to perceive or to be perceived." [400, p.161] How did Berkeley come to the conclusion that reality consists only of perception? He started by observing that no one would seriously contend that an idea such as "pain" or "itching" could exist independently from the one who experienced them. (Trees neither itch nor experience pain.) Similarly, ideas like "red" and "sweet" are inherently objects of perception. His *Treatise* challenges the skeptical reader to attempt to conceive of any object existing unperceived, as for example, a chair or tree. Berkeley contended that it was impossible to conceive of a tree existing unperceived since the person who perceived it, by the very fact of doing so, "constructed" the tree and brought it into "existence." Therefore, "to be is to perceive or to be perceived." Berkeley then had to address one of the issues that confronts every philosopher who contends that all reality is of the "constructed" variety: how to account for the "apparent" stability in the external world.   That is, are chairs and trees annihilated and then re-created during intervals when they are not being perceived? Berkeley's answer was most ingenious. Since to him nothing could exist without its being perceived, in the time intervals when chairs and trees are not being perceived by human beings, they must exist in some other mind, i.e., the mind of God. Moreover, the lawlike regularities among perceptions that are discovered and verified in science are simply the manifestations of God's purpose for the world.   Therefore, Berkeley's idealistic philosophy could "prove" the existence of God, and science could "prove" God's purpose.

Berkeley's idealism led him directly to embrace what we would now call an instrumentalist view of laws and theories. This view holds that scientific laws and theories are "merely instruments" to make computations or predictions. They do not in any significant sense *truly* describe the real world. Section 8.2.1 discussed the silencing of Galileo by the

Church in 1633. In that celebrated case, the Church was quite willing to allow Galileo to extol the virtue of the Copernican universe as a, perhaps, better *computational* device (an instrumentalist position). Galileo's "mistake" was to insist that the Copernican system was both a better computational device and a better model of how the universe *actually was* (a *realist* position). Berkeley chastised Newton on precisely the same grounds that the Church had silenced Galileo. Berkeley maintained that Newton's references to "attractive forces," "cohesive forces," and "dissolutive forces," as truly describing the external world were misleading, since these "forces" are mathematical entities only. [400, p.161] For Berkeley, since only *ideas* were "real," only *they* could be causal agents, not such things as "forces."   Given Berkeley's idealism and instrumentalism, it is easy to understand how Popper would conclude that Berkeley opposed "the very idea of rational scientific knowledge" and that "he feared its advance."[503, p.29]

8.4.2   Immanuel Kant

Immanuel Kant (1724-1804) was born in Konigsberg in East Prussia, studied at its university, and spent his entire life there, teaching physics, mathematics, physical geography, and philosophy.   Kant was aroused, in his words, from a "dogmatic slumber" by the radical implications of Humean skepticism, which Kant believed destroyed the intellectual foundations of both religion and science. Being both a confirmed deist and sympathetic supporter of science, Kant's philosophy attempted, through the *Critique of Pure Reason* (1781) and other works, to save both religion and science from skepticism. To understand how Kant "saved" science, one must start with how he "saved" mathematics.

Hume had contended that mathematical truths were both *analytic* and *a priori*. That is, the truths of mathematics depend only upon how terms and relationships are defined (analytic) and cannot be established or refuted by experience (*a priori*). On the other hand, to Mill the truths of mathematics were *synthetic* (about the real world) and *a posteriori* (inductive generalizations from the real world which can be established or refuted by experience). Kant contended that the truths of mathematics and (Euclidian) geometry were *synthetic a priori*. Kant proposed that mathematical truths, like "7 + 5 = 12," are *synthetic* because "12" contains "more knowledge" than "7 + 5." These truths were also *a priori* because they were "necessary truths" in the sense that mathematical and geometrical truths were true both in this world and in all possible worlds. Kant's philosophy thus "saved" mathematics and in the process, "saved" classical rationalism, since pure reason alone could generate both mathematical and geometrical truths.

Kant dismissed summarily what he referred to as Berkeley's "dogmatic idealism." The external world could not consist entirely of "mere imaginations," since, he argued, no one could possibly become aware of himself unless there were enduring material substances with which he could compare his own sense perceptions. Our sense perceptions *reflect* these enduring material substances. Therefore, all scientific knowledge of the real world must (consistent with the classical empiricists) *come from* or have their origin in sense perceptions. However, although "coming from" the world, sense perceptions alone do not *constitute* scientific knowledge. These sense perceptions must be organized, analyzed, and interpreted by the active consciousness of the human mind, and *only* organized sense perceptions deserve the status of *knowledge*.

What could possibly justify or legitimize the organizing, analyzing, and interpreting of the human mind? At this point, Kant was ready to contend with the Humean skepticism that had aroused him from "dogmatic slumber." Recall that Hume believed his own skepticism would not and could not be taken seriously since inferring causality from the constant conjunction of events (an unobservable inferred from observables) was firmly established or justified by "habit and custom." Further recall that Mill believed the concept of "cause" was justified as the most general of all inductive generalizations. Kant (and scores of philosophers since Kant) took Humean skepticism seriously and sought a stronger justification for causality than Hume's "habit and custom" or Mill's induction. Kant proposed that there were certain "categories" of ideas or concepts that were *synthetic a priori*, examples being "cause," "unity," "reciprocal relation," and "necessity." Just as *empirical* concepts, like "tree," *arrange* sensations from the real world, these "transcendent" categories of concepts enable us to arrange, analyze, and interpret empirical concepts to create scientific knowledge. Transcendent concepts like "cause" are *synthetic a priori* because they relate to the real world of sense perceptions (synthetic) and, contended Kant, the very fact of the possibility of perceptual experience presupposes concepts like "cause." Thus, a concept like "cause" was *a priori* and *necessarily* true because one cannot even imagine the existence of a world of empirical events where such events are uncaused.

But where do *synthetic a priori* concepts like "cause" come from, if not from habit and custom *a la* Hume, or inductively derived from experience, *a la* Mill? Kant's answer was to propose the existence of the "transcendental self." (Hence, Kant's idealism is referred to as "transcendental idealism.") The transcendental self provides us with categories of concepts such as "cause" and "necessity." However, nothing can be known about this "transcendental self" because it was a precondition for knowledge to exist and, therefore, could not possibly become an object of investigation for that knowledge. Thus, said Kant, science is "saved" from Humean skepticism.

In his day, Kant was known as the "all-destroyer." The rationalists felt betrayed because Kant concluded that pure reason alone could generate *only* mathematical and geometrical truths and not knowledge about the external world of objects and phenomena. The speculative metaphysicians were likewise infuriated by Kant's demonstration that metaphysics, since it relied only on pure reason, could not generate knowledge. Kant proposed that the truths of metaphysics (to the extent that there were any) should be accepted on "faith," an entirely unsatisfactory prospect for the metaphysicians. Empiricists were upset at the introduction of such idealistic concepts as the "transcendental self" into the justification of science. Finally, in the area of ethics, Kant himself claimed to have destroyed "utilitarianism" (although the doctrine would not acquire that label until the time of Mill) with his categorical imperative: Act only according to those maxims you could wish to become universal law.

Unfortunately for Kant's physical safety, his works deviated from orthodox Lutheran Protestantism. In particular, Kant's attacks on rationalism and metaphysics necessarily implied that the existence of God could not be proved by the standard ontological methods of rationalism. Although Kant claimed to have "saved" theology by showing that the existence of God could not be *disproved* by rationalist methods and claimed that the existence of God could be accepted as a practical commitment of morality, such a defense was unpersuasive to the Lutheran hierarchy. As a consequence, Kant received the following order from the Prussian government:

> Our highest person has been greatly displeased to observe how you misuse your philosophy to undermine and destroy many of the most important and fundamental doctrines of the Holy Scriptures and of Christianity. We demand of you immediately an exact account, and expect that in the future you will give no such cause of offense, but rather that, in accordance with your duty, you will employ your talents and authority so that our paternal purpose may be more and more obtained. If you continue to oppose this order you may expect unpleasant consequences. [491, p. 49]

Kant reflected on the precise nature of the threatened "unpleasant consequences," and, as Galileo had done before him, accepted the silencing.

8.4.3 Hegel

When philosophers and historians of philosophy speak of "German idealism," they generally refer not to the transcendental idealism of Kant, but to the idealism of Hegel. In fact, "Hegelian philosophy" is often used synonymously with "German philosophy": "He ruled the philosophic world as indisputably as Goethe the world of literature, and

Beethoven the realm of music." [161, p.222]   Many 20th century philosophies owe their origins to Hegel.   For example, the underlying philosophies of fascism (the myth of the "chosen race") and Marxism (the myth of the "chosen class") spring directly from Hegel. [506, p. 9]   Who was Hegel and how could his ideas become so powerful that his very name would be equivalent to the central philosophy of an entire nation?

Georg Wilhelm Friedrich Hegel (1770-1831) was born to a family of modest means in Stuttgart, Prussia, studied the ministry at the University of Tubingen, and wrote two of his most important books, *The Phenomenology of Mind* and *Logic*, before being appointed in 1817 to the Chair of Philosophy at the University of Heidelberg.   Hegel was upset by the liberal democratic views of the Enlightenment and the destruction of metaphysics by Kant.   The nature of his philosophical system came to him through a "mystical experience" which compelled him to reveal the "truths of idealism" to the world.

Essentially, Kant's transcendental idealism had held that we can comprehend the external world because the active mind forms or molds our sense-perceptions; that is, because "reality" is "mind-like."   Hegel's idealism claimed not that the world was "mind-like," but that the mind *is* the world: There is only one reality of minds and matter which is a holistic unity, called the "Absolute" mind, or *Geist*.   "The rational is the real and the real is the rational" claims Hegel's so-called "philosophy of the identity of reason and reality."   Proclaiming *only* reason (the rational) to be "real," gave Hegel the license, he argued, to construct a metaphysical philosophical system comprised of pure reason alone.   Knowledge about Absolute mind could not be gleaned from the method of science with its emphasis on observation and experimentation, since only reason is "real" and reason is unobservable.   Therefore, Hegel articulated and developed his alternative method, the method of dialectic.   In many respects Hegel's system and method was a direct descendant of medieval scholasticism [Neurath, in 472a, p. 7]

Hegel was a firmly committed historicist.   Since only "ideas" are "real," what needed explaining was the history of the progression of ideas.   Central to Hegel's dialectic was the concept of contradiction or contradictory ideas.   (Actually, the reader will note, Hegel's "contradictions" are often better described as "polar opposites.")   From the empirical observation that the history of ideas is filled with contradictory (polar opposite) concepts (e.g., freedom and slavery, democracy and totalitarianism, good and evil), Hegel propounded the radical *causal* proposition that every idea (or thesis) *produces* its contradiction (or antithesis). [505, p. 315]   The contradictory theses and antitheses engage in conflict and struggle, producing *syntheses* that contain elements of both contradictions.   Therefore, a good idea never wins over a bad idea and a true idea never refutes a false one, the synthesis is always an inexorable (Hegel is deterministic) combination of the two.   For example in any struggle between democracy and totalitarianism, one side cannot "win"; the conclusion (or synthesis) *must* contain elements of both.   Each dialectical process produces a synthesis which, in turn, becomes a thesis and produce its *own* antithesis.

According to Hegel, all the great writers in the history of ideas had been producing theses and antitheses like "stones on a pile." Because the process was inexorable and strictly determined by the *Zeitgeist* (the Spirit of the Age), the ideas could neither be objectively true nor objectively false, but only products of the Spirit of the Age. However, the dialectical progression of the history of ideas (the "pile of stones") comes to its final conclusion in Hegel's philosophical system, since he had "the good fortune to come last, and when he places his stone the arch stands self-supported." [161, p.225]

8.4.4　The Triumph of German Idealism

The firestorm of German idealism swept through the Western philosophical world and completely dominated it from 1850-1900. Even that bastion of empiricism, the British Isles, fell under the idealistic onslaught. The empiricism of Galileo, Bacon, Locke, Hume, Mill and Newton was considered so much rubbish to be swept from the idealist house of intellect. Indeed, claimed the idealists, how presumptuous of these scientists and philosophers to believe that knowledge about the external world could be gained from a method that conjoined hypothesis development with mathematics, observation, experiment, and "old logic" (as contrasted with the new logic of dialectic)? German idealism seemed to solve the major philosophical problems of such diverse groups as the speculative metaphysicians, organized religion, right-wing monarchists, and left-wing revolutionaries. That such a philosophy could serve well such diverse groups attests to its obtuseness. As Schopenhauer (1788-1860), Hegel's contemporary, noted: "But the height of audacity in serving up pure nonsense, in stringing together senseless and extravagant mazes of words, such as had previously been known only in madhouses, was finally reached in Hegel, and became the instrument of the most bare-faced general mystification that has ever taken place." [564a, p. 429]

A major problem of the speculative metaphysicians had been their disenfranchisement from the productive activity of knowledge-creation by not only the rapid advances of practicing scientists but also by the philosophical works of Kant. The metaphysicians could now rejoin the knowledge-generating enterprise by pejoratively attacking the knowledge-claims of science. After all, since only the "rational is real," only rationalist metaphysics could explore the "real" or important problems of knowledge. Examples of such "real" issues included: Is the Absolute beyond time? Does the Absolute transcend thought? Is it personal? Is it moral? Is it beautiful? Metaphysicians such as Francis Bradley (1846-1924), perhaps the most prominent English advocate of idealism, explored issues such as these in his famous work *Appearance and Reality*. I offer the reader the following long passage from Bradley's book (as quoted in Russell [544, p. 14]), as an example of how the 19th century idealists attempted to demonstrate that relationships between entities in the external world were "mere appearances," rather than "reality":

> But how the relation can stand to the qualities is, on the other side, unintelligible. If it is nothing to the qualities, then they are not related at all; and, if so, as we saw, they have ceased to be qualities, and their relation is a nonentity. But if it is to be something to them, then clearly we shall require a *new* connecting relation. For the relation hardly can be the mere adjective of one or both of its terms; or, at least, as such it seems indefensible. And, being something itself, if it does not itself bear a relation to the terms, in what intelligible way will it succeed in being anything to them? But here again we are hurried off into the eddy of a hopeless process, since we are forced to go on finding new relations without end. The links are united by a link, and this bond of union is a link which also has two ends; and these require each a fresh link to connect them with the old. The problem is to find how the relation can stand to its qualities, and this problem is insoluble.

Note the obtuseness of the preceding argument. Russell concludes that "most people will admit, I think, that it [Bradley's argument] is calculated to produce bewilderment rather than conviction, because there is more likelihood of error in a very subtle, abstract, and difficult argument than in so patent a fact as the interrelatedness of the things in the world." [544, p. 14]

In addition to the metaphysicians, organized religion warmly embraced Hegel's idealism. As will be recalled, Kant had argued that rationalist metaphysics could neither prove nor disprove the existence of God since all knowledge has its foundations in sense-perceptions. Hegel's claim that "the rational is the real," when combined with the concept of the Absolute, provides a rationalist "proof" for the existence of God. For organized religion, Hegel's Absolute became simply another label for God. Hegel himself encouraged religious leaders to so interpret his Absolute and late in his life attempted to destroy an earlier writing on religion (his *Life of Jesus*) that might have troubled them. [161, p. 221]

Right-wing monarchists also endorsed Hegelian idealism. Instead of focusing on "the rational is the real" (as did the metaphysicians), the monarchists emphasized "the real is the rational," because it implies that whatever state of affairs presently exists, exists because it is *necessarily* so and *ought* to exist. All existing governments are completely justified because none could be other than it is. Hegel had allied himself with the Prussian king and despised liberal democracy, as the following passage shows: "To hold that every single person should share in deliberating and deciding on political matters of general concern on the ground that all individuals are members of the state, that its concerns are their concerns, and that it is their right that what is done should be done with their knowledge and volition, is tantamount to a proposal to put the democratic element without any rational form into the organism of the state although it is only in virtue of the possession of such a form that the state is an organism at all." [Hegel, as quoted in 81, p.563] Note how Hegel's argument depends so heavily on the view that the state is "real" (it has "rational form") and individual people are "unreal" by comparison (the "democratic element [is] without rational form"), a thesis which was later to be forcefully argued by Bosanquet, the English idealist philosopher. The reader is urged at this point to pause and reflect on the implications, especially the moral implications, of *any* philosophy that claims individual people to be "unreal."

Left-wing revolutionaries also found solace and inspiration in Hegelian idealism. Eastern Marxist philosophers, such as Plekhanov, have historically downplayed the importance of idealistic concepts such as the Absolute in their use of Hegelian philosophy. On the other hand, Western Marxist philosophers, such as Lukacs and Mannheim, have *emphasized* the idealistic component that dominates much of Marx's writings. In any respect, Marx himself, in the preface to the second edition of *Das Kapital*, indicated he was "the pupil of that mighty thinker" Hegel and all Marxist writers have adopted Hegel's "method of dialectic." The idealistic ontology of Hegel's philosophy, as stated in "the real is the rational," argued for the status quo of the Prussian monarchy. Marx recognized that, on the contrary, Hegel's epistemology, as rooted in the "method of dialectic," argued for continuous revolutionary activity. Writing on the dialectical method in Marxism, Engels notes "What therefore is the negation of the negation? An extremely general . . . law of development of nature, history and thought; a law which holds in the animal and plant kingdoms, in geology, in mathematics, in history, and in philosophy." [Engels, as quoted in 505, p.333] For Marx, the dialectic implied that the monarchy (thesis) would give rise, or produce its own "contradiction" (antithesis). Thus, the monarchy and its contradiction, or "negation," would produce a new synthesis, and so on. Hegel thought the dialectical process ended with his own philosophy. Similarly, the dialectical materialism of Marx proposed that the history of political economy is an inexorable process ending with the ultimate socialist state.

Marxist philosophers have made great use of the concept of "contradiction" from Hegelian idealism and they, also, confuse "contradiction" with "polar opposite." Critics of Marxist philosophy in particular and German idealism in general often point out numerous instances of logical contradictions. That is, critics point out instances where such philosophies loudly proclaim that the statement "x is true" and the statement "x is false" are *both* "true" at the same time! As Popper cogently observes, when confronted by their critics with such obvious logical fallacies, Marxists and other idealists claim that the "criticism is mistaken because it is based on logic of the ordinary type instead of on dialectic." [505, p.328] Thus, if German idealism in general and Marxist philosophy in particular cannot be attacked on either logical grounds (because normal logic is "old logic" in contrast with the "new logic" of dialectic) or on empirical grounds (because only the "rational is real"), the reader should ponder the grounds that might remain. (Force? Power? Coercion?)

As noted previously, science grew out of general philosophy and for centuries scientific inquiry was a subdivision of philosophical inquiry. Scientists were in fact called natural philosophers until about 1800. By the middle of the 19th century German idealism had driven a mighty wedge between the child (science) and its parent (philosophy). Scientists viewed philosophical writings as irrelevant at best or mystical, metaphysical nonsense, at worst.   Philosophers, following Hegel, viewed mathematics with contempt and scorned empirical science. This "dangerous gulf," in Popper's terms [505, p. 69], between science and philosophy continued until the rise of Realism and Logical Positivism in the early part of the 20th century. But to understand the rise of these philosophies, we must first briefly examine the writings of Comte, Mach, and Frege, for they paved the way for Realism and Logical Positivism.

8.5   CLASSICAL POSITIVISM

During the early part of the 19th century, there arose in France a movement known as "social positivism" that had as its central objective the promotion of a more just society through the application of the knowledge generated by science and the scientific method. The movement was closely associated with the philosopher Saint-Simon (1760-1825), who coined the term "positivism." Saint-Simon's ideas heavily influenced August Comte (1798-1857), the French philosopher, mathematician, and historian. Comte's major work, the six-volume *Cours de Philosophie Positive*, elaborated and popularized the "positive philosophy of science," viewed by Laudan as "the most important single development in the last century" as to theories of the scientific method. [367, p. 29]

Comte was a confirmed historicist, believing that there were certain inexorable laws of history with respect to the stages of thinking that all disciplines go through. [505, p. 338] All sciences inevitably go through three stages of development: the theological, the metaphysical, and the "positive." [334, p.72] In the theological stage all events are caused by the exercise of the will of the gods, or the will of God. In the metaphysical stage abstract concepts, such as "essence", replace the will of the gods. In the final, or positive stage, the discipline gives up the quest for absolute knowledge in the sense of "final will" or "first cause" and, instead, turns toward attempting to discover the lawlike relationships of coexistence and succession by using the methods of observation, experimentation, and comparison.

Comte arranged the sciences in the hierarchy of (from bottom to top): astronomy, physics, chemistry, biology, and sociology. Comte, as a mathematician, viewed mathematics as a fundamental tool to be used in all the sciences and, therefore, was not "in" the hierarchy. Each discipline had either *gone* through the stages (like astronomy), or would have to *go through* the stages in the future (like sociology). Comte believed that social phenomena (when properly investigated) would follow lawlike patterns, coined the term *"sociologie"* to identify the scientific study of social phenomena and, thus, is considered the "father of sociology." [444, p. 299] Sociology is at the top of Comte's hierarchy because it gave meaning and purpose to the other sciences and because of the fundamental tenets of the social positivist movement. That is, scientific knowledge was not sought for its own sake, but to bring about a better life for all and a more just society through, among other things, the prediction and control of phenomena.

Many aspects of Comte's positivist philosophy were to influence the logical positivists in the next century. These aspects include: the emphasis on the explanation and prediction of observable phenomena, the disavowal of the search for "deeper" or "final" causes, the rejection of metaphysics, and the view that scientific knowledge and the use of the scientific method could be useful in bringing about a better society. In fact, the, so-called "verificationist theory of meaning" of the logical positivists has its roots in Comte: "Any proposition which is not reducible to the simple enunciation of the fact—either particular or general—can have no real or intelligible meaning for us." [Comte, as quoted in 334, p. 73]

8.5.1   Ernst Mach

Our second 19th century positivist, Ernst Mach (1838-1916), was an Austrian physicist and philosopher born in Moravia (now Czechoslovakia). While occupying a chair of physics at Prague University, he wrote his best known work, *The Science of Mechanics*, in which he attempted to reformulate Newtonian mechanics using a phenomenalist or sensationalist perspective.

Smitten with the "quest for certainty," Mach insisted that science should purge itself of metaphysical concepts. Since, for Mach, the only knowledge-claims that can be known with certainty are those related directly to sense-perceptions, or "sensations," science should restrict itself to laws and theories dealing directly with sensations. Mach held that "the aim of a theory is to correlate the facts, given that the process of correlation must take one beyond the facts, it should do so without postulating any other entities or processes that are not *necessary* for that task of correlation." [373, p. 208] Stated succinctly, Mach held that the purpose of laws and theories ought to be to give the most economical description of the phenomena. Thus, Mach (like Berkeley) embraced an *instrumentalist* view of scientific theory: The statements of a theory are mere instruments for summarizing phenomena in an efficient fashion. Laws and theories are not meant to be true descriptions of how the world is actually constructed, nor are the theoretical (nonobservable) concepts in a theory to be construed as having a real existence.

As is well known, Mach bitterly opposed the introduction of the concept of the atom into physics. He did so, not because of some objection that the atom could not be observed or that statements involving the atom could not be inductively generated from sense-data. Indeed, "contrary to popular mythology, there was nothing in 19th century positivism that was hostile to speculative theory construction." In fact, "all the major positivists from Comte to Mach, Poincare and Duhem enthusiastically accepted Kant's point about the active knower and were thoroughly contemptuous of that 18th-century brand of empiricism and inductivism which imagined that theories would somehow emerge mechanically from the data." [373, p.207] Mach opposed the introduction of the atom into physics because he believed that all the known laws about physics could be more economically stated without using the concept "atom." Thus, Mach was not opposed to the introduction into science of *all* concepts that transcend sensory experience. He himself considered "oxygen," "heat," and "center of gravity," as useful scientific concepts going beyond sensations. Rather, Mach believed that such concepts should be added to scientific knowledge only when necessary for the economical and efficient description of sensations. [373, p. 204] As we shall see later in this chapter, the logical positivists relied heavily on Mach's instrumentalist view of theories and his sensationalist epistemology. Further, we shall see that Mach's positivism influenced Einstein in developing his theories of relativity.

8.5.2   Gottlob Frege

Our third philosopher, the German mathematician Gottlob Frege (1848-1925) was not, strictly speaking, a classical positivist—his philosophical orientation was decidedly realist. Nevertheless, Frege's 19th century work in the area of the philosophy of mathematics was enormously influential on 20th century logical positivism. Therefore, it seems appropriate to discuss his views in this section, along with his 19th century colleagues.

Three fundamental questions have dominated the philosophy of mathematics for hundreds of years: (1) What is the fundamental nature of mathematics (the ontological question)? (2) How do we know mathematical truths (the epistemological question)? and (3) Why is it the case that mathematics is useful in empirical science (the pragmatical question)? Three different general approaches to these fundamental questions have been employed: intuitionism, formalism, and logicism. [361, p. 201]

Kant was one of the foremost exponents of the *intuitionist* approach. Kant believed that the sequence of natural numbers ("1," "2," "3," and so forth) are *synthetic a priori* concepts provided by our intuition. That is, in some meaningful sense mathematical numerals have a "real existence" (synthetic) and are known to us without the benefit of sense-perceptions (*a priori*).

Uneasiness about relying on vague concepts like "intuition" to explain the fundamental nature of mathematics have led many philosophers in the direction of *formalism*. Vigorous efforts to formalize the arithmetic of natural numbers culminated with the successful formulation of the Italian mathematician Giuseppe Peano (1858-1932) in 1899. As previously discussed in Chapter 6, Section 3, an axiomatic formal system (or calculus) contains elements, formation rules, definitions, transformation rules, and axioms. Peano showed that the fundamental nature of mathematics can be represented as a formal system with a minimum set of five axioms containing three primitive or undefined elements: "0," "number," and "successor." [626, p. 148] Thus, Peano's answer to the "fundamental nature" question was that mathematics was an uninterpreted formal system, or calculus. Further, Peano's answer to how we know the truths of mathematics was that we deductively derive them from the formal system. However, why should it be the case that mathematics should be useful to empirical science? Given that uninterpreted systems, by definition, "say nothing" about the real world, and given the fact that there are an infinite number of formal systems that could be constructed which would in fact be of little use to empirical science, is it simply an incredibly fortuitous occurrence that this particular formal system (mathematics) is so useful to empirical science? Or, alternatively, were the Pythagoreans correct that the gods had used mathematics as the pattern from which the cloth of the universe was cut? Now enter *logicism* and Gottlob Frege in an attempt to answer simultaneously all three fundamental questions concerning mathematics.

Systematic efforts to show the strong relationship between mathematics and logic go back at least as far as the English mathematician

George Boole (1815-1864). However, Boole's works always contained expressions that most writers would identify as purely mathematical, rather than logical in fundamental character. In a series of three famous publications, beginning with *Begrisschrift* in 1879, Gottlob Frege explored the fundamental nature of mathematics by showing that all mathematical concepts and operations could be replaced by purely logical concepts, while maintaining the truth-content of mathematical proofs. Frege maintained that the central notion for the conception of all cardinal numbers ("1," "2," etc.) is captured in the expression "just as many as there are things of some standard kind." Further, Frege defined the number "zero" as the "number of objects not identical with themselves." Thus, Frege's answers to the three fundamental philosophical questions about mathematics were: (1) The fundamental nature of all mathematics is logic; (2) We know the truths of mathematics because they can be derived from the truths of logic; and (3) Mathematics is useful to science on the same grounds that logic is useful to science. That is, it is inconceivable that science could exist without logic, since science necessarily includes statements containing both logical terms ("and," "or," etc.) and logical operations (for example, syllogistic reasoning). However, more important for our purposes than his concepts and definitions was his method of analysis. In order to analyze the logical character of mathematics, Frege found it necessary to create an entire system of notation and procedures that has come to be known as "mathematical logic," "modern logic," "symbolic logic," or, simply, "formal logic."

Another way of stating Frege's *methodological* achievement is to say that he *formalized* ordinary logic by explicitly creating a system of logical symbols (elements), rules for combining symbols meaningfully (formation rules), and rules for deriving certain combinations of symbols from other combinations (transformation rules). But why should he do this and what is its significance? The impetus for the formalization of logic stems from the impreciseness of logic as stated in any "ordinary" natural language. For example, English (a "natural" language) with its immense vocabulary (over twice the number of words as most other modern languages) is extraordinarily precise. Nevertheless, many English sentences containing logical terms are notoriously *imprecise*. For example, consider the following sentence: "Shopping goods or convenience goods may be used in the experiment." What is the meaning of "or" in the sentence? Does it mean "either/or" or "and/or"? One does not know unless given further information. Formal logic uses the symbol "v" to stand for the disjunctive connective "or." Therefore, since the symbol "v" is *always* used to mean "and/or," the meaning of any expression containing "v" is much more precise than an English sentence containing the word "or."

Frege's reduction of mathematics to logic was not to stand the test of time.[2] In a personal letter to Frege in 1901, Bertrand Russell pointed out a serious contradiction in one of Frege's axioms. This contradiction meant that the theorem which states that the series of natural numbers is infinitely large could no longer be proved in Frege's formal system. Nevertheless, Frege's work strongly influenced Russell's attempt to reduce mathematics to logic in his classic, *Principia Mathematica*. And Frege's method, formal logic, was to be adopted as a principal tool of analysis by the logical positivists in the 20th century.

This section has focused on the classical positivists in the 19th century, Comte and Mach, and the work of Frege in symbolic logic and mathematics. The reader should be reminded, however, that these philosophers did not dominate philosophical thought in their time. Rather, the philosophical world continued to be dominated by German idealism through the latter half of the 19th century. Only with the rise of classical realism, as exemplified by philosophers such as Moore, Russell, and Wittgenstein, accompanied by the pragmatism of Peirce, did the influence of German idealism begin to wane.

QUESTIONS FOR ANALYSIS AND DISCUSSION

1. The headnote at the beginning of Chapter 8 by John Kekes states: "If rationality is abandoned, then either 'anarchy is loosed upon the world,' or dogmatism supported by brute force would prevail." Why is this the case? What is the relationship of this headnote to the rest of the material in Part II? What does this have to do with the "fear" that many scholars have of relativism?

2. Section 8.1.2 contends that "Sage philosophy, by its very nature, lacks the capability for being cumulative, since the knowledge of the student cannot go beyond that of the master." It also points out that Sage philosophy "has the distressing tendency to deteriorate into cultism or mysticism." What do we mean by "cumulative"? Given your definition, under what circumstances can inquiry be cumulative? There is an underlying value-judgment in the word "deteriorate." What is this value judgment? Do you agree or disagree with it? Why?

3. Summarize the argument that Socrates used against Protagoras and his version of relativism that is discussed in Section 8.1.3. What does it mean for an

---

[2]The modern view in the philosophy of mathematics is that all mathematics can be formalized into Second Order Logic. (Frege & Russell used First Order Logic). The issues at debate are whether Second Order Logic is properly called "logic" and the implications of such a formalization for the epistemology of mathematics. [512, p. 386]

argument to be self-refuting? Why should we *care* whether an argument is self-refuting? Would your answer differ if you believed that science is "just another game"?

4. Someone has said that "the key to understanding many of the silly statements that are made about the 'demarcation issue' in science is to recognize that the term 'science' should be approached from a *taxonomical* perspective, rather than a *definitional* perspective. In particular, 'scientific method' should be approached this way." Evaluate. Hint: See Section 7.1.2 and Section 8.2.2.

5. Compare and contrast the views of the "mechanicians" concerning their opposition to the rise of science with the views of many marketing practitioners and their beliefs about the purpose of marketing research and marketing science.

6. Many people seem to define the purpose of others exclusively in terms of some particular role. For example, many children never see their mothers and fathers as "people." Rather, their mothers and fathers exist only as "parents." To what extent can this help us understand why there will always be conflict between marketing practitioners and marketing academicians? To what extent does the "fault" lie with both groups?

7. It is often pointed out that all research involves "interpretation." Section 8.2.1 pointed out that the "Hermeneutics" of today derives from the "scholasticism" of the Middle Ages. Select a recent article in marketing. To what extent does "interpretation" enter into the research? Where? To what extent is the research *exclusively* "interpretation"? If one chooses to claim that an instance of "interpretation" is "incorrect," what could be the various bases for such a claim? Is all research *just* "interpretation"? (For more on this issue, see the Calder and Tybout article and Hirschman's "Afterword" in reference 274a.)

8. Classical empiricism claims that experience and observation are the fundamental sources or "foundations" of our knowledge of the external world. On the other hand, classical rationalism claims that *a priori* reason alone is the fundamental source or "foundation" of our knowledge of the external world. What do we mean by "fundamental source"? Suppose we had a child who, most unfortunately, was born without any of the "five senses." Could such an individual gain knowledge of the external world? Consider, next, a child born with all the five senses but with absolutely zero reasoning capability. Could such a child gain knowledge? How does "foundationalism" as a doctrine differ from "all research has foundations"?

9. Summarize the empiricism-rationalism debate. To what extent does the "discovery/justification" distinction help us understand the debate? To what extent does the "fallible/infallible" distinction help us? In your judgment, which "side" of the debate had the better case?

10. What is "foundationalism"? Why should we be interested in distinguishing between "knowledge" and "opinion"? If all knowledge-claims are, ultimately, based on "faith," then are not all knowledge-claims "merely opinions"? Evaluate.

11. What is idealism? How does idealism relate to relativism? Many ethicists attack idealism on the basis that it is "morally corrupt." What does "morally corrupt" mean? Evaluate the thesis that idealism is morally corrupt.

12. What is Hegel's "philosophy of the idea of the identity of reason and reality"? Why does such a philosophy *necessarily* imply that observation and experimentation are useless for gaining knowledge? What is the relevance for epistemology of

Russell's argument against idealism: "There is more likelihood of error in a very subtle, abstract, and difficult argument than so patent a fact as the interrelatedness of the things in the world"? How does this relate to sophisty?

13. What is classical positivism? What is its relationship to the Enlightenment? Why did the classical positivists reject metaphysical concepts? Should they have? Should we?

9

THE DEVELOPMENT OF THE DISCIPLINE OF PHILOSOPHY OF SCIENCE: FROM CLASSICAL REALISM TO LOGICAL EMPIRICISM

Insofar as the revolt against science condemns science for making of itself the instrument of power, looks with dismay on the devastation to which science-based technology has given rise, rejects a world made grey by standardization or a world in which the individual counts for less and less, and seeks to reinstate the imagination and direct sensual enjoyment, one can sympathize with its motives even when one believes that its accusations rest on a misunderstanding of science. But the attack on disciplined thinking, the revival of occultism with its doctrine of "hidden truths" to be revealed by magical means, the demand for instant gratification in every area of human life, the rejection of the idea of learning, of discipleship, of tradition—these, I freely confess, fill me with horror and dismay. And it is not only science which suffers but all the activities which particularly distinguish human society, as compared with a society of bees and ants—art, history, philosophy, social innovation, technological achievement, the spirit of critical inquiry.

John Passmore

After having given "birth" to science in the 17th century, philosophy and science became estranged from each other in the latter half of the 19th century. In fact, philosophy adopted an antiscience orientation as a result of its entanglement in Hegelian idealism. This chapter traces the decline of idealism in philosophy under the attacks on it by the (classical) realists and the reconciliation of science with philosophy brought about by the logical positivists and logical empiricists. The chapter closes with a discussion of scientific knowledge and its progress.

9.1   THE EMERGENCE OF REALISM

As will be recalled, Western philosophy at the beginning of the 20th century had been dominated by German idealism for over fifty years. Hegel's dictum "The Real is the Rational" guided philosophical inquiry.

Arguing that "all cognition is judgment," idealists denied the existence of the world of tangible objects and phenomena and claimed that only Absolute Mind is real. The "doctrine of internal relations" also buttressed the case for idealism. This doctrine held that the nature of anything must be grounded in and constituted by the relations it has with other things. That is, the "parts" cannot exist independently from their relatedness to some "whole." Therefore, objects cannot exist independently from their "relation" to the mind that knows them and *the external world does not exist independently of its being perceived* (the central tenet of German idealism).

The revolt against idealism was led by many philosophers who, themselves, had been seduced by idealism in the early parts of their careers. In this section we shall discuss the emergence of classical realism, whose central tenet maintains, contra idealism, that *the external world exists independently of its being perceived.* Note that the realism being advocated by philosophers at the turn of this century was primarily ontological (the nature of existence), rather than epistemological (the nature of knowledge) in character. Modern philosophers of science who characterize themselves as "scientific realists" usually adopt realism in *both* an ontological and epistemological sense. We shall return to the issue of scientific realism in Chapter 11. For now, we shall examine the arguments that realist philosophers, such as Moore, Russell, and Wittgenstein employed in their debate with German idealism.

9.1.1 G.E. Moore

The opening salvo fired in the idealism/realism debate was the publication of Moore's "The Refutation of Idealism" in 1903. George Edward Moore (1873-1958), professional philosopher, ethicist, Cambridge University lecturer, and close friend of Bertrand Russell, had been a dedicated idealist in the early part of his career. In one of his early papers entitled "In What Sense, if Any, Do Past and Future Time Exist?" (1897), Moore argued that time does not exist and that if this conclusion outraged common sense, then common sense is simply wrong. By 1903 Moore's analysis of language led him to conclude that idealism was fundamentally mistaken. In fact, Moore's method of analysis presaged modern linguistic analysis, since he constantly delved into the nature of meaning in both ordinary and philosophical terminology. Both he and his realist contemporaries used several arguments to refute idealism. First, Moore claimed that sentences like "I think of X" describe (1) mental acts and (2) objects related to but distinct from those acts. Once the object of a mental act is distinguished from the awareness of it, there is no reason to deny the existence of the object independently from its being perceived. Idealism simply confused the act of perception with the object being perceived. Moreover, if the perception or the awareness of an object cannot provide satisfactory evidence of the object's existence, no awareness is ever awareness of anything, for we could not be aware of other persons or even of ourselves and our own sensations.   That is, *the very concept of "awareness" presumes that there are objects independent of that awareness.*

A second argument against idealism concerned the concept "real." The realists argued that idealism used the concept "real" in ways that violated fundamental principles of intelligible discourse.   That is, the fundamental meaning of the term "real" derives from such standard examples as "this chair is real" and "this table exists."   To deny the fundamental examples that give meaning to a term and at the same time, to continue to use the term in other contexts, produces unintelligible speech.   To continue to create pseudosentences, containing terms stripped of their meanings, constitutes farce, not profundity.   (Some writers on the social sciences today employ the same technique.)

A third argument against idealism had a distinctly pragmatic character to it.   The argument stemmed from the inconsistency between stated beliefs and actual behaviors.   Realists claimed that idealists were disingenuous in their claimed beliefs.   Although idealists would claim that objects like tables and chairs do not exist, their actual behaviors belied their claims.   When idealists entered rooms, they approached and sat on chairs, just as if the chairs actually existed.   When idealists ate their meals, they pulled their chairs to tables, just as if the tables actually existed.   Thus, the elaborate argumentation of idealism points toward sophistry, rather than genuine belief.

9.1.2   Bertrand Russell

Whereas G.E. Moore was a philosopher/ethicist, our second realist, Bertrand Russell (1872-1970), was a philosopher/mathematician at Cambridge University.   Russell argued powerfully and persuasively in a series of papers (later published as *Our Knowledge of the External World* in 1929 [544]) that there are nonmental facts that are independent of any mind becoming aware of them.   He further argued (contra the doctrine of internal relations) that these facts are "atomic" in the sense that the truth-content of propositions containing them could be determined "in isolation" on the basis of whether the propositions *correspond* with observations.   His arguments were so forceful and conclusive that he is often credited with bringing about the downfall of idealism throughout Europe (German philosophy excepted). [505, p. 69]

Russell's "logical atomism" (his ontology) licensed his philosophical method, i.e., analyzing philosophical problems by breaking them into their constituent parts or elements.   Idealism had contended that the analysis of anything was impossible because to understand the nature of a part is impossible without already knowing how it "fits" into the whole, which meant one had to already comprehend the whole, or "Absolute." Russell called his method "logical constructionism," which, stated briefly, entailed the following steps: (1) identify a body of knowledge about which there are unresolved philosophical questions concerning the status of the entities involved in the knowledge and the justification for knowledge-claims about the entities; (2) demonstrate how the body of knowledge could be reformulated in terms of simpler, more undeniable entities; and (3) analyze the philosophical problems in the original body of knowledge in terms of the language of the simpler, more rigorous, "ideal" language. The objective of the procedure would be to solve the philosophical problems by converting the problematic to the unproblematic and the obscure to the clear. The method of "logical constructionism" implies that the philosophical problems in the original, complex body of knowledge were "constructed" from simpler entities.

Russell, along with Alfred North Whitehead (1861-1947), applied the method of logical constructionism with vigor to mathematical knowledge. In the classic set of works *Principia Mathematica* (1910-1913), they proceeded to take up Frege's work of reformulating all of pure mathematics in terms of logic, alone. The Russell-Whitehead notation for formal logic survives today as one of a handful of notational systems. Based on the primitive term "class," they defined (or "constructed") numbers as "classes of classes." The number "0" was defined as the "class of all empty classes," and the number "1" was defined as the "class of all classes each of which is such that any member is identical with any other member."

More important than the details of how Russell translated mathematics into logic was what has come to be known as "Russell's paradox" and how Russell solved it. As will be recalled from the previous section, Russell had found a contradiction in the fifth axiom of Frege's efforts to reduce mathematics to logic. The contradiction had to do with the concept "class" and, in particular, the "class of all classes which are not members of themselves." Referring to this class as "X," Russell asked whether "X" was, or was not, "a member of itself." Either way the question is answered, a paradox arises: If "X" is a member of itself, then it satisfied the defining condition of such members, so it is not a member of itself; and if it is not a member of itself, it belongs to the class of such classes and so is a member of itself.

Russell solved the paradox (and showed how the same procedure could solve a large number of such paradoxes) by showing that the paradox stemmed from a vicious circle arising when we propose a collection of objects containing members definable only by means of the collection as a whole. In other words, the contradiction involved the treatment of *classes* as being on a par with the treatment of their constituent *members*. Russell's "theory of types" maintained that there was a hierarchy existing among the types of entities in his mathematical logic and that if this hierarchy were violated, contradictions would result from the ill-formed expressions.

By now, most readers are probably thoroughly confused. And for good reason. The reader has been asked to attempt to understand sentences such as "is the class of all classes that are not members of themselves a member of itself?" Russell showed that the "paradox" is, strictly speaking, an ill-formed, or *meaningless* expression. Readers, therefore, have been asked to comprehend (make meaningful) the incomprehensible (the meaningless). Could it be the case that most philosophical puzzles were *meaningless* in the same sense as Russell's paradox and could it be the case that using "logical constructionism" would make supposed problems of philosophy disappear? Could it be the case that most of the problems of philosophy resulted, simply, from philosophers phrasing their propositions and questions in an ill-formed, inconsistent, meaningless manner? Enter Ludwig Wittgenstein.

9.1.3   Ludwig Wittgenstein

Ludwig Wittgenstein (1889-1951) was born in Vienna, Austria, studied engineering at the Technische Hochschule in Berlin and at the University of Manchester in England. Upon reading Bertrand Russell's *Principles of Mathematics* (not to be confused with *Principia Mathematica*), he became enthused about mathematics and transferred to Cambridge in 1912. There he studied under, and was greatly influenced by, Bertrand Russell. Wittgenstein's sole published work during his lifetime was *Tractatus Logico-philosophicus* (published in German in 1921, followed by an English translation in 1922). His only other major published work was *Philosophical Investigations*, published posthumously (at his request) in 1953. In a terse 80 pages, *Tractatus* explicated a philosophy that was to be enormously influential in the 20th century. Most interestingly, his 1953 *Philosophical Investigations* represented a critique and rejection of *Tractatus*, and it also has been enormously influential. This section will focus exclusively on the content of *Tractatus*; *Philosophical Investigations* will be discussed in Chapter 10.

Tractatus starts with a theory of meaning and winds up being a comprehensive theory of philosophy. Historically, the philosophy of language has been concerned with the following question: "What are we saying about a linguistic expression when we specify its meaning?" [11, p.10] The many theories that have been advanced to answer the question of meaning can be loosely grouped into three types: referential, ideational, and behavioral. *Referential* theories identify the meaning of a word or expression with that to which the word or expression refers. For example, the word "cat" refers to a certain kind of animal existing in the world. *Ideational* theories indicate that the meaning of a word is equivalent to the ideas in the human mind that the word "stands for." The classic statement of the ideational theory was given by John Locke in his *Essay Concerning Human Understanding:* "The Use, Then, of Words is to be Sensible Marks of Ideas; and the Ideas They Stand For Are Their Proper and Immediate Signification." [Locke, in 11, p. 22] Drawing upon the stimulus-response theories of psychology, *behaviorist* theories of meaning specify the meaning of a linguistic form to be identical with "the situation in which the speaker utters it [the linguistic form] and the response which it calls forth in the hearer." [70, p. 139]

Central to understanding the *Tractatus* is comprehending Wittgenstein's picture theory of meaning. As previously indicated, Wittgenstein was heavily influenced by Bertrand Russell. Russell's version of realism led him to adopt a referential theory of meaning. In fact, at one time Russell even believed that logical terms, such as "and" and "or," had referents in the world of objects and phenomena. Wittgenstein's picture theory of meaning specifies that the meaning of any linguistic form is a "picture in the mind" that refers to reality. Moreover, the pictures are not restricted to individual words, but, most importantly, all meaningful sentences and propositions are pictures of reality. Thus, Section 4.01 of the *Tractatus* states: "A proposition is a picture of reality. A proposition is a model of reality as we think it to be." Note that Wittgenstein does not simply state that a sentence was *like* a picture. Rather, he believed a sentence to be *literally* a "picture in the mind."

Wittgenstein justified his picture theory of meaning as the only sensible way to explain the fact that people can understand the meaning of a sentence that is composed of familiar words even though they have never seen the sentence before, nor had it explained to them. To Wittgenstein, a sentence must be a picture in the mind because the sentence "shows its sense." A sentence composed of familiar words is able to communicate a new state of affairs by virtue of being a picture of that supposed state of affairs.

The implications of the picture theory of meaning were enormous. First of all, for an elementary, basic, or "atomic" linguistic expression to have meaning or sense, its picture must either represent reality truly or falsely. [30, p.41] That is, the meaning of a linguistic expression is *construed* to be either a true or false "picture" of reality. For Wittgenstein, logical terms in a language were "operators" that showed how meaningful atomic linguistic expressions could be combined to form complex sentences or propositions that were likewise meaningful. Furthermore, all significant sentences or propositions could be analyzed into truth-functional combinations of their atomic constituents.

The means by which all significant propositions in a language could be analyzed in terms of their atomic constituents was the method of *truth-tables*. Wittgenstein's method of truth-tables can be illustrated through a simple example. The following is a truth-table for the linguistic expression "P & Q":

	P	Q	P & Q
1.	T	T	T
2.	T	F	F
3.	F	T	F
4.	F	F	F

For example, the first row of the truth-table indicates that "if P is true and Q is true, then P & Q is also true." Other rows are similarly interpreted. Wittgenstein proposed that all meaningful propositions, no matter how logically complex, could be broken into their constituent parts, displayed in truth-tables, and *if those constituent parts were meaningful,* the meaningfulness (truth-content) of the complex proposition could be unequivocably determined.

Wittgenstein in his *Tractatus* claimed to have "solved" all the problems that had confronted philosophers from the dawn of time. All philosophical problems were dissolved, he contended, by showing them to be ill-formed, pseudo, or meaningless *answers* to ill-formed or meaningless *questions* or *pseudoquestions.* As Baker and Hacker put it, Wittgenstein claimed to dissolve philosophical puzzles by showing that:

> The cardinal proposition of philosophy, conceived since the dawn of the subject as revealing ultimate truths about the nature of reality, the metaphysical structure of the world, transpire to be ill-formed propositions which violate the rules of logical syntax. They are not bi-polar, since they are conceived as *necessary* truths about reality. But only bi-polar propositions picture reality; and only Tautologies are necessary truths, and they say nothing about the world. The typical philosophical 'propositions' employ illegitimate categorial concepts (substance, property, concept, etc.) as if they were genuine names, but analysis reveals them to be variables, not names. Consequently these metaphysical pronouncements are no more than pseudo-propositions. [30, p.45]

But if all the world's philosophical puzzles are nothing more than pseudoanswers to pseudoquestions, what is the function of philosophy in the modern world? Wittgenstein gives his answer in Section 4.0031 of *Tractatus*: "All philosophy is a critique of language."

Wittgenstein was cryptic, to say the least. He wrote in aphorisms and even spoke aphoristically. [459] In many respects, Wittgenstein was much like an Eastern "sage" philosopher. Indeed, entire philosophical careers have been made in philosophy through interpreting and reinterpreting Wittgenstein. Nevertheless, on two points there is philosophical consensus: Wittgenstein's *Tractatus* shifted the course of philosophical analysis toward the analysis of language (Baker and Hacker refer to his work as "the watershed" [30, p.39]), and Wittgenstein strongly influenced the movement that would come to be known as Logical Positivism. Who were the logical positivists, what were their beliefs, and why were they so influential in the 20th century? The next section addresses these questions.

9.2   EINSTEINIAN RELATIVITY, QUANTUM MECHANICS, AND LOGICAL POSITIVISM

Science in the 19th century was characterized not only by the quest for certainty with respect to scientific knowledge, but also by the general belief that science had indeed achieved that ambitious goal. Scientific discoveries multiplied exponentially based upon the absolutely secure bedrock of Newtonian physics. However, Einstein's Special Theory of Relativity (1905) and General Theory of Relativity (1916), combined with quantum mechanics, struck the foundations of physics like a lightning bolt.

Greatly influenced by Mach's positivism (see Section 8.5.1), Einstein became very suspicious of the "absolute" nature of Newtonian physics. [418, p. 248; 390, p. 35] Newtonian physics held that space, time, and mass were absolutes in nature; Einstein proposed that all three were relative. Therefore, Newton's laws of motion would hold only for velocities that are small compared with the speed of light. Whereas Newtonian physics held that energy and mass were separate entities, relativity held that energy and mass were *aspects* of the *same* reality, related through the equation, $E=mc^2$. Quantum mechanics also rejected the intuitive distinction between particulate matter and wave-like light and accepted the "wave-particle duality," which holds that under certain conditions light mimics the characteristics of waves and under other conditions behaves like particulate matter. The wave-particle duality is expressed in Heisenberg's Indeterminacy Principle that the position and momentum of a particle may not simultaneously be measured to arbitrary accuracy. Thus, the nature of subatomic particles appears to be fundamentally discontinuous (in quantum units), rather than continuous; indeterministic, rather than deterministic.

The fall of Newtonian mechanics and the rise of Einsteinian relativity sent shock waves through the scientific and philosophical communities, particularly those in Germany. At the turn of the century, four philosophies coexisted in the German philosophical and scientific communities: mechanistic materialism, Hegelian idealism, neo-Kantian idealism, and Machian neo-positivism. [606, pp. 8-10] Mechanistic materialism, with its commitment that all the laws of physics must be strictly deterministic in character, was incompatible with quantum mechanics.   Hegelian idealism was the "official philosophy of the German state and the state universities." [606, p.8] As will be recalled, Hegelian idealism held that the world does not exist independently of its being perceived, and, therefore, whatever is "known" is "relative to the mind that knows it."   As such, it was hostile to science in general and mathematics in particular and could not provide a satisfactory foundation for the "new physics"with its mathematical ontology. As the nuclear physicist Mermin points out, quantum mechanics is *just* mathematics, i.e., *just* a series of equations (this is the meaning of the expression "mathematical ontology"):

> The fact is that although the underlying quantum mechanical view of the world is extraordinarily confusing—Bohr is said to have remarked that if it doesn't make you dizzy then you don't understand it—quantum mechanics as a computational tool is entirely straightforward . . . the problem is that although the formalism of the quantum theory fits nature like a glove, nobody, not even Bohr or Heisenberg, has ever really understood what it means. The only concise picture the formalism offers the world prior to an act of measurement is the formalism itself. [441, pp. 655-6]

The dominant philosophy of the German scientific community was neo-Kantian idealism, which held that there is an "ideal world structure which exemplifies itself in structured phenomena," and "the job of science is to discover the structure of this ideal world." But, the deterministic orientation of neo-Kantianism "virtually precluded acceptance of both relativity-theory and quantum-theory." [606, p. 9]   Finally, there was a small minority of scientists (primarily in the Gottingen and Berlin schools) who embraced Machian neo-positivism, with an epistemology based on "sensations."   However, strict Machian positivism did not allow for the high place that quantum theory gave to mathematics. Clearly, a crisis in both philosophy and science had emerged. Stove succinctly summarizes the situation:

> The crucial event was that one which for almost 200 years had been felt to be impossible, but which nevertheless took place near the start of this century: the fall of the Newtonian empire in physics. This catastrophe, and the period of extreme turbulence in physics which it inaugurated, changed the entire climate of the philosophy of science. Almost all philosophers of the 18th and 19th centuries, it was now clear, had enormously exaggerated the certainty and the extent of scientific knowledge. What was needed, evidently, was a far less optimistic philosophy of science, a rigorously *fallibilist* philosophy, which would ensure that such fearful *hubris* as had been incurred in connection with Newtonian physics should never be incurred again. [603, p. 51]

The philosophy that was to emerge that could accommodate what the physicist Mermin calls the "bizarre" nature of Einsteinian relativity and quantum mechanics came to be called Logical Positivism (a label coined by Feigl [438]). It had its chronological origin with an informal discussion group at the University of Vienna in 1907.

9.2.1   The Origins of the Logical Positivist Movement

Following Ayer's historical account, Logical Positivism should be construed as a *movement*. [25, p. 3] As such, the logical positivist movement has an identifiable beginning, a specifiable group of members, a program of action, and an identifiable end. The movement began with an informal discussion group formed in 1907 comprised of the mathematician Hans Hahn, the physicist Philipp Frank, and the social scientist Otto Neurath. All three were on the faculty at the University of Vienna (hence, the group later referred to itself as the "Vienna Circle") and discussed the desultory state of affairs in philosophy and its estrangement from science. Although at one time science (under the designation "natural philosophy") had been a subdivision of philosophy, science and philosophy were now not only independent of each other, but also openly hostile. Science was progressing by developing and empirically testing theories; whereas, philosophy seemed mired in the metaphysical speculation of German idealism.   Two questions dominated the discussion group in Vienna: (1) Does philosophy have anything to contribute to the progress of the scientific enterprise, especially in light of recent developments in Einsteinian relativity and quantum mechanics? and (2) If philosophy *could* contribute to the scientific enterprise, what methods could be employed to make the contribution?

In 1922, the physicist Moritz Schlick joined the faculty at Vienna and the discussion group. Schlick immediately became a major discussion leader of the group and under his leadership it added the following members: Friedrich Waismann (a mathematician), Edgar Zilsel (a sociologist), Bela von Juhos (a physicist), Felix Kaufmann (a lawyer), Herbert Feigl (a physicist and chemist), Victor Kraft (an historian), Karl Menger (a mathematician), Kurt Godel (a mathematician), and Rudolph Carnap (a mathematician). Recognizing that the views of the members of the discussion group were similar to those of Ernst Mach, the discussion group formally became the Ernst Mach Society in 1928. All the members of the Society were German-speaking, and most were trained in logic, mathematics, and/or physics. No member was a "pure" or "professional" philosopher in the German idealistic tradition. In the main, these were philosophically oriented *scientists*, not scientifically oriented *philosophers*. Although Ludwig Wittgenstein, Bertrand Russell, and Karl Popper were not formal members of the society, they interacted extensively with its members and strongly influenced their views. In 1926, the group studied Wittgenstein's *Tractatus,* and although its mysticism was disquieting, "they accepted it, and it stood out as the most powerful and exciting, though not indeed the most lucid, exposition of their point of view." [25, p. 5]

In 1929, the Society published its manifesto entitled *Wissenschaftliche Weltauffassung, Der Wiener Kreis* ("The Scientific World View: The Vienna Circle"). The manifesto loudly proclaimed a new philosophy of science that eschewed the metaphysical excesses of German idealism in order to "further and propagate a scientific world view." [Joergensen, in 473, p. 850] The manifesto traced the historical origins of the new philosophy and set forth its program. As a result of the manifesto, the society came to be known as the "Vienna Circle." The label "logical positivism" was later coined by Herbert Feigl to identify the views of the circle. "Logical" signified the tremendous importance placed by members of the Circle on using formal logic to analyze philosophical problems, and "positivism" associated the Circle with the views of such classical positivists as Comte and Mach.

Logical positivism quickly became a truly international movement, and the members of the Vienna Circle began to rapidly propagate their views. They established a new journal (*Erkenntnis*) in 1930, and held world congresses in 1934 (Prague), 1936 (Copenhagen), 1937 (Paris), 1938 (Cambridge), 1939 (Harvard), and 1941 (Chicago). The congresses were heavily attended by both practicing scientists and philosophers. The Vienna Circle also helped establish the Philosophy of Science Association and its journal, the *Philosophy of Science.* The lead article in the inaugural issue of *Philosophy of Science* in January, 1934, Rudolph Carnap's "On the Character of Philosophic Problems," proposed the logical positivist perspective. Moreover, the inaugural issue's editorial stated a positivist objective: "Philosophy of science is the organized expression of a growing intent to clarify, perhaps unify, the programs, methods and results of the disciplines of philosophy and science." [117, p. 20]

Logical positivism and its legatee, logical empiricism, came to dominate Western philosophy of science in the first half of this century. Only (but very importantly) German philosophy stayed firmly committed to idealism. Formally speaking, logical positivism as a movement and the Vienna Circle as an organized group disintegrated in the 1930s. Although the members of the circle were not generally politically active, their views on freedom and scientific objectivity were incompatible with Nazism. Many members of the Circle escaped the clutches of the Nazis only by migrating to England and the United States. The Ernst Mach Society was formally dissolved in 1938; *Erkenntnis* was moved in 1938 to The Hague, where it took the name of *Journal of Unified Science*; it was discontinued in 1940 (to be revived in the 1970s). The Third Reich made publications of the Circle illegal. By 1940, the doctrines of logical positivism had been merged into, or had become, mainstream empiricism. Although the logical positivists did not completely develop their program, the views of the Circle changed the topography of the philosophical landscape. The precise nature of the Circle's program is our next topic.

9.2.2   The Logical Positivist Program

From the time of Aristotle to the 19th century, all inquiry was philosophy: Philosophy housed both our methods of inquiry and their applications. Philosophy gave us methods such as critical discussion, syllogistic logic, mathematics, observation, experimentation, and formal logic. Philosophy also applied its methods to such diverse areas as moral philosophy, political philosophy, social philosophy, and natural philosophy. Gradually, these application areas, the "children" of philosophy, matured and developed separate identities of their own: mathematics, physics, chemistry, sociology, political science, and so forth. One science after another separated from the mother—philosophy. [Neurath, in 472a, p. 10] As a response to the maturation of its children, philosophy in the latter half of the 19th century turned toward endless speculation about the ultimate nature of reality, i.e., German idealism. Even here, Einstein's theory of relativity somehow seemed to tell us much more about the ultimate nature of reality than did the "theories" proposed by idealist metaphysicians (compare $E=mc^2$ with "the first cause of the world is the Unconscious," or "there is an entelechy which is the leading principle in living being"). Given that philosophy and science were no longer coterminous, and given that science the child had co-opted the methods of philosophy the parent, was there any continuing role that the parent could play that would further assist the child's development? Stated succinctly, what could or should be the purpose of philosophy in the age of modern science? The logical positivists believed they had found the answer to this question in the works of Wittgenstein and Russell. Section 4.111 of Wittgenstein's *Tractatus* stated:

> The object of philosophy is the logical clarification of thoughts. Philosophy is not a theory, but an activity. A philosophical work consists essentially of elucidations. The result of philosophy is not a number of "philosophical propositions," but to make propositions clear. Philosophy should make clear and delimit sharply the thoughts which otherwise are, as it were, opaque and blurred.

Thus, the logical positivists followed Wittgenstein and claimed that the purpose of *philosophy* should be the "logical clarification" of language, and the purpose of the *philosophy of science* should be to clarify the language of science. In the lead article in the inaugural edition of *Erkenntnis* (1930), Schlick discussed the "turning point in philosophy." He contended that "philosophy is not a system of statements; it is not a science." Continuing his discussion, he proclaimed that "the great contemporary turning point is characterized by the fact we see in philosophy not a system of cognitions, but a system of *acts*; philosophy is that activity through which the meaning of different statements is revealed or determined. By means of philosophy statements are explained, by means of science they are verified." [Schlick in 25, p. 56]

How was the logical clarification of the language of science to be accomplished?   To buttress the traditional method of critical discussion, two tools were proposed for the task. First, following Wittgenstein, the positivists proposed the "verification theory of meaning" as an Ockham's Razor to expunge all metaphysical entities and propositions from the language of science. An early formulation of the verifiability principle stated that "the meaning of a proposition is the method of its verification." Given the positivists' penchant for clarity of expression, this ambiguous and vague formulation of their principle was both surprising and unfortunate, or as Feigl later reminisced, "brash and careless." [177, p. 5]   Essentially, the verifiability principle, following Wittgenstein, claimed that all the propositions, or statements, in science could fall into only one of three potential categories:

1. statements that are cognitively meaningful and true,
2. statements that are cognitively meaningful and false, and
3. statements that are meaningless.

Similar to Russell's "logical atomism," all cognitively meaningful statements, no matter how complex, could be subdivided into their elemental components that could be conclusively verified as either true or false. These elemental components could then be displayed in truth-tables, as developed by Wittgenstein, to determine the truth or falsity of the complex proposition. All statements, either elementary or complex, that could not be recast in the preceding manner were held to be meaningless, or "empty talk."

The second tool to be employed in the clarification of scientific language was formal logic, as originally developed by Frege and extended by Bertrand Russell in *Principia*. Given the notorious imprecision of natural languages (English, French, etc.), the precision of formal logic would enable the positivists to clarify the language of science in general, and its theories in particular, by reconstructing it from a natural, imprecise language into an ideal, precise one.

What would be the outcome of the clarification of the language of science through ridding it of meaningless assertions by means of the verifiability principle and reconstructing it through formal logic into a precise, ideal language? The ultimate outcome, the Vienna Circle believed, was to be an *Einheitswessenschaft*, i.e., "a unified science comprising all knowledge of reality accessible to man without dividing it into separate unconnected special disciplines, such as physics and psychology, natural science and letters, philosophy and the special sciences." [Joergensen, in 473, p. 850]

The logical positivists rejected the notion of Comte that there was a hierarchy of sciences. Rather, (following Mach) they embraced the "unity of science" thesis, which provided that, although there were numerous differences in terms of subject matter and techniques among the various sciences, they all shared a common belief that their knowledge-claims should be intersubjectively certifiable through empirical testing. Disciplinary objectives (i.e., the explanation of phenomena through laws and theories) separate the sciences from art and the humanities; whereas, method of verification (intersubjectively certifiable tests) separate the sciences from pseudosciences, such as astrology, palmistry, and phrenology.[1]

A second aspect of the "unity of science" thesis was that "scientists of different disciplines should collaborate more closely with each other and with philosophers than they usually do." [25, p. 29] This is why the positivists organized numerous congresses where they brought together both philosophers and scientists from all disciplines for the purpose of discussing common interests. (It is worth noting that most philosophy of science conferences today are attended almost exclusively by philosophers, historians, and sociologists of science, rather than practicing scientists.) The positivists believed that many of the problems separating the different sciences were brought about because practitioners in the various sciences were using concepts and terminology that inhibited communication. Therefore, they believed it very important that the unification of the various "special" sciences should take place through the formation of a universal language of science. [Joergensen in 473, p. 922]

Finally, the "unity of science" thesis entailed the objective of working toward "reducing" all the special sciences into a "unitary or monistic set of explanatory premises." [177, p. 21] In this regard, the positivists were encouraged by the partial success of reducing chemistry to physics; of biology to physics and chemistry; and of psychology to neurophysiology. To further all the goals of the unity of science movement, the positivists planned an ambitious program of developing an

---

[1]The reader should note how Anderson completely misses the point when he claims that "Hunt's demarcation standard depends entirely on the last criterion" (i.e., scientific method). "The first two requirements [a distinct subject matter and underlying uniformities] are specious since astrologers, parapsychologists, and scientific creationists also study subject matters which they presuppose to exhibit regularities." [13, p. 18] The objective of the first criterion is to distinguish marketing science from disciplines such as economics and psychology. The purpose of the second criterion is to distinguish the sciences from the arts, e.g., painting and music. (Note that neither painting nor music have "explanation" through "regularities" as an objective.) Therefore, the first two criteria are not "spurious." (See, also, Sections 10.2.2 and 11.2.1.)

International Encyclopedia of Unified Science. The encyclopedia was planned for 26 volumes and was to be a forum "where scientists of the special sciences and philosophers worked together in harmony, although being completely free to express varying opinions on questions of doubt." [Joergensen in 473, p. 928] Because of the war and other problems, only two volumes [472a and 473] of the encyclopedia were ever finished. (Interestingly—ironically—the second volume housed Kuhn's "Structure of Scientific Revolutions.") Obviously, although the Vienna Circle rejected idealism in the sense of a philosophy identified with speculative metaphysics (German Idealism), they were nonetheless "idealistic" in the sense of having lofty goals and noble ambitions. They were visionaries.

Stated succinctly, the logical positivists viewed the purpose of philosophy of science to be the clarification of the language of science through critical discussion, formal logic and the verifiability principle in order to create a unified science. In doing so, the positivists fostered the development of the academic discipline of the philosophy of science in the 1920s and 30s. By 1950, the professionalization and institutionalization of the discipline in university philosophy departments had become complete. [400, p. 174]

9.2.3   Implementing the Logical Positivists' Program

The first phase of implementing the logical positivists' program included the destruction of the metaphysics of German idealism. Historically, the hostility of German idealism toward science had been returned in kind by both practitioners and philosophers of science. Hume's beliefs about metaphysics are captured in the following famous quotation from his *Enquiry Concerning Human Understanding:*

> When we run over to libraries, persuaded of these principles, what havoc must we take? If we take in our hand any volume; of divinity or school metaphysics, for instance; let us ask, *Does it contain any abstract reasoning concerning quantity or number?* No. *Does it contain any experimental reasoning concerning matter of fact and existence?* No. Commit it then to the flames: for it can contain nothing but sophistry and illusion.

The positivists' position on metaphysics was similar to Hume's. They believed that the verification theory of meaning, when combined with formal logic, would be sufficient to show that all metaphysics was comprised of meaningless, pseudosentences.

In order to understand the assault on Hegel and his idealist successors, it is useful to have an example of exactly what was being "assaulted." The following passage comes from Heidegger's 1929 book entitled *Was Ist Metaphysik?,* as reproduced in Carnap's famous article "The Elimination of Metaphysics Through Logical Analysis of Language":

What is to be investigated is being only and—nothing else; being alone and further—nothing; solely being, and beyond being—nothing. What about this Nothing? . . . does the Nothing exist only because the Not, i.e. the Negation, exists? Or is it the other way around? Does Negation and the Not exist only because the Nothing exists? . . . We assert: the Nothing is prior to the Not and the Negation. . . where do we seek the Nothing? How do we find the Nothing. . . .we know the Nothing. . . . anxiety reveals the Nothing. . . that for which and because of which we were anxious, was "really"—nothing. Indeed: the Nothing itself—as such—was present. . . .What about this Nothing?—the Nothing itself nothings. [109, p.69 emphasis in original]

What should be made of the preceding paragraph? Is it profound truth, or odious falsity? Carnap and other positivists, essentially following Wittgenstein, claimed that it was as senseless to believe the quoted passage to be true as it was to believe it to be false. Rather, as Hume proposed, the passage should be "committed to the flames" as meaningless. Carnap's analysis was basically as follows.

According to the members of the Vienna Circle, all languages contain a vocabulary (words) and a syntax (rules for forming meaningful combinations of words, or sentences). Essentially, the positivists adopted a referential theory of the meaning of words. That is, words have meaning because they are associated with things in the external world to which they refer, i.e., "observables." All meaningful words either refer directly to these observables or can be explicitly defined through "correspondence rules" or "reduction sentences" in terms of the observables. By way of illustration, Carnap asks the reader to suppose "that someone invented the new word 'teavy' and maintained that there are things which are teavy and things which are not teavy." [109, p. 64] Carnap suggests that "in order to learn the meaning of this word, we ask him about its criterion of application: How is one to ascertain in a concrete case whether a given thing is teavy or not?" If the inventor of the new word could not provide "empirical signs of teaviness," the word would be described as meaningless. Using this line of reasoning, Carnap claimed as meaningless such familiar concepts of German idealism as: "the Idea," "the Absolute," "the Unconditioned," "the being of being," "thing in itself," "being-in-itself," and "being-in-and-for-itself."

Given that many of the concepts used in metaphysics were meaningless, all statements comprised of such concepts would be equally meaningless. Nevertheless, the more insightful and original aspect of Carnap's assault on the metaphysics of idealism as meaningless lay not in sentences comprised of meaningless words. Much more interesting was his claim that, even though all the terms might be meaningful, many of the statements in metaphysics were meaningless because the statements violated certain *syntactical* considerations. For example, all speakers of English would recognize the following (grammatically correct) sentence as meaningless: "Julius Caesar is a prime number." The sentence is meaningless because it violates the "type confusion" of terms; in this case, names of people and names of numbers belong to different logical types. Thus, although the sentence is grammatically "correct," it is nevertheless meaningless. It is as senseless to *deny* that "Julius Caesar is a prime number," as it is to affirm it.

Returning now to the passage by Heidegger concerning "the Nothing," Carnap proceeded to demonstrate, using formal logic and meaning analysis, that Heidegger's entire passage was meaningless on *syntactical* grounds. Although the English word "nothing" is meaningful, Heidegger had combined it with other words to form syntactically impermissible statements. That is, the very meaning of the word "nothing" implies nonexistence and, therefore, to assert (in a seemingly profound fashion) the existence of nonexistence and discuss its relationship with other concepts is as syntactically unintelligible as to assert "Caesar is a prime number."

The positivists were well aware of the fact that the word "meaning" can have several different "meanings." In particular, they differentiated between *cognitive* meaning (designative or referential) and non-cognitive meaning (expressive or emotive). Thus, they compared the works of the metaphysicians to poetry and art, but "Metaphysicians are musicians without musical ability." [109, p. 80] The danger of the metaphysics of German idealism was that their works of (bad) poetry and art were claimed by their proponents to have *cognitive* meaning and assertive force, representing a higher, more profound kind of "understanding" than science. Thus, Heidegger asserted (as being cognitively profound) statements such as: "[I]f thus the power of the *understanding* in the field of questions concerning Nothing and Being is broken, then the fate of the sovereignty of 'logic' within philosophy is thereby decided as well. But will sober science condone the whirl of counter-logical questioning?" [Heidegger in 109, p.72] Although positivist philosophers believed their arguments against the illogicality and meaninglessness of idealism to be conclusive (as did Socrates in his arguments against the relativism of the Sophists), as we shall see in Chapter 10, such was not to be the case.

A second part of implementing of the logical positivists' program centered on examining the nature of science. In particular, how could a philosophy of science be constructed that would be compatible with both the lessons of the metaphysical excesses of German idealism and the overthrow of the Newtonian empire by Einsteinian relativity and quantum mechanics? To understand how the positivists interpreted the "lessons" requires an understanding of what Watkins refers to as the "security pole," and its counterpart, the "depth pole," in science. [627, p. 133]

Ever since the time of Bacon and Descartes, science has embraced two aims that often appeared to conflict with each other. On the one hand, science strived toward developing theories about the world whose knowledge-claims could be known with absolute certainty (the "security pole"). On the other hand, science strived toward developing theories whose knowledge-claims progressed toward ever deeper, more fundamental, explanations (the "depth pole"). For the positivists, the lesson to be learned from both idealism and the fall of Newtonian mechanics was that science should virtually abandon the depth pole and move decisively toward the security pole. Only by adopting the very conservative procedure of restricting the knowledge-claims of science to directly observable phenomena and relationships among those phenomena could another Newtonian debacle be prevented. As the 1929 manifesto of the Vienna Circle emphasized, "in science there are no 'depths'; there is surface everywhere." [627, p. 137] Thus, the positivists adopted a form of *radical* empiricism with regard to science. (The positivist version of radical empiricism was similar to, but conceived and developed independently of, the version known as "operationalism," as discussed in Section 6.5.2.)

Following Suppe's summary [606], the radical empiricism of the Vienna Circle contained the following view of scientific theories. First, scientific theories should be capable of being axiomatized in accordance with the formal logic of Bertrand Russell. Second, the terms in theories should be comprised of (1) logical and mathematical terms, (2) theoretical terms, and (3) observational terms. Logical and mathematical terms were justified on the basis of their acceptance of Kant's analytic/synthetic dichotomy (see Section 4.3) and the reduction of mathematics to logic by Frege and Russell (Sections 8.5.2 and 9.1.2). Although "theoretical terms" were allowed, such terms were not to be in any sense "metaphysical." All theoretical terms must be explicitly definable through *correspondence rules* with "observable terms." The correspondence rules guaranteed the cognitive significance of the theoretical terms and specified "the admissible experimental procedures for applying a theory to phenomena" (empirical testing). [606, p. 102]

As a major "lesson" to be learned from Einsteinian relativity and quantum mechanics, the logical positivists, led by Schlick, proposed that both theories and their constituent theoretical terms were to be interpreted in a Machian *instrumentalist*, rather than *realist*, manner. [216] Although the positivists accepted the classical realist position that the world exists independently of its being perceived (Schlick referred to it as "empirical realism" [418, p. 247]), they rejected the much stronger thesis of *scientific realism* that theories may contain theoretical terms that are in principle unobservable and which cannot be reduced through definitions or correspondence rules to observable terms. Whereas, scientific realism holds that theories, including the postulated relationships among constituent theoretical terms, truly represent in some significant fashion how the world really is constituted, the positivists held that *only* relationships among observables "truly represent." Since it was believed (and continues to be held according to the "Copenhagen interpretation" in physics today—see Mermin [441]) that, in principle, there could not be anything in reality corresponding to the formalisms in quantum mechanics (the wave-particle duality), quantum theory *must* be interpreted instrumentally. That is, quantum theory is *just* a series of equations that can serve as an instrument to economically summarize the results of experiments. Since the "Copenhagen" version of quantum mechanics can only be interpreted instrumentally, the "lesson" for the logical positivists was (in a colossal act of inductive *hubris*) that *all* theories should be interpreted instrumentally.

As Bergman has observed, a fundamental, unifying belief of the positivists was the adoption of the Humean view of causality. [58, p. 2] The Humean view of causality and induction also suggests a strictly instrumentalist perspective of scientific theories. Hume observed that metaphysical concepts like "cause" can never be logically inferred from the observation of a series of correlated events. Thus, it is impossible to logically (deductively) go from a series of observable antecedents and consequents to any "unobservable," such as "cause." Since no amount of empirical support could possibly confirm a theory with certainty (here *certainty* implies the same degree of warrant as proof by deductive logic), theories should be construed as instruments to economically summarize observations, rather than postulated as truly representing the actual "hidden structure" of the world. Or, as we have previously noted, Humean analysis suggests science should stay as close as possible to the "security pole," as it is described by Watkins [627].

If the "lesson" of quantum mechanics for the positivists was to embrace instrumentalism for all scientific theories (and not just quantum mechanics), such was definitely not the view of scientists in general and the practicing physicists in particular who actually *developed* quantum mechanics. Physicists such as Planck, Einstein, Rutherford, Bohr, Heisenberg and Schrodinger believed that the world existed independently of its being perceived (ontological or classical realism) and that the purpose of science was to develop theories that in some meaningful sense truly explain how the world *really* is (scientific realism). (Of all the sciences, only the behaviorist branch of psychology embraced radical empiricism in preference to scientific realism.) To the developers of quantum theory, throwing out scientific realism for all science just because of the problems inherent in quantum mechanics would be analogous to "throwing out the baby with the bath water." In today's vernacular, throwing out scientific realism because of the anomaly of quantum mechanics would be tantamount to "naive" falsificationism (see Section 11.1).

Although the "early" Einstein was *positivistic* in perspective, in a famous letter to Schlick the "mature" Einstein emphatically expressed his *realist* views:

> I tell you straight out: Physics is the attempt at the conceptual construction of a model of the *real world* and its lawful structure. . . .in short, I suffer under the unsharp separation of Reality of Experience and Reality of Being . . . you will be astonished about the "metaphysicist" Einstein. But every four-and two-legged animal is de facto in this sense a metaphysicist. (Einstein 1930, in 280, p. 188)

The year after Einstein's letter, Planck expressed the same view:

> Now the two sentences: 1) *There is a real outer world which exists independently of our act of knowing* and 2) *the real outer world is not directly knowable* form together the cardinal hinge on which the whole structure of physical science turns. And yet there is a certain degree of contradiction between these two sentences . . . therefore, we see the task of science arising before us, an incessant struggle toward a goal which will never be reached, because by its very nature it is unreachable. It is of a metaphysical character, and, as such, is always and again beyond our achievement. [Planck 1931 in 280, p. 189]

The reader should note that Planck is specifically stating that the ultimate goal of science is, in principle, unrealizable. This position is in sharp contrast to those modern philosophers and historians of science who believe that all of the cognitive aims of science must be *realizable* if they are to be legitimate. Thus, Laudan argues against the acceptance of "utopian" aims in science. [375, p. 52]   We shall return to this issue in Section 11.2.2.

As previously indicated, logical positivism was a *movement*. It had its inception with a discussion group at the University of Vienna in the early '20s; it peaked in the late '20s with the manifesto; and it ended in the middle '30s with the dissolution of the Vienna Circle under the onslaught of Nazism. The legacy of logical positivism was not a movement, but what might be loosely called (in Lakatosian terms) a "research program." [86, p. 26] Many of the members of the Vienna Circle continued to explicate the nature of science with critical discussion through logical analysis, both formal (or "mathematical" in the spirit of Russell) and informal (or "traditional" in the spirit of Moore). They were joined in their efforts by scores of other philosophers of science, including, most prominently, Carl Hempel, Ernest Nagel, and Richard B. Braithwaite. Their writings dominated the philosophy of science literature in the 1940s and 1950s, and their views came to be known as *Logical Empiricism*. Neurath suggested in 1938 that "empirical rationalism" should be the preferred term since the approach represented a kind of synthesis of the rationalism of Descartes, Spinoza, and Leibniz (with its emphasis on deductive logic) and the empiricism of Bacon, Locke, Hume, and Mill (with its emphasis on observation). [Neurath in 472a, p. 1] Much of the logical empiricist research program involved not only the explication of science, but also a retreat from the rigid positions of the *radical* empiricism inherent in logical positivism. The next several sections will discuss how the logical empiricists modified the rigid positions of the logical positivists. (Chapters 10 and 11 discuss how, in turn, the views of the logical empiricists were attacked by advocates of scientific realism, historicism, and relativism.)

9.3   THE DEVELOPMENT OF LOGICAL EMPIRICISM

The logical empiricists shared many of the fundamental beliefs of the logical positivists concerning the nature of the world, science, and the philosophy of science. Indeed, many of the logical empiricists had themselves been members of the logical positivist movement. Most importantly, the logical empiricists shared beliefs with their positivist predecessors concerning the purpose of the philosophy of science and its appropriate method of inquiry. That is, the purpose of the philosophy of science was to clarify, or explicate, the language of science, using a method which conjoined critical discussion with formal logic. To fully understand logical empiricism and how it differs from logical positivism, we shall explore how the logical empiricists explicated four key concepts in the language of science: laws, explanation, theories, and verification.

9.3.1   Explicating Scientific Laws

Given the influence of Mach, the logical positivists had, quite naturally, given high status to the importance of science discovering and justifying laws and lawlike generalizations. Such laws were generally construed to be universal conditionals relating observable phenomena to other observable phenomena: "Every time phenomenon 'X' occurs, then phenomenon 'Y' will occur."

The positivists' construal of scientific laws as universal conditionals posed for them an embarrassing dilemma. Since the "verifiability principle" implied that all cognitively meaningful statements must be *verifiable* (the ability to be shown conclusively true or false), all scientific laws must be cognitively meaningless. This is because all statements having the form of universal conditionals *cannot* be conclusively verified. (Although observations in the past may have conformed to the universal conditional, it is always *possible* that some disconfirming observation might occur in the future.) Either the positivists would have to give up the verifiability principle or assert that scientific laws are meaningless. They, of course, chose to give up the verifiability principle.

Carnap in his 1936 paper entitled "Testability and Meaning," specifically addressed the problem that scientific laws posed for the verifiability principle and suggested that it be replaced with the, more liberal, "testability criterion." [108]   Brown suggests that Carnap's article "can reasonably be viewed as the founding document of logical empiricism." [86, p. 23] As stated by Feigl, the testability criterion indicated that "the differences between an assertion and its denial must in principle be open to at least partial and indirect observational tests, otherwise there is no factual meaning present in the assertion." [Feigl in 124, p. 13]

Recall that the logical positivists, as a reaction to the downfall of the Newtonian empire and the rise of relativity and quantum mechanics, had sought to secure the foundations of scientific knowledge in observable phenomena.   Statements concerning only observable phenomena had been thought to be capable of conclusive verification. According to Carnap, the adoption of the testability criterion necessarily implied the substitution of "gradually increasing confirmation" for the knowledge-claims of science. However, the abandonment of verification meant also that the knowledge-claims of science could no longer be considered "positive," hence the genesis of the label "logical empiricism" as a successor for logical positivism.   For the members of the Vienna Circle "positive knowledge" had implied a kind of knowledge capable of being known with the same certainty associated with the simple, atomistic assertions of Russell and Wittgenstein, e.g., "the cover of this book is red."

How the logical empiricists explicated Carnap's concept of "gradually increasing confirmation" will be addressed in Section 9.3.4. For now, we need to discuss the logical empiricist approach to scientific explanation, since the empiricist approach to scientific laws influenced their views on explanation.

9.3.2   Explicating Scientific Explanation

Much of the work of the logical empiricists focused on the nature of scientific explanation. Indeed, they held that "the *distinctive aim* of the scientific enterprise is to provide systematic and responsibly supported explanations." [464, p.15] Building upon the models of scientific explanation implicit in the works of Hume [293] and Kant [331], Hempel and Oppenheim in their 1948 article entitled "Studies in the Logic of Explanation" developed the Deductive-Nomological, or "covering law," model of explanation (see Section 2.3). Briefly, the covering law model of explanation proposes that a phenomenon is to be explained by showing that it can be *deduced* from a set of universal laws and a set of initial characteristics associated with the particular situation. Hempel and Oppenheim showed that the covering law model of explanation conforms well to many classical views on the topic. For example, Kant referred to "the laws from which reason explains the facts." [331, p.18]

Although the Deductive-Nomological model conforms well to many explanations in science, the logical empiricists came to realize that many scientific explanations involve statistical laws, rather than laws in the form of universal generalizations. Therefore, either they had to claim that explanations such as quantum mechanics based on statistical laws are not "scientific," or another model that incorporated statistical laws would be required. Hempel's 1962 article entitled "Deductive-Nomological vs. Statistical Explanation" developed the Deductive-Statistical and Inductive-Statistical models of explanation (see Sections 2.4.3 and 2.4.4). [Hempel, in 175] However, since statistical laws do not *deductively imply* the phenomenon to be explained, Hempel added the requirement that the statistical laws should confer a "high probability" on the likelihood of the occurrence of the phenomenon to be explained. The issue of what "high probability" implies will be returned to later.

Hempel and Oppenheim's original 1948 article also proposed that scientific explanation and scientific prediction had the same logical form. The "thesis of structural symmetry" (as it came to be called) asserted that (1) every adequate explanation is potentially a prediction, and (2) conversely, every adequate prediction is potentially an explanation (see Section 3.1). [262, p. 367] Articles by, among others, Scheffler [561] and Scriven [571] attacked Hempel's thesis of structural symmetry. The attacks centered on several fundamental issues, including the observation that if "adequate" means "accurate" then there are many instances where one can accurately predict the occurrence of a phenomenon that science would not claim as "truly explanatory." (For example, predicting the stock market through the rise and fall of the hemlines in women's skirts.) Hempel's 1965 book [262] reviews the charges of his critics, acknowledges that their criticisms pose significant problems for (at least) the second sub-thesis, but can only (lamely) conclude that the second sub-thesis must "be regarded here as an open question." [262, p. 376]

The reason why Hempel and other logical empiricists could not simply deny the second sub-thesis in the "symmetry" argument was that they were firmly committed to the logical positivist view that the concepts "cause" and "causal" were metaphysical and superfluous to science, i.e., they were firmly committed to the Humean view of causality [58; 334, p. 12] For example, Brodbeck defended the thesis of structural symmetry in 1962 by noting that critics had adopted the "causal idiom" and that the truth-content of "statements like 'C is the cause of E' is problematic." [Brodbeck in 175, p. 250] Discussing the concept of causal explanations, Hempel concludes, "it is not clear what precise construal could be given to the notion of factors 'bringing about' a given event, and what reason there would be for denying the status of explanation to all accounts invoking occurrences that temporally succeed the event to be explained." [262, pp. 353-4] As we shall see, the influence of Hume was also strongly evident in how the logical empiricists explicated the concept of theory.

9.3.3   Explicating Theory

The logical positivists had held that theories should be comprised of (1) logical and mathematical terms, (2) theoretical terms, and (3) observational terms.   Lawlike relationships between observational terms, or "observables," came to be called "empirical laws," and lawlike relationships between theoretical terms, or "theoreticals," came to be called theoretical laws. [464]   However, all theoretical terms, in order to be cognitively meaningful, had to be explicitly definable through correspondence rules with "observables."   The historical origin of the thesis that theoretical terms must be defined through observable terms traces back to Russell and Hume. [418]

Hume had contended (the "Humean problem of induction") that it was improper to infer the existence of an "unobservable" (like "cause") from observation, because such a procedure was inconsistent with *deductive* logic.   Russell, in a very influential 1914 essay entitled "The Relation of Sense-Data to Physics", accepted the Humean view that "correlation does not deductively imply causation" as necessarily implying that "whenever possible, logical constructions are to be substituted for inferred entities" and that "we may succeed in actually defining the objects of physics as a function of sense-data." [Russell, as quoted in 418, p. 250]   Following Hume and Russell, the logical positivists adopted a very limited realism as their ontology—the classical realism discussed in Section 9.1.   On this view, observational terms have a real existence, but, since theoretical terms were nonobservational terms (or the "inferred entities" of Hume and Russell), they were not accorded the status of "real."   Therefore, in order for the theoretical laws to be cognitively meaningful, all theoretical terms must be explicitly definable through observational terms.   The explicit definitions would make the relationship between the theoretical terms and observational terms *purely analytic.*   Thus enters the analytic/synthetic dichotomy into the construction of theories. (See Section 4.3.)

The reader should note that the preceding on "correspondence rules" is not the same thing as *measuring* a construct, or identifying empirical indicators of a construct.   Since the logical positivists believed that theoretical terms, or nonobservational terms, did not have a real existence, such terms could not in principle be measured in the customary sense. Rather, theoretical terms represented logical constructions, or a shorthand way of talking about "observables."   For those readers familiar with structural equations modeling and modern measurement theory, the logical positivists in effect assumed a *formative* measurement model between the theoretical terms and the observables, rather than a *reflective* measurement model. [288 and 209] For example, a reflective measurement model of the concept "intelligence" would claim that the concept is in some meaningful sense *real* and can be measured through a variety of instruments.   On the other hand, a formative measurement model might claim that intelligence is "whatever the Stanford-Binet IQ test measures and nothing more than what the test measures."

The logical empiricists recognized that there were at least three central problems with the criterion requiring all theoretical terms to be explicitly defined through correspondence rules with observation terms. We shall call these problems the problems of (1) extension, (2) dispositionals, and (3) theoretical dispensibility, and shall discuss each in turn.

The problem of *extension* points out that a major characteristic of *good* theories is that they be capable of predicting new phenomena. However, if the entire cognitive content of all theoretical terms is captured by a unique set of observational terms, then the theoretical laws would obviously be incapable of predicting new phenomena. In fact, the "explicit definition" requirement would logically imply that every time a theory predicts a new phenomenon (a new "observable"), the "meaning" of the theoretical terms has changed and, therefore, we have "new" concepts and a "new" theory. As the reader will no doubt note, this is exactly the argument that Hempel used in his 1950 and 1954 articles [reprinted in 262] that demonstrated the poverty of the underlying philosophy of operationalism. (See Section 6.5.2.)

The second problem, the problem of "dispositional terms," was addressed by Carnap in his 1936 article "Testability and Meaning." Carnap noted that there were many theoretical terms that could not in principle be explicitly defined through observables using the formal logic of *Principia*. For example, terms like "soluble" and "magnetic" state that certain entities have a dispositional ability and such an ability could not be explicitly defined in terms of observables.   Carnap's suggestion was that the explicit definition criterion should be abandoned and replaced with "partial interpretation." He proposed that theoretical terms were meaningful if they were partially interpreted through "reduction sentences" to observable terms.   Rather than providing general definitions of dispositional terms, the reduction sentences would show how such terms could be introduced in specific test conditions. [86, p. 41]

The third problem, theoretical dispensibility, focused on the role of theoretical concepts in theory construction and is summarized in Hempel's famous article, "The Theoretician's Dilemma." [1958, reprinted in 262] Hempel quotes the behaviorist psychologist B. F. Skinner that theoretical terms are unnecessary in science, since all meaningful theoretical terms can be replaced with observation terms. In short, paraphrasing Hempel, the "dilemma" is that if all theoretical terms can be explicitly defined or reduced to observation terms, then theoretical terms are "unnecessary," since they can be eliminated. On the other hand, if theoretical terms cannot be explicitly defined or reduced to observation terms then they surely are "unnecessary" because they are meaningless! Hempel resolves the dilemma by concluding:

> The theoreticians dilemma took it to be the sole purpose of a theory to establish deductive connections among observation sentences. If this were the case, theoretical terms would indeed be unnecessary. But if it is recognized that a satisfactory theory should provide possibilities also for inductive explanatory and predictive use and that it should achieve systematic economy and heuristic fertility, then it is clear that theoretical formulations cannot be replaced by expressions and terms of observables only; the theoreticians dilemma, with its conclusion to the contrary, is seen to rest on a false premise. [Hempel 1958, reprinted in 262, p. 222]

Why does not Hempel resolve the dilemma by affirming that, even with Carnap's reduction sentences, the cognitive content of a theoretical term cannot be captured by defining it through observables? Again, the influence of Hume on the logical empiricists is evident. To argue that theoretical terms are meaningful, yet undefined by observable terms, is tantamount to admitting that theoretical terms are "real." In Hempel's words, "to assert that the terms of a given theory have a factual reference, that the entities that they purport to refer to actually exist, is tantamount to asserting that what the theory says is true." [Hempel 1958, reprinted in 262, p. 221] Again, the reader should note the pervasive impact of Hume and the Newtonian debacle. Hempel is concerned that to accept a realist interpretation of theoretical concepts would be "tantamount to inferring" (improperly accordingly to Hume) that an empirically well-confirmed theory is true (and thus risking another Newtonian disaster should the theory later be disconfirmed).

By 1970, the logical empiricist version of scientific theories had concluded that the total cognitive content of theoretical terms could not be captured through any definitional system of correspondence rules or reduction sentences. Thus, Feigl proposed that the theoretical concepts are implicitly defined by the theoretical postulates or laws in which they occur and are "linked" by correspondence rules to observable concepts. His "orthodox view of theories" provides that there is an "upward seepage of meaning of the observational terms to the theoretical concepts." [Feigl, in 519, p. 7] Hempel provides an even more liberal view of the problem of the meaningfulness of theoretical terms. He notes that there has been a "steady retrenchment of the initial belief in, or demand for, full definability of all scientific terms by means of some antecedent vocabulary consisting of observational predicates or the like." But if we do not come to understand the meaning of theoretical terms through explicit definitions, how do we? Hempel responds:

> We come to understand new terms, we learn how to use them properly, in many ways besides definition: from instances of their use in particular contexts, from paraphrases that can make no claim to being definitions and so forth. The internal principles and bridge principles of a theory, apart from systematically characterizing its content, no doubt offer the learner the most important access to an "understanding" of its expressions, including terms as well as sentences. [Hempel, in 519, p. 162-3.]

9.3.4   Explicating Verification

As discussed in Section 9.3.1, the fact that scientific laws are often expressed in terms of universal conditionals necessarily implied that the "verifiability principle" would have to be modified. Carnap proposed that, rather than verifiability, the requirement ought to be that all scientifically meaningful assertions must be empirically testable and verification should give way to "gradually increasing confirmation." The logical empiricists then began the explication of "confirmation."

The epistemic problem of confirmation can be stated as a question: "How is it possible that observing a finite number of instances of a generalization (law or theory) can enable one to know that the generalization holds in all the unexamined cases (of which there normally is potential infinity)?" [606, p. 624] For the logical empiricists the question had both a qualitative and a quantitative dimension.

Qualitatively, what kind of observation or "instance" is to count as a bonafide confirmation? Analyzing this question from a purely logical, syntactical perspective generated the, so-called, "paradoxes of confirmation" concerning ravens and "grue." Hempel's 1945 paper developed the Paradox of the Ravens, which (paraphrased) states that the proposition P "all ravens are black" is logically equivalent to the statement $P*$ "all nonblack things are nonravens." Further, any observation or instance that tends to confirm $P*$ *must* logically tend to confirm P. Therefore, the fact that one observes a nonblack object (e.g., a red object) and determines that the nonblack object is a nonraven (the red object is a rose) must logically "tend to confirm" statement P that "all ravens are black."

Goodman in 1953 (reprinted in 1965 [231]) proposed the Paradox of "grue." Again briefly, Goodman starts by inquiring whether the observation that a particular emerald is green would be an instance of confirming the generalization "all emeralds are green." Goodman continues by defining the adjective "grue" as applying anytime an object is green before some arbitrary time t and blue after the arbitrary time *t*. Goodman notes that, since all observations of emeralds will occur before the arbitrary *t*, the observation that a particular emerald is green *equally* confirms both "all emeralds are green" and "all emeralds are *grue*." The "grue" paradox generated, according to Goodman, "a new riddle of induction." [231, p. 59]

Both the raven and "grue" paradoxes spawned a large number of papers that attempted their resolution. Specific efforts at resolution need not detain us here. Rather, we should note that in large measure the paradoxes stemmed from the general approach to confirmation that the logical empiricists used, i.e., approaching confirmation as a syntactical and logical problem. Even more specifically, one of the reasons the paradoxes occur is that "one of the characteristic features of *Principia* logic is that it is an extensional logic, that it does not take into account the *meaning* of the proposition involved in an argument." [86, p. 33] That is, just as using mathematics as a tool for analyzing certain problems in empirical science will, by itself, create problems, so will the use of *mathematical logic*.

Much more important than the qualitative dimension of confirmation, as exemplified in the "paradoxes," was the quantitative dimension. The logical empiricists interpreted the problem of finding a quantitative "degree of confirmation" that observed instances would confer on a generalization to be equivalent to solving the Humean problem of induction, or Humean skepticism. In order to understand the logical empiricist approach, it is time to formally state the basic propositions underlying Humean skepticism.

Following Watkins [627], Humean skepticism is not to be confused with Academic skepticism which states that "there is but one thing that one can know, namely that one can know nothing else." Neither is it Pyrrhonian skepticism, which claims that one cannot even know that one cannot know anything. Rather, Humean skepticism allows that each of us can have genuine knowledge about our own beliefs, feelings, and perceptual experiences in addition to allowing that logical and mathematical truths are possible. However, Humean skepticism "denies that one can progress by logical reasoning from perceptual experience to any genuine knowledge of an external world, if there is one." [627, p.3] Stated more formally, Humean skepticism denies that genuine knowledge of the external world can proceed from perceptual experience by asserting the following three fundamental propositions [627, p.3]:

HS1.   There are no synthetic *a priori* truths about the external world.

HS2.   Any genuine knowledge we have of the external world must ultimately be derived from perceptual experience.

HS3.   Only deductive derivations are valid.

These three propositions are sometimes referred to as the *anti-apriorist* thesis (HS1), the *experientialist* thesis (HS2), and the *deductivist* thesis

(HS3). As will be recalled, Kant's answer to Hume was to deny HS1 and assert that there exist concepts (like "cause") that are both synthetic and *a priori*. Further, Mill's answer to Hume was that "cause" is the most general of all inductive generalizations. That is, Mill denied HS3. We should note that Hume did not take his own skepticism seriously, but denied it on the grounds of "habit and custom." The logical empiricists took Humean skepticism seriously and attempted to overcome it by modifying HS3 with the claim that "probability logic, or the logic of partial entailment, is a legitimate extension or generalization of classical logic." [627, p. 4] That is, the logical empiricists attempted to develop the logic of probability so that they could show that finite instances of observable evidence could be combined in a logical fashion to generate a probability number between zero and one which would be logically related to the intuitive notion that the observable evidence, more or less strongly, confirmed the generalization.

The authors who are most closely associated with the attempt to develop probability theory into a logic of confirmation are Reichenbach [525], Carnap [106], and, more recently, the Finnish mathematicians Hintikka and Niiniluoto [274]. Reichenbach's approach to the problem used what are referred to as "self-corrective" procedures; Carnap's approach focused on system probabilities determined by state descriptions and structure descriptions; whereas Hintikka's approach was to modify the system of Carnap. Suppe reviews the effort to develop the logic of probability as a logic of confirmation and concludes:

> What is common to all the approaches to inductive logic is that in one way or another they make only a finite number of instances relevant to the testing of universal generalizations, and such means ultimately rest on various assumptions about the sorts of regularities characteristic of the world. Thus it would appear that one can obtain non-zero probability measures for generalizations only if one makes certain fairly metaphysical assumptions to the effect that certain patterns of regularity are characteristic of the world. Burks argues that such assumptions are pragmatic presuppositions of induction which can be established on neither *a priori* nor empirical grounds ... initially, logical positivism was concerned with global induction: Reichenbach's self-corrective method and Carnap's analytic inductive method were attempts to prove the truth of probabilistic induction hypotheses which would enable us to obtain general knowledge; both failed to do this. More recent work in inductive logic [e.g. Hintikka] has given up the attempt to develop a more global inductive logic. [607, p. 630]

Suppe points out that most of the recent works, rather than focusing on global induction, focus on "local induction," where one attempts to justify generalizations inductively in the context of specific scientific inquiries, given "deeply held metaphysical presuppositions or beliefs." [p. 630]

9.3.5 Misconceptions in Marketing about Logical Empiricism

We are now in a position to clear up at least a few of the many misconceptions concerning logical empiricism in the marketing literature. For example, Arndt claims that in logical empiricism "marketing systems are viewed as being equilibrium-seeking," and that "the real world is considered essentially as harmonious and conflict-free in the long run." [22, p. 199] As is abundantly clear from the preceding sections, there is nothing in logical empiricism which implies that marketing systems are necessarily "equilibrium-seeking." Similarly, there is nothing in logical empiricism which implies that the world must be considered "essentially as harmonious and conflict-free." It is true that some researchers choose to treat marketing systems as equilibrium-seeking, and it is true that some researchers choose to treat the world as conflict-free. However, there is nothing in the nature of logical empiricism which suggests, implies, demands, or impels researchers to do so. Arndt also claims that the influence of logical empiricism has resulted in marketing being an "applied discipline concerned with the improvement of management practice and research methodology." [22, p. 203] (In contrast, Dholakia now claims that the emphasis on marketing management has *prevented* the discipline from being dominated by logical empiricism. [149a, p. 13]) In any respect, it is surely the case that the marketing discipline has been historically very interested in problems concerning the improvement of marketing management. Furthermore, a good case can be made that the marketing discipline should be concerned with more societal, or "macro" issues concerning marketing. Nevertheless, to contend that logical empiricism *brought about* the emphasis on marketing management is simply untenable.

Anderson provides another example of a common error concerning logical empiricism. He states: "logical empiricism is characterized by the inductive statistical method. On this view, science begins with observation, and its theories are ultimately justified by the accumulation of further observations. . . ." [13, p. 19] As an example, Anderson uses the well-known PIMS studies. Although it is true that empirical testing and observation play significant roles in logical empiricism, it is not true that logical empiricism implies "the inductive statistical method" where "science begins with observation." That is, whereas the classical empiricism of Bacon viewed science as inducing generalizations from observations, logical empiricism (since it separated the context of discovery from the context of justification) did not propose a method for generating hypotheses, laws, and theories. Rather, it focused exclusively on the justification of hypotheses, laws, and theories.

Belk provides a third common misperception when he states that logical positivism focuses on "notions of linear causality." [p. 131] However, as we have seen, because of their commitment to Hume, the positivists and empiricists avoided the concept of cause in its entirety (whether "linear" or "nonlinear").

The logical empiricists approached Humean skepticism as both a problem to be solved and a problem that *could* be solved through the development of the logic of probability. Our next philosopher of science assumed that Humean skepticism was irrefutable and made it the basis for his entire philosophy; that philosopher is Sir Karl Popper.

9.4   POPPER, CRITICAL RATIONALISM AND FALSIFICATIONISM

Sir Karl Popper (1902-) was born in Austria and studied mathematics, physics, and philosophy at the University of Vienna. Although not a member of the Vienna Circle, he interacted frequently with its members. The German edition of his first book, *The Logic of Scientific Discovery*, was published in Vienna in 1935. He accepted a position as senior lecturer at Canterbury University in New Zealand in 1937, moved to England in 1945 to teach at the London School of Economics, and was knighted in 1964. At various times, and by numerous people, he has been called a logical positivist, a logical empiricist, an irrationalist, a relativist, and a realist. While he refers to his philosophy as "critical rationalism," others refer to it as "falsificationism." The reasons why different people come to different conclusions concerning Popperian philosophy will become evident as we trace the development of its major themes.

As a student of physics, Popper was immersed in the development of Einstein's theories of relativity. He recalls being "thrilled" at the results of Eddington's test of Einsteinian theory. [503, p. 34] Popper noted that Newtonian mechanics had been overthrown, or in his words "refuted," by Einsteinian theory even though Newtonian mechanics had been "confirmed," or "verified," by literally millions of observations over a span of time exceeding two hundred years. Popper also experienced, observed, and was greatly upset by, the rising tide of irrationalist philosophies in Europe, most notably, fascism and Marxism. He saw both these political philosophies as logical outgrowths of Hegelian idealism and its notion of the historical inevitability of social events and structure. On the one hand, fascism claimed that it was historically inevitable that the "chosen race" should rule. On the other hand, Marxism claimed the historical inevitability of the success of the "chosen class." [506, p. 9] Tracing Hegelian idealism and its irrationalism and historicism back to Plato, Popper was later to argue forcefully that such "closed" societies "are not inevitable; the future depends on ourselves." [506, p. 2] For Popper, the key to combatting totalitarianism and for maintaining an "open society" was the maintenance of a belief in reason, or rationalism, for "beginning with the suppression of reason and truth, we must end with the most brutal and violent destruction of all that is human." [506, p. 200]

But, was not the theory underlying Marxist philosophy "scientific"? Did it not "explain" thousands of observable social phenomena? In fact, was it not the case that *all* social phenomena could be "explained" by Marxist theory? Before turning the age of 18, Popper had formulated his answer to all those who claimed that theories could be verified through their confirming instances. He set about developing a book on the topic, which culminated in 1931 with a manuscript so massive that it was never to be published in that form. However, Popper's basic thesis concerning falsifiability was published in a letter to the editor of *Erkenntnis* in 1933, in which he attacks the logical positivists' "verifiability principle" and puts forth his own criterion of falsifiability. [503, p. 311] A shortened version of the 1931 manuscript was published in Vienna as *Logik der Forschung* (The Logic of Scientific Discovery) and translated into English in 1959. [503]

Given the pervasive concern of philosophy with Humean skepticism, it is not surprising that the very first section in Chapter 1 of *The Logic of Scientific Discovery* is "The Problem of Induction." Popper discusses the "widely accepted view" that the fundamental characteristic of the empirical sciences is that they use "inductive methods." These methods are usually considered to be procedures that allow one to go from "observations or experiments to universal statements, such as hypotheses or theories." [503, p. 27] Therefore, according to this widely accepted view, what is necessary is to find a procedure for justifying inductive inferences or a "principle of induction" that would enable us to "put inductive inferences into a logically acceptable form." [503, p. 29] Popper believed it was impossible to find a suitable principle of induction. Why? Because "I found Hume's refutation of inductive inference clear and conclusive." [505, p. 42] As recently as 1972, Popper notes "I regard Hume's formulation and treatment of the logical problem of induction ... as a flawless gem ... a simple, straightforward, logical refutation of any claim that induction could be a valid argument, or a justifiable way of reasoning." [507, pp. 86 and 88] At this point, the reader should carefully note Popper's words. He rejects inductive arguments because they could not be "valid arguments." In this case, he is using "valid" as synonymous with "deductive arguments." That is, Popper rejects inductive arguments because they are not valid, and they are not valid because they are not deductive arguments. But inductive arguments, by definition, are not deductive arguments. More importantly, note the phrase "or a justifiable way of reasoning." All reasoning in order to be "legitimate" must be deductive in nature. Popper would have us equate "good reasons to believe" in the truth of a proposition with "reasons that accord with deductive logic." We shall return to this issue later and shall see how restricting "good reasons" to "deductive logic" leads Popper to (ironically) irrationalism, rather than rationalism. [603]

Popper dismissed the program of the logical empiricists that attempted to find a probability formulation for the "degree of confirmation" of a lawlike generalization. (Indeed, over 25% of the original text of *The Logic of Scientific Discovery* was devoted to examining and refuting the position that the degree of confirmation could be equated with a probability.) Popper next considered whether the logical positivist verifiability principle could solve the "problem of demarcation" between science and pseudoscience. Popper points out, as he did in his letter to *Erkenntnis* in 1933, that the verifiability principle as a method of demarcation is untenable because lawlike generalizations can not be verified in the sense of being shown *deductively* true. (It is on the basis of the *Erkenntnis* letter pointing out the deficiencies of the verifiability principle and on the *Logic of Scientific Discovery* that Popper justifies the claim that he "killed" logical positivism. It is also why Popper deeply resents the fact that many of his critics call him a "positivist".)

Popper concludes that, since neither verifiability nor probability-confirmation will work, "the *falsifiability* of a system is to be taken as a criterion of demarcation." In other words, "it must be possible for an empirical scientific system to be refuted by experience." [503, pp. 40-41] As will be recalled, Popper refers to his philosophy as critical rationalism, and it is precisely the doctrine of falsifiability which to him justifies the label of "critical" in his philosophy.

Popper proposed that the *objectivity* of science is maintained through the falsifiability principle: "The objectivity of scientific statements lies in the fact that they can be inter-subjectively tested." [503, p. 44] But a scientific statement is not testable because one can find confirming instances. Rather, a statement is "more testable" the more things that it excludes from happening. (Some "theories" exclude nothing from happening and, therefore, are not testable. In particular, Popper held that such devices as the concept of "false consciousness" made all social phenomena consistent with Marxist theory and prevented it from being falsifiable.)

Theories, for Popper, cannot be confirmed, they can only be "corroborated." But corroboration is not to be found in terms of the number of times a theory has withstood attempts at falsification. Nor can the degree of corroboration be associated with a specific probability. Rather, a theory is more highly corroborated to the extent that it has passed *severe* tests. [503, p. 267]

Popper is often accused of proposing "dogmatic falsificationism" where a theory must be ruthlessly rejected on the basis of a single falsifying test. [see 362, p.181] Popper's writings belie that interpretation. Consider the following: "No conclusive disproof of a theory can ever be produced; for it is always possible to say that the experimental results are not reliable." [503, p. 50] Also, "a few stray basic statements contradicting a theory will hardly induce us to reject it as falsified." [503, p. 86] Furthermore, Popper recognized that we attempt to falsify "basic statements," and it is always possible in principle to deduce even *more* basic statements for further test. [503, p. 104] Therefore, for Popper, we "corroborate" that a theory is false by subjecting it to numerous severe tests, carefully examining the experimental requirements and characteristics of each test, and examining whether the basic statements being exposed to testing are truly the most appropriate.

How does science progress? Through "bold conjectures and refutations" is Popper's answer. [505] In this regard, Popper noted, Marxism is filled with bold conjectures, e.g., the absolute impoverishment of the working class, the first socialist revolution will occur in the most industrially developed country, and socialism will be free of revolutions. It was also abundantly clear to Popper that all the bold conjectures had been refuted and that Marxism as it was currently constituted was "saved" from further refutations only by ex post, ad hoc, auxiliary hypotheses.

Popper's philosophy is decidedly realist as far as the aims of science and the ontology of the concepts in scientific theories. It is not the *"possession* of knowledge, of irrefutable truth, that makes the man of science, but his persistent and recklessly critical *quest* for truth." [503, p. 281] Theories are "genuine conjectures—highly informative guesses about the world which although not verifiable . . . can be submitted to severe critical tests. They are serious attempts to discover the truth." [503, p. 115] Popper rejects the instrumentalist view of theories and the entities in them. He attributes the current allure of instrumentalism to the, so-called, "Copenhagen interpretation." Popper accepts the position that we cannot know both the position and the momentum of a subatomic particle, but he rejects the assertion that a subatomic particle cannot *have* both a position and a momentum. [508] Is the Hegelian idealist position correct that the world does not exist independently of its being perceived? No, claims Popper: "Some of these theories of ours can clash with reality; and when they do, we know that there is a reality; that there is something to remind us of the fact that our ideas may be mistaken. And this is why the realist is right." [503, p. 117] But because we never know for certain that our theories are correct, we should *proliferate* our theories as much as possible to encourage the growth of scientific knowledge. This proliferation of theories will lead to an "open society."

We opened this section on Popper with the observation that he and his philosophy have been called many, often contradictory, names. For Popper, falsifiability made his philosophy "critical," and the strong emphasis on conjectures made his philosophy similar to the rationalists. Hence, he refers to it as "critical rationalism." Even though Popper claims to have "killed" positivism by pointing out the problems of the verifiability principle, many writers, such as Barone [36] continue to refer to Popper as a positivist. Similarly, writers such as Laudan [371] refer to Popper as a logical empiricist, even though Popper strongly opposed the reliance on the formal logic of the logical empiricists and their program of formalizing scientific theories in terms of mathematical logic. He also sharply opposed the instrumentalist's view of theories held by most logical empiricists and clearly identified his falsifiability criterion as not being a "theory of meaning," (unlike the testability criterion of Carnap and Feigl). However, Popper did interact extensively with both the logical positivists and the logical empiricists and shared many of their values and views. In particular, he shared their views with respect to the unity of science, the importance of observation in science, the rationality of science, and the progress of science. In fact, the shared belief in the progress of science of Popper and the logical empiricists is of such importance that their concept of scientific progress warrants more detailed explication.

9.5   THE CONCEPT OF SCIENTIFIC PROGRESS

Implicit (and sometimes explicit) in the views of Popper and the logical empiricists was the belief that science progressed through four different means: (1) the development of new theories for phenomena not previously explained, (2) the falsification of existing theories and their replacement with new theories, (3) the expansion of the scope of a theory to include new phenomena, and (4) the reduction of specific theories into more general theories. We shall discuss each of these means of progress.

9.5.1   New Theories

With respect to the first method of progress (the development of new theories for phenomena not previously explained), the logical empiricists believed that this was beyond the scope of their endeavors. Specifically, the logical empiricists, following Whewell and Reichenbach, made a sharp distinction between the "context of discovery" and the "context of justification." They believed that there was no *logic* of discovery, but that discovery of new hypotheses and theories was an inherently psychological/sociological process, and the study of that process properly belonged within the psychology of science and/or the sociology of science. A second aspect of the discovery/justification thesis was that discovery was irrelevant to justification: "It is one thing to ask how we arrive at our scientific knowledge claims and what sociocultural factors contribute to their acceptance or rejection; and it is another thing to ask what sort of evidence and what general, objective rules and standards govern the testing, the confirmation or disconfirmation, and the acceptance or rejection of knowledge claims of science." [176, p. 472] Popper agreed that "the question how it happens that a new idea occurs to a man—whether it is a musical theme, a dramatic conflict, or a scientific theory—may be of great interest to empirical psychology; but it is irrelevant to the logical analysis of scientific knowledge." [503, p. 31]

Recently, it has become fashionable among many writers to deny the discovery/justification distinction. The reasons cited for denying the distinction usually fall under one or more of the following arguments: (1) the "argument from understanding science" [606, pp. 125-26], (2) Kuhn's "context of pedagogy" and "subjective factors arguments" [358, p. 327], and (3) Quine's argument for "naturalizing epistemology." [515] Seigel reviews and analyzes the various arguments that the discovery/justification distinction should be abandoned and concludes that "these distinctions are necessary for our overall understanding of the complexities of scientific knowledge—and, in particular, for our understanding of the way in which scientific claims purport to *appropriately* portray our natural environment." [580, p. 321] More recently, Hoyningen-Huene reviewed the current status of the discovery/justification debate and pointed out that "philosophers of the historicist orientation felt compelled, in order to legitimize their philosophical child, to argue against the distinction." [289, p. 501] He traces the historical origins of the distinction, analyzes the arguments both in favor and against it, and concludes "It is striking that none of the attacks on the context distinction has been directed against the distinction between the factual and the normative. But this difference seems to be the core of the context distinction as intended by its proponents." [289, p. 511] Stated simply, Hoyningen-Huene is pointing out that "Is does not imply ought."

The issue of the discovery/justification distinction has arisen in the marketing literature. For example, Peter and Olson claim that the "positivistic/empiricist" view of science is that "only the logic of justification is needed to understand science." [492, p. 119] Obviously, this is a "straw man" distortion of the actual views of the logical empiricists, for they simply restricted *their own studies* to justification.

9.5.2   Falsification of Theories

Continuing our discussion of the ways that science progresses, the second way is through the falsification of prior theories and their replacement by successors. A common example is the falsification of the view of Ptolemy that the Sun revolves around the Earth and its replacement with the Copernican view that the Earth revolves around the Sun. Essentially, this is a major part of the Popperian view of scientific progress. But, if science is an endless series of conjectures and their refutations, in what meaningful sense can we say that science has made "progress"? Indeed, this is a serious issue for "strict falsificationists." In mature sciences, such as physics, the issue seems to hinge on how one should answer the following question: "Is it more meaningful to claim that Newtonian physics was *false* and superseded by Einsteinian relativity; or is it more meaningful to claim that Newtonian physics was in some sense 'approximately true' or 'true within certain boundaries' "? On the one hand there are philosophers such as Laudan who claim that, "I am aware of no sense of approximate truth according to which highly successful, but evidently false, theoretical assumptions could be regarded as 'truth like.' " [372, p. 35] Others, both in physics and philosophy, contend that Newtonian physics is in some sense "approximately true" within its boundary conditions, citing as examples that it was the predictive accuracy of Newtonian physics that put man on the moon, rather than Einsteinian relativity. For example, Rohrlich and Hardin argue that "superseding theories do not falsify established theories" as long as the "validity limits" of the theories are appropriately identified. [537, p. 603]

Recall that the logical empiricists adopted an instrumentalist, rather than realist, approach to theories (one of the "lessons" of the downfall of Newtonian mechanics). The fact that the existence of particular theoretical terms in a theory was demonstrated to be false would pose no insurmountable problem to a logical empiricist conception of "approximate truth" so long as the "directly testable consequences were close to the observable values." [372, p. 33]

9.5.3   Expansion of Theories

A third method for science to progress is to expand the scope of a theory by showing that it can explain more, or different, phenomena. The logical empiricists believed that the formalization of theories through mathematical logic might be helpful in this regard. The formalization would clearly identify the underlying structure of the theory and perhaps show how the theory could be expanded to cover additional phenomena. An example of this kind of procedure is the extension of classical particle mechanics to rigid body mechanics. [606, p. 53]

9.5.4   Reduction of Theories

The fourth way that science progresses is the subsumption of specific theories (reduction) into more general theories. For example, "Galileo's

Two New Sciences was a contribution to the physics of freely falling terrestrial bodies; but when Newton showed that his own general theory of mechanics and gravitation (when supplemented by appropriate boundary conditions) entailed Galileo's laws, the latter were incorporated into the Newtonian theory as a special case." [463, p. 39] A strict or "naive falsificationist" would claim that the reduction of Galileo's laws to Newton's would not be an example of "progress" because Galileo's laws cannot be *deductively* derived from Newton's laws. (Galileo's laws provide that a body falls to the earth with constant acceleration; Newton proposed that acceleration is inversely proportional to the square of the distance of the body to the center of the earth.) The underlying issue at stake here is the *cumulativity* of scientific knowledge.

This section ends with what is perhaps the most fundamental question facing science and the issue of scientific progress today: "To what extent, if any, is scientific knowledge cumulative?" To what extent, if any, do we know more about the world as a result of the activities of science over, say, the last 400 years? Should we characterize Galileo's laws as "false" and Newton's laws as "false," and *generalizing* (inductively) that all of science is, simply, an endless succession of replacing "false" theories with *equally* "false" theories? Under such a construal, it would indeed be difficult (but perhaps not impossible) to make the case that science is cumulative, or even partially cumulative. Conversely, is it more meaningful to claim that we genuinely "knew more" about the world after Galileo's laws than before? Similarly, that we "knew more" after Newton's laws? Note that the issue here is not whether over the last 400 years all the knowledge-claims of science are *strictly* cumulative, analogous to bricks in a pile. Nor is the issue whether science has established, or even *could* establish, final or ultimate truths. The question is: Has there been *any* cumulative growth in scientific knowledge at all?

There are some authors who claim, or whose stated views logically imply, that there has been no scientific progress, no cumulativity at all in the knowledge-claims of science. These writers are generally referred to as "historical relativists" and are the topic of the next chapter. But to understand and evaluate the credibility of the historical relativists, we need first to examine more extensively what we mean by "knowledge" and the approaches to justifying knowledge-claims.

9.6   KNOWLEDGE, FOUNDATIONALISM AND FALLIBILISM

The purpose of this section is to explicate what we mean by scientific knowledge, starting from Plato's conceptualization that knowledge means "justified true belief." We shall then examine foundationalism, the "K-K thesis," the "philosophers' fallacy," and fallibilism as they relate to scientific knowledge.

9.6.1   Knowledge, Belief and Theories of Truth

Since the time of Plato, (see Section 8.1) philosophy has conceptualized knowledge to be "justified true belief." [607, p. 701]   On this view, knowledge implies belief.   That is, (unless the person is lying), a speaker of the English language cannot truthfully claim to "know that P" unless they "believe that P." Although philosophers have investigated the nature of knowledge and knowledge-claims extensively over thousands of years, they have paid little attention to the nature of belief or belief-claims. Generally, belief-claims have been thought to be non-problematical. The *locus classicus* concerning belief was *The Emotions and the Will* written by the Scottish philosopher Alexander Bain in 1859. Bain suggested that to know the beliefs of people is to examine their actions, since people may untruthfully respond to questions about their beliefs, or may not even truly know their own beliefs. Therefore, the beliefs of people are to be inferred from examining their actions. For example, if an individual truly believes that a water-well contains no poison, the person should be willing to drink from the well. As will be recalled, it is precisely this line of reasoning that G. E. Moore used in his attack on idealism, where he claimed that the stated beliefs of idealists were inconsistent with their behaviors (see Section 9.1.1).

A knowledge-claim is more than simply the statement of belief. Knowledge also implies a belief that is in some sense true. That is, if a speaker of the English language claims to "know that P" and subsequently claims to "know not P," the person does not speak of having previously had "false knowledge" and now having "true knowledge." Rather, the person would claim to have been *mistaken* in claiming to "know that P." For example, if a person claims to *know* that a water-well contains no poison and subsequently observes that many people have drunk from the well and immediately died, the person speaks of being mistaken in claiming to know that the well was safe. Therefore, the word "knowledge" in the English language always connotes some sense of the word "true," as well as "belief."

Finally, knowledge is more than a belief which is claimed to be true, it is a belief that can be *justified* as true. Although there have been many theories as to what justifies the truth-content of a belief, almost all fall within three major groupings: the correspondence theory of truth, the coherence theory of truth, and the pragmatic theory of truth. (Strictly speaking, the so-called "consensus theory of truth," held by relativists, is not really a "theory" of *truth*, since it simply states that whatever a person or group *believes* to be true, *is* true, i.e., "belief" equals "truth"—see Section 10.1.3.)

The correspondence theory of truth provides that the truth-content of any statement or proposition is the extent to which the statement corresponds, or represents, or is similar to, reality. Three problems are evident with any correspondence theory of truth. First, there may be no reality external to the human mind for establishing correspondence. The idealist position is that the external world does not exist unperceived (see Section 8.4). Therefore, in Hegelian terms, since only the "rational is the real," one cannot compare knowledge-claims with any external reality. Second, even if one accepts the fundamental premise of classical realism (that the external world exists unperceived), there are knowledge-claims that consist exclusively of terms that appear in principle to have no external referents. For example, the "entities" in mathematics and logic seem to have no reference in the external world, yet areas such as mathematics and logic contain knowledge-claims that have truth-content. Third, even if it is conceded that the external world exists unperceived, knowledge of the characteristics of this external world can only be gleaned through human senses. But we know that our perceptual processes are fallible and, therefore, what is *perceived* to be the "reality," may in fact be an illusion. One of the most complete expositions and defenses of the correspondence theory of truth in this century using formal logic has been the work of Alfred Tarski. [612] Tarski's formal development of the correspondence theory of truth was very influential on Popper. [503, p. 274]

The second theory of truth, the coherence theory, indicates that a statement is true or false to the extent it fits, is consistent with, or "coheres" with another statement or system of statements. This conceptualization of how one justifies the truth of a statement certainly accords with many examples of how people claim to know that a statement is true. For example, we may reject as false the claim that a particular consumer is brand-loyal to two different brands of the same product at the same time on the basis that it fails to *cohere* with our knowledge of how brand loyalty may be measured (e.g., if brand loyalty is defined as purchasing more than 50% of one's requirements of a particular product from a particular brand).

Infinite regress poses the major problem with the coherence theory of truth. That is, if statement A is to be justified as true by statement B, and statement B is to be justified by statement C, and statement C is to be justified by statement D, and so on, what is the justification for the statement at the end of the justificatory chain? Sometimes the last statement in the chain is justified through correspondence, as in the correspondence theory of truth. Sometimes the last statement in the chain is justified as a "necessary truth" (true in all possible worlds). For example, the axioms of Euclidian geometry were thought to be *necessarily true*. Similarly, the last statement in the justificatory chain might be a statement that is, on intuitive grounds, indubitably true (true for any normal person "beyond all reasonable doubt"). For example, the statement *cogito ergo sum* was considered by Descartes to be indubitably true (see Section 8.3.2). Finally, the last statement in the justificatory chain might, simply, be assumed to be true by stipulation or convention.

The third theory of truth, the pragmatic theory of truth, has its origins in the pragmatism of C. S. Peirce (1839-1914). Pragmatism is often considered to be the only unique philosophical system original to the United States. Peirce developed pragmatism as a rule or procedure for promoting conceptual clarity in science. (Thus, Peirce shared much with the logical positivists.) In his 1878 paper entitled "How to Make Our Ideas Clear," Peirce proposed that the meaning of scientific terms is entailed by their "practical consequences." The totality of practical consequences for a scientific term provides a conditional translation for the term or "sign." All terms for which there are no practical consequences have no "pragmatic meaning" or are "empty." Thus, the pragmatic theory of meaning of Peirce is very similar to the operational definitions proposed by the operationalists several decades later. It also foreshadowed the "verifiability theory of meaning" developed by the logical positivists.

Although Peirce restricted his pragmatic theory of meaning to *experimental* inquiry, William James (1842-1910) generalized pragmatism to a theory of truth. In particular, James proposed that the truth-content of statements must be evaluated on the basis of their "practical consequences," "usefulness," "workability," or "cash value." Thus, in a famous defense of faith, James noted: "On pragmatic principles, if the hypothesis of God works satisfactorily in the widest sense of the word, it is 'true'. " [315, p. 299]

The extension of pragmatism to such concepts as "truth" infuriated its originator, C. S. Peirce. In fact, Peirce objected so violently that he coined the label "pragmaticism" to differentiate his own philosophy from the pragmatism of William James. Other philosophers began to assail James' pragmatic theory of truth, most notably, Bertrand Russell and G. E. Moore. For example, Russell pointed out that the way James used the word "working" is at odds with how scientists use the term. When a scientist says a theory "works," the implication is that the theory "predicts correctly or some such thing and *not* that the theory is good for the scientist or for society." Further, the pragmatic theory of truth totally confuses sentences like "It is true that other people exist" with sentences like "It is useful and desirable to believe that other people exist." Although some recent writers (see Phillips [497a]) believe that James was "misunderstood," the pragmatic theory of truth has gained little acceptance.

9.6.2   Foundationalism, The K-K Thesis, The "Philosophers' Fallacy," and Fallibilism

The preceding section points out that, at least since the time of Plato, Western philosophy has considered knowledge to be "justified true belief." Further, the truth of a knowledge-claim was to be determined by its correspondence with reality and/or its coherence with other statements that we "knew." However, in *Theaetetus* Plato argued that genuine knowledge can only be had of those things that are eternal and unchanging, for example, the entities in geometry and his idealized "forms" (see Section 8.1.2). Since the objects in the existing external world were constantly changing and were only "imperfect copies" of the "forms," genuine knowledge of the existing external world could not be had. That is, Plato equated knowledge with true beliefs "justified-with-certainty." And for Plato, "certainty" meant the degree of certainty found in the truths of geometry.

Plato's view of restricting knowledge to claims "known-with-certainty" provided the historical genesis for the position known as *foundationalism*. Briefly, foundationalism provides that scientific knowledge must be based on a foundation which is known to be true with absolute certainty. [435, p. 124] Consider the classical rationalists. As previously discussed in Section 8.3.2., Descartes' "method of doubt" sought unquestionably true first principles for his science and arrived at *cogito ergo sum* for such a foundation. On the other hand, classical empiricists, such as Bacon, believed that direct observation and experience would provide a secure and certain foundation for the development of science. A modern variant of Plato's thesis is the so-called "K-K Thesis."

The K-K thesis holds that to "know that *P*" entails "one must *know* that one *knows* that *P*." (Hence, "K-K".) In other words, "one cannot know that *P* unless one knows that one's claim to know that *P* is correct." [607, p. 717][2] Thus, not only must science justify its knowledge claims with good reasons, but it must justify its method of justifying. The tacit acceptance of the K-K thesis has resulted in a slide into skepticism by many philosophers of science through two mechanisms. First, the K-K thesis involves infinite regress. "To know" entails "one must know that one knows," which entails "one must know that one knows that one knows," and so forth. Second, to "know that one knows" has often been interpreted as "to *know-with-certainty* that one knows."

For example, the K-K Thesis underlies Humean skepticism: "The heart of Hume's attack consists in showing that one cannot know the induction hypothesis needed to infer the derivative knowledge that *P*

---

[2] I am indebted to Michael Levin (Department of Philosophy, City University of New York) for helpful correspondence on the implications of the K-K thesis.

from what one already knows, hence that one does not know that one's evidence is adequate; but this yields his [Hume's] skeptical conclusions only if resort is made to the K-K Thesis." [607, p. 718] Furthermore, the logical positivists implicitly accepted the K-K Thesis and, therefore, attempted (unsuccessfully) to overcome Humean skepticism with an inductive logic substituting a known probability for "know-with-certainty." Similarly, Popper accepted the K-K Thesis and attempted to meet its resultant skepticism with the falsification doctrine, which "fails" because such procedures do not enable one to *know-with-certainty* that any particular theory is conclusively false. Finally, "the K-K Thesis crucially underlies Feyerabend's and Kuhn's extreme views on scientific knowledge." [607, p. 719]

Three options for dealing with the K-K Thesis are manifest. The first option is to follow in the footsteps of the classical rationalists, classical empiricists, logical positivists, logical empiricists, and falsificationists. This option implies the acceptance of the K-K Thesis and to continue the foundationalist search for incorrigible foundations and methods for the development of scientific knowledge. The second option is to reject the K-K Thesis and develop fallibilistic models and theories regarding science and the development of scientific knowledge. In this regard, *fallibilism* is an alternative to foundationalism. That is, fallibilism holds that, not only is scientific knowledge fallible, but also that genuine scientific knowledge may be built upon foundations which are themselves fallible. As Suppe has observed, the denial of the K-K Thesis and the acceptance of fallibilism "appears to accord more closely with the actual means whereby science evaluates putative knowledge claims in the attempt to undergo the objective growth in scientific knowledge." [607, p. 726] My own position on the K-K Thesis is in accord with Suppe and was implied in Section 7.4 where I stated "In science all knowledge claims are tentative, subject to revision on the basis of new evidence," and that "the concept 'certainty' belongs to theology, not science." I believe that the acceptance of fallibilism and its concomitant rejection of the K-K Thesis and foundationalism, is the preferred option.

There is a third option which is being put forth by many as the preferred path to follow. The third option is to (1) accept the K-K Thesis, (2) point out that neither science nor the philosophy of science can justify with certainty its own methods of justifying its knowledge-claims and (3) proceed to accept (reluctantly as with Kuhn or exuberantly as with Feyerabend) the resultant relativism, skepticism, and irrationalism.

This third option represents a classic example of what Harré has labeled the "philosophers' fallacy of high redefinition." [250, p. 4] This is the fallacy of defining a concept (e.g., scientific knowledge, truth, falsity, objectivity, or progress) in such a manner (e.g., must be "known with certainty" or "known with probability 'p' ") that the concept cannot be realized and then lapsing into relativism, nihilism, or skepticism.[3]

It is worth noting that examples of the philosophers' fallacy abound in marketing: Anderson claims that theories cannot be falsified because their falsity "can never be known with certainty" [14, p. 163]; purportedly agreeing with Kuhn, Anderson claims that "science is a process without a goal" on the basis that "there is no *guarantee* that it progresses toward anything—*least* of all toward 'truth'." [13, p. 22, emphasis added]; Popper's theory is faulty because "it is impossible to *conclusively* refute a theory" [13, p. 21, emphasis added]; since science cannot conclusively show that it produces "objective absolute meanings," then "all meanings" in science "are subjectively determined," and therefore "science is subjective." [492, p. 120-1]   Even the so-called "underdetermination thesis" is an example of the philosophers' fallacy: "Scientific methods underdetermine theory choice." [14, p. 158] All this claim really asserts is that we cannot know-with-certainty, i.e., *determine,* that our methods in science will yield a *unique* theory choice. That is, there may be theories other than the one in question that are consistent with the data. Laudan refers to assertions like the "underdetermination thesis" as "innocuous" doctrines. [377, p. 230] Although proponents of such doctrines put them forth as supposedly implying relativism, subjectivism, and irrationalism in science, such innocuous locutions imply nothing other than that science is fallible. It is to the subject of relativism that we now must turn.

Questions for Analysis and Discussion

1. Explain the relevance of John Passmore's quotation in the headnote to this chapter to the quest by the ancient Greeks to separate "knowledge" from "opinion." What does Passmore mean when he claims "its accusations rest on a misunderstanding of science"? Evaluate Passmore's thesis that the attack on science is, also, an attack on art, history, philosophy, and so forth. Do the humanities have a stake in the defense of science? Do the sciences have a stake in the defense of the humanities?

2. What is classical realism? To what extent is classical realism consistent/inconsistent with classical empiricism/rationalism? It is often claimed that all scientists are either classical realists or sophists. Evaluate this position.

3. What is Russell's method of "logical constructionism"? Do experience and observation play any role in logical constructionism? If so, what? If not, is this a deficiency of logical constructionism?

---

[3] I am indebted to David Stove, University of Sydney Philosophy Department, for pointing out that the "fallacy of high redefinition" was first discussed by Paul Edwards in his evaluation of Bertrand Russell's work on induction. See reference 162a.

4. What is the "picture theory of meaning" of Wittgenstein? How does this theory of meaning relate to classical realism? How does this theory of meaning relate to Russell's logical constructionism? What is the difference between attempting to build a "philosophical system" and Wittgenstein's claim that "all philosophy is critique of language"?

5. Why was Einsteinian relativity so disastrous for the philosophy of science at the turn of the century? Why could not Hegelian idealism be compatible with quantum mechanics? What problems for Machian neo-positivism did quantum mechanics pose? How does logical positivism accommodate both Einsteinian relativity and quantum mechanics?

6. What are the fundamental tenets of logical positivism? What is the difference between considering logical positivism to be a movement and considering it to be a research program? To what extent is the movement of logical positivism consistent with the aims of the Enlightenment? Why were the logical positivists so critical of Hegelian idealism? In your judgment, should they have been so critical?

7. What was the major "lesson" that the logical positivists learned from Einsteinian relativity and quantum mechanics? To what extent did the views of the logical positivists depart from classical realism? To what extent did the views of logical positivists accord with those of classical realism? Why was the "humean view of causality" consistent with the "lesson" that the logical positivists learned from Einsteinian relativity and quantum mechanics?

8. How does logical empiricism differ from logical positivism? How does Humean skepticism relate to the views of the logical empiricists concerning scientific explanation? How does Humean skepticism relate to the "theoretical term/observational term" distinction?

9. What is the difference between developing a "correspondence rule" for *defining* a construct and developing a "measure" of a construct? Are there circumstances under which "correspondence rules" and "measures" are identical? Are there research programs that imply that "correspondence rules" and "measures" are identical? *Should* all "measures" of constructs be "correspondence rules"?

10. Summarize Humean skepticism. Why does it require that "only deductive derivations are valid"? Speculate on why the discipline of philosophy has been so obsessed with Humean skepticism. What does Humean skepticism have to do with Plato, his conceptualization of knowledge, and his "theory of forms"?

11. To what extent is Popper's philosophy of "critical rationalism" consistent/inconsistent with the Enlightenment? To what extent does Popper's philosophy rely on Humean skepticism? How do Popper's philosophy and Humean skepticism relate to the Enlightenment?

12. Differentiate between "corroboration" for Popper and "confirmation" for the logical empiricists. Does the claim that theories are not, strictly speaking, *falsifiable* necessarily imply that all theories are "equally false"? Does the claim that theories are not, strictly speaking, *confirmable*, mean that all theories are "equally true"? If so, why? If not, why not? If we cannot show that our theories are true-with-certainty or, alternatively, that they are false-with-certainty, should we not (as relativists demand) dispense entirely with the notions of "truth" and "falsity"?

13. What does "scientific progress" imply?   Why should we be interested in whether science makes progress or not?   Do we really *know* more about marketing now than we did two decades ago?   How about four decades ago? In which areas are we making the most progress?   What definition of "progress" was implied in your answer to the previous question?

14. What is the difference between the claim that "only the logic of justification is needed to understand science," [492, p. 119] and the claim that "the logical empiricists focused exclusively on the logic of justification."   Why is this difference significant?   What does it mean to "understand" science?   What does the positive/normative dichotomy have to do with this issue?

15. What is the "philosophers' fallacy"?   How does it relate to Humean skepticism? How does it relate to the current discussions concerning relativism in marketing and the social sciences?   Why is the "philosophers' fallacy" a genuine fallacy?   How does the philosophers' fallacy inexorably lead to the destruction of our ability to make judgments on the merits of issues?   (Hint: Consider the extent to which the philosophers' fallacy *destroys* language. Remember, Orwell's world of "1984" had no word for "science".)

10
THE RISE AND FALL OF HISTORICAL RELATIVISM IN PHILOSOPHY OF SCIENCE

The cruelest fate which can overtake enfants-terribles is to awake and find that their avowed opinions have swept the suburbs.

David C. Stove

In the 1960s the philosophy of science turned toward historicism, relativism, and irrationalism. Indeed, the pejorative label of "Received View" was coined and used as an epithet to be hurled at anyone who dared hold any view that did not conform with an irrationalistic perspective of science.[1] But, to understand historical relativism requires a basic, working knowledge of *relativism*, itself. Therefore, this chapter begins with a discussion of relativism, then examines the versions of historical relativism provided by Kuhn and Feyerabend, and concludes with a discussion of why historical relativism was so quickly and passionately embraced in the sixties.

10.1 RELATIVISM vs. ABSOLUTISM

Although (as was pointed out in Section 8.1.3) relativism can be traced to the time of Socrates, modern relativism has its genesis in the works of certain cultural anthropologists at the turn of this century. Much of the cultural anthropology of the 19th-century, implicitly or explicitly, accepted the concept of the progressivity of culture, believing that cultures progressed from those of primitive tribes and peoples to those of modern societies. Similarly (as with August Comte), science was

---

[1]The term "Received View" was originally coined by Putnam [510] and referred to certain tenets of logical empiricism about the nature of theories in science. However, the meaning of the term became extremely pejorative in the 1960s, used by many to refer to *all* views on science other than the "new orthodoxy" of historical relativism.

considered to be an institution that progressed from beliefs based on magic and superstition to beliefs justified by scientific method. As a reaction to this cultural ethnocentrism, several anthropologists, led by Franz Boas and M. Herskovits, strongly argued that other cultures should not be evaluated in terms of Western norms. Rather, they argued that we should accept "the validity of every set of norms for the people whose lives are guided by them, and the values they represent." [270, p. 76] Thus, cultural relativism was born.

10.1.1   Cultural/Moral Relativism

Essentially, the *cultural relativism* proposed by the anthropologists embodied the acceptance of three theses: (1) the elements embodied in a culture can only be evaluated relative to the norms of that culture; (2) there are no transcultural or culture-neutral norms to evaluate different cultures or different elements within cultures, and (3) since there are no transcultural norms, no culture (and no element within a culture) can be claimed to be "better" or "more advanced" than any other culture (or any other element within another culture). For relativist anthropologists, cultures and elements within cultures are neither good nor bad, they simply "are."

Cultural relativism has come to be closely associated with *moral relativism,* so much so, in fact, that the terms are often used synonymously. As Krausz and Meiland put it, "cultural relativism is the position which begins with value relativism—the view that each set of values, *including moral values,* is as valid as each other set—and draws the conclusion that no society has a right to attempt to change or otherwise interfere with any other society." [350, p. 7, emphasis added] Moral relativism holds the following:

1. Whether an action is right or wrong can only be evaluated relative to some moral code (held by an individual, group, society or culture).
2. There are no objective, impartial, or nonarbitrary standards or criteria for evaluating different moral codes (across individuals, groups, societies, or cultures).

Therefore, since there are no objective criteria for evaluating codes, the holder of one moral code cannot praise, condemn, or interfere with the actions of another individual, group, society, or culture having a different moral code.

Cultural relativism was enthusiastically embraced by many liberal colonialists, most notably many British administrators in places such as West Africa. [Williams in 350, p. 171] Several academic disciplines have, either implicitly or explicitly, embraced cultural relativism. The discipline of social anthropology has come closest to being dominated by the cultural relativist perspective. [276, p. 1] Furthermore, many writers believe that cultural and ethical relativism are pervasive throughout American society. For example, Bloom believes:

> There is one thing a professor can be absolutely certain of: almost every student entering the university believes, or says he believes that truth is relative. If this belief is put to the test, one can count on the students' reaction: they will be uncomprehending. . . . The danger they have been taught to fear from absolutism is not error but intolerance. . . . The true believer is the real danger. The study of history and of culture teaches that all the world was mad in the past; men always thought they were right, and that led to wars, persecutions, slavery, xenophobia, racism, and chauvinism. The point is not to correct the mistakes and really be right; rather it is not to think you are right at all. If I pose the routine questions designed to confute them and make them think, such as, "if you had been a British administrator in India, would you have let the natives under your governance burn the widow at the funeral of a man who had died?," they either remain silent or reply that the British should never have been there in the first place. [69, p. 25-26]

So, cultural and moral relativism began with the observation of diversity, was nourished by hostility toward ethnocentrism, and was (often) motivated by a desire for pluralism and an enlightened tolerance toward non-Western cultures. Unfortunately, although individual relativists may advocate pluralism and enlightened tolerance, the *philosophy* of relativism does not *imply* these attributes. Since our focus in this book must be on cognitive relativism, we can only give a flavor of the arguments that show the deficiencies of cultural/moral relativism.

First we examine the claim that relativism leads to an "enlightened" viewpoint toward other cultures. Consider the fact that there still are several societies in the world today where the practice of slavery continues unabated. (The "market price" of a young child is $150-$250.) [483] Or, consider that in the late 1970s the Khmer Rouge slaughtered between one and two million of their fellow Cambodians (out of a population of approximately seven million). [617, 1988, p. 32] Or, consider that the Western estimates of "only" twenty million Soviet citizens being murdered during Stalin's purges have been revised upward by the Soviet historian Bestuzhevlada to 38-50 million. [509] (As a consequence of the revelations of Bestuzhevlada and others, the Soviet State Committee on Education canceled all traditional history exams so that the history books—which had maintained that, at most, a "few thousand" dissidents had been executed—could be revised to reflect the truth.) [85a, p. 74] This Orwellian approach to the facts of social reality and its accompanying list of atrocities could go on and on. Is it "enlightened" not to condemn such atrocities? Most of us would, rightly, claim "No." Yet, as the ethicist James Rachels has pointed out, cultural/moral relativism implies that none of these heinous actions and practices could be condemned under moral relativism:

Cultural Relativism would preclude us from saying that any of these practices were wrong. We would not even be able to say that a society tolerant of Jews is *better* than the anti-Semitic society, for that would imply some sort of transcultural standard of comparison. The failure to condemn *these* practices does not seem "enlightened"; on the contrary, slavery and anti-Semiticism seem wrong *wherever* they occur. *Nevertheless, if we took cultural relativism seriously, we would have to admit that these social practices are also immune from criticism.* [516, pp. 17-18]

When Rachels uses the phrase "if we took cultural relativism seriously," he is pointing out that many who refer to themselves as cultural relativists are engaging in self-delusion or sophistry.

Just as cultural/moral relativism does not imply an enlightened perspective, neither does it imply a tolerant pluralism, even though advocates such as Herskovits seem to believe that it does: "In practice, the philosophy of relativism is a philosophy of tolerance." [271, p. 31] A detailed analysis of why cultural relativism does not imply tolerance can be found in Harrison. [Harrison in 350] Briefly, suppose we have two societies, A and B, both of which are firmly committed to relativism, but which have different religions. Suppose further that society A has a norm that states that it has a moral obligation to impose, by force if necessary, its religion on all other societies of different religions. Such a norm, since it is consistent with the rest of its culture, is "right" and, given relativism, the norm cannot be challenged from outside the culture. What logically follows is that society A will be morally "correct" in invading society B to impose on B the religion of A. Not only can other countries (e.g., C and D) not morally condemn society A (since it is only following a norm of its culture), but (most ironically) society B cannot even condemn society A (since B is also firmly committed to relativism). In short, not only does relativism not *imply* tolerance, but also, relativism can easily be used to defend the most atrociously intolerant actions! As the sociologist Orlando Patterson observes: "Relativism, in fact, can be associated just as easily with a reactionary view of the world, and can easily be used to rationalize inaction, complacency, and even the wildest forms of oppression. It is all too easy for the reactionary white South African, or American, to say of the reservation Bantus or Indians, that it is wrong to interfere with their way of life since what might appear to be squalor and backwardness to us, may be matters of great virtue to them." [489, p. 126] Recognizing that cultural/moral relativism does not deliver on its implied benefits, most ethicists (such as Rachels [516]) reject it. Some ethicists point out that cultural relativism, just like cognitive relativism, is self-refuting and incoherent. [408] That is, the conclusion that one cannot (morally) interfere with the actions of another who holds a different moral code is inconsistent (self-refuting) with the thesis that there are no transcultural standards: "Critics find moral relativists maintaining the relativity of morals, while at the same time morally condemning in an absolute way any outside interference in other societies." [350, p. 9] On the other hand, many ethicists reject relativism on the basis that its second thesis is incorrect. Such ethicists hold that there exist criteria for appraising cultural values and norms, in general, and ethical values and norms, in particular. Such ethicists would subscribe to some form of *absolutism*. One should note that subscribing to the thesis that there exist appraisal criteria for evaluating ethical values (absolutism) does not imply that one must know-with-certainty that one's appraisal criteria are correct (what Siegel [586a] calls "vulgar absolutism"). Such a requirement would be akin to accepting the K-K Thesis and falling prey to the "philosophers' fallacy," as discussed in Section 9.6.2. In other words, one can hold that there exist appraisal criteria without holding that one *knows* for certain that one's appraisal criteria are true or correct.

Whereas moral relativism deals with matters of *value*, cognitive relativism deals with matters of *fact* (although any sharp distinction may be difficult to make). [276, p. 2] Both share the *relativity thesis* that "something is relative to something else" and both share the *evaluation thesis* that "there are no objective, impartial, or nonarbitrary criteria to make evaluations *across* the various kinds of 'something else.'" (Absolutism rejects the evaluation thesis, not the relativity thesis.) As we shall see, as with moral relativism, cognitive relativism also has historical roots in cultural relativism.

10.1.2   Rationality Relativism and the "Strong Thesis"

There are numerous kinds of cognitive relativism. For example, Muncy and Fisk discuss subjective relativism, objective relativism, aletheic relativism, conceptual relativism, and social relativism. [458] However, three major types have the greatest import for marketing: rationality relativism, reality relativism, and conceptual framework-relativism. To understand the nature and origins of these kinds of relativism requires a brief discussion of the sociology of science.

The sociology of science can trace its roots back to the French philosopher, August Comte. However, most sociologists ascribe to Robert K. Merton the distinction of "founding father of modern sociology of science." [Storer in 444, p. xi] Merton's 1935 doctoral dissertation was entitled *Science, Technology, and Society in 17th-Century England*. As a reaction to the fate of "non-Aryan science" in Hitler's Germany during the 1930s, Merton subsequently focused his attention on the various social conditions under which science can lose its autonomy in a 1937 paper entitled "Science and the Social Order." At that time, he also developed the concept of a "scientific community" that was later to be expanded on by Michael Polanyi and to become a basic concept in the sociology of science. [Storer, in 444, p. xvii] By 1942, Merton had developed his comprehensive analysis of the ideal norms of the various scientific communities:

1. Universalism (the knowledge-claims of science are to be subjected to preestablished impersonal criteria and are not to depend on attributes of the scientist such as race, nationality, and social class).
2. Communism (the knowledge gleaned from scientific activity is to be made available to all and is not to be the "private property" of the scientist).
3. Organized skepticism (all knowledge-claims are open to doubt and to be exposed to intense scrutiny).
4. Disinterestedness (in providing expert opinions on matters of controversy within the realm of the scientist's domain of knowledge, the scientist is to render an opinion based on the objective facts of the matter and not on the basis of the interests of a particular party in the controversy).

In 1945, Merton laid out a research program for studying the sociology of knowledge in an article entitled "The Paradigm for the Sociology of Knowledge." The paradigm has been enormously influential in guiding the research activities of sociologists of science. An implicit assumption of the paradigm was what Laudan now calls the "arationality assumption," which "amounts to the claim that the sociology of knowledge may step in to explain beliefs if and only if those beliefs cannot be explained in terms of their rational merits." [370, p. 202] The arationality thesis has to do with the following question: Are the beliefs and knowledge-claims of science to be explained by examining the *reasons* that scientists give for their knowledge-claims, or are they to be explained as being *caused* by such social factors as race, nationality, social class, social position, and culture? Most sociologists of science have thought it appropriate to explain the knowledge-claims of science by looking for "causes" only when it was evident that there were no rational reasons underpinning the scientists' claims. In recent years, some sociologists of science have put forth the so-called "strong thesis" that all knowledge-claims in science are to be explained as being caused, or determined, by social factors. In the sociology of science literature "the terms 'relativist' and 'strong thesis' are used almost interchangeably." [558a, p. 135]

The "strong thesis," or relativism in sociology has its origins in the work of Karl Mannheim (1893-1947). Mannheim's most famous work was *Ideology and Utopia*, published in English in 1936. Acknowledging the tremendous influence of Hegel on his views, Mannheim proposed that "a modern theory of knowledge which takes account of the relational as distinct from the merely relative character of all historical knowledge must start with the assumption that there are spheres of thought in which it is impossible to conceive of absolute truth existing independently of the values and position of the subject and unrelated to the social context." [Mannheim, in 81, p. 123] Given Mannheim's avowed Marxist orientation, it is not surprising that he focused on "values and position of the subject" and the "social context" as factors determinative of knowledge. A second source of Mannheim's views that knowledge was "socially determined" was his realization that the prevailing views of sociology, itself, were so determined:

> As Mannheim concedes, the entire discipline of the sociology of knowledge emerged as a generalization from the features of sociology itself. Early twentieth-century sociologists, examining the history of their own discipline, came to the conclusion that it was full of doctrines which owed more to the social background of their defenders than to their intrinsic rational merits. The general thesis of the sociology of knowledge (to wit, that ideas in most disciplines are socially determined) was founded on the hope that all other forms of knowledge might prove to be as subjective as sociology clearly was. [370, p. 244]

The impact of Mannheim on the development of the "strong thesis" in sociology has been great. Equally great, however, has been the work of the cultural anthropologists on the nature of rationality in primitive cultures. Recall that Merton and Laudan proposed that "social factors" should be used to explain *only* those knowledge-claims in science that could not be justified on rational grounds. However, suppose that what we in Western societies call "rational" were found to be a "purely local" formulation? Barnes and Bloor reviewed the works of the cultural anthropologists on primitive cultures and concluded that many such cultures do not exhibit a preference for what, by Western standards, would be called "rational." They, therefore, proposed that *rationality is relative:*

> For the relativists there is no sense attached to the idea that some standards or beliefs are really rational as distinct from merely locally accepted as such. Because he thinks that there are no context-free or super-cultural norms of rationality, he does not see rationally and irrationally held beliefs as making up two distinct and qualitatively different classes of thing . . . hence the relativist conclusion that they are to be explained in the same way. [Barnes and Bloor, in 276, pp. 27-28]

Our first major kind of cognitive relativism, *rationality relativism,* provides a major underlying rationale for the "strong thesis" that all knowledge-claims are to be treated equally and to be explained through the use of social factors, such as race, class, religion and position. Thus, rationality relativism provides the following:

1. The canons of correct, or rational reasoning are relative to individual cultures.
2. There are no objective, neutral, or nonarbitrary criteria to evaluate what is called "rational" across different cultures.

Therefore, if what counts as rational, or "good reasons," for accepting a knowledge-claim cannot be evaluated outside the confines of a particular culture, then *all* knowledge-claims are to be "explained" through social factors.

Several lines of criticism have been directed at rationality relativism and the "strong thesis." The first observation about rationality relativism is that it is self-refuting and incoherent. Rationality relativism asserts that there are no objective, impartial, nonarbitrary means to evaluate different canons of rationality across different cultures. We may, therefore, legitimately ask: Is this assertion true? In order to justify the assertion, the relativist will have to provide "good reasons" for believing the assertion. However, if the "good reasons" that demonstrate the truth of the assertion are objective, impartial, and nonarbitrary, then the doctrine of rationality-relativism is false. And if the "good reasons" to demonstrate the truth of rationality-relativism are nonobjective, biased, and arbitrary, then the "good reasons" beg the question, since they assume the assertion to be true in their premises. Either way, rationality relativism cannot be justified. Note that this is the same argument that Socrates used against Protagoras (see Section 8.1.3) and is similar to the self-refuting argument against moral relativism (see Section 8.12.1).

Second, some sociologists have examined the findings of the cultural anthropologists and have concluded, contra Barnes and Bloor, that the similarities between primitive societies' concept of "rationality" and that in the West were greater than the differences. Put more simply, the empirical evidence seems to support the assertion that what comes to be known or considered to be "rational" across diverse cultures is pretty much the same. [53, p. xxiii] The cultural anthropologists Cole and Scribner review the mass of studies that have been conducted on the reasoning processes of different cultures and conclude: "There is no evidence for different *kinds* of reasoning processes such as the old classic theories alleged—we have no evidence for a 'primitive logic.' " [125, p. 170] And why should anyone ever have *expected* that empirical studies of other cultures would yield any other conclusion? Stripped to its essence, the canons of rational thought hold that people can (inductively) learn from experience: We *generalize* (learn) that "alligators are unfaithful swimming companions" from *observing* (and being told that others have observed) that "alligators have a penchant for eating humans." Furthermore, we can *act* on the basis of our (deductive) reasoning: If it is true that "alligators are unfaithful swimming companions," then "don't swim with alligators!" Thus, those cultures that did not apply so-called "Western" canons of rational thinking would not have survived to be available for cultural anthropologists to study!

Laudan provides a third argument against rationality relativism. He points out that the historical record undercuts the thesis that major scientific theories can be explained by social factors. There has never existed a specifically "Bourgeois mathematics" (contra the Marxists), nor a "Jewish physics" (contra the fascists), nor a "specifically proletarian version of the special theory of relativity" (contra the Leninists). The reason for the failure of sociologists to make their "social factors" case (among other things) is "that the vast majority of scientific beliefs (though by no means all) seem to be of no social significance whatever." [370, p. 218]

A fourth argument against rationality relativism provides that, even if Western canons of rationality cannot be proved-with-certainty to be superior to those of primitive tribes, science may choose to work within those canons of rationality on the basis that they represent a significant intellectual achievement of Western civilization. [Hacking, in 276, p. 52] (Such a posture is much like the bumble bee, who, not knowing that it is impossible for him to fly, continues to fly anyway, or, "if others wish to 'swim with alligators,' let them.")

A fifth line of attack on rationality relativism is provided by Laudan who notes that such a relativism includes the belief that "all systems of belief, including science, are seen as dogmas and ideologies, between which objective, rational preference is impossible." [370, p. 3] Laudan believes that the rationality of science is to be found in its problem-solving ability, rather than its reliance on "good reasons." Therefore, for Laudan, since science has been manifestly successful in solving problems, its knowledge-claims are to be preferred.

A sixth line of attack has been to deny the assertion that there are no objective, impartial, nonarbitrary criteria for evaluating different conceptualizations of "rationality" across cultures. [Hollis in 276, p. 72] The reader should note that rationality relativists, such as Barnes and Bloor, *implicitly* accept the K-K Thesis and commit the "philosophers' fallacy." That is, they point out that we cannot know with certainty that our criteria for evaluating different conceptualizations of "rationality" across cultures are objective and impartial. They then implicitly place the know-with-certainty requirement and the K-K Thesis on all efforts to compare "rationality" across cultures. Given that we cannot know-with-certainty that our evaluative criteria are correct, they then conclude that *no such criteria exist!* However, if we reject the K-K Thesis with respect to rationality, we need only have "good reasons" to believe that our evaluative criteria are objective and impartial to claim that rationality is not relative. Further, even if some cultures *believe* in a different form of rationality, such criteria could still enable us to evaluate the relative merits of the different versions.

The force of arguments such as the preceding ones have resulted in the "strong thesis" remaining a minority view in the sociology of science, as Barnes and Bloor, themselves, point out. [Barnes and Bloor, in 276, p. 21]

10.1.3 Reality Relativism

Modern forms of relativism owe much to the later writings of Wittgenstein, notably his *Philosophical Investigations*, published posthumously in 1953. [643] The "early" Wittgenstein was decidedly realist in orientation (see Section 8.6.3), believing that the meanings of words and propositions were "pictures" in the mind that *referred* to the external world. The "later" Wittgenstein specifically rejects the view that the meanings of words, phrases, and propositions are to be found in their referential properties; rather, their meanings are to be found in the circumstances in which they are used. The idealism inherent in *Philosophical Investigations* provides that all language is a rule-governed activity (i.e., a "game"). Since language is a vehicle to communicate with someone else, the rules for various languages cannot be "private," they must be *shared* with other people (i.e., there are no "private languages"). The use of language to communicate with others is carried out in many different kinds of situations, contexts, or circumstances (i.e., "forms of life"). Within the same language, the particular rules that will govern the meanings of words, phrases, and propositions will vary depending upon the situations, contexts, and circumstances (i.e., there are numerous "language-games" that can be played). Therefore, the meaning of even scientific terms or words changes radically between contexts (between various "language-games").

The "later" Wittgenstein heavily influenced Winch and his 1958 monograph entitled *The Idea of a Social Science and Its Relation to Philosophy,* which "like Kuhn's book was short, polemical, provocative, and ambiguous." [60, p. 25] Winch's book and his 1964 article, "Understanding a Primitive Society," [639] analyzed the primitive society of the Azande and its reliance on witchcraft as detailed in the 1930s works of anthropologist Evans-Pritchard. From using Wittgenstein to analyze the witchcraft practices of the Azande, Winch concluded that (using Bernstein's paraphrase) these *"forms of life* may be so radically different from each other that in order to understand and interpret alien or primitive societies we not only have to bracket our prejudices and biases but have to suspend our own Western standards and criteria of rationality. We may be confronted with standards of rationality about beliefs and actions that are incompatible with or incommensurable with our standards." [60, p. 27] Thus, to Winch, Western rationality simply represents "our standards" and Azande rationality simply represents "their standards." Judging other people's standards of rationality by our own represents, simply, our own ethnocentrism.

If Wittgenstein is correct that words, phrases, and propositions do not in some meaningful sense *refer to reality,* then what is the nature of reality? Winch answers:

> Our idea of what belongs to the realm of reality is given for us in the language that we use. The concepts we have settle for us the form of the experience we have of the world. . . .the world *is* for us what is presented through those concepts. That is not to say that our concepts may not change; but when they do, that means that our concept of the world has changed too. [638, p. 15]

Essentially, Winch says that what comes to be considered "reality" is *constructed* by us as a result of the nature of the language we use. Hanson in his 1958 book *Patterns of Discovery* [248] comes to a similar conclusion through an analysis of our perceptual processes. Hanson wished to explore perception in science as "seeing" and to distinguish between *retinal-stimulation* and *interpretation*. Hanson argued that scientists who held different theories about the world would "see" different things even though each might be exposed to the same retinal stimulation. Hanson uses several examples to explore the issue, but he discusses most extensively the following:

> Let us consider Johannes Kepler: imagine him on a hill watching the dawn. With him is Tycho Brahe. Kepler regarded the sun as fixed: it was the earth that moved. But Tycho followed Ptolemy and Aristotle in this much at least: the earth was fixed and all other celestial bodies moved around it. *Do Kepler and Tycho see the same thing in the East at dawn?* [248, p. 5, emphasis added]

Hanson considered several answers to his question. He rejects the position that the "same retinal stimulation" justifies the claim that they "saw" the same thing. Hanson uses the Wittgensteinian example of the "duck/rabbit" from Gestalt psychology to argue the case that "seeing" *inherently* involves *interpretation*. (In this classic example of Gestalt, subjects are shown an ambiguous drawing in which some people "see" a duck, others "see" a rabbit, and some people can "switch" back and forth, "seeing" first one and then the other.) Hanson then argued that what scientists "see" (or perceive, or observe) is directly related to their knowledge, theories, and beliefs. He answered the question concerning Kepler and Tycho thusly:

> Tycho sees the sun beginning its journey from horizon to horizon. He sees that from some celestial vantage point the sun (carrying with it the moon and the planets) could be watched circling our fixed earth. Watching the sun at dawn through tychonic spectacles would be to see it in something like this way, ... but Kepler will see the horizon dipping or turning away, from our local fixed star. The shift from sunrise to horizon-turn is analogous to the shift-of-aspect [from "duck" to "rabbit"] phenomena already considered; it is occasioned by differences between what Tycho and Kepler think they knew. [248, pp. 23-24]

The preceding kinds of examples and analyses led Hanson to conclude that all observation in science is formed or directed by theory and, thus, is "theory-laden." Against the obvious response that the "duck" in his example was "really" an *interpretation* of an ambiguous set of pencil lines on paper, Hanson's reply would be that the "duck" is *precisely* the kind of "seeing" that is entailed in all scientific observation. That is, the "seeing" in all scientific observation *inherently* has an element of interpretation to it and is not "lines on paper."

The arguments of those, like Winch, who have proposed that it is our language which determines our "reality," and those, like Hanson, who have proposed that it is our theories that determine our "reality," have led many to what is now referred to as the "constructivist thesis," or *reality relativism*. Reality relativism holds that:

1. What comes to be known as "reality" is constructed by individuals *relative* to their language, group, social class, culture, theory, paradigm, world-view, or *Weltanschauung*.

2. What comes to count as "reality" cannot be objectively, impartially, or nonarbitrarily evaluated across different languages, individuals, groups, social classes, cultures, theories, paradigms, world-views, or *Weltanschauungen*.

The reader should note that reality relativism is *not* simply that different people perceive the *same phenomenon* differently. For this would mean that the perceptions of some of the people could be "right" and others could be "wrong." Further, reality relativism does *not* simply mean that our theories guide us, or inform us, or direct us in our observations and experiments. Rather, reality relativism implies that we cannot compare or evaluate or adjudicate different conceptualizations of "reality" across theories or whatever.

The constructivist thesis, or reality relativism, has been eagerly embraced by many writers. For example, Latour and Woolgar [366] have investigated the "construction of reality" in biochemistry laboratories. They propose that the purpose of the biochemists was to produce what they call literary inscriptions, "such as diagrams, figures, tables and other items contained in written reports." [p. 236] These literary inscriptions are constitutive of reality and the biochemists attempted to persuade their colleagues to accept their literary inscriptions as a scientific fact. How are the arguments among various biochemists settled? Is it not the case that the arguments are settled because one side can show that their "literary inscriptions" correspond better with the real world than other interpretations? No, according to Latour and Woolgar "argument between scientists transforms some statements into figments of one's imagination and others into facts of nature" and "*reality was the consequence* of the settlement of the dispute rather than its cause." [366, p. 236, emphasis added] That is, scientific reality was constructed in the laboratory independent of any relationship to a world external to the biochemists' "language-game." This conclusion corresponds well with the view of Collins about science: "The natural world in no way constrains what is believed to be." [127, p. 54]

Knorr-Cetina opts for a constructivist position very similar to Latour and Woolgar in her book *The Manufacture of Knowledge* [338]. Knorr-Cetina proposes that "the products of science have to be seen as highly internally structured through the process of production, *independent* of the question of their external structuring through some match or mismatch with reality." [338,p. 5, emphasis added] Similarly, the philosopher Nelson Goodman in his *Ways of Worldmaking* [232] also develops a constructivist thesis: "There are many different *equally true* descriptions of the world, and their truth is the only standard of their faithfulness," and "none of them tells us *the* way the world is, but each of them tells us *a* way the world is." [232, p. 30] (For an evaluation of Goodmanian relativism, see Siegel [585].)

Several writers in marketing recommend the adoption of reality relativism [481].   Thus Peter and Olson contend that "science creates many realities" and believe that "adopting the R/C [Relativistic/Constructionist] approach in marketing could produce more creative and useful theories," when compared with "the outdated P/E [Positivistic/ Empiricist] orientation that currently dominates marketing research." [492, pp. 119 and 123] Similarly, Sauer, Nighswonger, and Zaltman suggest: "Because realities are socially and psychologically constructed, the same event may have multiple realities, *each of which is valid.*" [557, p. 18, emphasis added] Anderson's "critical relativism" rejects the position "that there is a single knowable reality waiting 'out there' to be discovered via *the* scientific method." [14, p. 157] Similarly, Zaltman, LeMasters, and Heffring advocate what they call the "contemporary" view "that 'reality' may be structured in different yet equally valid ways." [649, p. 5] Hudson and Ozanne believe that interpretivist research in consumer behavior assumes that "reality is essentially mental and perceived," and that it is "also socially constructed." [p. 509] Many of the advocates of naturalistic, humanistic, and interpretivist approaches to research rely heavily on the work of Lincoln and Guba and their contention that "it is dubious whether there is a reality. If there is, we can never know it. Furthermore, no amount of inquiry can produce convergence on it." [396, p. 83]

Reality relativism is almost indistinguishable from *idealism,* its 19th century predecessor, whose central tenet was that "the external world does not exist unperceived." Thus, those who believe that the world exists unperceived (i.e., realism) and who believe that different conceptualizations of the nature of the world can be objectively, impartially, and nonarbitrarily evaluated (i.e., absolutism) frequently use many of the same arguments developed in Sections 8.6.1 and 8.6.2 against this modern version of idealism. Therefore, those arguments (e.g., the sophistry argument) need not be repeated here. Similarly, many of the criticisms leveled at rationality relativism in the previous section are equally applicable to reality relativism, e.g., both are self-refuting and incoherent. However, there is one argument against reality relativism that must be developed here—the argument from morality. Given that Hegelian idealism concluded that individual people are "unreal," but the state was "real" (see Section 8.4.3), is this modern version of idealism ethically troublesome, also?

Reality relativism starts innocently enough with the observation that different people have different perceptions of the real world. Reality relativists then (1) propose that these different perceptions constitute multiple realities; (2) argue that there are no neutral standards for comparing these multiple realities; (3) advance the view that the truth of any of the multiple realities is established by consensus, not by correspondence with any external reality; and (4) conclude that each of the many multiple realities is equally valid. Lincoln and Guba give numerous examples of such "constructed realities," including: "handicapped children," "social science," "Bobby Knight," "communism," "the Holocaust," "Watergate," and the "Vietnam Era." Each of these realities, they contend, is constructed, although some of them may in some way be related to what they call "tangible entities." As a parenthetical aside, they casually point out that "there are people who have argued, for instance, that the Holocaust never happened, but was merely a political construction to arouse world-wide sympathy for the Jews." [396, pp. 84] Their cavalier treatment of such a sober issue as the existence or nonexistence of the Holocaust provides a powerful example of the massive problems confronting the morality of reality relativism.

It is indeed true that one of the "multiple realities" that some people hold concerning the actions of the Nazis in World War II is that the Holocaust never occurred, but has been "manufactured," or "constructed," or "created" by those sympathetic to the Jews. An alternative "multiple reality" concerning World War II is that the Holocaust did in fact occur; the Nazis did in fact slaughter millions of Jews (and others) in their notorious concentration camps; and never again should such an atrocity be allowed to occur. What is to be said of these two "multiple realities"? Which "multiple reality" is correct? Where does truth lie? Sincere (non-sophist) advocates of reality relativism must stand mute when confronted with this question. Contending, as they do, that the two "multiple realities" cannot be objectively, impartially, or nonarbitrarily compared, they cannot evaluate which "reality" corresponds better with what actually occurred. Each is "equally valid." All consistent reality relativists can only (impotently) inquire whether the members of some group agree on a "reality." Thus, reality relativists such as Lincoln and Guba explicitly advocate a "consensus theory of truth" [396, p. 84] and others do so by implication. In contrast, absolutists have no problem addressing the question of which view of the Holocaust is correct, since they believe that the evidence (e.g. photographs, diaries, eyewitness accounts, concentration-camp records and the like) can provide an objective, impartial, nonarbitrary basis for evaluating which of the two claimed realities is closer to the truth. This is not to say that absolutists will always be correct when addressing questions such as this, for sometimes the evidence may lead them toward error. (And the task of epistemology in the philosophy of science has historically been that of trying to increase the odds of being right.) To those, and *only* to those, who prefer the *certainty* of moral impotence over the *possibility* of moral error, reality relativism has something to offer.

Some may think Lincoln and Guba's example of the Holocaust to be extreme or atypical. But such is not the case. Most of the truly important issues throughout all the social sciences have to do with genuine realities, not "essentially mental" constructs. Consider the many propositions and statements in the social sciences involving constructs such as racism, poverty, freedom, slavery, democracy, totalitarianism, fascism, and hunger. To contend that propositions and statements involving these kinds of constructs are "essentially mental," each being one example of a "multiple reality," and each being "equally valid" is disingenuous, or preposterous, or leads to moral impotence. Although absolutists, when facing the difficult decisions of our age, may at times choose incorrectly, at least they need not stand impotently mute. It is for this reason (among others) that ethicists condemn equally both *moral* relativism and *reality* relativism (note the similarity of the arguments against both). It is also for this reason that ethicists and others *fear* relativism and we can note how misguided are those in marketing who, following Feyerabend, contend that such fears are "unwarranted." [16, p. 137] In fact, Feyerabend's own works demonstrate the moral impotence of relativism.

Feyerabend has clearly seen the logical implications of his reality relativism concerning morality. He notes: "We certainly cannot assume that two incommensurable theories deal with one and the same objective state of affairs (to make the assumption we would have to assume that both at least *refer* to the same objective situation)." Therefore, "we must admit that they deal with different worlds and that the change (from one world to another) has been brought about by a switch from one theory to another." [190, p. 70] Feyerabend takes his reality relativism to its logical conclusion in his most recent book, *Farewell to Reason*. He notes: "My refusal to condemn even an extreme fascism and my suggestion that it should be allowed to survive. . .has enraged many readers and disappointed many friends." [194, p. 309] Although he points out that "fascism is not my cup of tea," he finds that his relativism does not allow him to condemn it. He asks, do his feelings toward fascism have "an 'objective core' that would enable me to combat fascism not just because *it does not please me*, but because *it is inherently evil*? And my answer is: we have an inclination—nothing more." [194, p. 309, emphasis in original] After recognizing that there are "philosophical systems" (e.g., realism, absolutism, and fallibilism) that might enable some people to justify their "inclinations," his own relativistic philosophy leads him to conclude: "And all I can find when trying to identify some content are different [philosophical] systems asserting different sets of values *with nothing but our inclination to decide between them*." [194, p. 309, emphasis added] Thus, we can see that Feyerabend sincerely believes in his reality relativism and accepts its logical implication of moral impotence.

Why have some philosophers (among many others) allowed themselves to be drawn into the moral morass of reality relativism? The philosopher Frederick L. Will believes that this, what he calls "perverse," position has resulted from philosophers' acceptance of the "relativist illusion." Thus:

> To recognize the role that practices and their governance play in the conduct of investigation [in science] is by no means to depreciate the role that the objects of investigation themselves play, in particular cases, in determining the course of investigation and, eventually, its results. . . . Recognition that knowledge of objects is gained through practices [in science] has led some philosophers to conclude that objects thus known are *produced* by the practices and are thus artifacts somehow dependent for their existence and character upon the practices themselves. Judged in the context of the history of human knowledge, and in particular the fabulous development of physical science in the past four centuries, *this is perverse*. Cognitive practices are designed to *discover and disclose* objects, not to produce them . . . Of course not all cognitive practices are *well designed* for the purpose; but as is indeed obvious to us *when we are not bemused by some potent philosophical illusion*, they are not all ill designed. [637, p. 18, emphasis added]

The third major form of relativism that we need to address is conceptual framework-relativism, alternatively referred to as, simply, conceptual relativism. Conceptual framework-relativism holds that:

1. Knowledge or knowledge-claims are relative to conceptual frameworks, theories, paradigms, worldviews, or *Weltanshauungen*.
2. Knowledge or knowledge-claims cannot be objectively, impartially, or nonarbitrarily evaluated across different conceptual frameworks, theories, paradigms, worldviews, or *Weltanshauungen*.

This version of relativism is most commonly associated with those philosophers subscribing to the view known as historical relativism, which can be traced to Thomas Kuhn's influential book, *The Structure of Scientific Revolutions*, published in 1962. We shall examine the views of the two most influential historical relativists, Kuhn and Feyerabend in the next section.

10.2   HISTORICAL RELATIVISM

Upon the rise of logical positivism in the 1920s and the birth of the philosophy of science as a distinct academic discipline, philosophers (at least in the Anglo-American tradition) viewed the purpose of philosophy of science as the clarification of the language of science. Although philosophers differed in the extent to which they used formal logic as an analytical tool, they agreed that "critical discussion" in the manner of Plato was the appropriate method for analyzing, evaluating and, thus, clarifying the nature of such scientific concepts as theory, explanation, laws, and models. The use of history and historical analysis was limited to providing examples for illustrative purposes.

Starting in the 1960s, a philosophical perspective known as historical relativism developed, having a different set of premises. First, instead of attempting to clarify the language of science, the historical relativists attempted to generate general theories of science. The historical relativists believed that from analyzing the historical development of science they could develop theories to explain (much like a social science) how scientists both discover and justify their knowledge-claims. The theories proposed by several of these historically oriented philosophers embraced one version or another of cognitive relativism, the theories of Kuhn and Feyerabend being the most influential. Since Kuhn is generally given credit for initiating the "historical turn" that philosophy of science took in the 1960s, we shall begin our discussion with him.

10.2.1 Kuhnian Relativism

Although Thomas S. Kuhn (1922-) received his Ph.D. in physics from Harvard University, most of his academic career has focused on the history and philosophy of science. Kuhn in his early years was heavily influenced by the works of Jean Piaget on the cognitive development of children, the Gestalt psychologists on perception, W. V. O. Quine on the analytic-synthetic distinction, and Ludwyk Fleck on the sociology of science. After publishing his first major book, *The Copernican Revolution,* in 1953, Kuhn accepted an invitation from the logical empiricists to develop a monograph on his emerging theory of science for inclusion in Volume II of their *Encyclopedia*, entitled the *Foundations of the Unity of Science* [473]. The resultant work, "The Structure of Scientific Revolutions," first appeared in the *Encyclopedia* in 1962 [473], was reprinted as a free-standing monograph shortly thereafter [354], and was revised with a *Postscript* in 1970. [355] Since that time Kuhn has published numerous articles explaining and clarifying his views, many of which are included in his 1977 book of readings, *The Essential Tension.* [358]

The origins of the central tenets of Kuhn's theory illustrate that the process of discovery is seldom neat and tidy. Although the concept of "paradigm" as it relates to the "worldview" or *Weltanschauung* of a community of scientists is usually considered to be the central construct of Kuhnian theory, the concept of "scientific revolution" was developed prior to his notions concerning the worldviews of scientists. In particular, the entire chapter on "scientific revolutions" (No. IX) was written before he had even begun its predecessors on "normal science." He relates:

The concept of paradigms proved to be the missing element I required in order to write the book. . . .unfortunately, in that process, paradigms took on a life of their own. . .having begun simply as exemplary problem solutions, they expanded their empire to include, first the classic books in which these accepted examples initially appeared and, finally, the entire global set of commitments shared by the members of a particular scientific community. [358, p. xix]

The preceding illustrates one reason why the concept of paradigm became so ambiguous in the original version of the *Structure of Scientific Revolutions,* resulting in Masterman finding 21 separate usages of the term. [425, pp. 59-90] In the 1970 edition of *Structure,* Kuhn recommends that the term paradigm be restricted to what he calls "exemplars," which are the concrete solutions to problems identified as important by the members of a specific scientific community. He suggested using the term "disciplinary matrix" (instead of paradigm) to identify the constellation of beliefs, values, and techniques (or "worldview") of a specific scientific community. In large measure, however, most writers continue to use the term paradigm in its broader context, and we shall follow that tradition in this section.

A paradigm, or *Weltanschauung* ("world-view"), contains three separate kinds of entities. First, there is a content, which includes theories, laws, concepts, "symbolic generalizations" (e.g., $F = ma$), and "exemplars." The exemplars represent standard examples of problems that the content of the paradigm solves. Second, a paradigm contains a methodology, which represents the procedures and techniques by which further knowledge within the paradigm is to be generated. Third, a paradigm contains an epistemology, which represents the set of criteria (Kuhn calls them "values" in his revised addition [355, p. 205]) for evaluating knowledge-claims.

Kuhn divides the historical development of all disciplines into three stages: the pre-paradigm stage, the normal science stage, and the revolutionary stage. In the pre-paradigm stage, there are many schools of thought within a discipline, none of which can be characterized as a full-fledged paradigm with well-developed "exemplars" that successfully solve important problems. Thus, scientists in the pre-paradigm stage spend much time in disputation regarding philosophical and methodological issues. The absence of well-developed paradigms means that research in this stage has a high random component and exhibits little, if any, cumulativity. Kuhn characterized the social sciences as being pre-paradigmatic (and would have, most assuredly, so characterized the marketing discipline had he been aware of it). [355, p. 15] Thus, Kuhn believed that his model of scientific change would not apply to the social sciences and marketing, which is ironic since his greatest impact has been there. [608]

Building upon his earlier work in the *Copernican Revolution,* Kuhn often uses Ptolemaic astronomy as an example of a paradigm. Kuhn proposed that the normal science stage of development occurs when one particular paradigm is viewed to be more successful than its "competitors in solving a few problems that a group of practitioners had come to recognize as acute." [355, p. 23] The members of the discipline then gradually coalesce around this single paradigm with its exemplars, and the paradigm uniquely dominates the entire scientific community. New members of the scientific community learn the details of the paradigm through studying its exemplars. That is, the learning of the paradigm is done *implicitly* through interacting with other members of the scientific community and learning how problems are to be solved in a manner similar to the exemplars. During normal science, scientists engage in activities, known as "puzzle-solving," to flesh out the paradigm; "Mopping-up operations are what engage most scientists throughout their careers." [358, p. 24] Research during periods of normal science is cumulative, but does not aim at the production of novelties of fact or theory. Such novelties are rare and generally unwelcome when they do appear. [355, p. 35]

Genuine scientific discovery only occurs when, contrary to their aims, scientists stumble upon "anomalies," i.e., "the recognition that nature has somehow violated the paradigm-induced expectations that govern normal science." [355, p. 52] For example, although Ptolemaic astronomy was extraordinarily successful in predicting the changing positions of both stars and planets when compared with any of its predecessors, "Ptolemy's system never quite conformed with the best available observations." [355, p. 68] Although the system was patched-up time and time again, "by the early 16th century an increasing number of Europe's best astronomers were recognizing that the astronomical paradigm [of Ptolemy] was failing in application to its own traditional problems. That recognition was prerequisite to Copernicus' rejection of the Ptolemaic paradigm and his search for a new one." [355, p. 69] Persistent anomalies will provoke a scientific "crisis" within the community, and it is only during this "crisis" period that all aspects of the dominant paradigm are explicitly examined, evaluated, and discussed. (It is from Kuhn that Shweder and Fiske [579] draw the label "crisis literature" discussed in Part II's Introduction.)

During crisis periods, and only then, is there a proliferation of rival theories, including some that are variations of the fundamental principles in the dominant paradigm. Paradigm-debate within any discipline is resolved in one of only three ways: (1) Some modifications of the dominant paradigm make it successful in accommodating the anomalies, (2) the problems presented by the anomalies are simply shelved to be solved by some future generation, or (3) "a crisis may end with the emergence of a new candidate for [the status of dominant] paradigm and with the ensuing battle over its acceptance." [247a, p. 84]

Kuhn likens the change to the new paradigm to a political revolution because both involve choices "between incompatible modes of community life," and both involve techniques of "mass persuasion." Furthermore, there will be "significant shifts in the criteria determining the legitimacy of both problems and proposed solutions," and the advocates of the competing paradigms "will inevitably talk through each other when debating the relative merits of their respective paradigms." [355, p. 109] One might wonder why techniques of "mass persuasion" would be needed. Why could there not be experimental tests or other investigations conducted to guide the choice between the rival paradigms? For Kuhn, however, such a rational resolution would only be possible "if there were but one set of problems, one world within which to work on them, and one set of standards for their solution, paradigm competition might be settled more or less" this way. [355, p. 148] Unfortunately, the two rival paradigms are "incommensurable" in three ways: (1) the list of problems to be solved by the paradigm, (2) how terms and concepts are to be defined, and (3) "in a sense that I am unable to explicate further, the proponents of competing paradigms practice their trades in different worlds." [355, p. 150] Therefore, relying heavily on the work of Wittgenstein and Hanson (as discussed in the previous section), the shift to the new paradigm is like a "Gestalt switch," from "duck" to "rabbit." Furthermore, "just because it is a transition between incommensurables, the transition between competing paradigms cannot be made a step at a time, forced by logic and neutral experience. Like the Gestalt switch, it must occur all at once. . .or not at all." Finally, "the transfer of allegiance from paradigm to paradigm is a *conversion* experience that cannot be forced." [358, pp. 150-151]

To what extent, for Kuhn, does the shift to a new paradigm after a revolution constitute scientific progress? Is there any meaningful way that we can state that we "knew more" after Newton than before? Or, did we know more after Einstein than before? Kuhn answers these questions in two ways. First, the scientific communities have *defined* their revolutions to be "progress." As Kuhn notes, "revolutions close with a total victory for one of the two opposing camps," and "Will that group [the victor] ever say that the result of its victory has been something less than progress?" [355, p. 166] Kuhn proposes that "the member of a mature scientific community is, like the typical character in Orwell's *1984*, the victim of a history rewritten by the powers that be." However, he believes the Orwellian analogy "is not altogether inappropriate," since "there are losses as well as gains in scientific revolutions, and scientists tend to be peculiarly blind to the former." [355, p. 167]

The second form of progress for Kuhn is the growth in the "list of problems solved by science and the precision of individual problem-solutions." [355, p. 170] Furthermore, "later scientific theories are better than earlier ones for solving puzzles in the often quite different environments to which they are applied." However, successive theories in science do not "grow ever closer to, or approximate more and more closely to, the truth, . . . there is, I think, no theory-independent way to reconstruct phrases like 'really there'; the notion of a match between the ontology of a theory and its 'real' counterpart in nature now seems to me illusive in principle." [355, p. 206] Using Darwinian evolution as a metaphor, Kuhn proposes that scientific knowledge is evolving, but it is not evolving toward truly understanding the world: "I can see in their succession no coherent direction of ontological development." [355, p. 206]

Kuhn, Paradigms, and Weltanshauungen: An Evaluation. The Kuhnian theory of science was obviously a radical and provocative departure from (in Kuhn's terms) the "image of science" put forth by the logical empiricists and the falsificationists: "Part of the reason for its [the book's] success is, I regretfully conclude, that it can be too nearly all things to all people." [358, p. 293] Most regrettably (as previously noted), Kuhn used his central construct, the "paradigm," in so many ways that for several years much discussion and debate focused on how to define this key term. Although Kuhn opted for restricting the term to refer to "exemplars," most other writers continued to use it in a broader context, often like the German construct, "*Weltanschauung*." Used in this manner, to posses a paradigm would imply that a scientist has a particular language where the belief in a certain theory or group of theories *uniquely determines*: (1) the meanings of the terms in the language, (2) the canons of experimental design and control, (3) standards for assessing the adequacy of the theory, (4) the relevance of information to the theory, and (5) which questions or problems the theory is committed to answer. Suppe reviews this *Weltanschauung*, or worldview, approach to interpreting the meaning of a Kuhnian paradigm and asks "how plausible is it to suppose that each person working with a theory possesses a *Weltanschauung*?" He notes that a central characteristic of scientific communities is the extreme *diversity* of the backgrounds, beliefs, and cultures of scientists practicing in the same scientific "community." Therefore, it is "exceedingly doubtful whether a *Weltanschauung* can be the joint possession of a group of scientists—as, for example, Kuhn's analysis requires. For there is every reason to suppose that there will be enough individual variation between individuals—even among individuals engaged in close cooperation in research—that no two persons will share exactly the same *Weltanschauung*." [606, p. 218] Thus, Suppe exhorts his fellow colleagues in the philosophy of science "to eschew *Weltanschauungen* talk and instead speak of languages, theory formulations, experimental canons, standards, and so on." [606, p. 220]

Although "strong form" versions of paradigms as *Weltanschauungen,* or world-views, are untenable, it is obviously the case that members of scientific communities and subgroups within those communities often share *some* beliefs about theories, methods, objectives, and epistemology. Therefore, it is reasonable to ask whether "weak-form" Kuhnian theory adequately describes the actual history of science wherein the concept of paradigm is viewed to mean a rough, or approximate, agreement on a set of theories, methods, aims, and evaluation procedures. We must remember that a central complaint of Kuhn (and all other historicists) about the logical empiricists' and falsificationists' "image of science" was that it did not adequately *describe* the actual development of science. Although the logical empiricists (adopting as they did a "reconstructionist" approach) neither claimed that their views *described* actual scientific practice, nor agreed that their views could be properly *evaluated* by examining historical events, those who adopt the historical method for understanding science (at the very least) claim that their "image of science" is accurately historical.

How well does Kuhnian theory accurately describe the actual history of science? The answer is: "very poorly indeed." For example, consider the Kuhnian notion that there exists a "pre-paradigm" stage that all the mature sciences passed through. Hull examined the various sciences that Kuhn himself used as evidence for the "stage" and concluded: "The periods which he [Kuhn] had previously described as pre-paradigm contained paradigms not that different from those of normal science." [291, p. 397] How about the claim that during "normal science" there is a single paradigm which is dominant and the subclaim that, during normal science, debate about the fundamental assumptions of the paradigm is absent? Laudan's review of the history of the sciences concludes that "virtually every major period in the history of science is characterized both by the co-existence of numerous competing paradigms, with none exerting hegemony over the field, and by the persistent and continuous manner in which the foundational assumptions of every paradigm are debated within the scientific community." Further, "Kuhn can point to no major science in which paradigm monopoly has been the rule, nor in which foundational debate has been absent." [370, pp. 74 and 151] How about the Kuhnian claim that paradigms are always "implicit"? If debate does exist during normal science on fundamental assumptions, then paradigms must have a significant degree of *explicitness*, otherwise such debate could not occur! [370, p. 75] Recall that Kuhnian theory claims that there is a cyclical pattern between long periods of "normal science," then a "crisis" and a short period of "revolutionary science." Hull examines the history of science on these counts and concludes "nor does normal science alternate with revolutionary science; both are taking place all the time. Sometimes a revolution occurs without any preceding state of crisis." [291, p. 397]

In short, the Kuhnian theory of science fails by its own standard of adequacy: It does not accurately describe the actual development of science nor the individual sciences to any significant extent. Therefore, "Kuhn belongs more to the history of the philosophy of science than to contemporary philosophy of science; for today few philosophers of science...believe that Kuhn's views are acceptable or even a near approximation to an adequate account." [608, p. 98]

Kuhnian Relativism: An Evaluation.   More important for our purposes than the fact that Kuhnian theory is historically inaccurate is his
(seeming) adoption of both reality relativism and conceptional framework-relativism. As Kuhn himself has acknowledged, his constant references to scientists who hold different paradigms as living in "different
worlds" and phrases like "the world changes according to different
paradigms" strongly implied reality relativism. [355, p. 192]   Thus,
Suppe asks "if one's only approach to the world is always through a disciplinary matrix which shapes and loads the data, how is it that the
world, which does not depend on the matrix, exerts an objectifying and
restraining influence on what some science accepts?   Put more flip-
pantly, if science always views the world through a disciplinary matrix
on Kuhn's view, then isn't Kuhn committed to some form of antiempiri-
cal idealism?" [606, p. 151] Similarly, Scheffler claims that, for Kuhn,
"reality is gone as an independent factor; each viewpoint creates its
own reality," and paradigms "are not only 'constitutive of science'
. . .but they are constitutive of nature as well." [562, p. 19]

Although many current-day advocates of reality-relativism cite
Kuhn to justify their positions, Kuhn, himself, has explicitly denied this
interpretation of his views. In the *Postscript* to the 1970 version of
Structure, Kuhn states: "We posit the existence of stimuli to explain
our perceptions of the world, and we posit their immutability to avoid
both individual and social solipsism. About neither posit have I the
slightest reservation." [355, p. 193] (Solipsism is the philosophical view
that either the "self" is the only reality or one can only claim to have
knowledge about one's self.)   Given that Kuhn specifically acknowledged [see 355, p. 167] the Orwellian implications of his theory of science, it is both surprising and sorrowful that he did not repudiate
reality relativism in 1962 rather than eight years later.

Although Kuhn has successfully defused his critics by denying the
charge of reality relativism, the charge of conceptual framework-
relativism continues to plague his "image of science." Recall that Kuhn
claimed that advocates of rival paradigms during revolutionary science
must undergo a "Gestalt switch" (from "duck" to "rabbit") or a "conversion process" because the rival paradigms are *incommensurable.* Thus,
Kuhn necessarily implies some form of conceptual framework-
relativism, since a "conversion process" would surely be unnecessary if
there were paradigm-neutral criteria for adjudicating the conflict between the dominant paradigm and its rivals. That is, Kuhnian theory
implies that (1) the knowledge-claims of a paradigm are relative to that
paradigm (or conceptual framework) and (2) they cannot be objectively,
impartially, or nonarbitrarily evaluated across rival paradigms.

Since Kuhnian conceptual-framework relativism depends crucially
on his concept of *incommensurability*, various writers began (soon after
the publication of his 1962 work) identifying precisely how incommensurability should be interpreted. Space limitations prevent a detailed

description of all the interpretations and their resultant analyses. Rather, we here shall only identify the three most prominent interpretations and point the reader toward the literature that evaluates them.

One of the earliest interpretations was the *meaning/variance* view that scientific terms change meaning from paradigm to paradigm. This view was critiqued by Shapere [574a and 574], Scheffler [562, Chapter 3] and Kordig [340a, Chapters 2 and 3]. A second analysis, the *radical translation* interpretation, suggests that in some meaningful way the actual terms involved in one paradigm cannot be translated into the language of its rivals. This interpretation was suggested by Kuhn, himself, in his *postscript* to the 1970 edition of *Structure* [pp. 200-204]. The radical translation view has been analyzed by Kitcher [337], Moberg [450] and Levin [394] (the radical translation view is also critiqued in my own [306a], pp. 368-372). A third interpretation of incommensurability has been the *incomparability* view that rival paradigms simply cannot be meaningfully compared. This interpretation was critiqued by Scheffler, Shapere, and Kordig in the references previously cited and also by Laudan [369], Jones [321] and Putnam [513].

Although, as previously mentioned, the details of the analyses cited in the preceding paragraph cannot be extensively developed here, some flavor of the arguments can certainly be presented. For example, consider the *incomparability* interpretation. Most assuredly, incommensurability *cannot* imply incomparability, for to recognize that the "revolutionary" paradigm is incommensurable with the rival "dominant" paradigm (as Siegel [581, p. 366] has noted) is at the very least to imply that the paradigms can be *compared*. How would one even know that the paradigms are *rival* if they could not be compared in some meaningful way? Two genuinely rival theories *cannot* be just solving self-contained, self-generated, encapsulated "puzzles" because one could not determine if they were rival unless they shared problems. Similarly, the *radical translation* thesis is fundamentally flawed. As Putnam points out, to contend that the language of one paradigm cannot be translated into the terms of another paradigm "and then to go on and describe [both paradigms] *at length* [in the same language] is totally incoherent." [513, p. 114]. Finally, the *meaning-variance* thesis (that some concepts or terms that are used in the revolutionary paradigm have a meaning that is different from how the concepts or terms are used in the dominant paradigm) may present difficulties in communicating, but it surely does not imply *incommensurability* in any meaningful sense. Again, how can the two paradigms be genuinely *rival* paradigms if they are "talking" about different phenomena? Roughly speaking, it's like "Aha! Here we have been arguing and all the time you were discussing apples and I was discussing oranges!"

The many detailed analyses of the concept of incommensurability over the last several decades have led most philosophers of science to agree with the summary evaluation most recently put forward by

Hintikka: "The frequent arguments that strive to use the absolute or relative incommensurability of scientific theories as a reason for thinking that they are inaccessible to purely scientific (rational) comparisons are simply fallacious." [273, p. 38] Ironically, advocates of the *meaning-variance* interpretation of incommensurability have demonstrated the cogency of the logical positivist view about the purpose of the philosophy of science. The logical positivists held that philosophers could and should clarify the language of science and, therefore, increase the ability of various scientists to talk with each other when working in different "paradigms."

A fundamental flaw of Kuhnian conceptual-framework relativism is its interpretation of the concept of a "theory-neutral observation language." Shapere examines what it means for an "observation-language" to be "theory-neutral" (as summarized in Suppe [606]) and points out the fatal flaw underlying most of Kuhn's (and his successors') confused discussions on this issue. Briefly, Shapere notes that most writers, since the time of Wittgenstein [643], have believed that in order for science to be objective and relativism to be avoided, have (correctly) noted that science needs a theory-neutral observation language to determine the extent to which its theories *correspond* with the external world. Many writers, such as Kuhn and Hanson, then note that our perceptual processes influence, inform, impart, or (more strongly) *determine*, our interpretations of what we observe. Therefore, they have concluded, observation is "theory-laden," and the absence of a "theory-neutral" observation language defeats the claimed objectivity of science, leading to conceptual framework-relativism.

As Shapere points out, the fatal flaw in the preceding analysis is the presumption that objectivity in science requires an observation-language that is neutral for *all* theories. However, it is *never* the case that the knowledge-claims of a theory are evaluated against *all* theoretically possible alternatives. Rather, the knowledge-claims of a theory are always compared against a limited number of genuine rivals. *What is required for objectivity in science is not an observation-language that is neutral with respect to all potential theories; rather, what is required is an observation-language that is neutral with respect to comparing the theories in question.* That is, what is required for objectivity is an observation-language that does not beg the question, or presume the truth-content, of the specific theories being evaluated. For example, both the Ptolemaic and Copernican theories base their predictions of the observed position of Mars on the *theory* that a certain light in the sky is actually a physical body millions of miles away that continues to exist when unobserved. However, that "theory" does not assume anything about the orbit of the object in question. So the fact that observations of Mars depend on a "theory of Mars" does not imply that the observations cannot be used to compare, evaluate, or potentially adjudicate between the Ptolemaic and Copernican theories. Thus, the absence of an observation-language that is neutral with respect to *all* theories in science does not imply cognitive relativism of any kind, nor does it imply that there cannot be objective, impartial, nonarbitrary criteria for evaluating the knowledge-claims across theories or (in Kuhn's case) paradigms. In fact, in the actual practice of science there appears to be no significant problem in finding theory-neutral terms for adjudicating claims across genuinely rival theories.

Kuhn's response to the many critiques of incommensurability is enlightening. Sensitive to the complex issues raised by the critiques, he has attempted to modify his positions accordingly. In his 1970 revision of *Structure,* he claimed that his critics had completely misinterpreted his views on incommensurability when they claimed that he believed "the proponents of incommensurable theories cannot communicate with each other at all; as a result, in a debate over theory-choice there can be no recourse to *good* reasons; instead theory must be chosen for reasons that are ultimately personal and subjective; some sort of mystical apperception is responsible for the decision actually reached." [pp. 198-199, emphasis in original] That is, the 1970 Kuhn wishes to deny his previous rhetoric about "conversions" and "Gestalt-shifts" from "ducks" to "rabbits." Rather, he emphasizes that science relies on "good reasons." Moreover, the reader should note that Kuhn does not just say "reasons," but *good* reasons, which would seem to necessarily imply that there are some paradigm-neutral standards that can be used to assess the adequacy of rival paradigms. However, Kuhn has not simply stopped with advocating *good reasons.* In his 1970 "Reflections on My Critics," he states:

> What I mean to be saying, however, is only the following. In a debate over choice of theory, neither party has access to an argument which resembles a proof in logic or formal mathematics. [356, p. 260]

In his 1976 work, he attempts to clarify his concept of incommensurability and again construes it as analogous to the concept of a *mathematical algorithm:*

> Most readers of my text have supposed that when I spoke of theories as incommensurable, I meant that they could not be compared. But "incommensurability" is a term borrowed from mathematics, and it there has no such implication. The hypotenuse of an isosceles right triangle is incommensurable with its side, but the two can be compared to any required degree of precision. What is lacking is not comparability but a unit of length in terms of which both can be measured directly and exactly. [pp. 190-1]

Note that, for Kuhn, incommensurability stems from the inability to adjudicate paradigm choice "exactly" because "any required degree of precision" is not enough, nothing resembling "a proof in logic or formal mathematics."

Why has Kuhn been so anxious to modify and thereby retreat from his earlier, highly provocative, "Gestalt-shift" position? It is precisely because Kuhn recognized that his earlier position implied relativism and irrationalism:

> My critics respond to my views. . .with charges of irrationality, relativism, and the defense of mob rule. These are all labels which I categorically reject. [356, p. 234]

Similarly, when Feyerabend defended Kuhn's theory of science as (like Feyerabend's) advocating irrationalism, Kuhn retorted that this was "not only absurd but vaguely obscene." [356, p. 264]

Given our previous analysis of both moral and cognitive relativism, it is easy to understand why Kuhn would want to disassociate himself from such positions (even though some readers might be offended that Kuhn would characterize such positions as "obscene"). How did one of the most eminent historians of science in the 20th century get himself into a position that necessitated a retreat from many of the views so provocatively argued in *Structure*? A clue to the answer to this question lies on page 171 of *Structure*. On this occasion, Kuhn discusses the "maze" of problems associated with the nature of science and scientific progress and concludes: "Somewhere in this maze, for example, must lie the problem of induction." In other words, Kuhn sees the Humean "problem of induction" as underlying his "maze" of problems. A second clue occurs fifteen years after *Structure* when Kuhn attempted to defend the fact that his views have often seemed to imply relativism and irrationalism. He states: "This is only another way of saying that I make no claim to have solved the problem of induction." [358, p. 332] Finally, the reader should carefully note that Kuhn's most recent attempt to define incommensurability as analogous to a mathematical algorithm essentially sets up the standard that we cannot "know" anything (paradigms are incommensurable) unless our method of knowing has the certainty of a *deductive* mathematical proof ("directly and exactly"). Thus, Suppe notes that "the K-K thesis crucially underlies Feyerabend's and Kuhn's extreme views on scientific knowledge." [606, p. 719] As we have seen before, Kuhn commits the "philosophers' fallacy." He sets for science an impossible standard: Science must know-with-certainty (i.e., a mathematical proof) that its procedures for justifying its knowledge-claims are correct. He then finds that certainty is unavailable to science and (rather than adopting fallibilism) opts for views that (to his lament) inexorably lead down the slippery slope to relativism and irrationalism.

Although Kuhn can be aptly described as a "reluctant relativist," our next author, Paul Feyerabend, is an *exuberant* relativist.

10.2.2   Feyerabend's Relativism

Paul K. Feyerabend (1924-) was born in Austria, studied theater, mathematics, history, and physics at the University of Vienna, where he received his doctorate in 1951. While in Vienna, he interacted extensively with Wittgenstein, from whom he got his "first doubts about the identification of science with the explicit features of its theories and its observational reports." [194, p. 294] In Vienna he also met Sir Karl Popper, studied under him at the London School of Economics and was strongly influenced by his philosophy. In 1955 Popper assisted him in getting a lectureship in the philosophy of science at the University of Bristol in England, after which Feyerabend joined the faculty at the University of California, Berkeley, in 1959. There, he interacted with Kuhn, who was also teaching at Berkeley at the time. Since 1979, he has taught at Berkeley and the Federal Institute of Technology in Zurich, Switzerland. He is widely known as one of the foremost advocates of relativism, having forcefully argued his relativistic approach to science in many articles and three major books translated into English: *Against Method* [186 and 187] (first presented at a conference at the University of Minnesota in 1966, published in its proceedings in 1970, and turned into a book in 1975), *Science in a Free Society* [190], and *Farewell to Reason* [194].

Although Feyerabend's advocacy of the historical method and relativism is widely known, less recognized is that he started his philosophical career as an ardent believer in scientific realism. [190, p. 113] Thus, one of his earliest papers was a 1958 article entitled "An Attempt at a Realistic Interpretation of Experience," and as recently as 1965 he could state "I for one am not aware of having produced a single idea that is not already contained in the realistic tradition and especially in professor Popper's account of it." [185, p. 251] However, we shall not review Feyerabend's realism; rather, we shall examine his relativistic approach to science.

A key to understanding Feyerabend's relativism is his ongoing attack on rationalism, which he (somewhat idiosyncratically) defines as "the idea that there are general rules and standards for conducting our affairs, affairs of knowledge included." [190, p. 16] Throughout Feyerabend's years as a realist, he attempted to find "general rules" that would assist scientists in the conduct of research. However, a discussion with professor C.F. von Weizacker in Hamburg in 1965 on the foundations of quantum mechanics convinced Feyerabend that the pursuit of general rules for all science was an illusion, that any such rules would only be "a hindrance rather than a help: a person trying to solve a problem whether in science or elsewhere *must be given complete freedom* and cannot be restricted by any demands, [or] norms, however plausible they may seem to the logician or the philosopher who has thought them out in the privacy of his study." [190, p. 117, emphasis in original] (We again note that a prominent philosopher has drawn a "lesson" from the downfall of Newton and the rise of quantum mechanics.)

Feyerabend believed that the discipline of the philosophy of science had become dictatorial in its relationship with science and *Against Method* was written in part "to defend scientific practice from the rule of philosophical law." [194, p. 316] In short, Feyerabend wanted philosophy to "leave science to the scientists!" [194, p. 317] His disdain for other philosophers of science is, to say the least, strong. He calls them "ratiofacists," "illiterates," "academic rodents," and a "gang of autistic intellectuals" who have gone from "incompetent professionalism to professionalized incompetence." [see 193, p. 191; 190, pp. 183, 195 and 209; and 194, p. 315] Notwithstanding his 1965 claim of admiration for Popper, his invective toward Popper in recent years has been particularly strong, referring to him as a "mere propagandist" and his philosophy as an "outhouse," a "dog hut," and a "tiny puff of hot air in the positivistic teacup." [190, p. 208; and 194, pp. 282-3]

A major thesis of *Against Method* is that science is not a rule-governed endeavor. Feyerabend cites numerous examples of rules that he believes the philosophy of science has attempted to introduce into the practice of science. These include such things as never using *ad hoc* hypotheses, never introducing hypotheses that contradict well-established, experimental results, and never introducing hypotheses whose content is smaller than the content of empirically adequate alternatives. [186, p. 22] He also attacks rules which he attributes to Popper's critical rationalism, including: (1) "theories of large content are to be preferred to theories of small content," (2) "increase of content is welcome; decrease of content is to be avoided," (3) "a theory that contradicts an accepted basic statement must be given up," and (4) "*ad hoc* hypotheses are forbidden." [186, p. 73] Feyerabend goes through several historical examples of actual scientific activity that almost any believer in science would accept as being episodes resulting in scientific progress. Most notably, Feyerabend focuses on Galileo and the Copernican Revolution and the replacement of Newtonian physics with Einsteinian relativity. His analysis of these historical episodes leads him to conclude that:

> The idea of a method that contains firm, unchanging, and absolutely binding principles for conducting the business of science gets into considerable difficulty when confronted with the results of historical research. We find, then, that there is not a single rule, however plausible, and however firmly grounded in epistemology, that is not violated at some time or other. It becomes evident that such violations are not accidental events, they are not the results of insufficient knowledge or of inattention which might have been avoided. On the contrary, we see that they are necessary for progress. [186, p. 21-22]

As the preceding quotation makes abundantly clear, at this point in Feyerabend's writings, he still believes in a nontrivial view of the progressivity of science, and he contends that the violation of methodological rules is absolutely essential for such progressivity.

Given the subtitle of his 1970 work ("An Outline of an Anarchistic Theory of Knowledge") and given his expression "anything goes," Feyerabend is often accused of being a "naive anarchist." Such an anarchist would observe that "both absolute rules and context dependent rules have their limits and infer that all rules and standards are worthless and should be given up." [190, p. 32] Feyerabend vigorously denies such a characterization of his views, and assails those he refers to as "lazy anarchists" who "accept the slogan and interpret it as making research easier and success more accessible." [194, p. 284] He states succinctly how "anything goes" should be interpreted:

> "Anything goes" does not express any conviction of mine, it is a jocular summary of the predicament of the rationalist: if you want universal standards, I say, if you cannot live without principles that hold independently of situation, shape of world, exigencies of research, temperamental peculiarities, then I can give you such a principle. It will be empty, useless, and pretty ridiculous—but it will be a "principle." It will be the "principle," "anything goes." [190, p. 188]

A similar elucidation of his use of "anything goes" is given in his most recent book. [194, p. 284]

Now that we have an "official" interpretation of "anything goes," one might wonder what all the fuss was all about. That is, Feyerabend originally attacked with logic, historical evidence, and substantial quantities of derision and scorn his fellow philosophers of science on the basis that they were proposing "universal" rules and "absolutely binding principles" for the conduct of science. To the charge that Feyerabend was claiming that rules and standards were "universally worthless," he now states that this is a "misinterpretation," since his intention all along was "to convince the reader that all methodologies, even the most obvious ones, have their limits," and that "I do not argue that we should proceed without rules and standards." [190, p. 32] Stated succinctly, Feyerabend attacked other philosophers of science with vim, vigor, and invective on the charge of advocating "naive universalism" regarding rules and standards for conducting science, and he now lashes out at those accusing him of "naive anarchism." However, any careful reading of the works of those philosophers that Feyerabend attacked will show that they were, and continue to be, as guiltless of the charge of naive universalism as is Feyerabend of the charge of naive anarchism.

The "anything goes" controversy directly relates to our previous discussions on fallibilism, the "philosophers' fallacy," the "search for certainty" and the K-K Thesis. That is, not only are the knowledge-claims of science fallible, but so also are the procedures and processes (method) that *produce* those knowledge-claims. In Feyerabend's terms, there are no *universal* rules and standards. The preceding analysis demonstrates, in part, how Suppe arrives at the conclusion that the search for certainty and the K-K Thesis underlie Feyerabend's "extreme view on scientific knowledge." [606, p. 719] Thus, this part of Feyerabend's philosophy poses no problem at all for those advocating *fallibilism* with regard to science. We turn now to examining Feyerabend's views on the incommensurability of theories and scientific progress.

Feyerabend on Incommensurability, Scientific Progress, and Reality Relativism. As previously discussed in Section 9.5, the logical empiricists and critical rationalists believed that science progressed through four different means: (1) the development of new theories for phenomena not previously explained, (2) the falsification of existing theories and their replacement with new theories, (3) the expansion of the scope of a theory to include new phenomena, and (4) the reduction of specific theories into more general theories. With respect to the fourth way that science progresses, the logical empiricists claimed that science made genuine progress (we knew more) both when Galileo discovered that the distance an object falls toward the earth is directly related to the square of the elapsed time, and that science made further progress (we knew more) when Newton proposed that the gravitational attractive force of two bodies increases as the distance between the two bodies decreases (implying that their mutual acceleration will increase). Finally, the logical empiricists held that science made genuine progress with the general theory of relativity of Einstein and its proposal that (among other things) space, time, and mass (which were considered to be absolutes in Newtonian mechanics) were relative to the observer. The standard treatment of the logical empiricist view is given by Nagel [463] and contends that these are genuine instances of scientific progress because the physics of Galileo can be "reduced" to Newton, and the physics of Newton can be "reduced" to Einsteinian relativity.

Feyerabend attacked the conception that science progresses through "reduction" in a series of articles and books. [183, 184, 186, 187, 190, 194] Basically, Feyerabend's early attempts [183] to show that science is not progressive proceeds by demonstrating that Galileo's "Law of Descent" cannot be mathematically *derived* from Newtonian mechanics. That is, since Galileo's Law of Descent assumes that the acceleration of the falling body is constant and Newtonian theory proposes that the acceleration increases as the falling body approaches the earth, Galileo's formula, formally speaking, cannot be derived from Newton's Laws. Simply put, if d is the distance of a body from the surface of the earth and D is the radius of the earth, Galileo's Law of Descent holds only if the ratio d/D equals zero. (The reason why Galileo's law predicts very well in most cases is that the ratio for most situations is "close" to zero). Thus, Galileo's Law does not "reduce" to Newton's because (unlike most mathematicians) Feyerabend does not consider derivations "in the limit" as legitimate derivations. Therefore, Feyerabend concludes, science does not "progress" through reduction.

Since the preceding argument lacks persuasiveness for most observers of science, Feyerabend's later attempts to demonstrate that science does not progress through "reduction" have focused on "meaning-change" in theory. For example, he claims that in relativity theory the concepts of "length" and "mass" change radically in their meaning from the same terms in Newtonian mechanics and, therefore, Newtonian mechanics does not "reduce" to quantum mechanics. This is the meaning-variance thesis regarding incommensurability discussed in Section 10.2.

Many writers have pointed out the severe deficiencies in the meaning-variance thesis (see the references in Section 10.2 for sources). Specifically with respect to the derivation thesis and its relationship to reduction, writers have pointed out that Galilean mechanics reduces to Newtonian mechanics *in the limit*. That is, the ratio d/D will approach zero (and thus approach Newtonian mechanics) as either d gets very small or D gets very large. Furthermore, in the limit the concepts of "relativistic length" and "relativistic mass" approach their Newtonian equivalents. Thus, Einsteinian Mass (M) is related to Newtonian "rest mass" (m_o) by $M = m_o \div \sqrt{1 - v^2/c^2}$. [394] Thus, it is the case that most philosophers of science (and practicing scientists) continue to claim (1) that the transitions from Galileo to Newton to Einstein represent genuine instances of scientific progress; (2) that we are warranted in claiming that we "know more" about the physical world now than we did in 1500; (3) that the best interpretation of Galilean mechanics is that it is a "limiting case" of Newtonian mechanics and, thus, we are warranted as referring to it as "approximately true," in many situations; and (4) that Newtonian mechanics is best interpreted as a "limiting case" of Einsteinian relativity and, thus, we are warranted in claiming that it is in some meaningful sense "approximately true," especially in cases where velocities are low. Feyerabend's analysis was and continues to be (1) that Galilean mechanics is *incommensurable* with Newtonian mechanics; (2) that Newtonian mechanics is *incommensurable* with Einsteinian relativity; (3) that no warranted claim to "progress" can be made in science; which, therefore, implies the nihilistic conclusion (4) that we cannot claim to "know more" about the physical world now than we did in 1500 A.D.

How can Feyerabend continue to reject the claim of scientific progress in general and, more specifically, the claim of "reduction"? The answer, in part, lies in Feyerabend's specific characterization of "incommensurability." Feyerabend (like Kuhn) now complains bitterly that his version of incommensurability has been misinterpreted by many writers as claiming that theories cannot be *compared*. Thus, for him, theories or paradigms are to be considered incommensurable only when they "use concepts that cannot be brought into the usual logical relations of inclusion, exclusion, and overlap," and that "when using the term 'incommensurable' I always meant deductive disjointedness, *and nothing else.*" [188, p. 363 and 365] Moreover, Feyerabend now states: "mere *difference* of concepts does not suffice to make theories incommensurable in my sense. The situation must be rigged in such a way that the conditions of concept formation in one theory forbid the formation of the basic concepts of the other." [190, p. 68] Consistent with these views, Feyerabend most recently states that "incommensurability as understood by me is a rare event. It occurs only when the conditions of meaningfulness for the descriptive terms of one language (theory, point of view) do not permit the use of the descriptive terms of another language (theory, point of view); mere difference of meanings does not lead to incommensurability in my sense." [195, p. 81]

Given Feyerabend's clarification of his version of incommensurability, we are now in a better position to evaluate the basis for his claim that science does not and cannot make progress through "reduction." The reader should note carefully the words "logical relations of inclusion, exclusion, and overlap" in the preceding paragraph. Basically, what Feyerabend is using as a standard is that (he claims) the examples of theory reduction cannot be shown using the tool of formal logic and therefore, such theories have "deductive disjointedness." In short, Feyerabend sets up the following standard: The progressivity of scientific knowledge can be warrantedly asserted only if we know with the certainty of formal logic that theories can be "reduced," (the K-K Thesis once again). He then purports to show that several examples of supposed theory-reduction cannot be shown with the conclusiveness of formal logic and proceeds to claim that this "incommensurability" dooms the claim of progress in science, thus committing the philosophers' fallacy.

There are at least three responses to Feyerabend's claim that his version of incommensurability leads to the conclusion that science is not progressive. First, one can simply show that, contra Feyerabend, formal logic is perfectly capable of accommodating the changes in meaning associated with different theories. This has been shown by Hintikka. [273] Second, one can deny that theory reduction needs to be warranted with the conclusiveness of formal logic. That is, reject the K-K Thesis and assert that we have good reasons to believe that the general theory of relativity better describes the characteristics of the world than does Newtonian mechanics, which itself better describes the world than Galilean mechanics, which itself better describes the world than Aristotelian mechanics. Such an approach implies that we are warranted in believing that not all theories are "equally false," or "equally true." Further, we are warranted in using phrases such as "true within certain boundary conditions" and "true in the limiting case." This, essentially, is the approach of Rohrlich and Hardin. [537]

A third approach is to deny the assertion that theory reduction is a necessary requirement for scientific progress. Many writers in the philosophy of science implicitly assume that highly general, hierarchical theories employing a few universal laws (such as those found in physics) are both necessary for, and the only constituent of, scientific progress. Yet, in many sciences such powerful, highly general, hierarchical theories are the exception, rather than the rule. Certainly, there exist no such powerful theories in any of the behavioral sciences at the present time, and the prospects for developing such powerful, hierarchical theories in the future are, to say the least, open to debate. (General theories in the behavioral sciences are more likely to be collections of subtheories. [165]) Thus, to require as a condition for scientific progress that a discipline be able to reduce all its knowledge claims to highly general and very powerful theories (like Newtonian mechanics) would seem to necessarily establish *in advance* that there has never been any "progress" in many sciences, including *all* of the behavioral sciences (for now at least and possibly forever). On the other hand, if we broaden the concept of scientific progress to include lower-level theories, propositions, and empirical findings, the claim of scientific progress could be warranted (and in my judgment *is warranted*) without the claim of "theory reduction." Siegel makes a point similar to this when he suggests that we should distinguish between what he calls "theoretical cummulativity" and "low-level empirical or experimental cummulativity." [583, p. 66]

Feyerabend is well aware of the many weaknesses of his views on incommensurability, theory reduction, and scientific progress. Nevertheless, he continues to advocate these positions because, in part, they are absolutely necessary for his version of reality relativism:

> [W]e certainly cannot assume that two incommensurable theories deal with one and the same objective state of affairs (to make the assumption we would have to assume that both at least *refer* to the same objective situation)....we must admit that they deal with different worlds and that the change (from one world to another) has been brought about by a switch from one theory to another.... We concede that our epistemic activities may have a decisive influence even upon the most solid piece of cosmological furniture—they may make gods disappear and replace them by heaps of atoms in empty space. [190, p. 70]

Another reason for Feyerabend maintaining his discredited views about incommensurability, theory-reduction, and scientific progress is that they are necessary to buttress his case that "Western science has now infected the whole world like a contagious disease." [194, p. 297] We must recall that many of Feyerabend's early works were, essentially, polemical attacks on his fellow colleagues in the philosophy of science (the "illiterates" and "academic rodents"). However, these attacks formed the foundation for his assault on science itself and to admit the deficiencies of his attacks on his philosophical colleagues would destroy the foundations for his claim that science is a "disease." To understand how Feyerabend arrives at the conclusion that science is a "disease," we need to trace the development of his own version of conceptual framework-relativism.

Feyerabend's Conceptual Framework-Relativism. In his 1978 and 1987 books, Feyerabend recounts the experiences that influenced the development of his thoughts. In both books, he identifies the "turning point" in his career as occurring in the turbulent 1960s when he was a professor at the University of California at Berkeley and had to teach courses having numerous "Mexicans, blacks and Indians." [194, p. 317] These students "wanted to know, they wanted to learn, they wanted to understand the strange world around them—did they not deserve better nourishment? Their ancestors had developed cultures of their own, colorful languages, harmonious views of the relation between man and man, and man and nature, whose remnants are a living criticism of the tendencies of separation, analysis, self-centeredness inherent in Western thought." [194, p. 317, reprinted from 190, p. 118] Feyerabend believed that Western science and culture was destroying other cultures or, in his words, "traditions." The Western "tradition" had its origins in the triumph of "rationalism" in 7th century Greece. [190, p. 120] Now, the Western "tradition," the descendants of Greek "rationalism," was asking him to teach to those whose "traditions" had been destroyed:

> I looked at my audience and they made me recoil in revulsion and terror from the task I was suppose to perform. For the task—this now became clear to me—was that of a very refined, very sophisticated slave driver. And a slave driver I did not want to be." [194, p. 317, reprinted from 190, p. 118]

Thus began Feyerabend's assault on "rationalism," Western science, and (ultimately) Western civilization.

Central to understanding Feyerabend's assault on Western science is his construct of a "tradition." This construct comes directly from Wittgenstein's "forms of life," [190, p. 66], discussed in Section 10.1.3. Of the many different kinds of traditions in life, some are given the designation of "knowledge-creating traditions." Science, Feyerabend contends, is but one of many knowledge-creating traditions. Throughout his 1978 book, Feyerabend discusses and defends examples of other such traditions: mysticism [p. 31], magic [p. 74] astrology [p. 74], rain dances [p.78], religion [p. 78], mythical world views [p. 78], tribal medicine [p.96], parapsychology [p. 103], all non-western belief traditions [p. 102], and witchcraft [p. 191]. One might suppose that some of these traditions might be better "ways of knowing" than others, but for

Feyerabend they are all equally valid. Feyerabend, like Winch before him, relies heavily on the work of Evans-Pritcherd concerning the primitive society of the Azande and its reliance on witchcraft. Science and witchcraft are equal, claims Feyerabend, because any argument of science that would tend to refute witchcraft, when "translated into Zande modes of thought would serve to support their entire structure of belief. For their mystical notions are eminently coherent, being interrelated by a network of logical ties and are so ordered that they never too crudely contradict sensory experience but, instead, experience seems to justify them." [194, p. 74]   Feyerabend approvingly quotes Evans-Pritcherd on the "rationality" of using the oracles of witchcraft for making day-to-day decisions: "I found this as satisfactory a way of running my home and affairs as any other I know of." [194, p. 74] Feyerabend then compares the Zande beliefs in witchcraft and the processes of justifying those beliefs as being no different from the processes used to settle disputes in science. In particular, he cites the dispute between Einstein and other physicists over the nature of quantum theory. He, therefore, justifies his all-encompassing relativism:

> For every statement, theory, point of view believed to be true (with good reasons) *there exists* [sic] arguments showing a conflicting alternative to be at least as good, or even better. [194, p. 76, emphasis in original]

Feyerabend's all-encompassing relativism includes (among others) all the versions we have discussed so far, i.e., cultural, moral, rationality, reality, and conceptual framework. Note that Feyerabend does *not* say there "may" exist, he states *there exists*. Note also that he does *not* say an alternative "may" be as good, but will be "as least as good, or even better." The reader may think that Feyerabend is simply engaging in sophistry to "make a point." One might suppose that Feyerabend's works are just academic gamesmanship and that he did not intend for his readers to take his views seriously. Brodbeck notes that relativists believe "science is in effect a game" [82, p. 3], which is consistent with the view in marketing that "the important question that we must ask is how I can convince my colleagues in the scientific community that my theory is correct?" [82, p. 15] As noted previously, the sophists in ancient Greece were among the first relativists in Western intellectual history. One test for the presence of sophistry is whether people behave consistently with their stated beliefs. On this criterion, Feyerabend is clearly no sophist. Consider the following response of Feyerabend to a critique of his work by a philosopher named Tibbets:

> [Tibbets] also asks: 'If *he* had a child diagnosed with Leukemia would he look to his witchdoctor friends or to the Sloan Kettering Institute?'

I can assure him that I would look to my 'witchdoctor friends' to use his somewhat imprecise terminology *and so would many other people in California* whose experience with scientific medicine has been anything but encouraging. The fact that scientific medicine is the only existing form of medicine in many places does not mean that it is the best and the fact that alternative forms of medicine succeed where scientific medicine has to resort to surgery shows that it has serious lacunae: numerous women, reluctant to have their breasts amputated as their doctors advised them, went to acupuncturists, faithhealers, herbalists and got cured. Parents of small children with allegedly incurable diseases, leukemia among them, did not give up, they consulted 'witchdoctors' and their children got cured. How do I know? Because I advised some of these men and women and I followed the fate of others. [190, pp. 205-206, emphasis in original]

Unfortunately, most relativists in marketing and other social sciences are not as consistent as Feyerabend. They wish to emphatically proclaim extreme relativist premises (like Feyerabend), but they wish to deny the logical consequences of those premises. Before continuing our discussion of Feyerabend's assault on Western science, a digression on the "nature of science argument" will reveal, in sharp relief, the implications of the preceding paragraphs.

The "Nature of Science Argument." A critique of relativism [308] developed the "nature of science argument" according to the premises advocated by relativists.[2] The argument may be concisely summarized as follows:

R1. *There are no fundamental differences separating the sciences and the nonsciences.* ("The search for [demarcation] criteria that separate science from nonscience"...has been "signally unsuccessful." [13, p. 18] Since there are no objective criteria separating science from nonscience, "science is whatever society chooses to call science." [13, p. 26])

R2. *The knowledge-claims of the nonsciences have as much epistemological warrant as the sciences.* (That is, we have no good reason to believe and act on the knowledge-claims of the sciences in preference to the nonsciences. Statement R2 is *logically implied* by R1 because, if we had good reasons to believe and act on the knowledge-claims of the sciences, such reasons would constitute "fundamental differences" that could be used to separate science from nonscience.)

R3. Therefore, statement R2 implies that if a palmist should diagnose a person as *not* having bone cancer (an example of a nonscience knowledge-claim), such a diagnosis would have equal warrant as the diagnosis of a medical doctor that the person *did* have bone cancer (an example of a science knowledge-claim).

Anderson reviewed the narrative version of the preceding argument and lamented that opponents of relativism often cast "proffered alternatives" as "relativistic flights of fancy that lead to epistemological anarchy and the abandonment of rationality and objectivity." [14, p. 156] He dismissed the argument as a "straw man," stating:

> The type of relativism attacked by Hunt (1984) has *never* been advocated by any of the participants in the current debate. The object of Hunt's critique is a straw man known as judgmental (Knorr-Certina and Mulkay 1983) or "nihilistic" relativism. In this view, all knowledge claims are equally valid and there is no basis on which to make judgments among the various contenders. (*Indeed, a careful reading of even the most radical of contemporary relativists will reveal that this does not even approximate their views*, e.g., Collins 126, 127; Feyerabend 187, 189). [p. 156, emphasis added]

Note the use of Feyerabend as an example of a relativist for whom the "palmistry argument" "does not even approximate their views." On the contrary, however, the preceding long quotation from Feyerabend in this section clearly shows that the "palmistry argument" about the nature of science very closely states the logical implications of relativist views about the nature of science ("science is whatever society chooses to call science") and that Feyerabend, being no sophist, accepts the logical implications of those views. However, the ongoing debate on the "nature of science" in marketing and the social sciences is not, and ought not to be, whether *Feyerabend* advocates "nihilistic" relativism, that "all ways of knowing are equal," or that palmistry is equivalent to medical science—for the record is clear that Feyerabend does so believe. Rather, the debate in marketing and the social sciences is, and ought to be, the extent to which the relativistic premises that are being advocated by many writers in marketing and the social sciences *imply* "nihilism," all "methods of knowing are equal," and so forth.

It is certainly the case that all advocates of relativism in marketing and the social sciences quote and reference Feyerabend liberally to justify the desirability of accepting relativism. More tellingly, advocates of relativism in marketing and the social sciences state Feyerabend-like relativist premises: "science is whatever society chooses to call science"; "there exists no privileged epistemological platform from which to assess competing knowledge claims" [14, p. 158]; "truth is a subjective evaluation that cannot be properly inferred outside of the context provided by the theory" [492, p. 119]; "truth plays no role in the ontology of critical relativism." [16, p. 134] All these look indistinguishable from the very premises of Feyerabend that (rightly) lead him to the irrationalism and "nihilism" that marketing and social science relativists so pejoratively dismiss.

Feyerabend on Science. The preceding discussion about the irrationalism implied by relativism becomes even clearer by examining precisely how Feyerabend uses relativism to attack science. As previously discussed, Feyerabend believes science is but one knowledge-creating tradition among many and that "traditions are neither good nor bad, they simply are." [190, p. 27] Feyerabend notes that in the 17th, 18th, and 19th centuries the scientific tradition was but one of the many competing ideologies and was in fact a "liberating force" because it "restricted the influence of other ideologies and thus gave the individual room for thought." [p. 75] However, he believes science today does not have a liberating effect, since it has turned into a "dogmatic religion." He believes "the very same enterprise that once gave man the ideas and the strength to free himself from the fears and prejudices of a tyrannical religion now turns him into a slave of its interests." [p. 75] How did the consensus emerge that the knowledge claims of science were preferred by society over the knowledge claims of competing traditions? Is it not because society rationally and reasonably determined that scientific knowledge-claims had more epistemological warrant, were more-likely to be true? Is not the "societal consensus" backed by good reasons? Emphatically not, asserts Feyerabend:

> It reigns supreme because some past successes have led to institutional measures (education; role of experts; role of power groups such as the AMA) that prevent a comeback of the rivals. Briefly, but not incorrectly: Today science prevails not because of its comparative merits, but because the show has been rigged in its favor. [p. 102]

Specifically, for Feyerabend, how did these other traditions lose out? "These myths, these religions, these procedures have disappeared or deteriorated not because science was better, but because *the apostles of science were the more determined conquerors,* because they *materially suppressed* the bearers of alternative cultures." [p. 102, emphasis in original] How was the material suppression of rival traditions and the triumph of the "apostles of science" accomplished? The suppression of rival traditions was accomplished, he contends, through the actions of scientists, both individually and through their collective associations, aided and abetted by such diverse groups as "liberal intellectuals, white missionaries, adventurers, and anthropologists." [p. 77]

As examples of suppressive tactics, Feyerabend notes that anthropologists "collected and systematized" knowledge about non-Western traditions and developed "interpretations" that "were simply a consequence of popular antimetaphysical tendencies combined with a firm belief in the excellence first, of Christianity, and then of science." [p. 77] Liberal intellectuals aided the suppression by first "loudly and persistently" proclaiming that they defend freedom of thought, while at the same time not recognizing that this freedom of thought only "is granted to those who have already accepted part of the rationalist (i.e., scientific) ideology." [p. 76] Feyerabend, himself, even contributed to the suppression while teaching at the University of California at Berkeley: "My function was to carry out the educational policies of the State of California, which means I had to teach people what a small group of white intellectuals had decided was knowledge." [p. 118]

Feyerabend concludes that "the prevalence of science is a threat to democracy" [p. 76] and proposes his "solution" to the problem of science in society. He addresses this issue by first proposing the following rhetorical questions:

> But—so the impatient believer in rationalism and science is liable to exclaim—is this procedure not justified? Is there not a tremendous difference between science on the one side, religion, magic, myth on the other? Is this difference not so large and so obvious that it is unnecessary to point it out and silly to deny it? [p. 78]

Feyerabend answers his rhetorical questions concerning the differences between science and other "traditions" with: "Rationalists and scientists cannot rationally (scientifically) argue for the unique position of their favorite ideology." [p. 79] Therefore, he proposes, in order to have a free society "is it not rather the case that traditions [mysticism, magic, astrology, rain dances, religion, mythical worldviews, tribal medicine, parapsychology, all non-Western belief traditions, and witchcraft] that give substance to the lives of people must be given equal rights and *equal access to key positions in society* no matter what other traditions think about them?" [p. 79, emphasis added]

So, Feyerabend's relativism began in the 1960s by attacking the philosophy of science and then progressed in the 1970s to attack science, itself. Feyerabend's 1980s efforts, like *Farewell to Reason*, continues by attacking all elements of Western culture and civilization. Briefly, *Farewell to Reason* states the case for relativism again and claims: "Western forms of life are found in the most remote corners of the world and have changed the habits of people who only a few decades ago were unaware of their existence. Cultural differences disappear, indigenous crafts, customs, and institutions are being replaced by Western objects, customs, and organizational forms." [194, p.2] He notes that the spread of Western culture has not been beneficial: "Many so-called 'Third World problems' such as hunger, illness and poverty seem to have been caused rather than alleviated by the steady advance of Western Civilization." [p. 4] He identifies the "two ideas that have often been used to make Western expansion intellectually respectable—the idea of Reason and the idea of Objectivity." [p.5] These ideas which come down to Western Civilization from the ancient

Greeks are fallacious and should be discarded in favor of accepting relativism because "there exist no 'objective' reasons for preferring science and Western rationalism to other traditions." [p. 297] Given that (1) "western science has now infected the whole world like a contagious disease"; and that (2) "western Civilization was either imposed by force,. . .or accepted because it produced better weapons"; and that (3) "its advance while doing some good, also caused enormous damage" [p. 297], what recourse is there left for the relativist Feyerabend? He contends that the concepts of Reason and Objectivity must be abandoned and, thus, he concludes his book with: "FAREWELL TO REASON." [p. 319]

Given the extreme nature of Feyerabend's philosophy, it is easy to understand and sympathize with Suppe's characterization of it as "hopeless." [607, p. 648] Nevertheless, Feyerabend's relativistic philosophy, though now thoroughly discredited in the philosophy of science, has had a warm and welcome reception throughout much of marketing and the social sciences and has left a legacy for society in general. To co-opt Feyerabend's metaphor, many scholars believe relativism has "infected" Western society.[3] Our next section explores why the relativism and irrationalism of Kuhn and Feyerabend were so influential in the 1960s.

10.3 THE RISE AND FALL OF HISTORICAL RELATIVISM

Kuhnian relativism totally dominated philosophical thought in the 1960s. [376] In fact, a good case can be made that Thomas Kuhn dominated the philosophy of science in the 1960s in a manner unparalleled in recent history. Given that many of its deficiencies seem painfully obvious today, how and why was Kuhnian relativism accepted so swiftly and passionately in the 1960s? One answer is that the seeds of relativism found fertile soil in the irrationalistic environment of that troubled and turbulent decade. As just one of the more sorrowful legacies of the Sixties, the irrationalistic manifesto "turn on, tune in, drop out" left behind a society dangerously (perhaps fatally?) dependent on drugs. Most shamefully, many university faculty preached that the Establishment had lied to its young about the dangers of drugs. Hallucinogenic drugs in particular were touted by prominent faculty as being safe, "mind expanding," and opening up "new ways of knowing." Alas, the education efforts of public and private health authorities have as yet been unsuccessful in reestablishing the pre-Sixties societal consensus that drugs,

---

[3]For a discussion by the physicists Theocharis and Psimopoulos of how the acceptance of relativism has severely damaged British science (including physics), see their article entitled "Where Science has Gone Wrong" in *Nature*, Vol. 329, Oct. 15, 1987.

far from "expanding minds," destroys them. In Pogo's words, "We have met the enemy and he is us."

Although all institutions of American society (representing the "Received Views" of the "Establishment") came under vigorous attack in the 1960s, universities may have suffered the greatest damage. Bloom has chronicled the revolutionary violence, both verbal and physical, that engulfed American universities in the Sixties: "Enlightenment in America came close to breathing its last during the sixties. The fact that the universities are no longer in convulsions does not mean that they have regained their health." [69, p. 314] All the fundamental values underlying Western universities (academic freedom, rational discourse, tolerance for the views of others, and the search for truth) came tumbling down when "students discovered that pompous teachers who catechized them about academic freedom could, with a little shove, be made into dancing bears." [69, p. 315]

In a section of his book entitled "The Decomposition of the University," Bloom recounts the behaviors of the faculties in the various departments in response to the siege of their universities. Unfortunately, "there was no solidarity in defense of the pursuit of truth." [69, p. 347] Distressingly, "the professional schools—engineering, home economics, industrial-labor relations and agriculture—simply went home and closed the shutters." Likewise, the natural scientists, believing themselves "not threatened," refused to speak out: "Only one natural scientist at Cornell spoke out against the presence of guns or the bullying of professors." [p. 347] This is because "the natural sciences were not a target, as they had once been in high-grade fascism and communism. There were no Lenins thundering against positivism, relativity or genetics, no Goebbels alert to the falseness of Jewish science." [p. 348] The humanities' faculty, on the other hand, not only capitulated to the revolutionary radicals, but warmly embraced them:

> To find hysterical supporters of the revolution one had, not surprisingly, to go to the humanities. Passion and commitment, as opposed to coolness, reason and objectivity, found their home there. The drama included a proclamation from a group of humanities teachers threatening to take over a building if the university did not capitulate forthwith. A student told me that one of his humanities professors, himself a Jew, had said to him that Jews deserved to be put in concentration camps because of what they had done to blacks. [p. 352]

Why were the faculty in the humanities such easy targets for the revolutionaries? Because, Bloom observes, of the overwhelming influence of relativism and such kindred as deconstructionism: "On the portal of the humanities is written in many ways and many tongues, 'There is not truth—at least here.' " [p. 372] He writes:

> The reasons for this behavior [embracing the irrationalism of the stu-
> dent revolutionaries] on the part of many humanists are obvious and
> constitute the theme of this book. Cornell was in the forefront of cer-
> tain trends in the humanities as well as politics. It had for years been
> a laundering operation for radical Left French ideas in comparative
> literature. From Sartre, through Goldmann, to Foucault and Derrida,
> each successive wave washed over the Cornell shores. These ideas
> were intended to give life to old books...and make them a part of
> revolutionary conscience. At last there was an active, progressive role
> [i.e., overthrowing the "Establishment"] for the humanists...[p. 352]

Given that the professional schools "closed their shutters," the natural scientists stood mute, and the humanities were co-opted, the social
sciences remained "the only place where any kind of stand was made."
[p. 353] Bloom recounts that, when (1) "historians were being asked to
rewrite the history of the world, and of the United States in particular,
to show that nations were always conspiratorial systems of domination
and exploitation"; when (2) "psychologists were being pestered to prove
the psychological damage done by inequality and the existence of nuclear weapons, and to show that American statesmen were paranoid
about the Soviet Union"; when (3) "political scientists were urged to interpret the North Vietnamese as nationalists and to remove the stigma
of totalitarianism from the Soviet Union"; and when (4) the "major student activity in social science was to identify heretics" who questioned
the truth of these positions, it was then that many social scientists
fought back. [pp. 354, 355] Seeing that "objectivity was threatened, and
without respect and protection for scholarly inquiry anyone of them
might be put at risk...social scientists of the Left, Right and
Center...joined together to protest the outrage against academic freedom and against their colleagues that took place there and continues in
more or less subtle forms everywhere." [p. 355]

Against the backdrop of the tidal wave of irrationalism sweeping
across the universities in the Sixties, the swift and passionate (some
have called it "mindless") acceptance of Kuhnian relativism was virtually ensured. It provided another superficially plausible (yet, due to
Kuhn's stature, very formidable) intellectual arrow in the revolutionary's quiver. Against attempts to defend university values, Kuhnian
relativism gave the revolutionary an arsenal of epithets: "Does not the
eminent historian Kuhn show that all *genuine* progress comes about
only through revolutionary activity?" "Doesn't Kuhn clearly show that
everything, even physics, is inherently just persuasion and politics?"
"Is not everything either the *irrelevant* puzzle-solving of the received
view of the Establishment, or *relevant* revolutionary change?" "Is it not
the case that there is no such thing as the rational pursuit of truth,
only the pursuit of power?"

Fortunately, tidal waves recede. The revolutionary irrationalism of
the 1960s gradually gave way to the more sober reflection and rational

discourse of the 1970s, both in universities in general and the philosophy of science in particular. As detailed in the previous sections, Kuhnian relativism began to crumble under the carefully reasoned analyses of Shapere, Scheffler, and Suppe (among many others). Many writers believe the turning point was the often-cited symposium on the structure of scientific theories held at the University of Illinois in 1969. Believing, in Suppe's words, that the philosophy of science was being "castigated for irrelevance," ("irrelevant" was a Sixties epithet) and that the entire discipline was in "an acute state of disarray," the symposium brought together many of the discipline's most prominent members, including: Peter Achinstein, Robert L. Causey, Bernard Cohen, Bas C. van Fraassen, Carl Hempel, Thomas Kuhn, Hillary Putnam, Dudley Shapere, Frederick Suppe, Patrick Suppes, and Stephen Toulmin. [606] Attesting to the importance of the symposium, many of the sessions drew audiences exceeding 1,000 people, most of whom represented disciplines other than philosophy. [606, p. viii] It was at this symposium that the deficiencies of the "Received View" of the logical empiricists (the "Establishment") concerning the nature of scientific theories were detailed. Also, the alternative *Weltanschauungen* theories of Hanson, Kuhn, and Feyerabend were explicated and evaluated. Thus, it was at this symposium that Kuhn began his steady retreat from relativism, noting that *incommensurability* "is a term I have used, although it is not one I have been very fond of." [606, p. 409] The proceedings of the symposium and the 240-page critical introduction written by Frederick Suppe provided significant input into the research agenda of the philosophy of science in the early 1970s.

By the late 1970s the verdict was in on the historical relativism of Kuhn and Feyerabend. As Causey, one of the participants in the 1969 symposium, cogently observes: "In the Sixties it appeared that there was a crisis in the foundations of science. Recent work indicates there was not really a crisis; instead the Sixties were a transitional period leading to significant modifications of earlier views." [111, p. 199] In 1977, Suppe prepared his "Afterward" to summarize the results of the research on Kuhn's and Feyerabend's theories of science conducted since the 1969 symposium. In a section entitled "The Waning of the *Weltanschauungen* Views," Suppe reviews a long list of "weighty objections" that had been brought to bear on Feyerabend's version of relativism. He concludes: "Collectively, these objections are weighty indeed, displaying how bizarre, implausible, and unattractive is Feyerabend's view of science." [607, p. 641] Suppe notes that Feyerabend's *Against Method* had moved toward a "subjective idealism," and other "than perhaps to the most fanatical Hegelian, Feyerabend's philosophy of science has little to recommend itself and is losing whatever importance and influence it once had within philosophy of science." [607, p. 643] As noted in the previous section, since Suppe's 1977 conclusion on Feyerabend's philosophy, Feyerabend has taken his relativism to its logical conclusion, i.e., there is no reason to prefer the knowledge-claims of science over mysticism, magic, astrology, rain dances; and, furthermore, Western civilization is a "disease."

Unlike Feyerabend, Suppe points out that Kuhn took the views of the other participants in the 1969 symposium quite seriously and in the ensuing years made numerous modifications and clarifications of his theory of science. In particular, as we have noted previously, he emphatically rejected relativism and irrationalism by attempting to redefine his concept of incommensurability. He now defines two theories as being incommensurable when there is no procedure (like a mathematical algorithm) to compare the theories on a "point by point" basis and know-with-certainty (the "philosophers' fallacy" again) which theory to choose. This is a far cry from his previous "Gestalt-shift" view and its radical implications.

Suppe reviews the work on Kuhn's relativism that had been conducted since the 1969 symposium and concludes that "since the symposium, Kuhn's views have undergone a sharply declining influence on contemporary philosophy of science," because (1) "as Kuhn has modified and attenuated his views, it has seemed to many that he was retreating toward a neo-positivistic view"; (2) "Kuhn's account unnecessarily but essentially shortchanges the role of rationality in the growth of scientific knowledge"; (3) "There is a growing skepticism over Kuhn's claims that the history of science exemplifies his views on how science oscillates between normal and revolutionary science"; and (4) "Kuhn's position commits him to a metaphysical and epistemological view of science which is fundamentally defective since it makes discovering how the world really is irrelevant to scientific knowledge." Therefore, "collectively, these factors have led increasing numbers of philosophers of science to reject Kuhn's approach as irredeemably flawed, although not as hopeless as Feyerabend's." [607, p. 648]

Since the rejection of relativism in the late 1970s, the trend in the philosophy of science has been toward *historical empiricism* and *scientific realism:*

> The directions in which contemporary philosophy of science is heading are profoundly influenced by the repudiated *Weltanschauungen* analyses: Like the *Weltanschauungen* analyses, they view the history of science, as well as contemporary scientific practice, as providing important evidence to be used in developing and evaluating their philosophical analyses. . . .further, contemporary work in philosophy of science increasingly subscribes to the position that it is a central aim of science to come to knowledge of how the world *really* is, that correspondence between theories and reality is a central aim of science as an epistemic enterprise and crucial to whatever objectivity scientific knowledge enjoys—in sharp repudiation of the "sociological" views of knowledge found in the more extreme *Weltanschauungen* [Kuhn and Feyerabend] analyses, while acknowledging the defects of positivistic and earlier empiricist treatments. [607, p. 649]

In the final chapter, we shall investigate the views of the two most prominent advocates of historical empiricism: Imre Lakatos and Larry Laudan. We shall then explore scientific realism and conclude by discussing the role that philosophy of science can play in furthering the development of marketing science.

QUESTIONS FOR ANALYSIS AND DISCUSSION

1. The headnote to this chapter states "the cruelest fate which can overtake *enfants-terribles* is to awake and find that their avowed opinions have swept the suburbs." When Stove made his comment, he was referring to the philosophy of Thomas Kuhn. Why would Stove suggest that it would be a "cruel fate" for Kuhn if, in fact, "the suburbs" truly accepted all of Kuhn's philosophy? There is an old expression that goes: "Sophistry is the most dangerous game you can play." What does this have to do with the headnote?

2. Rachels points out that "if we took cultural relativism seriously, we would have to admit that these social practices are also immune from criticism." What does he mean "if we took cultural relativism seriously"? Under what circumstances will individuals propose philosophies that are "not to be taken seriously"? How do we *know* when a philosophy is to be "taken seriously"? Is it *ever* appropriate to propose philosophies that one does not "take seriously"?

3. What is absolutism with respect to ethics? Critics of absolutism often spell it "Absolutism." What is the implication of capitalizing the "A"? Likewise, critics of truth often spell it "Truth," or even "TRUTH!" Evaluate the thesis that such critics fall prey to the "philosophers' fallacy."

4. Section 10.1.2 points out that the "strong thesis" is often used synonomously with "relativism" in sociology. What is "strong" about the "strong thesis"? In what way does the fear of ethnocentrism result in the "strong thesis"? One writer has claimed that it is actually ethnocentrism of the most vicious and condescending kind to claim that other people have "reasoning processes" that are radically different from so-called "Western reasoning processes." How could it be "ethnocentric" *not* to believe in rationality relativism and "viciously ethnocentric" to *believe* in rationality relativism?

5. As pointed out in Section 10.1.3, reality relativism has its historical origins, in part, in Winch's monograph entitled *The Idea of a Social Science and Its Relation to Philosophy*. In this monograph Winch analyzed the primitive society of the Azande and its reliance on witchcraft. Curiously, many modern advocates of relativism wish to deny their historical heritage: "Siegel dredges up the hackneyed example of witchcraft practices among the Zande people as Evans-Pritcherd found them in the late 1920s and early 1930s. Ever since Winch's misreading of Wittgenstein sparked the so-called 'rationality debates', philosophers have imagined that important epistemological issues were at stake in Azande ethnography." [16, p. 134] Why is it important for relativists to (now) deny their historical heritage? Under what circumstances is it appropriate (inappropriate) to deny the historical heritage of one's philosophy?

6. Section 10.1.3 contends that reality relativism is "morally impotent." Other writers have contended that reality relativism is "morally outrageous." What would be the difference between a philosophy being, simply, "morally impotent" and "morally outrageous"? The statement was made that the distinction between moral relativism and cognitive relativism is often "difficult to make." Why should this be the case? Why should, or should not, the morality of cognitive relativism be an issue?

7. Discuss the various usages of the term "paradigm." How does a "paradigm" differ from a *"Weltanschauung"*? What difference does it make if everyone uses the term "paradigm" in his or her own way? (Hint: reflect on the purpose of language.)

8. Thomas Kuhn believed that his theory of science did not apply to the social sciences because they were in the "pre-paradigm stage." Many writers, however, have pointed out that Kuhn's theory has been actually *applied* most often in the social sciences. Why has this been the case? Should it be the case?

9. Discuss the three major interpretations of the word "incommensurable." What does "rival" mean? Why is it important to recognize that it is only "rival" theories or paradigms for which the concept of "incommensurability" poses a potential problem for science? Why is it important to distinguish between theories and paradigms being "incommensurable" and being, simply, "different"?

10. What are the "Orwellian implications" of reality relativism? Why does the book claim that it is "surprising and sorrowful" that Kuhn did not repudiate reality relativism earlier? To what extent do you believe that current advocates of reality relativism have recognized its "Orwellian implications"?   Should they so recognize?

11. What does it mean and why is it important to recognize that "what is required for objectivity in science is not an observation-language that is neutral to all potential theories; rather, what is required is an observation-language that is neutral with respect to the theories in question." How have many philosophers erred by claiming that objectivity requires an observation-language that is "neutral" with respect to all theories? What does it mean to claim that an observation-language is "neutral" with respect to a *particular* theory? (Hint: What does "question begging" mean?)

12. Define the terms "objective" and "subjective" as they might apply to any method or procedure for justifying knowledge-claims.   Draw a continuum with your definition of objective at the left end of the continuum and your definition of subjective at the right. Now, place an "x" on the line where you believe "science" should go. Continue by positioning other societal institutions on the line, such as religion and politics. Use the continuum and your definitions to evaluate the thesis: "Science is subjective." It is often claimed that "relativism destroys language." What does this mean with reference to the objectivity/subjectivity issue? Is science subjective? Should it be?

13. Why do you believe that Kuhn stated that it was "obscene" for Feyerabend to claim that their views were advocating the same thing? Why is Kuhn referred to as a "reluctant relativist" and Feyerabend an "exuberant relativist"?

14. After the publication of Feyerabend's *Science in a Free Society*, Tibor Machan wrote a review for the *Philosophy of Social Science* [410]. Feyerabend then commented on the review of Machan, referring to Machan's views as "academic ratiofascism." [193, p. 191] Machan then replied:

> Oh my, what have I unleashed with my humble little review! A veritable Don Rickles of the journal circuit, only without the fun. But let me try, as hard as I can, to keep away from derision, not without saying first, however, that it does hurt. [411, p. 197]

Machan then proceeds to respond to the charges that he is a "ratiofascist" and concludes his response with:

> Feyerabend may wish to have us think that all he, but no one else, asks for is a tolerance for different lifestyles. But there is plenty of room in my own standard-ridden outlook. . .for enormous varieties of lifestyles within societies with the very same legal framework—the U.S. liberal melting pot is really far richer, though getting less so, than Feyerabend allows. What with his calling me a fascist for thinking and publishing my libertarian notions, I doubt that a polity of his conception would be anywhere near so open and pluralistic as one I have in mind. . . .It really makes me doubt that Feyerabend is a man with whom any kind of conversation that does not begin with total submission to his views could be carried out in a civilized fashion. [411, p. 199]

How does Machan's comment relate to the headnote of this chapter? Some writers have pointed out that many advocates of relativism, like Feyerabend, seem totally intolerant of others whose views may differ with their own. How does this relate to the acceptance of relativism in the 1960s? How does it relate today?

15. Suppe points out the distressing tendency for the behavioral sciences to uncritically accept many theories of science from the philosophy of science, even after those philosophies have been long repudiated: "Increasingly, behavioral and social sciences are reading and being influenced by Thomas Kuhn's *Structure of Scientific Revolutions*. Within anthropology, economics, political science, psychology, and sociology there has been a spate of publications attempting to view these disciplines from a 'Kuhnian' perspective, either in an attempt to discern the current state of the field or in an attempt to resolve various methodological disputes within the discipline." [608, p. 89] He goes on to relate that "I am dismayed and worried by the burgeoning influence Kuhn is having on behavioral and social scientists. My fears here rest not so much on the fact that Kuhn's structure of scientific revolutions is bad history of science and fundamentally defective philosophy of science, but rather on the *way* in which behavioral and social scientists are resorting to and relying on Kuhn's work." [608, p. 69] Suppe concludes that "science must approach philosophy of science with a critical eye" and:

> In short, scientific methodologies are strategies for ascertaining the likelihood that accepted theories or hypotheses are correct, and to the extent that science has been progressive it has involved the development of increasing more sophisticated strategies or cannons of rationality for deciding which theories to accept or reject on the basis of increasingly smaller data bases, in such a way that such strategies lead to increasingly higher success rates in the acceptance of true theories or hypotheses and the rejection of false ones. The methodologies codified by philosophers of science or methodologically-concerned scientists are codifications of such strategies, often coupled with assessments of the relative merits of these strategies compared to other available ones. [608, p. 102]

To what extent are Suppe's comments relevant to marketing today? To what extent is Suppe arguing that scientific *methodology* is progressive? Would it be possible to know-with-certainty that scientific methodology is progressive? Why is the issue of the progressivity of scientific methodology important, or not important?

16. Why is it a fallacy to restrict discussions of scientific progress to only hierarchical, general theories, such as Newtonian mechanics? To what extent has marketing science made progress? To what extend would it be *possible* for marketing science to exhibit progress if one adopts relativism?

17. Evaluate Peter and Olson's position that "truth is a subjective evaluation that cannot be properly inferred outside of the context provided by the theory." [492, p. 119]

18. Peter and Olson argue, following Feyerabend, that " 'anything goes'—i.e., any methodology or theory, no matter how unconventional, can contribute to scientific progress." [492, p. 121] What is the difference between "can contribute," and "may contribute," or "is likely to contribute," or "is likely not to contribute"? Does the phrase "can contribute" make the statement trivially true? Demonstrably false?

19. Peter and Olson state "alternatively, researchers with an R/C orientation conceive of many possible rationalities, each of which is relative to a specific context or frame of reference. According to this view, scientists *construct* 'realities' by developing a degree of social agreement about the meanings of their theories and empirical observations." [492, p. 120] Evaluate this position. How does it relate to the "consensus theory of truth"?or "is likely not to contribute"? Does the phrase "can contribute" make the statement trivially true? Demonstrably false?

11

POST-RELATIVISTIC
PHILOSOPHY OF SCIENCE

To say that truth is no part of the aim of science is on a par with saying that curing is no part of the aim of medicine or that profit is no part of the aim of commerce.
> *John W. N. Watkins*

In the 1980s, philosophy of science turned sharply toward historical empiricism and scientific realism. Advocates of historical empiricism share with Kuhn and Feyerabend a belief that philosophy of science should reflect and explain the actual history of science but reject Kuhn and Feyerabend's relativism/irrationalism. Advocates of scientific realism, though sensitive to the history of science, often place more emphasis on understanding science as it is currently practiced. As Suppes points out: "[A]bout ninety percent of all scientists who have ever lived are now alive, and the development of science since World War II is the most smashing success story in the history of thought. To be concerned only with the long historical perspective and not to understand the systematic details of modern science is as mistaken as the pursuit of empty formal methods that make no contact with developed scientific theories and their supporting experiments." [Suppes, in 23, p. 25] Kuhn himself has lamented the growing trend of historical critics of science (so-called "external studies") to be ill-informed about actual scientific practice ("internal studies"):

> [A] phenomenon which alarms me sometimes accompanies the increasing trend toward external studies. It is here and there possible these days to enter graduate school in the history of science without significant scientific training and to complete a degree without ever having to analyze a technical document in depth. That is a bit like studying the history of music without ever having heard a concert or examined a score. [Kuhn, in 23, p. 124]

We turn now to the historical empiricism of both Imre Lakatos and Larry Laudan. The chapter concludes with an examination of scientific

354

realism and a discussion of how the philosophy of science relates to marketing.

11.1   IMRE LAKATOS' HISTORICAL EMPIRICISM

Imre Lakatos (1922-1974) was a Hungarian philosopher of science and mathematics who changed his name from Imre Lipschitz to escape the Nazis during World War II. After the war, he was appointed Secretary, Hungarian Ministry of Education (1947-49), was imprisoned as a dissident (1950-53), and was able to flee from his homeland during the 1956 Hungarian uprising. He received his Ph.D. at Cambridge University in England in 1958 and taught at the London School of Economics as a Professor of Logic from 1960 to 1974. At the London School of Economics, he worked closely with Popper and "His philosophy helped me to make a final break with the Hegelian outlook which I had held for nearly twenty years. . . . Since Hegel each generation has unfortunately needed—and has fortunately had—philosophers to break Hegel's spell on young thinkers who so frequently fall into the trap of impressive and all-explanatory theories . . . which act upon weak minds like revelations." [363, p. 139]

Having seen the consequences of totalitarian regimes of both the Left and the Right, Lakatos was a determined opponent of authoritarianism. Sampson points out that Lakatos saw "the 'barren skepticism' that results from strict application of Popper's principle and the immature frivolity of Paul Feyerabend's intellectual anarchism (which, like the anarchism of the 1960s political movements, Lakatos saw as a front for a particularly intransigent form of authoritarianism)." [553, p. 313] Lakatos recognized that the falsificationism of his mentor Popper was not in accord with much of the actual history of science and, also, was inadvertently fostering skepticism and irrationalism. At the same time, he abhorred the position of "some sociologists of knowledge" that science is just "truth by (changing) consensus." [362, p. 92] Noting that Kuhn's historical theory of science promoted "truth by consensus" and had "authoritarian overtones," Lakatos states: "My concern is that Kuhn, having recognized the failure of both justificationism [foundationalism] and falsificationism in providing rational accounts of scientific growth, seems now to fall back on to irrationalism." [362, p. 93] Therefore, Lakatos adopted for himself the problem of developing a general theory of science that would be faithful to the actual history of scientific progress and, at the same time, would avoid the irrationalism implicit in Kuhnian relativism. He titled his theory "The Methodology of Scientific Research Programmes," and it drew heavily from Popperian falsificationism. We shall now develop and evaluate his general theory of science by first examining what Lakatos considered to be its rivals.

11.1.1   Justificationism, Dogmatic Falsificationism, and Naive Falsificationism

The Methodology of Scientific Research Programmes relies heavily on the concept of "sophisticated methodological falsificationism." But to understand how Lakatos defends this concept as central to understanding science, Lakatos first discusses and evaluates what he considers to be its major rivals: justificationism, dogmatic falsificationism, and naive methodological falsificationism. First, Lakatos points out that "for centuries knowledge meant proven knowledge—proven either by the power of the intellect [classical rationalism] or by the evidence of the senses [classical empiricism]." [362, p. 8] Therefore, like religious knowledge that was guaranteed to be certain by the Church, scientific knowledge must be justified (hence "justificationism") by methods that will guarantee with certainty its truth. Justificationism (or, alternatively, "foundationalism") was entirely credible for several hundred years because of the spectacular success of Newtonian mechanics. However, Lakatos observes, the downfall of the Newtonian empire showed that science cannot yield truth-with-certainty; justificationism is, therefore, untenable; and the Humean "problem of induction" shows precisely why justification is untenable. However, "one cannot simply water down the ideal of proven truth—as some logical empiricists do—to the ideal of 'probable truth.'" [362, p. 92] What is the answer to the "problem of induction"? For Lakatos, scientific knowledge could be guaranteed with the certainty of the *modus tollens* of deductive logic by adopting a sophisticated form of Popperian falsificationism.

Lakatos differentiates dogmatic falsificationism from both naive falsificationism and his "sophisticated" falsificationism. Dogmatic falsificationism demands that for a theory to be scientific it must forbid the occurrence of certain events and scientists must stipulate in advance of some test what kind of events in an experiment would constitute a "falsifier" to permit the theory to be refuted. There are three problems with dogmatic falsificationism. First, "there are and can be no sensations unimpregnated by expectations and therefore there is not a natural (i.e., psychological) demarcation between observational and theoretical propositions." [362, p. 99] That is, Lakatos (correctly) observes that there is no "observation language" that is neutral to all theories and (mistakenly) concludes that this poses an insurmountable problem for maintaining objectivity in science. (As has been discussed previously in Section 10.2.1, what is required to maintain objectivity in science is an observational language that is neutral to genuinely rival theories, not all potential theories.) A second problem for dogmatic falsificationism is that "the truth-value of the 'observational' propositions cannot be indubitably cited: no factual proposition can ever be proved from an experiment." [362, p.99] That is, formally speaking, deductive logic applies only to the relationships among sentences or propositions. Only a sentence can "disprove" another sentence; observing some real world event may in some sense be inconsistent with a sentence but it does not "refute" or "disprove" the sentence. Here we see the impact of formal logic and mathematics on Lakatos' analysis.

The third problem with dogmatic falsificationism is that "exactly the most admired scientific theories simply fail to forbid any observable state of affairs." [362, p. 100] Here, Lakatos is referring to what is normally called the "Quine-Duhem thesis." Named after the philosophers W.V. Quine and Pierre Duhem, this thesis holds that when one conducts a test of a theory one is actually "testing" a host of initial conditions, measuring instruments and auxiliary hypotheses that together form the *ceteris paribus* conditions. If a particular experiment yields results inconsistent with the theory, the researcher cannot know-with-certainty whether it is the theory, measures, procedures, or some auxiliary hypotheses at fault. Therefore, no theory can be conclusively disproved in the same sense as a mathematical proof/disproof. Again, we see Lakatos setting the standard for acceptability in science as that of the certainty of a mathematical proof.

Lakatos considers the three problems of dogmatic falsificationism to be conclusive, points out that many writers have falsely charged Popper with advocating such a falsificationist theory of science, and then discusses the actual version of falsificationism advocated by Popper, i.e., "naive methodological falsificationism." Naive falsificationism addresses the first problem of dogmatic falsificationism by having scientists make a methodological decision that some terms will be called "observation terms" and some sentences "observation sentences" or "basic sentences." These "basic sentences" are then accepted "by convention" (i.e., without proof) of the scientists as potential falsifiers of the theory in question. As a response to the second problem, "the methodological falsificationists separate action and disproof, which the dogmatic falsificationists had conflated." [362, p. 109] Therefore, scientific theories are not "disproved" with the certainty of mathematics. Rather they are *rejected* or *refuted*.

The third problem of dogmatic falsificationism is addressed by first subjecting all aspects of the *ceteris paribus* clause to "severe tests." That is, the scientist must carefully delineate all of the specific assumptions and auxiliary hypotheses associated with the theory in question and subject these assumptions and auxiliary hypotheses to empirical testing. The scientist then must devise an experiment to control for these assumptions and auxiliary hypotheses and stipulate in advance of conducting the experiment that certain events would constitute a conclusive falsification of the theory. Such an experiment would constitute a "crucial experiment," and the researcher is committed to rejecting the theory. What does "rejecting" mean? Lakatos contends: "Since, for our savage falsificationist, falsifications are methodologically conclusive, the fateful decision amounts to the methodological elimination of [a] theory, making further work on it irrational." [362, p. 111]

Being a firm believer in the "historical approach" to the philosophy of science, Lakatos compared the theory of science according to naive falsificationism with the actual behaviors of scientists in significant historical episodes. He found that when naive falsificationism was "tested" by comparing it with the history of science, the theory fared very poorly. Many of the "most celebrated crucial experiments" were "accepted as crucial for no rational reason or their acceptance rested on rationality principles radically different from the ones we have just discussed." [362, p. 114] Second, many "stubborn theoreticians" in the history of science seem to refuse to accept the "experimental verdicts" of crucial tests and continued to work on their theories. Third, many prominent scientists in history seemed to have been "irrationally slow" in accepting the falsification of a theory: "For instance, eighty-five years elapsed between the acceptance of the Perihelion of Mercury as an anomaly and its acceptance as a falsification of Newton's theory." [362, p. 114] Fourth, scientists often seem to be "irrationally rash" in accepting a theory in spite of apparent falsifications. For example, "Galileo and his disciples accepted Copernican heliocentric celestial mechanics in spite of the abundant evidence against the rotation of the earth." [362, p. 115] Fifth, on many occasions the history of science indicates that a single theory is not tested by some crucial experiment; rather, rival theories are tested against each other. Sixth, "some of the most interesting experiments result, *prima facie*, in confirmation rather than falsification." [362, p. 115]

Lakatos viewed the problems of a naive methodological falsificationism as devastating to the notion of scientific rationality and saw only two alternatives: "One alternative is to abandon efforts to give a rational explanation of the success of science." [362, p. 115] This alternative was "Kuhn's way" where the idea of scientific *progress* vanishes and is replaced by a series of "changes" in "paradigms," brought about by "Gestalt shifts" and "religious conversions." But this alternative inexorably leads to relativism, irrationalism, "mob rule," and "authoritarianism." Therefore, Lakatos opted for a *sophisticated* version of methodological falsificationism that would "rescue methodology and the idea of scientific *progress*." [362, p. 116] Lakatos called his general theory of science the "methodology of scientific research programmes."

11.1.2   Acceptance, Pursuit, and Rationality in Science

Before discussing Lakatos' general theory of science, we should point out a fundamental confusion in Lakatos' analysis of the problems of naive falsificationism and its lack of consistency with the history of science. As pointed out by his friend and colleague, John W. N. Watkins, throughout all of Lakatos's writings there is a confusion between a researcher "accepting" a theory and "working on" a theory. [627, p. 156] That is, it is one thing for a researcher "accepting" a theory as being the best theory of the day to truly explain some set of phenomena or, alternatively, the best theory to guide decision-making. It is another thing for a researcher to select a theory to "work on." Further, the decision to "work on" a theory may be totally rational *even though* it is not the "best" theory of the day in the sense of explaining phenomena and/or guiding decision-making. Laudan refers to this fundamental confusion as the difference between the "context of acceptance" and the "context of pursuit." [370, p. 108] In this regard, the "context of acceptance" is very similar to what is normally referred to as the "context of justification." The "context of pursuit" is analogous to, but certainly not identical with, the "context of discovery." In any respect, just like Kuhn and Feyerabend, Lakatos continually and consistently in his writings confuses "acceptance" with "working on," as in the following: "Since, for our savage falsificationists, falsifications are methodologically conclusive, the fateful decision amounts to the methodological elimination of [a] theory, *making further work on it irrational.*" [362, p. 111, emphasis added]

Lakatos interpreted naive falsificationism as a *logic of pursuit* and, when he found that the history of science was inconsistent with his logic of pursuit, he was faced with adopting Feyerabend's solution ("anything goes") or developing a logic of pursuit that would not (he thought) imply that science was irrational. Four observations are in order here. First, the logical empiricists, but not necessarily Popper, believed that there was no "logic of discovery," i.e., discovery was an inherently untidy process. Therefore, although they never wrote about the "context of pursuit," we may infer that they would have viewed it as being, similarly, untidy. Second, many writers, such as Laudan, do not believe that "anything goes" in the context of pursuit (see Section 11.2.1). Third, the fact that scientists often choose to "work on" theories that are not the "best" in their day, manifestly does not imply that science is irrational. Even if "anything goes" in the context of pursuit and/or discovery, such a conclusion does not imply that "anything goes" in the context of acceptance and/or justification. Fourth, as Toulmin points out, in the final analysis it is the rationality of the scientific community that counts. [607, p. 672] That is, even if individual scientists are demonstrably irrational in their acceptance of the "best" theory of the day with regard to a set of phenomena, this would not imply that the *community* of scientists is (or, most assuredly, ought to be) *collectively* irrational. We shall now turn to a discussion of Lakatos' general theory of science.

11.1.3 The Methodology of Scientific Research Programmes

Just as the key concept in Kuhn's general theory of science is the paradigm, the key concept in Lakatos' theory is the "research programme." A research program (American spelling) is a sequence of related theories: $T_1, T_2, T_3 \ldots$ In one sense a research program is similar to Kuhnian "normal science," since this is what the researchers "work on" or "pursue." Also like Kuhn, the existence of a research program (paradigm) separates *mature* science from *immature* science. Lakatos considers the latter to be "a mere patched up pattern of trial and error." [362, p. 175] However, unlike Kuhn, Lakatos believed that "one must never allow a research program to become a *Weltanschauung*," because "normal science is nothing other than a research program that has achieved monopoly" and "the history of science has been and should be a history of competing research programs (or, if you wish, paradigms), but it has not been and must not become a succession of periods of normal science: the sooner competition starts, *the better for progress*." [362, p. 661, emphasis added]

Every research program has a "positive heuristic" that contains a set of methodological rules that guide the development of the research program and a "negative heuristic" that suggests paths of research to avoid. Lakatos notes that a research program "at any stage of its development, has unsolved problems and undigested anomalies. All theories, in this sense, are born refuted and die refuted." He continues by asking the following question: "But are they equally good?" [363, p. 5] Lakatos believed (unlike Kuhn) that rival, or alternative, research programs could be evaluated in terms of their progressivity: Some research programs are *progressive*; others are *degenerating*. Thus, Lakatos' theory differs sharply from Kuhnian relativism and its "Gestalt shifts." However, Lakatos' theory also diverges from the naive falsificationism attributed to Popper: "Contrary to Popper, the difference [between rival research programs] cannot be that some are still unrefuted, while others are already refuted. When Newton published his *Principia*, it was common knowledge that it could not properly explain even the motion of the moon; in fact, lunar motion refuted Newton." [363, p. 5] But if Newton's theory was "refuted when it was born," why was Newton's theory *progressive*? For Lakatos, Newton's theory was progressive because it predicted "novel facts." In general, research programs that are *theoretically progressive* "all predict novel facts, facts which had been either undreamt of, or have indeed been contradicted by previous or rival programs." [363, p. 5] For example, Lakatos notes that Newton's theory predicted the existence and exact motion of small planets which had never been observed before.

How do theories change within a Lakatos research program? Successor theories in a research program are formed with the aid of the positive heuristic by adding additional clauses to predecessor theories with the proviso that each successor theory must have more "empirical content" than its predecessor. That is, a successor theory must predict everything that its predecessor predicted and, in addition, some novel, hitherto unexpected, facts. However, each research program has a "hard core" of assumptions and clauses that are not to be subjected to refutation, in fact "we must use our own ingenuity to articulate or even invent auxiliary hypotheses which form a *protective belt* around this core." [362, p. 133]

If each new theory in a research program eliminates its predecessor by virtue of having greater empirical content (and, thus, is progressive), how are entire research programs eliminated? For Lakatos, a research program can be eliminated "only if there is a better one to replace it." [363, p. 150] Thus:

> The idea of competing scientific research programs leads us to the problem: *how are research programs eliminated?* It has transpired from our previous considerations that a degenerating problemshift is no more a sufficient reason to eliminate a research program than some old-fashioned "refutation" or a Kuhnian "crisis." Can there be any objective (as opposed to socio-psychological) reason to reject a program, that is, to eliminate its hard core and its program for constructing protective belts? Our answer, in outline, is that such an objective reason is provided by a rival research program which explains the previous success of its rival and supersedes it by a further display of *heuristic power.* . . . I use "heuristic power" here as a technical term to characterize the power of a research program to anticipate theoretically novel facts in its growth. I could of course use "explanatory power." [362, p. 155]

Given that Lakatos uses "eliminate" to mean "cease working on," the preceding would seem to imply that Lakatos is counseling scientists that they should cease pursuing, or working on, a degenerating research program that has been "overtaken" by some rival. However, Lakatos claims such is not the case:

> One may rationally stick to a degenerating program until it is overtaken by a rival *and even after*. What one must *not* do is to deny its poor public record. Both Feyerabend and Kuhn conflate *methodological* appraisal of a program with firm *heuristic* advice about what to do. It is perfectly rational to play a risky game: what is irrational is to deceive oneself about the risk. [363, p. 117]

Why should it be rational to stick to a degenerating research program "even after" it has been overtaken by a rival? Because Lakatos' reading of the history of science led him to conclude that many research programs that had been overtaken had subsequently "staged a comeback." [363, p. 113] Once again, we see Lakatos getting into serious difficulty because he confuses "working on" with "acceptance." Therefore, he conflates the following two questions: (1) When is it rational for a scientist to work on, or cease working on, a research program? (2) When is it rational for a scientist, or a community of scientists, to accept a theory or research program as the best explanation for a set of phenomena? Given that Feyerabend's writings share the same confusion as Lakatos, it is no wonder that Feyerabend could claim that Lakatos' theory was "anarchism in disguise." [187, p. 181] Thus, Feyerabend endorsed Lakatos: "I also agree with two suggestions which form an essential part of Lakatos' theory of science. . . . Neither blatant internal inconsistencies, . . . nor massive conflict with experimental results should prevent us from retaining and elaborating a point of view that pleases us for some reason or other." [187, p. 183] Note that Feyerabend uses "retaining and elaborating" in his agreement with Lakatos.

There are numerous critiques of Lakatos' general theory of science, including: Suppe [606, pp. 659-70], Laudan [370, pp. 76-78] and the articles by Kuhn, Feigl, Hall, and Koertge in Buck and Cohen [89]. Many of the criticisms seem particularly devastating, which is not surprising given his confusion of "working on" with "accepting." Consider first, for example, that a Lakatosian research program exists only when there is a succession of theories where later theories entail earlier theories; every successor theory must explain *everything* that a predecessor theory explained and "more." However, what most scientific disciplines would call "research programs" often contain successor theories that do not have this characteristic. Second, Lakatos claims that "immature" disciplines do not have research programs and are nothing more than "patched up trial and error." Yet, many of the disciplines that Lakatos would characterize as "immature" seem to have research programs that exhibit a high degree of systematic inquiry, rather than "patched up" work. Third, the claim that research programs have a "hard core" that cannot be changed or modified seems inconsistent with actual practice in many sciences and, further, would certainly not seem to be a characteristic of "ideal" science. For example, Leong [387] claims that the "hard core" of marketing science are the "four fundamental explananda" identified in my own 1983 article. However, I certainly never intended the four explananda to be "hard core" in a Lakatosian sense. Rather, I advanced the four explananda as suitable candidates for organizing the structure of marketing science and specifically urged readers to attempt to find counter-instances.

Laudan reviewed Lakatos' general theory of science and concluded that it was "a decided improvement on Kuhn's" because it "stresses the historical importance of the co-existence of several alternative programs at the same time, within the same domain." Further, "unlike Kuhn, who often takes the view that paradigms are incommensurable and thus not open to rational comparison, Lakatos insists that we can objectively compare the relative progress of competing research traditions." [370, p. 76] However, Laudan found that "Lakatos' model of research programs shares many of the flaws of Kuhn's paradigms, and introduces some new ones as well." [370, p. 77] Therefore, Laudan developed his "theory of research traditions," while acknowledging his "great debt" to the "pioneering work" of Kuhn and Lakatos. [370, p. 78]

11.2   LAUDAN'S HISTORICAL EMPIRICISM

Larry Laudan was born in Austin, Texas in 1941, received his Ph.D. from Princeton University in the history and philosophy of science in 1965, and has taught at Cambridge University, the University of London, the University of Pittsburgh, the Virginia Polytechnic Institute and State University, and the University of Hawaii. A prominent advocate of the historical approach to the study of science, Laudan's major publications include: "Theories of Scientific Method from Plato to Mach" [367], "Two Dogmas of Methodology" [369], *Science and Hypothesis* [373], "Confutation of Convergent Realism" [372], and "Relativism, Naturalism and Reticulation" [377]. Drawing upon these works (among others), Laudan develops his general theory of science in *Progress and Its Problems* [370] and *Science and Values* [375].

Laudan developed his general theory of science to satisfy five objectives. First, a satisfactory theory of science should be consistent with the actual history of the development of science. In this regard, Laudan has been most critical of Kuhn for developing a theory of science that was radically at odds with actual historical episodes in science and of Lakatos for using a "rational reconstruction" approach to the history of science. [370, pp. 74-77] Second, an adequate theory of science must reveal that science is progressive in some meaningful sense, but that such progressivity *cannot* involve the acceptance of the "cumulativity postulate." That is, Laudan holds that science is progressive, but that changes from one theory to another are seldom, if ever, *strictly* cumulative in the sense of the successor theory being able to explain everything that its predecessor did and "more." The "cumulativity postulate," Laudan contends, was one of the (false) "two dogmas" of methodology. [368] Third, Laudan proposed that a satisfactory theory of science must show that progress in science is *rational*, in sharp contrast to the irrationalist, "Gestalt shift," and "incommensurable" versions of Kuhn and Feyerabend. Laudan held that a second of the "two dogmas" of methodology was that rival theories would be incommensurable because of the absence of an observation language that was "neutral" to all theories. Rather, he noted, all that was required for objectivity was an observation language that was "neutral" between the two rival theories (i.e., the observation language itself did not *presume* that one or the other of the two theories was true). [369] Fourth, an acceptable general theory of science must be non-relativistic because, he contends, there are a wide range of evaluative criteria that can be applied within science to rationally adjudicate disputes within science. Fifth, we should approach scientific progress and rationality "without presupposing anything about the veracity or verisimilitude of the theories we judge to be rational or irrational." [370, p. 125] Laudan insists that, although there may be many appropriate goals for science, such goals must not be "utopian," because, "to adopt a goal with the feature that we can conceive of no actions that would be apt to promote it, or a goal whose realization we could not recognize even if we had achieved it, is surely a mark of unreasonableness and irrationality." [375, p. 51] How does Laudan come to the conclusion that "veracity," "verisimilitude," and "truth" are "utopian"? Because, he claims:

> Philosophers and scientists since the time of Parmenides and Plato have been seeking to justify science as a truth-seeking enterprise. Without exception, these efforts have foundered because no one has been able to demonstrate that a system like science, with the methods it has at its disposal, can be *guaranteed* to reach the "Truth," either in the short or the long run. . . . Realizing this dilemma, some philosophers (notably Pierce, Popper, and Reichenbach) have sought to link scientific rationality and proof in a different way, by suggesting that although our present theories are neither true nor probable, they are closer approximations to the truth than their predecessors. Such an approach offers few consolations, however, since no one has been able even to say what it would mean to be "closer to the truth," let alone to offer criteria for determining how we could assess such proximity. [370, pp.125-6, emphasis added]

We shall return to the issue of truth and its role in science later. For now, the reader should carefully note Laudan's word "guaranteed."

Actually, Laudan has produced *two* general theories of science, since the theory in *Science and Values* repudiates several of the major positions taken in *Progress and Its Problems*. However, the five considerations developed in the preceding paragraph remain constant throughout both theories. We shall first develop the "early Laudan" theory and examine its strengths and weaknesses before developing the "later Laudan" theory and evaluating it.

11.2.1   The "Early Laudan" Theory of Science

The central theme of *Progress and Its Problems* is that there is one overriding goal, or aim, for science: the solution of problems. Thus, the very first sentence of the first chapter is "Science is essentially a problem-solving activity." [p. 11] Similarly, "it is the purpose of this short book to sketch what seem to be the implications, for both the history of science and its philosophy, of a view of scientific inquiry which perceives science as being—*above all else*—a problem-solving activity."

[p. 12, emphasis added] Likewise, "it has often been suggested in this essay that the solution of a maximum number of empirical problems, and the generation of minimum number of conceptual problems and anomalies is the *central aim* of science." [p. 111, emphasis added]

Laudan differentiates between two major kinds of problems: empirical problems and conceptual problems. Empirical problems are "anything about the natural world which strikes us as odd, or otherwise in need of explanation," and scientists recognize empirical problems as such because "our theoretical presuppositions about the natural order tell us what to expect and what seems peculiar or 'problematic' or questionable (in the literal sense of that term)." [p. 15] On the other hand, conceptual problems are "higher-order questions about the well-foundedness of the conceptual structures (e.g., theories) which have been devised to answer the first-order [empirical] questions." [p. 48] Conceptual problems spring from diverse sources. For example, some conceptual problems are "internal" problems, as when an individual theory is logically inconsistent or unclear. "External" problems come about when a theory is inconsistent with another theory or "worldview," or "areas as diverse as metaphysics, logic, ethics and theology." [p. 61]

If the "central aim" of science is problem-solving and "empirical problems" are those things about the world that strike us as "peculiar," how does science know when it has "solved" a problem? Laudan states that "generally, any theory, T, can be regarded as having solved an empirical problem, if T functions (significantly) in any schema of inference whose conclusion is a statement of the problem." [p. 25]

Four preliminary observations can immediately be made about Laudan's problem-solving theory. First, his concept of "problem-solving" does not necessarily imply that science seeks solutions to practical problems of society. That is, Laudan is not *justifying* science and scientific activity on the basis that it is useful for solving significant social problems. Rather, a "problem" is something that seems "peculiar" or unexpected as a result of some theory held (explicitly or implicitly) by the scientist. Although the solution of "the problem" may have some practical applications, it need not. Second, Laudan's conceptualization as to what is to count as a "solution" to a problem is indistinguishable from what traditional philosophy of science has characterized as an "explanation" of some phenomenon. Therefore, Laudan's conceptualization that science is essentially "problem-solving" differs very little from the traditional view that science is essentially "explanation giving." Third, given that Laudan's "empirical problem" does not mean a practical problem of society, his theory is consistent with the view that science (at least "basic" science) is concerned with "knowledge for knowledge's sake." Finally, given that Laudan specifically disavows "truth" and "approximate truth" as a goal or aim of science (on the basis that such goals would be "utopian"), his view *necessarily* implies that theories and explanations in science should be viewed *instrumentally,* rather than realistically.

Continuing with our development of Laudan's theory, solving conceptual problems is "at least as important in the development of science as empirical problem solving." [p. 45] Conceptual problems arise from some inconsistency or incompatibility of a theory within itself ("internal") or, more frequently, with some other theory. These other kinds of theories may be: (1) scientific theories, (2) theories of methodology, or (3) "world-view" theories, such as those in politics, theology, logic, or metaphysics. Such inconsistencies between theories produce a "tension" that demands resolution. Not all conceptual problems are equally important. Indeed, a specific "weight" can be given to the relative importance of each conceptual problem: "Other things being equal, the greater the tension between two theories, the weightier the problem will be." [p. 65] The conceptual problems are "solved" by modifying one or more of the theories. He notes: "[T]he *fact* [is] that a tension often exists between our 'scientific' beliefs and our 'nonscientific' ones, and that such a tension does pose a problem for *both* sets of beliefs. How that tension is to be resolved depends on the particularities of the case." [p. 64]

As will be recalled, Laudan wanted his theory of science to demonstrate that science was indeed progressive and rational, but that such progressivity and rationality could not depend on "truth." How is theory appraisal to be accomplished so that theory-change in science will be progressive? For Laudan, "the solved problem—empirical or conceptual—is the basic unit of scientific progress." [p. 66] Therefore, we should evaluate theories on the basis of their problem-solving effectiveness, where "overall problem-solving effectiveness of a theory is determined by assessing the number and importance of the empirical problems which the theory solves and deducting there from the number and importance of the anomalies and conceptual problems which the theory generates." [p. 68] Thus, scientific progress inherently involves comparing theories through time: "Progress can occur if and only if the succession of scientific theories in any domain shows an increasing degree of problem-solving effectiveness." [p. 68] Such a criterion gives specific guidance to practicing scientists since "anytime we modify a theory or replace it by another theory, that change is progressive if and only if the later version is a more effective problem-solver (in the sense just defined) than its predecessor." [p. 68]

But Laudan is not just interested in explicating the concept of scientific progress as it relates to a succession of individual theories. Like Kuhn before him, he is interested in the progress of some larger conceptual structure. For Kuhn, it was the paradigm; for Laudan, it is the "research tradition." A research tradition "is a set of assumptions: assumptions about the basic kinds of entities in the world, assumptions about how those entities interact, assumptions about the proper methods to use for constructing and testing theories about those entities." [p. 97] In other words, a specific theory within a research tradition "articulates a very specific ontology and a number of specific and testable laws about nature," and a research tradition "specifies a general ontology for nature, and a general method for solving natural problems within a given natural domain." [p. 84]

Laudan's "research tradition" differs from the "research programme" of Lakatos since, unlike Lakatos, the "core assumptions" of research traditions are in fact testable and can be modified through time, although enough core assumptions remain relatively constant through time to give the research tradition continuity. [p. 98] Furthermore, while the collection of theories in a research tradition are related to each other, each theory does not specifically *entail* some predecessor theory, as with Lakatos.

How should research traditions be appraised? Laudan splits the appraisal process into two different contexts: the context of acceptance and the context of pursuit. He affirms that there are many circumstances, such as when one is conducting an experiment or when one is going to take some "practical action," where it is absolutely necessary to *accept* a theory or research tradition, meaning *"to treat it as if it were true."* [p. 108, emphasis in original] Under such circumstances, his recommendation is to "choose the theory (or research tradition) with the highest problem-solving adequacy." [p. 109] Therefore, "the choice of one tradition over its rivals is progressive (and thus a rational) choice precisely to the extent that the chosen tradition is a better problem solver than its rivals." This choice criterion is better than other models of evaluation because "it is *workable*: unlike both inductivist and falsificationist models, the basic evaluation measures seem (at least in principle) to pose fewer difficulties." [p. 109] At first glance, Laudan's criterion for "acceptance" would seem to be largely tautological, i.e., "if you want to adopt a theory for the solution of a problem of 'practical action,' then choose the theory that is the best 'problem-solver.'" However, we must keep in mind that Laudan's "problem-solving" relates not to "practical" problems, but rather to the problems that a theory has in explaining phenomena (in addition to "conceptual" problems).

Laudan relates that both Kuhn and Feyerabend have pointed out numerous occasions in the history of science where scientists chose to work on or pursue theories or research traditions that were not the best confirmed or most acceptable: "Indeed the emergence of virtually every new research tradition occurs under just such circumstances." [p. 110] Both Kuhn and Feyerabend concluded that these instances made the history of science seem to be "largely irrational." For example, Kuhn claims that the decision to pursue a new theory or paradigm is a decision that "can only be made on faith." [254, p. 157] However, Laudan claims that "scientists can have good reasons for working on theories that they would not accept." [p. 110] What are these "good reasons"?

He claims that "it is always rational to pursue any research tradition which has a higher rate of progress than its rivals (even if the former has a lower problem-solving effectiveness)." [p. 111] That is, the scientist should calculate the *rate* at which a research tradition is progressing through time and pursue that tradition that has the highest rate because "the rationality of pursuit is based on relative progress rather than overall success." [p. 112]

Progress and Its Problems: An Evaluation.   Many aspects of Laudan's general theory of science have significant merit. Certainly, much of science has to do with problem-solving (both "practical" and empirical), and many of the activities of scientists involve the search for problem-solutions. Distinguishing the empirical problems that confront a theory from its conceptual problems is a useful step forward in our understanding of theories. Clearly distinguishing between the context of acceptance and the context of pursuit clarifies much of the confusion in the theories of Lakatos, Kuhn, and Feyerabend. That is, even if it should be the case that "anything goes" in the context of pursuit (or discovery), this most assuredly does not imply that "anything goes" in the context of acceptance (or justification). Laudan's contention that both acceptance and pursuit can be viewed as having a significant rational component also seems meritorious, especially in light of the implicit irrationalism of Kuhn and the explicit irrationalism of Feyerabend. Finally, Laudan's refutation of the view that rival theories are incommensurable and, hence, incapable of being objectively compared (relativism) is both convincing and consistent with other modern writers. Nevertheless, there are some major shortcomings in Laudan's theory, some of which are devastating. Many of these have been pointed out by McMullin [433], Musgrave [460], Kordig [342], Krips [351], Sarkar [558],and Leplin [388]. Given that Laudan in his *Science and Values* [375] has altered his theory of science in many important respects as a result of these criticisms, we shall only briefly review the major "problems" of *Progress and Its Problems*.

Recall that Laudan attacked all those "philosophers and scientists since the time of Parmenides and Plato" who had been "seeking to justify science as a truth-seeking enterprise" on the basis that such an aim is "utopian" because "we apparently do not have any way of knowing for sure (or even with some confidence) that science is true, or probable, or that it is getting closer to the truth." [pp. 125, 6, and 7] Therefore, Laudan defends his model of scientific progress on the following basis: "The workability of the problem-solving model is its greatest virtue." [p. 127] It is important to note that Laudan is *not* just claiming that science is involved in problem-solving nor that in some intuitive sense modern science solves "more problems" than the science of the 17th century. Rather, he claims his model is "workable" and that his system of "counting and weighting of problems" will yield a "calculus of problem weights" that can be objectively used to appraise theories and research traditions for both the context of acceptance and pursuit. [p. 32] But, is such a procedure of "counting and weighting" really "workable"? The reader should consider the following (very partial) list of activities that such a procedure would necessarily entail:

1. Determine in an unambiguous fashion what situation constitutes a "problem."
2. Determine what shall constitute the "solving" of a problem by a theory.
3. Separate the individual problems sufficiently sharply to enable one to count them.
4. Unambiguously assign relative weights to both empirical problem-solutions and conceptual problems.
5. Develop a measuring procedure with metrical properties powerful enough to be able to subtract the negative weight of conceptual problems from the positive weight of the solved empirical problems.
6. Unambiguously add up the problem-solving adequacy of all the theories in an entire research tradition to measure the problem-solving adequacy of the larger structure.
7. Identify over appropriate time periods the rate of change in the problem-solving adequacy of rival research traditions.

Contrary to the claims of Laudan, all the commentators on Laudan's theory have pointed out that his problem-solving model of "counting and weighting" is patently *unworkable*. Furthermore, the claim that scientists in the past have actually *used* such a procedure to guide their decisions in the contexts of acceptance and pursuit borders on pure fantasy. Most tellingly for an historian of science, in Laudan's entire book he gives not a single case history where he actually applies his "counting and weighting" procedure. One might choose to defend the problem-solving model on the basis that it is a "rational reconstruction" of historical episodes. For example, Lakatos always claimed that his theory represented a "rational reconstruction" of science and that his model of rationality could be used to appraise historical episodes as to "what actually happened in the light of the rational reconstruction, pointing out the discrepancies between them." [460, p. 457] However, Laudan specifically rejects the "rational reconstruction" procedure of Lakatos as being an inappropriate use of historical data. [pp. 168-70] (It should be pointed out that according to Musgrave, Laudan's discussion of Lakatos' method of "rational reconstruction" is grossly inaccurate and a "caricature." [460, p. 457])

Laudan's theory of science conclusively fails its own criteria of adequacy: (1) His theory is not in accord with the history of science, and (2) it provides no "workable" procedure for "acceptance" or "pursuit," for, in Laudan's own pejorative terms, his theory is "utopian." In fact, we can substitute "maximum problem-solving" for the word "truth" in Laudan's own criteria: "No one has been able to demonstrate that a system like science, with the methods it has at its disposal, can be guaranteed to reach [maximum problem-solving], either in the short or in the long run. Furthermore, "no one has been able even to say what it would mean to be 'closer to' [maximum problem-solving], let alone to offer criteria for determining how we could assess such proximity."

Why has Laudan's theory of science foundered? In part because he attempted to develop a general theory of science that would be non-relativistic and rational, while at the same time being truth-independent. First of all, although Laudan attempts to avoid the words "true" and "false," Musgrave [460] has shown that on numerous occasions throughout *Progress and Its Problems* Laudan implicitly appeals to truth. For example, a research tradition's problem-solving effectiveness, for Laudan, relies in part on recognizing and solving genuine (true) empirical problems, rather than pseudo (false) problems. Also in Laudan's "context of acceptance" the scientist is to "treat the theory as if it were true." [p. 108] *More generally, and much more importantly, there are good grounds for believing that any theory of science which ignores truth is unlikely to escape sophistry, relativism, and irrationalism.* An example from Laudan's own work will illustrate this.

In 1982, the Arkansas "scientific creationism" trial of *McLean vs. Arkansas* came to a close. Federal judge William R. Overton ruled that the Arkansas law requiring that "creation science" be taught along with the theory of evolution violated the "separation of church and state" clause in the United States Constitution.[1] Judge Overton's opinion found that creation science was not science since it did not satisfy five essential properties (suggested by numerous witnesses) that distinguish scientific knowledge from other forms: (1) guided by natural law, (2) explanation by reference to natural law, (3) testable against the empirical world, (4) conclusions that are tentative and not necessarily the final word, and (5) falsifiable.

In an article entitled "Commentary: Science at the Bar—Causes for Concern," [374] Laudan vigorously attacked the opinion of the judge. He did not disagree with the verdict: "The verdict itself is probably to be commended." [p. 16] However, he believed it was "reached for all the wrong reasons and by a chain of argument which is hopelessly suspect." [p. 16] Laudan then opines once again that there is no "universal" characteristic or set of characteristics to demarcate science from either nonscience or pseudoscience. However, given that Laudan agrees with the verdict of Judge Overton (but not with the reasoning), how does Laudan believe the "correct" verdict should have been justified? One

---

[1] See *Science, Technology, and Human Values*, Vol. 7, Summer 1982, for a complete discussion of the facts of the case, its verdict, and the testimony of witnesses. See: Michael Ruse, "Response to the Commentary," *Science, Technology, and Human Values*, Vol. 7, Fall 1982, pp. 19-23, for a response to Laudan [543].

might suppose that Laudan would be forced to argue, on the basis of *Progress and Its Problems*, that the theory of evolution should be accepted because it has a "higher problem-solving adequacy" than creation science. However, he does not resort to his own theory of science. We do not know for sure why. It may be because his theory of science specifically stated that "religious theories" are, and must be, considered legitimate conceptual problems for scientific theories. Or, it may be that by 1982 he had accepted the fact that "maximum problem-solving" was an untenable theory of science, as pointed out by his critics. In any respect, he did not use "problem-solving" for justification.

How did Laudan propose Judge Overton should have justified his ruling? Laudan persuasively argues that "to make the inter-linked claims that Creationism is neither falsifiable nor testable is to assert that creationism makes no empirical assertions whatever. *That is surely false.*" [p. 16, emphasis added] He then discusses many of the empirical assertions that creationism makes and reports: "In brief these claims are testable, they have been tested, and *they have failed those tests.*" [p. 16, emphasis added] He continues, "Indeed, if any doctrine in the history of science *has ever been falsified,* it is the set of claims associated with 'creation-science.'" [p.17] Therefore, "The real objection to such creationist claims as that of the (relative) invariability of species is not that such invariability has not been explained by scientific laws, but rather that the evidence for invariability is less robust than the evidence for its contrary, variability." [p. 18]

As the preceding quotations clearly show, Laudan argues that Judge Overton should have justified his decision on the fact that the evidence is overwhelming in favor of the truth or approximate truth of the theory of evolution against its rival, creation science. Note the phrases "is surely false," "have been tested," "failed those tests," and "been falsified." Indeed, as stated previously, it is almost impossible to speak intelligibly about science without using the concept of "truth," or some surrogate for it. A philosophy which states on the one hand that "Determinations of truth and falsity are irrelevant to the *acceptability* or the *pursuitability* of theories and research traditions," [370, p. 120, emphasis added] and on the other hand vigorously attacks a Federal Court judge for not using criteria based on truth and falsity in his judicial determination does not pass minimum standards of coherence and intelligibility.

As will be further discussed in Section 11.3.4, on at least two separate occasions Laudan commits the "philosophers' fallacy of high redefinition." Laudan claims that before we may distinguish science from nonscience, or pseudoscience, we must provide a "universal" demarcation criterion that will "guarantee" that we can unambiguously separate disciplines or research traditions into various categories. Finding no such universal, completely unambiguous criterion, he proposes that we discard the concept of "science" vs. "nonscience" altogether. Like-wise, Laudan claims that before we may warrantedly believe that a the-ory is true or false; or is approximately true; or has more truth-content than a rival theory; or is closer to the truth than a rival theory, we must demonstrate that we have a methodology that will *guarantee* our ability to know-with-certainty that a theory or knowledge-claim will be as described. Finding no such methodology to guarantee such results, Laudan claims (with unrecognized ironic certainty) that the concepts "truth" and "falsity" are "irrelevant" to science. Having already suc-cumbed to the philosophers' fallacy on these two important questions, it is no wonder that Laudan's general theory of science fails to produce in-telligible discourse about its subject. We turn now to a discussion of "later Laudan," i.e., his general theory of science proposed in *Science and Values.*

11.2.2   Laudan's Science and Values

Whereas problem solving was the focal construct in Laudan's first gen-eral theory of science, the central construct in *Science and Values* [375] is his "research tradition." All research traditions contain three major domains: (1) theories, (2) methods, and (3) aims. [375, p. 63] A Lau-dan "research tradition" is similar to a Kuhnian "paradigm", except that a research tradition does not have a *Weltanschauung*. To understand *Science and Values*, we need to recapitulate how relativism has been "moderated" in recent years. As will be recalled, the "early" Kuhn im-plied that each scientist had a *Weltanschauung* which completely deter-mined the scientist's theories, methods, and aims. Therefore, changes in theories and paradigms had to come about by way of "*Gestalt* shifts" and "religious conversions" because the theories and paradigms were incommensurable. The "later" Kuhn both recognized and rejected the reality relativism and conceptual framework-relativism implicit in his earlier work. Even such strong advocates of relativism as Gerald Dop-pelt began to recognize that both Kuhnian reality relativism and con-ceptual framework-relativism were simply untenable:

> If rival scientific paradigms are as insular, self-enclosed, and impris-oned within their own language as Kuhn maintains, in what sense can they be rivals or compete? If they cannot communicate or argue, how and on what can they disagree? If each is necessarily focused on its own data and problems, in what sense do they offer incompatible ac-counts of the *same* subject-matter or domain? The clear implication is that Kuhn's incommensurability cannot account for the evident facts of theoretical conflict in scientific development. . . . if rival paradigms can thus speak to the same empirical situation, they must share *some* common concepts, data and problems. How is this possible, given Kuhnian incommensurability? *The implication is clearly that Kuhn is inconsistent and must violate his own relativism in developing a half-*

way plausible account of scientific development. [Doppelt, in 350, p. 117, emphasis added]

Given the nonviability of both reality and conceptual framework-relativism, Doppelt advocates what he calls "moderate relativism." Basically, moderate relativism is a relativism with respect to the aims, values, and goals of science. Thus, cognitive value relativism holds the following:

1. The aims, goals, or values in science are relative to a paradigm, research program, or research tradition.
2. The aims, goals, or values cannot be objectively, impartially, or nonarbitrarily evaluated across different paradigms, research programs, or research tradition.

Doppelt maintains that this version of relativism was implicit in Kuhn's work and, although a much more "moderate" form of relativism than its reality and conceptual framework predecessors, it still justifies that science is irrational and there has been no progress in scientific knowledge. One of the major aims of Laudan's *Science and Values* was to address the issue of cognitive value relativism: "Indeed, when I set out to write *Science and Values*, I had the Doppelt-ized version of Kuhn's position very much in mind." That is, Laudan sought to "explore the question whether—once we factor scientists' aims and methods into a description of their work—it follows that, as Kuhn and Doppelt maintained, there could never be rationally compelling grounds for preferring one tradition of research to another." [377, p. 223]

How do scientists choose between genuinely rival theories? Laudan argues that relativists such as Hesse, Bloor, Kuhn, and Collins have fallaciously argued the "underdetermination thesis" that "since theory choice is undetermined by methodological rules, it follows that no rational preference is possible among rival theories, which entails, in turn, that every theory is as well supported as any other, and that every party to a scientific debate is thus as rational as every other." Therefore, he notes that advocates of the underdetermination thesis "confusedly take the fact that our rules fail to pick out a unique theory that satisfies them as a warrant for asserting the inability of the rules to make any discriminations whatever with respect to which theories are or are not in compliance with them." [375, p. 30] Therefore, Laudan takes the position that, in general, theory choice among genuinely rival theories is normally made by scientists in precisely the manner historically advocated, i.e., from among the rival theories, the scientists determine which is best supported by the evidence by using methodological rules.

Suppose there is a dispute concerning the most appropriate methodological rules? That is, how do methodological rules change in science? Laudan contends that methodological rules sometimes change as a result of the changing aims and goals of scientific communities and sometimes as a result of changes in our theories about the world. For example, Laudan recounts that the discovery of the so-called "placebo effect" brought about a change in a methodological rule in medical science. Medical researchers discovered that "many patients report an improvement upon being given an apparent medication, even if (unbeknownst to the patient) it is pharmacologically inert." [375, p. 38] Therefore, medical researchers adopted methodological rules to guide inquiry and went from simple, controlled experiments to "single-blind" and "double-blind" tests. Thus, Laudan claims that changes in methodological rules are not "underdetermined" in any strong sense but are the results of rational debate and "good reasons."

Do different research traditions entail different cognitive values? Do different research traditions have different aims, objectives, and goals? Laudan contends they do. Moreover, he contends that these cognitive aims change through time within the same research traditions. For example, at one point in time a particular research tradition may have the aim of "simplicity" and at a later point in time the aim of "mathematical elegance" may become much more important. Unlike Kuhn, Laudan contends that these changes in cognitive values can be rationally explained and disputes rationally adjudicated. He believes that several mechanisms are readily available and used by scientists to resolve disputes about goals and aims. If it were otherwise, the specter of relativism would emerge again: "In short, radical relativism about science seems to be an inevitable corollary of accepting a) that different scientists have different goals, b) that there is no rational deliberation possible about the suitability of different goals, and c) that goals, methods, and factual claims invariably come in covariate clusters." [375, p. 50]

What are the mechanisms or criteria that Laudan suggests can be used (and are used) to evaluate cognitive values in science? First, he claims (consistent with his previous work) the cognitive values in science must not be "utopian." Goals are "demonstrably utopian" when "a certain cognitive goal cannot possibly be achieved, given our understanding of logic or the laws of nature." [p.52] Laudan gives, as an example, the goal of "infallible knowledge." On the other hand, a goal suffers from "semantic utopianism" when a goal cannot be characterized in a "succinct and cogent way." Therefore, goals may not be "imprecise," or "ambiguous." As examples, he notes that "such familiarly cited cognitive goals as simplicity and elegance often have this weakness, because most advocates of these goals can offer no coherent definition or characterization of them." [p. 52] Third, a goal may suffer from "epistemic utopianism." That is, "it sometimes happens that an agent can give a perfectly clear definition of his goal state and that the goal is not demonstrably utopian, but that nonetheless its advocates cannot specify (and seem to be working with no implicit form of) a criterion for determining when the value is present or satisfied and when it is not." [p.53] As previously discussed, Laudan gave the goal of "truth" as an example of a utopian goal in *P & P* on the basis that we "do not have any way of knowing for sure (or even with some confidence) that science is true, or probable, or that it is getting closer to the truth." [370, p. 127] His 1982 comments about Judge Overton's "fallacious" reasoning notwithstanding, Laudan in 1984 again claims truth as a goal "cannot be rationally propounded." [375, p. 53]

Finally, Laudan suggests that the cognitive values in science can be evaluated on the basis of "reconciling theory and practice." That is, there should be a congruence between "explicit" and "implicit" goals. [p. 53] We can criticize a scientist or a scientific community that claims to be pursuing one goal, but whose actions and behaviors imply the pursuit of some other goal, or set of goals. Sophistry would seem to be an obvious example of lack of "congruence."

Given that Laudan specifically states that the goals of truth, simplicity, and elegance will fail on utopian grounds, what goal or set of goals does Laudan recommend for science? Given Laudan's previous general theory of science, one might suspect that "problem-solving" would be recommended as a central, or overriding goal. However, such is not the case: Problem solving does not even appear in the subject index of *Science and Values*. Whereas, the "early Laudan" general theory of science confidently proposed and persuasively (to some people) argued that problem-solving was the major aim of science, the "later Laudan," with equal confidence and great rhetorical skill, argues that there *is* no basic aim to science. Moreover, *Science and Values* contains not a single example of an aim or goal that Laudan argues would pass his own criteria for evaluating cognitive values. This should disturb those readers who recall the "early Laudan" theory proposing a "counting and weighting" procedure but never giving a single example using such a procedure.

If "maximal problem-solving" is no longer the goal toward which science is progressing, and if developing theory, lawlike statements and other knowledge-claims that truly represent the external world is "utopian," then how does science progress, if it progresses at all? Laudan's new view on progress is:

> Does a certain sequence of theories move scientists closer to realizing or achieving a certain goal state than they were before? Then progress (relative to that goal state) has occurred. If not, then not. The matter really is as simple as that. [p. 65]

We should note just how much Laudan has changed his position. Laudan's earlier theory claimed that any scientific community or research tradition was rational and making progress if it was progressing toward the overriding goal of maximal problem-solving. Laudan's new view is that any scientific community or research tradition is rational and making progress if it has achieved or is making progress toward achieving any (nonutopian) goal or set of goals that it self-selects. Laudan's new view will surely strike many readers as more irrational than even Kuhn, who (ironically) is Laudan's chief foil. Although Kuhn rejected the concept that "changes of paradigm carry scientists and those who learn from them closer and closer to the truth," he did claim that science makes progress in its problem-solving capabilities: "Yet despite these and other losses to the individual communities, the nature of such communities provides a *virtual guarantee* that both the list of problems solved by science and the precision of individual problem solutions will grow and grow." [355, p. 170, emphasis added] (Many commentators in marketing and the social sciences have misinterpreted Kuhn on this point. For example, "[f]or Kuhn, science progresses through revolutions, but there is no guarantee that it progresses toward anything. . .". [13, p. 22]) Laudan closes his discussion on scientific progress with: "There is simply no escape from the fact that determinations of progress must be relativized to a certain set of ends, and that there is no uniquely appropriate set of those ends." [p. 66]

Science and Values: An Evaluation.   How well does *S&V* achieve its stated objectives of being historically accurate, exhibiting the rationality of science, and being nonrelativistic, while at the same time avoiding having truth as an overriding value in science? Although *S&V* has a relatively short history, several critical analyses have appeared, including Lugg [405], Suppes [609], Doppelt [155], and Brown [87]. Briefly, these writers point out that (1) Laudan's historical examples often do not support his substantive positions, (2) he fails on numerous occasions to adequately differentiate between what constitutes a goal of science versus a methodological rule, (3) he confuses the pragmatics of theory choice with cognitive values related to theory choice, and (4) his theory may actually embrace relativism rather than avoid it (read carefully the quote in the last sentence of the preceding paragraph). Readers are urged to consult the above citations for elaborations on these views. Here, we shall focus exclusively on Laudan's view of the aims of science.

Laudan claims that there are many aims in science, but no overriding aim or unique set of aims. Nevertheless, some aims are appropriate and others inappropriate, the latter, having failed his criteria of realizability (being nonutopian) and/or congruency. The aims of truth, simplicity and elegance, he contends, fail these criteria. Laudan makes the task of evaluating his position difficult because he nowhere gives us a list of aims that he either shows conclusively (or even suggests) might pass his criteria of adequacy. Nevertheless, we must start somewhere, and perhaps using "maximum problem-solving" as a goal to evaluate would shed light on the issues involved. Such a goal would seem to serve as a useful example since Laudan held it in high regard in his earlier work and Kuhn believed that increasing problem-solving was, most assuredly, an *outcome* of science, if not its goal. Is maximum problem-solving an appropriate goal for science? Does it pass the realizability and congruency criteria? First, just like the goal of truth, no one could ever claim that any particular theory has achieved the goal of solving the *maximum* number of problems. There could always exist some (unknown) theory that solves more problems, just like there could always exist some (unknown) theory that more truly corresponds with the external world. However, this is much too facile a refutation. Is it not possible that we can give an explicit and rigorous explication of what it would mean for our theories to be progressing in the direction of solving the maximum number of problems? Could we not show we are coming "closer to" our goal? To answer this question, we can turn to Laudan's own "counting and weighting" methodology discussed in *P&P*. However, as has been demonstrated by numerous commentators on *P&P* (as previously discussed), any attempt to apply Laudan's "counting and weighting" methodology runs into the insurmountable difficulties of unambiguously identifying "problems," "problem-solutions," and differential weights on a common metric. These difficulties seem to doom the task of unambiguously identifying when one is "coming closer to" the goal of maximum problem-solving. In fact, the difficulties seem no less than those that Laudan attributes to the task of determining when one is "coming closer to" a theory that truly explains some aspect of reality. In short, a strong case can be made that "maximum problem-solving" fails Laudan's criteria for a goal to be appropriate for science. Thus, we have the highly curious situation where maximum problem-solving has gone from being the central, overriding aim of science in Laudan's earlier work to it's being an *impermissible* aim of science in his later theory of science. Should this give readers grounds to question what is going on here? Indeed it should.

A fundamental flaw in Laudan's general theory of science is that it confuses (in Rokeach's [538] terms) "terminal values" and "instrumental values." That is, Laudan confuses enduring, end-state values that are prized in and of themselves, with instrumental values that are short-range and valued because they tend to promote, or lead toward, terminal values. Examples abound of objectives in science that are demonstrably realizable, e.g., developing a computer program to shorten the time required to do a particular multiple regression from 5 seconds to 4 seconds, completing a research report within the minimum number of pages required by a scholarly journal, cleaning the laboratory before leaving for home, and so on. Nevertheless, no one would suggest that these "realizable" objectives warrant consideration for the *goals* of science. Rather, they may or may not be instrumentally efficacious objectives leading toward more enduring, more important goals. Furthermore, self-serving, sociological goals like Anderson's "to advance our own status within the field" [in 99, p. 15] hardly warrant consideration as goals worthy of scientific communities. Given Laudan's well-known objections to the "strong thesis" in the sociology of scientific knowledge (see 370, pp. 196-22], he would be (rightly) loath to give serious consideration to institutionalizing such goals. In short, Laudan conflates the long-range *mission* of science with its short-range, realizable, "nonutopian," *objectives*.

The points made in the preceding paragraph may be generalized even further. There is a strong *prima facie* case that any cognitive value or goal for individual scientific communities, or science in general, that would be considered *worthy* of pursuit would most likely fail Laudan's utopian criterion. And this is as it should be. The terminal values of all societal institutions are, and ought to be, "utopian." When Laudan claims that "determinations of truth and falsity are irrelevant to the acceptability or the pursuitability of theories and research traditions," he is making a claim analogous to "determinations of *justice* are irrelevant to the legal system." Both are "utopian" (and appropriately so). As Watkins has stated most succinctly: "[T]o say that truth is no part of the aim of science is on a par with saying that curing is no part of the aim of medicine or that profit is no part of the aim of commerce." [627, p. 126]

Many exasperated readers may by now be crying "Enough!" and asking: Is all philosophy of science either incoherent or useless to practicing researchers, or both? Is there not a view of science that is intelligible, non-sophist, takes both science and truth seriously, and, at the same time, addresses some of the obvious deficiencies in the logical empiricists' research program? Many philosophers and practicing scientists believe that the "ism" coming closest is what is often referred to as "modern realism" or "scientific realism."[2]

11.3   SCIENTIFIC REALISM

After the repudiation of Kuhnian relativism in the 1970s, the philosophy of science turned sharply toward a *realist* orientation: "Contemporary work in philosophy of science increasingly subscribes to the position that it is a central aim of science to come to knowledge of how the world *really* is, that correspondence between theories and reality is a central aim of science. . . ."[607, p. 649] Just as modern relativism and constructivism have their roots in Hegelian idealism, modern versions of realism stem from the classical realism of Russell, Moore, and (early)

---

[2] Our discussion of scientific realism follows that in Shelby D. Hunt, "Truth in Marketing Theory and Research," [312a]. See also Blair and Zinkham [67].

Wittgenstein (see Section 9.1). Whereas relativism/constructivism either explicitly or implicitly accepts the Hegelian view that "the world does not exist independently of its being perceived," modern realists accept the classical realist position that "the world exists independently of its being perceived." Modern realists reject Hegelian idealism on many of the same grounds as did their classical predecessors. That is, idealism is self-refuting; represents sophistry, rather than genuine belief; confuses the act of perceiving an object with the object so perceived; and violates fundamental principles of intelligible discourse (see Section 9.1.1). Modern realism, or "scientific realism," is usually associated with authors such as Maxwell [426], Sellars [573], Putnam [511], Bhaskar [63],MacKinnon [414], McMullin [434], Boyd [75], Levin [395], Leplin [389], and Harré [250]. Causey notes that "the majority of philosophers of science now profess to be scientific realists." [111, p. 192] Nevertheless, Leplin observes: "[S]cientific realism is a majority position whose advocates are so divided as to appear a minority." [389, p. 1] He lists ten "characteristic realist claims no majority of which, even subjected to reasonable qualification, is likely to be endorsed by any avowed realist." [p. 1] These are:

1. The best current scientific theories are at least approximately true.
2. The central terms of the best current theories are genuinely referential.
3. The approximate truth of a scientific theory is sufficient explanation of its predictive success.
4. The (approximate) truth of a scientific theory is the only possible explanation of its predictive success.
5. A scientific theory may be approximately true even if referentially unsuccessful.
6. The history of at least the mature sciences shows progressive approximation to a true account of the physical world.
7. The theoretical claims of scientific theories are to be read literally, and so read are definitively true or false.
8. Scientific theories make genuine, existential claims.
9. The predictive success of a theory is evidence for the referential success of its central aims.
10. Science aims at a literally true account of the physical world, and its success is to be reckoned by its progress toward achieving this aim.

In short, there is no standard "general theory of science" according to scientific realism. Although most philosophers of science adopt some kind of realist orientation to science, scientific realism does not constitute a "school" developed around a general theory of science, such as the provocative theories offered by Kuhn, Feyerabend, Lakatos, or Laudan. This situation has led to a proliferation of "mini-theories," representing versions of scientific realism: transcendental realism [63], ontic realism [414], methodological realism [390], evolutionary naturalistic realism [Hooker in 116], referential realism [250], constructive realism [Giere in 116], and internal realism [513], among others.

Aside from a rejection of idealism/relativism/constructivism, is there any common denominator for the many versions of scientific realism? Even given the radical heterogeneity of the various versions of realism, McMullin suggests the following statement as a consensus fundamental tenet: *"The basic claim made by scientific realism ... is that the long-term success of a scientific theory gives reason to believe that something like the entities and structure postulated by the theory actually exists."* [434, p. 26] McMullin points out that there are four important qualifications built into this version of the fundamental thesis of scientific realism. First, a theory must be successful over a significant period of time in order to give good reason for believing in the entities and structure implied by the theory. Second, the success of a theory gives "reason" to believe and not conclusive warrant to believe in the entities and structure. That is, McMullin wishes to avoid the philosophers' fallacy of providing that success warrants knowledge-with-certainty and the problems of the K-K thesis. Third, the success of a theory provides good reason to believe that "something like" the entities and structure postulated by the theory actually exists. Again, in order to avoid the philosophers' fallacy, the entities and structure believed to exist in the real world need not be *exactly* like the ones postulated by the theory. Four, the postulated entities do not have a special, privileged form of existence. That is, the entities are not like the "essences" of Aristotle. To some, the fundamental thesis of scientific realism may seem rather innocuous. However, this thesis is totally at odds with the views of the logical positivists, is significantly different from the perspective of the logical empiricists, is *anathema* to the relativists and constructivists, and has been completely rejected by historical empiricists such as Laudan. To understand why, we need to develop the implications of the fundamental thesis of scientific realism in more detail, starting with the relationship between the success of science and scientific realism.

11.3.1   Realism and the Success of Science

McMullin uses examples from geology and chemistry to examine the relationship between scientific realism and success in science. We shall use an example from medical science, the eradication of smallpox. Such an example would seem particularly pertinent for marketing, since both marketing and medicine have "basic" and "applied" dimensions and the claim is often made that marketing (and the marketing academic discipline) should be "more like" medicine.

The disease called smallpox has plagued the human community for thousands of years.[3] There are numerous references to a disease with symptoms much like smallpox in the records of ancient India and Africa. For example, an analysis of the remains of several Egyptian mummies shows evidence of smallpox. In any respect, by the Middle Ages smallpox was a scourge in most of Asia, Africa, and Europe: Three million people died of smallpox in India's 1769 epidemic; by the end of the eighteenth century, Europe was losing over four hundred thousand people each year to smallpox, and it was responsible for over one-third of all the blindness in Europe.

By the early part of the eighteenth century, it was widely recognized that people who once had smallpox seemed never to get the disease again. Furthermore, several European countries began adopting inoculation (as distinguished from "vaccination") procedures to prevent people from acquiring the disease during an epidemic. (Inoculation procedures had been used in Asia for several hundred years.) With the inoculation procedure, the subject was injected with material from a smallpox lesion obtained from an infected person. Inoculation became commonplace in England after a publication of the Royal Society, authored by James Jurian, showed that the risk of dying from smallpox from the inoculation was about one percent; whereas the overall risk of dying from smallpox was about twelve percent, and in times of epidemics the risk rose to about twenty percent. However, in addition to the risk of death, the inoculation procedure also had the disadvantage of the inoculated person spreading the disease to others. Furthermore, many religious groups were vigorously opposed to inoculation procedures on the basis that diseases were a result of God being angry and, therefore, inoculations were "thwarting God's will."

Edward Jenner (1749-1823) was a physician, living in Berkeley, England, who for years had heard rumors to the effect that "country girls" who had been infected by the mild disease called "cowpox" never contracted smallpox. Intrigued, Jenner began systematically gathering data on those who claimed to be immune from smallpox on the basis of having already had cowpox. The data seemed to confirm the claims of the "country girls." However, would someone *inoculated* with cowpox be immune from smallpox? On May 14, 1796, Jenner inoculated one James Phipps with cowpox taken from a sore on the hand of a milkmaid who had recently become infected. The child developed a mild reaction similar to that of a favorable smallpox inoculation. On July 1, Jenner inoculated the boy with smallpox taken from another patient, and the inoculation produced no significant reaction. Elated with the results of

---

[3] The information on smallpox in this section (and much more) can be found in Donald R. Hopkins *Princes and Peasants: Smallpox in History* (Chicago: University of Chicago Press: 1983) and Frank Fenner and David White, *Medical Virology* (New York: Academic Press: 1976).

his experiment, Jenner repeated his experiment on five more children in 1798, when a fresh outbreak of cowpox next made the virus available to him. After the experiments yielded the same positive results, Jenner triumphantly announced his findings in a small pamphlet. Within a few short years, Jenner's experiments were repeated on much larger samples, and "vaccination" procedures with cowpox virus became commonplace. Even so, smallpox continued to kill thousands of people over the next two hundred years.

It should be pointed out that, of course, Jenner never "saw" a virus in his entire life. Although the "germ theory" of contagious diseases was actively being promulgated during his time, it was not widely accepted. In 1836, using the recently invented achromatic microscope, Agostino Bassi (1773-1856) was the first person to isolate a specific microscopic organism that causes a disease. In this case, he isolated a parasitic fungus that causes a common disease in silkworms. In 1898 Loeffler and Frosch demonstrated that some diseases were caused by microorganisms so small that they would pass through a very fine filter. Such microorganisms came to be known as "filterable viruses," and the organism causing smallpox soon came to be known as one of these, as did the organism causing poliomyelitis. In fact, viruses are so small that it was not until the invention of the electron microscope in 1947 that anyone "saw" a virus. The advent of the electron microscope brought about rapid advances in our knowledge of the characteristics and properties of the smallpox virus, including its internal chemistry and how it is able to attack human cells and force them to reproduce the virus.

It was already well known by the time of the electron microscope that the smallpox virus could not reproduce itself outside a human host. Therefore, if there ever came a time when no one in the world had smallpox, the disease (theoretically) should be completely eradicated. This was the program adopted by the World Health Organization at its 1966 meeting in Geneva. At that time, forty-four countries were still reporting smallpox and the disease was endemic in thirty-three of them. The WHO set a deadline of ten years for the eradication of the disease through massive vaccination programs. The last known case of smallpox was in 1978, when the virus escaped from a laboratory in Birmingham, England. In 1980 the thirty-third World Health Assembly accepted the Final Report of the Global Commission for the Certification of Smallpox Eradication.

Most people would consider the eradication of smallpox to be a significant "success story" for science. How can this success story be explained? Scientific realism postulates the following theory to explain the success of the smallpox eradication program:

> If it is true that (1) something like the phenomenon denoted by "small-
> pox disease" exists, and (2) something like the entity denoted by

"smallpox virus" exists, and (3) the smallpox virus cannot exist outside human subjects, and (4) something like the "cowpox virus" exists and (5) vaccinating people with cowpox virus will cause the body to produce antibodies that can successfully attack the smallpox virus, then (6) vaccinating people with cowpox virus will prevent them from contracting smallpox, and therefore (7) instituting a massive vaccination program throughout all parts of the world where smallpox currently exists can eradicate smallpox.

The preceding argument shows (in highly summarized form) how scientific realism can explain the millions of "micro" success stories making up the "macro" success story of smallpox eradication by science. Note the crucial role that "entities" play, e.g., "something like the smallpox virus exists." Furthermore, "structures" of entities play a key role, e.g., "if injections of cowpox virus cause the body to produce antibodies." Now, although the smallpox eradication is a highly visible "macro" success story, over the last four hundred years science has produced, literally, countless such episodes where the knowledge obtained through science has been pragmatically successful in solving real-world problems and empirically successful in explaining and predicting phenomena. What else, other than some form of scientific realism, can explain the pragmatic and empirical success of science? That is, explaining the *failure* of a program like the smallpox eradication program would be easy. For example, if the injections of cowpox virus *do not* cause the body to produce antibodies, then the eradication program would likely fail. But, what other viable theory is there, except scientific realism, to explain the success of the smallpox eradication program in particular and the overall pragmatic success of science in general? Aside from divine intervention, there currently exists no rival theory. In Putnam's terms, "The positive argument for realism is that it is the only philosophy that doesn't make the success of science a miracle." [511, p. 69]

How does science progress? As will be recalled, most theories of science fail miserably in enabling us to understand both the nature and the mechanisms of scientific progress. First of all, scientific realism holds that science does progress by means of the four procedures discussed in Section 9.5, i.e., the development of new theories, the falsification of existing theories, the expansion of the scope of a theory, and the reduction of specific theories into more general theories. However, scientific realism goes much further. In particular, scientific realism maintains that science progresses by (1) discovering new entities, (2) describing better the attributes and characteristics of entities, (3) measuring entities better, and (4) discovering the structure of the relationships among entities, including, most importantly, *causal* relationships.

Given that the long-term success of a scientific theory gives scientists reason to believe that something like the entities postulated by the theory actually exists, scientific realism holds that science progresses when researchers explore for the existence of new entities. For example, the belief in the "germ theory" of disease warranted researchers to search for other entities that may cause other diseases. Thus, as mentioned, by 1909 medical science had isolated the causal agent of poliomyelitis as a "filterable virus." Likewise, the warranted belief that entities exist prompted researchers to explore (and find) the virus resulting in AIDS (Acquired Immunity Deficiency Syndrome disease). If one does not have "good reason" to believe that the entities in one's theory exist, why engage in a search for them?

Scientific realism also holds that science progresses by better descriptions and better measures of the entities postulated by its theories. For example, how large is the viral entity? What is its shape? What is its chemical composition? By what means does it penetrate the cells of humans? Only scientific realism warrants the exploration of these kinds of questions. To work toward "better" descriptions and "better" measures of *nonexisting* entities is irrational. Absent the belief in scientific realism, the questions could only be explored by the researcher doing the following: "Even though viruses do not exist, I shall attempt to explore precisely how large these nonexisting entities are." Scientific realism holds that researchers do not in fact engage in such elaborate rituals of self-deception.

Given that scientific realism holds that the long-term success of a theory is reason to believe that something like the *structure* postulated by the theory exists, scientific realism warrants the search for how the entities postulated by the theories interact with other entities. For example, how do viruses cause human cells to propagate the production of copies of the original virus? By what means does the viral entity produce the negative complications of the disease, i.e., high temperature, rash, and so forth. By what mechanism and through what route does the cowpox virus cause the human body to produce antibodies? By what mechanism do the antibodies protect the human body against the smallpox virus?

As can be seen, scientific realism dramatically expands the concept of scientific progress to include many of the "lower-level" aspects of science. But "lower-level" does not mean unimportant. On the contrary, by focusing exclusively on "grand theories," many commentators on science have missed much of the real progress in the development of science.

In summary, scientific realism recognizes that science has been enormously successful over the last four hundred years. This success, particularly the pragmatic and empirical aspects of this success, warrants the belief that "something like" the entities and structures postulated by scientific theories actually exist. Perhaps the easiest way to understand scientific realism is to start with "belief," rather than "success." Scientific realism holds that the *belief* that "something like" the entities and the structure postulated by a scientific theory exists provides *warrant* for using the theory to take action. For example, the belief that the cowpox virus exists and that vaccinating people with cowpox virus will protect them from smallpox *warrants* the action of vaccinating people. The action of vaccinating people results in certain consequences. These consequences may be favorable (success) or unfavorable (failure). This pragmatic success (failure) involved in the use of a scientific theory warrants the belief (disbelief) in the truth of the theory. By "truth of the theory" we mean that "something like" the entities and structure postulated by the theory exists. The "something like" becomes synonymous with the notion of "approximate truth." The reader should recognize that the preceding does *not* imply the acceptance of the much-maligned "pragmatic theory of truth." Scientific realism does not contend that the *meaning* of the statement "theory X is true" is the same as accepting the pragmatic consequences of "theory X." Rather, scientific realism holds that the pragmatic and empirical consequences of a theory (its "success") give *warrant* (good reason) for believing the theory to be true, i.e., the world is "something like" the theory.

11.3.2   Scientific Realism and Logical Empiricism

Although scientific realism and logical empiricism share a common belief that science does in fact make progress, scientific realism differs sharply from logical empiricism on two issues. First, most scientific realists do not share the logical empiricists' confidence in formal logic. As will be recalled, the logical empiricists and logical positivists were enamored with the formal logic developed by Russell and Frege. They believed that most philosophical problems could be solved (or at least should be addressed) through the application of formal logic and that science could be reconstructed using it. Although scientific realists certainly make use of the tool of formal logic, they have little confidence that science can be reconstructed using this tool. The second, and more important, difference between scientific realism and logical empiricism is the issue of the "theoretical term/observation term" dichotomy.

Following their logical positivist predecessors, the logical empiricists believed in a sharp distinction between "observation terms" and "theoretical terms" in a scientific theory. Adopting, essentially, the "early" Wittgenstein "picture theory" of meaning, observation terms referred in a nonproblematical manner to entities in the real world. Thus, the logical empiricists adopted a kind of "empirical realism" with respect to observation terms in a theory (see Section 9.2.3). However, some terms in some theories did not *refer* in a direct manner as did the observation terms. The logical empiricists labeled all terms that did not directly refer to some aspect of the observable world as "theoretical terms." In order for scientific theories to be "meaningful" (as opposed to meaningless metaphysics), theoretical terms would have to be given meaning by being defined through "correspondence rules" with observation terms. However, this posed an enormous problem for the logical empiricists: the problem of theoretical dispensibility. As discussed in Hempel's famous article, "The Theoretician's Dilemma," [1958, reprinted in 263], if all theoretical terms can be defined through correspondence with observation terms and if the purpose of science is to determine relationships among observation terms, then theoretical terms are "unnecessary" in science. (See Section 9.3.3 for a discussion of the "Theoretician's Dilemma".)

For scientific realism, the "theoretician's dilemma" is no dilemma at all. Scientific realism dismisses the theoretical term/observational term dichotomy as a false dichotomy. That is, scientific realism acknowledges that *all* the terms in a theory are, properly speaking, "theoretical terms." The phrase "theoretical term" means nothing more than "a term in a theory." For the scientific realists, some terms in a theory may denote something more observable, more detectable, more easily measurable than other terms. In fact, some terms may denote nothing *in principle* observable. However, all the terms in a theory (excepting, of course, mathematical and logical terms) can lay a legitimate claim to existence based on the senses (classical realism) and/or the success of the theory.

Consider, for example, the concept of "intelligence." For the logical positivists and empiricists, "intelligence" would always be a theoretical concept whose *meaning* was totally contained within its measure ("when I say 'intelligence,' this is to be interpreted as a 'shorthand' way of saying 'the results that a person has obtained on the Stanford-Binet intelligence quotient test' "). From the perspective of the scientific realist, the concept of "intelligence" refers to a real, existing, nontangible entity, whose characteristics can be measured or indicated through a variety of measuring devices. Stated in modern measurement terms, scientific realism assumes a *reflective* measurement model, whereas logical empiricism assumes a *formative* measurement model. [288 and 209]

Why could not the logical empiricists adopt the position that theoretical terms could be "real," yet "nonobservable"? Several factors made it impossible for them to adopt a realistic interpretation of theoretical terms. First, like Popper and most other philosophers, the logical empiricists were firmly convinced that Hume was correct: It is impermissible to go from "observables" to "unobservables" (like "cause"), because only deductive logic is an acceptable method of reasoning. Therefore, no "nonobservable" entity may be *inferred* from experience and observation. Second, the logical empiricists implicitly accepted foundationalism and the K-K Thesis. That is, in order for science to be secure, it must rest on incorrigible foundations (observation), and it must proceed by infallible methods. Third, the "lesson" that the logical empiricists had learned from the downfall of Newtonian mechanics was that never again should science allow itself to believe it had found genuine knowledge about nonobservable entities existing in the world. Fourth, and finally, the "lesson" of quantum mechanics was that, since no one knew how to interpret quantum mechanics realistically, all theories should be interpreted instrumentally. That is, theories are calculation devices for making predictions about observable phenomena and do not represent any "underlying reality." In fact, the impact of quantum mechanics on all the debates about the nature of science in the last few decades has been enormous but underappreciated. Therefore, the issue of quantum mechanics and its "lessons" deserve more attention.

11.3.3   Scientific Realism and Quantum Mechanics

Many of the major participants in the debate about the nature of science have had strong backgrounds in physics. For example, Thomas Kuhn's formal training was in physics and Feyerabend's background leaned heavily toward physics. In fact, Feyerabend acknowledges that it was a discussion with Professor C. F. von Weizacker on the foundations of quantum mechanics that played a decisive role in his turn toward relativism and irrationalism. [190, p. 117] As another example, consider the philosophy of Bas C. van Fraassen. Van Fraassen's "constructive empiricism" shares many of the same tenets of the logical positivists and logical empiricists, since constructive empiricism is decidedly antirealist. Ever since the famous paper by Maxwell [426], philosophy has recognized that the concept of "observation" should be interpreted as a continuum. On this view, we have a large number of sense-extending instruments that enable us to "see," e.g., microscopes and telescopes of varying powers. Actually, "observable" is often used, and most appropriately so, as roughly synonymous with "detectable" or "measurable" in modern literature. Van Fraassen's theory of science totally rejects the notion of observation being a continuum and contends that we do not "see" through a microscope. For van Fraassen, only those entities exist that can be, in principle, observed by the unaided human eye. Therefore, genes, bacteria, and viruses do not exist (but the "backsides" of the moon and stars do). [Hacking, in 116, p. 135] Van Fraassen proposes: "That the observable phenomena exhibit these regularities, because of which they fit the theory, is merely a brute fact, and may or may not have an explanation in terms of unobservable facts 'behind the phenomena'—it really does not matter to the goodness of the theory, nor to our understanding of the world." [623, p. 54] What is the aim of science? For van Fraassen's constructive empiricism, "science aims to give us theories which are empirically adequate; and acceptance of a theory involves as belief only that it is empirically adequate." [623, p. 12] How does van Fraassen reach his conclusion that "empirical adequacy" is the only appropriate aim for science? Because he interprets this to be the "lesson" of quantum mechanics: "He [van Fraassen] takes it that the realist is committed to finding hidden variables in quantum mechanics." [434, p. 34] As with most versions of antirealism, van Fraassen's philosophy is an impoverished one. He would have us believe, for example, that the Nobel Prize committee was somehow totally confused about the nature of science when they awarded the Nobel Prize in medicine in 1962 to James D. Watson for his discovery that DNA had the structure of a double helix. (How can nonexisting entities have any structure, let alone, a double helix?)

The "lesson" of quantum mechanics has also been highly influential in convincing many behavioral scientists to adopt reality relativism/constructivism. Because of the indeterministic nature of measurement in quantum mechanics, as postulated by the Heisenberg uncertainty principle, both the position and momentum of a subatomic particle cannot be known at the same time. As discussed previously, quantum mechanics is *just* a series of equations. Although the equations, within probability limits, predict well, no one understands the *meaning* of the equations. This has led to what the physicist Polkinghorne refers to as numerous cases of "quantum mechanical folklore." [501, p. 61] One such example of folklore is "Schrodinger's cat":

> The unfortunate animal in question is incarcerated in a closed box which also contains a radioactive atom with a 50-50 chance of decaying in the next hour, emitting a gamma-ray in the process. If this emission takes place it triggers the breaking of a vial of poison gas which instantaneously kills the cat. At the end of the hour, before I lift off the lid of the box, the orthodox principles of quantum theory bid me consider the cat to be in a state which is an even-handed superposition of the states "alive" and "dead." On opening the box the wave packet collapses and I find either a cooling corpse or a frisking feline. [501, pp. 61-2]

Many advocates of reality relativism cite such treatments of quantum mechanics as that found in Zukav's *The Dancing Wu-Li Masters*. [651] Such treatments emphasize one interpretation of "Schrodinger's Cat": By opening the box the "reality" (either a dead or live cat) has been "created." For example, Lincoln and Guba are prominent proponents of reality relativism/constructivism. They propose that "it is

dubious whether there is a reality. If there is, we can never know it."
[396, p. 83] On what do they base their position? Their conclusion rests
almost exclusively on citing examples such as "Schrodinger's Cat"
drawn from interpretations of quantum mechanics by authors such as
Zukav.

Now, if there is one thing we can say for sure about quantum mechanics, it is that there are *many* interpretations of what quantum mechanics means. In fact, there appear to be as many interpretations of
quantum mechanics as there are quantum "mechanicians." J.C. Polkinghorne reviews many of the possible interpretations in his book, *The
Quantum World*. With respect to Schrodinger's Cat, he notes: "It is
scarcely necessary to emphasize *the absurdity* of the proposition that
this state of affairs, whichever it is, has been brought about by my action in lifting the lid. It must surely be the case that the cat is competent to act as observer of its own survival or demise and does not need
me to settle the issue for it." [501, p. 62] In fact, Polkinghorne points
out that there is absolutely nothing in quantum mechanics that com-
pels us to abandon realism. "It is astonishingly anthropocentric . . . to
suppose that in the thousands of millions of years before conscious life
emerged in the world—and still today in those extensive parts of the
universe where no conscious life has yet developed—no wave packet
has ever collapsed, no atom for certain decayed. . .that quantum mechanics as we know it is a biologically induced phenomenon." [501, p.
66] Thus, he concludes: "If in the end science is just about the harmonious reconciliation of the behavior of laboratory apparatus, it is hard to
see why it is worth the expenditure of effort involved. *I have never
known anyone working in fundamental science who was not motivated
by the desire to understand the way the world is.*" [501, p. 79] Again, as
MacKinnon has noted, are we to assume that the Nobel Prize committee was hopelessly confused for awarding Nobel Prizes to the physicists
who discovered such subatomic particles as the pi-meson and anti-pro-
ton? [414]

Quantum mechanics has also strongly influenced the "relativist/
constructionist" perspective of Peter and Olson [492], and the "critical
relativism" of Anderson in marketing. For example, Anderson (in his
critique of Cooper [132a]) claims to have "demonstrated that 'truth' is
an inappropriate objective for science, and that consumer research will
do well to abandon such a quixotic ideal." [17, p. 405] Anderson justifies his conclusion concerning "truth" in sections attacking what he
calls (following Laudan) "convergent realism" and "motivational realism." His section attacking "motivational realism" is based *exclusively*
on the "lesson" of quantum mechanics as interpreted by the well-
known, antirealist philosopher, Arthur Fine. However, the very same
Fine who emphatically pronounces that "Realism is dead" [197, p. 83]
(relying on quantum mechanics), in the very same article confidently

asserts: "I certainly trust my senses, on the whole, with regard to the existence and features of everyday objects," and he continues by stating that he has no problem believing that "there really are molecules and atoms." [p. 95] Thus, Fine's *antirealism* looks similar to the *realism* espoused here and by others elsewhere. Moreover, Fine's version of antirealism, far from disparaging the role of truth in science, leads him to conclude that "truth is the fundamental semantical concept" [197a, p. 149] because "there is no form of life [using Wittgenstein's terms], however stripped down, which does not trade in truth," and this "redundancy property of truth makes truth a part of any discourse that merits the name." [197b, p. 170] Readers may rightly question what is going on here. A careful examination of Anderson's and Laudan's attacks on "convergent realism" and, more generally, their attack on truth and its role in science, may help clarify the situation.

11.3.4   Science, Truth, and Scientific Realism

Anderson's attack on truth in science stems from the analysis of Laudan in his often-cited article entitled "A Confutation of Convergent Realism."[4] [372] There, Laudan defines "convergent realism" as entailing (in Anderson's paraphrase):

> (1) "mature" scientific theories are approximately true; (2) the concepts in these theories genuinely refer; (3) successive theories in a domain will retain the ontology of their predecessors; (4) truly referential theories will be "successful," and, conversely, (5) "successful" theories will contain central terms that refer. [17, p. 403]

Anderson uses numerous historical episodes drawn from Laudan to show that there have been many instances in the past where (1) theories were very *unsuccessful*, but (2) we now take the theories' terms to be genuinely referential, e.g., chemical atomic theory and the theory of continental drift. On the other hand, he points out numerous examples of past theories that were thought in their day to be *successful* that we would no longer hold to be genuinely referential, e.g., the humoral theory of medicine and the phlogistic theory in chemistry. From these examples (among others) Anderson argues (with Laudan) that the evidence "demonstrates that the fourth and fifth assertions [of the theory of "convergent realism"] are false." [p. 404] Therefore, "if 'truth' is properly defined as that which is unequivocally the case, then there *can be no criterion* for absolute truth." [p. 404, emphasis in original] Moreover, the concept of "approximate truth" is "even more dismal" since

---

[4] Our analysis here follows the argument developed in reference 312a.

"how could we judge 'approximate' truth when we have no standard to assess absolute truth?" [p. 404]

Several comments are in order concerning the preceding attack on realism. First, Laudan's "convergent realism" differs substantially from the fundamental thesis of scientific realism. Again, the fundamental thesis of scientific realism is that the long-term success of a scientific theory gives reason to believe that something like the entities and structure postulated by the theory actually exists. Note how this thesis differs dramatically from Laudan's "convergent realism." As a matter of fact, the genesis of Laudan's attack on realism, as noted in the headnote to his article [p. 19], was Putnam's observation that "the positive argument for realism is that it is the only philosophy that doesn't make the success of science a miracle." As pointed out by Leplin, Laudan's "convergent" realism is a significant misrepresentation of Putnam's central idea: "Putnam does not infer the truth of realism from the predictive success of science; rather, he infers the truth of realism from its alleged, *unique* ability, to explain the predictive success of science." [388, p. 280] That is, Putnam's observation is that, once one acknowledges that science has been enormously successful over the last four hundred years, either the enormous success of science is a "miracle" *or* some version of realism is correct. In short, scientific realism is a theory that explains the success of science, and its only known rival is the "miracle theory."

Even though Laudan's convergent realism differs substantially from scientific realism, we can still treat it as a theory of science and examine Anderson's analysis of it. Anderson claims that truth and approximate truth are inappropriate objectives for science and counsels their abandonment. Why? Because, he contends, we have no standards for assessing truth or approximate truth. How do we know this to be the case? Because the history of science "demonstrates" that convergent realism's "assertions are false." [17, p. 404] As with our earlier analysis of Laudan (see Section 11.2.1), we have yet another example of how abandoning concepts like "truth" and "falsity" inexorably leads to totally unintelligible discourse. It is incoherent to argue that *truth* and *approximate truth* must be abandoned because a particular theory of science is *false*. The claim that some of the assertions of the theory of convergent realism are *false* necessarily implies that they could have been *true*, or at least *approximately true*. Thus, critical relativism's argument that truth is an inappropriate goal for marketing science is self-refuting.

The issue here is much more fundamental than, merely, a semantic "slip of the pen." Everyone grants that antirealists of all kinds can successfully avoid using the words "true" and "false" by creatively adopting euphemisms and surrogates, e.g., "history is not in accord with," "the facts are inconsistent with," and so on. But surely, neither realists nor antirealists wish their views to be interpreted as mere quibbles. Both sides claim to be arguing substantive issues. Therefore, the fundamental point is that coherent, intelligible, meaningful, or substantive discourse about science (and *in* science) seems to *require* the use of locutions similar to those normally associated with the concepts "true" and "false."

How do notable scholars reach such an incoherent and unintelligible philosophy? Because, as we have seen before, they have fallen victim to the "philosophers' fallacy of high re-definition," just as have many other critics of realism and, for that matter, as Giere observes, critics of science, itself. [226, p. 170] Note that critical relativism proposes that "truth" should be "properly defined as that which is unequivocally the case." Upon finding no criterion which will *guarantee* "absolute truth," it dismisses "approximate truth" on the absence of a standard for "absolute truth." Starting from such "high redefinition" beginnings, the slide into skepticism, incoherence, and unintelligible discourse is almost assured. But the concept of truth need not suffer high redefinition into unequivocable truth or absolute truth: "To claim that a scientific proposition is true is not to claim that it is certain; rather, it is to claim that the world is as the proposition says it is." [583, p. 82] Such a perspective on truth allows one, at the minimum, to engage in coherent, intelligible discourse about science.

11.3.5 Scientific Realism: Conclusion

What can we conclude about scientific realism? First of all, the thesis that "the long-term success of a scientific theory gives reason to believe that something like the entities and structure postulated by the theory actually exists" does not imply that in actual practice all the sciences and all individual scientists are committed to realism. Nevertheless, the "conventional wisdom" is that most sciences and most scientists embrace some version of it. As noted by Suppe, "Science is overwhelmingly committed to metaphysical and epistemological realism." [607, p. 716] Also, Meehl states:

> As to realism, I have never met any scientist who, when doing science, held to a phenomenalist or idealist view; and I cannot force myself to take a nonrealist view seriously even when I work at it. So I begin with the presupposition that the external world is really there, there is a difference between the world and my view of it, and the business of science is to get my view in harmony with the way the world really is to the extent that is possible. There is no reason for us to have a phobia about the word "truth." The idea that you shouldn't ask whether a scientific statement is true, separate from the anthropologists or the Hogo Bogos' belief in it, *because you can't be absolutely certain,* is a dumb argument ... [438, p. 322, emphasis added]

As we have seen, it is not only a "dumb" argument, but unintelligible, as well.

What does scientific realism imply? First, some parts of the actual workings of science are totally incomprehensible and irrational if not viewed from a realist prospective: Many research programs *require* scientific realism. [390, p. 38] If a scientist does not believe that viruses exist, then such activities as engaging in experiments to determine the size, shape, and structure of "nonexisting viruses" is irrational. Second, realism gives the practicing scientist prescriptive warrant for engaging in certain kinds of research activities. For example, the belief that viruses exist (ontological realism) and that they have caused smallpox and polio (epistemological realism) gives warrant for the practicing scientist to attempt to discover if there is a virus that may cause another disease (such as AIDS).

Third, many of the attacks on scientific realism seem to be either attacks on strawmen caricatures of scientific realism, or unintelligibly incoherent, or fundamentally misguided. It is very curious and highly suspect that antirealists rely so heavily on the difficulty of realistically interpreting one scientific theory (i.e., quantum mechanics) and then generalize (in a monumental act of inductive *hubris*) that the entire universe of scientific theories should, therefore, be treated in a nonrealist fashion. To consider the absurdity of this situation, how about if the facts of the matter were in reverse? Suppose that quantum mechanics were the *only* theory that could be interpreted realistically and that it was very difficult, if not impossible, to interpret the entire universe of other theories in a realist manner? Are we to believe that those who currently adopt the antirealist position would suddenly argue powerfully in favor of realism? My strong suspicion is that they would not. Although the "lesson" of quantum mechanics may truly motivate some antirealists, there is good reason to believe that many others have radically different agendas.

Fourth, scientific realism occupies a kind of "middle ground" among varying philosophical systems. At one extreme is the "naive realism" (Siegel refers to it as "vulgar absolutism" [586a]), characteristic of the Newtonians of the 19th century, which held that science had at its disposal methods which, when followed rigorously, would inevitably lead to the objective of truth-with-certainty and that the existing scientific theories had (essentially) achieved this objective. At the other extreme lies the various versions of relativism/constructivism and their attendants: nihilism and skepticism. Between these two positions lie scientific realism and logical empiricism. Because of its acceptance of Humean skepticism, logical empiricism lies "closer" to relativism and constructivism. Given its rejection of Humean skepticism and its optimistic (basically Enlightenment) outlook with respect to the possibility of obtaining genuine knowledge about the world, scientific realism lies "closer" to naive realism. Although scientific realism adopts a thoroughgoing fallibilist orientation toward both the methods and products of science, its fallibilism differs dramatically from the skepticism of relativism. Most unfortunately, as pointed out by Harré, relativism conflates the logical possibility of error with the real chance of being wrong: To abandon all claims to know because of the possibility of error is "absurd." [250, p. 62]

11.4   PHILOSOPHY OF SCIENCE AND MARKETING

Some readers, having followed our narrative from its beginnings in Platonism, classical empiricism, and classical rationalism through to its conclusion with historical relativism, historical empiricism, and scientific realism, may feel a sense of disappointment. In particular, those readers expecting a set of truths-with-certainty at the end of our discussion may feel let-down. Hopefully, however, most readers will by now have a greater appreciation and understanding of the fundamental differences among various philosophical perspectives and will, at least, no longer be bewildered about many of the ongoing discussions. If so, perhaps the level of debate on philosophical issues in marketing may rise to a more productive level.

As will be recalled, logical positivism started when a group of philosophically oriented scientists in Vienna asked the following question: "Does philosophy have anything to contribute to the progress of the scientific enterprise?" Likewise, we in marketing have every right to ask the following question: "Does philosophy of science and its literature have anything to contribute to the progress of marketing science?" Although I can understand those who would respond "no" to this question on the basis of recent debates about what is the most appropriate philosophy to guide marketing research, I believe a definitive "yes" to be the preferred response. This is not to say that "dabbling" in the philosophy of science literature by marketers is either easy or likely to be quickly productive. The philosophy of science discipline, not unlike many other academic disciplines, has developed a highly jargonized literature (as anyone who picks up a current issue of *The Philosophy of Science* can attest). Furthermore, the literature in the philosophy of science is not always what it seems to be. Because of the many nuances of how terms are used, even careful readers of the philosophy of science literature may be misled. For example (as previously mentioned), many antirealists fondly quote Arthur Fine's emphatic assertion that "Realism is dead." [197, p. 83] Yet, in the same article that Fine asserts, "Realism is dead;" he asserts "I certainly trust the evidence of my senses, on the whole, with regard to the existence and features of everyday objects," and he continues by stating that he has no problem believing "that there really are molecules, and atoms." [197, p. 95] Thus, it is difficult to distinguish Fine's emphatic *rejection* of scientific realism from most people's *acceptance* of realism. The implication is that readers should approach the philosophy of science literature with a careful eye for subtlety and, at times (I regretfully admit), sophistry.

The preceding caveats notwithstanding, I still contend that the philosophy of science literature can play a significant and positive role in marketing science because (if for no other reason) of the fact that all research activity *necessarily* implies some underlying "philosophy." When a scholar engages in a research project there are always underlying assumptions about the goal or goals of the project, the nature of reality relative to the project, the appropriateness of the underlying methodology, the role of theory, and so forth. Therefore, the philosophy of science literature can help the practicing researcher be aware of the underlying assumptions of the project. This *explicit* awareness and acknowledgment of the oftentimes *implicit* assumptions of research, in my judgment, is likely to lead to better, more effective research. In fact, we can use the philosophy of science literature to analyze the following question: "What philosophy of science currently dominates marketing?"

11.4.1   What Philosophy Dominates Marketing?

At a recent marketing conference one speaker sadly lamented that the marketing discipline was "too managerial."   Later that same day, on the other hand, another speaker angrily chastised the marketing discipline for not paying *more* attention to the needs of marketing managers. The only common ground that both speakers shared was the view that the underlying problem resulted from marketing being "dominated by logical empiricism!" Both speakers believed strongly in their positions and both speakers were well-intentioned. Nevertheless, as is now obvious, both speakers were ill-informed about the philosophy known as "logical empiricism," leading both speakers to be wrong. Logical empiricism neither directs research toward problems relevant to the marketing manager, nor away from such problems. Hopefully, we can elevate future discussions on this topic to the point where speakers do not feel compelled to throw out the "bogeyman" of logical empiricism as the cause of all the ills in marketing.

What philosophy dominates marketing? To even begin to address this question requires a recognition of the many different research programs, traditions, or "schools" of thought in marketing. Sheth, Gardner, and Garrett [577] identify twelve such "schools of thought": commodity, functional, functionalist, regional, institutional, managerial, buyer behavior, activist, macromarketing, organizational dynamics, systems, and social exchange. One way to address the issue of what philosophy dominates marketing would be to systematically analyze all the research programs in these twelve schools of thought according to their philosophical foundations. Although Sheth, Gardner, and Garrett evaluate the twelve schools, they do not explore the "dominant philosophy" issue. Furthermore, although their overall evaluations are insightful and useful, their evaluation criteria unintentionally perpetuate certain myths about logical positivism and relativism. They evaluate the schools of thought as follows:

> In this book we utilized a metatheoretical evaluation system with six criteria that *bridges the gap between the logical positivist perspective and the relativism perspective*. The syntax criteria of structure and specification evaluate the consistency of the nomological network of constructs in a theory. Semantics criteria evaluate a theory's relationship to reality by analyzing its testability and empirical support. Finally, the pragmatics or relevance criteria of richness and simplicity scrutinize the applicability of a theory to those who are actively involved in marketing practice.
>
> In short, the emphasis on *syntax and semantics represents preference for logical positivism* whereas the emphasis on *pragmatics represents preference for relativism*. In some sense, this is really a debate as to which is more important—rigor or relevance. [577, p. 185, emphasis added]

Two comments are required here. First, there is no doubt but that "rigor or relevance" is an issue much discussed in marketing. However, there is great doubt as to the relationship, if any, that logical positivism has on this debate.[5] Second, and more importantly, Sheth, Gardner, and Garrett (following Peter and Olson [492]) mistakenly equate "pragmatics" and "usefulness" with a "preference for relativism." Whatever benefits that relativism may allegedly have, in no meaningful sense can "pragmatics" or "usefulness" imply a "preference for relativism." In fact, just the opposite is the case. As we have seen, the adoption of any significant, nontrivial, coherent version of relativism would make miraculous the actual usefulness and pragmatic success of any research program in science. In short, if science actually "constructs" its own "reality" *independent* of an external world, how could science be *useful* to anyone other than the individual scientists and their respective scientific communities? That is, if science were actually characterized by reality relativism/constructivism, then the pragmatic success (usefulness) of science would, indeed, be a miracle.

Again, what philosophy dominates marketing? One way to approach this question would be to examine individual research programs

---

[5] In my judgment, much of the "rigor vs. relevance" debate is misguided because *both* sides seem to (mistakenly) equate "rigorous" with "mathematical" and at least one side (equally mistakenly) seems to equate "relevant" with "nonmathematical." See Hunt [312b] for a discussion of this issue.

in marketing and identify their underlying characteristics. In this regard, we should keep in mind that logical positivism and logical empiricism hold that all the "theoretical" terms in a theory must be *defined* in terms of "observables." (All measures are formative measures.) On the other hand, scientific realism holds that "theoretical" terms may denote a real existence and, therefore, our measures are reflective, i.e., they reflect the presence or absence (or level of) some unobservable, but genuinely existing, entity. For example, consider the concept called "stage in the family-cycle." Now the stages in the family life-cycle are normally identified by combining age, marital status, and the number of children living at home, e.g., the "empty nest" stage identifies a married, older couple, with no children at home. "Empty nest" appears to be a "shorthand" way of identifying a couple with a set of demographic characteristics and *nothing more*. On the contrary, consider the construct called "behavioral intention." It is often measured by a person stating the likelihood or probability of engaging in a particular behavior. Such a measure does not *define* "behavioral intention." Rather, it *reflects* the "unobservable" entity.

A research program *dominated* by logical positivism or logical empiricism would (in part) rely exclusively, or almost exclusively, on *formative* measures (i.e., operational *definitions*). On the other hand, a research program dominated by scientific realism would (again, in part) rely exclusively, or almost exclusively, on constructs whose measures are *reflective* in nature. To be sure, different research programs in marketing science rely on both kinds of measures. However, it would seem that realist measures predominate. Only the behaviorist program in consumer behavior specifically forbids the use of "internal constructs" in explaining consumer behavior, and, therefore, it is the research program coming closest to being "dominated" by logical positivism and logical empiricism. However, as Nord and Peter point out, "Marketing scholars have given little consideration to . . . the behavior modification approach." [478a, p. 36] Although it is easy to conclude that the one research program that is clearly dominated by logical positivism is not terribly influential in marketing, no one has done the kind of careful, systematic research on the numerous research programs in marketing that would enable one to conclusively identify their respective orientations. Nevertheless, my suspicion is that more research is philosophically consistent with scientific realism than any other specific, philosophical "ism." Certainly, the work of Bagozzi [29] and all others who use causal modeling techniques, like LISREL, are committed to realism. My own efforts reflect a blend of logical empiricism and realism.

With respect to specific research programs (other than behaviorism and causal modeling), only sketchy observations are possible. For example, those researchers firmly committed to mathematical modeling (in "management science" or operations research terms) seem to have adopted a "Pythagorean orientation" in their work. That is, their mathematical modeling efforts seem to imply a belief in "mathematical harmony" in the universe (see Section 8.1). Most marketing practitioners and those marketing academicians oriented toward case analysis and developing "rules of thumb" to guide marketing management seem closest to some version of pragmatism. These marketers focus exclusively on "what works" for solving immediate and pressing problems and concern themselves very little with more fundamental issues, such as understanding *why* some rules of thumb "work" and others do not. Finally, those marketers believing that no combination of man's reasoning and sensory abilities is capable of producing genuine knowledge about the world (including mankind itself) are closest to relativism, irrationalism, and skepticism.

To repeat, what philosophy dominates marketing? As with many questions, a clear understanding of the nature of the question provides significant input for answering it. The question *presumes* that marketing, in fact, is currently "dominated" by some philosophy. Furthermore, the use of the word "dominates" carries with it the pejorative overtone that whatever philosophy currently guides marketing ought not to do so. In point of fact, marketing seems to be very heterogeneous in its many research programs throughout the twelve schools of thought identified by Sheth, Gardner, and Garrett. Why would we have thought it to be otherwise? If the history of marketing thought tells us nothing else, the marketing discipline has been amazingly eclectic, borrowing from everywhere. [312 and 332a] Indeed, a recurring complaint about marketing over the last thirty years has been that we have continually transgressed by indiscriminately borrowing concepts, theories, and methods from other disciplines.

For the final time, what philosophy dominates marketing? The most accurate answer is: "No single philosophy dominates marketing."

11.5   MARKETING SCIENCE AND MARKETING ETHICS

The fact that no philosophical "ism" dominates the entire marketing discipline does not imply that there are not choices to be made. As previously discussed, each individual marketing researcher will, by necessity, have a personal "philosophy" about research. Such personal philosophies may, or may not, be totally consistent with some formal philosophical "ism." Furthermore, each marketing academician is a member of the marketing academic community, which is itself a subgroup within the university community. As such, these broader communities both guide and constrain, for good or for ill, marketing academicians in their teaching, research, and service activities.

Recently, the American Marketing Association has been taking numerous steps toward the professionalization of marketing practice. Most notably, the AMA has completely revised its code of ethics. Why? Because it has been long-recognized that one of the major distinguishing characteristics separating professions from other vocations is that all true professions have a degree of self-control through codes of ethics, either formal or informal. An underlying tenet of all such codes is that the true professional, when interacting with clients of any kind, is not totally guided by self-interest. When people go to physicians, they have a right to expect that their physicians will not adopt a method of treatment solely based on which method will best serve the physicians' interests. Because of the disparity in knowledge of diseases and their respective treatments, the social compact between laypeople and their physicians requires a significant element of *trust*. Many philosophers of science are coming to realize that this same element of *trust* is a (perhaps *the*) key to understanding scientific communities.

Rom Harré [250] has been at the forefront of those philosophers advocating the importance of, in his terms, "moral order" in science. Carefully avoiding the philosophers' fallacy, Harré defines scientific knowledge as "trustworthy knowledge," rather than truth-with-certainty: "Science is not a logically coherent body of knowledge in the strict, unforgiving sense of the philosophers' high redefinition, but a cluster of material and cognitive practices, carried on within a distinctive moral order, whose main characteristic is the trust that obtains among its members and should obtain between that community and the larger lay community with which it is interdependent." [250, p.6] What is "trust"? "To trust someone is to be able to rely on them in the matter in question . . . Scientists believe that things personally unknown to them are as *another scientist* says they are." However, "trust is not maintained by telling each other only literal truths. Under that constraint the members of the community would perforce remain forever silent. It is enough that they tell each other what they honestly believe to be the truth." [p. 12] In this regard, Harré is claiming that the moral order advocates, among other things, the avoidance of sophistry and deception, as well as outright fraud—sound counsel, indeed.

Harré points out that trust in all societies is most often role-related: "[I]t is because the trusted one is in the role of parent, guardian, policeman, research supervisor, and so on, that the trust is there until something happens to upset it." [p. 21] Therefore, scientists in their role as researchers producing "trustworthy belief" are required by their peers and by the lay community to maintain a moral order. This is because researchers are involved in producing "practically reliable scientific knowledge." This "reliance might be existential, concerning what there is or what might be, or it might be practical, concerning what can and cannot be done, or both. The moral quality of the product comes through clearly in the kind of outrage felt by the [scientific] community at the disclosure of scientific fraud." [p. 13] Harré asks: "Is *scientific method* ... and *scientific morality*, the fiduciary act of committing oneself to make one's scientific utterances fiduciary acts, the best way to discipline a community which exists to find out about the natural world?" [p. 26, emphasis added] Harré answers this question affirmatively on the basis that science is committed to what he calls "referential realism." This realism holds that "existence is prior to theory, and that while no ontologies for science could be absolute, nevertheless, ontologies (realized in referential practices) are always, at any moment, less revisable than their associated belief-systems....On this view, truth and falsity migrate from the epistemology of science to the morality of its human community." [p. 6] For Harré, *any view of science that claims that scientific knowledge is "constructed" or "created" by the scientific community independent of some external reality is to be rejected on moral grounds.* (See Section 10.1.3 for a similar analysis.) Harré summarizes his position as follows:

> Science has a special status, not because it is a sure way of producing truths and avoiding falsehood, but because it is a communal practice of a community with a remarkable and rigid morality—a morality at the heart of which is a commitment that the products of this community shall be trustworthy....Science is not just a cluster of material and cognitive practices, but is a moral achievement as well....Antirealism, which, like it or not, seeps out into the lay world as antiscience, is not only false, but morally obnoxious...[p. 7]

As members of the marketing academic profession, we have numerous clients for marketing knowledge, our product. In addition to the obvious constituencies of students, marketing practitioners and others in the academic community, there are consumers, members of government, and society-at-large. Concerning marketing knowledge, its development, and dissemination, does the *trust* that these constituencies have *in* us impose certain special responsibilities *on* us? If so, what is the nature of these responsibilities, and what does it imply about the most appropriate philosophy to guide marketing science? Philosophies based on, or leading to, skepticism, cynicism, irrationalism, self-serving gamesmanship, and sophistry would seem to be unlikely candidates for inspiring trust. Most assuredly, no philosophy of research can *guarantee* trustworthy knowledge. Nevertheless, those researchers whose values make them recoil from skepticism, cynicism, irrationalism, gamesmanship, and sophistry, can find comfort in the fact that there exist philosophies of science that, at the minimum, are not antithetical to truth and its surrogate, trustworthy knowledge, and, at the maximum, may (fallibly) yield knowledge that is, indeed, truly worthy of others' trust. To those marketers, I hope this book will help.

The debate continues over the most appropriate philosophical orientation for marketing in general and marketing science in particular.

The overriding objective of these last four chapters has been to provide the historical foundations for elevating debate to a higher, better informed, plane. Past discussions, though provocative, have been less productive than they might have been—factually inaccurate, impassioned polemics are seldom good substitutes for carefully reasoned analyses. Two decades ago, many university disciplines suffered bouts with irrationalism. Some areas, such as the philosophy of science, seem to have emerged stronger than ever after their eras of turbulence. Others can too. If anything distinguishes academia from other societal institutions, it is its high regard for Reason. Our constituencies trust us to deliver our, honest, Reasoned efforts. Although they can ask no more, they surely deserve no less.

APPENDIX A, CHAPTER 11
SHOULD MARKETING
ADOPT RELATIVISM?

By: Shelby D. Hunt
Paul Whitfield Horn Professor of Marketing
Texas Tech University

Several writers have recently presented carefully constructed, meticulously written arguments in favor of marketers adopting relativism as a philosophical foundation for marketing science (Anderson 1983, and Peter and Olson 1983). The purpose of this paper is to examine three issues related to relativism and the nature of marketing science: (1) Is there a fundamental difference between sciences and nonsciences? (2) Should we "market" marketing science? (3) Should marketing adopt relativism as its philosophical foundation?

SCIENCES VS. NONSCIENCES

Anderson points out that the search for criteria that would separate science from nonscience dates from the very beginnings of Western philosophy and that Popper has labeled the question "the problem of demarcation" (Anderson 1983, p. 18). Anderson analyzes the issue and proposes that "philosophers have been signally unsuccessful in their search for such criteria" and that many "consider the question to be a chimera" (Anderson 1983, p.18).

After rejecting the notion that sciences differ from nonsciences in any fundamental respect, Anderson proposes that marketing science should adopt a "relativistic stance" and distinguishes between two different ways that the term "science" can be used. He designates them as science$_1$ and science$_2$:

It is proposed that science$_1$ should refer to the idealized notion of science as an inquiry system which produces "objectively proven knowledge" (Chalmers 1976, p. 1). On this view, science seeks to discover "the truth" by the objective methods of observation, test, and experiment. Of course it should be clear that no such inquiry system has ever existed—nor is it very likely that such a system will ever exist (p. 26).

Source: Reprinted by permission from Scientific Method in Marketing, eds., Paul F. Anderson and Michael J. Ryan, Chicago: American Marketing Association, 1984, pp. 30-34.

Given his belief that science as a process that searches for "truth" by objective methods cannot exist, he proposes that marketing adopt the notion of science$_2$:

> The defining element here is that of societal consensus. On this view, science is whatever society chooses to call a science. In Western cultures this would include all of the recognized natural and social sciences (1983, p.26).

Is there no fundamental difference between sciences and nonsciences? Stated more precisely, do the knowledge-claims of the nonsciences have equal espistemological status to the knowledge-claims of the sciences? This is equivalent to asking whether there are good grounds for accepting the knowledge-claims of sciences in preference to the knowledge-claims of nonsciences. Perhaps an example using medical science can provide a clearer perspective on exactly the issue in question.

Suppose your father visited his family physician because he was feeling poorly. Suppose further that the physician conducted some tests and diagnosed your father's condition as a bone cancer that if left unattended would probably result in your father's death within a year. Upset with this diagnosis, your father visits his local palmist. The palmist reads your father's palm and tells him that he does not have bone cancer and that he will live a long life without any medical treatment. The fundamental question here is whether there are good reasons for accepting the knowledge-claim (the diagnosis) of the physician (and acting accordingly) and for rejecting the knowledge-claim (the diagnosis) of the palmist? Do medical science and palmistry justify their claims about knowledge by equally acceptable methods?

When asked to justify his diagnosis of bone cancer, the family physician would refer to the results of experiments which have found that when the results of certain medical test are "positive," then the patient usually has a kind of bone cancer. Furthermore, he would point out that through time medical scientists have observed that the "average" life expectancy of someone with this kind of bone cancer is approximately one year. When the palmist is asked to justify his diagnosis, he indicates that his knowledge is based on the "gift of reading." He was born with this "gift," and only others who have been similarly "blessed" with this gift can truly understand his knowledge or powers.

Modern empiricists (as well as logical empiricists and practicing scientists) would claim that the diagnosis of the physician is better justified than the knowledge-claim of the palmist. That is, modern empiricists believe that open empirical testing of the knowledge-claims of medical science provides good reasons for accepting the diagnosis of the physician in preference to those of the palmist. Elsewhere, I have referred to his procedure as "intersubjective certification" (Hunt 1983, p. 243).

Relativists reject (or their views logically imply rejecting) the claim that empirical testing provides good reasons for preferring the knowledge-claims of medical science over palmistry. Relativists point out that there is no "unique scientific method." Science is "subjective" and its "observations are always subject to measurement error." Furthermore, our observations are "theory laden." Relativists would point out that many times medical science conducts the same test and the patient turns out *not* to have bone cancer. Thus, the palmist's diagnosis will sometimes be "correct," and the diagnosis of medical science will be "incorrect." They would also point out that such terms as "disease" and even "death" are theory-laden. For example, perhaps what medical science calls a disease is in reality the "normal" state of affairs, and what is to be our definition of "death"? Finally, relativists would contend that science is a "social process" and that the primary reason that many people often accept the diagnoses of physicians over the diagnoses of palmists is that people have been in essence "brainwashed" by the self-serving interests and propaganda of the members of the scientific community. After all, isn't science "whatever society chooses to call as science" (Anderson 1983, p. 26)?

The relativists certainly raise interesting questions concerning the issue of whether the knowledge-claims of the nonsciences have equal claim to our acceptance as the sciences. Many sociologists of science and marketers come down squarely on the side that there is no fundamental difference between palmistry and medical science. On the other hand, there are many who subscribe to the modern empiricist position that medical science and palmistry are fundamentally different.

Should marketers accept the modern empiricist or relativist position on the issue of demarcation? Although I cannot speak for others, I personally believe that the relativists have not persuasively argued their position that the knowledge-claims of nonsciences are justified as well as those of sciences, that is, that the diagnoses of palmist should be given equal status with the diagnoses of medical science. Therefore, I personally will continue to consult physicians for my medical problems rather than palmists. Presumably, those who sincerely hold the contrary view on this issue will act in accordance with their beliefs. To do otherwise would be to engage in sophistry. As has been observed

by others (Krausz and Meiland 1982, p. 6), the Greek Sophists (who delighted in weaving disingenuous arguments) were among the first relativists in Western intellectual history.

SHOULD WE "MARKET" MARKETING SCIENCE?

After dismissing the notion that sciences differ from nonsciences in how they justify their knowledge-claims, Anderson proposes that marketing should accept science$_2$, which essentially suggests that the primary problem facing marketing science is to "market" the discipline of marketing to the outside world.

Anderson proposes that marketing should seek recognition from society that marketing is a science for both altruistic and self-serving reasons. The altruistic reason is that "an important goal of any area of inquiry with scientific pretensions is to insure that its knowledge base is widely dispersed through the greater society, so that this knowledge can be used to benefit society as a whole" (Anderson 1983, p. 27). The self-serving reason is that "as marketing improves its scientific status in society, the knowledge it generates will be more acceptable within the society and that additional resources will be made available for further development of its knowledge base" (Anderson 1983, p. 27).

Given that marketing has good reasons to attempt to become recognized as a science, what should it do to gain this recognition? Anderson compares marketing with other recognized social and natural sciences and has two suggestions. "First, it is clear that marketing must be more concerned with the pursuit of knowledge as knowledge. Rightly or wrongly, society tends to reserve full scientific legitimacy for those inquiry systems which are perceived to be operating in the higher interest of knowledge and general societal welfare." He then goes on to point out that historically marketers have "viewed their discipline as an applied area concerned largely with the improvement of managerial practice." This emphasis on the normative side of marketing, he contends, has retarded and will continue to retard the recognition of marketing as a science.

Anderson then goes on to observe that much research in marketing is scattered and fragmented. The gathering of scattered facts, he contends, will never develop recognition for marketing as a science. Rather, "what is required in marketing is a greater commitment to theory-driven programmatic research, aimed at solving cognitively and socially significant problems" (Anderson 1983, p. 28).

Anderson is certainly correct in that there are many honorific overtones to the label "science." Furthermore, it would probably be in marketing's best interest to have society in general, and other scientists in particular, believe that marketing is a science. He points out the very practical consequences of the National Science Foundation withdrawing its blanket exclusion of research in business areas from funding considerations. Likewise, those of us who care deeply about the role of universities in generating knowledge and dispersing that knowledge throughout society, can only agree with the altruistic motives behind wanting society to consider marketing to be a science.

Turning now to the suggestions for convincing society that marketing is a science, we should examine the recommendations of "knowledge for knowledge's sake" and "theory-driven research." Anderson is to be commended for pointing out that marketing will be perceived as a science only when the umbilical cord tying the discipline to the marketing manager is severed. However, it is only fair to point

out that many marketing academicians believe that all marketing academicians do not share this belief. Many marketing academicians believe that all marketing research should have direct relevance to the problems of the marketing manager. For example, my article "The Nature and Scope of Marketing" (Hunt 1976) was vigorously attacked by many who believed I was touting "knowledge for knowledge's sake." For example, Robin (1977) indicated that the positive/normative dichotomy discussed in that article was meaningless because the information derived from a positive "study is of little interest unless it is given prescriptive overtones. That is, the positive issues are barren except where they have prescriptive implications" (p. 136). In reply to Robin and others, I proposed the following:

> The prime directive for scholarly research in marketing is the same as for all sciences: *to seek knowledge*. The knowledge must be intersubjectively certifiable and capable of describing, explaining and predicting phenomena. Sometimes the knowledge will assist marketing managers in making decisions. Other times the knowledge will guide legislators in drafting laws to regulate marketing activities. At still other times, the knowledge may assist the general public in understanding the functions that marketing activities provide society. Finally, at the risk of 'waxing philosophical,' the knowledge may simply assist marketing scholars in *knowing*, a not inconsequential objective (Hunt 1978, p. 109).

Anderson wants marketers to promote marketing science by generating knowledge and then dispersing that knowledge to society. Presumably, the members of the other "recognized" sciences would be a primary target market for our efforts. Here a problem emerges. How are marketing scientists going to convince the members of the "recognized" sciences that our knowledge is truly worthy of their consideration? If all sciences had a common methodological foundation, marketers would only have to show that marketing was generated using the same kinds of procedures as the other "recognized" sciences. However, Anderson rejects the view that there is commonality among the methods of the various disciplines:

> Instead, different research programs (i.e., disciplines, subdisciplines, or collections of disciplines) will adhere to different methodological, ontological and metaphysical commitments. These research programs are highly 'encapsulated' and are immunized against attack from the outside (p. 25).

If each discipline has its own unique method for justifying its knowledge-claims, how can marketing gain recognition from other sciences? One solution might be to adopt a "patron" science and accept its methods as our own. Marketing could then shift patrons every few years to convince the various disciplines that marketing knowledge is truly worthy of respect.

The modern empiricist perspective is that there really is no problem here at all because the various sciences share a common methodological foundation. This foundation consists of developing theories that are capable of generating hypotheses that are susceptible to empirical testing. The open empirical testing process, therefore, provides a common methodological foundation for evaluating the knowledge-claims of all sciences. However, if one is a relativist and believes that there is no such thing as "the" scientific method, then the problems of "marketing" marketing science to society would seem to be enormous, indeed.

Finally, Anderson proposes that we move marketing science forward by em-

phasizing "theory-driven programmatic research aimed at solving cognitively and socially significant problems." All marketers seriously interested in marketing science must share his concern for theory-driven research. Both empiricists and relativists, alike, agree that marketing is in dire need of theories that purport to explain and predict phenomena. Marketing science is hardly advanced by scattered empirical studies without theoretical foundation.

Professor Anderson has done the discipline a service by pointing out the need to "market" marketing science. His suggestion that marketing science must break the umbilical cord tying marketing science to the marketing manager is long overdue. And his plea for marketing knowledge for the sake of knowledge itself is laudatory. Theory-driven programmatic research is what is needed. Nevertheless, recommendations for theory-driven research and knowledge for knowledge's sake are not unique to relativism. In fact, given the relativists' belief that *usefulness* (not truth) is the appropriate criterion for evaluating theory (Peter and Olson 1983, p. 121), these pleas seem almost more consistent with traditional empiricism than with relativism. Surely, marketing science has a right to expect some unique consequences flowing from the adoption of relativism rather than simply, "let's all do a better job of self-promotion."

SHOULD MARKETING ADOPT RELATIVISM?

The last major issue of this paper, is "Should Marketing Adopt Relatavism?" To do so requires an understanding of the nature of relativism and how it compares with alternative approaches. Peter and Olson (1983) provide a table purportedly displaying the major differences between the so-called "positivistic/empiricist" and "relativistic/constructionist" views of science. Appendix A, Table 1 (pp. 408-409) displays these perspectives and, also, a column labeled "Modern Empiricism" prepared by this author. At the outset, the reader should note that neither relativism nor empiricism represents a monolithic body of views. As I am sure Peter and Olson would be the first to agree, not all relativists would share all of the views of Column 3 of Table 1. Similarly, I am sure that many empiricists would not share all of the views in Column 2.

Since Peter and Olson are self-proclaimed relativists, I shall presume that Column 3 of Table 1 is a reasonably accurate representation of the views of many relativists. Nevertheless, the column which purportedly represents the views of the positivist/empiricist does not in any way resemble the views of modern empiricism. In fact, I know of no philosopher of science whose views are fairly represented in Column 1. Therefore, I have developed Column 2 in Table 1 to more accurately represent my impression of the views of modern empiricists. I believe that Column 2 fairly represents many of the views held by both philosophers of science and many practicing scientists concerning these issues.

I invite the reader to go through Table 1 line by line asking two question at each stage: (1) Which statement best characterizes the nature of marketing science? (2) Which statement *ought to* best characterize the nature of marketing science? That is, it is one thing to state that certain beliefs or practices actually exist in marketing science. It is entirely another thing to claim that certain beliefs and practices are in some sense optimal or even desirable. It is often not clear whether relativists claim that their views should be adopted

in a positive sense or normative sense, or both. Clearly, relativists such as Feyerabend want their views to be accepted in a normative sense, since the adoption of such views, it is held, is necessary for scientific progress. Anderson (1983, p. 25) seems to agree when he states "thus, a relativistic stance appears to be the only viable solution to the problem of scientific method."

Should marketing adopt relativism? Those readers, after reviewing Table 1, whose views and values lead them to reject relativism, should take comfort in the fact that they are not philosophically alone. All protestations by relativists to the contrary, many philosophers of science (as well as most practicing members of scientific communities) have not embraced relativistic dogma. In his highly regarded work, *The Structure of Scientific Theories* (1977), Frederick Suppe analyzes the works of Feyerabend and other relativists and uses the term *Weltanschauungen* to describe their views. Suppe's conclusion concerning relativism and the current views of the discipline of the philosophy of science merit restatement.

> Contemporary work in philosophy of science increasingly subscribes to the position that it is a central aim of science to come to knowledge of how the world *really* is, that correspondence between theories and reality is a central aim of science as an epistemic enterprise and crucial to whatever objectivity science enjoys—in sharp repudiation of the "sociological" views of knowledge found in the more extreme Weltanschauugen analyses, while acknowledging the defects of positivistic and earlier empiricist treatments. This has led to an emphatic belief that a "hard-nosed" metaphysical and epistemological realism wherein how the world *is* plays a decisive role in the epistemic efforts and achievements of science (p. 649).

Appendix A, Table 1

Positivistic/Empiricist Science	Modern Empiricism	Relativistic/Constructionist Science
1. Science discovers the true nature of reality.	There is a real world and, although science *attempts* to discover the nature of reality, the "true" nature of reality can never be known with certainty.	Science creates many realities.
2. Only the logic of justification is needed to understand science.	It is useful to distinguish between the procedures that science uses to *discover* its knowledge-claims from those that science uses to accept or reject (justify) its knowledge-claims. The academic discipline of philosophy of science historically focused on issues in justification.	The process by which theories are created, justified and diffused throughout a research community are needed to understand science.
3. Science can be understood without considering cultural, social, political and economic factors.	The prodedures that science uses to justify its knowledge-claims should be independent of cultural, social, political, and ecomonic factors.	Science is a social process and cannot be understood without considering cultural, social, political, and economic factors.
4. Science is objective.	Although complete objectivity is impossible, science is more objective in justifying its knowledge-claims than nonsciences, e.g., medical science is more objective than palmistry.	Science is subjective.
5. Scientific knowledge is absolute and cumulative.	Scientific knowledge is *never* absolute. Much of scientific knowledge is cumulative, i.e., we really do know more about the causes of infectious diseases today than we did 100 years ago.	Scientific knowledge is relative to a particular context and period of time in history.
6. Science is capable of discovering universal laws that govern the external world.	Science attempts to discover regularities among the phenomena in the real world. Some of these regularities are stated in universal form and others are stated in probablistic form.	Science creates ideas that are context dependent, i.e, relative to a frame of reference.

Appendix A, Table 1 (continued)

Positivistic/Empiricist Science	Modern Empiricism	Relativistic/Constructionist Science
7. Science produces theories that come closer and closer to absolute truth.	Much of scientific knowledge is cumulative. Absolute truth is not knowable by science.	Truth is a subjective evaluation that cannot be properly inferred outside of the context provided by the theory.
8. Science is rational since it follows rules of formal logic.	Science is rational since its purpose is to increase our understanding of the world. It does so through developing theories, models, lawlike generalizations and hypotheses which purport to describe, explain and predict phenomena.	Science is rational to the degree that it seeks to improve individual and societal well-being by following whatever means are useful for doing so.
9. There are specific procedures for doing good science (e.g., falsification).	There are norms for doing good science. For example, theories should be testable, measures should exhibit reliability and validity, and data should not be fabricated or otherwise fraudulently collected.	There are many ways of doing science validly that are appropriate in different situations.
10. Scientists subject their theories to potential falsification through rigorous empirical testing.	Theories are and should be subjected to the empirical testing process.	Scientists see supportive, confirmatory evidence in order to market their theories.
11. Measurement procedures do not influence what is measured.	Absolute perfection in measurement procedures is impossible.	Nothing can be measured without changing it.
12. Data provide objective, independent benchmarks for testing theories.	The empirical testing process provides good grounds for accepting some knowledge-claims and rejecting others.	Data are created and interpreted by scientists in terms of a variety of theories and thus are theory laden.

Both marketing technology and science have made significant progress in recent decades. This is not to say that there are no unresolved issues or problems—for there clearly are. Nevertheless, the discipline of marketing is hardly advanced by adopting a philosophy that sees no difference between astronomy and medical science, on the one hand, and astrology and palmistry, on the other. Neither individuals, nor academic disciplines, nor societies in general can make "progress" (in any meaningful sense of the word) by abjuring the importance of truth and its earnest pursuit. For marketing science to turn toward relativism in the year 1984 would be Orwellian irony incarnate.

REFERENCES

Anderson, Paul F. (1983), "Marketing, Scientific Progress, and Scientific Method," *Journal of Marketing*, 47 (Fall), 18-31.

Chalmers, A. F. (1976), *What Is This Thing Called Science?* St. Lucia, Australia: University of Queensland Press.

Hunt, Shelby D. (1976), "The Nature and Scope of Marketing," *Journal of Marketing*, 40 (July), 17-28.

Hunt, Shelby D. (1978), "A General Paradigm of Marketing: In Support of the Three Dichotomies Model," *Journal of Marketing*, 42 (April), 107-110.

Hunt, Shelby D. (1983), *Marketing Theory: The Philosophy of Marketing Science*, Homewood, IL: Irwin.

Krausz, Michael and Jack. W. Meiland (1982), *Relativism: Cognitive and Moral*, Notre Dame, IN: University of Notre Dame Press.

Peter, J. Paul and Jerry C. Olson (1983), "Is Science Marketing?" *Journal of Marketing*, 47 (Fall), 111-125.

Robin, Donald P. (1977), "Comment on the Nature and Scope of Marketing," *Journal of Marketing*, 41 (January), 136-138.

Suppe, Frederick (1977), *The Structure of Scientific Theories,* 2nd ed., Urbana, IL: University of Illinois Press.

1989 Postscript to "Should Marketing Adopt Relativism"

Since its publication five years ago, many readers have asked for clarification on the article's last sentence: "For marketing to turn toward relativism in 1984 would be Orwellian irony incarnate." As a partial response to these requests, consider the following quotation:

> Reality is inside the skull. . .you must get rid of the 19th century ideas about the laws of nature. We make the laws of nature (p. 268).

Note how the preceding quote is so (frighteningly) consistent with the standard relativist position that science does not discover reality, rather it "constructs" its own reality (Peter and Olson 1983; Lincoln and Guba 1985; Olson 1987). Yet, the quote does not come from any contemporary marketing or consumer behavior relativist nor even from a relativist sociologist of science. Rather, it comes from George Orwell's classic work, *1984* (in the section where Big Brother's goons are "breaking" the protagonist).

The Orwellian society of Big Brother found it imperative to adopt a relativist perspective on reality in order to maintain control of its citizens through "double-think," which was the practice of holding "two contradictory beliefs in one's mind simultaneously, and accepting both of them" (Orwell 1949, p. 215). Doublethink was necessary "to deny the existence of objective reality and all the while to take account of the reality one desires" (p. 216). Thus, it is remarkably similar to the incoherence, unintelligibility, and sophistry found in today's relativism. Further, it was necessary to destroy empirical science:

> The empirical method of thought, on which all of the scientific achievements of the past were founded, is opposed to [our] most fundamental principles. [Therefore], in Newspeak there is no word for "science" (Orwell 1949, p. 194).

Lest there be any misunderstanding, *this writer in no way implies that others in the debate over the appropriateness of relativism in marketing and consumer behavior advocate the monstrous world of Orwell's 1984.* Yet, the message is clear to be gleaned from both the *hypothetical* world of Orwell and the *actual* world of contemporary societies whose state policy—as the events following the massacre at Tiananmen Square in China in June 1989 should remind us—is to regularly and routinely rewrite history to "socially construct" reality for consistency with political views. First, ideas have "lives of their own" that cannot be controlled by their creators and advocates. Second, modern writers on the ethical dimensions of science hold that scientists and philosophers of science must assume some measure of responsibility for their knowledge-claims (Gaa 1977). Therefore, just as scientists and their philosophical advocates are increasingly being held responsible for their claims of explaining the world as it really is, so also must relativist researchers and their philosophical/sociological advocates be held responsible for advocating a social construction of reality. Indeed, a strong case can be made that those researchers and writers who dismiss the view that science is involved in the search for truth and who enthusiastically embrace the position that science is a kind of ritualized, sophistic gamesmanship, have *special* moral and ethical responsibilities for their claims.

The preceding explains what I meant by the last sentence in "Should Marketing Adopt Relativism?" It also shows one of the reasons why so many philosophers of science "fear" relativism. And well they should.

REFERENCES TO POSTSCRIPT

Gaa, James C. (1977), "Moral Autonomy and the Rationality of Science," *Philosophy of Science,* 44, 513-541.

Lincoln, Yvonna S. and Egon G. Guba (1985), *Naturalistic Inquiry,* London: Sage Publications.

Olson, Jerry (1987), "The Construction of Scientific Meaning," in *Marketing Theory,* proceedings of the 1987 A.M.A. Winter Educators' Conference, Chicago: American Marketing Association.

Orwell, George (1949), *1984,* New York: Harcourt, Brace and World, Inc.

Peter, J. Paul and Jerry C. Olson (1983), "Is Science Marketing?" *Journal of Marketing,* 47 (Fall), 111-125.

APPENDIX B, CHAPTER 11 NATURALISTIC, HUMANISTIC, AND INTERPRETIVE INQUIRY: CHALLENGES AND ULTIMATE POTENTIAL

By: Shelby D. Hunt[1]
Paul Whitfield Horn Professor of Marketing
Texas Tech University

ABSTRACT

Many researchers are now both advocating and adopting naturalistic, humanistic, and interpretive inquiry methods. The purpose of this paper is to provide a constructive and critical commentary on this developing trend in consumer research. This paper proposes that in order for naturalistic, humanistic, and interpretive methods to reach their ultimate potential, they must respond to (at least) four separate challenges. Although these challenges reveal that I find *some* of the positions (apparently) advocated by natu-

ralistic, humanistic, and interpretive researchers to be problematical, this does not mean that I do not admire and respect their efforts. Rather, I agree with Laudan when he states that in academia "healthy disagreement (unlike imitation) is the deepest sign of admiration" (1977, p. ix).

CHALLENGES AND ULTIMATE POTENTIAL

In recent years several researchers have been adopting naturalistic, humanistic, and interpretive inquiry methods for studying both marketing and consumer research phenomena. The volume in which this paper is published represents a natural outgrowth of interest in these procedures, and the purpose of this paper is to provide a constructive critique of them. Several factors severely delimit both the breadth and depth of the critique, including page limitations and (more impor-

[1]The author wishes to thank Professors Roy Howell, James B. Wilcox and Robert W. Wilkes of Texas Tech University and Professor Harvey Siegel of the University of Miami Philosophy Department for their helpful comments on an earlier draft of this paper.

Source: Reprinted by permission from *Interpretive Consumer Research*, ed. Elizabeth Hirschman, Provo, UT: Association for Consumer Research, 1989, pp. 185-198.

tantly) diversity and heterogeneity of the papers in the volume and the naturalistic, humanistic and interpretive methods.

At the outset, I should admit my own positive bias towards the humanities and their function in both academe and society. I strongly believe that naturalistic, humanistic and interpretive inquiry can play a positive role in developing both marketing and consumer research. At the same time, we must recognize that naturalistic, humanistic and interpretive research efforts are in their early, formative stages in marketing and consumer research. Therefore, the extent to which these methods can develop their ultimate potential depends in part on the paths taken by their "early adopters." This commentary is offered in the constructive spirit of one colleague's suggestions as to which "paths" advocates of these methods might take in order to maximize the likelihood that the potential will be fulfilled.

I suggest that the ultimate fulfillment of the potential of these methods depends in part on how advocates of naturalistic, humanistic and interpretive inquiry respond to four challenges. Each challenge poses its own set of problems, but each appears to be amenable to resolution.

CHARACTERIZATIONS, MISCHARACTERIZATIONS, AND CARICATURIZATIONS

Many of the discussions involving naturalistic, humanistic and interpretive inquiry (hereafter referred to as "N-H-I" methods) seem to start off with a ritualized bashing of those scholars who hold contemporary views as to the nature of science and scientific inquiry. These scholars are labeled "positivists," and their views are contrasted with the enlight-

ened views of N-H-I. Unfortunately, instead of *characterizing* the view of contemporary social science, the ritualized bashing degenerates into blatant *mischaracterizing* or (worse) *caricaturizing*.

The paper by Ozanne and Hudson typifies the procedure of both mischaracterizing and caricaturizing contemporary social science (hereafter referred to as C-S-S). First, consider that they label C-S-S as "positivist." Now, the term positivism was coined in the 19th century by the French philosopher Saint-Simon, one of the founders of a movement known as social positivism, which had as its central objective the promotion of a more just society through the application of the knowledge generated by science and the scientific method. August Comte, Saint-Simon's colleague, articulated and developed the movement's "positive philosophy of science," which has been claimed by Laudan to be "the most important single development in the last century" as to theories of the scientific method (1968, p.29). Later in the 19th century, the physicist Ernst Mach continued the development of positivist philosophy and strongly influenced Einstein in the development of relativity theory (Holton 1970). The positivist movement culminated with the logical positivists of the Vienna Circle in the 1920s. However, a key premise of logical positivism, the verifiability principle, was demonstrated to be untenable in the early 1930s. Thereafter, the Vienna Circle was disbanded (under pressure and persecution from the Nazi's), and logical positivism, formally speaking, ceased to be. Many of the logical positivists continued to work in the general area of empiricist philosophy and some became associated with the research program (in Lakatosian terms) now called logical empiricism.

Although many philosophers of science characterize their philosophy as being *empiricist*, I know of no contemporary philosopher of science who characterizes his/her work as "positivist." For example, Laudan calls his perspective "historical empiricism" (1979, p. 46). Furthermore, although many *practitioners* of C-S-S call their work "empirical," none characterize its nature as "positivistic." In fact, most philosophers of science and practitioners of C-S-S would object strongly to being labeled "positivist." Then why do Ozanne and Hudson (as well as many others in these debates) choose to identify practitioners of C-S-S with a label that not only mischaracterizes their views, (associating them with such discredited beliefs as, for example, the verifiability principle) but one which practitioners find objectionable? The answer lies in applying some concepts of the illuminating paper by Stern in this volume. In particular, Stern points out that words have both a denotative and a connotative meaning. Although "positivist" *denotes* a set of views (including the discredited verifiability principle) held by an identifiable set of people at a particular period of time, over the last several decades the term (rightly or wrongly) has taken on a highly pejorative *connotation*. Thus, by adopting a pejorative, rather than neutral, label for C-S-S, Ozanne and Hudson bring negative connotations into the debate.

Phillips (1987) has chronicled the ongoing diatribe being conducted by a host of writers (including, he notes, Lincoln and Guba) against contemporary social science. In a section entitled "Rampant Anti-Positivism," he concludes:

> [T]here have been many exaggerated claims about the evils of positivism, and about the beneficial effects of its de-

mise. . . . First, many factual errors are made when researchers refer to positivism. Indeed, without suggesting that those who make the errors are dishonest, it seems as if the word "positivism" arouses such negative feelings that it is often used in a blanket way to condemn any position at all that the writer in question disagrees with, irrespective of how positivistic that position really is (1987, p. 94).

Note that Ozanne and Hudson use "interpretive" to identify naturalistic, humanistic and interpretive inquiry. Although "interpretive" may not accurately denote all the characteristics of N-H-I inquiry (as Professor Belk has commented to me), it has to my knowledge no pejorative connotation. Furthermore, it at least is a label chosen by practitioners and advocates of N-H-I, themselves, and not "pinned" on them by advocates of C-S-S.

As a straightforward example of caricature, consider Ozanne and Hudson's claim that a fundamental premise of practitioners of C-S-S is that an "immutable social reality" (p. 5) exists, a "single unchanging reality" (p. 4). "Immutable" is a very strong word implying that social reality is *totally* unchanging. Can anyone seriously claim that practitioners of C-S-S believe that social reality (for example, the relationships among attitudes, intentions, and behaviors of consumers) is totally unchanging? Is this not a *caricature* of C-S-S? As another caricature example, Ozanne and Hudson paint C-S-S researchers as believing that human behavior is "entirely deterministic" (p. 17) rather than "entirely voluntaristic" and propose their own "middle ground position," since "humans seem to indicate some evidence of choosing freely and some evidence of being influenced by internal/external forces" (p. 17). Their discovery of the "middle ground" will hardly seem revelatory to practitioners of C-S-S who have long considered most human behavior to be indeterministic, to be explored through "tendency laws" (Hunt 1983, p. 200) and the like. Is there a better word than *caricature* to describe Ozanne and Hudson's assertions?

Although I have restricted my examples to those in this volume from Ozanne and Hudson, similar rhetorical devices seem all too commonplace throughout the literature. Most importantly, mischaracterizing through pejorative labeling and using caricatures both demean and damage the cause of those who advocate N-H-I. Such devices are normally adopted only by those whose positions are weak or unsound and, therefore, are surely unnecessary for advocates of N-H-I.

The preceding paragraphs point out that the first challenge for advocates of N-H-I is to raise the level of the debate by avoiding pejorative labeling and the caricaturizing of the views of their colleagues in C-S-S. The use of these rhetorical devices may serve well when "preaching to the committed." However, such techniques are unlikely to gain "converts."

DEMONSTRATE THE VALUE OF YOUR PRODUCT

The objective of all research is to produce *knowledge*, or (more epistemologically modest) knowledge-claims. Every university discipline has an extant body of knowledge and all scholarly journals associated with academic disciplines evaluate manuscripts according to whether each submitted manuscript contributes to, or extends, the extant body of knowledge as judged by a jury of one's peers. Essentially, the process of evaluating manuscripts for a scholarly journal involves answering three questions:

1) What is the *nature* of the purported contribution to knowledge of the manuscript? 2) What is the *extent* of the purported contribution to knowledge? 3) Is the purported contribution to knowledge *genuine*?

The first evaluative question categorizes the purported contribution. Does the manuscript fall within the domain of the journal? For example, is the manuscript truly in the area of consumer behavior, or is it marketing management, or is it personnel management, and so forth. The second question, identifying the *extent* of the purported contribution, is actually a composite of three sub-questions. First, to what extent is the purported contribution new? That is, has the contribution been previously reported in the literature? The second aspect of the extent criterion is, roughly speaking, a quantitative dimension. In the judgment of the reviewers is the contribution "large enough" to warrant publishing in the journal. Alternatively, is the contribution-to-page-length ratio large enough? The third aspect of the extent question has to do with the value of the contribution. Will the manuscript be valuable in encouraging further research? Does the manuscript have value for decision makers? Does the manuscript have value for government policy? In addition to the nature of the contribution and the extent of the contribution, the manuscript review process evaluates the *genuineness* of the contribution. How do we know that the knowledge-claims in the manuscript are true, or trustworthy, or verified, or confirmed, or (in philosophy of science terms) have "high epistemic warrant"?

It seems to me that the product, or output, or knowledge-claims of interpretive inquiry faces serious and significant (but not insuperable) difficulties with all three of the major criteria that scholarly journals impose on manuscripts. Consider the major knowledge-claim extensively discussed in the Holbrook, Bell and Grayson paper (originally developed in Holbrook and Grayson (1986)). As I understand their work, the major knowledge-claim resulting from their interpretive inquiry is that "consumption symbolism contributes to the development of character in a work of art" (p. 36). This knowledge-claim of interpretive inquiry provides an excellent illustration, since it has already been published in the *Journal of Consumer Research* and, therefore, has survived the peer-review process. (Presumably, the results of many interpretive studies, just like the results of many studies conducted using the methods of C-S-S, would not pass the peer-review process of major journals, such as *JCR*.)

How might reviewers have applied the first criterion to the Holbrook-Grayson contribution? The reviewers would obviously have to ask themselves whether the contribution was more about "consumption symbolism" (and therefore appropriate for *JCR*) or whether the contribution was more in the area of "art" (and therefore more appropriate for another journal)? My experience has been that most journals receive many manuscripts where, in the judgment of the reviewers, the nature of the contribution is outside the domain of the journal. Second, how would the *extent* criterion be applied to the Holbrook-Grayson contribution? I suspect that some reviewers might contend that, since works of art mirror society, and since it is "well known" (from the hundreds of life-style and psychographic studies) that many people significantly express their personalities through consumption symbols, that the Holbrook-Grayson contribution may not represent a "new" addition to the body of knowledge. Further, I suspect that some reviewers might contend that, even if the contribution is "new," it is not "large enough" for a journal such as *JCR*. Finally, with respect to *extent*, what is the value of the contribution? Will it encourage further research? If so, of what kind? Does the contribution have value to any of *JCR*'s publics in addition to researchers? (Although *JCR* does not purport to be a "managerial" journal, it does purport to be relevant to public policy and other societal issues.)

With respect to the third criterion, is the Holbrook-Grayson purported contribution *genuine*? To what extent is it true that "consumption symbolism contributes to the development of character in a work of art"? (For those who consider the word "true" to be naive, naughty or nefarious, they may substitute surrogates, such as warranted, justified, credible, or trustworthy. Notably Holbrook, Bell and Grayson do not avoid the word "truth," since they claim "the humanities in general and artworks in particular contain truths that escape procedures of the hypothetico-deductive method" (p. 31)). The reviewers will ask whether the Holbrook-Grayson knowledge-claim is in some meaningful sense *genuine*. After all, Holbrook and Grayson do not simply claim that it is *possible* to interpret consumption symbolism as contributing to the development of character. Rather, they claim that "consumption symbolism *contributes* to the development of character." This implies the necessity of demonstrating that the Holbrook-Grayson interpretation satisfies appropriate criteria for good, well-conducted, truly justificatory, interpretive research; and not bad, poorly conducted, nonjustificatory, interpretive research.

It is clear that the Holbrook-Grayson contribution satisfied the reviewers of *JCR* on all three criteria discussed in the preceding paragraphs. Nevertheless, I am sure the authors of that paper would be the first to admit that much needs to be done to smooth the way for publishing (and thus disseminating) the work of future research efforts. Therefore, interpretive researchers must consciously address the second challenge: clearly demonstrating that the nature of their purported contributions to knowledge reside within the domains of their chosen publishing outlets, both showing the *extent* of their contributions (i.e., their newness, significance and value) and justifying that their contributions are *genuine*. In this regard the paper by Wallendorf and Belk in this volume is exemplary. Contrary to the oft-cited claim that there are no universal standards or values (across different approaches or paradigms or "disciplinary matrixes"), they note that "trustworthiness" is to them considered "to be a scientific universal," although "the particular way that trustworthiness is evaluated will vary considerably depending on the research program and the philosophy within which the research operates" (p. 1). Their paper builds upon the criteria for evaluating humanistic inquiry developed by Hirschman (1986) and clearly demonstrates that there are both good procedures to adopt in actually conducting naturalistic inquiry and that these procedures can be used as evaluative criteria for assessing the justificatory warrant of the knowledge-claims generated by such research.

With respect to demonstrating the value of interpretive inquiry, it seems strange that advocates of N-H-I are characterizing their inquiry in such a manner as to render it fundamentally irrelevant to public policy and other significant social concerns. Ozanne and Hudson claim that "while interpretivists may identify patterns of behavior, they believe that the world is so complex and dynamic that causal relationships cannot be identified" (p. 5). Similarly, Hirschman, claims that "phenomenal aspects cannot be segregated into causes and effects" (1986, p.239).

As an implication of claiming that interpretive inquiry cannot yield causal knowledge, consider the issue of the impact of television advertising on children. This is currently a significant social issue about which there are direct public policy implications. It would seem that interpretive inquiry might have a role to play in identifying how children interpret the messages or "texts" received from the television screen. Further, such interpretive inquiry might yield knowledge, or at least some tentative hypotheses, about how children's interpretations of television advertising are formed (a causal imputation). Such interpretive inquiry might then give guidance to public policy in this important area. But, public policy decisions in this kind of area *inherently* involve causal imputations. That is, if television advertising has no *effect* on children's beliefs, attitudes, or values, then any government regulation would be unnecessary or ineffective. If television *does* have a (deleterious) effect on children, what kind of government regulation would negate or overcome the effect? *In fact, most government regulation necessarily implies that a particular law or regulation will bring about, or "cause," some desirable consequence.* Therefore, I question why advocates of N-H-I choose to define and circumscribe their inquiry to be irrelevant to public policy. Curiously, there is no reason for them to do so, except perhaps as a reaction (over-reaction?) to the strong emphasis on causal processes in C-S-S and the reliance (over-reliance?) on the views of those such as Lincoln and Guba (1985). Finally, it should be noted, substituting Hudson and Ozanne's "mutual, simultaneous shaping" (1988, p. 512) for "cause" does not save N-H-I from irrelevancy. To suggest that a child and a television set are engaged in "mutual simultaneous shaping" strains credulity beyond all reasonable limits. (Consider for starters the implications of the word *simultaneous* on the child/television set example.)

INTERPRETIVISM AND RELATIVISM

Both the Anderson paper and the Peter and Olson contribution present spirited defenses of the appropriateness of relativism for consumer research. Both position their papers as a reply to Calder and Tybout (1987), who adopt a sophisticated falsificationist perspective for analyzing various kinds of knowledge-claims. Much of the content of the Anderson, Peter and Olson papers contains rather standard arguments against falsificationism as a demarcation criterion to separate science from nonscience. In this section I shall not analyze their attack on falsificationism. Rather, I shall focus on the more fundamental issue of demarcation in general.

Consistent with his previously stated positions (1983, 1986), Anderson claims that "we currently have *no* universally applicable criterion by which we can demarcate scientific knowledge from any other kind of knowledge" (p. 1). He cites Laudan (1980) as a reference and notes that "unfortunately this is often thought to imply that all knowledge-claims are on an equal epistemic footing" (p. 1), referring to Hunt (1984). He claims that "very

little follows from the fact that philosophers have been unable to come up with a *universal* demarcation criterion" (p. 1), and speaks again in favor of what he calls "science$_2$—the definition of science by societal consensus" (p. 2). Is it the case that nothing of great importance follows from the demarcation issue? Stated more succinctly, is it the case that "societal consensus" alone constitutes the reason why there are astronomy departments in universities but not astrology departments, that there are medical science departments but not palmistry departments? I and many others believe that it is not just "societal consensus," but rather that *the societal consensus is backed by very good reasons*, as can be illustrated by analyzing what may be called the "nature of science argument."

The "nature of science argument" according to a fundamental premise (noted hereafter as "R1") of the relativist point of view, as stated by Anderson and detailed in Hunt (1984), may be concisely summarized as follows:

R1.   *There are no fundamental differences separating the sciences and the nonsciences.* ("The search for [demarcation] criteria that separate science from nonscience"...has been "signally unsuccessful" (Anderson 1983, p. 18). Since there are no objective criteria separating science from nonscience, "science is whatever society chooses to call science" (Anderson 1983, p. 26).)

R2.   *The knowledge-claims of the nonsciences have as much epistemological warrant as the sciences.* (That is, we have no good reason to believe and act on the knowledge-claims of the sciences in preference to the nonsciences. Statement R2 is *logically implied* by R1 because, if we had good reasons to believe and act on the knowledge-claims of the sciences, such reasons would constitute "fundamental differences" that could be used to separate science from nonscience).

R3. Therefore, statement R2 implies that if a palmist should diagnose a person as *not* having bone cancer (an example of a nonscience knowledge-claim), such a diagnosis would have equal warrant as the diagnosis of a medical doctor that the person *did* have bone cancer (an example of a science knowledge-claim).

A reconstruction of the "nature of science argument" according to modern empiricism (as detailed in Hunt (1984) and drawing upon works such as Hempel (1969), Radner and Radner (1982), Rudner (1966) and Siegel (1986)) would be:

E1. *There are fundamental differences separating the sciences and non-sciences.* (Sciences differ from non-sciences in their method of verifying knowledge-claims.)

E2. *The knowledge-claims of sciences have greater epistemological warrant than the knowledge-claims of the non-sciences.* (Since the knowledge-claims of the sciences are intersubjectively certifiable through open empirical testing, people have good reasons for accepting such claims and acting upon them in preference to the knowledge-claims of nonsciences.)

E3. Therefore, E2 implies that if a palmist should diagnose a person as *not* having bone cancer and a medical doctor should diagnose that same person as *having* bone cancer, the person has good reasons for believing the diagnosis of the medical doctor and acting accordingly. (Palmistry has not adopted the verification sys-

tem of open empirical testing and, therefore, is not a science.)

Anderson reviewed the narrative versions of the preceding nature of science arguments and lamented that empiricists often cast "proffered alternatives" as "relativistic flights of fancy that lead to epistemological anarchy and the abandonment of rationality and objectivity" (Anderson 1986, p. 156). He did not deny that the empiricist version accurately reflected the views of modern empiricism. Nor did he do a detailed analysis of the relativist version, pointing out logical flaws or empirical inadequacies. Rather, he dismissed the argument as a "straw man." To avoid the impression of possibly mischaracterizing Anderson's reasons for dismissing the argument, he is quoted at length:

> The type of relativism attacked by Hunt (1984) has *never* been advocated by any of the participants in the current debate. The object of Hunt's critique is a straw man known as judgmental (Knorr-Cetina and Mulkay 1983) or "nihilistic" relativism. In this view, all knowledge claims are equally valid and there is no basis on which to make judgments among the various contenders. (*Indeed, a careful reading of even the most radical of contemporary relativists will reveal that this does not even approximate their views*, e.g., Collins 1975, 1981; Feyerabend 1975, 1978a) (page 156 emphasis added).

Is it true that the above argument (indicating that the relativism advocated by Anderson and others inexorably leads one to be indifferent between the claims of palmistry and medical science) is a "straw man?" Is it truly the case that "a careful reading of *even the most radical* of contemporary relativists will reveal that this does not even *approximate* their views?"

Is the Nature of Science Argument a Strawman?

Since Anderson uses Feyerabend as an example of a contemporary relativist who would not subscribe to the so-called "nihilistic" relativism presented in the preceding argument, we shall examine Feyerabend's views on the subject. Feyerabend is one of the most prominent and widely cited supporters of a relativist view of science (Suppe 1977). Indeed, all of the relativist writers in consumer research draw heavily from his works for intellectual sustenance, reference him liberally, and even refer to him as a relativist "hero" (Olson 1987). In addition to many articles extolling the virtues of relativism, Feyerabend has published several books on the subject, including: *Against Method* (1975) and *Science In A Free Society* (1978b). In the 1978 book he extends and further clarifies the positions taken in the 1975 book. (All references to Feyerabend in the following sections refer to his 1978 work.) Further, he addresses and answers many criticisms of his work from other philosophers of science. He is quoted here at length (again, to avoid the charge of mischaracterization) concerning his answer to a critique by a philosopher named Tibbets:

> [Tibbets] also asks: 'If *he* had a child diagnosed with Leukemia would he look to his witchdoctor friends or to the Sloan Kettering Institute?' I can assure him that I would look to my 'witchdoctor friends' to use his somewhat imprecise terminology *and so would many other people in California* whose experience with scientific medicine has been anything but encouraging. The fact that scientific medicine is the only existing form of medicine in many places does not mean that it is the best and the fact that alternative forms of medicine succeed where scientific medicine has to resort to surgery shows that it has serious lacunae: numerous women, reluctant to have their breasts amputated as their doctors advised them, went to acupuncturists, faithhealers, herbalists and got cured. Parents of small children with allegedly incurable diseases, leukemia among them, did not give up, they consulted 'witchdoctors' and their children got cured. How do I know? Because I advised some of these men and women and I followed the fate of others (pp. 205-206, emphasis in original).

Recall that Anderson dismissed the "nature of science argument" on the basis that "a careful reading of even the most radical of contemporary relativists will reveal that this does not even approximate their views" (1986, p. 156). The above quote clearly shows that, to the contrary, any careful observer of relativists' writings knows that the relativist "nature of science argument" very closely reflects the logical implications of their views! How do relativists (such as Feyerabend) reach such extreme positions that even their followers (such as Anderson) dismiss relativist views as "nihilistic" nonsense? The answer lies precisely in Feyerabend's fundamental beliefs about the existence of many, equally viable, "ways of knowing" that he calls research "traditions." These fundamental beliefs are very similar, if not precisely the same, as those (supposedly) now championed by relativist consumer researchers.

Feyerabend on "Ways of Knowing"

Central to the relativist philosophy of Feyerabend is the construct of a knowledge-creating "tradition." Feyerabend notes that science is but one of many such traditions, each constituting a "way to know." What are these other traditions? Throughout his 1978 book he discusses and defends mysticism (p. 31), magic (p. 74), astrology (p. 74), rain dances (p. 78), religion (p. 78), "mythical world views" (p. 78), tribal medicine (p. 96), parapsychology (p. 103), all non-Western belief traditions (p. 102), and witchcraft (p. 191). Each "way of knowing" is equal, since "traditions are neither good nor bad, they simply are" (p. 27). (This is similar to Science$_2$ in Anderson's terms.)

Feyerabend notes that in the 17th, 18th, and 19th centuries the scientific tradition was but one of the many competing ideologies and was in fact a "liberating force" because it "restricted the influence of other ideologies and thus gave the individual room for thought" (p. 75). However, he believes science today does not have a liberating effect since it has turned into a "dogmatic religion." He believes "the very same enterprise that once gave man the ideas and the strength to free himself from the fears and prejudices of a tyrannical religion now turns him into a slave of its interests" (p. 75).

How did the consensus emerge that the knowledge-claims of science were preferred by society over the knowledge-claims of competing traditions? Is it not because society rationally and reasonably determined that scientific knowledge-claims had more epistemological warrant, were more likely to be true? (Science$_1$ in Anderson's terms.) Emphatically not, asserts Feyerabend:

> It reigns supreme because some past successes have led to institutional measures (education; role of experts; role of power groups such as the AMA) that prevent a comeback of the rivals. Briefly, but not incorrectly: Today science prevails not because of its comparative merits, but because the show has been rigged in its favor (p. 102).

Specifically, for Feyerabend how did these other traditions lose out? "These myths, these religions, these procedures have disappeared or deteriorated not because science was better, but because *the apostles of science were the more determined conquerors,* because they *materially suppressed* the bearers of alternative cultures" (p. 102, emphasis in original).

How was the material suppression of rival traditions and the triumph of the "apostles of science" accomplished? The suppression of rival traditions was accomplished, he contends, through the actions of scientists, both individually and through their collective associations, aided and abetted by such diverse groups as "liberal intellectuals, white missionaries, adventurers, and anthropologists" (p. 77).

As examples of suppressive tactics, Feyerabend notes that anthropologists "collected and systematized" knowledge about non-Western traditions and developed "interpretations" that "were simply a consequence of "popular antimetaphysical tendencies combined with a firm belief in the excellence first, of Christianity, and then of science" (p. 77). Liberal intellectuals aided the suppression by first "loudly and persistently" proclaiming that they defend freedom of thought, while at the same time not recognizing that this freedom of thought only "is granted to those who have already accepted part of the rationalist (i.e., scientific) ideology" (p. 76). Feyerabend, himself, even contributed to the suppression while teaching at the University of California at Berkeley: "My function was to carry out the educational policies of the State of California, which means I had to teach people what a small group of white intellectuals had decided was knowledge" (p. 118).

Feyerabend concludes that "the prevalence of science is a threat to democracy" (p. 76) and proposes his solution to the problem of science in society. He addresses this issue by first proposing the following rhetorical questions (concerning Science$_1$ and Science$_2$):

> But—so the impatient believer in rationalism and science is liable to exclaim—is this procedure not justified? Is there not a tremendous difference between science on the one side, religion, magic, myth on the other? Is this difference not so large and so obvious that it is unnecessary to point it out and silly to deny it? (p. 78)

Feyerabend answers his rhetorical questions concerning the differences between science$_1$ and science$_2$ thusly: "Rationalists and scientists cannot rationally (scientifically) argue for the unique position of their favorite ideology" (p. 79). Therefore, he proposes, in order to have a free society "is it not rather the case that traditions [mysticism, magic, astrology, rain dances, religion, mythical world views, tribal medicine, parapsychology, all non-Western belief traditions, and witchcraft] that give substance to the lives of people must be given equal rights and *equal access to key positions in society* no matter what other traditions think about them? (p. 79, emphasis added).

The preceding discussion of Feyerabend's relativist views on research traditions in society clearly shows how he arrives at conclusions so extreme as to be labelled "nihilistic" and "a straw man" by Anderson. One might suppose that Feyerabend is simply engaging in academic gamesmanship or sophistry and that he did not intend for readers to take his views seriously. Brodbeck notes that relativists believe "science is in effect a game" (1982, p. 3), which is consistent with Anderson's view that "the impor-

tant question we must ask is how can I convince my colleagues in the scientific community that my theory is correct?" (1982, p. 15). As Krausz and Meiland (1982, p. 6) have pointed out, the sophists in ancient Greece were among the first relativists in western intellectual history. From whom we get the term "sophistry," these philosophers delighted in weaving incredibly convoluted arguments that *they* knew to be false, but that the *less sophisticated* would (or could) not know.

Clearly, however, Feyerabend is not sophist! The preceding discussion demonstrates that he recognizes how extreme are his premises concerning the nature of the scientific "tradition" (the knowledge-claims of the sciences are no better than the knowledge-claims of the nonsciences) and is willing to accept their logical consequences (palmistry and medical science should have "equal rights" and "equal access to key positions"), no matter how extreme those consequences may appear to others. Most importantly, he not only intellectually accepts these extreme consequences, but (unlike a sophist) he also acts upon them (referring now to the first long quote of Feyerabend in this paper where he indicates he has both used and referred others to "witchdoctor friends").

Unfortunately, many relativists are not as consistent as Feyerabend. The issue was *never* (as Anderson and others have stated it) whether relativists embraced "nihilistic" conclusions (like R3), but whether relativist beliefs (like R1) *implied* nihilism. Relativist advocates wish to emphatically proclaim Feyerabend's extreme premises concerning the nature of science, yet unlike him, they wish to deny (indeed, pejoratively dismiss) the logical consequences of those premises. For the purposes of present discussion, let us label this position as "weak-form" relativism (consistent with Anderson's "weak-form incommensurability" (1986, p. 164)) and in order for its advocates to avoid the charges of nihilism, sophistry, and/or the pain of logical inconsistency, let us explore how they might defend such a position.

Weak-Form Relativism

Anderson and presumably (but not necessarily) other consumer behavior relativists do not share the extreme conclusions on the nature of science held by writers such as Feyerabend (such as statement R3). Yet, they wish to embrace Feyerabend-like premises on science (such as statement R1). Is it possible, therefore, to salvage the weak-form relativism championed by them? A satisfactory answer to this question lies not in them simply *denying* that they agree with the extreme conclusions of the relativist argument on the nature of science (that the diagnoses of palmists should be given equal epistemological status to the diagnoses of medical science). To do so is much like killing the messenger who brings bad news. Rather, since the conclusions of any argument are entailed in its premises, advocates of weak-form relativism must re-examine their premises in order to salvage their position, for extreme premises yield extreme conclusions.

Modifying statement R1 to make it less extreme might be a useful starting place for weak-form relativists. Such a modification might be as follows:

R1a. Although in most cases it is impossible to find fundamental differences separating what society chooses to call "science" from "nonscience," there are isolated instances (like medical science versus palmistry) where such differences are obvious.

Weak-form relativists would then have to identify and state the characteristics that so "obviously" differentiate science from nonscience in each such "isolated instance." Further, they would have to show how these differentiating characteristics lack commonality (each obvious instance is totally idiosyncratic) and defend this lack of commonality as a reasonable position. *Or* they would have to identify the *common* differentiating characteristics across the "isolated instances" and defend how these commonalities differ in some significant fashion from what practicing scientists (and those philosophers of science who live in the supposed "fairy tale" world of modern empiricism) call the *scientific method* of verification through open empirical testing. Otherwise, weak-form relativists would be forced to *deny* one of their most cherished precepts: that science does not differ from nonscience through its method of verification of knowledge-claims.

Clearly, the preceding procedure for salvaging weak-form relativism would seem to be an extraordinarily difficult task at best, or devastating to the relativist agenda at worst. Therefore, modifying statement R2 as a possibility to salvage weak-form relativism should be examined.

Statement R2 of the relativist argument indicates that the knowledge-claims of the nonsciences have as much epistemological warrant as the knowledge-claims of sciences. Anderson has already made a useful start in the direction of modifying R2 when he noted that "society bestows a high epistemological status on science because it believes that science generally functions in the best interests of society as a whole" (Anderson 1983, p. 26). Advocates of weak-form relativism could modify their position on R2 by *agreeing* with society:

> R2a. Society does bestow and *ought to bestow* a higher epistemological status on the knowledge-claims of the sciences than on knowledge-claims of the nonsciences.

Justifying statement R2a would pose a significant challenge for relativists. Although society may bestow a privileged epistemological position on science capriciously and arbitrarily (as Feyerabend states and Anderson implies in his science$_2$: "science is whatever society chooses to call a science"), weak-form relativists, as professed scholars of science, would have to explain exactly *why* society ought to bestow a superior position on the knowledge-claims of science. Precisely *why* is it reasonable to believe that science, in preference to nonscience, functions "in the best interests of society as a whole?" This would seem to necessarily imply that weak-form relativists would have to claim that the procedures that science uses to justify its knowledge-claims are somehow *better*. That is, its "way of knowing" or "tradition" is *superior*. But if the verification procedures for scientific knowledge-claims are better than the procedures used by nonsciences, then, on pain of continuing inconsistency, weak-form relativists would have to again give up their belief that there are no fundamental differences separating the sciences from the nonsciences. And therein lies the rub. In order to "save" relativism, the weak-form relativists have to destroy it.

Contrary to the verdict of Anderson (relying on Laudan's views), many philosophers of science continue to believe that there are fundamental differences

separating science from the nonscience, which provide good reasons for societal consensus (Grove 1985). For example, a recent article in the *Philosophy of Science* by Siegel reviewed the debate and notes that "Laudan's rejection of a unique SM [Scientific Method] depends on a failure to distinguish between general principles of appraisal and specific instantiations of such principles" [or "techniques"] (1985, p. 528). He goes on to note that the methodological criteria of science that collectively constitute the scientific method can best be expressed as a "commitment to evidence," as exemplified by "a concern for explanatory adequacy, however that adequacy is conceived; and insistence on testing, however testing is thought to be best done; and a commitment to inductive support, however inductive inference is thought to be best made" (p. 528). Thus, "science's commitment to evidence, by way of SM, is what justifies its claim to respect—science is to be taken seriously precisely because of its commitment to evidence" (p. 530). However, the preceding conclusions by Siegel about scientific method do not imply that he claims that science is the *only* domain in which the epistemic worthiness of beliefs, hypotheses, or claims may be putatively established on the basis of evidence. Rather, "SM extends far beyond the realm of science proper. But this is only to say that SM can be utilized widely. It is still properly labeled *scientific* method" (p. 530).

One of the problems with the entire demarcation issue in science is the word "demarcation," itself. This unfortunate choice of words (by Popper) tends to suggest (connote) that an *unequivocal* judgment can be made in all cases using a single, simple criterion (like "falsifiability"). Borderline cases, such as parapsychology, are then brought forth by relativists such as Anderson as examples that purportedly demonstrate the science/nonscience distinction to be just a societal convention rather than a societal consensus based on good reasons. The fallacy of such a ploy is evident as pointed out by Grove (1985). *Most, if not all, genuine and useful categorizational schemata have borderline cases.* Should biology dispense with the male/female distinction because some entities share characteristics of both sexes? Should consumer research dispense with consumer goods/industrial goods because some goods at some times can be either? Should advocates of N-H-I dispense with the trustworthy research/nontrustworthy research distinction just because the truth-content of its knowledge-claims cannot be known with certainty? How about rational/irrational? Objective/subjective? Or, I suggest, truth/falsity?

Should interpretivist consumer research adopt relativism as Anderson, Peter and Olson propose? The preceding analysis should (at the very least) sound a cautionary note: *Any philosophy* whose underlying premises lead to conclusions so extreme that they are dismissed as "nihilistic" nonsense *by the philosophy's own advocates* must be considered highly suspect, if not intellectually impoverished. Such a philosophy would seem to poorly serve the needs of researchers of any kind. Nevertheless, Hudson and Ozanne imply that consumer research should strongly consider relativism since it is "based on the premise that every approach to consumer research may have something to offer" (1988, p. 520). Hudson and Ozanne (mistakenly, as Muncy and Fisk (1987), Vallicella (1984), Margolis (1983), and Hacking (1982) point out) equate the premises of relativism with diversity, tolerance and pluralism. But relativism, as Feyerabend has so forcefully argued, implies epistemological anarchy, not a tolerant epistemological pluralism. And

just as ethical relativism does not imply the tolerance of ethical diversity (Harrison 1982), and just as political anarchy does not imply a tolerant, pluralistic democracy, epistemological anarchy does not imply a tolerant, pluralistic science. So, the third challenge for N-H-I inquiry is to advocate a tolerant pluralism, without relativism. The reasons for this challenge will become even clearer after we discuss incommensurability.

INTERPRETIVISM AND INCOMMENSURABILITY

Ozanne and Hudson evaluate the procedures for producing knowledge-claims in interpretivism and C-S-S, concluding that "the knowledge outputs of these two approaches are incommensurable" (in abstract). The notion that paradigms are incommensurable was first introduced by Kuhn in his influential 1962 book, *The Structure of Scientific Revolutions,* and was strongly argued by Feyerabend in his early work. It is most curious that Ozanne and Hudson would claim that interpretivism and C-S-S are incommensurable, since now even Feyerabend concedes that "incommensurability as understood by me is a rare event," and that "incommensurability is a difficulty for philosophers, not for scientists" (1987, p. 81).

Of the many new concepts that Kuhn introduced to the analysis of science in his 1962 work, incommensurability has been one of the most controversial and extensively discussed. Kuhn's original argument provided that in "normal" science (e.g., the paradigm of Ptolomy) all the members of a scientific community implicitly accept a common paradigm, which contains 1) a content (concepts, laws, theories, etc.), "exemplars" (standard examples of problems that the content of the paradigm solves), 2) a methodology (the procedures by which further knowledge within the paradigm is to be generated) and, 3) an epistemology (a set of criteria by which the knowledge generated within the paradigm is to be evaluated). Kuhn claimed that a new rival paradigm (e.g., Copernicus) emerges in "revolutionary" science only when the existing paradigm is faced with "anomalies." This rival or competing paradigm is considered *incommensurable* with the previous dominant paradigm.

Kuhn's claim of incommensurability rests upon Gestalt psychology and the work of Hanson (1958) and Wittgenstein (1953). Arguing by analogy, Kuhn compares the views of the advocates of the rival paradigms as being similar to the familiar "duck/rabbit" illustration in Gestalt psychology textbooks. (In this classic example of Gestalt, subjects are shown an ambiguous drawing in which some people "see" a duck, others "see" a rabbit, and some people can "switch" back and forth, "seeing" either.) Kuhn proposes that there are no paradigm-neutral criteria for adjudicating the conflict between the dominant paradigm and its rival. Rather, when the "revolutionary" paradigm is successful, the former adherents to the dominant paradigm undergo a "Gestalt switch" (from "duck" to "rabbit"), or a "conversion" process.

Exactly what does incommensurability mean? After Kuhn's 1962 work, various writers began pinning him down as to precisely how he proposed incommensurability should be interpreted. Space limitations prevent a detailed description of all the interpretations and their resultant analyses. Rather, we here shall only mention some of the most prominent interpretations and point the reader toward the literature that evaluates them.

One of the earliest interpretations was the *meaning/variance* view that scientific terms change meaning from para-

digm to paradigm. This view was critiqued by Shapere (1964 and 1966), Scheffler (1967, chapter 3) and Kordig (1971, chapters 2 and 3). A second analysis, the *radical translation* interpretation, suggests that in some meaningful way the actual terms involved in one paradigm cannot be translated into the language of its rivals. This interpretation was suggested by Kuhn, himself, in his *postscript* to the 1970 edition of *Structure* (pp. 200-204). The radical translation view has been analyzed by Kitcher (1978), Moberg (1979) and Levin (1979) (the radical translation view is also critiqued in my own 1983, pp. 368-372). A third interpretation of incommensurability has been the *incomparability* view that rival paradigms simply cannot be meaningfully compared. This interpretation was critiqued by Scheffler, Shapere and Kordig in the references previously cited and also by Laudan (1976) and Putnam (1981).

Although, as previously mentioned, the details of the analyses cited in the preceding paragraph cannot be extensively developed here, some flavor of the arguments can certainly be presented. For example, consider the *incomparability* interpretation. Most assuredly, incommensurability *cannot* imply incomparability, for to recognize that the "revolutionary" paradigm is incommensurable with the rival "dominant" paradigm (as Siegel (1980, p. 366) has noted) is at the very least to imply that the paradigms can be *compared*. How would one even know that the paradigms are *rival* if they could not be compared in some meaningful way? Similarly, the *radical translation* thesis is fundamentally flawed. As Putnam points out, to contend that the language of one paradigm cannot be translated into the terms of another paradigm "and then to go on and describe [both paradigms] *at length* [in the same language] is totally incoherent" (p. 114). Finally, the *meaning-variance* thesis (that some concepts or terms that are used in the revolutionary paradigm have a meaning that is different from how the concepts or terms are used in the dominant paradigm) may present difficulties in communicating, but surely does not imply *incommensurability* in any meaningful sense. Again, how can the two paradigms be genuinely *rival* paradigms if they are "talking" about different phenomena? Roughly speaking, it's like "Aha! Here we have been arguing and all the time you were discussing apples and I was discussing oranges!"

The many detailed analyses of the concept of incommensurability over the last several decades have led most philosophers of science to agree with the summary evaluation most recently put forward by Hintikka: "The frequent arguments that strive to use the absolute or relative incommensurability of scientific theories as a reason for thinking that they are inaccessible to purely scientific (rational) comparisons are simply fallacious" (1988, p. 38). Ironically, advocates of the *meaning-variance* interpretation of incommensurability have demonstrated the cogency of the logical positivist view about the purpose of the philosophy of science. The logical positivists held that philosophers could and should clarify the language of science and, therefore, increase the ability of various scientists to talk with each other when working in different (in today's vernacular) "paradigms."

Much more interesting for our purposes here than the fact that incommensurability has been discredited in the philosophy of science, is the reaction of Kuhn himself to critiques of incommensurability. Kuhn has been very sensitive to the complex issues raised by these critiques and has attempted to modify his position accordingly. In his 1970 revision of *Struc-*

ture, he claimed that his critics had completely misinterpreted his views on incommensurability when they claimed that "the proponents of incommensurable theories cannot communicate with each other at all; as a result, in a debate over theory-choice there can be no recourse to *good* reasons; instead theory must be chosen for reasons that are ultimately personal and subjective; some sort of mystical apperception is responsible for the decision actually reached" (pp. 198-199, emphasis in original). That is, Kuhn now wishes to deny the previous rhetoric about "conversions" and "Gestalt-shifts." Rather, he now emphasizes the reliance on "good reasons." Moreover, the reader should note that Kuhn does not just say "reasons," but "good" reasons, which would seem to necessarily imply that there are some paradigm-neutral standards that can be used to assess the adequacy of rival paradigms. However, Kuhn has not simply stopped with advocating *good reasons*. In his 1976 work, he has again attempted to further clarify his concept of incommensurability and now seems to be construing incommensurability as analogous to the concept of a mathematical algorithm:

> Most readers of my text have supposed that when I spoke of theories as incommensurable, I meant that they could not be compared. But "incommensurability" is a term borrowed from mathematics, and it there has no such implication. The hypotenuse of an isosceles right triangle is incommensurable with its side, but the two can be compared to any required degree of precision. What is lacking is not comparability but a unit of length in terms of which both can be measured directly and exactly (pp. 190-1).

Why has Kuhn been so anxious to modify and thereby retreat from his earlier, highly provocative, "Gestalt-shift" position? It is precisely because Kuhn has recognized that his earlier position implied relativism and irrationality:

> "My critics respond to my views. . .with charges of irrationality, relativism, and the defense of mob rule. These are all labels which I categorically reject" (1970a, p. 234).

But, why should one of the most eminent historians of science of this century wish to "categorically reject" the charge of relativism? Is not relativism roughly analogous to *diversity* and *pluralism*, as Ozanne, Hudson, Peter and Olson suggest? Isn't it *obviously* the case that "the way in which social and consumer behavior research is actually practiced is best construed from a critical relativist perspective" (Anderson 1986, p. 167)? No. As Barnes and Bloor (themselves strong advocates of relativism) point out: "In the academic world, relativism is everywhere abominated" (1982, p. 21). Generally speaking, most philosophers of science go to great lengths to avoid having their views associated with "abominated" relativism because they recognize the extreme conclusions that stem from relativistic doctrine. Capsulized in very succinct form, the argument that motivated Kuhn to retreat from incommensurability goes as follows:

1. It is difficult, if not impossible, to accept *incommensurability* (in any nontrivial, interesting, or meaningful sense) without accepting *relativism*.
2. It is difficult, if not impossible, to accept *relativism* (in any nontrivial, interesting, or meaningful sense) without accepting *irrationalism*.
3. It is difficult, if not impossible, to accept *irrationalism* (in any nontrivial, interesting, or meaningful sense) without denying that it is possible to have *knowledge* about the world.

4. It is difficult, if not impossible, to deny that we can have *knowledge* (in any nontrivial, interesting, or meaningful sense) about the world without denying that there has been scientific *progress*.
5. It is difficult, if not impossible, to deny that there has been scientific *progress* (in any nontrivial, interesting, or meaningful sense) without denying that we *know* more about the world now than we did before the rise of modern science in the 17th century.

Stove (1982) reviews the works of those he calls the "modern irrationalists," including Kuhn and Feyerabend, and states his own version of the conclusion of the preceding argument:

> Much more is known now than was known 50 years ago, and much more was known then than in 1580. So there has been a great accumulation or growth of knowledge in the last four hundred years. This is an extremely well-known fact, which I will refer to as (A). . . . So a writer whose position inclined him to deny (A), or even made him reluctant to admit it, would almost inevitably seem, to the philosophers who read him, to be maintaining something extremely implausible. . . .Everyone would admit that if there has *ever* been a growth of knowledge, it has been in the last four hundred years, so anyone reluctant to admit (A) must, if he is consistent, be reluctant to admit that there has ever been a growth of knowledge at all. But if a philosopher of science takes a position which obliges him, on pain of inconsistency, to be reluctant to admit *this*, then his position can be rightly described as irrationalism . . . (pp. 3 and 4).

The extreme nature of the conclusion of the preceding argument shows why Kuhn has been so anxious to demonstrate that one can accept *incommensurability* without accepting *relativism* and *irrationalism*. (Kuhn's philosophy, to his chagrin, is now used as a standard example of irrationalism in such reference works as the *Dictionary of the History of Science* (1981, p. 360).) Further, it explains why those, like Anderson (1986 and 1988), who willingly accept relativism take such great pains to attempt to show that "their version" of relativism is neither self-refuting, nor irrationalistic. It also shows clearly the consistency of Feyerabend when he denies that the knowledge generated from science differs in any meaningful or genuine way from magic, astrology, rain dances, religion, mythical world views, and witchcraft (as previously discussed in this paper). Indeed, as Siegel has noted, except for logically consistent relativists such as Feyerabend, by the time that others get through qualifying and modifying concepts such as incommensurability and relativism, often labels such as "critical pluralism" more appropriately characterize what is left (1988, p. 132).

Is Interpretivism Incommensurable?

We are now in a position to better assess the claim by Ozanne and Hudson that "the knowledge outputs of these two approaches [N-H-I and C-S-S] are incommensurable" (in abstract). The evidence for their conclusion comes from their examination of Bower's [C-S-S] approach to studying emotion defined as "a physiological, internal state". . . stored in memory in an associative network," and comparing it with Denzin's "interpretivist approach," where "emotions are defined as self-feelings; they are feelings of and for one's self (p. 7)." Thus, the claim of in-

commensurability is based on the assertion (which for the present purposes we shall assume to be true) that "it was clear that what was perceived to be the phenomenon of emotion changed when investigated" (p. 14) by the two researchers. Ozanne and Hudson then buttress their incommensurability claim by citing Shapiro (1973), who attempted to integrate "the data of a more interpretive methodology and the data of a more positivist methodology," and concluded that her problems "were the result of her measuring different things" (p. 14).

It is clear that Ozanne and Hudson are using the meaning-variance interpretation of incommensurability, as previously discussed. That is, although Bower and Denzin were using the same term (emotion), they were not referring to, or measuring, the same phenomenon. This is another "apples vs. oranges" example. Is this a nontrivial, interesting, or meaningful kind of incommensurability? Obviously, the (presumed) fact the Bower and Denzin mean very different things when using the same term poses significant problems for them in communicating with each other. But, in what meaningful way does this imply that "the knowledge outputs of these two approaches are incommensurable"?

As previously noted, the concept of incommensurability comes from such classic examples of Kuhn as the rival knowledge-claims of Ptolemy and Copernicus. One paradigm claimed that the Sun revolved around the Earth and its rival claimed that the Earth revolved around the Sun. Clearly, these are two *rival*, or competing, claims. The problems between Ptolemy and Copernicus were not, simply, a result of them using common terms (e.g. "Earth," "Sun" and "revolve") in different ways. In Ozanne and Hudson's example, however, the two researchers are using the same concept (i.e., "emotion") to mean very different things! Therefore, the knowledge-claims of Bower and Denzin, although *different,* cannot be considered to be "rival," or "competing" and are *not incommensurable* in any meaningful epistemic sense. (This is not to say that the research *programs* could not, or do not compete for resources or the interest of other researchers. But, although there have been numerous interpretations of the concept of incommensurability, to my knowledge no one has ever seriously advanced a "resources" interpretation.)

It may be possible that contemporary social science and naturalistic, humanistic and interpretive inquiry are incommensurable in some nontrivial, interesting and meaningful way. However, the work of Ozanne and Hudson provides no justification for the claim. Contrary to Ozanne and Hudson, the paper by Holbrook, Bell and Grayson in this very volume tacitly acknowledges *commensurability* when they develop an experimental test of the Holbrook-Grayson hypothesis using C-S-S methods. Although Holbrook, Bell and Grayson claim that the humanities contain "truths that escape procedures of the hypothetico-deductive method," (p. 31) such a claim does not imply incommensurability, (nor, it should be observed, do they claim it does).

The preceding analysis implies a fourth challenge: Practitioners and advocates of N-H-I, instead of retreating into purposely encapsulated, purportedly incommensurate, semantical cocoons, should make strong and continuing efforts to clarify the meanings of their major concepts, especially when such concepts are shared with C-S-S and are used differently. Only through such a careful process can it be shown where the knowledge outputs are genuinely competitive, or rival, with those of C-S-S. There is no reason to *assume* in advance that in the event of genuinely *rival* knowledge-claims between C-S-S and N-H-I such claims will be incommensurable. Most certainly, incommensurability would seem to be a curious and counter-productive goal for practitioners and advocates of N-I-H to pursue.

CONCLUSION

The purpose of this paper has been to present a constructive, yet critical commentary on the emerging areas of naturalistic, humanistic, and interpretive inquiry. I remain as firmly convinced as ever that N-H-I inquiry has significant potential for advancing knowledge in both the marketing and consumer research areas. Even though the challenges facing N-H-I inquiry are significant, they are not insuperable. Certainly, the N-H-I agenda is not furthered when the views of their colleagues who conduct C-S-S are presented in caricature form. It is difficult to keep discussions of the differences between C-S-S and N-H-I on a cognitive level when caricatures such as "single immutable reality" and "entirely deterministic" are employed. Just as obviously, practitioners and advocates of C-S-S should likewise avoid such caricatures. One useful step in this direction is for both sides, especially when each is being critical of the other, to use direct quotations in their critiques, rather than simple, paraphrased references. For example, why reference Lincoln and Guba (strong critics of C-S-S) when one purports to portray or characterize the beliefs of C-S-S? Why not quote, or cite, a practitioner or advocate of C-S-S?

A second challenge for N-H-I is to clearly demonstrate the value of its knowledge-claims and the truth-content (or validity or trustworthiness, or warrant or credibility) of same. This can only be done, as I've indicated, by developing appropriate criteria for evaluating the knowledge-claims of N-H-I. Further, although "knowledge for knowledge's sake" is indeed a characteristic of science, no commentator on science to my knowledge claims that *irrelevancy* of knowledge-claims is, or ought to be, a goal of science. By defining the nature of N-H-I inquiry to *preclude* the possibility of identifying causes and effects before such inquiry even begins, advocates of N-H-I (unnecessarily) make such inquiry irrelevant to major problems in society.

A third challenge facing N-H-I inquiry is to be pluralistic, without being relativistic. Although, as it has been shown, one can be both relativistic and pluralistic at the same time, relativism neither implies pluralism, nor does pluralism imply relativism. If advocates of N-H-I embrace relativism because they (mistakenly) believe that it implies (or is implied by) pluralism, they will either spend much valuable time (as do most relativists) defending that *their* highly modified version of relativism does not imply irrationalism or they will have to accept (as does Feyerabend) "nihilistic" nonsense.

A final challenge for N-H-I is to defend the proposition that the knowledge outputs of its inquiry are different in some meaningful sense from the knowledge outputs of C-S-S without advocating that such knowledge outputs are incommensurable with C-S-S. Simply put, the fact that knowledge-claims are *different*, whether by nature of subject-matter or means of production or verification, does not imply that they are *incommensurate*. Incommensurability is a very strong concept and its value and meaning are debased when it is used as a synonym for "different." Again, if advocates of N-H-I truly wish to characterize their method of inquiry as producing incommensurate knowledge outputs, much time will be wasted in defending the position that *their* incommensurable knowledge outputs do not imply relativism and irrationalism. It would be most curious and unfortunate if advocates of N-H-I were to adopt incommensurability at the same time that the originator of the concept (Kuhn) is retreating from it and when one of the concept's most radical defenders (Feyerabend) is conceding that incommensurability is a "rare event" and "is a difficulty for philosophers, not for scientists" (1987, p. 81).

Thirty years from now, how will scholars evaluate the history of naturalistic, humanistic and interpretative inquiry in marketing and consumer research? Will it be viewed as a significant addition to other methods in the quest for scientific progress? Or, will it be viewed as a "blip" in the scientific enterprise, much like the motivation research flap in the 1950s? The nature of the historical verdict on naturalistic, humanistic and interpretivist inquiry will be determined in large measure by how its practitioners and advocates respond to challenges such as those detailed in this paper. Until such time, interpretive inquiry is much more like a promissory note than a certified check.

REFERENCES

Anderson, Paul F. (1982), comments in "Current Issues in the Philosophy of Science: Implications for Marketing—A Panel Discussion," ed., J. Paul Peter, in *Marketing Theory: Philosophy of Science Perspectives*, eds., Ronald F. Bush and Shelby D. Hunt, Chicago, IL: American Marketing Association, 11-16.

_____"Marketing, Scientific Progress, and Scientific Methodology," *Journal of Marketing*, 47 (Fall), 18-31.

_____ (1986), "On Method of Consumer Research: A Critical Relativist Perspective," *Journal of Consumer Research*, 13 (September), 155-173.

_____ (1988), "Relative to What—That is the Question: A Reply to Siegel," *Journal of Consumer Research*, Vol. 15, No. 1 (June), 133-137.

_____ (1989), "On Relativism and Interpretativism—With a Prolegomenon to the 'Why' Question," in *Interpretive Consumer Research*, ed., Elizabeth Hirschman, Provo, UT: Association for Consumer Research.

_____ Barnes, Barry and David Bloor (1982),"Relativism, Rationalism, and the Sociology of Knowledge," in *Rationality and Relativism*, eds., Martin Hollis and Steven Lukes, Cambridge, MA: The MIT Press, 21-47.

Brodbeck, May (1982),"Recent Developments in the Philosophy of Science," in *Marketing Theory: Philosophy of Science Perspectives*, eds., Ronald F. Bush and Shelby D. Hunt, Chicago, IL: American Marketing Association, 1-6.

Calder, Bobby J. and Alice M. Tybout (1987), "What Consumer Research Is. . .,"*Journal of Consumer Research*, 14 (June), 136-140.

Collins, H.M. (1975), "The Seven Sees: A Study in the Sociology of a Phenomenon, or the Replication of Experiments in Physics," *Sociology*, 9, 205-224.

_____ (1981), "Son of the Seven Sees: The Social Destruction of a Physical Phenomena," *Social Studies of Science*, 11, 33-62.

Dictionary of the History of Science (1981), eds., Bynum, W.F., E.J. Browne, and Roy Porter, Princeton, NJ: Princeton University Press.

Feyerabend, Paul (1975), *Against Method*, Thetford, U.K.: Lowe and Brydone.

_____ (1978a), "From Incompetent Professionalism to Professionalized Incompetence—The Rise of a Breed of Intellectuals," *Philosophy of the Social Sciences,* 8 (March), 37-53.

_____ (1978b) *Science in a Free Society*, London, U.K.: Verso.

_____ (1987a), *Farewell to Reason*, London, U.K.: Verso.

_____(1987b), "Putnam on Incommensurability," *British Journal of the Philosophy of Science,* 38, 75, 92.

Grove, J.W. (1985), "Rationality at Risk: Science against Psuedoscience," *Minerva*, III (Summer), 216-240.

Hacking, Ian (1982), "Lanugage, Truth, and Reason," in *Rationality and Relativism*, eds., Martin Hollis and Stephen Lukes, Cambridge, MA: The MIT Press, 48-66.

Hanson, N. R. (1958), "The Logic of Discovery," *Journal of Philosophy*, 55, 1073-1089.

Harrison, Geoffrey (1982), "Relativism and Tolerance," in *Relativism: Cognitive and Moral*, eds., Michael Krausz and Jack W. Meiland, Notre Dame, IN: University of Notre Dame Press.

Hemple, Carl G. (1969), "Logical Positivism and the Social Sciences," in *The Legacy of Logical Positivism*, eds., Peter Achinstein and Stephen F. Borker, Baltimore, MD: John Hopkins Press, 163-194.

Hintikka, Jaakko (1988), "Two Dogmas of Methodology," *Philosophy of Science*, 55, 25-38.

Hirschman, Elizabeth C. (1986), "Humanistic Inquiry in Marketing Research: Philosophy, Method, and Criteria," *Journal of Marketing Research*, 23 (August), 237-249.

Holbrook, Morris B. and Mark W. Grayson (1986), "The Semiology of Cinematic Consumption: Symbolic Consumer Behavior in *Out of Africa*," *Journal of Consumer Research*, 13 (December), 374-381.

_____, Stephen Bell, and Mark W. Grayson, (1989), "The Role of the Humanities in Consumer Research: Close Encounters and Coastal Disturbances," in *Interpretive Consumer Research*, ed., Elizabeth Hirschman, Provo, UT: Association for Consumer Research.

Holton, G. (1970), "Mach, Einstein and the Search for Reality," *Ernest Mach, Physicist and Philosopher*, eds., R.S. Cohen and R.J. Seeger, Dordrecht: Reidel Publishing.

Hudson, Laurel Anderson and Julie L. Ozanne (1988), "Alternative Ways of Seeking Knowledge in Consumer Research," *Journal of Consumer Research*, 14 (March), 508-521.

Hunt, Shelby D. (1983), *Marketing Theory: The Philosophy of Marketing Science*, Homewood, IL: Irwin.

_____ (1984), "Should Marketing Adopt Relativism?" in *Scientific Method in Marketing*, eds., Paul F. Anderson and Michael J. Ryan, Chicago: American Marketing Association, 30-34.

Kitcher, P. (1978), "Theories, Theorists, and Theoretical Changes," *Philosophical Review*, 87, 510-547.

Knorr-Cetina, Karen D. and Michael Mulkey (1983), "Introduction: Emerging Principles in Social Studies of Science," in *Science Observed*, London: Sage Publications.

Kordig, C. R. (1970), "Feyerabend and Radical Meaning Variance,"*Nous*, 9, 399-404.

Krausz, Michael and Jack W. Meiland (1982), *Relativism: Cognitive and Moral*, Notre Dame, IN: University of Notre Dame Press.

Kuhn, Thomas S. (1962), *The Structure of Scientific Revolutions*, Chicago, IL: University of Chicago Press.

_____ (1970), The Structure of Scientific Revolutions, Enlarged ed., Chicago, IL: University of Chicago Press.

_____ (1970a) "Reflections on My Critics," in *Criticism and the Growth of Knowledge*, eds., Imre Lakatos and Alan Musgrave, Cambridge, U.K.: Cambridge University Press, 231-278.

_____ (1976), "Theory-Change as Structure-Change: Comments on the Sneed Formalism," *Erkenntnis*, 10, 179-199.

Laudan, Larry (1968), "Theories of Scientific Method From Plato to Mach: A Bibliographical Review," in *History of Science*, Vol. 7, eds., A.C. Crombie and M.A. Hoskins, Cambridge MA: W. Heffer and Sons Ltd., 1-63.

_____(1976), "Two Dogmas of Methodology," *Philosophy of Science*, 55, 25-38.

_____ (1977), *Progress and Its Problems*, Berkeley CA: University of California Press, Ltd.

_____ (1979), "Historical Methodologies: An Overview and Manifesto," in *Current Research in Philosophy of Science*, eds., Peter D. Asquith and Henry E. Kyburg, Jr., East Lansing, MI: Phliosophy of Science Association, 55-83.

_____(1980), "Views of Progress: Separating the Pilgrims From the Rakes," *Philosophy of the Social Sciences*, 10, 273-286.

Levin, M. E. (1979), "On Theory Change and Meaning Change," *Philosophy of Science*, 46, 407-424.

Lincoln, Yvonna S. and Egon G. Guba (1985), *Naturalistic Inquiry*, Beverly Hills, CA: Sage Publications.

Margolis, Joseph (1983), "The Nature and Strategies of Relativism," *Mind*, Vols. 42, 548-567.

Moberg, D. W. (1979), "Are There Rival, Incommensurable Theories?" *Philosophy of Science*, 46, 244-262.

Muncy, James A. and Raymond P. Fisk (1987), "Cognitive Relativism and the Practice of Marketing Science," *Journal of Marketing,* 51 (January), 20-33.

Olson, Jerry C. (1987), "The Construction of Scientific Meaning," presented in the *1987 Winter Marketing Educators' Conference,* Chicago, IL: American Marketing Association.

Ozanne, Julie L. and Laurel Anderson Hudson (1989), "Exploring Diversity in Consumer Research," in *Interpretive Consumer Research,* ed., Elizabeth Hirschman, Provo, UT: Association for Consumer Research.

Peter, J. Paul and Jerry C. Olson (1989), "The Relativist/Constructionist Perspective on Scientific Knowledge and Consumer Research," in *Interpretive Consumer Research,* ed., Elizabeth Hirschman, Provo, UT: Association for Consumer Research.

Phillips, O.C. (1987), *Philosophy, Science and Social Inquiry,* Oxford, U.K.: Pergamon Press.

Putnam, Hilary (1981), *Reason, Truth, and History,* Cambridge, U.K.: University of Cambridge Pres.

Radner, Daisie and Michael Radner (1982), *Science and Unreason,* Belmont, CA: Wadsworth Publishing Co.

Rudner, Richard S. (1966), *Philosophy of Social Science,* Englewood Cliffs, NJ: Prentice-Hall.

Scheffler, I. (1967), *Science and Subjectivity,* Indianapolis, IN: Bobbs Merrill.

Shapere, D. (1964), "The Sturcture of Scientific Revolutions," *Philosophical Review,* 73, 383-394.

_____(1966), Meaning and Scientific Change," in *Mind and Cosmos: Explorations* in the Philosophy of Science, ed., R. Colodny, Pittsburgh, PA: Univeristy of Pittsburgh Press, 41-85.

Shapiro, Edna (1973), "Educational Evaluation: Rethinking the Criteria of Competence," *School Review,* (November), 523-549.

Siegel, Harvey (1980), "Objectivity, Rationality, Incommensurability, and More," *British Journal of the Philosophy of Science,* 31, 359-384.

_____ (1985), "What is the Question Concerning the Rationality of Science?" *Philosophy of Science,* Vol. 52, No. 4 (December), 517-537.

_____ (1986), "Relativism, Truth, and Incoherence," *Synthese,* 68 (August), 255-259.

_____ (1988), "Relativism for Consumer Research? (Comment on Anderson)," *Journal of Consumer Research,* Vol. 15, No. 1 (June), 129-132.

Stern, Barbara B. (1989), "Literary Explications: A Methodology for Consumer Research," in *Interpretive Consumer Research* ed., Elizabeth Hirschman, Provo, UT: Association for Consumer Research.

Stove, David (1982), *Popper and After,* Elmsford, NY: Pergamon Press, Inc.

Suppe, Frederick (1977), *The Structure of Scientific Theories,* 2nd ed., Urbana, IL: University of Illinois Press.

Vallicella, William F. (1984), "Relativism, Truth, and the Symmetry Thesis," *The Monist* , Vol. 67, No. 3 (July), 452-467.

Wallendorf, Melanie and Russel W. Belk (1989), "Assessing Trustworthiness in Naturalistic Consumer Research," in *Interpretive Consumer Research,* ed., Elizabeth Hirschman, Provo, UT: Association for Consumer Research.

Wittgenstein, Ludwig (1953), *Philosophical Investigations,* Oxford, U.K.: Basil Blackwell.

APPENDIX C, CHAPTER 11 REIFICATION AND REALISM IN MARKETING: IN DEFENSE OF REASON

By: **Shelby D. Hunt**[1]
Paul Whitfield Horn Professor of Marketing
Texas Tech University

Over the last decade a provocative "crisis literature" has developed that questions the underlying philosophical foundations of the marketing discipline (Anderson 1983, 1986, 1988a, 1988b; Arndt 1985a, 1985b; Firat, Dholakia, and Bagozzi 1987; Hudson and Ozanne 1988; Hunt 1984; Hunt and Speck 1985; Olson 1981, 1987; Peter and Olson 1983; Sauer, Nighswonger and Zaltman 1982). A recent article in the *Journal of Macromarketing* by Monieson (1988) extends the crisis literature by attacking the "process of intellectualization" in macromarketing, which allegedly prevents the discipline from entering "the authentic age of macromarketing" (p. 9). In the same *JMM*

issue, Dholakia (1988) interprets Monieson's article and finds the situation serious but not "hopeless" as he contends Monieson implies. Dholakia's cautious optimism stems from "Hunt's powerful advocacy" of the "rigorous extreme" being "late in coming" to marketing; therefore, positivism does not *totally* dominate it (p. 12).

Monieson and Dholakia suggest several changes for marketing, including the demand that inquiry become more critical. This suggestion draws on one of the most fundamental philosophical traditions in Western philosophy: the Grecian view that genuine knowledge, or truth, can be found only by subjecting all knowledge-claims to Plato's "test of critical discussion." Perhaps because of marketing's youth, our literature has never developed a critical tradition. Although the call for more critical discussion motivates the present article, the approach here is not just to criticize or to defendmarketing's status quo. Rather, the crisis

[1]The author gratefully acknowledges the helpful comments of Professor Michael Levin (Philosophy Department, City University of New York) on an early draft of this article.

Source: Reprinted by permission from the *Journal of Macromarketing*, Vol. 9 (Fall 1989).

literature discussion is constructively extended by defending the importance of history and reason in scholarly inquiry. After briefly reviewing the attacks made by Monieson and Dholakia on the philosophical foundations of the marketing discipline, this article then subjects those attacks to the "test of critical discussion."

THE "INTELLECTUALIZATION" ATTACK

Drawing upon the works of Max Weber, Monieson (1988, p. 6) contends that marketing's fundamental problem is "intellectualization," which comes from the "continuous rationalization of society's activities and arrangements" and attempts to understand objectively the "mysteries of the world" through the use of logic and mathematics, or "technical rationality." This "positivistic social science" implies the search for order in the social world, that is, lawlike generalizations, and a necessary requirement for order is the "reification" of social science concepts, that is, treating concepts or ideas as real. Using examples from social marketing, he claims that reification is pernicious because social relations are then "forged into marketable traits, into commodities" (p. 7). Moreover, the goal of searching for lawlike generalizations is totally inappropriate: "The fact that such lawlike generalizations do not exist does not prevent the social scientist from laying claim to power based on their presumed existence and their ability to engineer social life" (p. 7).

Given that the *claimed* goals of social science are methodologically impossible to achieve, what will be the *actual* consequences of pursuing an "objective understanding" of the world? Intellectualization will result in a "golden age of macromarketing," characterized by a "mathematized rigor," as exemplified by "econometric simulations, input-output analysis, and general systems theory" (p.6). However, such a golden age will be "disenchanted," since it will have abandoned beauty, magic, mystery, subjectivity, values, ethics, morality, and religion, all characteristics of Monieson's preferred, "enchanted" world.

If contemporary social science cannot deliver on its claimed objective to understand the world, and if the resulting "disenchanted" world is so undesirable, then why would marketing take such a path? Because, Monieson claims, only those academic disciplines that are "rational and calculable" are "academically respectable" (p. 6). That is, marketing scholars are motivated by their ego-needs for "respectability" in their research. In fact, their ego-needs are so strong that marketers cannot adopt any other course: "The advancement of intellectualization is inexorable; just as it has been in the past in macromarketing, so it is in the present, and so it will be in the future" (p.6).

Even though intellectualization is "inevitable" and cannot be stopped, Monieson points out several changes that must take place before the "authentic age of macromarketing" can come: dialectic thinking, *verstehen*, critique, and de-reification. However, "the authentic age of macromarketing is not imminent," and he concludes: "The golden age of macromarketing will be with us for a long time to come." (p. 9).

THE "FUNDAMENTAL TENSIONS" ATTACK

Dholakia's (1988) dialectical analysis interprets Monieson as implying "three fundamental tensions" that "if in a state of taut balance, keep knowledge systems productive, honest, and meaningful": (1) science and conscience, (2) rigor and relevance, and (3) opulence and authenticity (p. 11). For Dholakia, Monieson's "intellectualization" occurs when "the knowledge system adopts unquestioningly the values of positive science, methodological rigor, and opulent conceptual schemata" (p. 11).

Dholakia agrees that the "quest for respectability" has motivated marketing scholars toward rigor, and that a major reason marketing is not in as bad a shape as economics is that the advocacy of a "positive empiricist framework" by Hunt (1983a, 1983b) came late. In the future marketing must give more attention to the moral dimensions of inquiry ("conscience") and turn toward creating knowledge that is relevant and authentic. Specifically, these goals will be accomplished by (1) adopting a different philosophy ("realism"), (2) avoiding grand theories ("opulent conceptual structures"), and (3) reinforcing certain rights of scholars (to "dissent," to "understand," and to be "simple"). By these means marketing can return to "the enchanted circle" (p. 13).

AN EVALUATION

At the outset, we should note that marketing's crisis literature is indeed making some progress. First, the "early" version emphatically proclaimed that the major reason marketing emphasized the needs of marketing management was that it was dominated, even "imprisoned," by positivism (Arndt 1985a). That claim was so demonstrably ahistorical and untenable (Hunt and Speck 1985) that these later contributions now fervently claim exactly the opposite. The interests of marketing management are now *preventing* marketing from being dominated by positivism: "Pragmatic concerns, albeit they are largely the concerns of business managers, keep pulling

marketing toward the relevance pole" (Dholakia 1988, p. 13). Therefore, on the "dominance of positivism" issue, the crisis literature has progressed from a demonstrably false position to one that is at least plausible. Its plausibility stems from the fact that the logical positivists and empiricists focused on the positive issues of empirical science, that is, on developing and testing theories to explain, predict, and, thus, understand phenomena. Yet, the pragmatic concerns of marketing managers lie primarily in developing normative models and heuristics to aid decision making. Therefore, one can plausibly argue that the pragmatic concerns of "managerial relevance" inhibit the development of a positive science of marketing.

A second encouraging aspect is the call for "authentic knowledge" (p. 13). This is refreshing, given that other crisis literature participants, most notably advocates of "critical relativism," are now contending that truth (genuine or authentic knowledge) is an impermissible aim for marketing inquiry and should be abandoned (Anderson 1988a, 1988b). With regard to "authentic knowledge," however, Dholakia implies that complex theories ("opulent conceptual structures") are necessarily less authentic than simple, "earthy" theories. Would that it were always so. Unfortunately, social reality often is extraordinarily complex, seemingly requiring equally complex theories. It probably would be more productive to advocate that our theories should be no more complex ("opulent") than necessary to explain truly ("authentically") the reality at which they are directed, that is, adopting what is often called the "criterion of simplicity." Nonetheless, the call for authentic knowledge constitutes progress.

Third, both writers emphasize the importance of ethics, social responsibility, and distributive justice ("conscience") in marketing. Although these concepts are certainly not new, it is helpful to keep in mind some of the underlying values that for many marketers distinguish macromarketing from micromarketing.

The preceding virtues notwithstanding, the papers by Monieson and Dholakia are problematical in several respects. Rather than critiquing them line for line, or point by point, we shall (after examining a preliminary issue) focus on three major themes: (1) lawlike generalizations, (2) rigor/relevance, and (3) reification/realism. First, however, we address a preliminary problem, the "motivational issue."

The Motivational Issue

Consider the following examples of what most scholars would consider to be rigorous inquiry in marketing: Bagozzi's work on causal modeling and LISREL (1980, 1984), Layton's work on trade flows (1981a, 1981b, 1985), Howard and Sheth's theory of buyer behavior (1969), and Churchill's model for measuring marketing constructs (1979). What motivated the rigorous work of these scholars? Both Monieson (1988, p.6) and Dholakia (1988, p. 12) contend that the motivation was the "quest for respectability." Thus, they continue one of the most distressing aspects of marketing's crisis literature: they attack the motivations rather than the substantive positions of those with whom they disagree.

Why could not Bagozzi have been motivated by the belief that causal modeling would truly extend the search for authentic knowledge in marketing? Similarly, why could not Layton, Howard, Sheth, and Churchill have been motivated by a genuine desire to advance their discipline? Even if these authors were in fact motivated by the ego-need of

personal or disciplinary "respectability," why not evaluate the substance of their rigorous contributions, rather than impugning their motives? This writer has no reason to believe that Monieson and Dholakia were motivated by anything other than an honest desire to advance marketing thought. Absent hard evidence to the contrary, would progress not be more likely if authors in the crisis literature adopted a similarly charitable view toward those with whom *they* disagree?

The Lawlike Generalizations Issue

Much of contemporary social science and marketing involves the search for relationships among phenomena, i.e., "lawlike generalizations." Typically, these are of the "tendency" kind; for example: "The greater the cost of the product considered, the greater the tendency for two or more family members to be involved in the decision process" (Hunt 1983a, p. 200). Monieson (1988, p.7) contends that the search for such generalizations is a "conceit emanating from the intellectualization process" and that in social science "law-like generalizations do not exist" (p. 7). Therefore, the methods of contemporary social science are doomed to fail and should be abandoned (to be replaced by "enchanted" inquiry).

The claim that lawlike generalizations in social science "do not exist" is highly curious, given: "Intellectualization will always generate a conceptual prowness for the field which its science can never deliver" (pp. 8-9) and "the advancement of intellectualization is inexorable; just as it has been in the past in macromarketing, so it is in the present, and so it will be in the future" (p. 6). To most readers these statements would qualify, if true, as examples of the kind of lawlike generalizations that contemporary social science pursues. Indeed, although most social science theories do not claim to contain "universal" lawlike generalizations (Hunt 1983a, p. 200), Monieson accords universality to *his* claims. (Note the paper's use of "always generate," "never deliver," "inexorable," and "inevitable".)

The preceding shows that a major theme of Monieson's paper is incoherent or unintelligible. One cannot claim that lawlike generalizations "do not exist" by using lawlike generalizations in one's own argument! It is difficult to see how the debate over the philosophical foundations of marketing inquiry is advanced through such unreasoned, unintelligible argumentation. Ironically, we may note, lawlike generalizations appear to be so central to serious social science inquiry that even those writers who are unalterably opposed to them (and who wish to deny their use to others) find them essential. Thus, if Monieson "makes the case" for anything, he (unintentionally) makes the case for contemporary marketing and social science and their emphasis on lawlike generalizations.

The Rigor/Relevance Issue

Dholakia's claim (1988, p. 12) of an inherent "tension" between rigor and relevance in "all systems of knowledge" (p. 12) necessarily implies that these attributes are at opposite ends of a continuum, that is, to increase relevance one must decrease rigor, and vice versa. (If one could have *both* rigor and relevance, there would be no "tension.") Although no specific examples of rigorous research are provided, Dholakia's previous article on this subject equated "rigorous" with "quantifiable results" guided by the "tenets of positive empiricism" (1985, p. 7), and he

now associates "technical rigor" with "positivist" methods and "relevance" with "realist" methods (1988, p. 12). Similarly, Monieson discusses "technical rationality" and "mathematized rigor" (1988, p. 6). Unfortunately, the rigor/relevance argument is ahistorical and fundamentally misguided.

There is no term in the crisis literature more abused than "positivism" (Phillips 1987) and the claim that positivism implies the use of quantitative methods is a classic example of historical abuse.[2] The logical positivists were a group of scientist/philosophers who articulated a particular philosophy of science, and there is much in that philosophy that can be legitimately criticized (see Suppe 1977). However, although the logical positivists were not fearful of mathematics, nothing in their philosophy mandated the use of quantitative methods in science. Marketing's crisis literature is not alone in falsely associating positivism with quantitative procedures. In his evaluation of the historical misuse of the term "positivism" in the social science crisis literature, D. C. Phillips notes in a section entitled "Rampant Antipositivism" that "a positivist, *qua* positivist, is not committed to any particular research design. There is nothing in the doctrines of positivism that necessitates a love of statistics or a distaste for case studies" (1987, p. 96).

Dholakia's implied claim that "realist" methods will be nonquantitative (and, therefore, "relevant") is refuted by Bagozzi's work (1990, 1984) on causal modeling. Bagozzi has been one of the most forceful advocates of scientific realism in marketing, and no one would deny that

---

[2] The historical material in this and the succeeding section is drawn from Manicas (1987), Ayer (1959), Phillips (1987), Hunt (1987), and Hunt (1990).

his work is rigorous. (Indeed, I and many others believe it is relevant as well.) However, Bagozzi's realism leads him to advocate LISREL, which is one of the most sophisticated mathematical/statistical procedures used in contemporary social sciences. Therefore, the claim that realism implies the use of nonquantitative methods, just like "positivism implies quantitative methods," is patently false.

Finally, equating "rigorous" with "quantitative" methods seems especially misguided for anyone wishing to oppose contemporary social science. Except for those who are viscerally opposed to mathematics and statistics, few scholars will be willing to accept either the claim (1) that rigorous work, like Bagozzi's, *necessarily* lacks relevance or (2) that the more nonrigorous a study is, the more relevant it somehow becomes. Therefore, by equating "rigorous" with "quantitative" methods, opponents of contemporary social science actually give comfort to those they oppose. Advocates of contemporary social science can now cite Monieson's and Dholakia's works to buttress their claim that qualitative methods, historical methods, hermeneutics, critical studies, and interpretive studies are "nonrigorous" by *necessity*. Thus, the rigor/relevance issue, as it is elaborated by Dholakia, serves no one well, least of all those for whom it is intended to support.

The Reification/Realism Issue

Monieson claims that "reification" is widespread in marketing, and contributes to "intellectualization" and "a world disenchanted." In order for marketing to enter the "authentic age of macromarketing," or the "enchanted" world, "de-reification must take place; intellectualization must stop" (p. 9). To reify a concept

means treating it as real, that is, such unobservable concepts as "racism," "love," "attitudes," and "intentions" are treated as having a real existence, much like "apples," "people," "space ships," and "stars." Unfortunately, Monieson equates "treat as real" (reification) with the pejorative "treat as a commodity." This simple confusion, which (understandably) contributes to the paper's tone of umbrage, is easily cleared by noting that one may claim that "love is real" without necessarily believing that "love is a commodity." That is, one reasonably may claim that people really do have a feeling, properly labeled "love," without there being an associated tangible substance (be it "commodity" or otherwise). In any respect, the philosophy of science that specifically reifies unobservable concepts is scientific realism (Bagozzi 1980, 1984). Therefore, Monieson is suggesting that scientific realism is widespread in marketing and "must stop" in order for the discipline to be re-enchanted.

Dholakia's interpretation of Monieson's article contends that the "positivist empiricist framework" is widespread in marketing and in order for the discipline to be re-enchanted the discipline must adopt realism. Citing Hooker (1987), a prominent philosophical advocate of scientific realism, Dholakia (1988, p. 12) maintains "the search for relevance drags a knowledge system into the messy reaches of realism," and "both realism and its advocacy in the form of relevance detract from the pursuit of systematic and disciplined programs of knowledge generation." Thus, we have the strange situation of Dholakia's supposedly favorable "interpretation" actually *contradicting* Monieson's central thesis. Which is correct? Is reification (realism) the major source of problems in the marketing discipline and its abandonment the solution, as per Monieson? Or is the *lack* of realism (reification) the source of marketing's problems and its acceptance our salvation, as per Dholakia? As we shall see, both theses are equally ill-informed. To understand why requires, again, an historical perspective.

At the turn of the century, Western philosophy was mired in the nihilistic, metaphysical excesses of Hegelian idealism; its guiding principle with respect to reality was the relativistic view that the world does not exist unperceived.[3] At best, this philosophy was irrelevant to modern science and at worst was openly hostile to it. The turn of the century also witnessed the shattering of the brash, deterministic certainty of Newtonian physics by Einsteinian relativity and quantum mechanics. In the 1920s a small group of scientist/philosophers, including Moritz Schlick, Otto Neurath, and Rudolph Carnap, met at the University of Vienna (hence, "the Vienna Circle") to discuss whether the discipline of philosophy could contribute to the development of science in the light of relativity and quantum mechanics. Heavily influenced by the theory of meaning in Wittgenstein's *Tractatus*, the symbolic logic in Russell's *Principia Mathematica*, and the positivistic philosophy of Ernst Mach (hence, "logical positivists"), they formulated the "verification theory of meaning," claiming that the meaning of a proposition is the method of its verification.

Two "lessons" were drawn by the logical positivists from the downfall of Newtonian mechanics and the rise of quantum mechanics: (1) All theories should be interpreted instrumentally, rather than realistically, and (2) science

should adhere strictly to Hume's views with respect to induction and the problem of "unobservables." That is, science should restrict itself to "observables," for example, concepts like "apples," "people," and "stars," and avoid so-called "theoretical terms,"or "unobservables," such as "attitudes," "atoms," "intentions," and "cause." The verification theory of meaning implied that the only time a "theoretical term" could be legitimately used in science was when it could be explicitly and unambiguously defined through correspondence rules with "observable terms." In short, theoretical terms had no real existence independent from the observable terms that defined them, and theories were to be construed as *instruments* for economically summarizing the lawlike regularities among observable terms. Since the search for "underlying causes" was impermissible according to Hume, to *explain* a phenomenon was only to be able to *predict* it, nothing more. The "symmetry thesis" of explanation and prediction contended that all theories that predicted a phenomenon with equal accuracy were equally explanatory.

Through time the rigid prescriptions and proscriptions of logical positivism were substantially modified, and the philosophy known as logical empiricism evolved. The differences between these "isms" need not be detailed here. What is important is the relationship between positivism and Monieson's claim that "positivistic social science" implies "reification" (the treatment of abstract concepts as having real existence). As our ruthlessly brief historical discussion demonstrates, "positivism" *implies exactly the opposite*. The positivists warned scientists *against* treating "unobservables" as having a real existence. Why did they do so? Because they feared another Newtonian debacle (Stove 1982). Thus, we

---

[3] Hegelian idealism provides the historical foundation for modern relativistic philosophies and their associated nihilistic conclusions (Suppe 1977).

see Monieson's thesis (positivism implies reification) to be historically ill-informed.

We now turn to Dholakia's thesis that marketing is dominated by the "positivist empiricist framework" and must accept realism to become re-enchanted. Again, history illuminates this thesis. It is certainly true that the logical positivists exerted significant influence on the social sciences. For example, as Dholakia correctly points out, positivist perspectives were used by Friedman (1953) to rebut those who were deeply concerned about the unrealistic assumptions of economics. (He contended that only predictive accuracy was important in science.) Moreover, positivism was highly influential on experimental psychology, "behaviorism," and the use of "operational definitions." However, Dholakia's thesis that marketing is dominated by the positivistic view with respect to "unobservables" and "unrealistic assumptions" cannot withstand scrutiny.

Dholakia uses the Hunt (1983a, 1983b) references as examples of a "positive empiricist framework" that denies realism. Nothing could be further from the truth. Not only does the first reference, Hunt (1983a), specifically adopt the views of the "realist school" (p. 4), but also its treatment of causation is realist in orientation (pp. 120-125), and it specifically rejects the positivist view on the symmetry of explanation and prediction: "Contrary to the thesis of structural identity, all adequate (accurate) predictions are not potential explanations" (p. 179). Furthermore, on general theories in marketing, Hunt (1983b) embraces the realist approach, favorably citing the realists Keat and Urry (1975). Much more important, Hunt (1983b) discusses the nature of such general theories in marketing as those proposed by Howard

and Sheth (1969), Engel, Kollat, and Blackwell (1973), Alderson (1965), Bartels (1968), and Bucklin (1966). Do any of these writers, as Dholakia implies, defend their theoretical efforts on the basis that "although my theory may have 'unrealistic assumptions,' it should be accepted on the basis of its extraordinarily high predictive accuracy"? Clearly, none do. And for good reason. Only the behaviorist research program in marketing specifically adopts the positivist perspective with respect to "unobservables," and as behaviorists themselves point out: "Marketing scholars have given little consideration to. . .the behavior modification approach" (Nord and Peter 1980, p. 36). Indeed, much of the historical development of the marketing discipline can be viewed as a reaction *against* the use of "unrealistic assumptions" in our mother discipline, economics.

Readers are cautioned not to misinterpret the preceding paragraphs on positivism. The preceding does not imply that many of the views of the logical positivists and logical empiricists do not inform contemporary social science—for they surely do. For example, their view that theories should be empirically testable most assuredly conforms with contemporary social science. Rather, the preceding focuses exclusively on the issues raised by Monieson and Dholakia, that is, realism, reification, and the use of "unobservables." Contra Monieson, the positivists did not advocate the reification of "unobservables." In fact, they strongly counseled against this practice. *If reification is marketing's problem, positivism is not the cause.* Contra Dholakia, contemporary marketing inquiry is not dominated by the positivist view with respect to "unobservables." In fact, most marketing theory is very "realistic" on this dimension. Moreover, "realism" does not imply "nonquantitative," as we have seen. Therefore, *"adopting realism" cannot be the solution to whatever problems Dholakia has with respect to the marketing discipline*. Thus, we must conclude that both Monieson's and Dholakia's positions are equally ill-informed.

CONCLUSION

The crisis literature continues in marketing. The examples discussed in this article show at least some progress is being made toward meaningful evaluation of the philosophical foundations of marketing inquiry. Unfortunately, however, although these articles push us one step forward, they then take two leaps backward. There is much to criticize about the current status of marketing inquiry. But until the crisis literature adopts a more historically informed, factually accurate, carefully reasoned approach, significant progress in addressing substantive issues will be thwarted. For starters, we should all be mindful that theory and research guided by "positivism" need not use quantitative methods, nor need it lack relevance, nor will it (most assuredly) reify concepts. Likewise, theory and research guided by "realism" need not use qualitative methods, nor will it necessarily have high relevance, but it will (most definitely) reify concepts. Finally, marketing theory and research are *not* dominated by a "positivist" view with respect to "unobservables," "theoretical terms," and "reification." On the contrary, marketing theory and research are very "realistic" on these issues.

Lamentedly, Monieson, in his zeal to attack "positivistic social science" and replace it with humanistic inquiry serving "distinctly human values," actually adopts a view much more extreme than the very one he abjures. Consistent with the historicism of Hegelian idealism, Monieson paints a dismal, deterministic picture of marketing, academic disciplines, and, by implication, society in general. His view that we are all prisoners of forces that "inexorably," "inevitably" control our destinies denies human agency, one of the central tenets of humanistic inquiry. Consistent with Western philosophical thought since the Enlightenment, human agency contends that society is now and can be in the future what people make of it, that is, people can "make a difference." So it is in marketing. Nothing is inexorable in the marketing discipline: not reification, intellectualization, quantitative methods, qualitative methods, positivism, realism, failure, success, nor, I might add, our very survival. Speaking for those who place high regard on reason and rational discourse as a preferred method for "making a difference," is it not time for the crisis literature to rise to a more historically informed level of debate? Perhaps the gulf separating those of different views in marketing is so great that no bridge can be built. If so, then so be it. But if common ground does exist, then a return to reasoned debate would seem to be a useful step toward spanning the gulf that divides us. Isn't the goal of disciplinary advancement worth maximum effort on *all* our parts?

REFERENCES

Alderson, W. (1965), *Dynamic Marketing Behavior*, Homewood, IL: Irwin.

Anderson, Paul F. (1983), "Marketing, Scientific Progress and Scientific Method," *Journal of Marketing*, 47 (Fall), 18-31.

_____ (1986), "On Method in Consumer Research: A Critical Relativist Perspective," *Journal of Consumer Research*, 13 (September), 155-173.

_____ (1988a), "Relative to What—That is the Question: A Reply to Siegel," *Journal of Consumer Research*, 15 (June), 133-137.

_____ (1988b), "Relativism Revidivus: In Defense of Critical Relativism," *Journal of Consumer Research*, 15 (December), 403-6.

Arndt, Johan (1985a), "The Tyranny of Paradigms: The Case for Paradigmatic Pluralism in Marketing," in *Changing the Course of Marketing: Alternative Paradigms for Widening Marketing Theory*, eds., Nikhilesh Dholakia and Johan Arndt. Greenwich, CT: J.A.I. Press, Inc.

_____ (1985b), "On Making Marketing Science More Scientific: Role of Orientations, Paradigms, Metaphors, and Puzzle Solving," *Journal of Marketing*, 49 (3), 11-23.

Ayer, A.J. (1959), *Logical Positivism*, Glencoe, Il: The Free Press.

Bagozzi, Richard P. (1980), *Causal Models in Marketing*, New York: John Wiley and Sons, Inc.

_____ (1984), "A Prospectus for Theory Construction in Marketing," *Journal of Marketing*, 48 (Winter), 11-29.

Bartels, R. (1968), "The General Theory of Marketing," *Journal of Marketing*, 32 (January), 29-33.

Bucklin, L.P. (1966) *A Theory of Distribution Channel Structure*, Berkeley: Institute of Business and Economic Research, University of California.

Churchill, Gilbert A., Jr. (1979), "A Paradigm for Developing Better Measures of Marketing Constructs," *Journal of Marketing Research*, 16 (February), 64-73.

Dholakia, Nikhilesh (1985), "Opposing Research Camps in Marketing: Rigor vs. Relevance," *Marketing Educator*, 4 (3), 3.

_____ (1988),"Interpreting Monieson: Creative and Destructive Tensions," *Journal of Macromarketing*, 8 (Fall), 11-14.

Engel, J., D.B. Kollat, and R. Blackwell (1973), *Consumer Behavior*, 2d ed., New York: Holt.

Firat, A. Fuat, Nikhilesh Dholakia, and Richard P. Bagozzi (1987), *Philosophical and Radical Thought in Marketing*, Lexington, MA: Lexington Books.

Friedman, M. (1953), *Essays in Positive Economics*, Chicago: University of Chicago Press.

Hooker, C.A. (1987), *A Realistic Theory of Science*, Albany, N.Y.: State University of New York Press.

Howard, John A. and Jagdish N. Sheth (1969), *The Theory of Buyer Behavior*, New York: John Wiley and Sons.

Hudson, Laural Anderson and Julie L. Ozanne (1988), "Alternative Ways of Seeking Knowledge in Consumer Research," *Journal of Consumer Research*, 14 (March), 508-521.

Hunt, Shelby D. (1983a), *Marketing Theory: The Philosophy of Marketing Science*, Homewood, IL: Irwin.

_____ (1983b), "General Theories and the Fundamental Explananda of Marketing," *Journal of Marketing*, 47 (Fall), 9-17.

_____ (1984), "Should Marketing Adopt Relativism?" in *Scientific Method of Marketing*, eds., Paul F. Anderson and Michael J. Ryan. Chicago: American Marketing Association, pp. 30-34.

_____ (1987), "The Logical Positivists: Beliefs, Consequences and Status," in *Pro-*

ceedings of the 17th Paul D. Converse Symposium, eds., Devanathan Sudharshan and Frederick W. Winter. Chicago: American Marketing Association, pp. 24-33.

_____ (1990), Modern Marketing Theory: Critical Issues in the Philosophy of Marketing Science, Cincinnati: South-Western Publishing Co.

Hunt, Shelby D. and Paul S. Speck (1985), "Does Logical Empiricism Imprison Marketing?" in Changing the Course of Marketing: Alternative Paradigms for Widening Marketing Theory, eds. Nikhilkesh Dholakia and Johan Arndt. Greenwich, CT: J.A.I. Press Inc., pp. 27-35.

Keat, R. and J. Urry (1975), Social Theory as Science, London: Routledge and Kegan Paul.

Layton, Robert A. (1981a), "Trade Flows in Macromarketing Systems: Part I, A Macromodel of Trade Flows," Journal of Macromarketing, 1 (Spring), 35-48.

_____ (1981b), "Trade Flows in Macromarketing Systems: Part II, Transforming Input/Output Tables into Trade Flow Tables," Journal of Macromarketing, 1 (Fall), 48-55.

_____ (1985), "Marketing Systems in Regional Economic Development," Journal of Macromarketing, 5 (Spring), 42-55.

Manicas, Peter T. (1987), A History and Philosophy of the Social Sciences. New York, NY: Basil Blackwell.

Monieson, David D. (1988), "Intellectualization in Macromarketing: A World Disenchanted," Journal of Macromarketing, 8 (Fall), 4-10.

Nord, Walter R., and J. Paul Peter (1980), "A Behavior Modification Perspective on Marketing." Journal of Marketing, 44 (Spring), 36-47.

Olson, Jerry C. (1981), "Towards a Science of Consumer Behavior," in Advances in Consumer Research, eds. Andrew A. Mitchell, Ann Arbor, MI: Association of Consumer Research, Vol. 9, v-x.

_____ (1987), "Construction of Scientific Meaning," presented at the 1987 Winter Marketing Educators' Conference, Chicago: American Marketing Association.

Peter, J. Paul and Jerry C. Olson (1983), "Is Science Marketing?" Journal of Marketing, Vol. 47 (Fall), 111-125.

Phillips, D.C. (1987), Philosophy, Science, and Social Inquiry, New York: Pergamon Press.

Sauer, William J., Nancy Nighswonger, and Gerald Zaltman (1982), "Current Issues in Philosophy of Science: Implication of the Study of Marketing," in Marketing Theory: Philosophy of Science Perspectives, eds. Bush and Hunt, Chicago: American Marketing Association.

Stove, D.C. (1982), Popper and After: Four Modern Irrationalists, New York: Pergamon Press.

Suppe, Frederick (1977), The Structure of Scientific Theories, 2d ed., Chicago: University of Illinois Press.

QUESTIONS FOR ANALYSIS AND DISCUSSION

1. A recent article in the *Journal of Marketing* by Siew Meng Leong [387] has attempted to apply a Lakatosian reconstruction to marketing science. This reconstruction proposes that there are four levels to any science: (1) the hard core, (2) the protective belt, (3) middle-range theories, and (4) working hypotheses. Leong proposes that the four fundamental explananda and the four guiding research questions proposed by Hunt form the "hard core" of marketing science. Accordingly, the "protective belt" is comprised of research programs in buyer behavior, seller and competitive behavior, institutional behavior, and environmental behavior.

   Suppose marketing science were to be comprised *exclusively* of marketing management. That is, suppose marketing were to be a completely (micro) *normative* discipline, rather than a discipline having both positive and normative dimensions. How could a Lakatosian reconstruction of marketing science be accomplished under these assumptions? What would be the implications for marketing researchers if these assumptions were true? In your judgment, is the marketing discipline moving closer to the acceptance of these assumptions? Should it?

2. In contrast to Anderson [13], who holds that logical empiricism is characterized by the "inductive statistical method," the late Johan Arndt [22] contended that the opposite was true: "A corollary of this view [empiricism] is that the hypothetico-deductive method of the unified science is elevated into being the only acceptable scientific approach." [22, p. 9] Arndt also stated that logical empiricism assumes: "Marketing relations have a concrete, real existence and systemic character producing regularities in marketing behavior." Furthermore, "marketing systems are viewed as being equilibrium seeking," and "the real world is considered essentially as conflict free." [22, p. 12] Evaluate these descriptions of logical empiricism. If you conclude that Arndt is not talking about logical empiricism, then what is he talking about? What set of circumstances has resulted in Arndt making these kinds of assertions?

3. Define the concept of "research programme" as the term is used by Lakatos. How does it differ from a "research tradition" for Laudan and a "paradigm" for Kuhn? Choose several of the "schools of thought" identified by Sheth, Gardner and Garrett in reference 577. To what extent are there one, or more, "research programs," "research traditions," and "paradigms" in each "school of thought"? Discuss the overall usefulness of these concepts for marketing.

4. Define and differentiate among "dogmatic falsificationism," "naive falsificationism," and "sophisticated methodological falsificationism." To what extent has marketing been characterized by these "isms"? How does the "context of acceptance" versus the "context of pursuit" distinction severely limit the ability of Lakatos' theory of science to adequately describe the process of scientific change?

5. What is the "historical approach" to the philosophy of science? How does the "historical approach" differ from the approaches used by the logical positivists and logical empiricists? Suppose that the methodology of science has truly been progressing over the last 400 years. That is, suppose that we have, in fact, developed better measurement procedures, better scientific instruments, better statistical methods, and more powerful mathematics. Under what circumstances could the "historical approach" explain this progressivity? Suppose, now, that there has been no progressivity in the methodology of science. That is, electron microscopes are not "better" than the human eye, and the mathematics of today, although different, is not more powerful. How could the "historical method" explain this circumstance? Which circumstance do you believe better describes reality?

6. How does the "context of pursuit" versus the "context of acceptance" relate to the issue of the rationality of science? Create a set of standards that would lead someone to conclude that "scientific communities are collectively irrational." Using the same set of standards, would *any* institution in society be "rational"? If there remain any "rational" institutions in your analysis, justify that these institutions are, indeed, "rational." If there do not remain "rational" institutions in your analysis, justify having a term, i.e., "rational," for which nothing applies. That is,

does not the term "irrational" imply that you should be able to find something that is "rational"?

7. Discuss how it could be the case that Feyerabend could claim that Lakatos and he were in agreement on essential issues. How do both fall prey to the "philosophers' fallacy"?

8. What are the major differences between Laudan's "early" theory of science and his "later" theory? How do each of these two theories differ from the theory of science proposed by Kuhn?

9. How does Laudan reach the conclusion that "truth" and "falsity" are "irrelevant" to science? Why has Laudan fallen victim to the "philosophers' fallacy" with respect to truth?

10. What is the difference between "problem solving" in the sense that Laudan uses the term and "problem solving" as the term is used pragmatically in society? Why is the issue of the differing uses of the term "problem solving" important?

11. How did science progress according to the "early" Laudan? How does science progress according to the "later" Laudan? Which of these two notions of "progress" is superior? Why? If, science does makes progress by "solving problems better," is it important to *explain* how this progressivity comes about? Why? What are the rival hypotheses as to the reasons for science making progress in the sense of solving problems better?

12. Evaluate the thesis of Laudan that "truth" is irrelevant to science and, at the same time, science should "treat theories as if they were true" for purposes of "practical action" and "testing theories."

13. Kuhn has now retreated to the point where "incommensurability" simply means that we do not have a procedure like a "mathematical proof" for deciding among various theories. Show how this is another example of the "philosophers' fallacy." Doppelt advocates "moderate relativism." His "moderate relativism" is virtually indistinguishable from "the underdetermination thesis." That is, since we have nothing like a mathematical proof for choosing among theories, such choice is "underdetermined." To what extent does the "underdetermination thesis" pose some significant problem for science? If you believe that it does not, why do so many writers believe they are saying something terribly provocative when they, in solemn tones, claim that theories are "underdetermined by the data"? If you believe that the "underdetermination thesis" poses significant problems for science, what are these problems and why are they important?

14. Why does Laudan claim that the goals of science must not be "utopian"? Evaluate his claim that the aims of science must not be "utopian."

15. Laudan desires that his theory of science should speak meaningfully about science and, at the same time, avoid both the concept of "truth," and being relativistic. Evaluate the inherent difficulties in attempting to achieve these objectives simultaneously.

16. What is scientific realism? How does it differ from logical positivism and logical empiricism? Many people believe that when the critics of science attack the logical positivists/empiricists, such critics are actually attacking scientific realism (but they do not realize it). Evaluate this thesis.

17. "Many critics claim to attack positivistic science. However, since most of science is not 'positivistic' in any true sense of the term, such critics are actually attacking science, itself." Evaluate this thesis.

18. Paul Meehl at a recent conference on social science states the following:
    It was agreed that logical positivism and strict operationism won't wash. . . .the last remaining defender of anything like logical positivism was Gustav Bergman, who ceased to do so by the late 1940's. Why, then the continued attack on logical positivism and its American behaviorists' near-synonym 'operationalism'? My answer to this is unsettling but, I think, correct. Our conference on social science came about partly because of widespread dissatisfaction about the state of the art, and we have always been more introspective methodologically than the physicists and biologists, who engage in this kind of thing only under revolutionary circumstances. My perhaps cynical diagnosis is that one reason the conference members spent needless time repeating that logical positivism and simplistic operationalism are incorrect views of scientific knowledge is that this relieves scientific guilt feelings or inferiority feelings about our disciplines. It is as if somebody said, 'Well, maybe clinical psychology isn't up to the standards of historical geology or medical genetics, let alone theoretical physics; but we need not be so fussy about our concepts and empirical support for them because logical positivism, which was so stringent on that score, is a nefarious doctrine and we are no longer bound by it.' [Meehl, in 579, pp. 315-16]
    Evaluate the thesis of Meehl. To what extent does it, or does it not apply to marketing?

19. How does scientific realism explain the success of science? In this respect, what does "success" mean?   What is the "miracle theory" of scientific success? Evaluate it as a genuine rival for scientific realism. Is it true that the "miracle theory" is the only genuine rival to scientific realism for explaining the success of science? Philosophers like to hypothesize a world where we are all "brains floating in a vat." In such a world, everything is "illusion." Is this a genuine rival for scientific realism?

20. Scientific realism expands the concept of scientific progress to include many of the "lower-level" aspects of science. What does "lower-level" mean? How have philosophers erred by focusing exclusively on "grand theories"? Is marketing making progress at the "lower-level"? Give examples.

21. Define and differentiate among the following theories of truth: pragmatic, correspondence, coherence, and consensus. How does the consensus theory of truth fail to address the issue of the pragmatic success of science? What is the relationship between the consensus theory of truth and reality relativism? Should marketing adopt the consensus theory? Why, or why not?

22. What is the difference between a correspondence rule *defining* a "theoretical term" and *measuring* a "theoretical term"? To what extent does marketing rely on "correspondence rules" versus "measures"? To what extent should it?

23. What is the most appropriate philosophy to guide marketing? Marketing science? Why?

24. J. Paul Peter contends: "While logical positivism is the dominant philosophical force in consumer research, it has been eschewed by philosophers since the late 1960's"...Evaluate. (Hint: see question 18).

25. Is the philosophy of science useful for marketing? Why, or why not?

26. If there ever is a fourth edition of *Marketing Theory,* what new issues should be addressed? What issues should be de-emphasized? All comments are welcome, in writing or otherwise.

REFERENCES

1. Aaker, David A. and George Day. *Consumerism*. New York: The Free Press, 1971.
2. Aaker, David A. "Visual Clustering Using Principal Components Analysis." In *Multivariate Analysis in Marketing*. Belmont, CA: Wadsworth Publishing Co., 1971.
3. Abel T. "The Operation Called Verstehen." *American Journal of Sociology*, 54 (1948), pp. 211-218.
4. Achinstein, Peter and Stephen F. Barker, eds. *The Legacy of Logical Positivism*. Baltimore: The Johns Hopkins Press, 1969.
5. Achinstein, Peter. "Approaches to the Philosophy of Science." In *The Legacy of Logical Positivism*. Eds. Peter Achinstein and Stephen F. Barker. Baltimore: The Johns Hopkins Press, 1969, pp. 259-291.
6. Achinstein, Peter. "Function Statements." *Philosophy of Science*, 44 (1977), pp. 341-367.
7. Addis, Laird. "The Individual and the Marxist Philosophy of History." In *The Readings in the Philosophy of the Social Sciences*. Ed. May Brodbeck. New York: Macmillan Co., 1968.
8. Adler, Lee. "Systems Approach to Marketing." *Harvard Business Review*, 45 (May-June 1967).
9. Alderson, Wroe. *Marketing Behavior and Executive Action*. Homewood, IL: Richard D. Irwin, Inc., 1957.
10. Alderson, Wroe. *Dynamic Marketing Behavior*. Homewood, IL: Richard D. Irwin, Inc., 1965.
11. Alston, William P. *Philosophy of Language*. Englewood Cliffs, NJ: Prentice-Hall, Inc., 1964.
12. Anderson, F. H. *The Philosophy of Francis Bacon*. Chicago: The University of Chicago Press, 1948.
13. Anderson, Paul F. "Marketing, Scientific Progress and Scientific Method." *Journal of Marketing*, 47 (Fall 1983), pp. 18-31.
14. Anderson, Paul F. "On Method in Consumer Research: A Critical Relativist Perspective." *Journal of Consumer Research*, 13 (Sept. 1986), pp. 155-173.
16. Anderson, Paul F. "Relative to What — That is the Question: A Reply to Siegel." *Journal of Consumer Research*, 15 (June 1988), pp. 133-137.
17. Anderson, Paul F. "Relativism Revidivus: In Defense of Critical Relativism." *Journal of Consumer Research*, 15 (Dec. 1988), pp. 403-6.
18. Andreason, Alan R. "Attitudes and Customer Behavior: A Decision Model." In *New Research in Marketing*. Ed. Lee Preston. Berkeley, CA: Institute of Business and Economic Research, University of California, 1965, pp. 1-16.
19. Arndt, Johan. "Perspectives for a Theory of Marketing." *Journal of Business Research*, 8 (1980), pp. 389-402.
20. Arndt, Johan. "The Conceptual Domain of Marketing: An Evaluation of Shelby Hunt's Three Dichotomies Model." *European Journal of Marketing* (Fall 1981).
21. Arndt, Johan. "The Political Economy of Marketing Systems: Reviving the Institutional Approach." *Journal of Macromarketing*, 1 (Fall 1981), pp. 36-47.

22. Arndt, Johan. "The Tyranny of Paradigms: The Case for Paradigmatic Pluralism in Marketing." In *Changing the Course of Marketing: Alternative Paradigms for Widening Marketing Theory*. Eds. Dholakia and Arndt. Greenwich, Connecticut: J.A.I. Press, Inc., 1985.

23. Asquith, Peter D. and Henry E. Kyburg, Jr. *Current Research in Philosophy of Science*. East Lansing, MI: Philosophy of Science Association, 1979.

24. Assael, J. and G. S. Day. " Attitudes and Awareness as Predictors of Market Share." *Journal of Advertising Research*, 8 (1968), pp. 3-12.

25. Ayer, A. J. *Logical Positivism*. Glencoe, Illinois: The Free Press, 1959.

26. Bagozzi, Richard P. "Marketing as an Organized Behavioral System of Exchange." *Journal of Marketing*, 38 (October 1974), pp. 77-81.

27. Bagozzi, Richard P. "Marketing as Exchange." *American Behavioral Scientist*, 21 (March-April 1978), pp. 535-536.

28. Bagozzi, Richard P. "Toward a Formal Theory of Marketing Exchanges." In *Conceptual and Theoretical Developments in Marketing*. Eds. O. C. Ferrell, Stephen Brown, and Charles Lamb. Chicago: American Marketing Association, 1979, pp. 431-447.

29. Bagozzi, Richard P. *Causal Models in Marketing*. New York: John Wiley & Sons, 1980.

30. Baker, G. P. and P. M. S. Hacker. *Language, Sense and Nonsense*. Oxford, England: Basil Blackwell Publisher, Ltd., 1984.

31. Balderston, Frederick E. "Communication Networks in Intermediate Markets." *Management Science*, 4 (January 1958), pp. 154-171.

32. Baligh, Helmy H. and Leon E. Richartz. *Vertical Marketing Structure*. Boston: Allyn and Bacon, Inc., 1967.

33. Barger, Harold. *Distribution's Place in the Economy Since 1869*. Princeton: Princeton University Press, 1955.

34. Barker, Stephen F. "Logical Positivism and the Philosophy of Mathematics." In *The Legacy of Logical Positivism*. Eds. Peter Achinstein and Stephen F. Barker. Baltimore: Johns Hopkins Press, 1969, pp. 229-257.

35. Barnes, Barry and David Bloor. "Relativism, Rationalism, and the Sociology of Knowledge." In *Rationality and Relativism*. Eds. Martin Hollis and Steven Lukes. Cambridge, MA: The MIT Press, 1982, pp. 21-47.

36. Barone, Francesco. *Il Neopositivismo Logico*. 2, Bari, Italy: Laterza, 1986.

37. Bartels, Robert. "Can Marketing be a Science?" *Journal of Marketing*, 15 (January 1951).

38. Bartels, Robert. *The Development of Marketing Thought*. Homewood, IL: Richard D. Irwin, 1962.

39. Bartels, Robert. "The General Theory of Marketing." *Journal of Marketing*, 32 (January 1968).

40. Bartels, Robert. *Marketing Theory and Metatheory*. Homewood: Richard D. Irwin, Inc., 1970.

41. Bartels, Robert. "The Identity Crisis in Marketing." *Journal of Marketing*, 38 (October 1974).

42. Bartels, Robert. *The Development of Marketing Thought*. 2d ed. Columbus, OH: Grid, 1976.

43. Bartels, Robert. *The History of Marketing Thought*. Columbus, OH: Grid, 1976.

44. Bass, Frank. "A New Product Growth Model for Consumer Durables." *Management Science* (January 1969).

45. Bass, Frank N. and W. Wayne Talarzyk. "An Attitude Model for the Study of Brand Preference." *Journal of Marketing Research,* 9 (February 1972), pp. 93-96.

46. Bass, Frank N. "The Theory of Stochastic Brand Preference and Brand Switching." *Journal of Marketing Research,* 11 (February 1974), pp. 1-20.

46a. Bass, Frank N. and Thomas L. Pilon. "A Stochastic Brand Choice Framework for Econometric Modeling of Time Series Market Share Behavior." *Journal of Marketing Research,* 17 (November 1980), pp. 486-97.

47. Bauer, Raymond. "Consumer Behavior and Risk Taking." *Proceedings:* 43d Conference of the American Marketing Association, 1960, pp. 389-98.

48. Bauer, Raymond. "A Revised Model of Source Effect." Presidential Address to the American Psychological Association Annual Meeting, 1965. Reprinted in *Buyer Behavior.* Eds. John A, Howard and Lyman E. Ostland. New York: Alfred A. Knopf, 1973, pp. 124-38.

49. Bauer, Raymond. "Games People and Audiences Play." Presented at Seminar on Communication in Contemporary Society. The University of Texas, 1967.

50. Bauer, Raymond. "Risk Taking in Drug Addiction: The Role of Company Preference." In *Risk Taking and Information Handling in Consumer Behavior.* Ed. Donald Cox. Boston: Harvard Business School, 1967.

51. Baumol, W.J. "On the Role of Marketing Theory." *Journal of Marketing,* 21 (April 1957).

52. Beckman, Theodore N. "The Value Added Concept as a Measurement of Output." *Advanced Management,* 22 (April 1957), pp. 6-8. Reprinted in *Managerial Marketing: Perspectives and Viewpoints.* Eds. William Lazer and Eugene J. Kelley. Homewood, IL: Richard D. Irwin, Inc., 1962, pp. 659-67.

52a. Belk, Russell. "Extended Self and Extending Paradigmatic Perspective." *Journal of Consumer Research,* 16 (June 1989), pp. 129-132.

53. Ben-David, Joseph. *The Scientist's Role in Society.* Chicago: The University of Chicago Press, 1984.

54. Berelson, Bernard and Gary Steiner. *Human Behavior: An Inventory of Scientific Findings.* New York: Harcourt Brace Jovanovich, 1964.

55. Berelson, Bernard. "The Cliché Expert Testifies on the Social Sciences." In *Theory Building.* Ed. Robert Dubin. New York: Free Press, 1969, pp. 259-64.

56. Bergman, Gustav. *Philosophy of Science.* Madison, WI: The University of Wisconsin Press, 1957.

57. Bergman, Gustav. *Meaning and Existence.* Madison: The University of Wisconsin Press, 1959.

58. Bergman, Gustav. *The Metaphysics of Logical Positivism.* Madison, WI: The University of Wisconsin Press, 1967.

59. Berkowitz, Leonard J. "Discussion: Achinstein on Empirical Significance: A Matter of Principle." *Philosophy of Science,* 46 (1979), pp. 459-465.

60. Bernstein, Richard J. *Beyond Objectivism and Relativism.* Philadelphia: The University of Pennsylvania Press, 1983.

61. Bettman, James R. and J. Morgan Jones. "Formal Models of Consumer Behavior: A Conceptual Overview." *Journal of Business* (October 1972), 544-62.

62. Bettman, James R. *An Information Processing Theory of Consumer Choice.* Reading, MA: Addison-Wesley Publications Co., 1979.

63. Bhasker, Roy. *The Possibility of Naturalism*. Brighton, England: Harvester Press, 1979.

64. Black, Max. "Is Induction an Acceptable Scientific Tool?" In *Philosophy and Science*. Ed. Frederick Mosedale. Englewood Cliffs, NJ: Prentice-Hall, 1979, pp. 154-161.

65. Blalock, Hubert M. *Theory Construction*. Englewood Cliffs, NJ: Prentice-Hall, 1969.

66. Blalock, Hubert M., ed. *Causal Models in the Social Sciences*. Hawthorne, New York: Aldine Publishing, 1971.

67. Blair, Edward and George M. Zinkham. "The Realist View of Science: Implications for Marketing." In *Scientific Method in Marketing*, Proceedings of the AMA Winter Educator's Conference. Eds. P. Anderson and M. Ryan. Chicago: American Marketing Association 1984, pp. 26-29.

68. Blanchard, C.H., C.R. Burnett, R.G. Stoner, and R.L. Weber. *Introduction to Modern Physics*. Englewood Cliffs, NJ: Prentice-Hall, 1972.

69. Bloom, Alan. *The Closing of the American Mind*. New York: Simon and Schuster, Inc., 1987.

70. Bloomfield, Leonard. *Language*. London: George Allen and Unwyn, Ltd., 1935.

71. Bock, R. D., and R. E. Borgman. "Analysis of Covariance Structures." *Psychometrics*, 31 (1966), pp. 507-534.

72. Bogart, Leo. "How Do People Read Newspapers." *Media / Scope*, 6 (January 1962).

73. Borden, Neil. *The Economic Effects of Advertising*. Homewood, IL: Richard D. Irwin, 1942.

74. Boyd, Harper W., and Ralph Westfall. *Marketing Research*. 3d ed. Homewood, IL: Richard D, Irwin, 1972.

75. Boyd, Richard N. "The Current Status of Scientific Realism." In *Scientific Realism*. Ed. J. Leplin. Berkeley: University of California Press 1984, pp. 41-82.

76. Braithwaite, Richard B. *Scientific Explanation*. Cambridge, England: Cambridge University Press, 1968.

77. Braybrooke, David. *Philosophical Problems of the Social Sciences*. New York: The Macmillan Company, 1965.

78. Bridgman, P.W. *The Logic of Modern Physics*. New York: Macmillan, 1927.

79. Bridgman, P.W. "Operational Analysis." *Philosophy of Science*, 5 (1938), pp. 114-31.

80. Bridgman, P.W. "The Nature of Some of Our Physical Concepts—I." *British Journal for the Philosophy of Science*, 1 (1951), pp. 257-72.

81. Brodbeck, May, ed. *Readings in the Philosophy of the Social Sciences*. New York: The Macmillan Company, 1968.

82. Brodbeck, May. "Recent Developments in the Philosophy of Science." In *Marketing Theory: Philosophy of Science Perspectives*. Eds. Ronald F. Bush and Shelby D. Hunt. Chicago: American Marketing Association 1982, pp. 1-7.

83. Brody, B.A. "Toward an Aristotelian Theory of Scientific Explanation." *Philosophy of Science*, 39 (1972), pp. 20-31.

84. Brody, Robert, and Scott Cunningham. "Personality Variables and the Consumer Decision Process." *Journal of Marketing Research*, 5 (February 1968), pp. 50-57.

85. Bromberger, S. "Why Questions." In *Mind and Cosmos: Explorations in the Philosophy of Science*. Ed. R. Colodny. Pittsburgh: University of Pittsburgh Press, 1966, pp. 86-111.

85a. Brown, Ezra. "A Fresh Breath of Heresy." *Time* (July 25, 1988), p. 74.

86. Brown, Harold I. *Perception Theory and Commitment*. Chicago: University of Chicago Press, 1977.

87. Brown, James Robert. "Unravelling Holism." *Philosophy of Social Science,* 17 (1987), pp. 427-33.

88. Brubacher, J. and M. Rudy. *Higher Education in Transition*. New York: Harper and Brothers, 1958.

89. Buck, R., and R. Cohen. "PSA 1970: In Memory of Rudolph Carnap." Boston Studies in *Philosophy of Science,* VIII. Dordecht, Holland: Reidel, 1971.

90. Bucklin, Louis P. *A Theory of Distribution Channel Structure.* Berkeley: University of California, Institute of Business and Economic Research, 1966.

91. Bucklin, Louis P. "Retail Strategy and the Classification of Goods." *Journal of Marketing,* 27 (January 1963), pp. 50-55.

92. Bucklin, Louis P. *Competition and Evolution in the Distributive Trades.* Englewood Cliffs, NJ: Prentice-Hall, 1972.

93. Bucklin, Louis P. *Productivity in Marketing.* Chicago: American Marketing Association, 1978.

94. Bunge, Mario. "Kinds and Criteria of Scientific Laws." *Philosophy of Science,* 28 (1961), pp. 260-281.

95. Bunge, Mario. *Scientific Research*. Vol. 1: *The Search for a System.* New York: Springer-Verlag, 1967.

96. Bunge, Mario. *Scientific Research*. Vol. 2: *The Search for Truth.* New York: Springer-Verlag, 1967.

97. Bunge, Mario. *Causality and Modern Science.* 3d ed. New York: Dover Publications, 1979.

98. Burian, Richard M. "More Than a Marriage of Convenience: On the Inextricability of History and the Philosophy of Science." *Philosophy of Science,* 44 (1977), pp. 1-42.

99. Bush, R.F. and S. D. Hunt. *Marketing Theory: Philosophy of Science Perspectives.* Chicago: American Marketing Association, 1982.

100. Butterfield, H. J. *The Origins of Modern Science: 1300-1800.* New York: Macmillan, 1958.

101. Buzzell, Robert D. "Is Marketing a Science?" *Harvard Business Review,* 41 (January-February 1963), pp. 32-40, 166-70.

102. Buzzell, Robert D., Donald F. Cox, and Rex V. Brown. *Marketing Research and Information Systems.* New York: McGraw-Hill, 1969.

102a. Calder, Bobby J. and Alice M. Tybout. "Interpretive, Qualitative, and Traditional Scientific Consumer Behavior Research." In *Interpretive Consumer Research.* Ed. E. Hirschman. Provo, UT.: Association for Consumer Research, 1989.

103. Campbell, N. R. *What is Science?* New York: Dover Publications, 1952.

104. Canton, Irving D. "A Functional Definition of Marketing." *Marketing News* (July 15), 1973.

105. Carmen, James M. "On the Universality of Marketing." *Journal of Contemporary Business,* 2 (Autumn 1973), pp. 1-16.

106. Carnap, Rudolf. *Logical Foundations of Probability.* Chicago: University of Chicago Press, 1950.

107. Carnap, Rudolf. "The Methodological Character of Theoretical Concepts." In *The Foundations of Science and the Concepts of Psychology and Psychoanalysis, Minnesota Studies in the Philosophy of Science.* Eds. Herbert Feigl and Michael Scriven. Vol. 1. Minneapolis: University of Minnesota Press, 1956, pp. 38-76.

108. Carnap, Rudolf. "Testability and Meaning." *Philosophy of Science,* 3 (1936), pp. 419-471.

109. Carnap, Rudolf. "The Elimination of Metaphysics Through the Logical Analysis of Language." *Erkenntnis,* 2 (1932). Reprinted in Ayer, A. J. *Logical Positivism.* Glencoe, IL: The Free Press, 1959.

110. Carnap, Rudolf. "The Aim of Inductive Logic." In *Logic Methodology and Philosophy of Science.* Eds. E. Nagel, P. Suppes, and A. Tarski. Stanford, CA: Stanford University Press, 1962, pp. 303-318.

111. Causey, Robert L. "Theory and Observation." In *Current Research in Philosophy of Science.* Eds. Asquith and Kyburg. East Lansing: Philosophy of Science Association, 1979, pp. 187-206.

112. Chisholm, Roderick M. *Theory of Knowledge.* Englewood Cliffs, NJ: Prentice-Hall, 1966.

113. Churchill, Gilbert A., Jr. "Comments on the AMA Task Force Study." *Journal of Marketing,* 52 (October 1988), pp. 26-31.

114. Churchill, Gilbert A. Jr., Neil M. Ford, and Orville C. Walker. "Organizational Climate and Job Satisfaction in the Salesforce." *Journal of Marketing Research,* 13 (November 1976), pp. 323-332.

115. Churchland, Paul M. *Scientific Realism and the Plasticity of Mind.* Cambridge: Cambridge University Press, 1979.

116. Churchland, Paul M. and Clifford A. Hooker. *Images of Science: Essays on Realism and Empiricism.* With a reply from Bas C. van Fraassen. Chicago: The University of Chicago Press, 1985.

117. Churchman, C. West. "Early Years of the Philosophy of Science Association." *Philosophy of Science,* 51 (March 1984), pp. 20-22.

118. Clagett, Marshall, ed. *Critical Problem in the History of Science.* Madison: The University of Wisconsin Press, 1969.

119. Clark, Desmond M. "Discussion: Teleology and Mechanism: M. Grene's Absurdity Argument." *Philosophy of Science,* 46 (1979), pp. 321-325.

120. Clark, J.M. "Competition and the Objectives of Government Policy." In *Monopoly and Competition and their Regulation.* Ed. E. Chamberlin. London: Macmillan, 1954, pp. 317-37.

121. Clark, Joseph T. "The Philosophy of Science and the History of Science." In *Critical Problems in the History of Science.* Ed. Marshall Clagett. Madison: University of Wisconsin Press, 1969, pp. 103-140.

122. Coffa, J. Alberto. "Probabilities: Reasonable or True." *Philosophy of Science,* 44 (1977), pp. 186-198.

123. Cohen, Morris R., and Ernest Nagel. *Logic and the Scientific Method.* New York: Harcourt Brace Jovanovich, 1934.

124. Cohen, Robert S. *Herbert Feigl, Inquiries and Provocations: Selected Writings 1929-1974.* Dordrecht: D. Reidell Publishing Company, 1981.

125. Cole, M., and S. Scribner. *Culture and Thought: A Psychological Introduction.* New York: Wiley, 1974.

126. Collins, H. M. "The Seven Sexes: A Study in the Sociology of a Phenomenon, or the Replication of Experiments in Physics." *Sociology,* 9 (1975), pp. 205-224.

127. Collins, H. M. "Son of Seven Sexes: The Social Destruction of a Physical Phenomenon." *Social Studies of Science,* 11 (1981), pp. 33-62.

128. Committee on Terms. *Marketing Definitions: A Glossary of Marketing Terms.* Chicago: American Marketing Association, 1960.

129. Converse, Paul D. "The Development of a Science of Marketing." *Journal of Marketing,* 10 (July 1945), pp. 14-23.

130. Converse, Paul D. "New Laws of Retail Gravitation." *Journal of Marketing,* 14 (October 1949), pp. 379-84.

131. Cooke, Roger M. "Discussion: A Trivialization of Nagel's Definition of Explanation for Statistical Laws." *Philosophy of Science,* 47 (1980), pp. 644-645.

132. Cooke, Roger M. "Discussion: A Paradox in Hempel's Criterion of Maximal Specificity." *Philosophy of Science,* 48 (June 1981), pp. 327-328.

132a. Cooper, Lee G. "Do We Need Critical Relativism?" *Journal of Consumer Research,* 14 (June 1987), pp. 126-127.

133. Copeland, Melvin T. "Relation of Consumers' Buying Habits to Marketing Methods." *Harvard Business Review,* 1 (April 1923), pp. 282-289.

134. Cox, Donald F. and Raymond Bauer. "Self Confidence and Persuasibility in Women." *Public Opinion Quarterly,* 27(Fall 1964), pp. 453-466.

135. Cox, Keith K., and Ben Enis. *Experimentation for Marketing Decisions.* Scranton, PA: International Textbook, 1969.

136. Cox, Keith K., and Ben Enis. *The Marketing Research Process.* Santa Monica, CA: Goodyear Publishing, 1972.

137. Cox, Reavis, Wroe Alderson, and Stanley J. Shapiro. *Theory in Marketing.* Homewood, IL: Richard D. Irwin, 1964.

138. Cox, Reavis. *Distribution in a High Level Economy.* Englewood Cliffs, NJ: Prentice-Hall, 1965.

139. Creath, Richard. "Discussion: A Query on Entrenchment." *Philosophy of Science,* 45 (1978), pp. 474-477.

140. Cunningham, Scott. "The Major Dimensions of Perceived Risk." In *Risk Taking and Information Handling in Consumer Behavior.* Ed. Donald Cox. Boston: Harvard Business School, 1967, pp. 82-108.

141. Cummins, Robert. "Programs in the Explanation of Behavior." *Philosophy of Science,* 44 (1977), pp. 269-287.

142. Cupples, Brian. "Three Types of Explanation." *Philosophy of Science,* 44 (1977), pp. 387-408.

143. Cupples, Brian. "Discussion: Four Types of Explanation." *Philosophy of Science,* 47 (1980), pp. 626-629.

144. Currie, Gregory. "The Role of Normative Assumptions in Historical Explanation." *Philosophy of Science,* 47 (1980), pp. 456-473.

145. Cyert, Richard M., and Garrel Pottinger. "Towards a Better Microeconomic Theory." *Philosophy of Science,* 46 (1979), pp. 204-222.

146. Darden, Lindley and Nancy Maull. "Interfield Theories." *Philosophy of Science,* 44 (1977), pp. 43-64.

147. Dawson, Leslie. "Marketing Science in the Age of Aquarius." *Journal of Marketing,* 35 (July 1971), pp. 66-72.

148. Derden, J.K. "Carnap's Definition of 'Analytic Truth' for Scientific Theories." *Philosophy of Science,* 43 (1976), pp. 506-522.

149. Dewey, John. *Logic: The Theory of Inquiry.* New York: Holt, Rinehart, and Winston, 1938.

149a. Dholakia, Nikhilesh. "Interpreting Monieson: Creative and Destructive Tensions." *Journal of Macromarketing,* 8 (Fall 1988), pp. 11-14.

150. *Dictionary of the History of Science.* Eds. W.F. Bynum, E.D. Browne, and Roy Porter. Princeton, NJ: Princeton University Press, 1981.

151. Dieks, D. "Discussion: On the Empirical Content of Determinism." *Philosophy of Science,* 47 (1980), pp. 124-130.

152. Dodd, S.C. "Systemmetrics for Evaluating Symbolic Systems." *Systemmatics,* 6 (1968), pp. 27-49.

153. Doehlert, David H. "Similarity and Preference Mapping: A Color Example." *Marketing and the New Science of Planning.* Ed. Robert L. King. Chicago: American Marketing Association, 1968, pp. 250-58.

154. Donagan, Alan. "The Popper-Hempel Theory Reconsidered." In *Philosophical Analysis and History.* Ed. W. Dray. New York: Harper and Row, 1966, pp. 127-59.

155. Doppelt, Gerald. "Relativism and the Reticulational Model of Scientific Rationality." *Synthese,* 69 (1986), pp. 225-52.

156. Drake, Stillman, and I.E. Drabkin. *Mechanics in Sixteenth-Century Italy: Selections from Tartaglia, Benedetti, Guido Ubaldo, and Galileo.* Madison, WI: University of Wisconsin Press, 1969.

157. Dray, William. *Laws and Explanation in History.* Oxford University Press, 1957.

158. Dretske, Fred. "Laws of Nature." *Philosophy of Science,* 44 (1977), pp. 248-268.

159. Dretske, Fred. "Discussion: Reply to Niiniluoto." *Philosophy of Science,* 45 (1978), pp. 440-444.

160. Dubin, Robert. *Theory Building.* New York: The Free Press, 1969.

161. Durant, Will. *The Story of Philosophy.* New York: Simon and Shuster, 1954.

162. Edwards, A.W.F., and L.L. Cavalli-Sforza. "A Method for Cluster Analysis." *Biometrics,* 52 (June 1965), pp. 362-375.

162a. Edwards, Paul. "Bertrand Russell's Doubts about Induction." In *Logic and Language.* Ed. A.G.N. Flew. Oxford: Basil Blackwell, 1951, pp. 55-79.

163. Eggert, Robert J. "Eggert Discusses Additional Goals for His Administration, Seeks Help in Defining Marketing." *Marketing News,* 8 (September 15), 1974.

164. Ehrenberg, A. S. C. "Laws in Marketing: A Tailpiece." In *New Essays in Marketing Theory.* Ed. G. Fisk. Boston: Allyn and Bacon, 1971, pp. 28-39.

164a. Einstein, Albert. *Sidelights on Relativity.* New York: E.P. Dutton Company, 1923.

165. El-Ansary, Adel. "The General Theory of Marketing: Revisited." In *Conceptual and Theoretical Developments in Marketing.* Eds. O. C. Ferrell, Stephen W. Brown, and Charles Lamb Jr. Chicago: American Marketing Association 1979, pp. 399-   407.

166. Elgin, C. Z. "Lawlikeness and the End of Science." *Philosophy of Science,* 47 (1980), pp. 56-68.

167. Engel, James E., David B. Kollat, and Roger Blackwell. *Consumer Behavior.* 2d ed. New York: Holt, Rinehart, and Winston, 1973.

168. Etgar, Michael. "Comment on the Nature and Scope of Marketing." *Journal of Marketing,* 41 (October 1977), pp. 14, 16, 146.

169. Farber, I.E. "Personality and Behavioral Science." In *Readings in the Philosophy of Social Sciences.* Ed. May Brodbeck. New York: The Macmillan Co., 1968, pp. 145-79.

170. Farley, John U. and L. Winston Ring. "An Empirical Test of the Howard-Sheth Model of Buyer Behavior." *Journal of Marketing Research,* 7 (November 1970), pp. 427-38.

171. Farley, John U. and Harold J. Leavitt. "Marketing and Population Problems." *Journal of Marketing,* 35 (July 1971), pp. 28-33.

172. Farley, John U. and L. Winston Ring. "On L and R and HAPPISIMM." *Journal of Marketing Research,* 9 (August 1972),pp. 349-53.

173. Feigl, Herbert, and Michael Scriven, eds. *The Foundations of Science and the Concepts of Psychology and Psychoanalysis, Minnesota Studies in the Philosophy of Science.* Vol. 1. Minneapolis: University of Minnesota Press, 1956.

174. Feigl, Herbert, Michael Scriven, and Grover Maxwell, eds. *Concepts, Theories and the Mind-Body Problem, Minnesota Studies in the Philosophy of Science.* Vol. 2. Minneapolis: University of Minnesota Press, 1958.

175. Feigl, Herbert, and Grover Maxwell, eds. *Scientific Explanation, Space and Time, Minnesota Studies in the Philosophy of Science.* Vol. 3. Minneapolis: The University of Minnesota Press, 1962.

176. Feigl, Herbert. "Philosophy of Science." In *Philosophy.* Ed. R.M. Chisholm. Englewood Cliffs, NJ: Prentice-Hall, 1965.

177. Feigl, Herbert. "The Origin and Spirit of Logical Positivism." In *The Legacy of Logical Positivism.* Eds. Peter Achinstein and Stephen F. Barker. Baltimore: Johns Hopkins Press, 1969, pp. 3-24.

178. Ferber, Robert. "The Expanding Role of Marketing in the 1970's." *Journal of Marketing,* 34 (January 1970), pp. 20-30.

179. Ferrell, O. C., Stephen W. Brown, and Charles W. Lamb, Jr., eds. *Conceptual and Theoretical Developments in Marketing.* Chicago: American Marketing Association, 1979.

180. Ferrell, O. C., and J. R. Perrachione. "An Inquiry into Bagozzi's Formal Theory of Marketing Exchanges." *Theoretical Developments in Marketing.* Eds., Lamb and Dunne. Chicago: American Marketing Association, 1980, pp. 158-61.

181. Festinger, Leon. *A Theory of Cognitive Dissonance.* Evanston: Harper and Row, 1957.

182. Fetzer, James H. Book review of Robert J. Ackerman. *The Philosophy of Karl Popper. Philosophy of Science,* 44 (1977), pp. 491-493.

183. Feyerabend, Paul K. "Explanation, Reduction, and Empiricism." *Minnesota Studies in the Philosophy of Science,* 3 (1962), pp. 46-8.

184. Feyerabend, Paul K. "On the Meaning of Scientific Terms." *Journal of Philosophy,* 62 (1965), pp. 267-71.

185. Feyerabend, Paul K. "Reply to Criticism." In *Boston Studies in the Philosophy of Science.* Eds. Cohen and Wartofsky. 2, New York: Humanities Press, 1965, pp. 223-261.

186. Feyerabend, Paul K. "Against Method." In *Analysis of Theories and Methods of Physics and Psychology.* Eds. Michael Radan and Stephen Winokur. Minneapolis, MN: University of Minneapolis Press, 1970.

187. Feyerabend, Paul K. *Against Method.* Thetford, England: Lowe and Brydone, 1975.

188. Feyerabend, Paul K. "Changing Patterns of Reconstruction." *British Journal of the Philosophy of Science,* 28 (1977), pp. 351-69.

189. Feyerabend, Paul K. "From Incompetent Professionalism to Professionalized Incompetence—The Rise of a New Breed of Intellectuals." *Philosophy of the Social Sciences,* 8 (March 1978), pp. 37-53.

190. Feyerabend, Paul K. *Science in a Free Society.* London: Verso, 1978.

191. Feyerabend, Paul K. *Problems of Empiricism.* Vol. 1. New York: Cambridge University Press, 1981.

192. Feyerabend, Paul K. *Problems of Empiricism.* Vol. 2. New York: Cambridge University Press, 1981.

193. Feyerabend, Paul K. "Academic Ratiofascism: Comments on Tibor Machan's Review." *Philosophy of Social Science,* 12 (1982), pp. 191-195.

194. Feyerabend, Paul K. *Farewell to Reason.* London: Verso, New Left Books, 1987.

195. Feyerabend, Paul K. "Putnam on Incommensurability." *British Journal of Philosophy of Science,* 38 (1987), pp. 75-81.

196. "50-50 Nuclear War Odds Seen Through Year 2000." *Wisconsin State Journal* (December 28), 1974.

197. Fine, Arthur. "The Natural Ontological Attitude." In *Scientific Realism.* Ed. Jarret Leplin. Berkeley, CA: University of California Press, 1984.

197a. Fine, Arthur. *The Shaky Game.* Chicago: The University of Chicago Press, 1986.

197b. Fine, Arthur. "Unnatural Attitudes: Realist and Instrumentalist Attachments to Science." *Mind,* 95 (1986), pp. 149-179.

198. Fischer, Robert B. "Definitions of Science." In *Philosophy and Science* Ed. Frederick Mosedale. Englewood Cliffs, NJ: Prentice-Hall, (1979), pp. 183-187.

199. Fishbein, Martin, and L. Ajzen. "Attitudes and Opinions." *Annual Review of Psychology,* 1972, pp. 487-543.

200. Fishbein, Martin, and Icek Ajzen. *Beliefs, Attitude, Intention, and Behavior: An Introduction to Theory and Research.* Reading, MA: Addison-Wesley, 1975.

201. Fisk, George. *Marketing Systems: An Introductory Analysis.* New York: Harper and Row, 1967.

202. Fisk, George. *New Essays in Marketing Theory.* Boston: Allyn and Bacon, Inc., 1971.

203. Fisk, George, and R. W. Nason, eds. *Macro-Marketing: New Steps on the Learning Curve.* Boulder, Colorado: Business Research Division, Graduate School of Business, University of Colorado, 1979.

204. Fisk, George, R. W. Nason, and P. D. White, eds. *Macromarketing: Evolution of Thought.* Boulder, Colorado: Business Research Division, Graduate School of Business, University of Colorado, 1980.

204c. Fisk, George. "Editor's Working Definition of Macromarketing." *Journal of Macromarketing,* 2 (Spring 1982), pp. 3-4.

205. Fleck, Ludwik. *Genesis and Development of a Scientific Fact.* Chicago: The University of Chicago Press, 1979.

206. Fodor, Jerry A. *Psychological Explanation: An Introduction to the Philosophy of Psychology.* New York: Random House, 1968.

208. Forge, John. "The Structure of Physical Explanation." *Philosophy of Science,* 47 (1980), pp. 203-226.

209. Fornell, Claes, and Fred L. Bookstein. "Two Structural Equation Models: LISREL PLS Applied to Consumer Exit-Voice Theory." *Journal of Marketing Research,* 19 (November 1982), pp. 440-452.

210. Frank, Ronald E., and Paul Green. "Numerical Taxonomy in Marketing Analysis: A Review Article." *Journal of Marketing Research* (February 1968), pp. 83-94.

211. Frankel, Henry. "Discussion: Harré on Causation." *Philosophy of Science,* 43 (1976), pp. 560-569.

212. Frankel, Henry. Book review of Thomas S. Kuhn, *The Essential Tension. Philosophy of Science,* 44 (1977), pp. 649-652.

213. Friedman, Milton. "The Methodology of Positive Economics." In *Essays in Positive Economics.* Chicago: University of Chicago Press, 1953, pp. 3-43.

214. Friedman, Milton. *Essays in Positive Economics.* Chicago: University of Chicago Press, 1958.

215. Friedman, Michael. *Foundations of Space-Time Theories*. Princeton, NJ: Princeton University Press, 1983.

216. Friedman, Michael. "Critical Notice: Moritz Schlick, Philosophical Papers." *Philosophy of Science*, 50 (September 1984), pp. 498-514.

217. Frost, W.A.K. "The Development of a Technique for TV Programming Assessment." *Journal of Marketing Research Society*, 9 (January 1969), pp. 25-44.

218. Fumerton, R.A. "Induction and Reasoning to the Best Explanation." *Philosophy of Science*, 47 (1980), pp. 589-600.

219. Gaa, James C. "Moral Autonomy and the Rationality of Science." *Philosophy of Science*, 44 (1977), pp. 513-541.

220. Gabor, Andre, Clive Granger, and Anthony Sowter. "Comments on Psychophysics of Prices." *Journal of Marketing Research*, 8 (May 1971), pp. 251-52.

221. Gaski, John F. "Nomic Necessity in Marketing: The Issue of Counterfactual Conditionals." *Journal of The Academy of Marketing Science*, 13 (1985), pp. 320-21.

222. Garb, Gerald. "Professor Samuelson on Theory and Realism: Comment." *American Economic Review* (December 1965), pp. 1151-53.

223. Garda, Robert A. "Comments on the AMA Task Force Study." *Journal of Marketing*, 52 (October 1988), pp. 32-41.

224. Gardner, M. "On the Fabric of Inductive Logic." *Scientific American*, 234 (1976), pp. 119ff.

225. Gardenfors, Peter. "A Pragmatic Approach to Explanations." *Philosophy of Science*, 47 (1980), pp. 404-423.

226. Giere, Ronald N. *Explaining Science: A Cognitive Approach*. Chicago: University of Chicago Press, 1988.

227. Gieryn, Thomas F. "Boundary-Work and the Demarcation of Science from Non-Science." *American Sociological Review*, 48 (December 1983).

228. Gist, Ronald R. *Marketing and Society*. New York: Holt, Rinehart, and Winston, 1971.

229. Glymour, Clark. "Discussion: Hypothetico-Deductivism is Hopeless." *Philosophy of Science*, 47 (1980), pp. 322-325.

230. Goble, Ross L. and Roy Shaw. *Controversy and Dialogue in Marketing*. Englewood Cliffs, NJ: Prentice-Hall, 1975.

231. Goodman, Nelson. *Fact, Fiction, and Forecast*. Indianapolis, IN: Bobbs-Merrill, 1965.

232. Goodman, Nelson. *Ways of Worldmaking*. Indianapolis, IN: Hackett Publishing Company, 1978.

233. Granbois, Ronald H. "Decision Processes for Major Durable Goods." In *New Essays in Marketing Theory*. Ed. G. Fisk. Boston: Allyn and Bacon, 1971, pp. 172-205.

234. Granger, C.W.J. "Investigating Causal Relationships by Econometric Methods." *Econometrics*, 37 (July 1969), pp. 424-438.

235. Green, Paul E., Roland Frank, and Patrick Robinson. "Cluster Analysis in Test Market Selection." *Management Science*, 13 (April 1967), pp. B-387-400.

236. Green, Paul, and Donald Tull. *Research for Marketing Decisions*. 2d ed. Englewood Cliffs, NJ: Prentice-Hall, 1970.

237. Greeno, James G. "Explanation and Information." In *The Foundations of Scientific Inference*. Ed. W. Salmon. Pittsburgh: University of Pittsburgh Press, 1966, pp. 89-104.

238. Grene, Marjorie. "Reducibility: Another Side Issue." In *Interpretations of Life and Mind*. Ed. Marjorie Grene. London: Routledge and Kegan Paul, 1971, pp. 14-37.

239. Grene, Marjorie. *The Understanding of Nature*. Holland: Reidel, 1974.

240. Grene, Marjorie. "To Have a Mind . . . ." *Journal of Medicine and Philosophy*, 1 (1976), pp. 177-199.

241. Grene, Marjorie. "Discussion: Comment on Desmond Clarke, 'Teleology and Mechanism: M. Grene's Absurdity Argument.'" *Philosophy of Science*, 46, pp. 326-327.

242. Guthrie, W.K.C. *History of Greek Philosophy*. Cambridge University Press, 1962.

243. Halbert, M. *The Meaning and Sources of Marketing Theory*. New York: McGraw-Hill, 1965.

244. Hall, D. "Review of Kuhn's the Structure of Scientific Revolutions." *Systematic Zoology*, 24 (1975), pp. 395-401.

245. Hall, Rupert. "The Scholar and the Craftsman in the Scientific Revolution." In *History of Science*. Madison: University of Wisconsin Press, 1959.

246. Hamilton, Edith, and Huntington Cairns, eds. *The Collected Dialogues of Plato*. London: Pantheon Books, 1961.

247. Hansen, Flemming. *Consumer Choice Behavior*. New York: The Free Press, 1972.

248. Hanson, Norwood R. *Patterns of Discovery*. Cambridge: Cambridge University Press, 1958.

249. Hanson, Norwood R. *The Concept of Positivism, A Philosophical Analysis*. Cambridge: Cambridge University Press, 1963.

250. Harré, Rom. *Varieties of Realism*. Oxford, UK: Basil Blackwell Ltd., 1986.

251. Harré, Rom, and E.H. Madden. *Causal Powers*. Totawa, NJ: Rowman and Littlefield, 1975.

252. Harré, Rom. "Discussion: Science as Representation: A Reply to Mr. MacKinnon." *Philosophy of Science*, 44 (1977), pp. 146-158.

253. Harré, Rom. *Great Scientific Experiments: Twenty Experiments That Changed Our View of the World*. Oxford: Phaidon Press, 1984.

254. Harris, Henry, ed. *Scientific Models and Man*. Oxford, England: Clarendon Press, 1979.

255. Harvey, David. *Explanation in Geography*. New York: St. Martin's Press, 1969.

256. Headen, Robert S., Jay Klompmaker, and Roland Rust. "The Duplication of Viewing Law and Television Media Schedule Evaluation." *Journal of Marketing Research*, 16 (August 1979), pp. 333-40.

257. Hempel, Carl G. "Studies in the Logic of Confirmation." *Mind*, 54 (1945), pp. 1-26, 97-121.

258. Hempel, Carl G. "Fundamentals of Concept Formation in Empirical Science." In *Foundations of the Unity of Science*. Eds. Otto Neurath, Rudolf Carnap, and Charles Morris. Chicago: University of Chicago Press, 1970, pp. 651-745.

259. Hempel, Carl G. "A Logical Appraisal of Operationism." *Scientific Monthly*, 79 (1954), pp. 215-220.

261. Hempel, Carl G. "The Logic of Functional Analysis." In *Symposium on Sociological Theory*. Ed. Llewellyn Gross. New York: Harper and Row, 1959, pp. 271-307.

262. Hempel, Carl G. "Aspects of Scientific Explanation." In *Aspects of Scientific Explanation and Other Essays in the Philosophy of Science*. New York: The Free Press, 1965, pp. 331-496.

263. Hempel, Carl G. "The Theoretician's Dilemma." In *Aspects of Scientific Explanation*. Ed. Carl Hempel. New York: The Free Press, 1965.

264. Hempel, Carl G. *Philosophy of Natural Science*. Englewood Cliffs, NJ: Prentice-Hall, 1966.

265. Hempel, Carl G. "Maximal Specificity and Lawlikeness in Probabilistic Explanation." *Philosophy of Science*, 35 (1968), pp. 116-133.

266. Hempel, Carl G. "Logical Positivism and the Social Sciences." In *The Legacy of Logical Positivism*. Eds. Peter Achinstein and Stephen F. Borker. Baltimore: Johns Hopkins Press, 1969, pp. 163-194.

267. Hempel, Carl G., et al. *The Isenberg Memorial Lecture Series, 1965-1966*. East Lansing, MI: The Michigan State University Press, 1969.

268. Hempel, Carl G. "Methods of Concept Formation in Science." In *Formations of the Unity of Science*. Eds. Otto Neurath, Rudolf Carnap, and Charles Morris. Chicago: University of Chicago Press, 1970.

269. Herschel, J.F.W. *Preliminary Discourse on the Study of Natural Philosophy*. London, 1830.

270. Herskovits, Melvile J. *Man and His Works*. New York: Alfred Knopf, 1947.

271. Herskovits, Melvile J. *Cultural Relativism*. New York: Random House, 1972.

272. Hesse, Mary. "A Revised Regularity View of Scientific Laws." In *Science, Belief and Behaviour*. Ed. D.H. Mellor. Cambridge: Cambridge University Press, 1980, pp. 87-103.

273. Hintikka, Jaakko. "On the Incommensurability of Theories." *Philosophy of Science*, 55 (1988), pp. 25-38.

274. Hintikka, Jaakko, and I. Niiniluoto. "An Axiomatic Foundation for the Logic of Inductive Generalization." In *Formal Methods of the Methodology of Science*. Eds. Prezelecki, Szaniawski and Wojcicki. Wroclaw: Ossolineum, 1976.

274a. Hirschman, Elizabeth C., ed. *Interpretive Consumer Research*. Provo, Utah: Association for Consumer Research, 1989.

275. Hollander, Stanley. "The Wheel of Retailing." *Journal of Marketing* (July 1960), pp. 37-42. Reprinted in *Marketing Classics*. Eds. Ben M. Erin and Keith Cox. Boston: Allyn and Bacon, Inc., 1969, pp. 331-39.

276. Hollis, Martin, and Steven Lukes. *Rationality and Relativism*. Cambridge, MA: The MIT Press, 1982.

277. Holloway, Robert J., and Robert S. Hancock. *The Environment of Marketing Behavior*. New York: John Wiley and Sons, 1964.

278. Holloway, Robert J., and Robert S. Hancock. *Marketing in a Changing Environment*. New York: John Wiley and Sons, 1968.

279. Holloway, Robert J., and Robert S. Hancock. *Marketing in a Changing Environment*. 2d ed. New York: John Wiley and Sons, 1973.

280. Holton, G. "Mach, Einstein and the Search for Reality." In *Ernest Mach, Physicist and Philosopher*. Eds. Kohen, R. S. and R. J. Seeger. Dordrecht: Reidel Publishing 1970.

281. Holton, Richard H. "The Distinction Between Convenience Goods, Shopping Goods, and Specialty Goods." *Journal of Marketing*, 23 (July 1958), pp. 53-56.

282. Homans, George C. *The Nature of Social Science*. New York: Harcourt, Brace, and World, 1967.

283. Hooker, C.A. "Discussion Review: Hollis and Nell's *Rational Economic Man: A Philosophical Critique of Neo-Classical Economics.*" *Philosophy of Science,* 46 (1979), pp. 470-490.

284. Hostiuck, K., Tim Kurtz, and David L. Kurtz. "Alderson's Functionalism and the Development of Marketing Theory." *Journal of Business Research,* 1 (Fall 1973), pp. 141-56.

285. Houghton, Walter E. *The Victorian Frame of Mind.* New Haven: Yale University Press, 1957.

286. Howard, John A. *Marketing Theory.* Boston: Allyn and Bacon, 1965.

287. Howard, John A., and Jagdish N. Sheth. *The Theory of Buyer Behavior.* New York: John Wiley and Sons, Inc., 1969.

288. Howell, Roy. "Covariance Structure Modeling and Measurement Issues: A Note." *Journal of Marketing Research,* 24 (February 1987), pp. 119-126.

289. Hoyningen-Huene, Paul. "Contexts of Discovery and Contexts of Justification." *Studies in the History and Philosophy of Science,* 18 (1987), pp. 501-505.

290. Hudson, Laural Anderson, and Julie L. Ozanne. "Alternative Ways of Seeking Knowledge in Consumer Research." *Journal of Consumer Research,* 14 (March 1988), pp. 508-521.

291. Hull, D. "Review of Hempel, Kuhn and Shapere." *Systematic Zoology,* 24 (1975), pp. 395-401.

292. Hume, David. *An Enquiry Concerning Human Understanding.* Chicago: The Open Court Publishing Company, 1927.

293. Hume, David. *A Treatise of Human Nature.* New York: E. P. Dutton, 1911.

294. Hume, David. *Writings on Economics.* Ed. Eugene Rotwein. Madison: The University of Wisconsin Press, 1970.

295. Hunt, Shelby D. "Post Transaction Communications and Dissonance Reduction." *Journal of Marketing,* 34 (July 1970), pp. 46-51.

296. Hunt, Shelby D. "The Morphology of Theory and the General Theory of Marketing." *Journal of Marketing,* 35 (April 1971), pp. 65-68.

297. Hunt, Shelby D., and James L. Pappas. "A Crucial Test for the Howard-Sheth Model of Buyer Behavior." *Journal of Marketing Research,* 9 (August 1972), pp. 346-48.

298. Hunt Shelby D. "Lawlike Generalizations and Marketing Theory." *Journal of Marketing,* 37 (July 1973), pp.69-70.

299. Hunt, Shelby D., and John R. Nevin. "Power in a Channel of Distribution: Sources and Consequences." *Journal of Marketing Research,* 11 (May 1974), pp. 186-93.

300. Hunt, Shelby D. *Marketing Theory: Conceptual Foundations of Research in Marketing.* Columbus, OH: Grid, Inc., 1976.

301. Hunt, Shelby D. "The Nature and Scope of Marketing." *Journal of Marketing,* 40 (July 1976), pp. 17-28.

302. Hunt, Shelby D. "The Three Dichotomies Model of Marketing: An Evaluation of Issues." In *Proceedings of Macro-Marketing Conference.* Ed. Charles C. Slater. Boulder: University of Colorado, 1976, pp. 52-56.

303. Hunt, Shelby D. "A General Paradigm of Marketing: In Support of the Three Dichotomies Model." *Journal of Marketing,* 42 (April 1978), pp. 107-110.

304. Hunt, Shelby D. "In Support of the 'Three Dichotomies Model,' Replying to Criticism by Gumucio, Robin, Ross, and Etgar." *Journal of Marketing,* 42 (April 1978), pp. 107-110.

305. Hunt, Shelby D., James A. Muncy, and Nina M. Ray. "Alderson's General Theory of Marketing: A Formalization." In *Review of Marketing 1981.* Eds. Ben M. Enis and Kenneth J. Roering. Chicago: American Marketing Association, 1981.

306. Hunt Shelby D., and R.F. Bush. *Marketing Theory: Philosophy of Science Perspectives.* Chicago: American Marketing Association, 1982.

306a. Hunt, Shelby D. *Marketing Theory: The Philosophy of Marketing Science.* Homewood, IL: Richard D. Irwin, Inc., 1983.

307. Hunt, Shelby D. "General Theories and the Fundamental Explananda of Marketing." *Journal of Marketing,* 47 (Fall 1983), pp. 9-17.

308. Hunt, Shelby D. "Should Marketing Adopt Relativism?" In *Scientific Method of Marketing.* Eds. Paul F. Anderson and Michael J. Ryan. Chicago: American Marketing Association (1984), pp. 30-34.

309. Hunt, Shelby D., and Paul S. Speck. "Does Logical Empiricism Imprison Marketing?" In *Changing the Course of Marketing: Alternative Paradigms for Widening Marketing Theory.* Eds. Nikhilkesh Dholakia and Johan Arndt. Greenwich, CT: JAI Press Inc. 1985, pp. 27-35.

310. Hunt, Shelby D. "The Logical Positivists: Beliefs, Consequences and Status." In *Proceedings of the 12th Paul D. Converse Symposium.* Eds. Devanathan Sudharshan and Fredrick W. Winter. Chicago: American Marketing Association, 1987, pp. 24-33.

311. Hunt, Shelby D. "Naturalistic, Humanistic, and Interpretive Inquiry: Challenges and Ultimate Potential." In *Interpretive Consumer Research.* Ed. Elizabeth Hirschman. Provo, UT: Association for Consumer Research, 1989.

312. Hunt, Shelby D. "Comments on the AMA Task Force Study." *Journal of Marketing,* 52 (October 1988), pp. 42-47.

312a. Hunt, Shelby D. "Truth in Marketing Theory and Research." *Journal of Marketing,* 54 (July 1990).

312b. Hunt, Shelby D. "Reification and Realism in Marketing." *Journal of Macromarketing,* 9 (Fall 1989).

313. Hutchinson, Kenneth D. "Marketing as a Science: An Appraisal." *Journal of Marketing,* 16 (January 1952), pp. 286-93.

314. Jacobson, Robert, and Franco M. Nicosia. "Advertising and Public Policy: The Macroeconomic Effects of Advertising." *Journal of Marketing Research,* 18 (February 1981), pp. 29-38.

315. James, William. *Pragmatism.* New York: Harper Brothers, 1907.

316. Janis, A. L., and P. B. Field. "Sex Differences and Personality Factors Related to Persuasibility." In *Personality and Persuasibility.* Ed. C. I. Hovland. New Haven: Yale University, 1959, pp. 55-68.

317. Jastram, Roy W. "A Treatment of Distributed Lags in the Theory of Advertising Expenditure." *Journal of Marketing,* 20 (July 1955), pp. 36-46.

318. Jeffrey, Richard C. "Statistical Explanation vs. Statistical Inference." In *The Foundations of Scientific Inference.* Ed. W. Salmon. Pittsburgh: University of Pittsburgh Press, 1966, pp. 89-104.

319. Jeffrey, Richard C. "Statistical Explanation vs. Statistical Inference." In *Essays in Honor of Carl G. Hempel.* Ed. N. Rescher. Dordrecht-Holland: D. Reidel Publishing Co., 1970, pp. 104-113.

320. Jevons, William Stanley. "Philosophy of Inductive Reference." In *Philosophy of Science.* Ed. Joseph J. Kockelmans. New York: The Free Press, 1968, pp. 137-46.

321. Jones, Gary. "Kuhn, Popper, and Theory Comparison." *Dialectria,* 35 (1981), pp. 389-97.

322. Joreskog, K.G. "A General Method for Analysis of Covariance Structure." *Proceedings.* Psychometric Society, Chapel Hill, NC: University of North Carolina Press, 1968.

323. Joreskog, K.G. "A General Method for Estimating a Linear Structural Equation System." In *Structural Equation Models in the Social Sciences.* Ed. A. S. Goldberger. New York: Seminar Press, 1973, pp. 85-112.

324. Jobe, Evan K. "Discussion: A Puzzle Concerning D-N Explanation." *Philosophy of Science,* 43 (1976), pp. 542-549.

324a. Jobe, Evan K. "Explanation, Causality, and Counterfactuals." *Philosophy of Science,* 52 (1985), pp. 357-389.

325. Johnson, Richard M. "Market Segmentation: A Strategic Marketing Tool." *Journal of Marketing Research* (February 1971), pp. 13-18.

326. Joyce, G. and C. Channon. "Classifying Market Survey Respondents." *Applied Statistics,* 15 (November 1966), 191-215.

327. Kamen, Joseph M. and Robert Toman. "Psychophysics of Prices." *Journal of Marketing Research,* 7 (February 1970), pp. 27-35.

328. Kamen, Joseph M. "Quick Clustering." *Journal of Marketing Research,* 7 (May 1970), pp. 199-204.

329. Kamen, Joseph M., and Robert Toman. "Psychophysics of Prices: A Reaffirmation." *Journal of Marketing Research,* 8 (May 1971), pp. 252-57.

330. Kangun, Norman. *Society and Marketing.* New York: Harper and Row, 1972.

331. Kant, Immanuel. *Prolegomena and Metaphysical Foundations of Natural Science (1783).* In *Philosophy of Science.* Ed. Joseph J. Kockelmans. New York: The Free Press, 1968, pp. 17-27.

332. Kaplan, Abraham. *The Conduct of Inquiry.* Scranton, PA: The Chandler Publishing Company, 1964.

332a. Kassarjian, Harold H. "Book Review." *Journal of Marketing,* 53 (Jan. 1989), pp. 123-126.

333. Katoma, George. *The Powerful Consumer.* New York: McGraw-Hill Book Company, 1960.

334. Keat, Russell, and John Urry. *Social Theory as Science.* London: Routledge and Kegan Paul, 1975.

335. Kekes, John. *A Justification of Rationality.* Albany: State University of New York Press, 1976.

336. Kernan, Jerome B. and Montrose S. Sommers. *Perspectives in Marketing Theory.* New York: Appleton-Century-Crofts, 1968.

337. Kitcher, P. "Theories, Theorists, and Theoretical Changes." *Philosophical Review,* 87 (1978), pp. 519-47.

338. Knore-Cetina, K. *The Manufacturer of Knowledge: An Essay on the Constructivist and Contextual Nature of Science.* New York, 1981.

339. Kockelmans, Joseph J., ed. *Philosophy of Science: The Historical Background.* New York: The Free Press, 1968.

340. Kordig, Carl R. "Feyerabend and Radical Meaning Variance." *Nous,* 9 (1970), pp. 399-404.

340a. Kordig, Carl R. *The Justification of Scientific Change.* Dordrecht, Holland: D. Reidel Publishing Company, 1971.

341. Kordig, Carl R. "Discovery and Justification." *Philosophy of Science,* 45 (1978), pp. 110-117.

342. Kordig, Carl R. "Progress Requires Invariance." *Philosophy of Science,* 47 (1980), p. 141.

343. Kotler, Philip. *Marketing Management.* Englewood Cliffs, NJ: Prentice-Hall, 1967.

344. Kotler, Philip. *Marketing Management.* 2d ed. Englewood Cliffs, NJ: Prentice-Hall, 1972.

345. Kotler, Philip, and Sidney J. Levy. "Broadening the Concept of Marketing." *Journal of Marketing,* 33 (January 1969), pp. 10-15.

346. Kotler, Philip, and Sidney Levy. "A New Form of Marketing Myopia: Rejoinder to Professor Luck." *Journal of Marketing,* 33 (July 1969), pp. 55-57.

347. Kotler, Philip and Gerald Zaltman. "Social Marketing: An Approach to Planned Social Change." *Journal of Marketing,* 35 (July 1971), pp. 3-12.

348. Kotler, Philip. "A Generic Concept of Marketing." *Journal of Marketing,* 36 (April 1972), pp. 46-54.

349. Kotler, Philip. "Defining the Limits of Marketing." *Marketing Education and the Real World, 1972 Fall Conference Proceedings.* Eds. Boris W. Becker and Helmut Becker. Chicago: American Marketing Association, 1972, pp. 48-56.

350. Krausz, Michael and Jack W. Meiland. *Relativism: Cognitive and Moral.* Notre Dame, IN: University of Notre Dame Press, 1982.

351. Krips, H. "Some Problems for 'Progress and Its Problems.'" *Philosophy of Science,* 47 (1980), pp. 601-616.

352. Kruger, Lorenz. "Are Statistical Explanations Possible?" *Philosophy of Science,* 43 (1976), pp. 129-146.

353. Krugman, Herbert E. "The Impact of Television Advertising: Learning Without Involvement." *Public Opinion Quarterly,* 29 (1965), pp. 349-356.

354. Kuhn, Thomas S. *The Structure of Scientific Revolutions.* Chicago: The University of Chicago Press, 1962.

355. Kuhn, Thomas S. *The Structure of Scientific Revolutions.* 2d ed. Chicago: University of Chicago Press, 1970.

356. Kuhn, Thomas S. "Reflections on My Critics." In *Criticism and the Growth of Knowledge.* Eds. Imre Lakatos and Alan Musgrave. Cambridge, UK: Cambridge University Press, 1970, pp. 231-278.

357. Kuhn, Thomas S. "Theory-Change as Structure-Change: Comments on the Sneed Formalism." *Erkenntnis,* 10 (1976), pp. 179-99.

358. Kuhn, Thomas S. *The Essential Tension.* Chicago: University of Chicago Press, 1977.

359. Kukla, Andy. "Discussion: On the Empirical Significance of Pure Determinism." *Philosophy of Science,* 45 (1978), pp. 141-144.

360. Kukla, A. "Discussion: Determinism and Predictability: Reply to Dieks." *Philosophy of Science,* 47 (1980), pp. 131-133.

361. Kyburg, Henry E. Jr. *Philosophy of Science.* New York: The Macmillan Company, 1968.

362. Lakatos, Imre. "Falsification and the Methodology of Scientific Research Programmes." In *Criticism and the Growth of Knowledge.* Eds. Imre Lakatos and Alan Musgrave. Cambridge, UK: Cambridge University Press, 1970, pp. 91-196.

363. Lakatos, Imre. *The Methodology of Scientific Research Programmes.* Cambridge, UK: Cambridge University Press, Vol. 1, 1978.

364. Lamb, Charles and Patrick M. Dunne, eds. *Theoretical Developments in Marketing*. Chicago: American Marketing Association, 1980.

365. Lambert, Karel and Gordon G. Brittan, Jr. *An Introduction to the Philosophy of Science*. Englewood Cliffs, NJ: Prentice-Hall, 1970.

366. Latour, B. and S. Woolgar. *Laboratory Life: The Social Construction of Scientific Facts*. Beverly Hills, 1979.

367. Laudan, Larry. "Theories of Scientific Method from Plato to Mach." In *History of Science*. Eds. A. C. Crombie and M. A. Hoskin. Cambridge: W. Heffer and Sons, Ltd., Vol. 7 (1968), pp. 1-63.

369. Laudan, Larry. "Discussion: Two Dogmas of Methodology." *Philosophy of Science,* 43 (1976), pp. 585-597.

370. Laudan, Larry. *Progress and Its Problems: Towards a Theory of Scientific Growth*. Berkeley: University of California Press, 1977.

371. Laudan, Larry. "Historical Methodologies: An Overview and Manifesto." In *Current Research in the Philosophy of Science*. Eds. Peter D. Asquith and Henry E. Kyburg, Jr. East Lansing, MI: Philosophy of Science Association, 1979, pp. 40-54.

372. Laudan, Larry. "A Confutation of Convergent Realism." *Philosophy of Science,* 48 (1981), pp. 19-49.

373. Laudan, Larry. *Science and Hypothesis*. Dordrecht, Holland: D. Reidel Publishing, 1981.

374. Laudan, Larry. "Commentary: Science at the Bar—Causes for Concern." *Science, Technology, and Human Values,* 7 (Fall 1982), pp. 16-19.

375. Laudan, Larry. *Science and Values*. Berkeley: University of California Press, 1984.

376. Laudan, Larry; Arthur Donovan; Rachel Laudan; Peter Barker; Harold Brown; Jarrett Leplin; Paul Thagard; Steve Wykstra. "Scientific Change: Philosophical Models and Historical Research." *Synthese,* 69 (1986), pp. 141-223.

377. Laudan, Larry. "Relativism, Naturalism and Reticulation." *Synthese,* 71 (1987), pp. 221-34.

379. Lavidge, Robert J., and Gary A. Steiner. "A Model for Predictive Measurements of Advertising Effectiveness." *Journal of Marketing,* 25 (October 1961), pp. 59-62.

380. Lavidge, Robert J. "The Growing Responsibilities of Marketing." *Journal of Marketing,* 34 (January 1970), pp. 25-28.

381. Lazer, William. "The Role of Models in Marketing." *Journal of Marketing,* 26 (April 1962), pp. 9-14.

382. Lazer, William, and Eugene Kelly. "Systems Perspective of Marketing Activity." In *Managerial Marketing Perspectives and Viewpoints*. Rev. ed. Eds. William Lazer and Eugene Kelly. Homewood, IL: R.D. Irwin, 1962, pp. 191-98.

383. Lazer, William. "Marketing's Changing Social Relationships." *Journal of Marketing,* 33 (January 1969), pp. 3-9.

384. Lazer, William and Eugene Kelly. *Social Marketing*. Homewood, IL: R.D. Irwin, 1973.

385. Leftwich, Richard H. *The Price System and Resource Allocation*. New York: Holt, Rinehart, and Winston, 1966.

386. Lehman, Donald R., Terrence V. O'Brien, John Farley, and John Howard. "Some Empirical Contributions to Buyer Behavior Theory." *The Journal of Consumer Research,* 1 (December 1974), pp. 43-55.

387. Leong, Siew Meng. "Metatheory and Metamethodology in Marketing: A Lakatosian Reconstruction." *Journal of Marketing,* 49 (Fall 1985), pp. 23-40.

388. Leplin, Jarrett. "Truth and Scientific Progress." *Studies in the History and Philosophy of Science,* 12 (1981), pp. 269-91.

389. Leplin, Jarrett. *Scientific Realism.* Berkeley: University of California Press, 1984.

390. Leplin, Jarrett. "Methodological Realism and Scientific Rationality." *Philosophy of Science,* 53 (1986), pp. 31-51.

391. Lerner, Abba P. "Professor Samuelson on Theory and Realism: Comment." *American Economic Review* (December 1965), pp. 1153-55.

392. Levi, Isaac. *The Enterprise of Knowledge.* Cambridge, MA: The MIT Pres, 1980.

393. Levin, Michael E. "The Extensionality of Causation and Causal Explanatory Contexts." *Philosophy of Science,* 43 (1976), pp. 266-277.

394. Levin, Michael E. "On Theory-Change and Meaning-Change." *Philosophy of Science,* 46 (1979), pp. 407-424.

395. Levin, Michael E. "What Kind of Explanation is Truth?" In *Scientific Realism.* Ed. J. Leplin. Berkeley: University of California Press, 1984, pp. 124-139.

396. Lincoln, Yvonna S. and Egon G. Guba. *Naturalistic Inquiry.* Beverly Hills: Sage Publications, 1985.

397. Little, John D. C. "Models and Managers: The Concept of a Decision Calculus." *Management Science* (April 1970), pp. 466-485.

398. Lockley, Lawrence C. "An Approach to Marketing Theory." In *Theory in Marketing.* Eds. Reavis Cox, Wroe Alderson, and Stanley Shapiro. Homewood, IL: Richard D. Irwin, Inc., 1964, pp. 37-50.

399. Longman, Kenneth A. "The Management Challenge to Marketing Theory." In *New Essays in Marketing Theory.* Ed. George Fisk. Boston: Allyn and Bacon, Inc., 1971, pp. 9-19.

400. Losee, John. *A Historical Introduction to the Philosophy of Science.* Oxford: Oxford University Press, 1980.

401. Louch, A.R. "Human Conduct Requires Ad Hoc Explanations." In *Philosophy and Science.* Ed. Frederick Mosedale. Englewood Cliffs, NJ: Prentice-Hall, 1979, pp. 281-285.

402. Luck, David J. "Broadening the Concept of Marketing—Too Far." *Journal of Marketing,* 33 (July 1969), pp. 53-55.

403. Luck, David J., Hugh G. Wales, and Donald A. Taylor. *Marketing Research.* Englewood Cliffs, NJ: Prentice-Hall, 1970.

404. Luck, David J. "Social Marketing: Confusion Compounded." *Journal of Marketing,* 38 (October 1974), pp. 70-74.

405. Lugg, Andrew. "Discussion: An Alternative to the Traditional Model? Laudan on Disagreement Consensus in Science." *Philosophy of Science,* 53 (1986), pp. 419-24.

406. Lutz, Richard J., and Robert W. Resek. "More on Testing the Howard-Sheth Model of Buyer Behavior." *Journal of Marketing Research,* 9 (August 1972), pp. 344-45.

407. Lutz, Richard J. "Opening Statement." In *Conceptual and Theoretical Developments in Marketing.* Eds. O. C. Ferrell, S. W. Brown, and C. W. Lamb. Chicago: American Marketing Association, 1979, pp. 3-6.

408. Lyons, David. "Ethical Relativism and the Problem of Incoherence." In *Relativism: Cognitive Moral.* Eds. Michael Krause and Jack W. Meiland. Notre Dame: University of Notre Dame Press, 1982, pp. 209-225.

409. MacDonald, Margaret. "The Natural Laws and Natural Rights." In *Readings in the Philosophy of the Social Sciences.* Ed. May Brodbeck. New York: Macmillan, Inc., 1968, pp. 719-36.

410. Machan, Tibor R. "The Politics of Medicinal Anarchism." *Philosophy of Social Science,* 12 (1982), pp. 183-189.

411. Machan, Tibor R. "Anarchosurrealism Revisited: Reply to Feyerabend's Comments." *Philosophy of Social Science,* 12 (1982), pp. 197-99.

412. Machlup, Fritz. "Professor Samuelson on Theory and Realism." *American Economic Review* (September 1964), pp. 733-36.

413. Mackie, J.L. "Causes and Conditions." *American Philosophical Quarterly,* 2 (1965), pp. 245-264.

414. MacKinnon, Edward. "Scientific Realism: The New Debates." *Philosophy of Science,* 46 (1979), pp. 501-532.

415. Malinowski, Bronislaw. "Anthropology." *Encyclopedia Britannica.* Suppl., Vol. 1, Chicago, 1936.

416. Malinowski, Bronislaw. "The Functional Theory." In *A Scientific Theory of Culture.* Chapel Hill, NC: 1944, pp. 145-76.

417. Malinowski, Bronislaw. *Magic, Science, and Religion.* New York: Doubleday and Company, Inc., 1954.

418. Manicas, Peter T. *A History and Philosophy of the Social Sciences.* New York: Basil Blackwell, Inc., 1987.

419. Marketing Staff of the Ohio State University. "Statement of Marketing Philosophy." *Journal of Marketing,* 29 (January 1965), pp. 43-44.

420. Markin, Rom J. *Consumer Behavior: A Cognitive Orientation.* New York: Macmillan Publishing Co., Inc., 1974.

421. Martilla, J.A. "Word of Mouth Communication in Industrial Adoption Process." *Journal of Marketing Research,* 8 (May 1971), pp. 173-78.

422. Martin, Raymond. "Beyond Positivism: A Research Program for Philosophy of History." *Philosophy of Science,* 48 (1981), pp. 112-121.

423. Masey, Gerald J. "Professor Samuelson on Theory and Realism: Comment." *American Economic Review* (December 1965), pp. 1153-63.

424. Massey, William, and Barton Weitz. "A Normative Theory of Market Segmentation." In *Behavioral Models for Marketing Action.* Eds. M. Nicosia and Y. Wind. Hinsdale, IL: Dryden Press, 1977, pp. 121-44.

425. Masterman, Margaret. "The Nature of a Paradigm." In *Criticism and the Growth of Knowledge.* Eds. I. Lakatos and A. Musgrave. Cambridge: Cambridge University Press (1970), pp. 59-90.

426. Maxwell, Grover. "The Ontological Status of Theoretical Entities." In *Scientific Explanation, Minnesota Studies in the Philosophy of Science.* Vol. 3. Eds. Feigl and Maxwell. Minneapolis: University of Minnesota, 1962.

427. McCarthy, E. J. *Basic Marketing.* Homewood, IL: R.D. Irwin, 1960.

428. McCarthy, E. J. *Basic Marketing.* Homewood, IL: R.D. Irwin, 4th ed. 1971.

429. McCarthy, Timothy. "Discussion: On an Aristotelian Model of Scientific Explanation." *Philosophy of Science,* 44 (1977), pp. 159-166.

430. McCauley, Robert N. "Discussion: Hypothetical Identities and Ontological Economizing: Comments on Causey's Program for the Unity of Science." *Philosophy of Science,* 48 (1981), pp. 218-227.

431. McGarry, Edmund D. "The Importance of Scientific Method in Advertising." *Journal of Marketing,* 1 (October 1936), pp. 82-86.

432. McMullin, Ernan. "Reactions to the Logical Positivist Conception of Science." In *Philosophy and Science*. Ed. Frederick Mosedale. Englewood Cliffs, NJ: Prentice-Hall, Inc., 1979, pp. 229-237.

433. McMullin, Ernan. "Discussion Review: Laudan's Progress and Its Problems." *Philosophy of Science*, 46 (1979), pp. 623-644.

434. McMullin, Ernan. "A Case for Scientific Realism." In *Scientific Realism*. Ed. J. Leplin. Berkeley: University of California Press, 1984, pp. 8-40.

435. McMullin, Ernan. "Empiricism at Sea." In *A Portrait of Twenty-five Years*. Eds. Cohen and Wartofsky. Dordrecht: D. Reidel Publishing, 1985, pp. 121-132.

436. McMullin, Ernan. "Empiricism at Sea." In *A Portrait of Twenty-Five Years: Boston Colloquium for the Philosophy of Science 1960-1985*. Eds. Cohen and Wartofsky. Dordrecht: D. Reidel Publishing Co., 1986.

437. McNair, Malcolm P. "Competitive Trends and Developments to the Postwar Period." In *Competitive Distribution in a Free, High Level Economy and Its Implications for the University*. Ed. A.B. Smith. Pittsburgh: University of Pittsburgh Press, 1958.

438. Meehl, Paul E. "What Social Scientists Don't Understand." In *Metatheory in Social Science*. Eds. Fiske and Shweder. Chicago: University of Chicago Press, 1986, pp. 315-338.

439. Meixner, John. "Homogeneity and Explanatory Depth." *Philosophy of Science*, 46 (1979), pp. 366-381.

440. Mellor, D.H., ed. *Science, Belief, and Behavior*. Cambridge: Cambridge University Press, 1980.

441. Mermin, N. D. "The Great Quantum Muddle." *Philosophy of Science*, 50 (December 1983).

442. Merrill, G. H. "The Model-Theoretic Argument Against Realism." *Philosophy of Science*, 47 (1980), pp. 69-81.

443. Merton, Robert K. *Social Theory and Social Structure*. New York: The Free Press, 1968.

444. Merton, Robert K. *The Sociology of Science*. Chicago: The University of Chicago Press, 1973.

445. Merton, Robert K. "Science, Technology and Society in Seventeenth Century England." *Osiris*, 4 (1938), pp. 360-362.

446. Meyer, Stuart L. "Discussion Urning a Resolution of Hempel's Paradox." *Philosophy of Science*, 44 (1977), pp. 292-296.

447. Meyers, James H. and William Reynolds. *Consumer Behavior and Marketing Management*. New York: Houghton Mifflin Co., 1967.

448. Mindak, William A, and H. Malcolm Bybee. "Marketing's Application to Fund Raising." *Journal of Marketing*, 35 (July 1971), pp. 13-18.

449. Mitroff, Ian. Book review of Stuart S. Blume, ed. *Perspectives in the Sociology of Science*. *Philosophy of Science*, 44 (1977), pp. 334-335.

450. Moberg, D. W. "Are There Rival, Incommensurable Theories?" *Philosophy of Science*, 46 (1979), pp. 244-62.

451. Monroe, Kent B. "Psychophysics of Prices: A Reappraisal." *Journal of Marketing Research*, 8 (May 1971), pp. 248-50.

452. Monroe, Kent, et. al. "Developing, Disseminating, and Utilizing Marketing Knowledge." *Journal of Marketing*, 52 (October 1988), pp. 1-25.

453. Morris, Charles W. "Scientific Empiricism." In *Foundations of the Unity of Science*. Vol. 1. Eds. Otto Neurath, Rudolf Carnap, and Charles Morris. Chicago: University of Chicago Press, 1955, pp. 63-75.

454. Morrison, Donald G. "The Use and Limitations of Brand Switching Models." In *Behavioral and Management Science in Marketing.* Eds. Harry L. Davis and Alvin J. Silk. New York: John Wiley and Sons, 1978, pp. 5-11.

455. "Motel 6's Ads Push Chain's Budget Concept." *Advertising Age* (December 4), 1972.

456. Moyer, Reed. *Macro-Marketing.* New York: John Wiley and Sons, 1972.

457. Mukherjee, Bishwa Nath. "A Factor Analysis of Some Qualitative Attributes of Coffee." *Journal of Advertising Research,* 5 (March 1965), pp. 35-38.

458. Muncy, James A., and Raymond P. Fisk. "Cognitive Relativism and the Practice of Marketing Science." *Journal of Marketing,* 51 (January 1987), pp. 20-23.

459. Munz, Peter. "Bloor's Wittgenstein of the Fly in the Bottle." *Philosophy of Social Science,* 17 (1987), pp. 67-96.

460. Musgrave, Alan. "Problems With Progress." *Synthese,* 42 (1979), pp. 443-464.

461. Myers, John G., Stephen A. Greyser, and William F. Massey. "The Effectiveness of Marketing's 'R&D' for Marketing Management: An Assessment." *Journal of Marketing,* 43 (January 1979), pp. 17-29.

462. Myers, John G., William F. Massey, and Stephen A. Greyser. *Marketing Research and Knowledge Development: An Assessment for Marketing Management.* Englewood Cliffs, NJ: Prentice-Hall, 1980.

463. Nagel, Ernest. "The Meaning of Reduction in the Natural Sciences." In *Philosophy of Science.* Eds. Danto and Morgenbesser. New York: Meridian Books, 1960.

464. Nagel, Ernest. *The Structure of Science.* New York: Harcourt Brace Jovanovich, 1961.

465. Nagel, Ernest. "Assumptions in Economic Theory." *American Economic Review,* 53 (May 1963), pp. 211-219.

466. Nagel, Ernest, and Richard B. Brandt. *Meaning and Knowledge.* New York: Harcourt Brace Jovanovich, 1965.

467. Nagel, Ernest. "Social Science Defended." In *Philosophy of Science.* Ed. Frederick Mosedale. Englewood Cliffs, NJ: Prentice-Hall (1979), pp. 286-293.

468. Nakamoto, Kent and Shelby D. Hunt. "Deterministic Theory and Marketing." In *Theoretical Developments in Marketing.* Eds. Charles W. Lamb, Jr. and Patrick M. Dunne. Chicago: American Marketing Association, 1980, pp. 244-47.

469. Nason, Robert W., and Phillip D. White. "The Visions of Charles C. Slater: Social Consequences of Marketing." *Journal of Macromarketing,* 1 (Fall 1981), pp. 4-18.

470. Neidell, Lester A. *Physician Perception and Evaluation of Selected Ethical Drugs: An Application of Nometric Multidimensional Scaling to Pharmaceutical Marketing.* Ph.D. dissertation, University of Pennsylvania, 1969.

471. Newman, Joseph W., and Richard A. Werbel. "Multivariate Analysis of Brand Loyalty for Major Household Appliances." *Journal of Marketing Research* (November 1973), pp. 404-9.

472. Newman, Peter. *The Theory of Exchange.* Englewood Cliffs, NJ: Prentice-Hall, 1965.

472a. Neurath, Otto, Rudolf Carnap, and Charles Morris, eds. *Foundations of the Unity of Science.* Vol. 1. Chicago: University of Chicago Press, 1955.

473. Neurath, Otto, Rudolf Carnap, and Charles Morris, eds. *Foundations of the Unity of Science.* Vol 2. Chicago: University of Chicago Press, 1970.

474. Nickles, Thomas. "Beyond Divorce: The Current Status of the Discovery Debate." *Philosophy of Science,* 52 (June 1985), pp. 177-206.

475. Nickels, William, G. "Conceptual Conflicts in Marketing." *Journal of Economics and Business,* 26 (Winter 1974), pp. 140-43.

476. Nicosia, Francesco W. *Consumer Decision Processes.* Englewood Cliffs, NJ: Prentice-Hall, Inc., 1966.

477. Nicosia, Francesco M., and Yoram Wind. *Behavioral Models for Market Analysis: Foundations For Marketing Action.* Hinsdale, IL: The Dryden Press, 1977.

478. Niiniluoto, Ilkka. "Discussion: Dretske on Laws of Nature." *Philosophy of Science,* 45 (1978), pp. 431-439.

478a. Ford, Walter R., and J. Paul Peter. "A Behavior Modification Perspective on Marketing." *Journal of Marketing,* 44 (Spring 1980), pp. 36-47.

479. O'Brien, Terrence. "Stages of Consumer Decision Making." *Journal of Marketing Research* (August 1971), pp. 283-289.

480. Olson, Jerry C. "Towards a Science of Consumer Behavior." In *Advances in Consumer Research.* Ed. Andrew A. Mitchell. Ann Arbor, MI: Association of Consumer Research, 9 (1981), v-x.

481. Olson, Jerry C. "The Construction of Scientific Meaning." Presented at the 1987 Winter Marketing Educators' Conference, Chicago: American Marketing Association, 1987.

482. Orwell, George. *1984.* New York: Harcourt, Brace and World, Inc., 1949.

483. Palacios, Joel. "Slaver up Among Maranos." *Dallas Morning News.* (Reuters) 1987.

484. Palda, Kristian S. "The Hypothesis of a Hierarchy of Effects: A Partial Evaluation." *Journal of Marketing Research* (February 1966), pp. 13-24.

485. Palmer, R. E. *Hermeneutics.* Evanston: Northwestern University Press, 1969.

486. Papineau, David. *Theory and Meaning.* Oxford: Clarendon Press, 1979.

487. Parsons, Talcott. *Essays in Sociological Theory.* Glencoe, IL, 1949.

488. Passmore, John. *Science and its Critics.* New Brunswick: Rutgers University Press, 1978.

489. Patterson, Orlando. "Guilt, Relativism, and Black-White Relations." *American Scholar,* 43 (1973).

490. Pauling, Linus. *College Chemistry.* San Francisco: W.H. Freeman and Co., 1956.

491. Paulsen, John. *Immanuel Kant.* New York: Harper Brothers, 1910.

492. Peter, J. Paul, and Jerry C. Olson. "Is Science Marketing?" *Journal of Marketing,* 47 (Fall 1983), pp. 111-125.

493. Peter, J. Paul. "Is Science Marketing?" *Journal of Marketing,* 47 (Fall 1983), pp. 111-125.

494. Pierce, David A., and Larry D. Haugh. "Causality in Temporal Systems." *Journal of Econometrics,* 5 (May 1977), pp. 265-293.

495. Pinson, Christian R.A., and Edward L. Roberto. "Simplicity, Parsimony, and Model Building." *Proceedings of the Midwest AIDS Conference,* April 1972, pp. C-31-C-33.

496. Pinson, Christian R.A., Reinhard Angelmar, and Eduardo L. Roberto. "An Evaluation of the General Theory of Marketing." *Journal of Marketing,* 36 (July 1972), pp. 66-69.

497. Phillips, D. C. "Was William James Telling the Truth?" In *The Monist,* 67 (July 1984).

497a. Phillips, D. C. *Philosophy, Science, and Social Inquiry.* Oxford: Pergamon Press, 1987.

498. Plato. *Republic: Book II, in Five Great Dialogues.* Ed. Louise R. Loomis. Roslyn: New York: Walter J. Block, Inc., 1942.

499. Polli, Rolando, and Victor Cook. "Validity of the Product Life Cycle." *Journal of Business* (October 1969), pp. 395-400.

500. Plekhanov, Georgi. *The Materialistic Conception of History.* New York: Random House, 1940.

501. Polkinghorne, J. C. *The Quantum World.* New York: Longman, 1984.

502. Pondy, Louis R. "Organizational Conflict: Concepts and Models." *Administrative Science Quarterly,* 12 (September 1967), pp. 296-320.

503. Popper, Karl R. *The Logic of Scientific Discovery.* New York: Harper and Row, 1959, German version, 1935.

504. Popper, Karl R. *The Poverty of Historicism.* 2d ed. London: Routledge and Kegan Paul, Ltd., 1960.

505. Popper, Karl R. *Conjectures and Refutations: The Growth of Scientific Knowledge.* New York: Harper and Row, 1963.

506. Popper, Karl R. *The Open Society and Its Enemies.* 5th ed. Princeton: Princeton University Press, 1966, originally published in 1945.

507. Popper, Karl R. *Objective Knowledge.* Oxford: Oxford University Press, 1972.

508. Popper, Karl R. *Quantum Theory and the Schism in Physics.* Totowa, NJ: Rowan and Littlefield, 1982.

509. "Purge Toll Under Stalin Revised." *Dallas Morning News.* (Reuters) 1988, April 17.

510. Putnam, Hilary. "What Theories are Not." In *Proceedings of the 1960 International Congress.* Eds. Nagel, Suppes and Tarski. Stanford: Stanford University Press, 1962, pp. 240-51.

511. Putnam, Hilary. *Mathematics, Matter and Method.* Cambridge: Cambridge University Press, 1975.

512. Putnam, Hilary. "Philosophy of Mathematics: A Report." In *Current Research in Philosophy of Science.* Eds. Asquith and Kyburg. East Lansing, MI: Philosophy of Science Association, 1979, pp. 386-9.

513. Putnam, Hilary. *Reason, Truth and History.* Cambridge,: University of Cambridge Press, 1981.

514. Quine, W. V. "Two Dogmas of Empiricism." *Philosophical Review,* 60 (1951), pp. 20-43.

515. Quine, W. V. "Epistemology Naturalized." In Quine, *Ontological Relativity and Other Essays.* New York: Columbia Press, 1969.

516. Rachels, James. *The Elements of Moral Philosophy.* New York: Random House, 1986.

517. Radcliffe-Brown, A.R. *Structure and Function in Primitive Society.* London, 1952.

518. Radner, Daisie, and Michael Radner. *Science and Unreason.* Belmont, CA: Wadsworth Publishing Co., 1982.

519. Radner, Michael, and Stephen Winokur, eds. *Analysis of Theories and Methods of Physics and Psychology, Minnesota Studies in the Philosophy of Science.* Vol. 4. Minneapolis, University of Minnesota Press, 1970.

520. Railton, Peter. "A Deductive-Nomological Model of Probabilistic Explanation." *Philosophy of Science,* 45 (1978), pp. 206-226.

521. Rapport, Anatol. *Operational Philosophy.* San Francisco: International Society for General Semantics, 1969.

522. Ravetz, Jerome R. *Scientific Knowledge and Its Social Problems*. Oxford: Oxford University Press, 1971.

523. Ray, Michael. "Marketing Communication and the Hierarchy of Effects." In *New Models for Mass Communications Research*. Ed. Peter Clark. Vol. 2. Beverly Hills: Sage Publications, 1973, pp. 147-76.

524. Reed, Virgil. *Planned Marketing*. New York: Ronald Press, 1930.

525. Reichenbach, Hans. *The Theory of Probability*. Berkeley: The University of California Press, 1949.

526. Rescher, Nicholas, ed. *Essays in Honor of Carl G. Hempel*. Dordrecht-Holland: D. Reidel Publishing Co., 1970.

527. Rescher, Nicholas. *Scientific Explanation*. New York: The Free Press, 1970.

528. Rescher, Nicholas. "Lawfulness as Mind-Dependent." In *Essays in Honor of Carl G. Hempel*. Ed. Nicholas Rescher. Dordrecht-Holland: D. Reidel Publishing Co., 1970, pp. 179-197.

529. Rewoldt, Stewart H., James D. Scott, and Martin R. Warshaw. *Introduction to Marketing Management*. Homewood, IL: Richard D. Irwin, 1973.

530. Reynolds, Paul Davidson. *A Primer in Theory Construction*. Indianapolis: The Bobbs-Merrill Co., Inc., 1971.

531. Rigby, Paul. *Conceptual Foundations of Business Research*. New York: John Wiley and Sons, Inc., 1965.

532. Ringen, Jon D. "Explanation, Teleology, and Operant Behaviorism: A Study of the Experimental Analysis of Purposive Behavior." *Philosophy of Science*, 43 (1976), pp. 223-253.

533. Robicheaux, Robert and Adel El-Ansary. "A General Model for Understanding Channel Member Behavior." *Journal of Retailing*, 52 (Winter 1975), pp. 13-30, 90-94.

534. Robin, Donald P. "Success in Social Marketing." *Journal of Business Research*, 3 (July 1974), pp. 303-10.

535. Robin, Donald P. "Comment on the Nature and Scope of Marketing." *Journal of Marketing*, 41 (January 1977), pp. 136-138.

536. Robin, Donald P. "Comment on the Nature and Scope of Marketing." *Journal of Marketing*, 42 (July 1978), 6, 42.

537. Rohrlich, Fritz, and Larry Hardin. "Established Theories." *Philosophy of Science*, 50 (1983), pp. 603-607.

538. Rokeach, Milton. *Beliefs, Attitudes, and Values*. San Francisco: Jossey Bass, 1968.

539. Rolston, Howard L. "Discussion: A Note on Simplicity as a Principle for Evaluating Rival Scientific Theories." *Philosophy of Science*, 43 (1976), pp. 438-440.

540. Rothschild, Michael L. "The Effects of Political Advertising on the Voting Behavior of a Low-Involvement Electorate." Ph.D. Dissertation, Stanford University: Graduate School of Business, 1974.

541. Rozeboom, William W. "Discussion: Nicod's Criterion: Subtler Than You Think." *Philosophy of Science*, 47 (1980), pp. 638-643.

542. Rudner Richard. *Philosophy of Social Science*. Englewood Cliffs, NJ: Prentice-Hall, Inc., 1966.

543. Ruse, Michael. "Response to the Commentary: Pro Judice." *Science, Technology, and Human Values*, 7 (Fall 1982), pp. 19-23.

544. Russell, Bertrand. *Our Knowledge of the External World.* New York: The New American Library, 1929.

545. Russell, Bertrand. *A History of Western Philosophy.* New York: Simon and Schuster, 1945.

546. Ryle, G. *The Concept of the Mind.* London: Hutchinson, 1949.

547. Salmon, Wesley C. *Logic.* Englewood Cliffs, NJ: Prentice-Hall, Inc., 1963.

548. Salmon, Wesley C. *Statistical Explanation and Statistical Relevance.* Pittsburgh: University of Pittsburgh Press, 1971.

549. Salmon, Wesley C. "An 'At-At' Theory of Causal Influence." *Philosophy of Science,* 44 (1977), pp. 216-224.

550. Salmon, Wesley C. "Hempel's Conception of Inductive Inference in Inductive-Statistical Explanation." *Philosophy of Science,* 44 (1977), pp. 180-185.

551. Salmon, Wesley C. "Indeterminism and Epistemic Relativism." *Philosophy of Science,* 44 (1977), pp. 199-202.

552. Salmon, Wesley C. *Scientific Explanation and the Causal Structure of the World.* Princeton: Princeton University Press, 1984.

553. Sampson, Geoffrey. *Thinkers of the Twentieth Century.* 2nd ed. Ed. Roland Turner. Chicago: St. James Press, 1987.

554. Samuelson, Paul A. "Problems of Methodology—Discussion." *American Economic Review* (May 1963), pp. 231-236.

555. Samuelson, Paul A. "Theory and Relativism: A Reply." *American Economic Review* (September 1964), pp. 736-739.

556. Samuelson, Paul A. "Professor Samuelson on Theory and Realism: A Reply." *American Economic Review* (December 1965), pp. 1164-72.

557. Sauer, William J., Nancy Nighswonger, and Gerald Zaltman. "Current Issues in Philosophy of Science: Implication of the Study of Marketing." In *Marketing Theory: Philosophy of Science Perspectives.* Eds. Bush and Hunt. Chicago: American Marketing Association, 1982.

558. Sarkar, H. "Truth, Problem-Solving and Methodology." *Studies in History and Philosophy of Science,* 12 (1981), pp. 61-73.

558a. Sayers, Brian. "Wittgenstein, Relativism, and the Strong Thesis in Sociology." *Philosophy of Social Science,* 17 (1987), pp. 133-45.

559. Sayre, Kenneth M. "Statistical Models of Causal Relations." *Philosophy of Science,* 44 (1977), pp. 203-214.

560. Sarker, Husain. "Discussion: Musgrave's Appraisals and Advice." *Philosophy of Science,* 45, (1978), pp. 478-483.

561. Scheffler, I. "Explanation, Prediction, and Abstraction." *The British Journal for the Philosophy of Science,* 7 (1957), pp. 293-309.

562. Scheffler, I. *Science and Subjectivity.* Indianapolis: Bobbs Merrill, 1967.

563. Schiffman, Leon G., and Vincent Gaccione. "Opinion Leaders in Institutional Markets." *Journal of Marketing,* 38 (April 1974), pp. 49-53.

564. Schlaifer, Robert. *Probability and Statistics for Business Decisions.* New York: McGraw-Hill Book Company, 1959.

564a. Schopenhauer, Arthur. *The World as Will and Representation.* New York: Dover Publications, 1969 (original 1818).

565. Schmidt, Stuart M., and Thomas A. Kochon. "Conflict: Toward Conceptual Clarity." *Administrative Science Quarterly,* 17 (September 1972), pp. 359-370.

566. Schuette, Thomas F. "On the Development of a Propositional Inventory to Marketing." In *Marketing and the New Science of Planning.* Ed. Robert L. King.

Chicago: American Marketing Association Fall Conference Proceedings, 1968, pp. 154-162.

567. Schwartz, George. *Development of Marketing Theory*. Cincinnati: South-Western Publishing Co., 1963.

568. Schwartz, George. "Nature and Goals of Marketing Science." In *Science in Marketing*. Ed. George Schwartz. New York: John Wiley and Sons, Inc., 1965, pp. 1-19.

569. Schwartz, George, ed. *Science in Marketing*. New York: John Wiley and Sons, Inc., 1965.

570. Scott, Richard A. and Norton E. Marks. *Marketing and Its Environment*. Belmont, CA: Wadsworth Publishing Co., 1968.

571. Scriven, Michael. "Explanation and Prediction in Evolutionary Theory." *Science*, 130 (1959), pp. 477-82.

572. Scriven, Michael. "Logical Positivism and the Behavioral Sciences." In *The Legacy of Logical Positivism*. Eds. Peter Achinstein and Stephen F. Barker. Baltimore: Johns Hopkins Press, 1969, pp. 195-209.

573. Sellars, Wilfrid. *Science, Perception and Reality*. New York: Humanities Press, 1963.

574a. Shapere, D. "The Structure of Scientific Revolutions." *Philosophical Review*, 73 (1964), pp. 383-394.

574. Shapere, D. "The Structure of Scientific Change." In *Mind and Cosmos: Explorations in the Philosophy of Science*. Ed. R. Colodny. Pittsburgh, PA: University of Pittsburgh Press, 1966, pp. 41-85.

575. Shapiro, Benson P. "Price Reliance: Existence and Sources." *Journal of Marketing Research*, 10 (August 1973), pp. 286-293.

576. Sheth, Jagdish N., and W. Wayne Talarzyk. "Perceived Instrumentality and Value Importance as Determinants of Attitudes." *Journal of Marketing Research*, 9 (February 1972), pp. 6-9.

577. Sheth, Jagdish N., David M. Gardner, and Dennis E. Garrett. *Marketing Theory: Evolution and Evaluation*. New York: John Wiley and Sons, Inc., 1988.

578. Shrader, Douglas W. "Discussion: Causation, Explanation, and Statistical Relevance." *Philosophy of Science*, 44 (1977), pp. 136-145.

579. Shweder, Richard A., and Donald W. Fiske. "Introduction: Uneasy Social Science." In *Metatheory in Social Science*, Eds. Fiske and Shweder. Chicago: University of Chicago Press, 1986.

580. Siegel, Harvey. "Justification, Discovery, and the Naturalizing of Epistemology." *Philosophy of Science*, 47 (1980), pp. 297-321.

581. Siegel, Harvey. "Objectivity, Rationality, Incommensurability, and More." *British Journal of the Philosophy of Science*, 31 (1980), pp. 359-84.

582. Siegel, Harvey. "Truth, Problem Solving and the Rationality of Science." *Studies in the History and Philosophy of Science*, 14 (1983), pp. 89-112.

583. Siegel, Harvey. "Brown on Epistemology and the New Philosophy of Science." *Synthese*, 56 (1983), pp. 61-89.

585. Siegel, Harvey. "Goodmanian Relativism." *The Monist*, 67 (July 1984).

586. Siegel, Harvey. "Relativism, Truth, and Incoherence." *Synthese*, 68 (Fall 1986), pp. 225-259.

586a. Siegel, Harvey. *Relativism Refuted*. Dordrecht: D. Reidel Publishing Co., 1987.

587. Siegel, Harvey. "Relativism for Consumer Research? (Comments on Anderson)." *Journal of Consumer Research*, 15 (June 1988), pp. 129-132.

588. Siegfried, Tom. "Questioning the Existence of Scientific Truth." *Dallas Morning News.* Editorial Section, (November 2, 1987).

589. Simon, Julian. *Basic Research Methods in Social Science.* New York: Random House, 1969.

590. Sims, C.A. "Money, Income, and Causality." *American Economic Review,* 6 (September 1972), pp. 540-552.

591. Slater, Charles C. "Marketing Processes in Developing Latin American Societies." *Journal of Marketing,* 32 (July 1968), pp. 50-55.

592. Slater, Charles C., ed. *Macromarketing: Distributive Processes from a Societal Perspective.* Boulder, Colorado: Business Research Division, Graduate School of Business, University of Colorado, 1977.

593. Smelser, Neil J., ed. *Readings in Economic Sociology.* Englewood Cliffs, NJ: Prentice-Hall, Inc., 1965.

594. Smelser, Neil J. *The Sociology of Economic Life.* Englewood Cliffs, NJ: Prentice-Hall, Inc., 1963.

595. Smith, Robert E. and William R. Swinyard. "Information Response Models: An Integrated Approach." *Journal of Marketing,* 45 (Fall 1982), pp. 81-93.

596. Snyder, Paul. *Toward One Science.* New York: St. Martin's Press, Inc., 1978.

597. Sokal, R.R. and P. Sneath. *Principles of Numerical Taxonomy.* San Francisco: W.H. Freeman and Co., 1963.

598. Sosa, Ernest, ed. *Causation and Conditionals.* London: Oxford University Press, 1975.

599. Stallo, J.B. *The Concepts and Theories of Modern Physics (1882).* Ed. Percy W. Bridgeman. Cambridge, MA, 1960.

600. Steiner, Robert L. "Does Advertising Lower Consumer Prices?" *Journal of Marketing,* 37 (October), pp. 19-26.

601. Stewart, Paul W. *Does Distribution Cost Too Much?* New York: Twentieth Century Fund, 1939.

602. Stinchcombe, Arthur L. *Constructing Social Theories.* New York: Harcourt, Brace, and World, Inc., 1968.

603. Stove, David. *Popper and After.* Oxford, UK: Perganon Press, Ltd., 1982.

604. Stroetzel, Jean. "A Factor Analysis of Liquor Preferences of French Consumers." *Journal of Advertising Research,* 1 (December 1960), pp. 7-11.

605. Stuewer, Roger H., ed. *Historical and Philosophical Perspectives of Science, Minnesota Studies in the Philosophy of Science.* Vol. 5. Minneapolis: University of Minnesota Press, 1970.

606. Suppe, Frederick. *The Structure of Scientific Theories.* 2d ed. Chicago: University of Illinois Press, 1977.

607. Suppe, Frederick. "Afterword—1977." In *The Structure of Scientific Theories.* Ed. Frederick Suppe. 2d ed. Urbana, IL: University of Illinois Press, 1977, pp. 614-730.

608. Suppe, Frederick. "Beyond Skinner and Kuhn." *New Ideas in Psychology,* 2 (1984), pp. 89-104.

609. Suppes, Patrick. "Book Review, Science and Values." *Philosophy of Science,* 53 (1956), pp. 449-51.

610. Swinyard, William R. and Kenneth A. Coney. "Promotional Effects on a High Versus Low-Involvement Electorate." *Journal of Consumer Research,* 5 (June 1978), pp. 41-48.

611. Swoyer, Chris. "Relative Truth." In *Philosophy*. Ed. Robert Solomon. New York: Harcourt, Brace, and Jovanovich, 1984, pp. 194-201.

612. Tarski, Alfred. *Logic, Semantics, Metamathematics*. Translated by J.H. Woodger. Oxford: Claredon Press.

613. Taylor, C. "Teleological Explanation—A Reply to Dennis Noble." *Analysis*, 27 (1967), pp. 141-143.

614. Taylor, Weldon J. "Is Marketing a Science? Revisited." *Journal of Marketing*, 29 (July 1965), pp. 49-53.

615. Tellis, Gerald J. and C. Merle Crawford. "An Evolutionary Approach to Product Growth Theory." *Journal of Marketing*, 45 (Fall 1981), pp. 125-32.

616. Theocharis, T. and M. Psimopoulos. "Where has Science Gone Wrong?" *Nature*, 329 (October 15, 1987), pp. 595-98.

617. *Time*, 1988, July 11, p. 32.

618. Tucker, W.T. "The Development of Brand Loyalty." *Journal of Marketing Research*, 1 (August 1964), pp. 32-35.

619. Tucker, W.T. *Foundations for a Theory of Consumer Behavior*. New York: Holt Rinehart, and Winston, Inc., 1967.

620. Twedt, Dik Warren. "A Multiple Factor Analysis of Advertising Readership." *Journal of Applied Psychology* (June 1952).

621. Utz, Stephen. "Discussion: On Teleology and Organisms." *Philosophy of Science*, 44 (1977), pp. 313-320.

622. Vallicella, William F. "Relativism, Truth and the Symmetry Thesis." *The Monist*, 67 (July 1984), pp. 452-467.

623. Van Fraassen, Bas C. *The Scientific Image*. Oxford: Clarendon Press, 1980.

624. Venkatesan, M., and Robert J. Holloway. *An Introduction to Marketing Experimentation*. New York: The Free Press, 1971.

625. Walker, Jr., Orville C., and Richard F. Santer. "Consumer Preferences for Alternative Retail Credit Terms." *Journal of Marketing Research* (February 1974), pp. 70-78.

626. Wartofsky, Marx W. *Conceptual Foundations of Scientific Thought*. New York: The Macmillan Company, 1968.

627. Watkins, John. *Science and Skepticism*. Princeton, NJ: Princeton University Press, 1984.

628. Webster, Frederick E., Jr. *Social Aspects of Marketing*. Englewood Cliffs, NJ: Prentice-Hall, 1974.

629. Webster, Frederick E., Jr. "Comment on the AMA Task Force Study." *Journal of Marketing*, 52 (October 1988) pp. 48-51.

630. Weitz, Barton. "Effectiveness in Sales Interaction: A Contingency Framework." *Journal of Marketing*, 45 (Winter 1981).

631. Weld, L. D. H. *The Marketing of Farm Products*. New York: Macmillan, 1920.

632. Werskey, P. G., ed. *Science at the Cross Roads*. London, 1971, (originally published in 1931).

633. Whewell, William. *The Philosophy of the Inductive Sciences*. London: Longwans, Green and Company, Ltd., 1840. Reprinted in *Philosophy of Science*. Ed. Joseph J. Kockelmans. New York: The Free Press, 1968, pp. 51-79.

634. White, P., and W. S. Hayward. *Marketing Practice*. New York: Doubleday, Page, and Co., 1924.

635. White, P. D. and C. C. Slater, eds. *Macro-Marketing: Distributive Processes from a Societal Perspective: An Elaboration of Issues.* Boulder, Colorado: Business Research Division, Graduate School of Business, University of Colorado, 1978.

636. Wicker, A. W. "Attitudes vs. Actions." *Journal of Social Issues,* 25 (1969), pp. 41-78.

637. Will, Frederick L. "Reason, Social Practice, and Scientific Realism." *Philosophy of Science,* 48 (1981), pp. 1-18.

638. Winch, Peter. *The Idea of a Social Science and Its Relation to Philosophy.* London: Routledge and Kegan Paul, 1958.

639. Winch, Peter. "Understanding a Primitive Society." *American Philosophical Quarterly,* 1 (1964), pp. 307-24. Reprinted in *Ethics and Action.* London: Routledge and Kegan Paul, 1972.

640. Wind, Yoram, and Frederick E. Webster, Jr. "Industrial Buying as Organizational Behavior: A Guideline for Research Strategy." *Journal of Purchasing* (August 1972), pp. 5-16.

641. Wish, John R. and Stephen H. Gamble. *Marketing and Social Issues.* New York: John Wiley and Sons, 1971.

642. Wittgenstein, Ludwig. *Tractatus Logico-Philosophicus.* London: Routledge and Kegan Paul, 1922.

643. Wittgenstein, Ludwig. *Philosophical Investigations.* Translated by G. E. Moore. Anscombe, Oxford: Blackwell, 1953.

644. Worrall, John and G. Currie. *The Methodology of Scientific Research Programs: Philosophical Papers of Imre Lakatos.* Vol. I. Cambridge: Cambridge University Press, 1978.

645. Wright, Larry. "Explanation and Teleology." *Philosophy of Science,* 39 (1972), pp. 204-218.

646. Wright, Larry. "Discussion: Rejoinder to Utz." *Philosophy of Science,* 44 (1977), pp. 321-325.

647. Zaltman, Gerald, Christian R. A. Pinson, and Reinhard Angelmar. *Metatheory and Consumer Research.* New York: Holt, Rinehart, and Winston, Inc., 1973.

648. Zaltman, Gerald and Alan Vertinsky. "Health Services Marketing: A Suggested Model." *Journal of Marketing,* 35 (July 1971), pp. 19-27.

649. Zaltman, Gerald, Karen LeMasters, and Michael Heffring. *Theory Construction in Marketing: Some Thoughts on Thinking.* New York: John Wiley and Sons, 1982.

650. Zikmund, William G., and William J. Stanton. "Recycling Solid Wastes: A Channels of Distribution Problem." *Journal of Marketing,* 35 (July 1971), pp. 34-39.

651. Zukav, Gary. *The Dancing Wu-Li Masters.* New York: Bantam, 1979.

NAME INDEX

SUBJECT INDEX